Praise for *What Liberals Believe*

"What a wonderful collection of invaluable quotes!"
—Katrina vanden Heuvel, editor and publisher of *The Nation* and author of *Taking Back America: And Taking Down the Radical Right*

"Every speaker needs great quotes. And if you're like me, you can use a little progressive inspiration now and then. William Martin's book provides both."
—Gloria Feldt, author, lecturer, women's rights activist, and former president of the Planned Parenthood Federation of America

"William Martin has become the ultimate quotographer of the American Left! Revel in these quotations. Spread them liberally. Take them to heart. And then act on them!"
—Jim Hightower, national radio commentator and author of *Thieves in High Places*

"A treasure chest of wisdom from the port side."
—Alfie Kohn, author of *No Contest: The Case Against Competition* and *Punished by Rewards*

"Wow. What a research job. What a resource!"
—Eric Alterman, author of *When Presidents Lie* and *What Liberal Media?* and columnist for *The Nation*

"A quotation book that is pro-choice, pro-environment, pro-civil rights, pro-civil liberties, pro-union, and 'pro' all the things that really matter. In short, a quote book that won't just sit on the shelf."
—Frances Kissling, former president of Catholics for a Free Choice

"An invaluable resource for spreading the word and for understanding the progressive legacy."
—Tom Hayden, anti-war activist, author of the Port Huron Statement, and one of the founders of the Students for a Democratic Society

"From A to Z, this book covers the tumultuous political waterfront with quotations that often go to the eye of the storm. William Martin has gathered thousands of quotes that speak to us with concise clarity. . . . Turn to any page and start reading; you'll probably be hooked within seconds."
—Norman Solomon, author of *War Made Easy: How Presidents and Pundits Keep Spinning Us to Death*

"This marvelous collection of progressive insights is bound to provoke much-needed inspiration, thought, and action."
—Joel Bakan, professor of law at the University of British Columbia, filmmaker, and author of *The Corporation: The Pathological Pursuit of Profit and Power*

"An entertaining and convenient resource for all who seek to convey progressive values, the nastiness of the Far Right, or the moral mushiness of the so-called 'center.' With abundant material to inspire or outrage, this is an essential collection of quotations for progressive speakers, writers, and thinkers."
—Mayor Ross C. "Rocky" Anderson, Salt Lake City, Utah

"Words well-assembled give us good maps for our lives in the world. William Martin does skillful service in assembling quotations that capture the dangerous half-hidden reality in today's America, teetering as it is on the edge of losing us our American heritage as citizens in a constitutional democracy."
—Andrew Bard Schmookler, author of *The Parable of the Tribes: The Problem of Power in Social Evolution*

"Grist for the debate. This is a valuable resource for progressive advocates."
—Robert L. Borosage, co-director of the Campaign for America's Future

"This comprehensive compendium of quotations should be within arm's reach of any progressive concerned about the corporate takeover of the Democratic Party, indeed of our entire society."
—Charlie Cray, director of the Center for Corporate Policy and coauthor of *The People's Business: Controlling Corporations and Restoring Democracy*

"William Martin's collection of enlightening and energizing quotations illustrates the storied history of our liberal values while providing a roadmap for a strong progressive future. Read it, quote it yourself, but most importantly, take action."
—Amy Isaacs, national director of Americans for Democratic Action (ADA)

"An indispensable reference tool for writers, researchers, and reformers . . . William Martin has done a public service by giving us a window into the soul of liberalism."
—David Morris, columnist and co-founder of the Institute for Local Self-Reliance

"William Martin's new compendium of progressive voices reflecting the values that inform our work and our politics is a timely reminder that no political party or social movement has a monopoly on values—even explicitly religious values."
—Rev. Dr. Katherine Hancock Ragsdale, executive director of Political Research Associates, board member of NARAL Pro-Choice America, and former chair of the Religious Coalition for Reproductive Choice

WHAT LIBERALS BELIEVE

Also by
WILLIAM MARTIN

The Best Liberal Quotes Ever: Why the Left Is Right

WHAT
LIBERALS
BELIEVE

The Best Progressive Quotes Ever

Edited by
WILLIAM MARTIN

WITH A NEW INTRODUCTION BY THE EDITOR

SKYHORSE PUBLISHING

Skyhorse Publishing books may be purchased in bulk at special discounts
for sales promotion, corporate gifts, fund-raising, or educational purposes. Special editions can also
be created to specifications. For details, contact the Special Sales Department,
Skyhorse Publishing, 307 West 36th Street, 11th Floor, New York, NY 10018 or
info@skyhorsepublishing.com.

Skyhorse® and Skyhorse Publishing® are registered trademarks
of Skyhorse Publishing, Inc.®, a Delaware corporation.

www.skyhorsepublishing.com

10 9 8 7 6 5 4 3 2 1

Library of Congress Cataloging-in-Publication Data available on file.

ISBN: 978-1-61608-883-5

Printed in the United States of America

For Mar,
lover of nature, protector of underdogs,
and collector of small shiny objects

CONTENTS

THE PROMISE OF LIBERALISM

THE UNCHECKED POWER OF CORPORATIONS

THE CULTURE WAR

THE DEMAND FOR JUSTICE

THE STRUGGLE FOR EQUALITY

THE CORRUPTION OF PUBLIC SERVICE

THE COMMITMENT TO EDUCATION

THE HUMAN CONDITION

THE PUBLIC'S RIGHT TO KNOW

THE NATURE OF RIGHT AND WRONG

THE MEANING OF PATRIOTISM

THE POLITICAL PARTIES

THE THREAT OF RELIGIOUS EXTREMISM

THE ASSAULT ON SCIENCE AND THE ENVIRONMENT

THE INSANITY OF WAR AND VIOLENCE

THE BETTER ANGELS OF OUR NATURE

CALLOUS AND CLUELESS
QUOTES FROM THE RIGHT

THE BEST OF THE OBAMA YEARS AND MORE

INTRODUCTION:
WHAT DO LIBERALS BELIEVE?

Liberals value equality, justice, compassion, and purpose. We are unequivocally pro-choice, pro-environment, pro-jobs, pro-union, and pro-marriage equality. We love our country enough to criticize it and believe that we are all in this society together. If you scan the pages of this book, you'll see that this is not just a book about politics, but about the many issues that determine how we can improve our lives and the lives of others. *What Liberal's Believe: The Best Progressive Quotes Ever* is a resource for keeping hope alive in an increasingly conservative society.

Much has happened since the original 2008 publication of *What Liberals Believe,* some of it very good. To the amazement of the world, we elected our first African American president. We enacted a historic national health care law, ended the Iraq War, repealed "Don't Ask, Don't Tell," and through the Stimulus Bill made the largest investment in green technology in history. Several states now allow same-sex marriages. These accomplishments are impressive, but they don't tell the whole story. Overall, the arc of recent history has not bent toward justice. America has taken a hard turn to the right.

The reckless financial deregulation and risk-taking of the Reagan-Bush era finally came home to roost, causing the largest financial meltdown since the Great Depression. To prevent disaster, the political establishment bailed out the banks and large corporations, but left ordinary citizens to largely fend for themselves. This mismanaged crisis not only helped create the Occupy Movement, it spawned a Tea Party uprising so ideologically rigid and reactionary that it has caused the Republican Party to come unhinged. The Tea Party-dominated GOP has purged itself of all moderation. It's now so extreme that it would reject the policies of such conservative icons as Ronald Reagan or George W. Bush. The big tent of the Grand Old Party has been taken hostage by market fundamentalists who write the checks, and by religious fundamentalists who do their bidding.

The disastrous years of the Bush-Cheney presidency have not brought repudiation of the Radical Right, but rather even more passionate intensity, much of it fixated on Barack Obama. America has not become more thoughtful or temperate; instead, it has become an upside-down country where citizens who were swindled by bankers now demand that bankers have even less scrutiny. It's a country where billionaires whine and complain that they are the poor and oppressed. It's a country of bizarre birth certificate conspiracies and shameless inequality, where down is up, war is peace, freedom is slavery, ignorance is strength, and science is considered a left-wing plot.

To make matters worse, in 2010 the most brazenly political Supreme Court of all time (remember Bush v. Gore) delivered an unprecedented blow to our political system. (The corporate media gave it scant attention, preferring to cover *American Idol* and *Dancing with the Stars*.) In the case of Citizens United v. Federal Election Commission, the court's 5 – 4 decision opened the floodgates for corporations to spend unlimited amounts of money to buy elections. By striking down the decades-long prohibition on corporate financing of elections, the GOP Five (Alito, Kennedy, Roberts, Scalia, and the strangely mute Thomas) corrupted a system already dominated by the super rich. No candidate, no election, and no issue are now safe from secretive Super PACs and their limitless dark money. Without a constitutional amendment to repeal *Citizens United,* the richest 1% will continue to accrue power and wealth at the expense of the rest of us.

The Republicans have also doubled down on their assault on women. Around the country there are new mandatory ultrasound "shame" requirements for women seeking abortions, attempts to ban insurance companies from providing contraceptives, threats to eliminate Planned Parenthood funding, schemes to cut Head Start funding to force women to become stay-at-home mothers, and even plans for hospitals to let pregnant women die rather than perform life-saving abortions. What's more, when women speak out for themselves, Republican leaders call them "sluts" and "prostitutes," while rank and file Republicans look at their fingernails. The depth and scope of this misogyny boggles the mind.

What Liberals Believe: The Best Progressive Quotes Ever will not just highlight politics. It has plenty to say about other core topics such as love, humility, courage, tolerance, marriage, children, and God. This newly expanded book has hundreds of new quotations that go to the heart of being liberal. It even has a special section of "Callous and Clueless Quotes from the Right" to remind readers just how ridiculous and extreme the right wing has become. A perfect resource for writers, bloggers, researchers, activists, speechwriters, teachers, and students, *What Liberals Believe* is a bible of progressive insight. This book will help you appreciate that the cause of social and economic justice is still worth fighting for.

A free and equal democratic society is worth your struggle. Don't lose faith. Don't be silent. Don't be afraid to call yourself "liberal."

William Martin
April 2012

THE RIGHTS OF CITIZENS
IN A DEMOCRACY

Abortion

Abortion is not just a women's issue.
—Bob Burnett, "Why Don't Men Write About Abortion?" *Common Dreams* (March 29, 2006)

The conservatives' fondest dream—overturning Roe—will be the Republicans' worst nightmare.
—James Carville and Paul Begala, *Take It Back* (2006)

Among the first things the Nazis did upon seizing power in 1933 was to outlaw abortion.
—Steven Conn, "In Struggle for Women's Freedom, Which Side is U.S. On?" *St. Paul Pioneer Press* (June 23, 2006)

Democrats aren't pro-abortion. . . . We do believe that a woman has a right to make up her own mind.
—Howard Dean, quoted in "Democrats Elect Dean as Committee Chairman," *New York Times* (February 12, 2005)

What better way to discourage abortion than to encourage and facilitate humane family planning.
—Editorial, *New York Times* (April 2, 1993)

Frankly, I adore your catchy slogan, "Adoption, not Abortion," although no one has been able to figure out, even with expert counseling, how to use adoption as a method of birth control.
—Barbara Ehrenreich, *The Worst Years of Our Lives* (1991)

Democrats do not support coerced childbirth.
—Don Hazen, "Power Play," AlterNet (January 7, 2005)

Being pro-choice is an expression of our deepest-held moral values.
—George A. Hill and Nancy Mosher, "Pro-choice supporters not ceding anything," *Maine Today* (January 25, 2005)

History teaches that abortions do not stop because they are made illegal.
—Edward M. Kennedy, in his address to the National Press Club, "A Democratic Blueprint for America's Future" (January 12, 2005)

If men could get pregnant, abortion would be a sacrament.
—Florynce Kennedy, quoted in "The Verbal Karate of Florynce R. Kennedy, Esq." *Ms.* magazine (March 1973)

The Republicans want to criminalize the right of women to choose, take us back to the days of back alleys, gag doctors and deny families the right to plan and be aware of their choices. We Democrats want to protect the constitutional right of privacy.
—John Kerry, in his keynote address to the Massachusetts Democratic Issues Convention (June 7, 2003)

Women soldiers who are raped . . . and who subsequently get pregnant presently cannot end their pregnancies in a military hospital, because abortions are not permitted there.
—George Lakoff, *Don't Think Like an Elephant* (2004)

Pro-choice people understand that there are two lives involved in an abortion—one born (the pregnant woman) and one not (the fetus)—but that the born person must be allowed to decide what is right.
—Anne Lamott, "The Rights of the Born," *Los Angeles Times* (February 10, 2006)

The principles that underlie a pro-choice position are the principles of dignity and privacy for women. Abortion rights and reproductive freedom and choice need to be seen in the larger context of individual liberties, of women determining the course of their lives and having control over their lives.
—Kate Michelman, appearing with Kate O'Beirne on NBC's *Meet the Press*, (January 8, 2006)

Many "pro-lifers" are really pro-sperm. Basically, they insist that the sperm has an inalienable right to try to get to the egg.
—David Morris, "The Pro-Life Continuum," AlterNet (December 19, 2005)

We will not return to the back-alley, wire-hanger abortions.
—Deborah Morse-Kahn, on states such as South Dakota who have criminalized abortion even in cases of rape or incest, "Another State's Giant Step Backward for Women," *Minneapolis Star Tribune*, (March 7, 2006)

No one is pro-abortion.
—Barack Obama, in his speech at Benedictine University (October 5, 2004)

The pro-life movement is really no longer the anti-abortion movement. . . . It has turned itself into the anti–birth control movement, the anti-sex movement, and, indeed, the anti-modern family movement.
—Cristina Page, *How the Pro-Choice Movement Saved America* (2006)

Until 1869, even the Catholic Church supported legalized abortion until quickening, at approximately nineteen weeks of pregnancy, which is when it considered the fetus was given a soul.
—Cristina Page, *How the Pro-Choice Movement Saved America* (2006)

The Bible doesn't mention abortion even once. . . . That so many Christians are firmly persuaded that the Bible condemns abortion suggests that God's politics tend to be the politics of the people who claim to speak for him.
—Katha Pollitt, "Jesus to the Rescue?" *Nation* (January 20, 2005)

I believe that in a contest between the living and the almost living, the latter must, if necessary, give way to the will of the former.
—Anna Quindlen, *New York Times* (March 13, 1991)

A woman is a person; a zygote or a fetus is not.
—Michael Schwalbe, "Reproductive Freedom 101," *Common Dreams* (April 11, 2006)

The same groups who so forcefully denounce abortion have cheapened their claims to morality by actively opposing policies that might help poor, single mothers support their children. . . . They love children fiercely right up until the time they leave the womb.
—Cynthia Tucker, "Theocrats Losing Their Rigid Hold on Evangelical Christians," *Yahoo! News* (December 22, 2006)

To conservatives, abortion isn't so much about the welfare of fetuses as it is about the status of women and the nature of sex.
—Paul Waldman, "Why Rudy Giuliani Is Destined to Fall," *TomPaine.com* (March 1, 2007)

If two-thirds of all women who seek abortions say they cannot afford a child, improving economic conditions by providing viable job opportunities for both men and women should greatly decrease the number of abortions. Raising the minimum wage is an abortion issue.
—Elizabeth Wardle, "Reflections from a Former Anti-Abortion Activist," AlterNet (October 14, 2006)

Civil Liberties

Everything we stand for is under assault in this country, and not from some outside force. Our rights, liberties and economic security are threatened by the Republican Party as it operates today.
—Alec Baldwin, "We Cannot Fight Everyone," *Huffington Post* (April 28, 2006)

This administration has shredded the Bill of Rights. We have people in cages for going on two years now—no papers, no visitors, no phone calls, no lawyers, no nothing.
—Phil Donahue, on the Bush administration, "Out in Left Field," interviewed by Bruce Kluger in *Time Out New York* (November 24-30, 2005)

It's too bad, really, that Americans don't pledge allegiance to the Constitution—and don't revere it as they do the Stars and Stripes. If they did, they'd see the folly in defending a rectangle of cloth at the expense of the parchment's promises.
—Editorial, "Shielding the Flag, Shattering Liberty," *Minneapolis Star Tribune* (June 22, 2006)

It makes no more sense to launch an assault on our civil liberties as the best way to get at terrorists than it did to launch an invasion of Iraq as the best way to get at Osama bin Laden.
—Al Gore, quoted in "Gore Urges Repeal of Patriot Act," *Los Angeles Times* (November 10, 2003)

Surely the right to die in a manner and at a time one's own choosing is the ultimate civil liberty.
—Derek Humphry, quoted in "The Other Pro-Choice Movement," *Common Dreams* (January 21, 2006)

I believe in the Bill of Rights the way some folks believe in the Bible.
—Molly Ivins, quoted in "Molly Ivins, In Memoriam," *Progressive* (February 1, 2007)

Civil rights and civil liberties are in grave danger. . . . Preserving them will mean having to fight against some of our fellow citizens. We can fight with nonviolent methods, but there has to be a fight.
—Margaret Kimberley, "Civil War in America," *Black Commentator* (March 16, 2006)

Our freedoms are guaranteed only as long as ordinary, everyday people are willing to claim them—indeed, to insist on them.
—Patricia J. Princehouse, "Science and the First Amendment," *Nation* (May 16, 2006)

With the exception of a few stalwarts, such as the ACLU, we have witnessed the sorry spectacle of most civil libertarians remaining silent or actively supporting the most sweeping and ill-considered assault on civil liberties since the roundup of Japanese Americans during World War II.
—Robert Scheer, regarding post–September 11 hysteria, "Liberty Is Dying, Liberal by Liberal," *Nation* (November 20, 2001)

The main building block of a democratic society is that everyone is equal before the law, innocent until proved otherwise, and has the right to legal representation. If the guilt of the prisoners in Guantanamo Bay is beyond doubt, why are the Americans afraid to bring them to trial?
—Archbishop John Sentamu, quoted in "The Americans Are Breaking International Law . . . It Is a Society Heading Towards Animal Farm," *Independent (UK)* (February 16, 2006)

The real threat to our nation currently comes from within, when we begin taking away the very civil rights and civil liberty protections that made us great.
—Hilary Shelton, quoted in "Kucinich Leads Move in Congress to Curb Controversial Patriot Act," *Cleveland Plain Dealer* (September 25, 2003)

There is a long and unfortunate history of cooperation between government security agencies and powerful corporations to deprive individuals of their privacy and other civil liberties.
—Jay Stanley, *The Surveillance-Industrial Complex*, American Civil Liberties Union (August 2004)

There is one tiny corner of Cuba . . . where innocent people are held without charge for years, beyond international law, human decency and the mythical glow of Lady Liberty's torch. It is a place where torture is common, beating is ritual and humiliation is routine. They call it Guantanamo Bay.
—Gary Younge, "A Fantasy of Freedom," *Guardian (UK)* (January 24, 2005)

Dignity

An employee's dignity is violated when she isn't paid a living wage, when her right to bargain collectively is not recognized, when she is forced to work overtime against her will, and when she is forced to work in unsafe conditions.
—Robert Hinkley, quoted in "A Corporate Lawyer Speaks Out," *Common Dreams* (March 22, 2002)

Here is the real political story, the one most politicians won't even acknowledge: the reality of the anonymous, disquieting daily struggle of ordinary people . . . searching for dignity and fairness against long odds in a cruel market world.
—Bill Moyers, "For America's Sake," *Nation* (January 22, 2007)

People want politicians to STAND FOR THE PEOPLE, not grovel beneath the corporations.
—Ralph Nader, "Democrats Finally Wake Up to Need for Minimum Wage Hike," *Common Dreams* (June 24, 2006)

Our values ground us in respect for the inherent worth and dignity of every person, and our experience tells us that our diversity is to be celebrated rather than feared.
—Rev. William G. Sinkford, "Family Values for Diverse Families," *UU World* (December 6, 2005)

Our economic and political systems place more value in the accumulation of wealth than in the dignity of people.
—David Taylor, quoted in "Globalization's Diverse Foes," *Washington Post* (September 5, 2001)

I believe that women, and men, cannot live in dignity and equality if they cannot render for themselves their most intimate family decisions.
—Rev. Carlton W. Veazey, "On the Brink of Theocracy," Center for American Progress (May 6, 2005)

Free Speech

If we don't believe in freedom of expression for people we despise, we don't believe in it at all.
—Noam Chomsky, *Guardian (UK)* (November 23, 1992)

When liberals disagree with me, they send in long, logical e-mails explaining all my errors. I hardly ever get well-reasoned articles from the right. People just tell me to shut up.
—Roger Ebert, in an interview with Matthew Rothschild, *Progressive* (August 2003)

The best remedy for free speech to which you object is not squelching that speech, but countering it with speech that upholds your point of view.
—Editorial, "The Reagans' Controversy—Must Not See TV?" *Philadelphia Inquirer* (November 9, 2003)

So it has come down to this: You are at liberty to exercise your First Amendment right to assemble and to protest, so long as you do so from behind chain-link fences and razor wire, or miles from the audience you seek to address.
—Dahlia Lithwick, regarding so-called "free-speech zones" at political conventions, "Muzzling Free Speech," *Minneapolis Star Tribune* (August 16, 2004)

What's the point of free speech if we're always afraid to speak freely?
—Anna Quindlen, in her commencement address at Colby College (May 28, 2006)

A chill wind is blowing in this nation. . . . Every day, the air waves are filled with warnings, veiled and unveiled threats, spewed invective, and hatred directed at any voice of dissent.
—Tim Robbins, in his speech to the National Press Club, *Common Dreams* (April 16, 2003)

Free speech is the whole thing, the whole ball game. Free speech is life itself.
—Salman Rushdie, interview in *Guardian (UK)* (November 8, 1990)

The right to offend is far more important than any right not to be offended.
—Andrew Sullivan, quoted in "Aphorisms 2006," *Yahoo! News* (December 25, 2005)

Freedom

Liberty is always unfinished business.
—American Civil Liberties Union, annual report (1955–56)

Each generation must recreate liberty for its own times. Whether or not we establish freedom rests with ourselves.
—Florence Ellinwood Allen, *This Constitution of Ours* (1940)

Control of our own lives and destinies is what freedom is about, what democracy is about, and at a very fundamental level, what life itself is about.
—Caroline Arnold, "Status and Syntax: Who Controls? Who's Controlled?" *Common Dreams* (November 13, 2005)

Freedom is perhaps the most resonant, deeply held American value.
—Robert Bellah, et al., *Habits of the Heart* (1985)

Freedom for the wolves means death for the sheep.
—Isaiah Berlin, quoted in "Lib Dems Oppose Civil Service BNP Ban," *Guardian (UK)* (September 20, 2004)

I call that mind free, which jealously guards its intellectual rights and powers, which calls no man master, which does not content itself with a passive or hereditary faith, which opens itself to light whensoever it may come.
—William Ellery Channing, in his sermon entitled "Spiritual Freedom" (1830)

So long as man remains free he strives for nothing so incessantly and so painfully as to find someone to worship.
—Fyodor Dostoevsky, *The Brothers Karamazov* (1879–1880)

The cost of liberty is less than the price of repression.
—W. E. B. Du Bois, *John Brown* (1909)

We do love our freedom, and we will fight to keep it. We will fight to defeat the terrorists who threaten the safety and security of our families and loved ones. And we will fight to protect the rights of law-abiding Americans against intrusive government power.
—Russ Feingold, "On the President's Warrantless Wiretapping Program," *Common Dreams* (February 8, 2006)

The history of liberty has largely been the history of the observance of procedural safeguards.
—Felix Frankfurter, *McNabb v. United States* (1943)

They that can give up essential liberty to obtain a little temporary safety deserve neither liberty nor safety.
—Benjamin Franklin, in his speech to the Pennsylvania Assembly (November 11, 1755)

Freedom, the ability to preserve one's integrity against power, is the basic condition for morality.
—Erich Fromm, *Man for Himself* (1947)

Nothing so denies a person liberty as the total absence of money.
—John Kenneth Galbraith, quoted in "John Kenneth Galbraith Interview,"
Progressive (October 2000)

The emancipation of belief is the most formidable of the tasks of reform, the
one on which all else depends.
—John Kenneth Galbraith, quoted in "J. K. Galbraith's Towering Spirit,"
Washington Post (May 3, 2006)

Freedom includes the freedom to marry whomever you choose and to make
decisions about reproduction.
—Ellen Goodman, "Amen, Dubya," *Working For Change* (January 26, 2005)

The government has no claim on the time and life of anyone, except the peo-
ple who volunteer for military service . . . and convicted criminals.
—Father Andrew Greeley, "Moral Health Tip to America: Stay out of the
Draft," *Chicago Sun-Times* (December 1, 2006)

Libertarians argue that the state . . . is the greatest threat to individual freedom. . . . Liberals counterclaim that the libertarian critique ignores the reality of other organized forms of power—such as corporations, private militias,
and intractably racist state governments.
—Ryan Grim, "Liberalism's Brain on Drugs," *In These Times* (October 31,
2005)

Keep fighting for freedom and justice, beloveds, but don't forget to have fun
doin' it. . . . Rejoice in all the oddities that freedom can produce.
—Molly Ivins, quoted in "Molly Ivins's Joyful Outrage," *Washington Post*
(February 2, 2007)

One's right to life, liberty, and property, to free speech, a free press, freedom
of worship and assembly, and other fundamental rights may not be submitted
to vote; they depend on the outcome of no elections.
—Robert Jackson, *West Virginia State Board of Education v. Barnette*, quoted in
"Strong First Amendment Tradition Relies Upon Those Willing to Fight,"
Casper Star-Tribune (February 28, 2000)

Freedom of religion, freedom of the press, freedom of person under the protection of the habeas corpus, and trial by juries impartially selected. These principles form the bright constellation which has gone before us.
—Thomas Jefferson, inaugural address, Washington, D.C. (March 4, 1801)

If a nation expects to be ignorant and free . . . it expects what never was and never will be.
—Thomas Jefferson, letter to Charles Yancey (January 6, 1816)

The most disturbing threat to freedom of assembly isn't from the ways in which police officers restrict movement in public space, but from the disappearance of public space itself. . . . Today the space that is most public is privatized: the shopping mall.
—Robert Jensen, "Amendment I: Freedom of Assembly," *Fredericksburg Free Lance-Star* (December 5, 2005)

Freedom lies beyond conformity or rebellion.
—Sam Keen, *To a Dancing God* (1970)

Freedom is like taking a bath: you got to keep doing it every day.
—Florynce Kennedy, quoted in "Laughing All the Way to the Polls," *Bitch* magazine (January 5, 2006)

Liberty lies in the hearts of men and women; when it dies there, no constitution, no law, no court can save it.
—Learned Hand, in a speech in Central Park, New York City (May 21, 1944)

Is life so dear, or peace so sweet, as to be purchased at the price of chains and slavery? Forbid it, Almighty God! I know not what course others may take; but as for me, give me liberty or give me death!
—Patrick Henry, in a speech to the Virginia Convention (March 23, 1775)

Expansions of voting rights, civil rights, education, public health, scientific knowledge, and protections from fear and want . . . These were the ideals of freedom that I grew up with. They are now all under threat, not by guns or bombs, but an under-the-radar redefinition of freedom and liberty to suit right-wing ideology.
—George Lakoff, "Understanding the Meaning of Freedom," *Boston Globe* (July 4, 2006)

The function of freedom is to free someone else.
—Toni Morrison, quoted in *Bird by Bird* (1994)

We cannot defend freedom abroad by deserting it at home.
—Edward R. Murrow, quoted in "I Am a Liberal. There, I Said It!" *Huffington Post* (March 13, 2006)

We fight for liberty by having more liberty, not less.
—Keith Olbermann, MSNBC's *Countdown* (November 30, 2006)

If liberty means anything at all, it means the right to tell people what they do not want to hear.
—George Orwell, *Animal Farm* (1945)

The conscious mind is like a monkey riding a tiger of subconscious decisions and actions in progress, frantically making up stories about being in control.
—Dennis Overbye, "Free Will: Now You Have It, Now You Don't," *New York Times* (January 2, 2007)

Liberty requires opportunity to make a living—a living decent according to the standard of the time, a living which gives a man not only enough to live by, but something to live for.
—Franklin D. Roosevelt, quoted in *The Wit and Wisdom of Franklin D. Roosevelt, Government and Democracy* (1982)

We look forward to a world founded upon four essential freedoms [freedom of speech, freedom of worship, freedom from want, freedom from fear].
—Franklin D. Roosevelt, in a speech (January 6, 1941)

To renounce liberty is to renounce being a man.
—Rousseau, *The Social Contract* (1762)

The human person has a right to religious freedom . . . immune from coercion from individuals or of social groups and of any human power, in such ways that no one is to be forced to act in a manner contrary to his own beliefs.
—Second Vatican Council, Declaration on Religious Freedom (December 7, 1965)

There is reason why those seeking control and power consider true education and knowledge the enemy, for free thought . . . invariably leads to questioning of authority, to dissent, protest and debate of myths, beliefs, and propaganda.
—Manuel Valenzuela, "The Poisoning of the Well," *Information Clearing House* (January 19, 2006)

Homeland Security

In the era when the federal government sees "homeland security" as a slogan rather than a responsibility, allowing the nation's working waterfronts to be run by private firms just doesn't work.
—John Nichols, "Corporate Control of Ports Is the Problem," *Nation* (February 21, 2006)

Welcome to the American Gestapo. Be careful what you say and do. They are watching and they will be watching from now on.
—Doug Thompson, "Welcome to the American Gestapo," *Capitol Hill Blue* (November 20, 2002)

If you're reading this on the Internet, the FBI may be spying on you at this very moment.
—Nick Turse, "Bringing It All Back Home," *TomDispatch.com* (January 29, 2005)

Human Rights

America did not invent human rights. In a very real sense . . . human rights invented America.
—Jimmy Carter, in his farewell address (January 14, 1981)

The CIA is holding an unknown number of prisoners in secret detention centers abroad. In violation of the Geneva Conventions, it has refused to register those detainees with the International Red Cross or to allow visits by its inspectors. Its prisoners have "disappeared," like the victims of some dictatorships.
—Editorial, "Vice President for Torture," *Washington Post* (October 26, 2005)

How can we claim to promote human rights around the world when we are attacking basic rights at home?
—Matt Foreman, in a news release, "Bush Administration's Orwellian Logic," National Gay and Lesbian Task Force (June 25, 2003)

We once stood for something good in this world. . . . We once upheld the Geneva Conventions.
—Joseph L. Galloway, "We've Sunk to Bin Laden's Level," *Miami Herald* (September 23, 2006)

We stand for the rights of property, but we stand even more for the rights of man.
—Theodore Roosevelt, quoted in "Is Wal-Mart a Person?" *BuzzFlash* (January 28, 2005)

Human rights is not a religious idea. It is a secular idea, the product of the last four centuries of Western history. . . . The basic human rights documents— the American Declaration of Independence and the French Declaration of the Rights of Man—were written by political, not religious, leaders.
—Arthur M. Schlesinger, Jr., in his 1989 speech at Brown University, quoted in *2000 Years of Disbelief* (1996)

Progressive multiculturalism is about respecting and celebrating difference, but . . . human rights are universal and indivisible.
—Peter Tatchell, "Why Has the Left Gone Soft on Human Rights?" *Independent (UK)* (March 22, 2007)

All human beings are born free and equal in dignity and rights. They are endowed with reason and conscience and should act towards one another in the spirit of brotherhood.
—Universal Declaration of Human Rights, United Nations, Article 1 (December 10, 1948)

Police State

Your policies in Iraq are reprehensible.
—Steve Howards, to Dick Cheney. Howards was taking his eight-year-old son for a walk. The Secret Service arrested him for "assaulting" the vice president. Quoted in "Criticizing Cheney to His Face Is Assault?" *Progressive* (October 4, 2006)

Is America becoming what it most fears: a big brother state ruled by dictator, where no one is protected from eavesdropping by the secret police, and everything is permitted in defense of the homeland, including torture?
—Philip James, "The American Nightmare," *Guardian (UK)* (December 22, 2005)

The most common characteristics of all police states is intimidation by surveillance. Citizens know they are being watched and overheard. Their mail is being examined. Their homes can be invaded.
—Vance Packard, *The People Shapers* (1977)

The Republican majority is using its power to expand, not contract, the role of the government, replacing the welfare state with a far more costly and intrusive police state.
—James Ridgeway, "Attention, Small-D Democrats: The Party's Over," *Village Voice* (November 12, 2002)

Wal-Mart Turns in Student's Anti-Bush Photo, Secret Service Investigates Him
—Matthew Rothschild, article headline (October 4, 2005). The photo was for a homework assignment asking students to take photographs to illustrate their rights in the Bill of Rights."

I am going to tell you how we are not going to fight communism. We are not going to transform our fine FBI into a Gestapo secret police. . . . We are not going to turn the United States into a right-wing totalitarian country in order to deal with a left-wing totalitarian threat.
—Harry Truman, in a 1950 speech, quoted in "Excerpt: How Would a Patriot Act?" AlterNet (May 11, 2006)

America is undergoing its greatest metamorphosis. It has been severed from its constitutional moorings and is drifting towards a police state.
—Mike Whitney, "Drifting Towards a Police State," OpEdNews (November 3, 2005)

Privacy

The right to be let alone—the most comprehensive of rights and the most valued by civilized men.
—Louis D. Brandeis, *Olmstead v. United States* (1928)

If the right of privacy means anything, it is the right of the individual, married or single, to be free from unwarranted governmental intrusion into matters so fundamentally affecting a person as the decision whether to bear or beget a child.
—William J. Brennan, Jr., *Eisenstadt v. Baird* (1972)

Even people in public life are entitled to some zone of privacy.
—Bill Clinton, when he was the governor of Arkansas, interviewed on "ABC This Week" (August 18, 1991)

Big Brother in the form of an increasingly powerful government and in an increasingly powerful private sector will pile the records high with reasons why privacy should give way to national security, to law and order, to efficiency of operations, to scientific advancement, and the like.
—William O. Douglas, *Points of Rebellion* (1969)

We are rapidly entering the age of no privacy, where everyone is open to surveillance at all times; where there are no secrets from government.
—William O. Douglas, *Osborn v. United States* (1966)

Other than telling us how to live, think, marry, pray, vote, invest, educate our children, and, now, die, I think the Republicans have done a fine job of getting government out of our personal lives.
—Editorial page, *Portland Oregonian* (June 19, 2005)

The right of the people to be secure in their persons, houses, papers, and effects, against unreasonable searches and seizures, shall not be violated.
—Fourth Amendment to the U.S. Constitution (1791)

Let all men know thee, but no man know thee thoroughly.
—Benjamin Franklin, *Poor Richard's Almanack* (May 1738)

All violations of essential privacy are brutalizing.
—Katherine Fullerton Gerould, *Modes and Morals* (1920)

More than ever before, the details about our lives are no longer our own. They belong to the companies that collect them and the government agencies that buy or demand them.
—Robert Harrow, quoted in "HP and The Privacy Erosion," *Common Dreams* (September 30, 2006)

Political bodies have no business making medical decisions.
—Molly Ivins, "Fatuous Politicians Have No Business Here," *Daily Camera* (March 23, 2005)

Every man should know that his conversations, his correspondence, and his personal life are private.
—Lyndon B. Johnson, *Public Papers of the Presidents of the United States: Lyndon B. Johnson* (1967)

Part of the genius of the American way is its preservation of a personal sphere where government's writ cannot reach.
—Kate Michelman, "Alito's Fantasy World," *Boston Globe* (January 9, 2006)

Politicians at all levels of government show an increasing willingness to invade the most sacred areas of private life—from decisions about the beginning and end of life to the books we check out of the library.
—Kate Michelman, "This Time, Alito, It's Personal," *Los Angeles Times* (November 13, 2005)

I oppose outing. I don't believe any gay man or lesbian, no matter how prominent, should be forced to retire privacy for the good of the cause, although I believe that openness does the cause good.
—Anna Quindlen, *Thinking Out Loud* (1993)

[Privacy is] a primal demand for a personal sense of control in the face of intrusive government, intrusive medicine, and intrusive strangers who think holding a crucifix like a blunt instrument makes them righteous when it really only makes them sanctimonious.
—Anna Quindlen on the Terry Schiavo Case, "The Culture of Each Life," *Newsweek* (April 4, 2005)

Civilization is the progress toward a society of privacy. The savage's whole existence is public, ruled by the laws of his tribe. Civilization is the process of setting man free from men.
—Ayn Rand, *The Fountainhead* (1943)

Sifting through the lives of hundreds of millions of people is an inefficient, highly unreliable means of discovering a one-in-a-billion terrorist.
—Jay Stanley, *The Surveillance-Industrial Complex*, American Civil Liberties Union (August 2004)

The state has no business in the bedrooms of the nation.
—Pierre Elliott Trudeau, *Globe & Mail* (Toronto) (December 22, 1967)

Privacy is dying in America—not with a fight but a yawn.
—Jonathan Turley, "Americans Let Right of Privacy Slip Away," *Albany Times Union* (July 2, 2006)

Reproductive Rights

The pharmacists who want "freedom of conscience" to refuse to fill legal prescriptions for women seeking contraceptive devices are no different from the diner owners who wanted "freedom of conscience" not to serve blacks.
—Jon Carrol, *San Francisco Chronicle* (April 25, 2005)

Free societies allow their citizens to make their own reproductive decisions; repressive ones restrict them.
—Steven Conn, "In Struggle for Women's Freedom, Which Side Is U.S. On?" *St. Paul Pioneer Press* (June 23, 2006)

No one should tell a woman she has to bear an unwanted child.
—Walter Cronkite, quoted in *Newsweek* (December 5, 1988)

The stealth anti-choice strategy pursued by the Bush Administration has been premised on the expectation that a gradual whittling away of women's reproductive rights will have little political consequence.
—Editorial, "Post-Feminism, R.I.P.," *Nation* (April 29, 2004)

Birth control frees women to forge their own paths by separating sex from procreation. This strikes fear into those who, underneath it all, oppose the increased social power women attain from expanded equality and justice.
—Gloria Feldt, "Core Issue Missing in Birth-Control War Reports," *Women's eNews* (June 28, 2006)

I'm against forced childbirth. I don't think the state should be forcing women to give birth against their will.
—Joshua Holland, "Dempublicans and the Forced Childbirth Movement," *AlterNet* (January 18, 2006)

Forced motherhood should not be the punishment for failed contraception or a contraceptive lapse, or for being human. Women are more than their wombs.
—Adele Horin, *Sydney Morning Herald* (August 7, 2004)

There is something vicious and violent about coercing a woman to carry to term an unwanted child, to force the unwanted on the unwilling, to use a woman's body against her will and choice, is morally repugnant.
—Rabbi Steven B. Jacobs, "Defining 'Moral Values' for the Next Four Years," Religious Coalition for Reproductive Choice (2004)

The preservation of life seems to be rather a slogan than a genuine goal of the anti-abortion forces; what they want is control. Control over behavior: control over women.
—Ursula K. Le Guin, in her address to the National Abortion Rights Action League (1982)

We seek to create a world where abortion is safe, legal, accessible, and rare.
—Letter to Religious Leaders, Religious Institute on Sexual Morality, Justice, and Healing (2005)

It is an obscenity—an all-male hierarchy, celibate or not, that presumes to rule on the lives and bodies of millions of women.
—Robin Morgan, on the Roman Catholic Church, *Sisterhood Is Powerful* (1970)

[A] woman's right to practice birth control is under siege. Pharmacists and health care providers want the right to refuse to fill prescriptions for birth control pills and morning-after pills, and insurance companies don't want to pay for them.
—Susan Reimer, on the 40th anniversary of the Griswold v. Connecticut Supreme Court decision, *Baltimore Sun* (June 14, 2005)

No woman can call herself free who does not own and control her own body.
—Margaret Sanger, *Woman and the New Race* (1920)

Men presume themselves fit to make decisions that have life-and-death consequences for millions of people—decisions about economic policy, agricultural policy, health policy, and war. Anti-abortion laws imply that women, in

contrast to men, are not capable of making wise decisions in matters related to life and death.
—Michael Schwalbe, "Reproductive Freedom 101," *Common Dreams* (April 11, 2006)

The simple truth is that a woman who cannot control her own reproduction has no more freedom than a slave.
—Sunsara Taylor, "Last Clinic Standing," Truthdig (July 13, 2006)

Emergency contraception . . . is available over-the-counter in all fifty states, but women in the U.S. military cannot count on accessing the medication on military bases.
—Beccah Golubock Watson, "Democrats Shy Away from Emergency Contraception," *In These Times* (June 14, 2007). A 2003 Defense Department survey found that almost a third of military women reported being the victim of rape or attempted rape during their time in the military.

Same-Sex Marriage

Two gay people getting married has nothing to do with marriage as an institution. It has to do with homophobes who are so insecure about their own marriages (or sexuality) that they have to obsess over others.
—Steve Almond, quoted in *What Do We Do Now* (2004)

Same-gender marriage harms no one, whereas prohibiting civil marriage for gays and lesbians harms these couples and their children.
—American Academy of Pediatrics, report quoted in "Decision on Gay Marriage Is Absurd," *Newsday* (July 12, 2006)

Civil unions are a civil right.
—Bumper sticker

Same-sex families pose no threat to this country or to other couples. The threat to families is a proposed amendment, which would write discrimination into the Constitution for the first time ever.
—Gary Buseck, "Same-Sex Marriage Ban of 'National Importance,'" *San Francisco Chronicle* (February 25, 2004)

To define the wish of homosexuals for equal access to marriage rites and rights as a mortal threat to the social order . . . is to put gay people themselves in an unprecedented position of jeopardy.
—James Carroll, "The Risks of Waging 'Culture War,'" *Boston Globe* (March 9, 2004)

Gay marriage does nothing to threaten you or your marriage, but the anti-gay right-wing wants to make you feel that way in order to consolidate their power.
—Bob Cesca, "Bigotry in the Name of Jesus H. Christ," *Huffington Post* (September 24, 2005)

The religious argument against same-sex marriage ignores a fundamental historical fact about marriage in the United States: It has always been a civil matter.
—George Chauncey, *Why Marriage?* (2004)

Bill Bennett: Look, it's a debate about whether you think marriage is between a man and a woman.
Jon Stewart: I disagree. I think it's a debate about whether you think gay people are part of the human condition or just a random fetish.
—Exchange on "The Daily Show," quoted in "Jon Stewart's Gandhian Struggle," *Common Dreams* (January 8, 2007)

Marriage is a civil right that should be granted to gay and lesbian couples based on their commitment to one another and should have nothing to do with society's outdated religious definitions.
—Hank Kalet, "Time to Redefine the Family," *South Brunswick Post* (February 19, 2006)

Most people under forty think love-and-let-love is the right reaction to same sex marriage.
—Martin Kaplan, "Here Come the Culture War Games," *Huffington Post* (June 4, 2006)

We cannot—and should not—require any religion or any church to accept gay marriage. But it is wrong for our civil laws to deny any American the basic right to be part of a family, to have loved ones with whom to build a future

and share life's joys and tears, and to be free from the stain of bigotry and discrimination.
—Edward M. Kennedy, in his address to the National Press Club, "A Democratic Blueprint for America's Future" (January 12, 2005)

The same rhetoric that's being used today against the gay community was used . . . against interracial couples . . . It is as shameful now as it was then.
—Gavin Newsom, quoted in "The Politics of Fear," *Rolling Stone* (June 29, 2006)

Love and commitment are rare enough; it seems absurd to thwart them in any guise.
—Anna Quindlen, "Evan's Two Moms," *New York Times* (February 5, 1992)

Civil unions are a step in the right direction. But they almost always offer less than the full roster of rights that marriage entails—and they still stigmatize same-sex relationships as deserving only second-class recognition.
—Kenneth Roth, in a press release entitled "U.S.: Full Marriage Rights for Same-Sex Partners," Human Rights Watch (September 4, 2003)

It is up to the individual and not the state to define the essence of the human experience when it comes to love and marriage.
—Robert Scheer, "Scandal's Shame, Massachusetts' Pride," AlterNet (May 18, 2004)

What kind of values removes my ability to provide health care coverage for my family?
—Dan Sturgis, commenting on the Michigan same-sex marriage ban, "Where's the Family in These Values?" *Common Dreams* (December 16, 2004)

How is the institution of marriage being "violated" when rights to marry between consenting adults are being extended rather than restricted?
—Pierre Tristam, "Piety's Ruse: Invoking Sanctity to Label Different as Second Class," *Daytona Beach News-Journal* (November 25, 2003)

Gay marriage doesn't . . . contribute to the decline of heterosexual marriage. (We haven't needed any help with that.)
—Cynthia Tucker, "Bush's Strategy: Pander to Prejudice," *Baltimore Sun* (February 2, 2004)

The Patriot Act

The Surveillance-Industrial Complex: How the American Government is Conscripting Businesses and Individuals in the Construction of a Surveillance Society
—American Civil Liberties Union, report title (August 9, 2005)

The Patriot Act has gone too far. Secret renditions should be stopped. Torture must be outlawed. Our military should not spy on our own people.
—Robert Byrd, remarks delivered on the U.S. Senate floor, "Securing America Without Destroying Liberties" (December 16, 2005)

Yesterday we heard reports that the military has spied on Americans simply because they exercised their right to peaceably assemble and to speak their minds. Today we hear that the military is tapping phone lines in our own country without the consent of a judge.
—Robert Byrd to the U.S. Senate, "Securing America Without Destroying Liberties" (December 16, 2005)

Instead of cherishing our role as the great champion of human rights, we now find civil liberties and personal privacy grossly violated under some extreme provisions of the Patriot Act.
—Jimmy Carter, "This Isn't the Real America," *Los Angeles Times* (November 14, 2005)

In America today, Big Brother is watching.
—Editorial, "Big Brother Is Watching," *Oakland Tribune* (December 27, 2005)

Whatever their politics, Americans today should be appalled that law enforcement agencies are . . . creating files on people simply for expressing their views. Such spying on citizens can only undermine our democracy, not strengthen it.
—Editorial, "Spying on Citizens," *Florida Today* (March 23, 2005)

Chances are that your employer has already been monitoring you—not for ties to terrorist organizations, but for signs of insubordination, drug use, mental illness, or any other symptom of a "bad attitude."
—Barbara Ehrenreich, "Snooping Bosses," *Progressive* (February 2006)

The Patriot Act gives the FBI the power to collect information on people who are not suspected of committing a crime.
—Ivan Eland, "Surveillance Society," *Consortium News* (November 9, 2005)

I can't imagine a more shocking example of an abuse of power, to eavesdrop on American citizens without first getting a court order based on some evidence that they are possibly criminals, terrorists, or spies.
—Russ Feingold, "Remarks on Ending Debate on Reauthorization of the USA Patriot Act," *Common Dreams* (December 16, 2005)

There is no doubt that if we lived in a police state, it would be easier to catch terrorists. . . . But that probably would not be a country in which we would want to live.
—Russ Feingold, in a statement on the Senate floor opposing the Patriot Act (October 25, 2001). Feingold was the only senator to vote against the act.

This administration reacts to anyone who questions this illegal [wiretapping] program by saying that those of us who demand the truth and stand up for our rights and freedoms have a pre-9/11 view of the world. In fact, the President has a pre-1776 view of the world.
—Russ Feingold, "On the President's Warrantless Wiretapping Program," *Common Dreams* (February 8, 2006)

It's scary to think that it may just be a matter of time before Googling will invite an FBI agent to tap your phone or interrogate you.
—Katie Hafner, "After Subpoenas, Internet Searches Give Some Pause," *New York Times* (January 25, 2006)

We have gone from being lied to about the war to being spied on for protesting the war.
—Rev. Jesse Jackson, interviewed by Amy Goodman, "Jesse Jackson on Samuel Alito, Domestic Spying and Poverty in America," *Democracy Now!* radio (January 9, 2006)

Spying on citizens for merely executing their constitutional rights of free speech and peaceful assembly is chilling and marks a troubling trend for the United States. . . . If the government has avowed pacifists under surveillance, then no one is safe.
—Joyce Miller, Assistant General Secretary for Justice and Human Rights, "The AFSC Sues the U.S. Defense Department for Unlawful Surveillance," American Friends Service Committee (Quaker) news release (June 14, 2006)

Almost four hundred communities across the United States and seven states . . . have passed resolutions condemning the assaults on civil liberties and the rule of law contained in the Patriot Act.
—John Nichols, "Feingold to Fight Patriot Act Reauthorization," *Nation* (December 10, 2005)

Domestic spying attracts folks that suffer from a kind of obsessive compulsive disorder. Once they begin collecting information on fellow citizens, they can't stop themselves.
—Stephen Pizzo, "Spying and Torture: Don't Go There," *News for Real* (December 20, 2005)

Big brother isn't coming—he's already here.
—Protest sign

Why has a legitimate effort to identify suicide bombers metastasized into the massive surveillance of protest politics?
—Christopher Pyle, "Checking Big Brother," *American Prospect* (January 20, 2006)

In American work places, bosses routinely snoop into underlings' personal e-mails and monitor our web-surfing practices. How did it come about that so many Americans have grown to accept such demeaning intrusions into our privacy?
—Phil Rockstroh, "To Hell with Centrism," *Thomas Paine's Corner* (November 15, 2006)

Word to the wise: If you're a peace activist, the government may be watching you and reading your e-mails.
—Matthew Rothschild, "Peace Activists Beware: Homeland Security May Be Reading Your E-Mail, and Passing it on to the Pentagon," *Progressive* (October 13, 2006)

The Patriot Act mandates that companies transform themselves into surrogate agents for the government.
—Jay Stanley, *The Surveillance-Industrial Complex*, American Civil Liberties Union (August 2004)

Some legal questions are hard. This one is not. The President's authorizing of NSA to spy on Americans is blatantly unlawful.
—Geoffrey Stone, University of Chicago law professor quoted in editorial entitled "King George," *Progressive* (January 31, 2006)

It's one of the basics of librarianship, to respect privacy, to understand that what people read isn't necessarily what they believe, and to give them the ability to come in and find information without any chilling effect.
—Gail Weymouth, of the Vermont Library Association on the encroachments of the Patriot Act, quoted in "Defender of the Free Word," *Mother Jones* (January/February 2004)

[George] Orwell's fear was government monitoring, but the real danger today is corporate monitoring: companies using technology to keep track of everything about you.
—Dave Wilson, "Corporate Monitoring Is a Growing Privacy Woe," *Los Angeles Times* (July 12, 2001)

THE CONSERVATIVE IMPULSE

Absolutes

Absolutism means never having to say you're sorry.
—Rosa Brooks, "The Dark Side of Faith," *Los Angeles Times* (October 1, 2005)

There is no absolute knowledge. And those who claim it, whether they are scientists or dogmatists, open the door to tragedy. All information is imperfect. We have to treat it with humility.
—Jacob Bronowski, *The Ascent of Man* (1973)

Long before cultural relativism appeared, tribes were killing each other in the cheerful, absolute certainty that their god or gods wanted them to massacre their neighbors. That's the reality of those "moral absolutes" right-wingers proclaim as the grounding of decent behavior.
—John Dolan, "Why Did We Let Bush Try to Bring Wal-Mart to Iraq?" AlterNet (September 16, 2006)

In the United States . . . reason is on the defensive as we head backward toward creationism and religious absolutism . . . Never before has an American chief executive worked deliberately to foment a fundamentalist absolutism that is ultimately tribal, theocratic, antiscientific, and incompatible with pluralist democracy.
—Robert Kuttner, "An Attack on American Tolerance," *Boston Globe* (November 17, 2004)

Thuggish absolutism explains why America has become a dark and ominous place.
—Dennis Loy Johnson, *What Do We Do Now* (2004)

Religion is so frequently a source of confusion in political life, and so frequently dangerous to democracy, precisely because it introduces absolutes into the realm of relative values.
—Reinhold Niebuhr, quoted in "Forgetting Reinhold Niebuhr," *New York Times* (September 18, 2005)

The Bill of Rights decoupled religion from the state, in part because so many religions were steeped in an absolutist frame of mind—each convinced that it alone had a monopoly on the truth and therefore eager for the state to impose this truth on others.
—Carl Sagan, *The Demon-Haunted World: Science as a Candle in the Dark* (1995)

Liberalism regards all absolutes with profound skepticism, including both moral imperatives and final solutions.
—Arthur M. Schlesinger, Jr., *The Crisis of Confidence* (1969)

Religion is absolutism, and absolutism goes to war with anything it abuts. Turn on the Christian television—cable is full of it—and listen to them denounce "humanistic relativism." What is relativism? It is moderation, it is accommodation, it is the rule of reason.
—Nicholas von Hoffman, "Democrats Should Oppose Empowering the Pious," *New York Observer* (December 1, 2004)

People escape into absolutism the way they retreated into fallout shelters during the Cold War.
—Lauren Sandler, *Righteous* (2006)

If believers feel that their faith is trivialized and their true selves compromised by a society that will not give religious imperatives special weight, their problem is not that secularists are antidemocratic but that democracy is anti-absolutist.
—Ellen Willis, "Freedom from Religion," *Nation* (February 1, 2001)

Fundamentalists deal with absolutes. Their eternal certainties make them formidable campaigners and awful negotiators—it is difficult to cut a bargain with divine truth.
—Gary Younge, "God Help America: U.S. Law Insists on the Separation of Church and State. So Why Does Religion Now Govern?" *Guardian (UK)* (August 25, 2003)

Arrogance

How can we humans imagine that we are the crowning achievement of an Intelligent Designer?
—Caroline Arnold, "Pros and Cons, and Our National Agenda," *Common Dreams* (October 7, 2005)

There is a sense that tells us it's wrong to presume to speak for God or to claim God's sanction of our particular legislation and his rejection of all other positions. Most of us are offended when we see religion being trivialized by its appearance in political throw-away pamphlets.
—Mario Cuomo, in his speech at the University of Notre Dame (September 13, 1984)

One of the central features of what I call a phallic stance is the denial of weakness—the repudiation of dependency and the need for collaboration in all its forms. . . . Instead of this kind of behavior being pigheaded arrogance, it's framed as manly resoluteness.
—Stephen J. Ducat, quoted in "The Wimp Factor," AlterNet (October 29, 2004)

We don't want to force you to have an abortion or to marry someone of the same gender, whereas you do want to close out those possibilities for us. Which is more arrogant?
—Michael Kinsley, "Am I Blue? I Apologize for Everything I believe In. May I Go Now?" *Los Angeles Times* (November 7, 2004)

The most unattractive trait of the American empire is American arrogance, which the president embodies. . . . It is not simply that we have a good system. It is the system everyone else should have. It is the best system, and we are the best people.
—Anna Quindlen, "We've Been Here Before," *Newsweek* (October 31, 2005)

We have judges who talk about the framers as though they played squash with them regularly: It reminds you of the proprietary, slightly arrogant way in which born-again Christians talk about God. They know Him; you don't.
—Anna Quindlen, "Justice and Mercy," *New York Times* (July 29, 1990)

I guess when you believe you're driving God's car, and when you believe He's giving you global positioning, and when you believe He's right there in the back seat blurting out directions, you don't care so much if you run people over in the process.
—Matthew Rothschild, "Bush's Press Conference Betrays Callousness," *Progressive* (January 29, 2005)

There is no greater human presumption than to read the mind of the Almighty, and no more dangerous individual than the one who has convinced himself that he is executing the Almighty's will.
—Arthur M. Schlesinger, Jr., "Forgetting Reinhold Niebuhr," *New York Times* (September 18, 2005)

When people in the name of religion claim to have sole possession of truth, they have crossed the line from faith to arrogance.
—Paul Simon, *P.S.: The Autobiography of Paul Simon* (1999)

There were unconfirmed reports yesterday that the United States is not the center of the world.
—Norman Solomon, "Is the USA the Center of the World?" AlterNet (December 13, 2006)

If God is ultimately unknowable, then how can we be so certain of what God's real position is on, say, the fate of Terri Schiavo? Or the morality of contraception? Or the role of women? Or the love of a gay couple?
—Andrew Sullivan, "My Problem with Christianity," *Time* (May 15, 2006)

A troubling arrogance is in the air among the nation's most fortunate.
—Jim Webb, "Class Struggle," *Wall Street Journal* (November 15, 2006)

Our leaders have taken it for granted, and planted that belief in the minds of many people, that we are entitled, because of our moral superiority, to dominate the world.
—Howard Zinn, "America's Blinders," *Progressive* (April 2006)

Authoritarianism

Authoritarianism . . . constitutes the prevailing thinking and behavior among conservatives.
—John Dean, *Conservatives Without a Conscience* (2006)

It makes no sense to fight religious authoritarianism abroad while letting it take over at home.
—Michelle Goldberg, "Saving Secular Society," *In These Times* (May 16, 2006)

Women's liberation, if it abolishes the patriarchal family, will abolish a necessary substructure of the authoritarian state.
—Germaine Greer, *The Female Eunuch* (1970)

In child rearing it would unquestionably be easier if a child were to do something because we say so. The authoritarian method does expedite things, but it does not produce independent functioning. If a child . . . merely conforms out of coercion or conditioning, he has no tools to use, no resources to apply in the next situation that confronts him.
—Elaine Heffner, *Mothering* (1978)

America today is in danger. It faces the threat by a radical, authoritarian right wing that refers to itself as "conservative," as if it were preserving and promoting American values. In fact, it has been trampling on them.
—George Lakoff, *Thinking Points: Communicating Our Values and Vision* (2006)

However sugarcoated and ambiguous, every form of authoritarianism must start with a belief in some group's greater right to power, whether that right is justified by sex, race, class, religion or all four.
—Gloria Steinem, *Outrageous Acts and Everyday Rebellions* (1983)

Certainty

People want certainty. The right offers it. The left doesn't. And we can't. Certainty isn't part of our package.
—Rev. Clare Butterfield, "Religious Left Needn't Be Ashamed to Speak Up," *Chicago Sun-Times* (November 24, 2004)

After 9/11, good old moral certainty was back—or so it seemed. Conservatives could once again insist that there was only one moral code in our world, as eternally true as $2 + 2 = 4$.
—Ira Chernus, "Voting Their Fears," *ProgressiveTrail.org* (December 15, 2004)

People who live by religious certainties don't have to waste time with recalcitrant facts or moral doubts.
—Maureen Dowd, "Casualties of Faith," *New York Times* (October 12, 2004)

Certainty is the narcotic of the right wing.
—Rev. Howard Gordon, quoted in "I Want My Faith Back," *Arkansas Times* (December 23, 2004)

The spirit of liberty is the spirit which is not too sure that it is right.
—Learned Hand, in a speech in Central Park, New York City (May 21, 1944)

It's one thing to be certain. But you can be certain and wrong. . . . Certainty sometimes can get you in trouble.
—John Kerry, in his first presidential debate with George W. Bush, Coral Gables, Florida (September 30, 2004)

Changing one's mind is not a sin. Indeed, it is a way of saying that I'm wiser today than I was yesterday.
—George McGovern, *The Essential America: Our Founders and the Liberal Tradition* (2004)

Men insist most vehemently upon their certainties when their hold on them has been shaken. Frantic orthodoxy is a method for obscuring doubt.
—Reinhold Niebuhr, *Does Civilization Need Religion?* (1927)

Conformity

Has there ever been a society which has died of dissent? Several have died of conformity in our lifetime.
—Jacob Bronowski, *Science and Human Values* (1961)

The reward for conformity was that everyone liked you except yourself.
—Rita Mae Brown, *Venus Envy* (1993)

Whoso would be a man must be a nonconformist.
—Ralph Waldo Emerson, *The Essay on Self-Reliance* (1908)

Conformity is the jailer of freedom and the enemy of growth.
—John F. Kennedy, in his address to the U.N. General Assembly (September 25, 1961)

Orthodoxy means not thinking—not needing to think.
—George Orwell, *1984* (1949)

The voices of conformity speak so loudly out there. Don't listen. People will tell you what you ought to think and how you ought to feel. They will tell you what to read and how to live. They will urge you to take jobs that they themselves loathe, and to follow safe paths that they themselves find tedious.
—Anna Quindlen, in a commencement address at Colby College (May 28, 2006)

As corporations grow larger and advertising grows more sophisticated, culture in general glides more than ever into groupthink.
—Anneli Rufus, *Party of One* (2003)

When you think of the long and gloomy history of man, you will find more hideous crimes have been committed in the name of obedience than have been committed in the name of rebellion.
—C. P. Snow, *The Moral Un-Neutrality of Science* (1961)

The hired preachers of all sects, creeds, and religions never do, and never can, teach any thing but what is in conformity with the opinions of those who pay them.
—Frances Wright, *Course of Popular Lectures* (1829)

Conservatism

What is it about conservative administrations that lead them into disgrace and indictment? Incompetence isn't at the core of these scandals—ideology is.
—Robert L. Borosage, "Why Conservatives Can't Govern," *TomPaine.com* (March 19, 2007)

Who knew, in 2000, that "compassionate conservatism" meant bigger government, unrestricted government spending, government intrusion in personal matters, government ineptitude, and cronyism in disaster relief?
—Christopher Buckley, son of conservative icon William F. Buckley, "Let's Quit While We're Behind," *Washington Monthly* (October 2006)

Conservatism clings to what has been established, fearing that, once we begin to question the beliefs we have inherited, all the values of life will be destroyed.
—Morris Raphael Cohen, *The Faith of a Liberal* (1946)

This is the real danger of conservatism—not so much its resistance to change, but its denial of even the possibility of change.
—Jane Fonda, "A Powerful Media Can Stop a War," Women's Media Center (January 16, 2007)

These are the days when men of all social disciplines and all political faiths seek the comfortable and the accepted; when the man of controversy is looked upon as a disturbing influence; when originality is taken to be a mark of instability; and when, in minor modification of the scriptural parable, the bland lead the bland.
—John Kenneth Galbraith, *The Affluent Society* (1958)

[Conservatism] is centrally dependent upon hatred of an Enemy, foreign or domestic—the Terrorist, the Immigrant, the Faggot, the Raghead, and most of all, the Liberal.
—Glen Greenwald, "Ann Coulter's 'Faggot' Remark Smears Mitt Romney Too," *AlterNet* (March 3, 2007)

Beginning with President Ronald Reagan in the 1980s, conservative governments have focused on reducing the obligations of the wealthy and increasing the burdens on the poor.
—Rev. Jesse Jackson, "Time to Push New Congress to Revive U.S.," *Chicago Sun-Times* (January 2, 2007)

If you think government is part of the problem, you can't govern well when there's a crisis.
—Joe Klein, interviewed by Onnesha Roychoudhuri, "Faking It: How America Lost Politics," AlterNet (May 2, 2006)

The political axis that currently controls Congress and the White House is an alliance between the preachers and the plutocrats—between the religious right, which hates gays, abortion, and the theory of evolution, and the economic right, which hates Social Security, Medicare, and taxes on rich people.
—Paul Krugman, "Things Fall Apart," *New York Times* (October 2, 2006)

Why do I want to see movement conservatism crushed? Partly because the movement is fundamentally undemocratic; its leaders don't accept the legitimacy of opposition.
—Paul Krugman, "The Great Revulsion," *New York Times* (November 10, 2006)

The central political agenda of America's conservative forces is to protect corporate power.
—Rabbi Michael Lerner, "Faith-Based Defunding of the Public Sector," *Tikkun* (May/June 2001)

Orthodox religious thinking invariably subscribes to power relations and ideologies that society as a whole has rejected. Women must bow their heads to their husbands' commands; homosexuals must transcend their unholy lust; children must submit to physical discipline.
—Carol Lloyd, "Two Nations under God," *Salon* (January 26, 1999)

American conservatism [has become] the primary author of the very social disorder that it routinely rails against, and that Republicans have the gall to run against. The party of family values? Please.
—Harold Meyerson, regarding pro-business, anti-family policies making workers more economically insecure, "'Family Values' Chutzpah," *Washington Post* (March 7, 2007)

American conservatism defends the right of corporations to ship jobs overseas.
—Harold Meyerson, "Card Check's Reality Check," *American Prospect* (June 21, 2007)

Please identify one right-wing idea that has moved American society forward.
—Ted Rall, *Wake Up, You're Liberal!* (2004)

No intellectual phenomenon has been more surprising in recent years than the revival in the United States of conservatism as a respectable social philosophy.
—Arthur M. Schlesinger, Jr. quoted in "A Historian Who Saw Beyond the Past," *Washington Post* (March 2, 2007)

No one, not even conservatives, doubts that conservatism is now in deep trouble: divided, uncertain of itself, and with a lot of explaining to do for the fiasco in Iraq. Yet the exhaustion of conservatism is not tantamount to a liberal revival.
—Paul Starr, "Why Liberalism Works," *American Prospect* (April 4, 2007)

All conservatism begins with loss. If we never knew loss, we would never feel the need to conserve.
—Andrew Sullivan, *The Conservative Soul* (2006)

The reactionaries hold that government policies should be designed for the special benefit of small groups of people who occupy positions of wealth and influence. Their theory seems to be that if these groups are prosperous, they will pass along some of their prosperity to the rest of us. This can be described as the "trickle-down theory."
—Harry S. Truman, in his speech in St. Paul as part of the Truman Day Celebration (November 3, 1949)

Conservative governance failed not because of a run of bad luck or a few bad apples, but because it is deficient at its core.
—Paul Waldman, "Democrats, Don't Wimp Out," *TomPaine.com* (November 15, 2006)

Democracies feature free presses, free speech, the rule of law, independent judiciaries, legislative oversight, and other measures to ensure that laws and treaties are followed. This is, to the conservative mind, a weakness.
—Matthew Yglesias, "Rogue State," *American Prospect* (September 26, 2006)

The Conservative Character

Too many people of a generally conservative temperament, people who value traditions, customs, and institutions, have been fooled by the current cynical use of the word "conservative" into identifying their own interests with those of the political right, which today . . . actually espouses a program of radical change.
—Brooke Allen, "What Orwell Saw," *Los Angeles Times* (May 1, 2006)

The idea that conservatives trust the market while progressives want the government is a myth. Conservatives simply are not honest about the ways in which they want the government to intervene to distribute income upwards.
—Dean Baker, *The Conservative Nanny State: How the Wealthy Use the Government to Stay Rich and Get Richer* (2006)

A philosophical conservative is someone willing to pay the price of other people's suffering for his principles.
—E. L. Doctorow, in a commencement address at Brandeis University (May 21, 1989)

Men are conservatives when they are least vigorous.
—Ralph Waldo Emerson, *Essays, Second Series* (1844)

The people who are calling themselves conservative have actually become the radicals in this society.
—Bob Herbert, quoted in interview "Times Columnist Bob Herbert Views the American Dream: But Can It Still Be Found?" *BuzzFlash* (May 3, 2005)

Conservatives have historically seen people falling through the cracks in society and said that's the way things work, survival of the fittest.
—Jim Hightower, quoted in "Texas Talker," *Pacific Sun* (March 20, 1992)

Conservatives command the presidency, Congress, the courts, major news outlets, and the majority of corporations; they appear to have the country comfortably in their pocket. What fuels their rage?
—Russell Jacoby, "The New PC: Crybaby Conservatives," *Nation* (March 16, 2005)

At their essence, conservatives are on guard, bristling, armed with a righteous anger, prone to mockery of their enemies, sure of themselves, unwilling to criticize America, especially by comparing it to anyplace else. The attacks of Sept. 11 only confirmed their world view: We are constantly at risk.
—Roland Merullo, "A Puzzling America," *Boston Globe* (September 20, 2004)

Conservatives are driven by rage. Progressives are driven by guilt. Conservatives suffer no moral qualms when they engage in dirty tactics. The ends justify the means. Civilization is at stake. Progressives worry that if they do evil, they will become evil.
—David Morris, "Fighting Dirty," AlterNet (December 20, 2004)

If conservatives had carried the day, blacks would still be in the back of the bus, women would be barefoot and pregnant, medical care would be on a cash-only basis, there'd be mouse feet in your breakfast cereal, and workers would still be sleeping next to their machines.
—Katha Pollitt, "Let's Not Devalue Ourselves," *Nation* (July 29, 2004)

Honest conservatives believe in the decentralization of power.
—Bernie Sanders, quoted in interview "Independent Congressman Bernie Sanders of Vermont," *BuzzFlash* (June 15, 2005)

Conservatives seem ready to throw everything away in order to maintain dominance—the Constitution, the good opinion of the rest of the world, the lives and limbs and sanity of our soldiers, the health and habitability of the Earth, and their own claims to common sense and decency.
—Jane Smiley, "Conservatives Cost a Lot of Money," AlterNet (March 22, 2007)

Conservatives supported slavery, conservatives opposed women's suffrage, conservatives supported Jim Crow, conservatives opposed the forty-hour work week and the abolishment of child labor . . . all the major advancements of freedom and justice in our history were . . . opposed by conservatives.
—Paul Waldman, "It's The Conservatism, Stupid," *TomPaine.com* (July 12, 2006)

Unlike liberals, conservatives don't simply criticize specific candidates or pieces of legislation, they attack their opponents' entire ideological worldview.
—Paul Waldman, "The Liberal Moderates," *American Prospect* (October 18, 2005)

Contemporary conservatism is a walking contradiction. Unable to shrink government but unwilling to improve it, conservatives attempt to split the difference, expanding government for political gain.
—Alan Wolfe, "Why Conservatives Can't Govern," *Washington Monthly* (July/August 2006)

Conservative Persecution Complex

The operative condition for the twenty-first-century American "conservative" is false indignation.
—R. J. Eskow, "Pick Your Favorite Phony Conservative Outrage," *Huffington Post* (March 21, 2006)

Understanding themselves as victims besieged by a hateful world absolves conservatives of responsibility for what goes on around them. It excuses them for their failures . . . blaming it all on a deprived liberal elite.
—Thomas Frank, *What's the Matter with Kansas?* (2004)

Wealth is today concentrated in fewer hands than it has been since the 1920s; workers have less power over the conditions under which they toil than ever before in our lifetimes; and the corporation has become the most powerful actor in our world. Yet that rightward shift . . . sells itself as a war against elites, a righteous uprising of the little guy against an obnoxious upper class.
—Thomas Frank, "The America That Will Vote for Bush," *Le Monde Diplomatique* (February 2004)

Conservatives shouldn't assert the prerogatives of victory and then claim the compensations of defeat as well. You can't oppress us and simultaneously complain that we are oppressing you.
—Michael Kinsley, "Am I Blue? I Apologize for Everything I Believe In. May I Go Now?" *Los Angeles Times* (November 7, 2004)

Remember the whiny, insecure kid in nursery school, the one who always thought everyone was out to get him, and was always running to the teacher with complaints? Chances are he grew up to be a conservative.
—Kurt Kleiner, from a study in the *Journal of Research into Personality*, "How to Spot a Baby Conservative," *Toronto Star* (March 19, 2006)

Conservatives have an odd persecution complex. They control Congress, the White House, and intelligence agencies; soon will dominate the Supreme Court; and can buy just about any conservative journalist for hire. Still not good enough. Greed is a sin, guys.
—Rhonda Chriss Lokeman, "How Right-Wing Grinches Try to Steal Christmas," *Knight Ridder* (December 14, 2005)

Conservatives—whether they're creationists or intelligent design theorists—probably represent a majority in our society. But they also love to present themselves as martyrs.
—Ronald Numbers, interviewed by Steve Paulson, "Seeing the Light—of Science," *Salon* (January 2, 2007)

The Christian Taliban is going too far . . . When your claim to be victims of secularism rests on Wal-Mart greeters wishing shoppers "Happy Holidays," you are clearly a bunch of great big babies.
—Katha Pollitt, "It Wasn't All Bad," *Nation* (January 9, 2006)

Happy holidays! Have I just offended you? If you are a member of the American Family Association, the Catholic League for Religious and Civil Rights, or the Committee to Save Merry Christmas, I probably have.
—Mary Zeiss Stange, "Christmas, Pagans and Religious Divergence," *USA Today* (December 11, 2006)

The angry cry of the victim is the lexicon of the conservative media.
—Paul Waldman, "The Right's Siege Mentality," *TomPaine.com* (April 25, 2005)

Many Christians are joining today's scramble for the status of victims.
—George Will, conservative columnist, "Religious Americans' Persecution Complex Is Unrealistic," *Deseret Morning News* (May 15, 2005)

Conservatives are apparently threatened by the rather sensible ongoing effort to acknowledge that not everyone on earth celebrates Christmas or considers it a religious holiday. Such defensiveness smacks of insecurity and seems to indicate that poor, beleaguered Christmas would collapse without incessant buoying by retail chains and the government.
—Dianne Williamson, "Christmas Declared Under Siege; Conservatives Oppose Inclusive Holiday Cheer," *Telegram & Gazette* (December 6, 2005)

Since contemporary conservatives get their political energy from angry voices of rage and revenge, they will always blame others for the failures built into their ideology.
—Alan Wolfe, "Why Conservatives Can't Govern," *Washington Monthly* (July/August 2006)

Domination

No nation can make itself secure by seeking supremacy over all others.
—Kofi A. Annan, "What I've Learned," *Washington Post* (December 11, 2006)

Controlling others through force, fear, coercion, or deceit is what war and imperialism are about, what racism, homophobia, anti-abortionism, religious fanaticism, slavery, and torture are about.
—Caroline Arnold, "Status and Syntax: Who Controls? Who's Controlled?" *Common Dreams* (November 13, 2005)

In every age of this world's history, the kings and emperors and czars and potentates, in alliance with the priests, have sought by all the means at their command to keep the people in darkness that they might perpetuate the power in which they riot and revel in luxury while the great mass are in a state of slavery and degradation.
—Eugene Debs, in a 1908 speech, quoted in *Debs: His Life, Writings and Speeches* (2002)

The increasing domination of corporations over virtually every dimension of our lives—economic, political, cultural, even spiritual—poses a fundamental threat to the well-being of our society.
—Lee Drutman and Charlie Cray, "The People's Business," *In These Times* (February 18, 2005)

Domination—either in a personal or a global context—can never be a permanent condition. It's a relational state. It's dependent on having somebody in a subordinate position. That means you could be manly today, but you're not going to be manly tomorrow unless you've got somebody to push around and control, whether that is an abused wife or another country.
—Stephen J. Ducat, *BuzzFlash* (March 2, 2005)

All domination involves invasion—at times physical and overt, at times camouflaged, with the invader assuming the role of helping friend.
—Paulo Freire, *Pedagogy of the Oppressed* (1970)

Respect . . . implies the absence of exploitation. I want the loved person to grow and unfold for his own sake, and in his own ways, and not for the purpose of serving me.
—Erich Fromm, *The Art of Loving* (1956)

Week by week, month by month, year by year, [the modern corporation] exercises a greater influence on our livelihood and the way we live than unions, universities, politicians, the government.
—John Kenneth Galbraith, *The Age of Uncertainty* (1977)

Fearful people are more dependent, more easily manipulated and controlled, more susceptible to deceptively simple, strong, tough measures and hard-line postures . . . They may accept and even welcome repression if it promises to relieve their insecurities.
—George Gerbner, quoted in "So Far, No Good," AlterNet (March 16, 2006)

One of the most crucial tasks in a democratic society is the act of limiting the power that corporations have in determining what happens in, and to, our schools.
—Alfie Kohn, "The 500-Pound Gorilla," *Phi Delta Kappan* (October 2002)

This is the era of entrenched exploitation. All sacrifices will be made by working people and the poor, and the vast bulk of the benefits will accrue to the rich.
—Bob Herbert, "The Era of Exploitation," *New York Times* (March 25, 2005)

Where a system of oppression has become institutionalized, it is unnecessary for individuals to be oppressive.
—Florynce Kennedy, "Institutionalized Oppression vs. the Female," *Sisterhood Is Powerful* (1970)

Employers are getting away with murder, underpaying and overworking people too vulnerable to complain.
—Betsy Leondar-Wright, "Widening the Racial Wealth Gap," *Common Dreams* (May 31, 2006)

The fatherland is abusing the motherland.
—Casey Martin, protest sign used at an anti-war rally in Lancaster, Pennsylvania (March 9, 2006)

However muted its present appearance may be, sexual dominion obtains nevertheless as perhaps the most pervasive ideology of our culture and provides its most fundamental concept of power.
—Kate Millett, *Sexual Politics* (1970)

The life-fate of the modern individual depends not only upon the family into which he was born or which he enters by marriage, but increasingly upon the corporation in which he spends the most alert hours of his best years.
—C. Wright Mills, *The Power Elite* (1956)

The "otherizing" of women is the oldest oppression known to our species, and it's the model, the template, for all other oppressions.
—Robin Morgan, *The Word of a Woman* (1992)

Corporations have become the dominant institution of our time, occupying the position of the church of the Middle Ages and the nation-state of the past two centuries.
—Richard Pascale, "The False Security of Employability," *Fast Company* (April 1996)

Silence is the voice of complicity.
—Protest sign

The worried young white men I've met on college campuses in the last year have internalized the newest myth of American race relations, and it has made them bitter. It is called affirmative action, a.k.a. the systematic oppression of white men.
—Anna Quindlen, "The Great White Myth," *New York Times* (January 15, 1992)

As the project of corporate globalization increases the disparity between the rich and the poor, as the world grows more and more restive, corporations on the prowl for sweetheart deals need repressive governments to quell the mutinies in the servants' quarters.
—Arundhati Roy, *An Ordinary Person's Guide to Empire* (2004)

Loan sharking is an odious practice whether it is performed by street corner thugs or the CEOs of large banks. Charging economically vulnerable Americans outrageous interest rates and fees is simply not acceptable.
—Bernie Sanders, "The Great Credit Card Scam," *TomPaine.com.* (December 3, 2004)

The forces now dominating America are moving relentlessly to shift power from the weak and vulnerable to those already mighty, and to transfer wealth from those who have less to those already rich beyond any rational need for more.
—Andrew Bard Schmookler, "The Concept of Evil," *Common Dreams* (November 9, 2005)

To exploit a person is to make money out of her without giving her an equivalent return.
—George Bernard Shaw, *The Intelligent Woman's Guide to Socialism, Capitalism, Sovietism, and Fascism* (1928)

2,245 Dead. How Many More?
—Cindy Sheehan's T-shirt message, referring to the number of U.S. troops killed in Iraq. This shirt prompted police to drag her out of the U.S. Capitol and arrest her just prior to Bush's State of the Union address (January 31, 2006)

If ever an industry needed to be more tightly regulated, it's credit card lending. A shark is a shark, even if it wears a suit and works in a building with marble floors.
—Jim Sollisch, "Credit Card Sharks," *Washington Post* (February 5, 2006)

I freed a thousand slaves. I could have freed a thousand more if only they knew they were slaves.
—Harriet Tubman, quoted in "Purchased Pulpits and Spiritual Exploitations," *Black Commentator* (March 3, 2005)

The ultraconservatives want control of the country. They want to tell the rest of us how to live, where to pray, what to think, how to love.
—Cynthia Tucker, "Right-Wing Extremists Turn Against Public," *Atlanta Journal-Constitution* (February 21, 1999)

False Piety

The louder he talked of his honor, the faster we counted our spoons.
—Ralph Waldo Emerson, *Worship in the Conduct of Life* (1860)

It is time we recognized the boundless narcissism and self-deceit of the saved. It is time we acknowledged how disgraceful it is for the survivors of a catastrophe to believe themselves spared by a loving God, while this same God drowned infants in their cribs.
—Sam Harris, *Letter to a Christian Nation* (2006)

Democrats should focus not on the public display of their faith, but on the will to fight for what they believe in.
—Rev. Jesse Jackson, "False Piety Is Wrong Cure for Dems," *Chicago Sun-Times* (July 18, 2006)

One of the most powerful ways of bypassing critical rationality in America has long been the posture of religious piety and moralism.
—Andrew Bard Schmookler, "A Nation Deceived," *Baltimore Sun* (October 27, 2004)

In the current political milieu, private beliefs and personal prayer aren't sufficient. To really do the trick, faith must be flaunted. What good is religiosity if you don't wear it on your sleeve and get a lot of good press?
—Norman Solomon, "Holy Smoke & Mirrors: Lieberman and the Rise of Centrist Theocrats," FAIR's "Media Beat" (August 10, 2000)

As the pietistical pose becomes the single stance in public life, brace yourself for the . . . phony reverential attitude, the lowering of the eyes, the clasping of the hands in a way which denotes piety and pure living.
—Nicholas von Hoffman, "Democrats Should Oppose Empowering the Pious," *New York Observer* (December 1, 2004)

Fascism

[Fascism is] a system of government that exercises a dictatorship of the extreme right, typically through the merging of state and business leadership, together with belligerent nationalism.
—*American Heritage Dictionary* (1983)

The exaltation of big business at the expense of the citizen was a central characteristic of government policy in Germany and Italy in the years before those countries were chewed to bits and spat out by fascism.
—Paul Bigioni, "The Real Threat of Fascism," *Common Dreams* (September 30, 2005)

If there will be a "revolution" in America today, it will no doubt be a move towards some variety of fascism.
—Noam Chomsky, *American Power and the New Mandarins* (2002)

One aspect of modern life which has gone far to stifle men is the rapid growth of tremendous corporations. Enormous spiritual sacrifices are made in the transformation of shopkeepers into employees. . . . The disappearance of free enterprise has led to a submergence of the individual in the impersonal corporation in much the same manner as he has been submerged in the state in other lands.
—William O. Douglas, quoted in *Democracy and Finance* (1940)

Fascists strut, while conservatives lounge.
—Terry Eagleton, "A Carnival of Unreason," *New Statesman* (May 3, 2004)

Totalitarian thought cannot bear to be disputed.
—André Glucksmann, "Clash of Civilizations? No, of Philosophies," *Le Monde* (March 3, 2006)

Hitler and Mussolini each came to power through democracy.
—Robert D. Kaplan, "Was Democracy Just a Moment?" *Atlantic Monthly* (December 1997)

While communism is the control of business by government, fascism is the control of government by business.
—Robert F. Kennedy, Jr., "Kennedy: Fascist America," *Common Dreams* (January 22, 2005)

The rise of fascism across Europe in the 1930s offers many informative lessons on how corporate power can undermine a democracy. In Spain, Germany, and Italy, industrialists allied themselves with right-wing leaders who used the provocation of terrorist attacks, continual wars, and invocations of patriotism and homeland security to tame the press, muzzle criticism by opponents, and turn government over to corporate control.
—Robert F. Kennedy, Jr., "Crimes Against Nature," *Rolling Stone* (December 11, 2003)

You have to understand the difference between free-market capitalism . . . and the kind of corporate crony capitalism where you have large corporations running our government. There's a name for that, and the name is fascism.
—Robert F. Kennedy, Jr., quoted in "RFK Jr. Uses the F-Word," *National Review Online* (July 27, 2004)

Aaron Sarver: "How does the America of George W. Bush differ from the Italy of Mussolini or the Spain of Franco?"
Lewis Lapham: "We don't yet have as many parades."
—Interview exchange in "Lapham's Way," *In These Times* (December 14, 2005)

Under fascism, the goodness of humanity is replaced by the goodness of Us in opposition to Them.
—Rabbi Michael Lerner, *The Left Hand of God* (2006)

When fascism comes to America, it will be wrapped in the flag, carrying the cross.
—Sinclair Lewis, *It Can't Happen Here* (1935)

I now refer to the "military-industrial-religious complex." That's what we're fighting.
—George E. Lowe, quoted in interview "Can 'It' Happen Here? Hasn't 'It' Already? A Fascist Christian America," *BuzzFlash* (June 10, 2005)

What qualities would one find in a Christo-Fascist? Greed, hubris, and self righteousness would probably top the list.
—Jason Miller, "The Iron Fist of Jesus," OpEdNews (December 8, 2005)

Fascism is on the ascendant in the USA, rising cloaked under the mantle of the Grand Old Party.
—Amanda Osborne, "Fascism on the Rise in America," *Washington Dispatch* (November 9, 2004)

Fascism is an ideology that favors dictatorial government, the obsessive creation of an economic climate favorable to big business, repression of political opposition, scapegoating of political enemies and ethnic minorities, and extreme nationalism channeled into a policy of military expansionism.
—Ted Rall, *Wake Up, You're Liberal!* (2004)

The liberty of democracy is not safe if the people tolerate the growth of private power to a point where it becomes stronger than the democratic state itself. That, in essence, is fascism.
—Franklin D. Roosevelt, in a message to Congress (April 29, 1938)

Fascism is the ultimate code of the hoodlum.
—George Steiner, *Language and Silence* (1967)

The best safeguard against fascism is to establish social justice to the maximum possible extent.
—Arnold J. Toynbee, *The Toynbee-Ikeda Dialogue* (1976)

[Fascists] claim to be super-patriots, but they would destroy every liberty guaranteed by the Constitution. They demand free enterprise, but are the spokesmen for monopoly and vested interest.
—Henry Wallace, vice president of the United States, "Wallace Defines American Fascism," *New York Times* (April 9, 1944)

The American fascist would prefer not to use violence. His method is to poison the channels of public information.
—Henry Wallace, "Wallace Defines American Fascism," *New York Times* (April 9, 1944)

Fearmongering

The phrase "Islamo-fascists" has spread around the [mainstream media] like a bad case of clap in a Texas whorehouse. Once again, the Republicans are being allowed to create a brand new scary enemy just in time for elections.
—John Atcheson, "What We Learned from Mainstream Media Last Week (and What We Didn't)," *Common Dreams* (August 14, 2006)

When quasi-hysterical fear-mongering replaces reasonable debate, dark forces can be set in motion that outrun anyone's intentions.
—James Carroll, "The Risks of Waging 'Culture War,'" *Boston Globe* (March 9, 2004)

Why have most people submitted so willingly to a new political order organized around fear? Other nations have confronted terrorism of a more sustained nature without coming thoroughly unhinged.
—William Greider, "Under the Banner of the 'War' on Terror," *Nation* (June 3, 2004)

Whether it's the specter of North Korean nukes or Iraqi insurgents making their way to Main Street, USA, fear is a powerful, universal emotion—always there to be exploited.
—Arianna Huffington, "freeSpeech: Arianna Huffington," *CBS Evening News* (October 24, 2006)

Fear and fear mongering have had a long history in America, stretching back to the witchcraft hysteria in colonial Salem, Massachusetts.
—George McGovern, *The Essential America: Our Founders and the Liberal Tradition* (2004)

Deceiving your entire nation and frightening children and adults with images of nuclear explosions in order to get them to support a bloody invasion of another country is not politics; it is a crime.
—James Moore, "The Criminalization of Criminals," *Huffington Post* (October 28, 2005)

As long as Americans remain susceptible to easily provoked fears—of losing their jobs to immigrants, their kids to perverts, their lives to terrorists—and as long as there are wealthy corporations and religious control freaks eager to exploit them—the Republican Party and its allies have a bright future.
—Ted Rall, "Conservatism Is Dead. Long Live Fictional Conservatism!" *Common Dreams* (March 21, 2007)

Greed and Selfishness

Conservatism, in the lump, is a euphemism for selfishness.
—Grant Allen, quoted in the *Westminster Gazette* (1894)

It's nearly impossible for the average citizen to grasp the scale of ExxonMobil Corp.'s huge profits. . . . Overall 2005 revenues of $371 billion amounted to more than $1 billion a day!
—Gar Alperovitz, "Return Oil Profits to American People," *Baltimore Sun* (February 9, 2006)

We believe the mortal sin of the Republicans under Bush is that in the end, they appeal to our selfishness.
—James Carville and Paul Begala, *Take It Back* (2006)

Throughout the 1980s, we did hear too much about individual gain and the ethos of selfishness and greed. We did not hear enough about how to be a good member of a community, to define the common good, and to repair the social contract.
—Hillary Rodham Clinton, quoted from a commencement address at the University of Pennsylvania, *New York Times* (May 18, 1993)

An extravagant narcissism marks our cultural age.
—Marie Cocco, "Narcissism Ascendant," *Truthdig* (December 21, 2006)

Greed is a bottomless pit which exhausts the person in an endless effort to satisfy the need without ever reaching satisfaction.
—Erich Fromm, *Escape from Freedom* (1941)

Wealthy nations are greedier than ever and increasingly dependent on poor ones to stay poor and powerless in order to provide cheap labor and resources.
—Rachel Giese, "Our Greed Causes Third World Suffering," *Toronto Star* (July 19, 2001)

It is not good to take from the poor and give to the rich, and that's exactly what this country is doing today.
—Father Andrew Greeley, "America's Disease *is* Greed," *Chicago Sun-Times* (August 20, 2004)

The selfish spirit of commerce knows no country, and feels no passion or principle but that of gain.
—Thomas Jefferson, in a letter to Larkin Smith (1809)

The pursuit of corporate profit should no longer come at the expense of various elements of the public interest including the environment, human rights, the public safety, the dignity of employees, and the welfare of our communities.
—Robert C. Hinkley, "Corporate Values," *Common Dreams* (March 12, 2002)

Tens of millions of Americans feel betrayed by a society that seems to place materialism and selfishness above moral values.
—Rabbi Michael Lerner, "The Democrats Need a Spiritual Left," *Common Dreams* (November 4, 2004)

Predatory lending pumps wealth out of communities that can least afford it and into the coffers of some of the wealthiest companies in the country.
—Bobbi Murray, "Hunting the Predators," *Nation* (June 27, 2002)

Creation is God's gift to all. . . . To allow the appropriation of the world's resources by a small minority of persons betrays the gift of creation and the giver of the gift.
—Ronald D. Pasquariello, quoted in *Voices of the Religious Left* (2000)

Since the "War on Terror" began, the CEOs of the top thirty-four defense contractors have enjoyed average pay levels that are double the amounts they received during the four years leading up to 9/11.
—Sam Pizzigati, ed. *Executive Excess 2006* (August 30, 2006)

I should like to have it said of my first administration that in it the forces of selfishness and of lust for power met their match.
—Franklin D. Roosevelt, quoted in "Time Machine," *American Heritage* (October/November 1986)

We live in a culture where the primacy of the self and its satisfactions is everything. We are bombarded with messages telling us that we should have what we want because we're worth it.
—Jenni Russell, "The Selfish Generation," *Guardian (UK)* (December 6, 2003)

The original sin of Republicanism is greed.
—John Scalzi, quoted in *Wake Up, You're Liberal!* (2004)

We now live in a time in America where the rich are richer than any time in history. There is more money going into corporate profit than any time in history, and less money going into wages.
—Andy Stern, "Changing How America Works," AlterNet (November 2, 2006)

Bushian philosophy overtly encourages us, as a national mission, to concern ourselves only with our families, not our fellow citizens. Save for your own retirement. Educate your own kids. Worry about your own productivity. Let your fellow Americans fend for themselves.
—Robert Steinback, "Privatizing American Unity," *Miami Herald* (March 2, 2005)

We have people in this country who are richer than whole countries.
—Kurt Vonnegut, quoted in "Kurt Vonnegut's Stardust Memory," *Columbus Free Press* (March 5, 2006)

Selfishness is not living as one wishes to live; it is asking others to live as one wishes to live.
—Oscar Wilde, "The Soul of Man Under Socialism," *Fortnightly Review* (1891)

Americans have decided the most important person in their lives is . . . them, and our culture is now built upon that idea.
—Brian Williams, "Enough About You," *Time* (December 25, 2006)

We face not a clash between cultures or between red and blue states in this nation, but a clash between justice and greed. We worship the God of the Bible, not the god of wealth.
—Jim Winkler, "Defining "Moral Values" For the Next Four Years," Religious Coalition for Reproductive Choice (2004)

Homophobia

Homophobic men showed an increase in penile erection to male homosexual stimuli. . . . Homophobia is apparently associated with homosexual arousal that the homosexual individual is either unaware of or denies.
—H. E. Adams, et al. "Is Homophobia Associated with Homosexual Arousal?" *Journal of Abnormal Psychology* (1996)

Scouting has lost its moral compass. Current leaders of the Boy Scouts of America pervert the meaning of "morally straight" in the Scout Oath. They wrongly equate "morally straight" with having a heterosexual orientation.
—Frank Edward Allen, "Boy Scouts of America: A Symbol of Prejudice," *San Francisco Chronicle* (September 24, 2000)

It's time for Republicans to embrace their own gay wing and stop fueling the sickness of suppression that drives men like [U.S. Senator] Larry Craig into airport bathroom stalls.
—Nina Burleigh, "Why the GOP's Gay Wing Is Forced to Hide in the Bathroom," *Huffington Post* (August 30, 2007)

The open affirmation of gay identity can pose a mortal threat to people whose own sexual identity is insecure.
—James Carroll, "War, Religion, and Gay Rights," *Boston Globe* (November 13, 2006)

We treat racism and homophobia as delusional disorders.
—Shama Chaiken, at a meeting of the American Psychiatric Association, quoted in "Psychiatry Ponders Whether Extreme Bias Can Be an Illness," *Washington Post* (December 10, 2005)

Homophobia knows no party. Either party is happy to tap into anti-gay undercurrents in our society to ingratiate themselves to the homophobic masses.
—Sally Kohn, "Larry Craig's Pullout Strategy," *Common Dreams* (September 7, 2007)

In many ways contemporary homophobia is more virulent than contemporary racism. . . . A moral consensus now exists in this country that discriminating against blacks as teachers, priests, or tenants is simply wrong. (That doesn't mean it doesn't happen.) For much of the country, however, the moral legitimacy of homosexuals remains very much in question.
—Henry Louis Gates, Jr., "Backlash?" *New Yorker* (May 17, 1993)

Are all homophobic Republicans secretly gay? The leaders of the party with a penchant for condemning others would do well to look inward.
—Headline introducing an article by Nathaniel Frank, "Haggard, Foley and GOP Preach Against the Vices They Can't Shake," AlterNet (November 4, 2006)

Homophobia is like racism and anti-Semitism and other forms of bigotry in that it seeks to dehumanize a large group of people, to deny their humanity, their dignity, and personhood.
—Coretta Scott King, quoted in "Mrs. King Commends Lambda for Leadership at 25th Anniversary Celebration," *Lambda Legal* (March 31, 1998)

Homophobia is replacing the set of flag and race issues of a generation ago. It's the last refuge of the scoundrel.
—Kevin Phillips, quoted in "The Politics of Fear," *Rolling Stone* (June 29, 2006)

Not that long ago, it was considered consistent to be a Christian, and yet, hold slaves . . . I want to suggest that the day has come when Christians must declare that gay bashing is an attack on the gospel and that real Christians do not participate in any form of discrimination.
—Rev. Jim Rigby, "Real Christians Fight Intolerance," AlterNet (July 14, 2006)

The heart and soul of the prejudice against gays . . . is the knee-jerk equivalence of gays as pedophiles and recruiters for the "lifestyle."
—Pierre Tristam, "Homophobia as National Sport: Marriage by Constitutional Writ," *Daytona Beach News Journal* (July 15, 2003)

Conservatives are on a perpetual sexual hair-trigger, their heterosexuality hanging by a thread . . . The slightest provocation might drive them insane with desire, a too-friendly gaze from a man with washboard abs liable to give them feelings they're ashamed to admit they have.
—Paul Waldman, "Courting the Bigot Vote," *TomPaine.com* (November 1, 2006)

We cannot forget that when Hitler came to power in 1933, one of the first things that he did was ban gay organizations.
—Rabbi Eric Yoffie, quoted in "Jewish Leader Blasts 'Religious Right,'" the Associated Press (AP) (November 19, 2005)

Hypocrisy

And when thou prayest, thou shalt not be as the hypocrites are: for they love to pray standing in the synagogues and in the corners of the streets, that they may be seen of men.
—Matthew 6:6

Most on the Religious Right aren't even really pro-life—they are merely pro-birth.
—Brent Borgeois, "The Network of Spiritual Progressives," *Common Dreams* (May 23, 2006)

All too often I have seen a "personal relationship with God" used to justify behavior that is a radical departure from the life of Jesus.
—David Batstone, "God-Talk and Moral Values," *Sojourners* (November 2004)

It is strange but true that the country's most prominent spokesmen for the Prince of Peace and for tradition and morality are also its most outspoken proponents of torture.
—Joe Conason, "Opponents of Torture Are True Patriots," *New York Observer* (September 25, 2006)

Halliburton is crowing about getting a new Homeland Security contract to build detention camps for illegal immigrants just a few months after its subcontractors were caught using illegal immigrants.
—Charlie Cray, "More Halliburton Hypocrisy," *Huffington Post* (January 25, 2006)

If the GOP's moral compass is so steady, then where is the call from them for a constitutional amendment to outlaw divorce?
—Ed Danover, letter to the editor, "Right Is Oh, So Moral, but Oh, so Hypocritical," *Rocky Mountain News* (December 22, 2004)

If a politician doesn't feel comfortable talking about religion, that's going to show. If you don't feel it, then for God's sake don't fake it.
—Paul Greenberg, "If It Ain't Got That Swing," *Joplin Globe* (December 23, 2004)

If the religious right is so convinced that, here on earth, God's work must truly be our own, then why are they not spending their time and energy on vanquishing the poverty that exists in this country and all over the world?
—Andrew Hammond, "Religious Rhetoric Isn't Bad; Hypocrisy Is," *Chicago Maroon* (January 20, 2005)

Aside from Rush Limbaugh's drug scandal, Newt Gingrich's extramarital affairs, and William Bennett's gambling problem, money seems to be the most common moral corrupter of those on the far right who so loudly profess to be America's arbiters of proper behavior.
—Jim Hightower, "The Glass Houses of Right-Wing Moralists," AlterNet (January 22, 2005)

It's up to us to finger them as hypocrites for claiming to follow the Prince of Peace by serving the God of War.
—Todd Huffman, "How the Christian Left Can Get It Right," *Common Dreams* (November 10, 2005)

The church allows people to believe that they can be good Christians and yet draw dividends from armament factories.
—Aldous Huxley, *Ends and Means* (1937)

The Religious Right frowns on adultery, but they have offered no constitutional amendments to stop it. In fact the Bible assails adultery on a much more consistent basis than it does homosexuality.
—Paul Jeter, "Cherry Picking the Bible," *Dissident Voice* (December 24, 2004)

While Jesus berated those who worship money, or mammon, most contemporary "conservatives" embrace free-market capitalism and the accumulation of wealth with almost religious fervor.
—David R. Keller, "Terms 'Liberal' and 'Conservative' Are Just Too Fuzzy," *Salt Lake Tribune* (October 30, 2005)

He had grown up in a country run by politicians who sent the pilots to man the bombers to kill the babies to make the world safer for children to grow up in.
—Ursula K. Le Guin, *The Lathe of Heaven* (1971)

Chickenhawks . . . individuals who favor military solutions to political problems but who themselves avoided military service during wartime.
—Jim Lobe, "Chickenhawk Groupthink?" *Asia Times* (May 13, 2004)

Businesses criticize the job our schools are doing and then proceed to nail down every tax break they can get, further eroding the school's ability to do the job.
—Howard Metzenbaum, quoted in "Desperate for Dollars," *American School Boards Journal* (September 1992)

Is there a difference between Democrats and Republicans? Sure. The Democrats say one thing ("Save the planet!") and then do another—quietly holding hands behind the scenes with the bastards who make this world a dirtier, meaner place. The Republicans just come right out and give the bastards a corner office in the West Wing. That's the difference.
—Michael Moore, *Stupid White Men* (2002)

Regrettably, many religious conservatives act as if life begins at conception and ends at birth.
—David Morris, "The Pro-Life Continuum," AlterNet (December 19, 2005)

How often we hear the most vigorous argument for war from those who count on others of valor to fight it.
—Bill Moyers, "Message to West Point," *TomPaine.com* (November 29, 2006)

[Radical conservatives] would rather police bedrooms than board rooms.
—Robert Reich, *Reason: Why Liberals Will Win the Battle for America* (2004)

Today's church lifts its arms to praise Christ wearing liturgical garments woven in sweatshops.
—Rev. Jim Rigby, "Christians Who Want Democracy Must Stop Bowing to a Dictator Christ," *Huffington Post* (June 13, 2006)

Even the people who most loudly denounce government interference depend on it every day.
—Cass Sunstein, *The Second Bill of Rights: FDR's Unfinished Revolution and Why We Need It More Than Ever* (2004)

Blessed are the meek, for they shall inherit the Earth.
Blessed are the merciful, for they shall obtain mercy.
Blessed are the peacemakers, for they shall be called the children of God. . .
And so on. Not exactly planks in a Republican platform.
—Kurt Vonnegut, "Cold Turkey," *In These Times* (May 10, 2004)

Conservatism is Bill Bennett lecturing you about self-denial, then rushing off to feed his slot habit at the casino.
—Paul Waldman, "It's the Conservatism, Stupid," *TomPaine.com* (July 12, 2006)

Market Fundamentalism

Market fundamentalism ultimately rests on a fairy tale in which each person's pursuit of his or her self-interest automatically serves the common good.
—Fred Block, "Reframing the Political Battle: Market Fundamentalism vs. Moral Economy," Longview Institute (January 30, 2007)

It is the unfettered free market . . . that now poses the gravest threat to the morals of our society.
—David Callahan, *The Moral Center* (2006)

When television networks and Hollywood exploit sex to make money, why aren't liberals asking why the free market so revered by the right wing promotes values the very same right wing claims to despise?
—E. J. Dionne, Jr., "Lessons for Democrats," *Washington Post* (December 31, 2004)

If ever there was a time when the sovereignty of the market posed a mortal danger, it is surely now.
—Jonathan Freedland, "When It Comes to Global Warming, Market Rule Poses a Mortal Danger," *Guardian (UK)* (October 25, 2006)

Religious fundamentalisms, whether Christian, Jewish, or Muslim, are based on the threat of damnation and prescribe obedience to the will of God as the means to salvation. Secular fundamentalisms are based on the threat of scarcity and prescribe obedience to the Free Market as the redemptive path.
—Matt and Dan Hamburg, "Fundamentalisms in Collision," *Common Dreams* (September 28, 2001)

The concept of a free market that people simply trade things in an absolute vacuum is a fantasy. Every market is created by government, and the parameters of that market are defined by government.
—Thom Hartmann, interviewed by Mark Karlin, "Thom Hartmann Comes to the Defense of the Embattled, and Shrinking, Middle Class," *BuzzFlash* (September 25, 2006)

Given a choice between democracy without free markets or free markets without democracy, many conservatives would gladly choose the latter.
—Christopher Hayes, "Who's Afraid of Democracy?" *In These Times* (May 25, 2007)

Corporate capitalists do not want free markets, they want dependable profits, and their surest route is to crush competition by controlling government.
—Robert F. Kennedy, Jr., "Crimes Against Nature," *Rolling Stone* (December 11, 2003)

My conservative friends . . . tell me the market is the divine hand at work on earth. At the same time they deplore the crudity, vulgarity, and violence of popular culture. . . . Yet the very thing they deplore is market driven.
—Bill Moyers, "Address to PBS Annual Meeting," *Working For Change* (May 31, 2006)

We have always known that heedless self-interest was bad morals; we know now that it is bad economics.
—Franklin D. Roosevelt, in his second inaugural address on January 20, 1937, quoted in *Public Papers* (1941)

The project of corporate globalization has cracked the code. Free elections, a free press, and an independent judiciary mean little when the free market has reduced them to commodities on sale to the highest bidder.
—Arundhati Roy, *Public Power in the Age of Empire* (2004)

It is evident that the free market does not provide health care for millions of our people, does not ensure full employment, does not protect the natural environment, does not improve our schools, does not clean up our inner cities, and does not stop global warming.
—Arthur M. Schlesinger, Jr., "Opportunity Knocks," *American Prospect* (December 2004)

Markets are amoral. . . . But society cannot function without some distinction between right and wrong.
—George Soros, *On Globalization* (2002)

Markets can only serve the allocation of resources among private needs. But there are public needs which require cooperation and markets are not designed to provide public goods.
—George Soros, quoted in "Take Back America Conference Reflects a Fired-up, Unified Movement," *Common Dreams* (June 7, 2004)

Free-market competition works fine for those capable of competing. But children, the elderly, the mentally ill, the unemployed, and other groups can't effectively compete for their own prosperity.
—Robert Steinback, "Privatizing American Unity," *Miami Herald* (March 2, 2005)

If contractual commitments cannot be enforced by government, free markets will not operate. A strong and active government is indispensable.
—Cass Sunstein, *The Second Bill of Rights: FDR's Unfinished Revolution and Why We Need It More Than Ever* (2004)

There is no such thing as a "free market" because every corporation in America profits thanks to subsidized public goods like education, roads, [and] the electric power grid.
—Jonathan Tasini, "A 10-Step Program for Democrats," *TomPaine.com* (January 2, 2007)

Free-market fundamentalism—just as dangerous as the religious fundamentalisms of our day—trivializes the concern for public interest.
—Cornel West, "Democracy Matters Are Frightening in Our Time," *Logos* (Summer 2004)

Materialism

That happiness is to be attained through limitless material acquisition is denied by every religion and philosophy known to mankind, but is preached incessantly by every American television set.
—Robert Bellah, *The Broken Covenant* (1975)

The love of money is the root of all evil.
—I Timothy 6:10

Too many of us now tend to worship self-indulgence and consumption. . . . But we've discovered that owning things and consuming things does not satisfy our longing for meaning. We've learned that piling up material goods cannot fill the emptiness of lives which have no confidence or purpose.
—Jimmy Carter, in his address on national malaise (July 15, 1979)

The United States is a place where the prevailing instinct is to want it all, no matter the consequences.
—Andrew Gumbel, "Americans Want It All, and Hang the Consequences," *Independent (UK)* (October 11, 2006)

Our affluent society contains those of talent and insight who are driven to prefer poverty, to choose it, rather than to submit to the desolation of an empty abundance.
—Michael Harrington, *The Other America* (1962)

As a nation obsessed with money and possessions, celebrity and sport, we are not advanced morally or spiritually.
—Todd Huffman, "This Christmas, Where Is Our National Conscience?" *Common Dreams* (December 20, 2004)

In a consumer society there are inevitably two kinds of slaves: the prisoners of addition and the prisoners of envy.
—Ivan Illich, *Tools of Conviviality* (1973)

Few rich men own their own property. The property owns them.
—Robert Green Ingersoll, in his address to the McKinley League, New York (October 29, 1896)

We live in a culture that produces books like "God Wants You to Be Rich" and "Jesus, CEO."
—Molly Ivins, "Book Exposes the Real New Economy," *Charleston Gazette* (August 8, 2005)

Material possessions not only focus people toward private and away from communal life but also encourage docility. The more possessions one has, the more compromises one will make to protect them.
—Robert D. Kaplan, "Was Democracy Just a Moment?" *Atlantic Monthly* (December 1997)

America has enough brainy people ready to serve the interests of the ruling elite, but not enough caring people to challenge its materialism and militarism.
—Colman McCarthy, "Test-Driven Teaching Isn't Character-Driven," *Philadelphia Inquirer* (June 7, 2006)

Materialism alone will not fulfill the possibilities of your existence.
—Barack Obama, in a speech delivered at Brown Chapel A.M.E. Church in Selma, Alabama (March 4, 2007)

A way of life that bases itself on materialism, i.e., on permanent limitless expansionism in a finite environment, cannot last long.
—E. F. Schumacher, *Small Is Beautiful* (1973)

There really are some things that money can't buy.
—Mark E. Smith, "You Still Doing What Bush Told You to Do?" OpEdNews (October 18, 2006)

What would happen if we began to take matters into our own hands regarding our own lives and actions? . . . What if we learned to slow down, simplify, savor and make the best of our lives with a little less?
—Catherine Sundberg, "What They Can't Control," *Common Dreams* (April 6, 2005)

This idea that God wants everybody to be wealthy? There is a word for that: baloney. It's creating a false idol. You don't measure your self-worth by your net worth.
—Rick Warren, on the preaching of growing numbers of fundamentalist ministers, "Does God Want You to Be Rich?" *Time* (September 18, 2006)

The biggest test of America's moral values is whether we and our leaders find the courage to say that liberty for all means liberating ourselves from materialism before it drives us mad and makes us a target for the world's next madman.
—Derrick Z. Jackson, "Materialistic Madness," *Boston Globe* (November 12, 2004)

Misogyny

Admitting violence against women is pervasive does not make me a victim. It makes me a realist.
—Kim Antieau, "Have We Come a Long Way?" *Common Dreams* (March 3, 2004)

Anti-feminism is a direct expression of misogyny; it is the political defense of women hating.
—Andrea Dworkin, *Right-Wing Women* (1978)

Femiphobia is the male fear of being feminine. . . . The most important thing about being a man is not being a woman. This imperative to repudiate everything feminine—whether it's external or internal—is played out as much in politics as in personal life.
—Stephen J. Ducat, quoted in interview "The Wimp Factor," AlterNet (October 29, 2004)

The kind of hyper-masculine strutting that we see on display by right wing males is a defense. It's a defense against this anxious masculinity, against their fear of the feminine.
—Stephen J. Ducat, quoted in interview "Stephen J. Ducat Dissects 'Anxious Masculinity,' Making Sense of America's Strutting, in a Psychoanalytic Kind of Way," *BuzzFlash* (March 2, 2005)

I won't name names, but there are women out there who serve as ventriloquists for patriarchy.
—Jane Fonda, "A Powerful Media Can Stop a War," Women's Media Center (January 16, 2007)

The misogyny that shapes every aspect of our civilization is the institutionalized form of male fear and hatred of what they have denied and therefore cannot know, cannot share: that wild country, the being of women.
—Ursula K. Le Guin, *Dancing at the Edge of the World* (1989)

Punishment

The U.S. has the highest incarceration rate in the world. Higher even than Russia with its notorious Gulag system. One in thirty-seven of our adults are in prison.
—Bob Burnett, "Tookie Williams—On the Killing Floor," *Common Dreams* (December 12, 2005)

America has found one very successful method for dealing with black rage: massive incarceration of people who were never trained nor expected to be a part of "mainstream" society.
—Farai Chedeya, "USA: The Vast Sucking Sound of White Collar Crime," *CorpWatch* (September 18, 2002)

We cannot allow anyone who is incarcerated to be victimized by other prisoners, abused by officers, or neglected by doctors. We must remember that our prisons and jails are part of the justice system, not apart from it.
—*Confronting Confinement: A Report of the Commission on Safety and Abuse in America's Prisons* (June 2006)

What happens inside jails and prisons does not stay inside jails and prisons. It comes home with prisoners after they are released and with corrections officers at the end of each day's shift.
—*Confronting Confinement: A Report of the Commission on Safety and Abuse in America's Prisons* (June 2006)

When we tolerate abuse in U.S. prisons and jails, it should not surprise us to find U.S. soldiers using similar methods in Iraq.
—Anne-Marie Cusac, "Abu Ghraib," *Progressive* (July 2004)

I hear much of people's calling out to punish the guilty, but very little few are concern'd to clear the innocent.
—Daniel Defoe, *An Appeal to Honour and Justice, Tho' it be of His Worst Enemies* (1715)

The degree of civilization in a society can be judged by entering its prisons.
—Fyodor Dostoevsky, quoted in "The Attica of the Americas," ZNET (August 28, 2004)

The most effective way to create an ever-growing number of victims is to further dehumanize convicts in prison, the majority of whom will eventually be released to an unsuspecting public.
—Sean Gonsalves, "An Exercise in Mental Fitness," AlterNet (January 24, 2006)

The more seriously you take liberty as the bedrock of a liberal society the more seriously you have to take the deprivation of liberty.
—Ryan Grim, "Liberalism's Brain on Drugs," *In These Times* (October 31, 2005)

America has become a country that imprisons those it fails, blaming poverty, drug addiction, or homelessness on individuals rather than recognizing and addressing the conditions that give rise to them.
—Beverly Henry, "Reclaiming the Red, White and Blue for All Americans," *Baltimore Sun* (January 5, 2006)

It's perhaps fitting that I write this introduction in jail—that graduate school of survival.
—Abbie Hoffman, *Steal This Book* (1971)

Studies confirm that the punishment blacks receive when the victim is white is far more severe than if the victim is black.
—Earl Ofari Hutchinson, "Black Homicides Fuel Nation's Murder Surge," New America Media (February 21, 2007)

The punishment should not only fit the crime, it should also fit the age of the person that committed it, and the circumstances that drove them to commit their offenses.
—Earl Ofari Hutchinson, "No-Parole Sentences Hurt Black Teens," AlterNet (November 16, 2005)

Infinite punishment is infinite cruelty, endless injustice, immortal meanness.
—Robert G. Ingersoll, *The Great Infidels* (1881)

Half of all public housing built in the last ten years has been jail cells.
—Rev. Jesse Jackson, "Let Katrina Become Symbol of Revival," *Chicago Sun-Times* (January 9, 2007)

We Democrats are at our worst when we try to emulate Republicans as we did in signing onto the "war" on drugs that has ruined so many young lives. . . . There are more folks in prison for marijuana than for violent crimes.
—Garrison Keillor, "A Foul Tragedy: Democrats Fled in the Face of Danger," *In These Times* (November 2, 2005)

Punishment and reward proceed from basically the same psychological model, one that conceives of motivation as nothing more than the manipulation of behavior.
—Alfie Kohn, *Punished by Rewards* (1999)

I say that if Bush doesn't pardon him, at least he should give him a new nickname, because if you have "Scooter" on the back of your jumpsuit, you are asking for it.
—Bill Maher, on the rumor that President Bush will pardon Cheney's convicted chief of staff Lewis "Scooter" Libby, quoted in "Punchlines," *Newsday* (March 15, 2007)

Prison is designed to break one's spirit and destroy one's resolve . . . exploit every weakness, demolish every initiative, negate all signs of individuality.
—Nelson Mandela, quoted in *The Impossible Will Take a Little While Longer* (2003)

The United States has now become the world leader in its rate of incarceration, locking up its citizens at five to eight times the rate of other industrialized nations.
—Marc Mauer, "America Has Become Incarceration Nation," AlterNet (December 22, 2006)

Who built the moral cesspool into which this nation has sunk with its secret prisons and secret prisoners, legalized torture, indefinite imprisonment without trial or counsel?
—Floyd J. McKay, "Calling for Truth and Dignity in the Nation's Conduct," *Seattle Times* (November 16, 2005)

If we were to judge the United States by its penal policies, we would perceive a strange beast: a Christian society that believes in neither forgiveness nor redemption.
—George Monbiot, "Routine and Systematic Torture Is at the Heart of America's War on Terror," *Guardian (UK)* (December 12, 2006)

Distrust everyone in whom the impulse to punish is powerful.
—Friedrich Nietzsche, *Thus Spoke Zarathustra* (1885)

The reformative effect of punishment is a belief that dies hard, I think, because it is so satisfying to our sadistic impulses.
—Bertrand Russell, *Unpopular Essays* (1951)

We could build a million new prisons and we could fill them up, but we'll never stop the cycle of violence if we don't invest in people's health and education.
—Paul Wellstone, quoted in "Radical Realist; Bill Clinton Wasn't the Only Comeback Story of 1996," *Washington Post* (January 19, 1997)

Social Darwinism

We believe that while survival of the fittest may be a good working description of the process of evolution, a government of humans should elevate itself to a higher order.
—Mario Cuomo, in his speech to the Democratic National Convention (July 16, 1984)

Most civilized nations compensate for the inadequacy of wages by providing relatively generous public services such as health insurance, free or subsidized child care, subsidized housing, and effective public transportation. But the United States, for all its wealth, leaves its citizens to fend for themselves.
—Barbara Ehrenreich, "On the Outside Looking In: How Low-Wage Workers Get Squeezed," *Record* (Bergen County, New Jersey) (September 2, 2001)

Let us dedicate ourselves to what the Greeks wrote so many years ago: to tame the savageness of man and make gentle the life of this world.
—Robert F. Kennedy on hearing of the assassination of Rev. Martin Luther King, Jr. (April 4, 1968)

When conservatives say you're on your own, we liberals know we're all in this together.
—George Lakoff, *Thinking Points: Communicating Our American Values and Vision* (2006)

Sink-or-swim conservatism is not in the American tradition, or the American heart. Empathy, mutual responsibility, fairness, and community—all progressive values—are part of this heritage.
—George Lakoff and John Halpin, "Framing Katrina," *American Prospect* (October 7, 2005)

America was not meant to be a country where the winner takes all.
—Bill Moyers, "America 101," *TomPaine.com* (November 1, 2006)

You are on your own to buy your own health care, to buy your own retirement security, to buy your own roads and levees.
—Barack Obama, characterizing the Republicans' "ownership society," quoted in "Obama Says Republicans Practice 'Social Darwinism,'" Reuters (December 12, 2005)

The Conservative Movement . . . is now mounting a full-throttled attack on Darwinism even as it has thoroughly embraced Darwin's bastard child, social Darwinism.
—Robert Reich, "Of Darwinism and Social Darwinism," *Common Dreams* (November 29, 2005)

What do conservatives believe? Well, they believe that we're all on our own, and we're all out for ourselves.

—Paul Waldman, interviewed by Mark Karlin, "Paul Waldman Knows Progressives Can Win—and Here's How," *BuzzFlash* (May 25, 2006)

THE PROMISE OF LIBERALISM

Authority

I believe in a lively disrespect for most forms of authority.
—Rita Mae Brown, *Starting from Scratch* (1989)

I am against the illegitimate structure of authority called the corporation. I want to see different forms of economic organization emerge.
—Robert Jensen, "Critical Hope: Radical Citizenship in Reactionary Times," *Common Dreams* (December 17, 2001)

Authority has every reason to fear the skeptic, for authority can rarely survive in the face of doubt.
—Robert Lindner, *Must You Conform?* (1956)

When we blindly adopt a religion, a political system, a literary dogma, we become automatons.
—Anaïs Nin, quoted in *The Diaries of Anaïs Nin* (1976)

Revolt against authority was, and remains to this day, the original sin, the classic crime, of the individual.
—Thomas Szasz, *The Manufacture of Madness* (1970)

It is dangerous to be right in matters on which the established authorities are wrong.
—Voltaire, quoted in *A Cynic's Breviary* (1925)

Charity

It is more blessed to give than to receive.
—Acts 20:35

Too many people have decided to do without generosity in order to practice charity.
—Albert Camus, *The Fall* (1956)

Charity is a matter of personal attribute; justice is a matter of public policy. Never can the first be a substitute for the second.
—Rev. William Sloan Coffin, quoted in "Charity Is Not Enough," AlterNet (December 7, 2004)

Perform individual acts of charity and you're a good Christian. Inquire about why there's a need for charity in the first place, and you're a good communist.
—Sean Gonsalves, "An Exercise in Mental Fitness," AlterNet (January 24, 2006)

You burn yourselves out doing charitable work. But if you get into politics and get to the cause of these problems, you will have a just society where you don't need so much charitable work.
—Ralph Nader, quoted in a Mary McGrory editorial, *Boston Globe* (October 14, 2000)

Only an estimated 10 percent of all charitable deductions this year will be directed at the poor.
—Robert Reich, "When Charity Shouldn't Begin at Home," *Common Dreams* (December 20, 2006)

Charity knows neither race nor creed.
—Talmud, rabbinical writings in *The Talmudic Anthology* (1945)

Common Good

The truth is that runaway capitalists, environmental know-nothings, irresponsible accountants, amoral drug runners, and antimodern terrorists all flourish because we have diminished the power of the public sphere.
—Benjamin R. Barber, "A Failure of Democracy, Not Capitalism," *New York Times* (July 29, 2002)

Although corporations act only through people, these people are forced to play roles that in some ways make them more like machines than human beings. Every employee is aware that his or her job is only to help the company make money. Protecting the public interest is not part of the job description.
—Robert C. Hinkley, "Profits vs. Public Interest," *Miami Herald* (June 11, 2002)

We can make corporations more responsible to the public good by amending the law that says the pursuit of profit takes precedence over the public interest.
—Robert C. Hinkley, "How Corporate Law Inhibits Social Responsibility," *Business Ethics: Corporate Social Responsibility Report* (January/February 2002)

To the cheater, there is no such thing as honesty, and to Republicans the idea of serving the public good is counterfeit on the face of it—they never felt such an urge, and therefore it must not exist.
—Garrison Keillor, *Homegrown Democrat* (2004)

When you take a public trust, the most important thing is to defend the public interest.
—Dennis Kucinich, interviewed by Joshua Scheer, "The Charge of the Muny Light Brigade," *Truthdig* (December 14, 2006)

Our President Should Be Elected by Voters, Not Dollars
—Slogan from Public Citizen, a national nonprofit public interest organization (2006)

Compassion

No act of kindness, no matter how small, is ever wasted.
—Aesop, *The Lion and the Mouse* (6th century B.C.)

What is most needed is a loving heart.
—Buddha, *The Three Baskets of Wisdom* (6th century B.C.)

God builds his temple in the heart on the ruins of churches and religions.
—Ralph Waldo Emerson, *The Conduct of Life* (1860)

Treat men as pawns and ninepins and you shall suffer as well as they. If you leave out their heart, you shall lose your own.
—Ralph Waldo Emerson, *Essays: First Series* (1841)

The tiny flame that lights up the human heart is like a blazing torch that comes down from heaven to light up the paths of mankind.
—Kahlil Gilbran, *The Voice of the Master* (1958)

True kindness presupposes the faculty of imagining as one's own the suffering and joys of others.
—André Gide, *Pretexts* (1903)

In my experience, people are often kinder than their ideologies.
—Michelle Goldberg, *Kingdom Coming* (2006)

Human kindness is deeply subversive to totalitarian creeds, which seek to thwart all compassion toward those deemed unworthy of moral consideration.
—Chris Hedges, *American Fascists* (2006)

We are made kind by being kind.
—Eric Hoffer, *The Passionate State of Mind* (1954)

Liberal religion must come from the heart.
—Jim Kelley, "Democrats Must Reclaim Moral Ground," *Atlanta Journal-Constitution* (March 9, 2005)

A big heart is both a clunky and delicate thing; it doesn't protect itself and it doesn't hide.
—Anne Lamott, *Bird by Bird* (1994)

The holiest of holidays are those
Kept by ourselves in silence and apart;
The secret anniversaries of the heart.
—Henry Wadsworth Longfellow, "Holidays," *Sonnets* (1876)

Kindness is the mark of faith; and whosoever has not kindness has not faith.
—Muhammad, founder of the Islam religion, *The Sayings of Muhammad* (1941)

It doesn't interest me what you do for a living. I want to know what you ache for, and if you dare of meeting your heart's longing.
—Oriah Mountain Dreamer, *Dreams of Desire* (1995)

The heart has its reasons, which reason does not know.
—Blaise Pascal, *Pensées* (1670)

Be kind, for everyone you meet is fighting a great battle.
—Philo of Alexandria, first-century philosopher, quoted in *Writing to Change the World* (2006)

Better a bleeding heart than no heart at all.
—Anonymous

Competence

If elections were only about competence, then right about now we'd be dedicating the Michael Dukakis Presidential Library.
—Kenneth S. Baer and Andrei Cherny, "Wake Up, Democrats: Ideas and Vision Do Matter," *Los Angeles Times* (July 10, 2006)

I recalled the image of Mr. Bush sitting in a Sarasota, Fla., classroom after being informed of the Sept. 11 attacks. Instead of reacting instantly, commandingly, he just sat there for long wasted moments, with a bewildered look on his face, holding a second-grade story called *The Pet Goat*.
—Bob Herbert, "Failure upon Failure," *New York Times* (July 27, 2006)

No president in your lifetime or mine has seen his fundamental competence—his ability to think clearly and manage the government—so doubted by the voting public as Mr. Bush has. This is humiliation of a rare sort.
—Garrison Keillor, "Message to White House Co-Pilot: Eject Now," *Chicago Tribune* (March 22, 2006)

Government is competent when all who compose it work as trustees for the whole people.
—Franklin Delano Roosevelt, in his second inaugural address (January 20, 1937)

Conscience

Never do anything against conscience, even if the state demands it.
—Albert Einstein, quoted in *Albert Einstein: Philosopher-Scientist* (1949)

The still small voice within you must always be the final arbiter when there is a conflict of duty.
—Mahatma Gandhi, quoted in *Young India* (August 4, 1920)

Corporations, by their form, have no social conscience. Because their first obligation is—by law—to enhance profit, they are not committed to a community or a nation, or even to the basic humanity of the rest of us.
—Thom Hartmann, "Why Wal-Mart Is Not a Person," *BuzzFlash* (January 28, 2005)

Nothing is more powerful than individuals acting out of their own conscience.
—Vaclav Havel, quoted in *Writing to Change the World* (2006)

I cannot and will not cut my conscience to fit this year's fashions.
—Lillian Hellman, in a 1952 letter to the House Un-American Activities Committee, quoted in *Writers at Work* (1967)

Any attempt to replace the personal conscience by a collective conscience does violence to the individual and is the first step toward totalitarianism.
—Hermann Hesse, *Reflections* (1974)

The most effective way to silence a guilty conscience is to convince ourselves and others that those we have sinned against are indeed depraved creatures, deserving every punishment, even extermination.
—Eric Hoffer, *The True Believer* (1951)

We've seen the results of capitalism without conscience: the pollution of the air we breathe, the water we drink, and the food we eat; the endangerment of workers; and the sales of dangerous products—from cars to toys to drugs. All in pursuit of greater and greater profits.
—Arianna Huffington, "Capitalism without Conscience," *Huffington Post* (July 23, 2002)

Our greatest challenge if we are to remain a great nation is not terrorism, and not Iraq. Our greatest challenge is to recover our national conscience.
—Todd Huffman, "This Christmas, Where Is Our National Conscience?" *Common Dreams* (December 20, 2004)

It behooves every man who values liberty of conscience for himself to resist invasions of it in the case of others.
—Thomas Jefferson, in a letter to Benjamin Rush (April 21, 1803)

Vanity asks the question—is it popular? Conscience asks the question—is it right?
—Rev. Martin Luther King, Jr., in a sermon at the National Cathedral (March 31, 1968)

After watching the steady drift to the right of the Democratic Party under Clinton, I have come to the realization that I would rather vote my conscience than vote strategically.
—Tim Robbins, explaining his vote for Ralph Nader, "What I Voted For," *Nation* (August 6, 2001)

To obey God means, in practice, to obey one's conscience.
—Bertrand Russell, *Marriage and Morals* (1929)

Conscience is God's presence in man.
—Emmanuel Swedenborg, *Arcana Coelestia* (1856)

Courage

I'm tired of blaming Republicans for everything. We have a two-party system. When is the other party going to suit up?
—Andrew Foster Altschul, "Why the Democrats Aren't Going to Take Back Congress in 2006," *Huffington Post* (July 20, 2006)

You still are more likely to find someone willing to stand up to the big money boys among Democrats than Republicans. But the gap is narrowing. Voters sense it.
—Russ Baker, "The Top 10 Corporate Democrats-for-Hire," AlterNet (August 24, 2006)

We shouldn't be afraid of speaking out and putting ourselves at risk, even if it means getting arrested.
—Medea Benjamin, interviewed by Elizabeth DiNovella, *Progressive* (December 2004)

What about the opposition [Democratic] party? Too often they're not in opposition. With some notable exceptions, they've been absent without leave in this battle for America's soul. When one party is shameless, the other can't afford to be spineless.
—Julian Bond, quoted in "Take Back America Conference Reflects a Fired-Up, Unified Movement," *Common Dreams* (June 7, 2004)

I was raised to stand up to the bully in the schoolyard, and you don't lose that.
—Barbara Boxer, interviewed by Ruth Conniff, *Progressive* (July 2005)

If there is one single trait that persuades American voters that a candidate is a manipulative, cynical "elitist," it is the unwillingness to take clear-cut, unambiguous positions on the matters of gravest concern.
—Roger Bybee, "Kansas, Conviction, and the Future of the Dems," Democratic Underground (March 11, 2005)

A thousand men will march to the mouth of the cannon where only one man will dare espouse an unpopular cause.
—Clarence Darrow, *Resist Not Evil* (1903)

No phallic hero, no matter what he does to himself or to another to prove his courage, ever matches the solitary, existential courage of the woman who gives birth.
—Andrea Dworkin, *Our Blood* (1976)

Being able to work with the opposition party . . . is hardly a sign of moral courage when the opposition party controls the White House, Senate, and House of Representatives.
—Editorial, "The Senate Race in Connecticut," *New York Times* (October 29, 2006)

Democrats are fed up with fence-straddling and triangulation.
—Arianna Huffington, "Hillary's Too 'Vane' to Be President," *Los Angeles Times* (December 7, 2006)

It was involuntary. They sank my boat.
—John F. Kennedy, responding to a question on how he became a World War II hero, quoted in *A Thousand Days* (1965)

Moral courage is a rarer commodity than bravery in battle or great intelligence.
—Robert F. Kennedy, quoted in *Seeds of Peace* (1986)

Courage is the ladder on which all the other virtues mount.
—Clare Boothe Luce, *Reader's Digest* (May 1979)

Life shrinks or expands in proportion to one's courage.
—Anaïs Nin, quoted in *The Diaries of Anaïs Nin* (1966)

Some of us were ambivalent, but we don't do ambivalence well in America. We do courage of our convictions.
—Anna Quindlen, *Thinking Out Loud* (1993)

The ultimate act of bravery doesn't usually take place on a battlefield. It takes place in your heart when you have the courage to honor your character, your intellect, your inclinations, and your soul by listening to its clean, clear voice of direction instead of following the muddied messages of a timid world.
—Anna Quindlen, in her commencement address at Colby College (May 28, 2006)

It's better to have the courage of bad convictions than no courage or convictions at all.
—Frank Rich, "Karl Rove Beats the Democrats Again," *New York Times* (June 18, 2006)

A bully can be stopped, and so can a mob. It takes one person with the courage and a resolute voice.
—Tim Robbins, speech to the National Press Club, *Common Dreams* (April 16, 2003)

Scared Democrats vote away our rights: fearing attack ads showing them as soft on terror, not recognizing that a posture of supine submission wins far fewer votes than a principled stand.
—Maia Szalavitz, "How Torture Became Law, How Outrage Dies," *Huffington Post* (September 29, 2006)

When Democrats start demonstrating courage, voters stop thinking of them as weaklings. . . . When you stand up for what you believe in without fear and show how you're different from your opponents, Americans come to see you as principled and strong.
—Paul Waldman, "The Progressive Identity Complex," *TomPaine.com* (May 4, 2006)

To align yourself with the powerful and then take aim at the powerless takes not one ounce of valor.
—Gary Younge, "Take a Potshot at the Powerless, and You Too Can Win a Medal of Valor," *Guardian (UK)* (March 6, 2006)

Decency

I would as soon be descended from that heroic little monkey . . . as from a savage who delights to torture his enemies, offers up bloody sacrifices, practices infanticide without remorse, treats his wives like slaves, knows no decency, and is haunted by the grossest superstitions.
—Charles Darwin, *The Descent of Man* (1871)

There's no way to teach someone not to shoot an unarmed woman or child. If somebody doesn't already know why they shouldn't murder a baby, it's not clear that a refresher course will help.
—Maureen Dowd, on a U.S. Marine plan to teach an ethics course after U.S. troops were found to have murdered innocent civilians, "Teaching Remedial Decency," *New York Times* (June 3, 2006)

I believe that the essence of government lies with unceasing concern for the welfare and dignity and decency and innate integrity of life for every individual.
—Lyndon B. Johnson, remarks at a civil rights symposium in Austin, Texas (December 12, 1972)

Every time we turn our heads the other way when we see the law flouted—when we tolerate what we know to be wrong—when we close our eyes and ears to the corrupt because we are too busy, or too frightened—when we fail to speak up and speak out—we strike a blow against freedom and decency and justice.
—Robert F. Kennedy, quoted in *A New Day: Robert F. Kennedy* (1968)

To come together as a people we must acknowledge the basic human decency of people unlike ourselves.
—Rosa Maria Pegueros, "Charity Begins at Home," *Common Dreams* (January 5, 2005)

Until this moment, Senator, I think I had never gauged your cruelty or your recklessness . . . Have you no sense of decency, sir, at long last? Have you left no sense of decency?
—Joseph N. Welch, to Senator Joseph McCarthy at the Army-McCarthy hearings (June 9, 1954)

There was a time when America was looked up to by the rest of the world, a symbol of decency and caring.
—Dave Zweifel, "Our Nation Could Use a Better Year," *Capital Times (Madison, Wisconson)* (January 2, 2006)

Doubt

A belief which leaves no place for doubt is not a belief; it is a superstition.
—José Bergamín, *The Rocket and the Star* (1923)

A liberal never stops doubting himself, for self-doubt is precisely what allows us to make room in our minds for someone else's views and to keep the possibility of communication between us alive. A fundamentalist, on the other hand, is someone to whom the very idea of point of view is immaterial, or worse—the foundation of relativism.
—Nick Bromell, "Scooter Libby and Me," *American Scholar* (Winter 2007)

Who knows most, doubts most.
—Robert Browning, quoted in *2000 Years of Disbelief* (1996)

I respect faith, but doubt is what gets you an education.
—Wilson Mizner, quoted in *The Legendary Mizners* (1953)

Doubt is not a pleasant condition, but certainty is an absurd one.
—Voltaire, in a letter to Frederick II (April 6, 1767)

Empathy

Strong political leadership that emphasizes empathy over confrontation and solidarity over self-righteousness is essential to setting things in motion at home and abroad.
—Jeffrey Alexander and Ron Eyerman, "A Test of Moral Conscience," *Newsday* (November 30, 2003)

One of the most devastating consequences of unearned privilege . . . is the death of empathy.
—Robert Jensen, "The Consequences of the Death of Empathy," *Working For Change* (November 3, 2006)

In a world where women work three times as hard for half as much, our achievement has been denigrated, both marriage and divorce have turned against us, our motherhood has been used as an obstacle to our success, our passion as a trap, our empathy for others as an excuse to underpay us.
—Erica Jong, *Fear of Fifty* (1994)

Progressive/liberal morality begins with empathy, the ability to understand others and feel what they feel.
—George Lakoff, *Don't Think Like an Elephant* (2004)

If we could read the secret history of our enemies, we should find in each man's life sorrow and suffering enough to disarm all hostility.
—Henry Wadsworth Longfellow, *Driftwood* (1857)

Learning is a result of listening, which in turn leads to even better listening and attentiveness to the other person. . . . We must have empathy, and empathy grows as we learn.
—Alice Miller, *For Your Own Good* (1990)

Surely our empathy can transcend race.
—Anna Quindlen, "Somalia's Plagues," *New York Times* (September 6, 1992)

The human journey is, at its core, about the extension of empathy to broader and more inclusive domains.
—Jeremy Rifkin, "Man and Other Animals," *Guardian (UK)* (August 16, 2003)

Humanism

Humanism is a progressive philosophy of life that, without supernaturalism, affirms our ability and responsibility to lead ethical lives of personal fulfillment that aspire to the greater good of humanity.
—American Humanist Association, Humanist Manifesto III, a successor to the Humanist Manifesto of 1933

I feel no need for any other faith than my faith in human beings.
—Pearl S. Buck, *I Believe* (1939)

In our raucous democracy, fundamentalist religious belief has organized itself with political acumen to promulgate law that would undermine just those secular humanist principles that encourage it to flourish in freedom.
—E. L. Doctorow, "Why We Are Infidels," *Nation* (May 8, 2003)

What's wrong with being accused of humanism? . . . Why wouldn't we want to place human well-being at the center of our concerns?
—Gregory D. Foster, "Our -isms or Theirs?" *Common Dreams* (July 9, 2006)

Humanism is the creed of those who believe that in the circle of enwrapping mystery, men's fates are in their own hands.
—John Galsworthy, quoted in *The Philosophy of Humanism* (1997)

Our problems are manmade. Therefore, they can be solved by man.
—John F. Kennedy, in his speech at American University (June 10, 1963)

We must rapidly begin the shift from a "thing-oriented" society to a "person-oriented" society. When machines and computers, profit motives, and property rights are considered more important than people, the giant triplets of racism, materialism, and militarism are incapable of being conquered.
—Rev. Martin Luther King, Jr., in his speech delivered at Riverside Church in New York City, "A Time to Break Silence" (April 4, 1967)

The rehabilitation of humanism would be the religious right's worst nightmare.
—David A. Niose, "The Religious Right's Worst Nightmare," *Vermont Guardian* (November 11, 2005)

The ultra-right would have us believe that families are in trouble because of humanism, feminism, secular education, or sexual liberation, but the consensus of Americans is that what tears families apart is unemployment, inflation, and financial worries.
—Letty Cottin Pogrebin, *Family and Politics* (1983)

The Left

The next left will have to acknowledge, and even celebrate, the socialist spirit.
—Ronald Aronson, "The Left Needs More Socialism," *Nation* (March 31, 2006)

The great popular movements of our nation's history—against the slave trade, for the abolition of slavery, for women's suffrage, for trade union rights, for restraints on the power of big business in the Progressive Era, and extending to the civil rights movement, the New Left, and the environmental movement—can all be understood as efforts to align our economic and political institutions with our deepest moral commitments.
—Fred Block, "A Moral Economy," *Nation* (March 20, 2006)

The American left—or at least a broad swath of it—is more alienated from its own national institutions than its counterparts in any other developed nation. Even its own national symbols have become anathema (what a warning signal when you cannot tolerate the sight of your own flag).
—Marc Cooper, "Liberals Stuck in Scold Mode," *Los Angeles Times* (October 14, 2001)

The Moral Left spans a broad band of religious and secular organizations. It is an ecumenical movement where nuns and nonbelievers find common ground and the rich support policies helping the poor.
—Edward Cuddy, "Campaign 2004—A Battle for the Nation's Soul," *Buffalo News* (June 27, 2004)

When Republicans win, the Religious Right wins big. When Democrats win, the Moral Left, at best, gets a modest boost.
—Edward Cuddy, "Campaign 2004—A Battle for the Nation's Soul," *Buffalo News* (June 27, 2004)

The left must do what it has always done in American history . . . stake out a clear position in favor of social and economic justice, at home and abroad, and articulate it as clearly and forcefully as possible.
—Eric Foner, quoted in *What Do We Do Now* (2004)

The American left has won when it has cast its arguments in moral terms.
—Terry Curtis Fox, "The Immoral Veto," *Huffington Post* (July 20, 2006)

We forget sometimes that the values we treasure—equality, fairness, justice, dignity, and ultimately kindness and love—inspired the greatest moral and political achievements of the 20th century: civil rights, women's equality, the right to organize, and the growth of the environmental movement.
—Don Hazen, "Bring the Sixties Out of the Closet," AlterNet (March 23, 2006)

Instead of a left, America has a right wing that has proven powerful enough to pull both major parties significantly in its direction over the past twenty years.
—Mark Hertzgaard, *The Eagle's Shadow* (2002)

The arc of the moral universe is long but it bends towards justice.
—Rev. Martin Luther King, Jr., in his speech in Montgomery, Alabama, on March 25, 1965, quoted in "Torture and the 'Controversial' Arc of Injustice," *Common Dreams* (September 29, 2005)

We need to get out of issue silos that isolate arguments and keep us from the values and principles that define an overall progressive vision.
—George Lakoff, *Thinking Points: Communicating Our Values and Vision* (2006)

All those I know who voted blue . . . are law-abiding, respectful, reflective, thoughtful, spiritual people. Mostly, they believe in "live and let live."
—Karen Landers, "Blue Nation, Red Nation, and a Run for Democracy," *Common Dreams* (November 9, 2004)

It's the spirit of fighting back throughout American history that brought an end to sweatshops, won the eight-hour working day and a minimum wage, delivered suffrage to women and blacks from slavery, inspired the Gay Rights movement, the consumer and environmental movements, and more recently stopped Congress from enacting repressive legislation against immigrants.
—Bill Moyers, "A Time for Anger, a Call to Action," *Common Dreams* (March 22, 2007)

Ideas espoused by the Left stand for the little guy, the planet, and humanity as a whole.
—William Rivers Pitt, "Pressing Moral Imperative for the American Left," Truthout (April 27, 2002)

Those of us who reside in Gore Blueland cannot live without irony, which is to say, we cannot live without a filter of distance. We see the absurdity in everything, and we struggle to believe. . . . Bush Red is a simpler place.
—John Podhoretz, "The Two Americas: Ironic Us, Simple Them," *New York Post* (March 13, 2001)

I hate to say it, but pro-choicers really could learn some things from the antis, and I don't mean the arts of arson, murder, and lying to the Judiciary Committee. Lots of right-wing Christians tithe—how many pro-choicers write significant checks to pro-choice and feminist organizations?
—Katha Pollitt, *Virginity or Death!* (2006)

It took over a hundred years of advocacy to eliminate slavery, over a hundred years to put an end to child labor and over a hundred years to establish the minimum wage. This movement is in its infancy, but it is alive and it's not going away.
—Tim Robbins, "What I Voted For," *Nation* (August 6, 2001)

Let's get this straight: there are no "leftists" in modern-day America. Or, rather, there about ten of them.
—Matt Taibbi, "The Low Post: 101 Ways to Lie About Iraq," *Rolling Stone* (February 7, 2007)

What we haven't yet seen from the left is a sustained critique, not just of a particular politician or a particular policy, but of the entire ideology and worldview of conservatism.
—Paul Waldman, "It's the Conservatism, Stupid," *TomPaine.com* (July 12, 2006)

What you have on the left is a series of movements that are allied in some ways—an environmental movement, a pro-choice movement, a labor movement. These share some things in common, but they're not unified and working for one single goal.
—Paul Waldman, interviewed by Mark Karlin, "Paul Waldman Knows Progressives Can Win—and Here's How," *BuzzFlash* (May 25, 2006)

With the Republicans offering war overseas and corporate dominance at home, and the Democrats failing to offer any real alternatives, who will raise a prophetic voice for social and economic justice and for peace?
—Rev. Jim Wallis, "God's Politics: A Better Option," *Sojourners* (February 2005)

Many little lefts.
—James Weinstein, lamenting the fragmented, single-issue nature of the American Left, quoted in his obituary "James Weinstein: 1926–2005," *In These Times* (June 20, 2005)

If you are concerned about structural violence, if you're concerned about exploitation at the workplace, if you're concerned about institutionalized contempt against gay brothers and lesbian sisters, if you're concerned about organized hatred against peoples of color, if you're concerned about a subordination of women . . . That's what it means, in part, to be a leftist.
—Cornel West, "What It Means to Be a Leftist in the 21st Century," AlterNet (March 21, 2007)

The Left examines capitalism from the standpoint of such critical ideals as justice and freedom, rather than from the point of view of immediate selfinterest.
—Eli Zaretsky, "The Need for a Critical Left," *Tikkun* (November/December 2004)

The Left, Criticized

The basic posture of the Left . . . has been one of moral accommodation.
—Steve Almond, quoted in *What Do We Do Now* (2004)

One of the major failings of liberals (and liberalism in general) is an attitude that reeks of smugness, of arrogance, and of a sense of intellectual and cultural superiority. They're enlightened, the rest of us are not.
—Tom Bevan, "Liberal Snobbery v9.0," RealClearPolitics (July 19, 2006)

Until the American left decides to take a long, unprejudiced look at deepest America, at the kind of people who think voting for George Bush constitutes a blow against the elite, they are fated to continue their slide to oblivion.
—Thomas Frank, "The America That Will Vote for Bush," *Le Monde Diplomatique* (February 2004)

While leftists sit around congratulating themselves on their personal virtue, the right understands the central significance of movement-building, and they have taken to the task with admirable diligence.
—Thomas Frank, "Red-State America Against Itself," *TomDispatch.com* (July 16, 2004)

Hatred for Bush is no substitute for sound policy.
—Headline, *Charleston Daily Mail* (July 17, 2006)

Whereas the liberal mistake is to think that there is a program or policy to alleviate every problem in the world, the conservative flaw is to be vigilant against concentrations of power in government only—not in the private sector, where power can be wielded more secretly and sometimes more dangerously.
—Robert D. Kaplan, "Was Democracy Just a Moment?" *Atlantic Monthly* (December 1997)

Liberalism is dead, so dead that Democrats have all become moderate Republicans.
—Garrison Keillor, "You Say Potato," *Time* (April 22, 1996)

Conservative populists see themselves as oppressed by elitist liberals who look down their noses at them, when they are just ordinary, moral, right-thinking folks. They see liberals as trying to impose an immoral "political correctness" on them, and they are angry about it.
—George Lakoff, *Thinking Points: Communicating Our Values and Vision* (2006)

The major deficit of the Left is not inadequate money, but inadequate compassion for and understanding of the spiritual needs of the American people.
—Rabbi Michael Lerner, quoted in interview "Finding Spirit Among the Dems," AlterNet (February 10, 2006)

The right has been remarkably successful in pigeonholing liberalism as a white upper-middle-class affectation.
—Geoffrey Nunberg, *Talking Right: How Conservatives Turned Liberalism into a Tax-Raising, Latte-Drinking, Sushi-Eating, Volvo-Driving, New York Times-Reading, Body-Piercing, Hollywood-Loving, Left-Wing Freak Show* (2006)

The principal feature of American liberalism is sanctimoniousness. By loudly denouncing all bad things—war and hunger and date rape—liberals testify to their own terrific goodness.
—P. J. O'Rourke, *Give War a Chance* (1992)

All left-wing parties in the highly industrialized countries are at bottom a sham, because they make it their business to fight against something which they do not really wish to defeat.
—George Orwell, quoted in *The Collected Essays, Journalism and Letters of George Orwell* (1968)

A major barrier to the left reinventing itself and being effective is that we enjoy the cheap unity of critiquing the country and do not take responsibility for inspiring the country.
—Anjula Razdan, "Learning from the Right," *Utne* (March/April 2003)

People perceive the Democratic party as chardonnay-sipping, latte-drinking, Volvo-driving, Harvard-and-Yale-educated liberals.
—Andy Stern, "Changing How America Works," AlterNet (November 2, 2006)

Liberalism

Liberalism is too often misconceived as a new set of dogmas taught by a newer and better set of priests called "liberals." Liberalism is an attitude rather than a set of dogmas—an attitude that insists upon questioning all plausible and self-evident propositions.
—Morris Raphael Cohen, *The Faith of a Liberal* (1946)

Reality has a well-known liberal bias.
—Stephen Colbert, quoted "In Politics, Comedy Is Central," *In These Times* (August 4, 2006)

Over the long haul, America zigzags to the left. Principles once condemned as left wing heresies—abolition of slavery and equal rights for women and minorities—now form the core of American democracy.
—Edward Cuddy, "Campaign 2004—A Battle for the Nation's Soul," *Buffalo News* (June 27, 2004)

Liberalism will rise again and again because renewing the public sphere and reviving concern for the less privileged and less powerful are inevitably what free citizens demand.
—E. J. Dionne, Jr., describing Arthur M. Schlesinger's belief that history runs in cycles, "A Historian Who Saw Beyond the Past," *Washington Post* (March 2, 2007)

Once trade unionism, regulation of the market, and various welfare measures were the litmus tests of secular liberalism. Later, desegregation and racial justice were the litmus tests. Today the litmus test is abortion.
—E. J. Dionne, Jr., quoted in "With God on Our Side?" *Nation* (March 20, 2006)

Liberalism, above all, means emancipation—emancipation from one's fears, his inadequacies, from prejudice, from discrimination . . . from poverty.
—Hubert H. Humphrey, in a speech in New York City (March 29, 1967)

Liberalism is, I think, resurgent. One reason is that more and more people are so painfully aware of the alternative.
—John Kenneth Galbraith, review of *The Resurgent Liberal* (1991)

I believe that . . . liberalism is the best and only hope in the world today.
—John F. Kennedy, accepting the New York Liberal Party nomination (September 14, 1960)

If by a "liberal" [opponents] mean someone who looks ahead and not behind, someone who welcomes new ideas without rigid reactions, someone who cares about the welfare of the people—their health, their housing, their schools, their jobs, their civil rights, and their civil liberties . . . if that is what they mean by a "liberal," then I'm proud to say I'm a "liberal."
—John F. Kennedy, in accepting the New York Liberal Party nomination

Liberty-loving liberals founded our country and enshrined its freedoms. Dedicated, fair-minded liberals ended slavery and brought women the vote. Hardworking liberals fought the goon squads and won workers' rights: the eight-hour day, the weekend, health plans, and pensions.
—George Lakoff, *Thinking Points: Communicating Our American Values and Vision* (2006)

The heart of progressive-liberal values is simple: empathy (caring about and for people) and responsibility (acting responsibly on that empathy).
—George Lakoff, "The Post-Katrina Era," *Huffington Post* (September 8, 2005)

Don't let it be forgot,
That once there was a spot,
For one brief shining moment
That was known as Camelot.
—Alan Jay Lerner, the play "Camelot" (1960)

Liberalism by definition stands upon the elemental principal that change is necessary for survival, and that new ideas are not inherently dangerous.
—William Rivers Pitt, "Pressing Moral Imperative for the American Left," Truthout (April 27, 2002)

Every substantial improvement in the lives of the American people has been initiated by liberals and opposed by conservatives.
—Ted Rall, *Wake Up, You're Liberal!* (2004)

Liberal environmental laws have made the air safer to breathe, liberal food safety legislation has forced manufacturers to tell us what's in our food, and liberal education reformers have created a national network of public colleges and educations where the sons and daughters the poor and middle class may obtain a college degree.
—Ted Rall, *Wake Up, You're Liberal!* (2004)

There is perhaps no better measure of how radical and disruptive liberalism truly is than the ferocity of American elites' resistance to it. It took more than a half-million lives to eliminate slavery. American workers suffered more strike-related violence than workers in Western Europe—just to get an eight-hour day, freedom of association and a weekend.
—Corey Robin, "The Fear of the Liberals," *Nation* (September 8, 2005)

The essence of the Liberal outlook lies not in what opinions are held, but in how they are held: instead of being held dogmatically, they are held tentatively, and with a consciousness that new evidence may at any moment lead to their abandonment.
—Bertrand Russell, *Unpopular Essays* (1950)

The object of liberalism has never been to destroy capitalism . . . only to keep the capitalists from destroying it.
—Arthur M. Schlesinger, Jr., *The Age of Jackson* (1945)

That's why I'm a liberal. I believe in ambiguity, in risk, in uncertainty. I never have any doubts about the love of God and the sovereignty of God.
—Bishop Bennett Sims, quoted in "Religious Left Finds Its Voice," *Atlanta Journal-Constitution* (August 14, 2004)

The proposition that each of us has a right to "life, liberty, and the pursuit of happiness" remains as good a definition as anyone has ever come up with of liberalism's first principle and America's historic promise.
—Paul Starr, "Why Liberalism Works," *American Prospect* (April 4, 2007)

Liberalism is secular Christianity.
—Anonymous

The Liberal Character

Here is the liberals' problem in a nutshell: More than 30 percent of Americans happily answer to the appellation "conservative," while 18 percent call themselves "liberal."
—Eric Alterman, "Corrupt, Incompetent and 'Off Center,'" *Nation* (October 21, 2005)

Liberal: Not limited to or by established, traditional, orthodox, or authoritarian attitudes, views, or dogmas; free from bigotry. . . Favoring proposals for reform, open to new ideas for progress, and tolerant of the ideas and behavior of others; broad-minded. . . . Tending to give freely; generous.
—*The American Heritage Dictionary of the English Language* (2000)

The challenge we liberals face today is to match the fundamentalists' passionate intensity while still remaining true to our deepest convictions: a preference for tolerance over righteousness, fairness over success, and communication over certitude.
—Nick Bromell, "Scooter Libby and Me," *American Scholar* (Winter 2007)

Liberals are wary of regulating personal behavior, but would give government a powerful say over the shape of social and economic life.
—E. J. Dionne, Jr., *The War Against Public Life: Why Americans Hate Politics* (1991)

We need to be actually liberal, to view the world as being made up of varying points of view and to court those we would not normally meet for coffee.
—Percival Everett, quoted in *What Do We Do Now* (2004)

Liberals stand for tolerance, magnanimity, community spirit, the defense of the weak against the powerful, love of learning, freedom of belief, art and poetry, city life, the very things that make America worth dying for.
—Garrison Keillor, *Homegrown Democrat* (2004)

I like liberals. They gave us the five-day workweek; ended child labor; invented unemployment insurance, Social Security and Medicare; and led us, despite fierce opposition from "America First" pseudo-patriots on the political right, to victory over fascism in World War II.
—Robert Scheer, "Kerry a Bleeding Heart? Hardly," *Los Angeles Times* (October 12, 2004)

I remain to this day a New Dealer, unreconstructed and unrepentant.
—Arthur M. Schlesinger, Jr., *A Life in the 20th Century* (2000)

White men produced the Constitution. Liberals assert that what they produced is primary, while conservatives assert that who they were is primary.
—Jane Smiley, "Conservatives Cost a Lot of Money," AlterNet (March 22, 2007)

Liberals have more questions than answers; conservatives have more answers than questions.
—Anonymous

As Mankind becomes more liberal, they will be more apt to allow that all those who conduct themselves as worthy members of the community are equally entitled to the protections of civil government.
—George Washington, quoted in *God and Other Famous Liberals* (1991)

Why is it that right-wing bastards always stand shoulder to shoulder in solidarity, while liberals fall out among themselves?
—Yevgeny Yevtushenko, quoted in *Observer (UK)* (December 15, 1991)

Populism

Rich and powerful people generally encounter the law only as an irritant. Preventing them from developing wetlands. Or dumping toxic wastes from their factories.
—Larry Beinhart, "The Great Experiment in (Neo-con) Freedom," *Huffington Post* (February 2, 2007)

I'm tired of seeing the people who work hard and play by the rules get the shaft.
—Bill Clinton, quoted in *Talking Right: How Conservatives Turned Liberalism into a Tax-Raising, Latte-Drinking, Sushi-Eating, Volvo-Driving, New York Times-Reading, Body-Piercing, Hollywood-Loving, Left-Wing Freak Show* (2006)

Right-wing populism never applied to economics. While bravely championing chastity, fetuses and heterosexual marriage, the right has pursued an unabashedly elitist economic program: cutting taxes for the wealthy and services for everyone else.
—Barbara Ehrenreich, "It's the (Tanking) Economy, Stupid," AlterNet (September 13, 2006)

This long-running conservative revolt is rife with contradictions. It is an uprising of the common people whose long-term economic effect has been to shower riches upon the already wealthy and degrade the lives of the very people who are rising up.
—Thomas Frank, "Why They Won," *New York Times* (November 5, 2004)

It is not in the nature of elites to acknowledge people in the streets.
—Tom Hayden, "Anti-War Movement Deserves Some Credit," *San Francisco Chronicle* (November 26, 2006)

Even the smallest dog can lift its leg on the tallest building.
—Jim Hightower, *Thieves in High Places* (2003)

Everyone does better when everyone does better.
—Jim Hightower, quoted in "Race Card Backfires on Republicans," Truthdig (May 3, 2006)

While liberals offer a populism that promises underserved groups that "We will stand with you against the heartless and powerful," the central theme of the Ownership Society is . . . forget about a semblance of economic justice, it's about giving you, the individual, the tools you need to beat your neighbor. And if you can't beat him, he'll beat you.
—Joshua Holland, "Corporate Americans," AlterNet (January 18, 2005)

The right-wing has always used social issues to blunt populist uprisings. Racism, homophobia, abortion, cultural conflict, and the cynical manipulation of patriotism and religion have always worked to divide movements for reform.
—Marty Jezer, "Our Country Is on a Collision Course: Reform or War?" *Common Dreams* (July 19, 2002)

Now, more than ever, we need people who will stand up against the follies and lies of the powerful.
—Paul Krugman, "Missing Molly Ivins," *New York Times* (February 2, 2007)

Year after year . . . working-class voters fall for fire-breathing crusaders who promise to crack down on abortion, gay rights, porn, Darwin, and so on, but once in office all they do is cut the taxes of rich people and shovel favors to corporations.
—Katha Pollitt, "Earthly Rewards for the Christian Voter," *Nation* (November 18, 2004)

The notion that average folks need a party to defend their interests against corporations and the rich remains the [Democratic] party's guiding principle.
—Ted Rall, *Wake Up, You're Liberal!* (2004)

Populism is ultimately the way back for Democrats.
—David Sirota, "The Democrat's Da Vinci Code," *American Prospect* (January 2005)

Since when was your pocketbook—a.k.a. your ability to provide a decent standard of living for you and your family—not a moral issue?
—David Sirota, "The Failure of Populism?" *TomPaine.com* (April 12, 2001)

Progress

Political change in this country doesn't come from the center.
—Craig Aaron, "The Plot to Elect Kerry," *In These Times* (May 3, 2005)

I cannot escape my conviction that God is interested in the progress of mankind, individually and collectively.
—Bono, "The Constant Charmer," *Time* (January 2, 2006)

We win by being the party of progress, not by blurring differences with the new reactionaries.
—Robert L. Borosage & Katrina vanden Heuvel, "Progressives: Get Ready to Fight," *Nation* (November 11, 2004)

All progress has been an enlargement of the liberties of the individual with a corresponding decrease of the authority wielded over him by external forces.
—Emma Goldman, *The Individual, Society, and the State* (1936)

Martin Luther King Jr. Day: A paid federal feel-good holiday in which America congratulates itself on how "far" we've come.
—Sean Gonsalves, "Be Your Own King," AlterNet (January 15, 2007)

I find the great thing in this world is not so much where we stand, as in what direction we are moving.
—Oliver Wendell Holmes, *The Autocrat at the Breakfast Table* (1858)

The history of progress is written in the lives of infidels.
—Robert Ingersoll, in his speech in New York City (May 1, 1881)

The moment we choose to shape our love is the first, most critical step in shaping the whole God damn world.
—Courtney E. Martin, "Love Is Our Most Powerful, Lasting Form of Activism," AlterNet (February 14, 2007)

The test of our progress is not whether we add to the abundance of those who have much. It is whether we provide enough to those who have little.
—Franklin Delano Roosevelt, in his second inaugural address (January 20, 1937)

All progress means war with society.
—George Bernard Shaw, *Getting Married* (1908)

All progress has resulted from people who took unpopular positions.
—Adlai Stevenson, in a speech at Princeton University (March 22, 1954)

There is a constant trend in human affairs toward the perfectibility of mankind.
—Charles E. Merriam, *The New Democracy and the New Despotism* (1939)

Progressives

Progressives have always been torn between two impulses: to smash or to sustain.
—Richard Goldstein, "Looking for Lefty," *Village Voice* (September 13–19, 2000)

Conservatives, at their very best, draw lines that should never be crossed. Progressives, at their very best, tear down walls that should never have been built.
—Bill Clinton, at the dedication of his presidential library, "A Nation of Intolerance," *Denver Post* (December 5, 2004)

The fundamental challenge today is not to move the Democratic Party to the left, it is to educate "mainstream" Americans about the need and potential for progressive economic and social policies.
—Christopher D. Cook, "The Next Campaign: Ideas," *In These Times* (January 2005)

Progressive Christians believe in most things typical leftists believe in. But unlike liberals, progressive Christians' beliefs are informed by the word of Christ. So if they're environmentalists, they believe in preserving what God gave us. If they're for health care reform, it's because Christ wants his children healthy.
—Amanda Coyne, "No Christian Left Behind," *Anchorage Press* (November 18, 2004)

I think that progressive refers to a process based way of political thinking that believes if we organize, plan, and pull together in informed, honest, and open debate, and make reasonable accommodation for honest differences, we can improve our society.
—Robert Harris, "So What is '(a) Progressive,'" *BlueOregon* (October 26, 2005)

We're for the average working stiff in America . . . and keeping government from being a honey pot for either churches or corporations.
—Thom Hartmann, "Progressives and Democrats: Assert Your Brand!" *Common Dreams* (February 10, 2005)

A progressive believes that society can be made . . . "better" only when it's better for everybody.
—Garret Keizer, "Left Alone," *Mother Jones* (November 2005)

Progressives cannot continue to play defense in the battle of ideas. The stakes are too high.
—Edward M. Kennedy, quoted in "Kennedy's Other Speech," *Nation* (March 10, 2004)

The Democratic Party needs our help to regain its soul. If this is to be the party of peace, of universal, single-payer healthcare, of fair trade, then it needs people to speak out on those issues.
—Mimi Kennedy, quoted in news release "New Political Organization to Be Launched in Boston: Progressive Democrats of America" (July 20, 2004)

Progressives say, "We're all in this together," while conservatives say, "You're on your own."
—George Lakoff, "Building on the Progressive Victory," *Common Dreams* (December 14, 2006)

America is, and has always been, a progressive country. We care. We act responsibly. We want a level playing field for all to succeed, and a sense of national community. That is what makes us progressives.
—George Lakoff and John Halpin, "Framing Katrina," *American Prospect* (October 7, 2005)

Most of the leading Democrats in the country refer to themselves as progressives, a way in their case of avoiding the dreaded "liberal" tag. . . . It has become a way of appearing slightly left of center and at the same time not being of the left in any fundamental philosophical sense.
—Wayne O'Leary, "Distorting Progressive Legacy," *Progressive Populist* (December 15, 2005)

Movement progressives need to continue to see the Democratic Party as a means to an end—not an end unto itself.
—David Sirota, "Embracing Populism," *In These Times* (November 28, 2006)

If progressives don't have the will to fight, they don't deserve to govern.
—Paul Waldman, *Being Right Is Not Enough* (2006)

Progressives should start talking about the Bush administration's failures not as those of a president, but of an ideology.
—Paul Waldman, "It's the Conservatism, Stupid," *TomPaine.com* (July 12, 2006)

Progressives have been better at denunciation than annunciation. We need both. People are as interested in what you're for as what you're against.
—Paul Wellstone, "Winning Politics," *Nation* (February 19, 2001)

Who do you want to be—Mr. Potter or George Bailey?
—Oliver Willis, "I Am a Progressive," *Huffington Post* (March 10, 2006)

I should say that a progressive is one who insists upon recognizing new facts as they present themselves.
—Woodrow Wilson, in his speech in New York City (January 29, 1911)

Progressivism

Democrats should not agree to partial torture, partial violations of the Constitution, partially honest elections, or partial right of *habeas corpus* or right to counsel. These involve practices and policies that are so radical, so extreme, so violative of American tradition, that they simply must be stopped.
—Brent Budowsky, "New Congress: Americanism Means No Torture, Eavesdropping with Warrants, Honest Elections, Habeas Corpus," *Huffington Post* (November 13, 2006)

In the end, the future of liberalism/progressivism depends not on identifying and vilifying an enemy . . . but on espousing a positive vision for the future around which a movement, a party, and an American consensus can be built.
—Wes Boyd, interviewed by Don Hazen, "MoveOn Muscles Up," AlterNet (April 26, 2005)

We must become the change we wish to see in the world.
—Mahatma Gandhi, quoted in the *Los Angeles Times* (July 30, 1989)

Progressives need to systematically expand the universe of access points to the progressive worldview. . . . There are three main ways this can be achieved: the development of a vibrant progressive mass media, a revived labor movement, and the organizing of large-scale grassroots social movements.
—Christopher Hayes, "How to Turn Your Red State Blue," *In These Times* (March 22, 2005)

American values are inherently progressive.
—George Lakoff, *Thinking Points: Communicating Our American Values and Vision* (2006)

The six modes of progressive thought: (1) socioeconomic, (2) identity politics, (3) environmentalists, (4) civil libertarians, (5) spiritual, and (6) anti-authoritarian.
—George Lakoff, *Don't Think Like an Elephant* (2004)

The great progressive struggles in our history have been waged to make sure ordinary citizens, and not just the rich, share in the benefits of a free society.
—Bill Moyers, "Saving Democracy," *Common Dreams* (February 24, 2006)

Are you for everyone having health care, a fair wage, solid retirement, and being able to live in a democratic system that allows the people to decide how corporations behave?
—Jonathan Tasini, "A 10-Step Program for Democrats," *TomPaine.com* (January 2, 2007)

Progressive politics is remembering its own religious history and recovering the language of faith.
—Rev. Jim Wallis, "The Religious Right's Era Is Over," *Time* (February 16, 2006)

Responsibility

Our responsibility as privileged human beings is to pay back for the opportunities we've received.
—Kathryn Anastos, quoted in *New York* magazine (December 21, 1992)

We can't escape responsibility, there's no sitting out moral decisions, and whenever we refuse to stand up against wrongdoing we're actually supporting the status quo.
—Rocky Anderson, "The Other Rocky," *Nation* (January 1, 2007)

Unto whom much is given, of him shall be much required.
—Luke 12:48

If God exists, all depends on him and we can do nothing against his will. If he does not exist, everything depends on us.
—Albert Camus, *The Myth of Sisyphus* (1942)

If I drive a gas-guzzling 12-cylinder vehicle knowing what I know now about carbon emissions and our dependence on foreign oil, I am basically saying that I don't care about the planet I leave behind for your or my kids.
—Sheryl Crow, "On Deception, Spin, and Losing Our Way," *Huffington Post* (May 4, 2007)

It's always somebody else's fault. It's the gays' fault. It's the immigrants' fault. It's the liberals' fault. It's the Democrats' fault. It's Hollywood people.
—Howard Dean, on Republican tactics, quoted in "Dean Calls Iraqi PM an Anti-Semite," *AccessNorthGa.com* (July 26, 2006)

Liberals should be unafraid to embrace the language of personal responsibility.
—E. J. Dionne, Jr. "'Family Values' for All of Us," *Washington Post* (October 7, 2006)

It was a mistake to vote for this [Iraq] war in 2002. I take responsibility for that mistake.
—John Edwards, "The Right Way in Iraq," *Washington Post* (November 13, 2005)

Our privileges can be no greater than our obligations. The protection of our rights can endure no longer than the performance of our responsibilities.
—John F. Kennedy, in a speech (May 18, 1963)

We must strive to become good ancestors.
—Ralph Nader, *The Good Fight* (2004)

That's what happened to Jimmy Carter—he asked Americans to take responsibility for their profligate ways, and promptly lost to Ronald Reagan, who told them once again that they could do anything they wanted.
—Jane Smiley, "The Unteachable Ignorance of the Red States," *Slate* (November 4, 2004)

Secular Society

Not a few secular progressives subscribe to an extreme relativism. . . . They suppose all morality is culture-dependent and has no reference to any fixed standard, a view that would let Adolf Hitler off the hook.
—Jay Ambrose, "Religion and the Presidency," *Naples Daily News* (June 21, 2004)

Living without God means turning toward something. To flourish we need coherent secular popular philosophies that effectively answer life's vital questions.
—Ronald Aronson, "The New Atheists," *Nation* (June 25, 2007)

A secular society, not a fundamentalist society, is the only kind where religious freedom is available for all and secure for any.
—Kimberley Blaker, *The Fundamentals of Extremism* (2003)

For those who value secular society, apprehending the threat of Christian nationalism is tricky. It's like being a lobster in a pot, with the water heating up so slowly that you don't notice the moment at which it starts to kill you.
—Michelle Goldberg, "Saving Secular Society," *In These Times* (May 16, 2006)

The Democrats would be in trouble if they tried to be a purely secular party, but they would also be wasting their time trying to woo the most traditional religious voters, because they are firmly Republican, and they would have to give up a lot to go for them.
—John Green, quoted in "God and the Blue States," *Nation* (August 12, 2004)

I think atheism and secularism are . . . names that ultimately we don't need. We don't need a name for disbelief in astrology. I don't think we need anything other that rationality and reason and intellectual honesty.
—Sam Harris, interviewed by Laura Sheahen, "Why Religion Must End," Beliefnet (May 10, 2006)

The pendulum has swung completely. There's a push-back by many conservative Christians, perhaps emboldened by . . . the increasing presence of evangelical Christianity in the public arena. They're saying the secularization of our society and public schools has gone too far and become hostility to their religion.
—Charles Haynes, quoted in "Evangelicals Use Courts to Fight Restrictions on Christmas Tidings," *Washington Post* (December 20, 2004)

The government of the United States is secular. It derives its power from the consent of man.
—Robert Ingersoll, quoted in *What's God Got To Do With It?* (2005)

Secularists are not value-free; their values are simply grounded in earthly concerns rather than in anticipation of heavenly rewards or fear of infernal punishment.
—Susan Jacoby, *Freethinkers* (2004)

Appeal to the 60 or 70 percent of the American people who aren't fundamentalists—who may have lots of religious beliefs, but who also believe in secular government. Don't waste time trying to persuade people who believe that the earth was created in seven days.
—Susan Jacoby, quoted in *BuzzFlash* interview (February 14, 2005)

History, I believe, furnishes no example of a priest-ridden people maintaining a free civil government.
—Thomas Jefferson, in a letter to Alexander von Humboldt (December 6, 1813)

Secularists are often wrongly accused of trying to purge religious ideals from public discourse. We simply want to deny them public sponsorship.
—Wendy Kaminer, "The Last Taboo," *New Republic* (October 14, 1996)

Religions do not have a monopoly on ethics or morality. Secularism itself would be a good place to start our search for a stronger public debate on values.
—Thornton McCamish, "Secularism Is No Moral Vacuum," *The Age* (November 19, 2004)

The secular fundamentalism of the left is as much a problem as the religious fundamentalism of the right.
—Rev. Jim Wallis, quoted in "Focus on Moral Values Drove Bush's Win," *Patriot-News* (November 4, 2004)

A genuinely democratic society requires a secular ethos: one that does not equate morality with religion, stigmatize atheists, defer to religious interests, and aim over others to make religious belief an informal qualification for public office.
—Ellen Willis, "Freedom from Religion," *Nation* (February 19, 2001)

Self-Improvement

The only effective discipline is self-discipline, motivated by the inner desire to act meritoriously in order to do well in one's own eyes, according to one's own values.
—Bruno Bettelheim, *A Good Enough Parent* (1987)

You can't change the world, but you can change yourself. That adage suits consumer capitalism perfectly, since the illusion of changing ourselves is successfully maintained through shopping.
—Madeleine Bunting, "The End is Nigh," *Guardian (UK)* (August 27, 2001)

In place of obsessively changing yourself, let's change the world.
—Johann Hari, "The Selfishness of the Self-Help Industry," *Independent (UK)* (April 12, 2007)

If I am not for myself, who will be for me?
If I am not for others, what am I?
And if not now, when?
—Rabbi Hillel, quoted in *Soul of a Citizen* (1999)

There is only one corner of the universe you can be certain of improving, and that is your own self.
—Aldous Huxley, *Time Must Have a Stop* (1945)

If you bring forth what is within you, what you bring forth can save you. If you do not bring forth what is within you, what you do not bring forth will destroy you.
—Jesus, Gnostic Gospel of Thomas, quoted in *The Gnostic Gospels* (1989)

I have tried to learn from my mistakes and sought to be better in the course of my life—better husband, better brother, better father, better grandfather, better senator.
—Edward M. Kennedy, quoted in "At 74, Sen. Edward Kennedy Still Roars," Reuters (April 22, 2006)

This is the moment freedom begins, the moment you realize someone else has been writing your story, and it's time you took the pen from his hand and started writing it yourself.
—Bill Moyers, quoted "Media Reform: Arming the Lambs," *Common Dreams* (January 16, 2007)

Learn what you are and be such.
—Pindar, *Odes* (5th century B.C.)

Personal transformation is a political act. Until we change ourselves, we cannot change the world.
—Marianne Williamson, "Toward a Holistic Politics," *Tikkun* (July/August 2003)

I believe the only truly radicalizing force is people's desire to change their own lives for the better.
—Ellen Willis, quoted in "Bully in the Pulpit?" *Nation* (February 22, 2001)

Men can starve from a lack of self-realization as much as they can from a lack of bread.
—Richard Wright, *Native Son* (1940)

Service

The soul is awakened through service.
—Erica Jong, *Fear of Fifty: A Midlife Memoir* (1994)

Service is the rent that you pay for room on this earth.
—Shirley Chisholm, quoted in *I Dream a World: Portraits of Black Women Who Changed America* (1989)

Ask not what your country can do for you, ask what you can do for your country.
—John F. Kennedy, in his inaugural address (January 20, 1961)

[The Bush administration] has reduced the honorable profession of public service to an opportunity for plunder and self-enrichment.
—Robert F. Kennedy, Jr., *Crimes Against Nature* (2004)

The country is in deep trouble. We've forgotten that a rich life consists fundamentally of serving others, trying to leave the world a little better than you found it.
—Cornel West, quoted in *The Impossible Will Take a Little While: A Citizen's Guide to Hope in a Time of Fear* (2004)

Strength

We're . . . sick of Democrats whining about Republicans' hardball tactics. We want our party to toughen up, smarten up, and listen up.
—James Carville and Paul Begala, *Take It Back* (2006)

Strength and wisdom are not opposing values.
—Bill Clinton, in his address to the Democratic National Convention (July 27, 2004)

Memo to Democrats . . . If you are not as tough as [Bush] is, he will crush you—again.
—E. J. Dionne, Jr., "Lessons for Democrats," *Washington Post* (December 31, 2004)

We need to be blunt about what distinguishes Democrats from Republicans on the issues that matter.
—Dick Durbin, quoted "Dick Durbin: Bush Fighter," *Nation* (January 27, 2005)

Don't expect Jimmy Carter or Ronald Reagan or John Lennon or Yoko Ono or Bob Dylan or Jesus Christ to come and do it for you. You have to do it yourself.
—John Lennon, in an interview, *Playboy* (January 1981)

Waffling rarely wins campaigns. The people want straight talk and real action.
—Ralph Nader, *In Pursuit of Justice: Collected Writings 2000–2003* (2004)

What does not kill me makes me stronger.
—Friedrich Nietzsche, *Twilight of the Idols* (1889)

It is a mistake to give the right a monopoly on values by agreeing with them in a half-baked, yes-but, wishy-washy way.
—Katha Pollitt, "Let's Not Devalue Ourselves," *Nation* (July 29, 2004)

O! it is excellent to have a giant's strength; but it is tyrannous to use it like a giant.
—William Shakespeare, *Measure for Measure* (1604)

Liberals have rediscovered their moral backbone.
—Amy Sullivan, "Fightin' Words," *Sojourners* (September 2004)

Strength doesn't flow from a policy proposal, and it can't be demonstrated with a hawkish vote. The public will be convinced that Democrats are strong when they stand up for their beliefs, take political risks, and don't run scared every time they get attacked by Republicans.
—Paul Waldman, "Elections Aren't About Issues," *Boston Globe* (September 6, 2006)

Tolerance

Judge not, and ye shall not be judged: condemn not, and ye shall not be condemned: forgive, and ye shall be forgiven.
—Luke 6:37

Being tolerant does not mean that I share another one's belief. But it does mean that I acknowledge another one's right to believe, and obey, his own conscience.
—Victor Frankl, *The Will to Meaning* (1969)

Tolerance is a virtue, but tolerance coupled with passivity is a vice.
—Chris Hedges, *American Fascists* (2006)

Respect—not tolerance—must be our goal if we would diminish prejudice in our time. For tolerance is often but a gentle disguise for prejudice: the tolerant often behave as self-appointed connoisseurs of weaknesses in others, or self-appointed protectors of those whom they deem to be their inferiors.
—Selma G. Hirsch, *The Fears Men Live By* (1955)

The highest result of education is tolerance.
—Helen Keller, *Optimism* (1903)

Liberalism teaches us to be tolerant of other people's religious beliefs, so long as those beliefs don't cause anyone harm or impinge on another's right to believe differently.
—Barack Obama, *The Audacity of Hope* (2006)

If we extend unlimited tolerance even to those who are intolerant, if we are not prepared to defend a tolerant society against the onslaught of the intolerant, then the tolerant will be destroyed, and tolerance with them.
—Karl Popper, *The Open Society and Its Enemies* (1945)

I pledge to have respect for people whose abilities, beliefs, culture, race, sexual identity, or other characteristics are different from my own.
—Tolerance Pledge, attacked by conservatives as "pro-homosexual propaganda," quoted in "Safe Harbor for Gay Bigotry," *Boston Globe* (February 2, 2005)

THE UNCHECKED POWER OF CORPORATIONS

Bankers

What is robbing a bank compared to founding one?
—Bertolt Brecht, *The Threepenny Opera* (1928)

Conservatives worry that kids today grow up wanting to be porn stars; liberals fear they want to be investment bankers.
—David Callahan, *The Moral Center* (2006)

A power has risen up in the government greater than the people themselves, consisting of many and various and powerful interests, combined into one mass, and held together by the cohesive power of the vast surplus in the banks.
—John C. Calhoun, in a speech (May 27, 1836)

There are 22 times in the Old Testament which speak of the sin of charging interest on a loan. . . . I am surprised that so many Christians who are fighting to keep the commandments on the wall are not fighting as hard to have them implemented.
—Karen Horst Cobb, "Ye Shall Know the Truth: Profits of the New World Order," *Common Dreams* (July 29, 2005)

I sincerely believe . . . that banking establishments are more dangerous than standing armies.
—Thomas Jefferson, in a letter to John Taylor (May 28, 1816)

What can citizens do when the banks start robbing them—and the political system fails to protect them from corporate abuses?
—Jake Lewis, "Taming the Banking Predators," *Multinational Monitor* (January/February 2004)

I have the Confederacy before me and the bankers behind me, and I fear the bankers most.
—Abraham Lincoln, quoted in "Crimes against Nature," *Rolling Stone* (December 11, 2003)

Big Business

The exaltation of big business at the expense of the citizen was a central characteristic of government policy in Germany and Italy in the years before those countries were chewed to bits and spat out by fascism.
—Paul Bigioni, "Fascism Then. Fascism Now?" *Toronto Star* (November 28, 2005)

Men err when they think they can be inhuman exploiters in their business life, and loving husbands and fathers at home.
—Smiley Blanton, *Love or Perish* (1956)

Mankind was my business. The common welfare was my business; charity, mercy, forbearance, and benevolence were all my business. The dealings of my trade were but a drop of water in the comprehensive ocean of my business!
—The ghost of Jacob Marley, in Charles Dickens's *A Christmas Carol* (1843)

Businesses don't say the Pledge of Allegiance anymore, they don't consider themselves American. Their goal is to produce in China, sell in America, and run the income through the Cayman Islands to avoid paying taxes.
—Byron L. Dorgan, U.S. senator from North Dakota, in an interview with Mark Karlin, *BuzzFlash* (August 24, 2006)

We all know bad things are happening to our political and social universe; we know that business is colonizing ever larger chunks of American culture; and we know that advertising tells lies. . . . And yet we do nothing.
—Thomas Frank, quoted in *Conglomerates and the Media* (1997)

These men of the technostructure are the new and universal priesthood. Their religion is business success; their test of virtue is growth and profit. Their bible is the computer printout; their communion bench is the committee room.
—John Kenneth Galbraith, *The Age of Uncertainty* (1977)

Why is Wall Street so infatuated with cigarettes? . . . They are addictive. They are inexpensive to make, require almost no innovation, there is a global market for them, and cigarette makers can raise prices without seeing much of a drop in business.
—Andrew Martin, "Tobacco's Stigma Aside, Wall Street Finds a Lot to Like," *New York Times* (January 31, 2007)

We have a government of big business, by big business and for big business.
—Ralph Nader, "Corporate Socialism," *Washington Post* (July 18, 2002)

What the credit card industry has been doing the last ten years is akin to sending free samples of alcohol to alcoholics.
—Travis Plunkett, quoted in "Bankruptcy Bill is Congress' Shame," *Capital Times* (Madison, Wisconson) (March 7, 2005)

It is a shameful and inhuman thing to treat men as mere chattels for profit.
—Pope Leo XIII, *On the Condition of Workers* (May 15, 1891)

Pharmaceutical companies sell disease. Every state and stage of existence has become a pathology in need of pharmaceutical "intervention."
—Jonathan Rowe, "Drug Ads Sell a Problem, Not a Solution," *Christian Science Monitor* (August 21, 2006)

Anti-intellectualism has long been the anti-Semitism of the businessman.
—Arthur M. Schlesinger, Jr., *Partisan Review* (March 4, 1953)

Perpetual devotion to what a man calls his business is only to be sustained by perpetual neglect of many other things.
—Robert Louis Stevenson, *Virginibus Puerisque* (1881)

In an effort to eliminate the possibility of any rival growing up, some monopolists would sacrifice democracy itself.
—Henry Wallace, vice president of the United States, "Wallace Defines American Fascism," *New York Times* (April 9, 1944)

Microsoft has decided (and publicly confirmed this summer) that anyone in China doing a search containing the words "freedom" or "democracy" will be shown a message explaining that those words are banned and the requested search query will not be processed.
—G. Pascal Zachary, "See No Evil: How American Businesses Collaborate with China's Repressive Government," *In These Times* (October 24, 2005)

Commercialism

We support the right of parents to raise their children in an environment free from corporate manipulation. So many parents I talk to are fed up with the continual commercial assault on their children.
—Enola Aird, quoted in press release, "New Name for National Coalition on Marketing to Children," Campaign for a Commercial-Free Childhood (November 10, 2004)

Junk-food marketers' claim to innocence is about as plausible as the tobacco industry's long-standing position that cigarette advertising does not increase smoking.
—Joe Badaracco, quoted in *The Corporation: The Pathological Pursuit of Profit and Power* (2004)

There are no models, in the mainstream media, suggesting that anything less than middle-class affluence might be an honorable and dignified condition, nor is there any reason why corporate advertisers should promote such a subversive possibility.
—Barbara Ehrenreich, *Fear of Falling* (1990)

The people who make advertising are, in a very real sense, the ideologues of the corporate revolution: They are architects of dissatisfaction and of perpetual obsolescence.
—Thomas Frank, quoted in *Conglomerates and the Media* (1997)

In a time, not so very long ago, America was a commercial giant. But today we seem to be a giant of commercials. . . . Commercials and commercialism have become ubiquitous, cacophonous, intrusive, and overbearing.
—Jim Hightower, *Thieves in High Places* (2003)

Corporations put ads on fruit, ads all over the schools, ads on cars, ads on clothes. The only place you can't find ads is where they belong: on politicians.
—Molly Ivins, "Is Absolutely Everything For Sale in America?" *St. Louis Post-Dispatch* (July 19, 2000)

[Advertising] . . . makes women believe that their chief role is to please men.
—Lucy Komisar, quoted in *Women in Sexist Society* (1971)

Angels we have heard on high, tell us to go out and buy.
—Tom Lehrer, in a Christmas parody, quoted in "Media May Ignore War, but It Goes On," *Binghamton Press & Sun-Bulletin* (December 2, 2005)

There can be no solution to the commercialization of public education until public schools are adequately and equitably funded.
—Steven Manning, "The Littlest Coke Addicts," *Nation* (June 7, 2001)

The rise of commercialism is an artifact of the growth of corporate power.
—Gary Ruskin and Juliet Schor, "Every Nook and Cranny: The Dangerous Spread of Commercialized Culture," *Multinational Monitor* (March 25, 2005)

What was once a trickle of advertising to children has become a flood. . . . Children have few legal protections from corporate marketers in the United States.
—Gary Ruskin and Juliet Schor, "Every Nook and Cranny: The Dangerous Spread of Commercialized Culture," *Multinational Monitor* (March 25, 2005)

Americans spend three to four times as many hours a year shopping as their counterparts in Western European countries. Once a purely utilitarian chore, shopping has been elevated to the status of a national passion.
—Juliet Schor, quoted in "The People's Business," *In These Times* (February 18, 2005)

We cannot allow marketeers to establish our social norms.
—Jenni Russell, "The selfish generation," *Guardian (UK)* (December 6, 2003)

Advertising is the false spirituality of materialism.
—Rev. Jim Wallis, *The Soul of Politics* (1994)

Corporate Crime

Passing the Corporate Three Strikes law would demonstrate that California is willing to get tough on crime in the suites, not just crime in the streets. It would create a climate where law-abiding companies thrive and give the public a means of cracking down on recidivist corporate criminals.
—Lee Drutman, "What About Three-Strikes-and-You're-Out for Corporate Criminals?" *Common Dreams* (March 7, 2003)

Great is the mischief of the legal crime.
—Ralph Waldo Emerson, address in Concord, Massachusetts (May 3, 1851)

Yes, as through this world I've wandered
I've seen lots of funny men;
Some will rob you with a six-gun,
And some with a fountain pen.
—Woody Guthrie, from his 1939 "The Ballad of Pretty Boy Floyd," *American Folksong* (1961)

It's time for the IRS to stop coddling corporate crooks and start going after tax shelter thieves with a vengeance. To do any less is a slap in the face of all the hardworking taxpayers who, however grudgingly, pay their fair share.
—Arianna Huffington, "Corporate Tax Cheats Wreak Havoc on the Neediest Among Us," *Arianna Online* (July 23, 2003)

Corporate criminals should not be given a special pass.
—Russell Mokhiber and Robert Weissman, "Corporate Crime Without Shame," *Common Dreams* (July 28, 2003)

Most of the leading federal agencies responsible for pursuing corporate criminals . . . remain woefully understaffed, underfunded, and undermotivated.
—Ralph Nader, "How to Curb Corporate Power," *Nation* (October 10, 2005)

Corporate killers rarely see the inside of a jail cell, let alone face real consequences for their deplorable behavior.
—Karyn Strickler, "Is It Time for a Corporate Death Penalty Act?" *Common Dreams* (January 28, 2005)

We have a system in America that encourages companies to violate the law because it's a tiny cost of doing business.
—Jonathan Tasini, "Wal-Mart's Sweetheart Deal," *TomPaine.com* (February 16, 2005)

Just once, I'd like to see a corporate executive whose company has knowingly hired illegal immigrants doing the perp walk for his offenses—handcuffed, disgraced, chaperoned by law enforcement officials.
—Cynthia Tucker, "Secure Border by Going After Employers," *Atlanta Journal-Constitution* (May 21, 2006)

Crime is a logical extension of the sort of behavior that is often considered perfectly respectable in legitimate business.
—Robert Rice, *The Business of Crime* (1956)

Corporate Power

The twentieth century has been characterized by three developments of great political importance: the growth of democracy, the growth of corporate power, and the growth of corporate propaganda as a means of protecting corporate power against democracy.
—Alex Carey, quoted in "Democracy Falters as Corporate Power Grows," *Toronto Star* (April 1, 2001)

How did corporations gain so much power with so little social accountability?
—Chuck Collins, "Oversight Hearings: What Should Congress Do?" *Nation* (January 4, 2007)

Corporations are great and appalling things. They take you and shape you in nearly nothing flat.
—Don DeLillo, *Underworld* (1998)

Of the one hundred largest economies in the world, fifty-one are corporations and forty-nine are nations.
—Lee Drutman and Charlie Cay, "The People's Business," *In These Times* (February 18, 2005)

Corporate America and the Republican Party have forged a partnership that currently decrees the contours of our economic and cultural life. If progressives ever want to counter this corporate hegemony, they must learn from the past and embrace the strength and potential of the union movement.
—Jeff Epton, "Labor's Future Is Ours," *In These Times* (January 21, 2005)

What is called corporate welfare is a minor detail. Far more important is the full-fledged takeover by private industry of public decision-making and government spending.
—John Kenneth Galbraith, "Free Market Fraud," *Progressive* (January 1999)

Corporations cause harm every day. Why do their harms go unchecked? How can they dictate what we produce, how we work, what we eat, drink, and breathe? How did a self-governing people let this come to pass?
—Richard L. Grossman and Frank I. Adams, *Taking Care of Business: Citizenship and the Charter of Incorporation* (1993)

Practically every progressive struggle . . . is being fought against one cluster of corporations or another.
—Jim Hightower, *If the Gods Had Meant Us to Vote They Would Have Given Us Candidates* (2001)

I hope we shall . . . crush in its birth the aristocracy of our moneyed corporations, which dare already to challenge our government to a trial of strength and to bid defiance to the laws of their country.
—Thomas Jefferson, in a letter to George Logan (November 12, 1816)

Merchants have no country. The mere spot they stand on does not constitute so strong an attachment as that from which they draw their gains.
—Thomas Jefferson, in a letter to Horatio G. Spafford (March 17, 1814)

The biggest threat to American democracy is corporate power.
—Robert F. Kennedy, Jr., "Kennedy: Fascist America," *Common Dreams* (January 22, 2005)

I see in the near future a crisis approaching that unnerves me and causes me to tremble for the safety of my country. Corporations have been enthroned and an era of corruption in high places will follow, and the money power of the country will endeavor to prolong its reign by working upon the prejudices of the people until all wealth is aggregated in a few hands and the Republic is destroyed.
—Abraham Lincoln, in a letter to Col. William F. Elkins, dated November 21, 1864, The *Lincoln Encyclopedia* (1950)

Corporations are stifling our lives . . . aesthetically speaking, culturally speaking, spiritually speaking. They flatten everything. They are the Big Empty.
—Norman Mailer, "The Big Empty," *Adbusters* (January/February 2005)

The corporate conservatives and their allies in the political and religious right are achieving a vast transformation of American life. . . . They are systematically stripping government of all its functions except rewarding the rich and waging war.
—Bill Moyers, in his keynote address to the Inequality Matters Forum, New York University (June 3, 2004)

The men and women who have mastered the money game have taken advantage of this fundamental weakness in our system—the high cost of campaigns—to sell democracy to the highest bidder.
—Bill Moyers, "A Time for Heresy," AlterNet (March 24, 2006)

It is precisely because religion takes the problem of evil so seriously that it must always be suspicious of too much concentrated power—politically and economically—either in totalitarian regimes or in huge multinational corporations which now have more wealth and power than many governments.
—Rev. Jim Wallis, *God's Politics: Why the Right Gets It Wrong and the Left Doesn't Get It* (2005)

A specter of despair haunts late twentieth-century America. The quality of our lives and the integrity of our souls are in jeopardy. Wealth inequality and class polarization are escalating—with ugly consequences for the most vulnerable among us. The lethal power of global corporate elites and national managerial bosses is at an all-time high.
—Cornel West, quoted in *The Impossible Will Take a Little While: A Citizen's Guide to Hope in a Time of Fear* (2004)

Men are the servants of corporations.
—Woodrow Wilson, *The New Freedom* (1913)

Corporations

If you're looking to defraud, delude, double-cross, dupe, embezzle, fleece, gouge, hoodwink, hornswoggle, mislead, mug, rig, rip off, sandbag, scam, screw, shaft, shortchange, snooker, or just plain sucker the public in the Grand American Tradition, you've got to have a corporation.
—Kenny Ausubel, "Mighty Corporate," *Huffington Post* (November 4, 2005)

The corporation's legally defined mandate is to pursue relentlessly and without exception its own economic self-interest, regardless of the harmful consequences it might cause to others.
—Joel Bakan, *The Corporation: The Pathological Pursuit of Profit and Power* (2004)

Corporation. An ingenious device for obtaining individual profit without individual responsibility.
—Ambrose Bierce, *Collected Works of Ambrose Bierce* (1911)

A new rebelliousness haunts the world. With each day, more and more people are challenging the institutions that exert control over our lives. The new rebels have set their sights on that force which during the last generation has nearly supplanted the nation-state as the possessor of true power: the transnational corporation.
—Kevin Danaher and Jason Mark, *Insurrection: Citizen Challenges to Corporate Power* (2003)

The corporation has become a site for internal predation, where one person can advance by eliminating another one's job.
—Barbara Ehrenreich, *Bait and Switch* (2005)

Corporations were not originally created to maximize profit to stockholders, as most people today believe. They were first created to serve the public interest, the public purpose.
—Ralph Estes, *Tyranny of the Bottom Line* (1996)

Corporations . . . were designed by law, set up by the state, to serve the people, to build bridges and tunnels and roads. And now they are this Goliath that's eating up the very entities, and having more power than the very entities, that set them up.
—Robert Greenwald, quoted in interview "Robert Greenwald Tackles Wal-Mart: Just How Have Americans Paid for Those Low Prices?" *BuzzFlash* (October 27, 2005)

A corporation today can have an infinite lifespan. It doesn't fear death. It doesn't fear pain or incarceration. It doesn't need fresh water to drink or clean air to breathe. It doesn't need health care or retirement. It can own others of its own kind. It can change citizenship in a day. It can tear off a part of itself and create a new corporation in an hour. It can amass virtually infinite wealth.
—Thom Hartmann, "Is Wal-Mart a Person?" *BuzzFlash* (January 28, 2005)

Corporations are like the feudal domains that evolved into nation-states; they are nothing less than the vanguard of a new Darwinian organization of politics.
—Robert D. Kaplan, "Was Democracy Just a Moment?" *Atlantic Monthly* (December 1997)

Corporations are shredding the social compact, pensions are disappearing, median incomes are flattening, and healthcare costs are soaring. In many ways, the average household is generally worse off today than it was thirty years ago,
—Bill Moyers, "For America's Sake," *Nation* (January 22, 2007)

American corporations are set up not to "create wealth," but to plunder the wealth of everyone not powerful enough to stop them.
—Jane Smiley, "CEO President," *Huffington Post* (August 20, 2006)

Cult of the CEO

Times of war call for a spirit of shared sacrifice, not greed.
—Sarah Anderson, "Put an End to CEO Excess" (December 17, 2005)

Crack down on stock option plans that give corporate leaders an incentive to cook the books. End sweetheart deals that protect executive pensions but leave workers with empty promises.
—Robert L. Borosage and Robert Loper, eds., *Straight Talk: Common Sense for the Common Good* (2006)

Income inequality is the worst ever recorded. The top 5 percent make as much as the bottom 60 percent.
—Robert L. Borosage and Robert Loper, eds., *Straight Talk: Common Sense for the Common Good* (2006)

Our factories are all overseas. All we produce here are rich executives.
—Bumper sticker

CEOs now earn more than their employees at a ratio of more than 400 to 1.
—Stephen Dick, "Toward a New Moral Majority," *Herald Bulletin* (January 24, 2007)

Shame on the CEOs who make eight-figure incomes while their lowest-paid employees trudge between food banks.
—Barbara Ehrenreich, "Workers' Rights Are About Dignity as Much as Wages," *Progressive* (October 27, 2006)

There is zero correlation between CEO pay and CEO performance.
—Barney Frank, quoted in "Poll Shows Americans Distrust Corporations," *New York Times* (December 10, 2005)

In America, workers aren't being rewarded for productivity and CEOs aren't being punished for poor performance. What's wrong with this picture?
—Ellen Goodman, "Bob the Un-Builder," Truthdig (January 11, 2007)

CEOs Get the Pie, Workers, Crumbs
—Headline to David Moberg's story, *Newsday* (September 17, 2006)

Public companies spend 10 percent of their earnings compensating their top five executives.
—Clara Jeffery, "A Look at the Numbers: How the Rich Get Richer," *Mother Jones* (May/June 2006)

In 1974 the ratio between what a factory worker earned and what a CEO of the same company earned was something in the neighborhood of fourteen to one. Today it's closer to 431 to one.
—Lewis Lapham, interviewed by Aaron Sarver, "Lapham's Way," *In These Times* (December 14, 2005)

Soulless GOP warmongering oil execs see this planet as merely one giant oil well to be sucked dry.
—Mark Morford, "If We All Vanished Tomorrow," *San Francisco Chronicle* (October 20, 2006)

Is it morally acceptable for the head of a corporation to pay himself $40 million the same year his company lays off ten thousand people?
—Ted Rall, *Wake Up! You're Liberal!* (2004)

Many corporate executives earn more money in a couple of hours than the average factory worker makes in a year.
—John Robbins, "The Health Costs of Wealth Inequality," *Common Dreams* (October 1, 2006)

Those positions of real power—the bankers, the CEOs—are not vulnerable to the vote.
—Arundhati Roy, *Public Power in the Age of Empire* (2004)

In today's corporate America, workers see gutted paychecks and pensions despite rising worker productivity, while CEOs get golden pay, perks, pensions, and parachutes.
—Holly Sklar, "Economy Booming for Billionaires," *Common Dreams* (September 28, 2006)

This was the true mark of a "CEO President"—do what you can get away with, dare the others to stop you, act always as a predator rather than as a custodian of the common good, because according to theorists of the "free market", there is no common good.
—Jane Smiley, "CEO President," *Huffington Post* (August 20, 2006)

Just about every paper has a "Business" section, where the focus is on CEOs, company managers, profit reports and big-time investors. But a lot more readers are working people—and a daily "Labor" section would be a welcome addition.
—Norman Solomon, "Media New Year's Resolutions for 2006," *Common Dreams* (January 3, 2006)

CEOs in the oil and defense industries are making out like profiteering bandits. Wages for American workers are declining while their productivity is rising.
—Katrina vanden Heuvel, "Lessons for Labor Day," *Nation* (September 1, 2006)

When I graduated from college in the 1960s, the average CEO made twenty times what the average worker made. Today, that CEO makes four hundred times as much.
—Jim Webb, "Class Struggle," *Wall Street Journal* (November 15, 2006)

Democratic Leadership Council

I can't tell the difference between the positions the DLC puts forward and Republican policy.
—Jack Blum, quoted in "Centrist Democrats Warn Liberals," *Washington Times* (April 4, 2005)

There is this sub-culture within a small faction of the Democratic Party, often embodied by the Democratic Leadership Council . . . attacking other Democrats, falsely accusing them of being weak on national defense, and directly contributing to the far right attacks.
—Brent Budowsky, "Centrist Democrats Must Call on Senator Lieberman to Support Lamont," *Huffington Post* (August 9, 2006)

The Republican wing of the Democratic Party.
—Howard Dean, characterizing the Democratic Leadership Council, quoted in "DLC: Wolves in Democrats' Clothing," *San Francisco Chronicle* (January 5, 2004)

I see the DLC [Democratic Leadership Council] as, to some extent, taking the soul away from the Democratic Party. And I see the DLC as having sold American workers down the river.
—Russ Feingold, in an interview with Matthew Rothschild, *Progressive* (May 2002)

There once was a Democratic Party that stood for something, before the Democratic Leadership Council convinced Democrats to feed from the same trough as Republicans if they hoped to win.
—Ed Garvey, "Howard Dean Perfect to Revive Dems' Spirit," *Capital Times* (Madison, Wisconson) (February 22, 2005)

The DLC stands for nothing, nada, zero, except that it is anti-union.
—Robert Reich, "The Democrats Aren't Just Resting," *Washington Post* (March 11, 2001)

The DLC is really just a group of Beltway-insulated corporate-funded hacks who have spent the better part of the last decade trying to undermine the Democratic Party's traditional working class base.
—David Sirota, "The Democrats 2008 Choice: Sell Out and Lose, or Stand Up and Win," *TomPaine.com* (July 27, 2005)

Anybody who claims to be a Democrat and is cozy with the Chamber of Commerce is not a Democrat; he's a Republican in drag.
—Harley Sorensen, "DLC: Wolves in Democrats' Clothing," *San Francisco Chronicle* (January 5, 2004)

The DLC are the lowest kind of scum; we're talking about people who are paid by the likes of Eli Lilly and Union Carbide to go on television and call suburban moms and college kids who happen to be against the war commies and jihadists.
—Matt Taibbi, "The Low Post: The Mansion Family," *Rolling Stone* (August 4, 2006

Food Industry

Over 5,000 schools in the United States have contracts to sell soda pop and candy from vending machines and fast food in school cafeterias. I urge parents, teachers, legislators, and students to stand up to corporate venders of type 2 diabetes, osteoporosis, heart disease, and empty calories, and tell them, "Our children are not for sale."
—John F. Borowski, "Commercialism in a Can," *Common Dreams* (October 21, 2002)

Just as surely as the tobacco industry tried for years—and succeeded—in hooking young kids on its deadly weed, the food industry is spending billions to advertise products that will make the next generation look and live like its porky parents: overweight, and at great risk of debilitating disease and early deaths linked to obesity.
—Marie Cocco, "Forget Big Tobacco—Big Food Kills," Truthdig (March 29, 2007)

Today just four or five corporations control nearly every aspect of food, from seeds to commodity crops like grains, food processing, meat production, and supermarkets.
—Christopher D. Cook, "Voting Beyond Our Forks," *Common Ground* (February 2007)

The soaring increase in obesity and type 2 diabetes among children is a public-health crisis, plausibly linked to the "toxic environment" created in large part by the food industry.
—Editorial, "Selling to—and Selling Out—Children," *The Lancet* (September 28, 2002)

How can we even begin to talk about making better food choices when the food industry is spending $36 billion a year to market the wrong kind of food? It seems rather disingenuous for a company to spend that kind of money and then turn around and blame the consumer when that marketing actually works.
—Michelle Simon, in an interview with Matthew Wheeland, "Agribusiness' Endless Appetite for Profit," AlterNet (January 29, 2007)

Globalization

It's time to rethink unlimited free trade and globalization. Do we want a country of millionaire lawyers and entertainers and everyone else works at Wal-Mart and Burger King?
—Larry Beinhart, "A Manifesto (for Democrats and Liberals)," *Common Dreams* (December 15, 2005)

Corporate America's brand of globalization includes elements that inflame a broad swath of the electorate: the export of U.S. jobs to low-wage dictatorships, the chartering of U.S. firms in offshore tax havens, and the surrender of democratic governance to international bodies composed of corporate representatives.
—Roger Bybee, "Kansas, Conviction, and the Future of the Dems," *Democratic Underground* (March 11, 2005)

The global marketplace is not a substitute for global civil society.
—Bob Burnett, "A Liberal Foreign Policy: Ten Maxims," *Huffington Post* (March 1, 2007)

Businesses, whether global or local, must recognize that as agents of global change they are acting not simply as economic but also as moral agents.
—Jane Collier and Lilian Wanderley, "Thinking for the Future: Global Corporate Responsibility in the Twenty-First Century," World Business Council for Sustainable Development (March 11, 2005)

There are two basic worldviews: Their worldview is that you subordinate society and nature to the economy. And we say, subordinate the economy to society and nature.
—Kevin Danaher, anti-globalization activist quoted in "Globalization's Diverse Foes," *Washington Post* (September 5, 2001)

Are we to absolutely turn back the clock on every achievement that we've made to improve the lives of our citizens in order for a U.S. multinational to get cheaper labor? . . . I don't think so.
—Lou Dobbs, in an interview with Bill Moyers, "Outsourcing and Patriotism," Alternet (August 21, 2004)

Free trade is just a mantra created by the multinational corporations and their friends in politics to describe an opportunity to ship American jobs overseas.
—Byron L. Dorgan, U.S. senator from North Dakota, in an interview with Mark Karlin, *BuzzFlash* (August 24, 2006)

Globalization: . . . the international flows of money and information across borders, the power and reach of multinational corporations that often override the interests of nation-states.
—Susan J. Douglas, "The New Globetrotters," *Nation* (April 28, 2003)

We should think of moral globalism parallel with economic globalism.
—Amitai Etzioni, quoted in "Globalization's Onward March," *Progressive Populist* (November 15, 2000)

Globalization poses a basic question: are people only consumers, and is the Earth only a cache of resources to be consumed?
—Roger Gottlieb, in an interview with Nelson Harvey, "Not Just for Hippies," *American Prospect* (April 19, 2006)

The World Trade Organization and NAFTA, it now turns out, are really outsourcing agreements. They give corporate America an opportunity to move plant, production, and, yes, jobs to Mexico, to any part of the world, and ship back into this market.
—Lou Dobbs, in an interview with Bill Moyers, "Outsourcing and Patriotism," Alternet (August 21, 2004)

Who is to rule the world's future—global markets or national governments?
—William Greider, "Military Globalism," *Nation* (March 31, 2003)

War is an extension of corporate globalization by other means.
—Joshua Holland, on the thesis of Antonia Juhasz's book *The Bush Agenda*, "Bush Clears the Way for Corporate Domination," AlterNet (May 5, 2006)

Corporate globalists and the corporate empires they serve may be at the cutting edge of technological innovation, but socially and environmentally they are relics of a bygone era of imperial colonial rule, elite privilege, and state-sanctioned plunder.
—David C. Korten, *When Corporations Rule the World* (1995)

Business insists that trading nations respect its property rights. What about human rights and social rights?
—Robert Kuttner, "Globalism, Democracy, and the Ports Deal," *Boston Globe* (March 11, 2006)

Everybody talks about globalization; nobody ever does anything about it. . . . The process of harnessing it, of writing enforceable rules that would benefit not just investors but most of our citizens, is hard to even conceive.
—Harold Meyerson, "NAFTA and Nativism," *American Prospect* (February 9, 2006)

These days, anybody who insists on a higher wage can be replaced by someone in another country who'd be happy to have the job at a fraction of that wage.
—Robert Reich, "The Shrinking Nest Egg," *American Prospect* (April 5, 2006)

Those of us who are "leftist" and who belong to the "anti-globalization" movement are put on notice. We are now terrorist suspects in the eyes of the U.S. intelligence community.
—Matthew Rothschild, "A Closer Reading of the National Intelligence Estimate," *Progressive* (September 27, 2006)

I think people haven't yet understood the extent of deprivation and the extent of desperation that is being created by feeding this capitalist machine.
—Arundhati Roy, interviewed by Terrence McNally, "Finding Justice with Arundhati Roy," AlterNet (September 21, 2004)

Brand logos and slogans are more famous worldwide than most national anthems and flags.
—Anneli Rufus, *Party of One* (2003)

Globalization is a violent system, imposed and maintained through use of violence. As trade is elevated above human needs, the insatiable appetite of global markets for resources is met by unleashing new wars over resources.
—Vandana Shiva, "Violence of Globalization," *The Hindu* (March 25, 2001)

Globalization is war by other means.
—Rebecca Solnit, *Hope in the Dark* (2004)

Companies—not countries—are making the rules in the global economy.
—Andy Stern, "Changing How America Works," AlterNet (November 2, 2006)

America doesn't need to try harder. China needs to stop using slave labor.
—Matt Taibbi, "'Competition' with China Is Killing U.S.," *Rolling Stone* (October 3, 2006)

The first page of every trade agreement should state that trade should take place for the benefit of the people, not corporations.
—Jonathan Tasini, "Democrats: Get a Real Economic Agenda or Become the Minority Party Again," *Huffington Post* (December 5, 2006)

Free trade allows factories and capital to move across borders, in a global race to the bottom. At the bottom, they find the lowest wages, least restrictive health and safety laws, and the greatest opportunities to profit by polluting air, water, soil, and communities.
—Mary Turck, "Triangle Shirtwaist Fire—Then and Now," *Common Dreams* (March 23, 2006)

Health Insurance Industry

In the current U.S. system, there are literally tens of thousands of different, and overlapping, health care organizations generating a blizzard of paperwork in an administrative wilderness creating enormous waste—thousands, if not millions of people pushing paper around . . . A single payer system would eliminate all that.
—Stephen Fleischman, "National Health Insurance Now, Not Later," AlterNet (February 2, 2007)

Modern medicine has morphed from a healing profession into a business where the primacy of profit takes precedence over greater human needs.
—Joanna Garritano, "U.S. Health Care Puts Profit over People," *Seattle Post-Intelligencer* (January 10, 2007)

The insurance industry's business model is darkly cynical: Spend enormous amounts of money identifying who most needs health insurance in order to deny them coverage. Profits are generated by insuring the healthy, not the sick.
—Ezra Klein, "Healthy Bottom Lines," *American Prospect* (January 24, 2007)

Health care for children, or subsidies for insurance companies. Which will it be?
—Paul Krugman, "Children versus Insurers," *New York Times* (April 6, 2007)

The free market doesn't work for health insurance, and never did.
—Paul Krugman, "Health Economics 101," *New York Times* (November 14, 2005)

Why are we keeping a hopeless, for-profit health insurance system alive?
—Phil Mattera, "Private Health Insurance Is Not the Answer," AlterNet (February 23, 2007)

Hospitals should be healing centers, not-for-profit corporations beholden to shareholders.
—Ted Rall, "250,000,000 Insured but Still in Trouble: The Healthcare Crisis for the Rest of Us," *Common Dreams* (January 17, 2006)

Insurance companies make money when they don't pay claims. They'll do anything to avoid paying, because if they wait long enough, they know the policyholders will die.
—Mary Beth Senkewicz, senior executive at the National Association of Insurance Commissioners, quoted in "Aged, Frail and Denied Care by Their Insurers," *New York Times* (March 26, 2007)

Management

Shame on Ford and GM for putting all their eggs in the SUV basket and then laying off thousands.
—Barbara Ehrenreich, "Workers' Rights Are About Dignity as Much as Wages," *Progressive* (October 27, 2006)

I wish to challenge the hubris of management, the presumptuous belief that everything is, can be and must be predicted, planned for, and controlled.
—Yiannis Gabriel, "The Hubris of Management," Symposium of the International Society for the Psychoanalytic Study of Organizations, New York City Marriott Financial Center (June 1996)

Corporate power lies with management—a bureaucracy in control of its task and its compensation. Rewards can verge on larceny.
—John Kenneth Galbraith, "Corporate Power is the Driving Force Behind U.S. Foreign Policy—and the Slaughter in Iraq," *Guardian (UK)* (July 15, 2004)

The first myth of management is that it exists. The second myth of management is that success equals skill.
—Robert Heller, *The Great Executive Dream* (1972)

Corporatism demands employees render themselves fecklessly pleasant. One doesn't want to be caught being "negative" nor be accused of the treachery of not being "a team player."
—Phil Rockstroh, "To Hell with Centrism," *Thomas Paine's Corner* (November, 2006)

Outsourcing

We've outsourced our slavery now, so we don't see the children working on our behalf in factories, the women in textile bondage, the indentured farmers picking our grapes in Chile.
—Kay Campbell, "Chew on Some Collective Guilt before the Turkey This Year," *Common Dreams* (November 13, 2006)

There's a stark logic to outsourcing: jobs will go wherever they cost employers less.
—Michelle Chen, "Exporting Blame," *Common Dreams* (October 10, 2004)

The despicable art of shipping jobs overseas has become the rage of American business practice.
—Amy F. Isaacs, "Outsourcing Sacrifices Many U.S. Jobs on Altar of Corporate Greed," *Augusta Chronicle* (June 7, 2004)

The government has essentially been outsourced to corporate America.
—Lawrence Goodwyn, "The Coming Party Realignment," *Nation* (April 30, 2007)

There is no reason to have U.S. taxpayers subsidize business decisions that harm American workers . . . Corporate tax laws should be modified to increase the cost of exporting jobs and decrease the cost of maintaining jobs in America.
—Edward M. Kennedy, in his address delivered at the City University of New York, "Creating a Genuine 'Opportunity Society'" (March 1, 2004)

We have to stop outsourcing. If we don't stop it, we're going to see the elimination of the middle class.
—John Sweeney, "AFL-CIO Head Blasts Corporate Policies," the Associated Press (AP) (January 19, 2006)

In almost every U.S. corporation, U.S. employees are being dismissed and replaced by foreigners who work for lower pay.
—Paul Craig Roberts, "Bush's Con Jobs," CounterPunch (January 10, 2006)

Technology

With the machine came the capitalist.
—Eugene Debs, in a 1908 speech, quoted in *Debs: His Life, Writings and Speeches* (2002)

Things are in the saddle, and ride mankind.
—Ralph Waldo Emerson, *Ode* inscribed to W. H. Channing (1847)

Modern technology has led . . . to the development of a society controlled (ruthlessly in the totalitarian states, politely and inconspicuously in the democracies) by Big Business and Big Government.
—Aldous Huxley, *Brave New World* (1958)

You can use the Internet to promote anti-evolutionism just as easily as you can use it to promote pro-evolutionism. . . . Technology itself is not a liberating force.
—Susan Jacoby, quoted in *BuzzFlash* interview (February 14, 2005)

Ours is the age which is proud of machines that think, and suspicious of men that try to.
—Elbert Hubbard Jones, quoted in "Thoughts on the Business of Life," *Forbes* (March 1989)

Our scientific power has outrun our spiritual power. We have guided missiles and misguided men.
—Rev. Martin Luther King, Jr., *Strength to Love* (1963)

The promise of technology was that we could do things five times as fast, so we would have more time to play with our children and enjoy life. Instead, we do five times more than we used to.
—John Buffalo Mailer, *The Big Empty* (2006)

The technology we need most badly is the technology of community—the knowledge about how to cooperate to get things done.
—Bill McKibben, "How Close to Catastrophe?" *New York Review of Books* (November 16, 2006)

Technology follows corporate power. . . We need a much broader public debate about the purposes of technology and the harm of technology.
—Ralph Nader, quoted in "Nader Shows Real Byte in His Campaign Against 'Techno-Twits,'" *Los Angeles Times* (September 4, 2000)

The telephone and cable companies would like to transform our Internet from a medium that allows people to connect to one another, engage in debate, and learn about the world into little more than a portal to sell goods and transmit television programs, films, and games.
—Chellie Pingree, "Keep Internet Free, Fast," *Miami Herald* (May 9, 2006)

Industrialism produced a new man . . . one adapted to the demands of the machine. In contrast, today's emerging consciousness seeks a new knowledge of what it means to be human.
—Charles A. Reich, *The Greening of America* (1970)

The Internet has been the place where Davids can take on Goliaths, where someone without resources but with brains and guts and information can skewer the high and mighty.
—Robert Reich, "The War of Internet Democracy," *Common Dreams* (May 11, 2006)

Men have become the tools of their tools.
—Henry David Thoreau, *Walden* (1854)

Our children have inherited technologies whose by-products, whether in war or peace, are rapidly destroying the whole planet as a breathable, drinkable system for supporting life of any kind.
—Kurt Vonnegut, "Vonnegut's Blues for America," *Sunday Herald* (Scotland) (February 5, 2006)

Wal-Mart

The Wal-Mart Stores Inc. Political Action Committee for Responsive Government earmarks the vast majority of its contributions to Republican Party political candidates and Republican political committees.
—Bill Berkowitz, "Wal-Marting Philanthropy," Inter Press Service (October 22, 2005)

Intimidation, strong-arming, and flagrant unfair labor practices are company policy at Wal-Mart.
—Ruth Conniff, "Wal-Mart Wins," *Progressive* (March 1, 2005)

Wal-Mart is both a beneficiary and a driver of the race to the bottom in the global economy. It has enormous leverage, and how it uses that leverage in the pursuit of ever cheaper labor has enormous consequences.
—Alejandra Domenzain, quoted in "Wal-Mart Nation," *Time* (June 27, 2005)

Wal-Mart has more employees than Wyoming has people and annual revenues that equal the combined revenues of ten states.
—Mark Green, *Losing Our Democracy* (2006)

The Wal-Mart story is the story of economic injustice, and it's the story of corporate greed and corporate unfairness.
—Robert Greenwald, quoted in interview "Robert Greenwald Tackles Wal-Mart: Just How Have Americans Paid for Those Low Prices?" *BuzzFlash* (October 27, 2005)

The world's most controversial company . . . locks its workers in overnight while they stock shelves and aggressively resists the formation of unions among its employees.
—Katherine Griffiths, "Fat? Over 40? Don't Bother Applying for a Wal-Mart Job," *Independent (UK)* (October 27, 2005)

Wall Street's powerhouse investors are now demanding that every corporation and the overall American economy be organized on the low-wage, no-benefit, anti-union model of Wal-Mart.
—Jim Hightower, "How the Social Glue of America is Being Dissolved," *Hightower Lowdown* (January 2006)

Wal-Mart makes its low prices by exploiting its own workers.
—Jim Hightower, interviewed by Matthew Rothschild, *Progressive* (November 2003)

Wal-Mart is the largest private employer in the U.S. . . . It's also one of the most controversial, by now virtually synonymous with low wages, workplace discrimination, union-busting, and right-wing Christianity.
—Michal Lumsden, "Selling Women Short," *Mother Jones* (February 2, 2005)

Wal-Mart captures one out of every ten dollars that Americans spend in retail stores.
—Stacy Mitchell, "The Big Box Swindle: The True Cost of the Mega-Retailers," *Multinational Monitor* (September/October 2006)

Wal-Mart [is] the most famously offensive, town-destroying, junk-purveying, labor-abusing, sweatshop-supporting, American-job-killing, soul-numbing, seizure-inducing, hope-curdling retailer in the known universe.
—Mark Morford, "Can You Still Hate Wal-Mart?" *San Francisco Chronicle* (May 24, 2006)

Wal-Mart is devilishly ingenious in thinking up ways to have taxpayers fill in its wage gap. Put them on partial welfare, says the very well-paid company bosses who make millions of dollars each per year. These workers are given advice on how to apply so that taxpayers subsidize Wal-Mart's profits.
—Ralph Nader, "Wal-Mart Ways," *Common Dreams* (November 28, 2004)

Does America really want to change Wal-Mart? If the answer truly is yes, then Americans need to change themselves first.
—Joseph Nocera, "To Change Wal-Mart, First Change America," *New York Times* (November 4, 2005)

Why can't a company that had a quarter-trillion dollars in sales and earned $10.3 billion in fiscal 2005 provide affordable health coverage for its lowest-paid workers?
—Robert Steinback, "Wal-Mart's Health Keeps People Sick," *Miami Herald* (January 18, 2006)

Wal-Mart is the world's largest employer and one of the worst abusers of its women employees in the U.S. It isn't just that Wal-Mart doesn't pay a living wage; it's that they pay women even less than men in the same positions.
—Thalia Syracopoulos, "Wal-Mart Abuses Female Employees," *Seattle Post-Intelligencer* (December 6, 2006)

Welfare for Corporations

Corporate welfare—an array of direct subsidies, tax breaks and indirect assistance created for the special benefit of businesses—is one of those things that politicians would rather criticize than abolish.
—Steve Chapman, "Corporate Welfare as We Know It: No End in Sight," *Baltimore Sun* (July 16, 2004)

Across the country, more and more fans, small businessmen, and community leaders say using public money to build sports arenas for major league teams is "corporate welfare."
—Ron Kampeas, "Sports Fans Organizing to Protest 'Corporate Welfare,'" The Associated Press (AP) (April 27, 2001)

Instead of cutting out school lunches, let us cut off tax subsidies that are nothing more than food stamps for the rich.
—Edward M. Kennedy, speech to the Democratic National Convention (August 12, 1980)

Citizens should be given standing to sue in order to challenge corporate welfare abuses—to restrain agencies that reach beyond their statutory powers to dole out corporate welfare.
—Ralph Nader, "Ethics Reform Package: Time to Address All Problems," *Common Dreams* (January 21, 2006)

Most big American companies these days are global anyway. They're developing products all over the planet. . . . It's simply wrong to claim that by [government] subsidizing basic research in America we're somehow improving "American competitiveness."
—Robert Reich, "Bad Planning," *Common Dreams* (February 9, 2006)

America is not a capitalistic society. America is a corporate welfare state.
—Jane Stillwater, "Corporate Welfare: How Come Lockheed Gets Food Stamps and We Don't?" OpEdNews (February 10, 2005)

Welfare reform won't truly be considered a success until Big Business is told it will have to upgrade its skills, go into the marketplace and compete on its own merits.
—Rod Watson, "End Corporate Welfare to Achieve True Reform," *Buffalo News* (July 6, 2000)

THE CULTURE WAR

Art

Artists are often the canary in the coal mine.
—Robert Atkins, in an interview with Onnesha Roychoudhuri, "Facing Up to Modern Censorship," AlterNet (April 14, 2006)

There is not a single true work of art that has not, in the end, added to the inner freedom of each person who has known and loved it.
—Albert Camus, quoted in *Resistance, Rebellion, and Death* (1961)

We are a little bit out of touch in Hollywood every once in a while. We were the ones who talked about AIDS when it was being whispered. We talked about civil rights when it wasn't really popular. I'm proud to be part of this Academy. I'm proud to be part of this community. I'm proud to be out of touch.
—George Clooney, accepting his Academy Award for the film *Syriana*, Reuters (UK) (March 6, 2006)

Progressive art can assist people to learn not only about the objective forces at work in the society in which they live, but also about the intensely social character of their interior lives. Ultimately, it can propel people toward social emancipation.
—Angela Davis, *Women, Culture, and Politics* (1984)

Why this silence in the face of what's happening in our country and in the world? . . . Who or what has silenced our artists at this time in our history?
—Cathy Pagano, "Where Are All Our Artists?" OpEdNews (October 2004)

All art is subversive.
—Pablo Picasso, quoted in *Thoughts in a Dry Season: A Miscellany* (1978)

Artists hear what no one else hears. They see what no one else sees. They say what no ones else says. They must.
—Anneli Rufus, *Party of One* (2003)

A primary function of art and thought is to liberate the individual from the tyranny of his culture . . . and to permit him to stand beyond it in an autonomy of perception and judgment.
—Lionel Trilling, *Beyond Culture* (1965)

Practicing any art is a way to make your soul grow.
—Kurt Vonnegut, quoted in "Kurt Vonnegut: A Requiem for the USA," *Sunday Herald* (Scotland) (February 5, 2006)

Books

Among the less well-known aspects of the Patriot Act are provisions permitting the Justice Department to obtain information secretly from booksellers and librarians about customers' and patrons' reading, Internet and book-buying habits. . . . The act prohibits librarians and booksellers from disclosing these subpoenas, so the objects of investigation don't know and therefore cannot defend themselves.
—Joan E. Bertin, "Now They Check the Books You Read," *Newsday* (September 16, 2002)

Most people in this world believe that the Creator of the universe has written a book. We have the misfortune of having many such books on hand, each making exclusive claim as to its infallibility.
—Sam Harris, *The End of Faith* (2005)

I cannot live without books.
—Thomas Jefferson, in a letter to John Adams (June 10, 1815)

Sit down and read. Educate yourself for the coming conflicts.
—Mother Jones, quoted in *Ms.* magazine (November 1981)

A book must be the ax for the frozen sea within us.
—Franz Kafka, letter to Oscar Pollak (January 27, 1904)

Incredibly, we are now in an era where reading a controversial book may be evidence of a link to terrorists.
—Edward M. Kennedy, "On Wiretapping, Bush Isn't Listening to the Constitution," *Boston Globe* (December 22, 2005)

This . . . is the most pressing question of our time: How to get the vast majority of Americans to care? To pay attention? To read? To effect change and demand accountability from bumbling spoon-fed leaders.
—Mark Morford, "Why Don't Americans Care?" *San Francisco Chronicle* (October 6, 2004)

Wear the old coat and buy the new book.
—Austin Phelps, *The Theory of Preaching* (1881)

Books are getting dumber and shallower and safer, and a huge wide swathe of opinion [is] not represented in mainstream publishing at all.
—Colin Robinson, interview quoted in "Changing the Country, One Book at a Time," AlterNet (January 26, 2006)

I think that it's society's outcasts who will continue to treasure and reproduce literature.
—Mark Schurmann, "Who Reads in America?" Pacific News Service (January 9, 2006)

People get nothing out of books but what they bring to them.
—George Bernard Shaw, quoted in *George Bernard Shaw: His Life and Personality* (1963)

Books matter.
—Rebecca Solnit, "Welcome to the Impossible World," *TomDispatch.com* (May 14, 2006)

Go home to Crawford. We'll help you raise the money for a library, and you won't even ever have to read a book. We're not cruel. We just want to get rid of you.
—Gore Vidal, to President Bush in "Gore Vidal's State of the Union," *Democracy Now!* radio (January 31, 2006)

Our daily sources of news, papers and TV, are now so craven, so unvigilant on behalf of the American people, so uninformative, that only in books can we find out what is really going on.
—Kurt Vonnegut, "I Love You, Madame Librarian," *In These Times* (August 6, 2004)

Liberals may write best-selling books about why George W. Bush is a terrible president, but conservatives write best-selling books about why liberalism is a pox on our nation . . . Indeed, large portions of the conservative movement can be understood as an effort to crush liberalism in all its manifestations.
—Paul Waldman, "The Liberal Moderates," *American Prospect* (October 18, 2005)

There is no such thing as a moral or immoral book. Books are well written, or badly written. That is all.
—Oscar Wilde, in the preface to *The Picture of Dorian Gray* (1945)

Culture War

The crucial distinction in political culture in the world today is between God and the Enlightenment; that is, imposed theology or reason.
—Eric Alterman, "God Is a Concept," *Media Matters for America* (December 19, 2006)

Culture war has become the organizing principle of the right.
—Kevin Baker, "The Past and Future of a Right-Wing Myth," *Harper's* (July 15, 2006)

Politicians who spark a culture war for the sake of their own power are playing with fire.
—James Carroll, "The Risks of Waging 'Culture War,'" *Boston Globe* (March 9, 2004)

People know things are out of whack, that fundamentally the order of, the rhythm of public life and our common life as Americans has been severely disturbed.
—Bill Clinton, quoted in "Clinton Says Republican Extremists Divided Country," Reuters (October 15, 2006)

At a time when ethnic and religious warfare is bloodying much of the world, Americans should count the blessings of the religious pluralism that has made their country so great and so stable. The Christian right wants to end all of this and bring religious warfare to our shores.
—Alan Dershowitz, *The Vanishing Jew* (1996)

Today's real battles in the halls of government are about the survival of democracy itself.
—Thom Hartmann, "The Robber Baron's Party," *Common Dreams* (January 20, 2005)

I am on the side of the "culture wars" that believes that morality exists outside of religion, and that most religions, when literally followed, have little relevance in the modern world.
—Laina Farhat-Holzman, "Whatever Happened to Morality Outside Religion?" *Santa Cruz Sentinel* (November 7, 2004)

The proponents of competing paradigms practice their trades in different worlds.
—Thomas Kuhn, *The Structure of Scientific Revolutions* (1962)

Conservatives understand the importance of fighting culture wars, and have managed to focus huge amounts of resources on the public development of ideas.
—Rabbi Michael Lerner, "Hostile Takeover: Theocracy in America," *Tikkun* (January/February 2006)

The culture war is real, and it's about to go nuclear. This is not a war that the American people want, but it's one that the Religious Right seems determined to fight.
—Rev. Barry Lynn, "Religious Coalition for Reproductive Choice Leaders Assert That War, Jobs—Not Cultural Divide—Motivated Voters," U.S. Newswire (November 9, 2004)

So strong is this propensity of mankind to fall into mutual animosities, that where no substantial occasion presents itself, the most frivolous and fanciful distinctions have been sufficient to kindle their unfriendly passions and excite their most violent conflicts.
—James Madison, *The Federalist*, No. 10 (1787)

This sense of otherness is the single most pernicious force in American discourse. Its not-like-us ethos makes so much bigotry possible: racism, sexism, homophobia. It divides the country as surely as the Mason-Dixon Line once did.
—Anna Quindlen, "The Politics of Meanness," *New York Times* (November 16, 1994)

The culture war is supposed to be about morality, but really it's a crusade to compel Americans to follow certain norms of private behavior that some social and religious conservatives believe are mandated by sociology, nature, or God.
—Eugene Robinson, "'Values' Choice for the GOP," *Washington Post* (October 10, 2006)

Even some liberals have apparently bought the Big Lie . . . that a liberal, permissive, secular, coastal culture has perverted the otherwise pristine heartland of our nation.
—Robert Scheer, "The Invisible Hand Holds the Remote," AlterNet (November 30, 2004)

I think most of us know that the season's deeper meaning has nothing to do with whether retailers hang banners saying "Merry Christmas" or "Happy Holidays." It has much more to do with how we treat one another—including the most vulnerable among us.
—Cynthia Tucker, "We Have Little Patience with the Poor," *Atlanta Journal-Constitution* (December 24, 2005)

Most of the culture-war issues that matter to conservatives have something to do with sex.
—Paul Waldman, "Why Rudy Giuliani Is Destined to Fall," *TomPaine.com* (March 1, 2007)

If an ambivalent public hears only one side of a question, the conservative side, passionately argued . . . and they perceive that the putative spokespeople for feminism and liberalism are actually uncomfortable about advancing their views—the passionate arguers will carry the day.
—Ellen Willis, "Escape from Freedom: What's the Matter with Tom Frank (And the Lefties Who Love Him)?" *Situations: Project of the Radical Imagination*, Volume 1, No. 2 (2006)

The culture wars are not just about competing world views of people who read different books and watch different films. They are waged by people who, for the most part, occupy entirely different worlds.
—Gary Younge, "Culture War Casualties," *Guardian (UK)* (April 5, 2004)

Hate

He who says he is in the light and who hates his brother is in the darkness still.
—1 John 2:9

I am a proud liberal, feminist woman, and the hate mail I get for those three things is not about me. It's about those signifiers, and about what the right in this country has managed to do to perpetuate anger over what they mean.
—Janeane Garofalo, interviewed by Elizabeth DiNovella, *Progressive* (April 2003)

America is full of good people, but something dark is loose. There's a free-floating anxiety that easily metastasizes into paranoia and hatred for the same enemies always targeted by authoritarian populist movements—homosexuals, urbanites, foreigners, intellectuals, and religious minorities.
—Michelle Goldberg, *Kingdom Coming* (2006)

The best defense against hate is a strong, diverse and democratic civic culture that respects human rights and civil liberties.
—Elizabeth Hartmann, "America's Climate of Fear and Loathing," *Boston Globe* (April 19, 2002)

There was a time in American history when candidates appealed to our hopes and dreams rather than our fears and prejudices, our divisions and hates.
—Sybil Hinkle, "Beware the Stain of Atwater's, Rove's Tactics," *Napa Valley Register* (July 24, 2006)

Haters are always a menace, and those who turn political differences into jihads are not helping this country.
—Molly Ivins, "Rabid Rightists Are Leninists of Today," *Boulder Daily Camera* (February 7, 2003)

Hate destroys a man's sense of values and his objectivity. It causes him to describe the beautiful as ugly and the ugly as beautiful.
—Rev. Martin Luther King, Jr., *Strength to Love* (1963)

No one is born hating another person because of the color of his skin, or his background, or his religion.
—Nelson Mandela, *Long Walk to Freedom* (1994)

Hatred has gotten out of control. Who are we being taught to hate? African-American rappers? Abortion doctors? Scientific researchers? College professors? Bloggers? The list goes on and on, and it's being drummed into our dear little ears on a daily basis.
—Joyce Marcel, "Love the Other as Yourself," *Common Dreams* (August 9, 2006)

Language

There is nothing inherently conservative in Christian language. It can point in any political direction, even the most radical.
—Ira Chernus, "Praise the Lord and Pass the Petition," *TomDispatch.com* (March 1, 2006)

It's time for liberals to stand up and embrace the very word that represents who they are and what they believe.
—Alan Colmes, *Red, White & Liberal* (2003)

The Democratic Party will not win elections or build a lasting majority solely by changing its rhetoric, nor will we win by adopting the other side's positions. We must say what we mean—and mean real change when we say it.
—Howard Dean, announcing his candidacy for the Democratic Party chair, quoted in "Dr. Dean Calling," *Nation* (January 12, 2005)

We can change our vocabulary, but I don't think we ought to change our principles.
—Howard Dean, quoted in "Democratic Leadership Rethinking Abortion," *Los Angeles Times* (December 23, 2004)

There is no greater power than the power to define. If you can determine how people use language, you really are able to determine how they think. If you can fill the word liberal with the meaning that you want it to have, which nowadays is weak, feminine, cowardly, so much so that even liberals want to run away from it, then you've won an enormous battle for control.
—Stephen J. Ducat, quoted in interview "Stephen J. Ducat Dissects 'Anxious Masculinity,' Making Sense of America's Strutting, in a Psychoanalytic Kind of Way," *BuzzFlash* (March 2, 2005)

The corruption of man is followed by the corruption of language.
—Ralph Waldo Emerson, *Nature* (1836)

The right has rhetorically outflanked the pro-choice movement, hijacking the words "family" and "life" and "human" to devastating effect.
—Laura Flanders, "Not by Spin Alone," *In These Times* (May 29, 2007)

There's been a long-needed discussion about how the Democrats lost the verbal high ground, how the blue people became tongue-tied in the language of values.
—Ellen Goodman, "Amen, Dubya," *Working For Change* (January 26, 2005)

It is simply no longer possible to ignore the strangeness of our public discourse. I know I am not alone in feeling that something has gone fundamentally wrong.
—Al Gore, *The Assault on Reason* (2007)

The smartest, easiest and most fruitful step we can take today is to label ourselves the progressives we in fact are, and our adversaries the regressives we know them to be.
—David Michael Green, "What's in a Name? Everything. How Progressives Can Start Winning Again by Renaming Their Opponents and Reframing the Debate," *Common Dreams* (February 8, 2005)

The word [atheist] is . . . conceptually unnecessary. We don't have words for people who are not astrologers or alchemists; we don't have words for people who doubt that Elvis is still alive.
—Sam Harris, interviewed by Blair Golson, Truthdig (April 3, 2006)

Words matter because they express ideas, and ideas matter because they present a picture of what's real and what's right.
—George Lakoff, "It's Escalation, Stupid," AlterNet (February 15, 2007)

The message of Bush's rhetoric is simple: Be afraid. Be very afraid. But trust me.
—William D. Lutz, "The Rhetoric of Fear," *Newsday* (September 7, 2003)

In recent years, the word "underprivileged" has fallen out of use. Too bad; the word was helpful. It captured the fact that what separated the poor from the rest of society was mostly just privilege—the advantage of being born into the right family.
—Linda McQuaig, "The Poor Haven't Changed—We Have," *Toronto Star* (January 2, 2005)

The left has lost the battle for the language itself.
—Geoffrey Nunberg, *Talking Right: How Conservatives Turned Liberalism into a Tax-Raising, Latte-Drinking, Sushi-Eating, Volvo-Driving,* New York Times-Reading, Body-Piercing, Hollywood-Loving, Left-Wing Freak Show (2006)

In our time, political speech and writing are largely the defense of the indefensible.
—George Orwell, quoted in *The Collected Essays, Journalism and Letters of George Orwell* (1968)

Political language . . . is designed to make lies sound truthful and murder respectable, and to give an appearance of solidity to pure wind.
—George Orwell, quoted in *The Collected Essays, Journalism and Letters of George Orwell* (1968)

If you control the language, you control the debate.
—Katha Pollitt, on the Right's substitution of "Islamo-fascism" for the "war on terrorism," "Wrong War, Wrong Word," *Nation* (September 11, 2006)

When [Republicans] wanted to let energy companies release more pollution into the air, they called it the "Clear Skies Initiative." When they wanted to let loggers cut down more trees and weaken environmental laws, they called it the "Healthy Forests Initiative."
—Harry Reid, quoted in "Democrats Assail Republicans on Ethics," Reuters (January 21, 2006)

The language of business is not the language of the soul or the language of humanity.
—Anita Roddick, founder of the beauty company Body Shop, quoted in *The Corporation: The Pathological Pursuit of Profit and Power* (2004)

The world does not speak. Only we do. . . . It cannot propose a language for us to speak. Only other human beings can do that.
—Richard Rorty, *Contingency, Irony, and Solidarity* (1989)

Sometimes I wonder if we shall ever grow up in our politics and say definite things which mean something, or whether we shall always go on using generalities to which everyone can subscribe, and which mean very little.
—Eleanor Roosevelt, in her syndicated newspaper column, "My Day," United Feature Syndicate (July 1, 1940)

Where one begins by corrupting language, worse corruptions swiftly follow.
—Salman Rushdie, "Ugly Phrase Conceals an Uglier Truth," *Sydney Morning Herald* (January 9, 2006)

Religious experience is highly intimate and, for me, ready words are not at hand.
—Adlai Stevenson, in his speech in Libertyville, Illinois (May 21, 1954)

"Fair" and "unfair" have become the wimp words of modern, mousy liberalism.
—Nicholas von Hoffman, "Here's a Capital Idea: Make the Rich Pay Taxes!" *New York Observer* (March 26, 2001)

Language is clearly important in politics, but the message remains more important than the messaging.
—Rev. Jim Wallis, "The Message Thing," *New York Times* (August 4, 2005)

Polarization

The visual representation of the nation's voters isn't a nicely shaped bell with most voters in the moderate middle. It's a sharp V.
—Alan Abramowitz and Bill Bishop, "The Myth of the Middle," *Washington Post* (February 28, 2007)

The Bush Administration has now become the first government in our nation's history to fight a major war without seeking any sort of national solidarity. Far from it. The whole purpose of the war in Iraq—and the "war on terrorism"—seems to have been to foment division and to win elections.
—Kevin Baker, "The Past and Future of a Right-Wing Myth," *Harper's* (July 15, 2006)

I would like to suggest that the split is not between right and left but between the faith-based and reality-based communities.
—Larry Beinhart, *Fog Facts* (2005)

There is no gravitational pull from the masses to some center. We don't avoid moving to the center because of ideology. We simply are not hearing that from America.
—Wes Boyd, in an interview with Don Hazen, "MoveOn Muscles Up," AlterNet (April 26, 2005)

I think it's a healthy thing in a democracy to have people disagreeing, but if you're screaming or demonizing, then the very people you want to reach— which is those who don't agree with you—can't hear you.
—Bill Clinton, quoted in "Clinton Calls for Kinder, Gentler Political Talk," *USA Today* (November 21, 2005)

Mankind likes to think in terms of extreme opposites. It is given to formulating its beliefs in terms of Either/Ors, between which it recognizes no intermediate possibilities.
—John Dewey, *Experience and Education* (1938)

When big chunks of the country begin to view their political adversaries as something close to traitors, we have arrived at a very dangerous time.
—E. J. Dionne, Jr., "What Readers Taught Me," *Washington Post* (December 30, 2005)

Republicans use big things to divide America. I think we can use big things to unite America.
—John Edwards, "Cornbread and Roses," *Nation* (November 28, 2005)

Dialogue is impossible without some shared sense of reality. . . . What's lacking isn't just truth, it's the entire social mechanism by which truth is distinguished from falsehood.
—Michelle Goldberg, on the enormous communication gap between the Left and Right, *Kingdom Coming: The Rise of Christian Nationalism* (2006)

The neutral language of polarization, with its implication of equivalence, is a fundamentally misleading description of contemporary American politics. . . . It has benefited Republicans far more than it has benefited Democrats.
—Jacob S. Hacker and Paul Pierson, *Off Center: The Republican Revolution and the Erosion of American Democracy* (2005)

I don't think it was liberals that polarized this country. Liberal Democrats got along well with moderate Republicans. I was there in the seventies in the Senate. You could compromise. You could reach agreement. It is when a different kind of Republican began to be elected that the divisiveness set in.
—Gary Hart, in an interview with Mark Karlin, *BuzzFlash* (December 21, 2005)

America is as fundamentally divided today . . . as it has been since the last civil war.
—Tom Hayden, "Learning from the Loss," AlterNet (November 8, 2004)

Movements draw people into something larger than themselves and show them who their friends and enemies are.
—Christopher Hayes, "How to Turn Your Red State Blue," *In These Times* (March 22, 2005)

The big split [is] . . . between the powerful and the angry, between those basking in power and those fighting for change.
—Don Hazen, "Stephen Colbert: New American Hero," AlterNet (May 9, 2006)

The reason we have so much bitter partisanship these days is that that's the way the radicals who have taken over the Republican Party want it.
—Paul Krugman, "Don't Make Nice," *New York Times* (October 23, 2006)

There is no appropriate scale available with which to weight the merits of alternative paradigms: they are incommensurable.
—Thomas Kuhn, *The Structure of Scientific Revolutions* (1962)

The two Americas, conservative and liberal, worship two very different gods.
—Roland Merullo, "A Puzzling America," *Boston Globe* (September 20, 2004)

Our public discourse has become the verbal equivalent of mud wrestling.
—Bill Moyers, *New York Times* (March 22, 1992)

The central rift in the religious landscape is no longer between members of competing denominations—Catholics versus Protestants versus Jews—but between traditionalists in all of these faiths, on the one hand, and Americans who are less pious on the other.
—Eyal Press, "God and the Blue States," *Nation* (August 12, 2004)

Americans have vastly different ways of looking at the world, of deciding what is important, even of defining what it means to be American.
—Ted Rall, "What's the Matter with Manhattan?" Universal Press Syndicate (January 5, 2005)

When ideological division replaces informed exchange, dogma is the result and education suffers.
—Hunter Rawlings, quoted in "Is the United States Becoming Hostile to Science?" Reuters (October 28, 2005)

There's still a huge reservoir of racism, sexism, and homophobia in our country, as well as terrible economic inequality. Much like the civil-rights activists of forty and fifty years ago, we're usually up against opponents who are clever, ruthless, rich, and determined to crush us.
—John Sweeney, quoted in "King's Message Rings True Today, Say Activists," *OneWorld* (January 19, 2004)

I think it's time for all of us to admit that something extremely sinister is happening in the American media landscape. We are being split up into rigid camps and kept doped up on fear, hate and invective.
—Matt Taibbi, "The Low Post: Keep on Hatin'," *Rolling Stone* (December 28, 2006)

The country is more divided, less secure, less free, more universally reviled abroad than at any point in history. . . . If only we recognized who the true hijackers of American values really are.
—Pierre Tristam, "How Long Will America Spill Blood for Liberty's Hijackers to Save Face?" *Daytona Beach News-Journal* (August 28, 2006)

The religious and political Right gets the public meaning of religion mostly wrong—preferring to focus only on sexual and cultural issues while ignoring the weightier matters of justice. And the secular Left doesn't seem to get the meaning and promise of faith for politics at all—mistakenly dismissing spirituality as irrelevant to social change.
—Rev. Jim Wallis, *God's Politics: Why the Right Gets It Wrong and the Left Doesn't Get It* (2005)

The world is divided into people who think they are right.
—Anonymous

The Sixties

We were right about civil rights; we were right about human rights; we were right about peace. . . . But I think we didn't know our butt from a hole in the ground about drugs, and that bit us pretty hard.
—David Crosby, "Rock Survivor," *Time* (October 30, 2006)

Hypercritical then, we are hypocritical now. Those who refused to serve when it was our turn are now among the most strident, hawkish flag wavers around. And most of those who were vehemently anti-establishment then have now sold out to (or bought into) "the system."
—Gregory D. Foster, "Baby Boomers: The Ungreatest Generation," *Common Dreams* (July 16, 2006)

We are people of this generation, bred in at least modest comfort, housed now in universities, looking uncomfortably to the world we inherit.
—Tom Hayden, "The Port Huron Statement" (1962)

It is time to resurrect the good sixties. . . . It was an era when millions of people were clear about their values—especially nonmaterial aspirations, and sharing, and ways of living simply that have long since been steamrollered by the nonstop tsunami of global consumer culture.
—Don Hazen, "Bring the Sixties Out of the Closet," AlterNet (March 23, 2006)

The lesson of the sixties—which very few of us have ever really learned—is not just to try to change what's wrong with the world, but to change your own life.
—Gary Kamiya, "Were the Sixties a Fraud?" *Salon* (December 22, 1997)

The thing the sixties did was to show us the possibilities and the responsibility that we all had. It wasn't the answer. It just gave us a glimpse of the possibility.
—John Lennon, interviewed on KFRC RKO Radio (December 8, 1980)

Measuring ourselves against the masters of the present, we regret nothing except our failure to prevail.
—Robert Stone, *Prime Green: Remembering the Sixties* (2007)

The 1960s are the last time the nation really questioned itself about its role in the world and its purpose as a nation.
—Pierre Tristam, "Past Due: Constructive National Self-Examination," *Daytona Beach News Journal* (March 27, 2007)

I think that many people who were touched deeply by the spirit of the sixties feel the same quickening of conversation beginning again. And this time we're sober.
—Marianne Williamson, quoted in "Holistic Politics: An Interview with Marianne Williamson," *Kindred Spirit (UK)* (Spring 1999)

Writers and Intellectuals

Fiction never exceeds the reach of the writer's courage.
—Dorothy Allison, *Skin* (1994)

One of my greatest pleasures in my writing has come from the thought that perhaps my work might annoy someone of comfortably pretentious position. Then comes the realization that such people rarely read.
—John Kenneth Galbraith, quoted in his obituary entitled "John Kenneth Galbraith, 97, Dies; Economist Held a Mirror to Society," *New York Times* (April 30, 2006)

The job of the writer is to kiss no ass, no matter how big and holy and white and tempting and powerful.
—Ken Kesey, *Paris Review* (Spring 1994)

In this dark and wounded society, writing can give you the pleasures of a woodpecker, of hollowing out a hole in a tree where you can build your nest and say, "This is my niche, this is where I live now, this is where I belong."
—Anne Lamott, *Bird by Bird* (1994)

My gratitude for good writing is unbounded; I'm grateful for it the way I'm grateful for the ocean.
—Anne Lamott, *Bird by Bird* (1994)

When it comes to the lifeblood of the left, the writers and artists, the men and women who fashion public opinion, the intellectuals—I found a curious lifelessness, a peculiar streak of timidity or irritability.
—Bernard-Henri Lévy, "A Letter to the American Left," *Nation* (February 8, 2006)

Literature is a form of permanent insurrection.
—Mario Vargas Llosa, *Literature Is Fire* (1967)

People have the right to the Truth as they have a right to life, liberty, and the pursuit of happiness.
—Frank Norris, *The Responsibilities of a Novelist* (1903)

The writer is the Faust of modern society, the only surviving individualist in a mass age.
—Boris Pasternak, quoted in the *London Observer* (December 20, 1959)

The writers who matter most to us are those who enlarge our consciences and our sympathies and our knowledge.
—Susan Sontag, in a speech at the Los Angeles Public Library (April 7, 2004)

A true piece of writing is a dangerous thing. It can change your life.
—Tobias Wolff, *Old School* (2004)

THE DEMAND FOR JUSTICE

Capitalism

Most of the world's main problems today are inseparable from the dynamics of the capitalist system itself.
—Ronald Aronson, "The Left Needs More Socialism," *Nation* (April 17, 2006)

The genius of contemporary capitalism is not simply that it gives consumers what they want but that it makes them want what it has to give. It's that core logic of ever-expanding desires that is unsustainable on a global scale.
—Timothy Garton Ash, "Global Capitalism Now Has No Serious Rivals. But It Could Destroy Itself," *Guardian (UK)* (February 22, 2007)

Pure capitalism invites astute investors to relocate businesses to optimize returns, even at the cost of neighborhoods and communities. It invites shareholders to streamline and profit-maximize, even at the expense of loyal workers.
—Eva Bertram and Kenneth Sharpe, discussing effects of capitalism ignored by conservatives, "Capitalism, Work, and Character," *American Prospect* (September 11, 2000)

Capitalism's problem is that it has nothing to say about how to combat greed.
—Lewis Black, "Lewis Black Interview," *Progressive* (April 2007)

Democracy is not synonymous with capitalism.
—Bob Burnett, "A Liberal Foreign Policy: Ten Maxims," *Huffington Post* (March 1, 2007)

Capitalism is basically a system where everything is for sale.
—Noam Chomsky, quoted in *Language and Politics* (1974)

Unrestrained free-market capitalism is not the friend of average Americans. It's not the friend of tradition and of small town values. It's quite the opposite. It's the great destroyer.
—Thomas Frank, quoted in an interview entitled "Recapturing Kansas," *In These Times* (January 12, 2005)

The capitalist system is not going to be destroyed by an outside challenger like communism—it will be destroyed by its own internal greed.
—Molly Ivins, "The Politics of Greed," Truthdig (July 10, 2006)

Capitalism is admittedly an incredibly productive system that has created a flood of goods unlike anything the world has ever seen. It also is a system that is fundamentally (1) inhuman, (2) anti-democratic, and (3) unsustainable.
—Robert Jensen, "Anti-Capitalism in Five Minutes or Less," *Common Dreams* (April 30, 2007)

Today, more than ever, it is critical for American citizens to understand the difference between the free-market capitalism that made our country great and the corporate cronyism that is now corrupting our political process, strangling democracy and devouring our national treasures.
—Robert F. Kennedy, Jr., "Crimes Against Nature," *Rolling Stone* (December 11, 2003)

Capitalism is the astounding belief that the most wickedest of men will do the most wickedest of things for the greatest good of everyone.
—John Maynard Keynes, quoted in "Mercury in U.S. Lakes; Cyanide in India—Trust the CEOs!" *Progreso Weekly* (September 8, 2004)

The new capitalism disdains stability; human beings, on the whole, don't.
—Harold Meyerson, "A Gentler Capitalism," *Washington Post* (January 4, 2006)

We're selling our harbors to an Arab government. Our biggest Internet companies are complicit in the Chinese government's censorship of information and suppression of dissidents. Welcome to American capitalism in the age of globalization.
—Harold Meyerson, "Wanna Buy a Port?" *American Prospect* (February 23, 2006)

Democracy has been made subservient to capitalism, and the great ideals of the American Revolution as articulated in the Preamble to the Constitution are being sacrificed to the Gospel of Wealth.
—Bill Moyers, "America 101," *TomPaine.com* (November 1, 2006)

Advocates of capitalism are very apt to appeal to the sacred principles of liberty, which are embodied in one maxim: The fortunate must not be restrained in the exercise of tyranny over the unfortunate.
—Bertrand Russell, *Skeptical Essays* (1928)

The necessity of capitalism does not argue for subservience to the capitalists. Private ownership gives wealthy capitalists quite enough power. They do not need to own the public government as well.
—Arthur M. Schlesinger, Jr., new introduction to *The Vital Center* (1998)

Capitalism has always been a failure for the lower classes. It is now beginning to fail for the middle classes.
—Howard Zinn, *A People's History of the United States* (1995)

Class

The horror of class stratification, racism, and prejudice is that some people begin to believe that the security of their families and communities depends on the oppression of others.
—Dorothy Allison, *Skin* (1994)

It's hard to concentrate in classrooms that were cleaned during the night by people who can barely make rent. You tend to choke on your chicken fingers when the cafeteria is staffed by men and women who have to work a second job in order to feed their own children.
—Barbara Ehrenreich, "Class Struggle 101," *Progressive* (November 2003)

Privileges based on position and property have always seemed to me unjust and pernicious.
—Albert Einstein, in a 1932 speech delivered to the German League of Human Rights, quoted in *Einstein: A Life in Science* (1994)

The main reason conservatives have been able to annex the language of social class so completely is that their opponents have been silent on the subject. The Democratic leadership decided years ago not to talk class anymore.
—Thomas Frank, "Let's Talk Class Again," *London Review of Books* (March 21, 2002)

We are in an environment where Republicans talk constantly about class—in a coded way, to be sure—but where Democrats are afraid to bring it up.
—Thomas Frank, "Red-State America Against Itself," *TomDispatch.com* (July 16, 2004)

The "middle class" is the creation of government intervention in the market-place, and won't exist without it.
—Thom Hartmann, "Democracy—Not 'The Free Market'—Will Save America's Middle Class," *Common Dreams* (March 12, 2004)

The gap between the rich and everybody else in this country is fast becoming an unbridgeable chasm.
—Bob Herbert, "The Mobility Myth," *New York Times* (June 6, 2005)

Corporations and the millionaire class already have a party—and notice that it is relentless in its devotion to their interests. . . . These fortunate few are doing fine; they don't need another party's help.
—Jim Hightower, "What I Want For Christmas," *Hightower Lowdown* (December 2005)

Corporations . . . have declared class war on working people.
—Marty Jezer, "Economic Recovery: Losers and Winners," *Common Dreams* (April 9, 2004)

It's easier for a poor child to make it into the upper-middle class in just about every other advanced country . . . than it is in the United States.
—Paul Krugman, "The Great Wealth Transfer," *Rolling Stone* (November 30, 2006)

If a society advertises itself as a meritocracy, but in practice allocates success based on hereditary advantage, how are those who are not winners supposed to respond?
—Jennifer Ladd and Felice Yeskel, "Class in America," *Common Dreams* (June 2, 2005)

When it comes to talking about class, it's as if we stumble and go speechless when confronted with the most basic of American divides.
—Jennifer Ladd and Felice Yeskel, "Class in America," *Common Dreams* (June 2, 2005)

Ask any waitress or waiter to tell you who tips them better, the wealthy or the working class.
—David Morris, "Why All Tax Credits Should Be Refundable," AlterNet (February 20, 2007)

In America's increasingly vicious class war, one reason the wealthy are winning is corporate media's insistence (all evidence to the contrary) that no such war exists.
—Geov Parrish, "Media Follies 2006!" *Working for Change* (December 21, 2006)

A renewed commitment to end the limitations born of class does hold this promise: It reaches Americans of all colors, from white single mothers in rural Georgia to brown high-school dropouts in Los Angeles to black men struggling to find jobs in Newark.
—Cynthia Tucker, "Class Is Harder Line to Cross Than Color," *Yahoo! News* (February 4, 2006)

Those who don't choose their parents wisely often find their achievements limited. This country is more class-oriented than many of us would like to believe.
—Cynthia Tucker, "We Have Little Patience with the Poor," *Atlanta Journal-Constitution* (December 24, 2005)

The Republicans yell "class warfare!" whenever the subject of tax justice is raised because the phrase is meant to remind us of Marxism—and therefore something beyond the pale of civilized thought.
—Nicholas von Hoffman, "Here's a Capital Idea: Make the Rich Pay Taxes!" *New York Observer* (March 26, 2001)

The security of middle-class life has disappeared. The new reality is millions of families whose grip on the good life can be shaken loose in an instant.
—Elizabeth Warren, "The Middle Class on the Precipice," *Harvard* magazine (January/February 2006)

The most important—and unfortunately the least debated—issue in politics today is our society's steady drift toward a class-based system.
—Jim Webb, "Class Struggle," *Wall Street Journal* (November 15, 2006)

There is indeed class warfare in this country. The problem is, only one class seems to know it.
—Michael Zweig, "Working-Class Majority Needs a Hero," *Newsday* (September 1, 2000

Crime

Marijuana isn't a harmless substance, and those who argue for a change in the drug's legal status do not claim it to be. However . . . pot's relative risks to the user and society are arguably fewer than those of alcohol and tobacco, and they do not warrant the expenses associated with targeting, arresting, and prosecuting hundreds of thousands of Americans every year.
—Paul Armentano, "It's Been an 'All Out War' on Pot Smokers for 35 Years," AlterNet (March 21, 2007)

Hunger makes a thief of any man.
—Pearl S. Buck, *The Good Earth* (1931)

There are few better measures of the concern a society has for its individual members and its own well-being than the way it handles criminals.
—Ramsey Clark, in his address to the American Correctional Association conference (August 1967)

It is better, so the Fourth Amendment teaches us, that the guilty sometimes go free than that the citizens be subject to easy arrest.
—William O. Douglas, *Henry v. United States* (1959)

The criminal justice system is both the most dysfunctional aspect of American democracy and the most insulated from reform.
—Editorial, "Does Prison Harden Criminals? Yes." *Nation* (December 14, 2006)

Crime seems to change character when it crosses a bridge or a tunnel. In the city, crime is taken as emblematic of class and race. In the suburbs, though, it's intimate and psychological—resistant to generalization, a mystery of the individual soul.
—Barbara Ehrenreich, *The Worst Years of Our Lives* (1991)

If marijuana were a new discovery rather than a well-known substance carrying cultural and political baggage, it would be hailed as a wonder drug.
—Lester Grinspoon, "Marijuana as Wonder Drug," *Boston Globe* (March 1, 2007)

A President can commit no more serious crime against our democracy than lying to Congress and the American people to get them to support a military action or war.
—Elizabeth Holtzman, "The Impeachment of George W. Bush," *Nation* (January 30, 2006)

A criminal is a person with predatory instincts without sufficient capital to form a corporation.
—Howard Scott, quoted in the *Idaho Observer* (December 2001)

I would call an end to the war on drugs—yesterday. I would take the police out of the business of popping people for the possession of small quantities of drugs, and I would devote much of that attention and money to prevention, education, and treatment.
—Norm Stamper, interviewed by Laura Barcella, "Seattle Confidential," AlterNet (June 15, 2005)

Lawmakers getting caught smoking crack in a Vegas whorehouse is embarrassing. Lawmakers endorsing a counterfeit war that has killed almost 2,100 American soldiers and more than 30,000 Iraqis . . . those things aren't embarrassing; they're criminal.
—Pierre Tristam, "Justice Deficit America's Grossest Domestic Product," *Daytona Beach News-Journal* (November 22, 2005)

During the Vietnam War, Abbie Hoffman announced that the new high was banana peels taken rectally. So then FBI scientists stuffed banana peels up their asses to find out if this was true or not.
—Kurt Vonnegut, Jr., *A Man Without a Country* (2005)

Conservatives have spent more than twenty years demonizing lawyers and ridiculing victims in order to eliminate a uniquely American right . . . that allows juries to assess damages in civil courts for corporate misbehavior.
—Dan Zegart, "Tort 'Reform' Triumphs," *Nation* (February 17, 2005)

Economic Justice

Shame on us. Those of us who work with the religious community have not adequately made the connection between economic disparity and moral values.
—Kim Bobo, quoted in "Pushing Poverty into 'Moral-Values' Debate," *San Francisco Examiner* (December 12, 2004)

There are those who believe that if you just legislate to make the well-to-do prosperous, that their prosperity will leak through on those below. The Democratic idea has been that if you legislate to make the masses prosperous, their prosperity will find its way up and through every class that rests upon it.
—William Jennings Bryan, in his famous "Cross of Gold" speech (1896)

Progressives should champion a bold and inclusive new wealth-broadening program that speaks to the aspirations of people left behind in our apartheid economy.
—Chuck Collins, "Oversight Hearings: What Should Congress Do?" *Nation* (January 4, 2007)

If there is a man on this earth who is entitled to all the comforts and luxuries of this life in abundance, it is the man whose labor produces them. If he is not, who is? Does he get them in the present system?
—Eugene Debs, quoted in *Debs: His Life, Writings and Speeches* (1908)

The more equally wealth is distributed the better the health of that society.
—Editorial, "The Big Idea," *British Medical Journal* (April 20, 1996)

People getting their fundamental interests wrong is what American political life is all about. . . . This derangement has put Republicans in charge of all three branches of government.
—Thomas Frank, *What's the Matter with Kansas?* (2004)

Trickle-down theory—the less than elegant metaphor that if one feeds the horse enough oats, some will pass through to the road for the sparrows.
—John Kenneth Galbraith, *The Culture of Contentment* (1992)

Although the system we call "meritocracy" is presumed to be more democratic and egalitarian than aristocracy, it is in fact reproducing that which it was intended to dislodge.
—Lani Guinier, in an interview with Rebecca Parrish, "The Meritocracy Myth," *Dollars & Sense* (January/February 2006)

One of the main activities of American executives these days is figuring out ways to cut the pay of their workers while at the same time hanging on to all they have.
—Richard Gwyn, "'American Dream' Turning into a Nightmare," *Toronto Star* (June 27, 2006)

In the good book, Jesus talks more about economic justice than nearly any other subject, and the apostles make clear that the most important ethical/religious test of Judeo-Christian faith is in how we treat the least wealthy, least important among us.
—Jim Hightower, "The Political Jesus," AlterNet (December 25, 2004)

Today, the top 1 percent controls 38 percent of our total wealth.
—Bill Moyers, "America 101," *TomPaine.com* (November 1, 2006)

The forces of capitalist society, if left unchecked, tend to make the rich richer and the poor poorer.
—Jawaharlal Nehru, *New York Times Magazine* (September 7, 1958)

An imbalance between rich and poor is the oldest and most fatal ailment of all republics.
—Plutarch, Greek philosopher, quoted in *Pacific Northwest* (July 25, 2004)

It's hard to run as an economic populist when corporate donors are paying your bills.
—Katha Pollitt, "Let's Not Devalue Ourselves," *Nation* (July 29, 2004)

We can create an economic system that is not at war with human beings or nature, and we can get from here to there by democratic means.
—Charles A. Reich, in his new preface to the twenty-fifth anniversary edition, *The Greening of America* (1995)

Democrats . . . once did have a progressive economic agenda. But in an age of money-drenched politics, they too have been increasingly co-opted by the same corporate agenda that control the Republicans.
—David Sirota, "The Failure of Populism?" *TomPaine.com* (April 12, 2001)

America has four hundred billionaires—and thirty-seven million people below the official poverty line.
—Holly Sklar, "Economy Booming for Billionaires," *Common Dreams* (September 28, 2006)

Wealth isn't trickling down. It's flooding up—from workers to bosses, small investors to big, poorer to richer.
—Holly Sklar, "Economy Booming for Billionaires," *Common Dreams* (September 28, 2006)

Economic trends have strained working families to the breaking point. Workers are not sharing in the wealth they helped create.
—John Sweeney, president of the AFL–CIO, quoted in "Lessons for Labor Day," *Nation* (September 1, 2006)

Islands of wealth are being created in a sea of misery.
—John J. Sweeney, quoted in "Labor chief Sees 'Sea of Misery,'" *Buffalo News* (April 12, 2005)

Last year was the first year on record . . . that a full-time worker at minimum wage could not afford a one-bedroom apartment anywhere in the country at average market rates.
—Ian Urbina, "Keeping It Secret as the Family Car Becomes a Home," *New York Times* (April 2, 2006)

Basic justice calls for the establishment of a floor of material well-being on which all can stand.
—U.S. Catholic Bishops, *Economic Justice for All: Pastoral Letter on Catholic Social Teaching and the U.S. Economy* (1986)

Reviving workers' living standards requires direct challenges to out-of-control corporate greed and unrestricted market power.
—Michael Zweig, "Stand up For Moral Value of Economic Justice," *Baltimore Sun* (November 19, 2004)

Economics

A moral economy does not require any heroic assumptions about human nature; it does not assume that people are always cooperative and kind. On the contrary, it starts from the idea that the individual pursuit of self-interest has to be controlled or it will turn destructive.
—Fred Block, "A Moral Economy," *Nation* (March 20, 2006)

Politics is simply the reflex of economics. The material foundation of society determines the character of all social institutions—political, educational, ethical, and spiritual.
—Eugene Debs, quoted in *Debs: His Life, Writings and Speeches* (1908)

Americans can hardly find time to sit down to eat together anymore. Is our economy just for raising the Dow Jones average, or is it to provide healthy and happy kids, families, and communities?
—John de Graaf, "The Big Question on This Labor Day: What's The Economy for Anyway?" *Common Dreams* (September 4, 2006)

Budgets are so much more than dry bureaucratic formalities. They are society's moral ledgers. . . . They are the X-ray-like instruments that strip the false sanctimony from our pious posturings to reveal to the world who we really are.
—Robert Freeman, "Bush's Budget Proposal: Is This Who We Really Are?" *Common Dreams* (February 10, 2006)

The economic game is not supposed to be rigged like some shady ring toss on a carnival midway.
—Arianna Huffington, *Pigs at the Trough* (2003)

A job for every person willing and able to work—this is the definition of a decent economy.
—Rev. Jesse Jackson, "A Job for the U. S.: Make Economy Fair," *Chicago Sun-Times* (March 20, 2007)

How did it happen today that a two-income family has less disposal income than a one-income family did thirty years ago?
—Bernie Sanders, "If You Are Concerned About Health Care, Iraq, the Economy, Global Warming You Must Be Concerned About Corporate Control of the Media," *Democracy Now!* radio (January 22, 2007)

John F. Kennedy said, "A rising tide lifts all boats," but right now we're only raising the luxury liners.
—Andy Stern, "Changing How America Works," AlterNet (November 2, 2006)

What we have in this country is socialism for the rich and free enterprise for the poor.
—Gore Vidal, quoted in *Pigs at the Trough* (2003)

Fiscal Responsibility

Maybe it's time to tie congressional pay raises to comparable percentage raises in the federal minimum wage.
—Steven P. Alpert, "Congress Gives Itself a Raise, but What About the Minimum Wage?" *USA Today* (June 20, 2006)

It is a moral value to make sure that we do not leave our own debts to be paid by the next generation.
—Howard Dean, "Democratic Moral Values," YubaNet (December 13, 2004)

Moderates and liberals alike are mystified by budget policies saddling our kids with debt tomorrow to pay for tax cuts for the wealthy today.
—E. J. Dionne, Jr., "The Positive Power of Negative Thinking," *Working for Change* (March 9, 2006)

The huge budget deficit is conservatism's Waterloo.
—E. J. Dionne, Jr., "The GOP's Shrinking Middle," *Washington Post* (March 21, 2006)

A corporate-driven consumer culture has led millions of Americans into personal debt, and alienated millions more by convincing them that the only path to happiness is through the purchase and consumption of ever-increasing quantities of material goods.
—Lee Drutman and Charlie Cray, "The People's Business," *In These Times* (February 18, 2005)

When the richest nation in the world has to borrow hundreds of billions of dollars to pay its bill, when its middle-class citizens sit on a mountain of debt to maintain their living standards, when the nation's economy has difficulty producing secure jobs or enough jobs of any kind, something is amiss.
—Norton Garfinkle, *The American Dream vs. the Gospel of Wealth* (2006)

Today, the average American's share of the national debt is $27,000 and rising . . . Every day we ignore the problem, we increase the chances that the problem will have severe, if not catastrophic, consequences.
—John F. Ince, "Crumbling Under Debt," AlterNet (April 8, 2006)

Last year's savings rate was negative—meaning American households saved nothing and went into debt—for the first time since the Great Depression.
—Robert Reich, "The Shrinking Nest Egg," *American Prospect* (April 5, 2006)

Credit cards have gone from a luxury to a necessity to a noose.
—Danny Schechter, quoted in "Young Borrowers Face a Life of Debt," AlterNet (November 18, 2006)

We don't want our kids getting out of college, spending their first ten years of life paying off their debt.
—Andy Stern, "Changing How America Works," AlterNet (November 2, 2006)

Where are the Good Republicans? Where are the fiscal grownups who think that an $8.38 trillion national debt is maybe several trillion too much?
—Ellis Weiner, "A Public Presentation of My New Theory," *Huffington Post* (April 19, 2006)

Our grandchildren's generation will be in hock up to its ears. Any historian or economist could have told our "deciders" that it wasn't prudent to launch a huge tax cut and a costly war at the same time.
—Jim Wright, "A Deaf Ear for America's Concerns," *Fort Worth Star-Telegram* (April 24, 2006)

Justice

What the poor and downtrodden need is not piecemeal charity but wholesale justice.
—Rev. William Sloane Coffin, quoted in "The Legacy of William Sloane Coffin," *Boston Globe* (April 15, 2006)

The requirement of "due process" is not a fair weather or timid assurance. It must be respected in periods of calm and in times of trouble; it protects aliens as well as citizens.
—Felix Frankfurter, *Joint Anti-Fascist Refugee Committee v. McGrath* (1951)

I believe that a core of justice is within us, and that it's yearning to come out, to become the guiding principle of our society.
—Jim Hightower, quoted in *The Impossible Will Take a Little While Longer* (2003)

We shall awaken from our dullness and rise vigorously toward justice.
—Hildegard of Bingen, twelfth-century magistra, quoted in *Writing to Change the World* (2006)

Every great struggle for justice in human history began as a lost cause.
—Robert Jensen, "Critical Hope: Radical Citizenship in Reactionary Times," *Common Dreams* (December 17, 2001)

What the worst people in the world fear most is justice.
—Angelina Jolie, "Justice for Darfur," *Washington Post* (February 28, 2007)

The absence of brutality and unregenerate evil is not the presence of justice.
—Rev. Martin Luther King, Jr., *Where Do We Go from Here: Chaos or Community?* (1967)

Doing justice cannot be separated from hating injustice; loving kindness cannot be separated from despising cruelty.
—Rev. Robin Myers, *Why the Christian Right is Wrong* (2006)

I had become a liberal largely through religion. Loving your neighbor as yourself, giving your cloak to the man who had none, blessed are the peacemakers: taken together, all of it seemed a clarion call to social justice.
—Anna Quindlen, "At the Left Hand of God," *Newsweek* (March 8, 2004)

Each person posses an inviolability founded on justice that even the welfare of society cannot override.
—John Rawls, *A Theory of Justice* (1971)

You have to understand that more important than anything else is justice.
—Arundhati Roy, in an interview with Terrence McNally, "Finding Justice with Arundhati Roy," AlterNet (September 21, 2004)

Justice is always in jeopardy.
—Walt Whitman, *Democratic Vistas* (1870)

It is justice, not charity, that is wanting in the world.
—Mary Wollstonecraft, *A Vindication of the Rights of Women* (1792)

Labor Unions

We have lost any effective right to form unions and bargain collectively . . . in America.
—Stewart Acuff, "Globalization and the American Labor Movement," *Common Dreams* (April 6, 2006)

Once upon a time, organized labor served as a crucial counterweight to the corporate right. Unions provided much more than a bigger paycheck for workers.
—Craig Aaron, "How the Right Has Won," *In These Times* (October 27, 2005)

The decline of labor is one of the central reasons traditional liberal strategies are in decline.
—Gar Alperovitz, "Another World Is Possible," *Mother Jones* (January/ February 2006)

With all their faults, trade unions have done more for humanity than any other organization of men that ever existed.
—Clarence Darrow, quoted in *The Railroad Trainman* (1909)

Anyone in the United States can join a political party, a faith group or a community organization simply by signing up. . . . When workers try to form a union under current rules, they run a gantlet of antiunion intimidation and propaganda.
—Editorial, "Recognizing Labor," *Nation* (January 1, 2007)

The underlying reason for organized labor's decline is that our labor laws do not let people join unions, freely and fairly, without being fired.
—Barbara Ehrenreich and Thomas Geoghegan, "Lighting Labor's Fire," *Nation* (December 5, 2002)

Organized labor is still the best-funded and organized progressive force in the country.
—Jeff Epton, "Labor's Future Is Ours," *In These Times* (January 21, 2005)

Labor unions are on the wane today. . . . Their decline goes largely unchecked by a Democratic Party anxious to demonstrate its fealty to corporate America, and unmourned by a therapeutic left that never liked those Archie Bunker types in the first place.
—Thomas Frank, "Red-State America Against Itself," *TomDispatch.com* (July 16, 2004)

There is no social theory on earth short of the divine right of kings that justify a five-hundred-fold [income] gap between management and labor.
—Thomas Frank, *One Market Under God* (2001)

Strong unions are the only thing standing between you and serfdom at the hands of corporate masters, and without the unions of the past there would be no American middle class today.
—Thom Hartmann, "Free Yourself from Conservative Talk Radio," *Common Dreams* (November 4, 2003)

Before the labor movement, a dangerous workplace, low wages, and arduously long workdays were just crappy things about a person's life.
—Christopher Hayes, "How to Turn Your Red State Blue," *In These Times* (March 22, 2005)

It's a concrete possibility we will wake up one morning and there won't be a single American labor union left. For thirty straight years, American organized labor has been hemorrhaging members, power and influence.
—Christopher Hayes, "The Fight for Our Future," *In These Times* (January 21, 2005)

Collective bargaining is how we built the middle class in this country.
—Andy Levin, quoted in "GOP Governors Cut State Workers' Rights," the Associated Press (AP) (March 12, 2005)

The right to organize in the United States is on the verge of extinction.
—Andy Levin, quoted in "Symbol of the System," *In These Times* (November 6, 2005)

No tin-hat brigade of goose-stepping vigilantes or Bible-babbling mob of blackguarding and corporation paid scoundrels will prevent the onward march of labor.
—John L. Lewis, president of the United Mine Workers, in a speech in Washington, D.C. (September 3, 1937)

Labor is prior to, and independent of, capital. Capital is only the fruit of labor, and could never have existed if Labor had not first existed. Labor is superior to capital, and deserves much the higher consideration.
—Abraham Lincoln, first annual message to Congress (December 3, 1861)

Of more than 1,400 Target stores employing more than 300,000 people nationwide, not one has a union.
—Kari Lydersen, "Target: Wal-Mart Lite," *CorpWatch* (April 20, 2006)

Solidarity—an injury to one is an injury to all. That is the basic principle of the labor movement, the understanding that we're all in it together.
—David Newby, "Securing the Common Good Underlies Labor Movement," *Capital Times* (Madison, Wisconson) (September 4, 2006)

Free trade is tantamount to a massive increase in the rich country's labor supply, since the products made by poor country workers can now be imported.
—Thomas Palley, "The Global Labor Threat," *TomPaine.com* (September 29, 2005)

The trouble with unregulated free trade is that it throws the balance between labor and management out of whack.
—Ted Rall, *Wake Up, You're Liberal!* (2004)

Bashing organized labor is a Republican pathology.
—David Sirota, "The War on Workers," *San Francisco Chronicle* (September 4, 2006)

In an era when government is a wholly own subsidiary of Corporate America, unions are one of the few strong voices left to defend ordinary Americans' economic interests.
—David Sirota, *Hostile Takeover* (2006)

An injury to one is an injury to all.
—Dan Sturgis, "Where's the Family in These Values?" *Common Dreams* (December 16, 2004)

No one may deny the right to organize without attacking human dignity it-self. Therefore, we firmly oppose organized efforts, such as those regrettably now seen in this country, to break existing unions and prevent workers from organizing.
—U.S. Catholic Bishops, *Economic Justice for All: Pastoral Letter on Catholic Social Teaching and the U.S. Economy* (1986)

Labor is an occasion for self-realization, not a mere factor of production.
—Stefano Zamagni, quoted in "Capitalism That Works for All," AlterNet (June 23, 2006)

Poverty

So long as people go to bed starving and without a home in this, the world's most prosperous country, there will always be a need for liberalism.
—Evan L. Balkan, "Though It's Often Bashed, Liberalism's Day Has Not Quite Passed," *Baltimore Sun* (February 15, 2001)

The world teems with elemental wants and is peopled by billions who are needy. They do not need iPods, but they do need potable water, not colas but inexpensive medicines, not MTV but their ABCs.
—Benjamin R. Barber, "Overselling Capitalism with Consumerism," *Baltimore Sun* (April 15, 2007)

How can you worship a homeless man on Sunday and ignore one on Monday?
—Coalition for the Homeless, caption under a drawing of Jesus, *New York Times* (January 16, 1994)

The Republican "War on the Poor" approach to government is disgusting when contrasted with their strong push for tax cuts for the very wealthiest of the wealthy.
—Stephen Crockett, "Republicans to Poor: 'Freeze to Death'," OpEdNews (December 25, 2005)

If the misery of our poor be caused not by the laws of nature, but by our institutions, great is our sin.
—Charles Darwin, *Voyage of the Beagle* (1840)

If you feed the poor, you're a saint. If you ask why they're poor, you're a communist.
—Dorothy Day, quoted in "Entertaining Angels: The Dorothy Day Story," *Christian Century* (February 26, 1997)

Poverty is the great moral issue of our time.
—John Edwards, quoted in "Survival of the Richest," *Boston Globe* (June 24, 2006)

You can make ending poverty in America the cause of your generation.
—John Edwards, "Cornbread and Roses," *Nation* (November 28, 2005)

The working poor neglect their own children so that the children of others will be cared for. They live in substandard housing so that other homes will be shiny and perfect; they endure privation so that inflation will be low and stock prices high.
—Barbara Ehrenreich, *Nickel and Dimed* (2001)

To live in poverty is to live with constant uncertainty, to accept galling indignities, and to expect harassment by the police, welfare officials, and employers, as well as by others who are poor and desperate.
—Barbara Ehrenreich, *Fear of Falling: The Inner Life of the Middle Class* (1990)

People who are much too sensitive to demand of cripples that they run races ask of the poor that they get up and act just like everyone else in society.
—Michael Harrington, *The Other America: Poverty in the United States* (1962)

The poor are increasingly slipping out of the very experience and consciousness of the nation.
—Michael Harrington, *The Other America: Poverty in the United States* (1962)

We punish people in this country for being poor and we punish homosexuality. When both are combined, it does more than double the effect.
—Amber Hollibaugh, "They Are Everywhere. But We Refuse to See Them. Queers Without Money," *Village Voice* (June 20, 2001)

36 million Americans live below the poverty line—12.9 million of them children.
—Arianna Huffington, "2005: Things I Want to Forget (Part Two)," *Huffington Post* (December 22, 2005)

First to feel God's wrath will be the elders and the princes, for they have defrauded the poor. They have filled their barns with grain extorted from the helpless peasants.
—Isaiah 3:14

My constituency is the desperate, the damned, the disinherited, the disrespected, and the despised.
—Rev. Jesse Jackson, in his address to the Democratic National Convention in San Francisco (July 17, 1984)

Will you join in the battle to give every citizen an escape from the crushing weight of poverty? . . . Will you join in the battle to build the Great Society, to prove that our material progress is only the foundation on which we will build a richer life of mind and spirit?
—Lyndon B. Johnson, in his speech at the University of Michigan (May 22, 1964)

Accepting the persistence of widespread poverty even as the rich get ever richer is a choice that our politicians have made. And we should be ashamed of that choice.
—Paul Krugman, "Helping the Poor, the British Way," *New York Times* (December 25, 2006)

Give me your tired, your poor,
Your huddled masses yearning to be free.
The wretched refuse of your teeming shore,
Send these, the homeless, tempest-tossed, to me,
I lift my lamp beside the golden door.
—Emma Lazarus, inscription on the Statue of Liberty, "The New Colossus," (1883)

I always give homeless people money and my friends yell at me, "He's only going to buy more alcohol and cigarettes." And I'm thinking, "Oh, and like I wasn't?"
—Kathleen Madigan, quoted in "For Duff, It's 'Kiss' and Tell," *Dallas Morning News* (February 7, 2007)

The poor are still largely invisible to the complacent majority. Most Americans don't see the everydayness of poverty. It is segregated in "bad neighborhoods" and in impersonal government waiting rooms.
—Jack Newfield, "How the Other Half Still Lives," *Nation* (February 27, 2003)

70 percent of the world's poorest people are women.
—Anne Penketh, "International Women's Day: Struggle for Equality and Freedom in Developing Countries," *Independent (UK)* (March 8, 2007)

America is not so beautiful when one's bed is a cardboard box.
—Richard Pretorius, "What Are the Priorities in a Land of Wealth?" *Baltimore Sun* (February 7, 2001)

We think of ourselves as an incredibly rich country, but we are beginning to realize that we are also a desperately poor country—poor in most of the things that throughout the history of mankind have been cherished as riches.
—Charles A. Reich, *The Greening of America* (1970)

We shouldn't push the poor out of sight; we should push them out of poverty.
—Reggie Rivers, "Don't Stop Giving Change to Beggars," *Denver Post* (August 26, 2005)

I see one-third of a nation ill-housed, ill-clad, ill-nourished.
—Franklin D. Roosevelt, in his second inaugural address on January 20, 1937, quoted in Public Papers (1941)

If you walk down the street and see someone in a box, you have a choice. That person is either the other and you're fearful of them, or that person is an extension of your family.
—Susan Sarandon, in an interview with Laura Sheahen, "Nobody Is a Stranger," *Beliefnet* (December 20, 2005)

A hungry man is not a free man.
—Adlai Stevenson, in a speech (September 6, 1952)

A generation of politicians and pundits has told us that the poor are lazy and irresponsible and undeserving of our help. Indeed, trying to help them would only make them worse off, we're told.
—Cynthia Tucker, "We Have Little Patience with the Poor," *Atlanta Journal-Constitution* (December 24, 2005)

When people are without a chance to earn a living, and must go hungry and homeless, they are being denied basic rights. Society must ensure that these rights are protected.
—U.S. Catholic Bishops, *Economic Justice for All: Pastoral Letter on Catholic Social Teaching and the U.S. Economy* (1986)

American women are 40 percent more likely than men to be poor.
—Jessica Valenti, "A Good Job Is Hard to Find," AlterNet (April 5, 2006)

God's politics remind us of the people our politics always neglect—the poor, the vulnerable, the left behind.
—Rev. Jim Wallis, "God's Politics: A Better Option," *Sojourners* (February 2005)

Poverty is indeed a religious issue, and the failure of political leaders to help uplift those in poverty will be judged a moral failing.
—Rev. Jim Wallis, quoted in "I Want My Faith Back," *Arkansas Times* (December 23, 2004)

When the poor are defended on moral or religious grounds it is certainly not "class warfare," as the rich often charge.
—Rev. Jim Wallis, *God's Politics: Why the Right Gets It Wrong and the Left Doesn't Get It* (2005)

The belief that we are responsible for each other's social, economic, and political well-being, that we will care for our weakest members compassionately, should be the keystone in the moral architecture of a democratic culture.
—Chip Ward, "What They Didn't Teach Us in Library School: The Public Library as an Asylum for the Homeless," *TomDispatch.com* (April 1, 2007)

If you want to reduce poverty, stop scapegoating people. Start focusing on a good education and a good job.
—Paul Wellstone, quoted in "Radical Realist; Bill Clinton Wasn't the Only Comeback Story of 1996," *Washington Post* (January 19, 1997)

Social Security

The richest country in the history of the world should be increasing, not decreasing, its support for those in the final years of life.
—Gar Alperovitz, "Time for Moral Outrage About Social Security," *Common Dreams* (January 31, 2005)

I don't believe the way to fix Social Security is to have Wall Street run it so that it can be invested in Enron and Tyco and MCI.
—Howard Dean, quoted in "Liberal Groups Keeping Close Eye on Dean," the Associated Press (AP) (February 25, 2005)

The president's proposal to privatize part of Social Security was . . . part of a larger effort to reorganize government and bring the New Deal era to a definitive close.
—E. J. Dionne, Jr., "Rove's New Mission: Survival," *Washington Post* (April 21, 2006)

Social Security, Medicare, private health insurance, traditional guaranteed pensions—all sent the same reassuring message: someone is watching out for you, all of us are watching out for you, when things go bad. Today, the message is starkly different: You are on your own.
—Jacob Hacker, quoted in "Live at Your Own Risk," *In These Times* (November 28, 2006)

Let's get this straight. The Republicans do not want to fix Social Security, they want to kill it. They don't want to "partially privatize" Social Security, they want to end it.
—Molly Ivins, "Lynching Social Security," AlterNet (January 6, 2005)

Why should people who make more than $90,000 have their higher income exempted, when every nickel made by people below the poverty level is taxed?
—Molly Ivins, "Noble Ideals, Nasty Actions," AlterNet (February 3, 2005)

We will not let any President turn the American dream into a nightmare for senior citizens and a bonanza for Wall Street.
—Edward M. Kennedy, in an address to the National Press Club, "A Democratic Blueprint for America's Future" (January 12, 2005)

Social Security is a government program that works, a demonstration that a modest amount of taxing and spending can make people's lives better and more secure.
—Paul Krugman, "Inventing a Crisis," *New York Times* (December 7, 2004)

The politics of privatization depend crucially on convincing the public that the system is in imminent danger of collapse, that we must destroy Social Security in order to save it.
—Paul Krugman, "Inventing A Crisis," *New York Times* (December 7, 2004)

Social Security is a true success story . . . returning more than ninety-nine cents in benefits for every dollar that it takes in. Its administrative costs are far lower than those in any private program.
—George McGovern, *Social Security and the Golden Age* (2006)

Social Security is like a car with a flat tire. There is a problem. We need to fix the flat tire. But we don't need to replace the car.
—Peter Orszag, quoted in "White House—Bush Criticized Over Social Security Plan," the Associated Press (AP) (December 21, 2004)

Social Security "privatization" would funnel trillions of dollars into the U.S. stock market and thus put more money in the hands of Wall Street investment firms, which already are big underwriters of the Republican Party.
—Robert Parry, "Bush & the Rise of 'Managed-Democracy,'" *Consortium News* (February 13, 2005)

Social Security taxes are taken out of only the first $87,900 of income. [The figure in 2007 was $97,500.] So Bill Gates pays the exact same amount in Social Security taxes as a middle manager making $87,900. Let Gates and his cohorts kick in all the way, and the Social Security shortfall four decades from now virtually vanishes.
—Matthew Rothschild, "Bush's BS on SS," *Progressive* (December 18, 2004)

The president [Bush] seems to find it distasteful that we set aside a portion of our earnings for people other than ourselves. But that is the glory of the system, its moral core.
—Jonathan Rowe, "The 'We' in Social Security," *Christian Science Monitor* (March 10, 2005)

After seven decades of unmitigated success in protecting seniors from the vagaries of market forces, the White House now wants to turn Social Security itself over to the vagaries of market forces.
—Robert Scheer, "Sabotaging Social Security," AlterNet (December 21, 2004)

One quarter of the [Iraq] war budget would have fixed Social Security for the next seventy-five years.
—Charles M. Young, "The $2 Trillion War," *Rolling Stone* (December 28, 2006)

Socialism

There can be no future social movements without key socialist themes: the importance of economic class, the centrality of labor and workers in shaping the world, the idea that people must act to create their own destiny.
—Ronald Aronson, "The Left Needs More Socialism," *Nation* (April 17, 2006)

In a world with such obscene disparities of wealth between nations and peoples, we desperately need a new ethos, based upon the fulfillment of human needs and social equality, rather than on the pursuit of private profit.
—Ken Brociner, "Utopianism, Human Nature, and the Left," *Dissent* (Winter 2001)

From each according to his ability, to each according to his needs.
—Karl Marx, *Critique of the Gotha Program* (1875)

Capitalism didn't create all human problems, and socialism can't solve all human problems. But moving toward a democratic socialist society is one step toward the discovery of what a human society might actually be.
—David McReynolds, "Socialism Yes. (What's Left?)" *Progressive* (April 1993)

Socialism is an effort to make every human being an end in himself or herself.
—David McReynolds, "Socialism Yes. (What's Left?)" *Progressive* (April 1993)

I don't mind really if millionaires vote against me; they probably should.
—Bernie Sanders, self-described socialist, quoted in "New Vermont Senator Not Standard Fare," *Seattle Post-Intelligencer* (November 9, 2006)

Society is divided into warring groups and classes, based upon material interests.
—Socialist Party Platform of 1912, quoted in *Dissent in America* (2006)

Doesn't anything socialistic make you want to throw up? Like great public schools, or health insurance for all?
—Kurt Vonnegut, Jr., *A Man Without a Country* (2005)

Society

Our Founding Fathers . . . knew that the only way to escape a closed society was to accept the risk of living in an open one.
—Frank Church, quoted in "Frank Church's Quixotic Vision," *Nation* (June 13, 2006)

We dwindling numbers of feminists and progressives need to get our act together and start arguing for a more humane, child-friendly society instead of taking the side of profit-mad business.
—Ruth Conniff, "Stop Feeding the Work Monster," *Progressive* (March 23, 2006)

I claim that human mind or human society is not divided into watertight compartments called social, political, and religious. All act and react upon one another.
—Mahatma Gandhi, *Young India* (1930)

Reporter: "Mr. Gandhi, what do you think of Western civilization?"
Gandhi: "I think it would be a very good idea."
—Mahatma Gandhi in 1930, quoted in *Good Work* (1979)

The shopping mall has replaced the church and town square as the center of our social life.
—Mark Hertzgaard, *The Eagle's Shadow* (2002)

Cities across the country are facing rising hunger and homelessness, a growing shortage of affordable housing, overcrowded schools, underpaid teachers, inadequate health care, an aged and declining infrastructure.
—Rev. Jesse Jackson, "Poor Get Cuts as Rich Get Tax Cuts," *Chicago Sun-Times* (June 6, 2006)

The permissive society has been allowed to become a dirty phrase. A better phrase is the civilized society.
—Roy Jenkins, in his speech in Abingdon, Oxfordshire, England (July 19, 1969)

We live in a society that prefers productive but passive people.
—Robert Jensen, "Critical Hope: Radical Citizenship in Reactionary Times," *Common Dreams* (December 17, 2001)

An elite with little loyalty to the state and a mass society fond of gladiator entertainments form a society in which corporate Leviathans rule and democracy is hollow.
—Robert D. Kaplan, "Was Democracy Just a Moment?" *Atlantic Monthly* (December 1997)

The liberal society is a free society, and it is at the same time and for that reason a strong society. Its strength is drawn from the will of free people committed to great ends and peacefully striving to meet them.
—John F. Kennedy, accepting the New York Liberal Party nomination (September 14, 1960)

The society to which we belong seems to be dying or is already dead. I don't mean to sound dramatic, but clearly the dark side is rising.
—Anne Lamott, *Bird by Bird* (1994)

We no longer live in a truly civilized society, but in one which revels in its arrogance, wealth, brutish conquest, denial of civil liberties, and torture.
—Joyce Marcel, "Life and Taxes," *Common Dreams* (March 23, 2006)

Can we plan ahead as a society so we know our priorities and where we wish to go? Or do we continue to let global corporations remain astride the planet, corporatizing everything, from genes to education to the Internet to public institutions, in short, planning our futures in their image?
—Ralph Nader, quoted in *The Ralph Nader Reader* (2000)

People are falling between the cracks and the cracks are growing wider.
—Rosa Maria Pegueros, "Charity Begins at Home," *Common Dreams* (January 5, 2005)

Bush's ownership society turns out to be the on-your-ownership society. The rising tide that was supposed to lift all boats is actually a flood that only those who already have a boat can escape.
—Katha Pollitt, "Intelligible Design," *Nation* (October 3, 2005)

Entire cultures are judged by how well they take care of those who can't take care of themselves. By that measure, America was once a very moral society.
—Beth Quinn, "Bush's Budget Reflects New Low in Moral Values," *Record Online* (February 14, 2005)

How is it possible that there may exist over time a stable and just society of free and equal citizens profoundly divided by reasonable though incompatible religious, philosophical, and moral doctrines?
—John Rawls, *Political Liberalism* (1996)

What a state of society is this in which freethinker is a term of abuse, and in which doubt is regarded as sin?
—W. Winwood Reade, *The Martyrdom of Man* (1972)

Society properly wants everyone to succeed. Do we really want some children to win while others lose? Is it desirable for some elderly people get adequate food and medical care while others don't?
—Robert Steinback, "Privatizing American Unity," *Miami Herald* (March 2, 2005)

My definition of a free society is a society where it is safe to be unpopular.
—Adlai Stevenson, in a speech in Detroit (October 7, 1952)

The mass of men lead lives of quiet desperation.
—Henry David Thoreau, *Walden* (1854)

Tax Giveaways to Millionaires

Tax loopholes continue to reward corporations that pollute the air and water, drill for oil and gas, and cut down forests.
—Brian Dunkiel, news release, "Tax Breaks for Polluters Growing More Expensive," *Friends of the Earth* (December 15, 1998)

We must reject billions in giveaways to the rich masquerading as economic stimulus. For the cost of the massive new tax breaks, we could provide health insurance for all our children and provide Head Start to every eligible child who needs it to succeed in school.
—Marian Wright Edelman, Children's Defense Fund president, in the press release "Senate Tax Bill Enough to Pay for Essential Protections for Children" (May 14, 2003)

America does not have a money problem—it has a priorities problem. . . . We give tax cuts to the wealthy, and budget cuts to the poor.
—Todd Huffman, "This Christmas, Where Is Our National Conscience?" *Common Dreams* (December 20, 2004)

We give tax credits to very large SUVs. I mean, this is public policy made in a lunatic asylum. And it only makes sense when you look at the millions of dollars in lobbying that the three Detroit automakers pay every year in political contributions.
—Arianna Huffington, interview entitled "Who Are the Pigs at the Trough?" *BuzzFlash* (March 6, 2003)

Companies that reincorporate offshore to avoid their fair share of taxes should have their tax and other benefits curtailed.
—Sheila Jackson Lee, "Accountable Corporations," *Nation* (February 6, 2006)

If some person defecates on your lawn, we throw him in jail, but if a corporation does it, they get a tax break.
—Bill Maher, "A Re-Look-See at the Constitution," *Boston Globe* (November 17, 2006)

Tax breaks are taking money from kids as sure as the schoolyard bully stealing classmates' lunch money—just on a scale so large that few have been willing to call it by name.
—Russell Mokhiber and Robert Weissman, "Stealing Money from Kids," *Common Dreams* (January 28, 2003)

Abolishing the outrageous forms of corporate welfare—subsidies, handouts, giveaways, and bailouts of largely big business—should become a trademark of the Democratic Party.
—Ralph Nader, "Go On Offensive Against the Republicans," *Common Dreams* (May 21, 2005)

Companies dangle office buildings, hotels, retail chain stores, or factories before state development agencies and ask for bids. The bids are a race to the bottom for exempting or abating these companies from paying their fair share to support the communities' services. . . . These companies are shameless freeloaders.
—Ralph Nader, "Protecting Public Education from Tax Giveaways to Corporations," *Common Dreams* (January 24, 24, 2003)

When the super-rich use offshore tax havens to avoid paying what they owe in taxes, they're reneging on their duties as citizens. It seems only fair to me that the consequence of that kind of tax avoidance ought to be loss of citizenship.
—Robert Reich, "What to Do About America's Rich Who Use Offshore Tax Havens," *Common Dreams* (May 23, 2007)

Why are millionaires getting big tax breaks while Congress cuts tuition aid for kids whose families can't afford to pay for college? Why are millionaires getting tax breaks while soldiers are killed and maimed in Iraq for lack of adequate armor?
—Holly Sklar, "Warning: Tax Cuts for Rich Harm Nation's Health," *Common Dreams* (April 17, 2006)

Taxes

I have been waiting my whole life to pay taxes. This is how it's supposed to work. This is how we are able to fund the things that make this country work—like roads and schools.
—Lewis Black, "Lewis Black Interview," *Progressive* (April 2007)

The federal budget is . . . a moral document.
—Bishop Frank T. Griswold, "Budget Is a Moral Document, Bush Warned," *Episcopal News Service* (January 27, 2005)

Taxes are what we pay for a civilized society.
—Oliver Wendell Holmes, *Compania General de Tabacas de Filipines v. Collector of the Internal Revenue* (1904)

It puzzles me that the well-off complain so much about taxes when they pay so little relative to their wealth.
—Molly Ivins, "Now That's Class Warfare," *Baltimore Sun* (September 5, 2002)

The only way to real economic strength and security is to provide real tax relief to those who need it most, workers and families.
—Dennis J. Kucinich, press release, "Kucinich Proposes Progressive Tax Reform to Assist Workers and Families" (December 8, 2003)

For patriots like me, paying taxes give a feeling of responsibility, of being a part of the fabric of our country, of contributing to the common good.
—Joyce Marcel, "Life and Taxes," *Common Dreams* (March 23, 2006)

The last Democratic president to effectively explain to the American people how the collection of taxes allows government to do important things—pave roads, defend borders, help poor people—was Lyndon B. Johnson.
—Ted Rall, *Wake Up, You're Liberal!* (2004)

Taxes are how we pool our money for public health and safety, infrastructure, research, and services—from the development of vaccines and the Internet to public schools and universities, transportation, courts, police, parks, and safe drinking water.
—Holly Sklar, "Warning: Tax Cuts for Rich Harm Nation's Health," *Common Dreams* (April 17, 2006)

The Democratic Party . . . has to stop pandering to people on the question of taxes. Taxes are a membership fee we pay for schools, roads, safe food, a clean environment, and a whole host of things that make our daily lives so much better than many other people around the world.
—Jonathan Tasini, "Why Were Democrats Applauding?" *Huffington Post* (January 24, 2007)

The Internet, which has so captivated and transfixed American business, was developed with taxpayer money.
—Nicholas von Hoffman, "Here's a Capital Idea: Make the Rich Pay Taxes!" *New York Observer* (March 26, 2001)

Republicans spend their time trying to rig the tax system so that the kinds of income rich people get—capital gains, inheritances, and the like—get taxed at a lower rate than the kind of income you get when you work for a living.
—Paul Waldman, "Paying A Fair Share," *TomPaine.com* (January 31, 2007)

I believe we should cut taxes for working families . . . especially when we're talking about education for our children, for our young people. But I don't think we need to have tax breaks for large multinational corporations and wealthy people.
—Paul Wellstone, quoted in "Radical Realist; Bill Clinton Wasn't the Only Comeback Story of 1996," *Washington Post* (January 19, 1997)

Unemployment

Of all the aspects of social misery nothing is so heartbreaking as unemployment.
—Jane Addams, *Twenty Years at Hull-House* (1910)

If anyone can testify credibly to the disappearance of the American dream, it is the white-collared unemployed—the people who "played by the rules," "did everything right," and still ended in ruin.
—Barbara Ehrenreich, *Bait and Switch* (2005)

There is no reason to have U.S. taxpayers subsidize business decisions that harm American workers . . . Corporate tax laws should be modified to increase the cost of exporting jobs and decrease the cost of maintaining jobs in America.
—Edward M. Kennedy, in his address delivered at the City University of New York, "Creating a Genuine 'Opportunity Society'" (March 1, 2004)

Universal Health Care

Americans must take a moral stand on changing the health care system. . . . Care must be accessible and affordable for everyone.
—George Askew, "A Snapshot of the Uninsured Life," *Washington Post* (January 1, 2006)

No one should have to suffer the health damaging effects of someone else's smoking in their home, school, or workplace.
—Susan J. Blumenthal, "Clear the Air of Secondhand Smoke," *Huffington Post* (August 1, 2006)

Universal, affordable and comprehensive health care is America's great, unfinished agenda.
—Robert L. Borosage and Robert Loper, eds., *StraightTalk: Common Sense for the Common Good* (2006)

Health care costs put American automakers at a serious competitive disadvantage with foreign competitors. A single-payer health care system would be the best thing the federal government could do to help U.S. manufacturers.
—Bill Gallagher, "Treasonous Bush Fostering Fascism," *Niagara Falls Reporter* (January 31, 2006)

Are you aware that for forty years, the United States has had a universal single-payer healthcare system that allows every participant to choose their own doctor, its administrative cost is one-tenth the cost of private insurance. . . . It is Medicare, and no one calls it socialized medicine.
—John Garamendi, quoted in "Medicare for All: The Only Sound Solution to Our Healthcare Crisis," AlterNet (January 16, 2007)

Universal care is a moral issue.
—Jim Hightower, "Our System, Designed by Big Business, Is Ranked 37th in the World," *Hightower Lowdown* (June 2006)

We profess to pollsters a high regard for "moral values," and yet why isn't poverty immoral? Why isn't lack of medical care immoral?
—Todd Huffman, "This Christmas, Where Is Our National Conscience?" *Common Dreams* (December 20, 2004)

Countries with national health plans, like Canada, France, and England, wouldn't dream of trading their free universal coverage, with all its imperfections, for our system, where millions lack any healthcare at all.
—Susan Jhirad, "The Public Cost of Privatization," *Boston Globe* (December 3, 2004)

An essential part of our progressive vision is an America where no citizen of any age fears the cost of health care, and no employer refuses to create new jobs or cuts back on current jobs because of the high cost of providing health insurance.
—Edward M. Kennedy, in his address to the National Press Club, "A Democratic Blueprint for America's Future" (January 12, 2005)

Let us resolve that the state of a family's health shall never depend on the size of a family's wealth.
—Edward M. Kennedy, in his speech at the Democratic National Convention (August 12, 1980)

There is no earthly reason for employers to control not just their workers' salaries, but their health security, too. . . . In every way, the employer-based system is unjust, inefficient, and unwise.
—Ezra Klein, "Healthy Bottom Lines," *American Prospect* (January 24, 2007)

When my daughter breaks her arm, my first thought should be concern for her well-being, not dread at how much it will cost and anxiety about how to get time off from work in order to fit in all the doctor's appointments.
—Cynthia Peters, interviewed by Tim Allen, "Youth, Parenting, & the Left," *Z* magazine (January 2002)

Should American citizens be permitted to die because they're too poor to see a doctor?
—Ted Rall, *Wake Up, You're Liberal!* (2004)

Should we be giving tax cuts to billionaires and millionaires or should we be giving health care to children?
—Edward Rendell, quoted in "Universal Health Care Gets a Bump," *Progressive* (February 28, 2007)

What does it take for Americans and their elected representatives to get past the socialized-medicine scare talk and come to grips with reality?
—David Rossie, "Nation Needs a More Affordable Health Care System," *Binghamton Press & Sun-Bulletin* (November 16, 2005)

Medicine is supposed to be about science, not huckstering; about healing people, not persuading more of them that they are sick. There are far better ways to inform the public about health issues than to spend billions of dollars a year pushing pills.
—Jonathan Rowe, "Drug Ads Sell a Problem, Not a Solution," *Christian Science Monitor* (August 21, 2006)

We are a nation obsessed with pharmaceuticals. We spend vast sums to manage our health, and we pop pills to address every conceivable symptom.
—Elizabeth Royte, "Drugging Our Waters," *OnEarth* (Fall 2006)

The American people continue to pay by far the highest prices in the world for prescription drugs. . . . The result is that millions of Americans suffer, and some die, because they are unable to afford the medicine they need.
—Bernie Sanders, "A Year of Contrasts: Courage, Sacrifice and . . . Corporate Greed," *Common Dreams* (December 24, 2001)

For the first time in history, a generation of children may not live as long as their parents.
—Hilda L. Solis, "Battling Health Disparities—A Call to Action," *Huffington Post* (July 7, 2006)

It's a disgrace that in the twenty-first century in America, we still have so many people who get sick and die—not because their illnesses aren't treatable, but because they are too poor to see a doctor.
—Andy Stern, "Horse-and-Buggy Health Coverage," *Huffington Post* (July 17, 2006)

We cannot compete in the global economy and be the only country that puts the price of healthcare on the cost our products.
—Andy Stern, "Changing How America Works," AlterNet (November 2, 2006)

Nothing else will solve the crisis in health care . . . until we wrench the system entirely out of the hands of the leeches in the drug and insurance industries.
—Jonathan Tasini, "Democrats: Get a Real Economic Agenda or Become the Minority Party Again," *Huffington Post* (December 5, 2006)

The system is broken. Nothing but universal health care, preferably through a non-profit, single-payer system, will begin to fix it.
—Pierre Tristam, "Compassion's Toll on Society of 'Owners' Too Poor to Be Sick," *Daytona Beach News-Journal* (November 8, 2005)

America's black children are twice as likely as whites to die before their first birthday.
—Paul Vallely, "UN Hits Back at U.S. in Report Saying Parts of America are as Poor as Third World," *Independent (UK)* (September 8, 2005)

The United States of America ought to have a system in which all citizens are provided an identical, taxpayer-financed, publicly administered health insurance system.
—Matthew Yglesias, "By the Slice," *American Prospect* (January 30, 2007)

Wages

There is no moral justification for a minimum wage lower than a living wage.
—Barbara Ehrenreich, "Minimum Wage Rises, Sky Does Not Fall," AlterNet (January 23, 2007)

While corporate profits soar, individual wages stagnate.
—Harold Meyerson, "Can Free Trade Be a Fair Deal?" *American Prospect* (February 23, 2007)

What happens to wages when two billion people from low-wage countries join the global labor market?
—Thomas Palley, "The Global Labor Threat," *TomPaine.com* (September 29, 2005)

Most Americans don't save because they can't save. Despite the surge in corporate profits . . . wages and benefits have been dropping.
—Robert Reich, "The Shrinking Nest Egg," *American Prospect* (April 5, 2006)

Despite an explosion of technology, huge increase in worker productivity, tens of millions of our fellow Americans have seen a decline in their real wages and are working longer hours for lower wages.
—Bernie Sanders, "If You Are Concerned About Health Care, Iraq, the Economy, Global Warming You Must Be Concerned About Corporate Control of the Media," *Democracy Now!* radio (January 22, 2007)

Until we reign in corporations, no one's wages, benefits, or job security are safe.
—Jonathan Tasini, "Democrats: Get a Real Economic Agenda or Become the Minority Party Again," *Huffington Post* (December 5, 2006)

Wealth

Behind every great fortune there is a crime.
—Honore de Balzac, quoted in "Others to Choose From," *Common Dreams* (March 2, 2007)

It is easier for a camel to go through the eye of a needle, than for a rich man to enter into the kingdom of God.
—Matthew 19:24

You cannot serve both God and Money.
—Matthew 6:24

We can have democracy in this country, or we can have great wealth concentrated in the hands of a few, but we can't have both.
—Louis Brandeis, quoted in "How to Curb Corporate Power," *Nation* (October 10, 2005)

The poor have sometimes objected to being governed badly; the rich have always objected to being governed at all.
—G. K. Chesterton, *The Man Who Was Thursday* (1908)

There is nothing so characteristic of narrowness and littleness of soul as the love of riches.
—Cicero, *De officitis*, translated, 1913.

The thunderous, relentless, organized spending of millions and millions of dollars by the radical Republican conservative fringe—in cahoots with evangelical, messianic Christians—has marginalized the liberal, progressive, left-speaking members of our populace.
—Phil Donahue, "Out in Left Field," in an interview with Bruce Kluger in *Time Out New York* (November 24–30, 2005)

Wealth is a great insulator.
—Byron L. Dorgan, *Take This Job and Ship It*, 2006)

How is it . . . that we became so totally, and apparently wrongly, fixated on the idea that our main goal, as individuals and as nations, should be the accumulation of more wealth?
—Bill McKibben, *Deep Economy: The Wealth of Communities and the Durable Future* (2007)

Because of the great disparities in wealth, the "shining city on the hill" has become a gated community whose privileged occupants . . . are removed from the common life of the country.
—Bill Moyers, "For America's Sake," *Nation* (January 22, 2007)

The great welfare scandal of the age concerns the dole we give rich people.
—William O. Douglas, *Points of Rebellion* (1969)

Wealth is the relentless enemy of understanding.
—John Kenneth Galbraith, quoted in "The Affluent Galbraith," *Boston Globe* (May 2, 2006)

The top 1 percent in this country now have as much wealth as the bottom 90 percent combined. That doesn't make a lot of sense to me.
—Bob Herbert, quoted in an interview entitled "Times Columnist Bob Herbert Views the American Dream: But Can It Still Be Found?" *BuzzFlash* (May 3, 2005)

It is inexcusable that, in a land of so much plenty, poverty forces some citizens to go without shelter, medical care, education, retirement benefits, and the other essential needs of life.
—Ted Rall, *Wake Up, You're Liberal!"* (2004)

It's very important for people with extraordinary wealth combined with phenomenal selfishness to know that they too are going to die . . . They're hoarding for the future. What future?
—Kathleen Reardon, "The Courage to Be Less Wealthy," *Huffington Post* (April 27, 2006)

The more money, the less virtue.
—Henry David Thoreau, "Civil Disobedience," *The Writings of Henry David Thoreau* (1906)

Plutocracy: 1: government run by the wealthy class 2: A controlling class of the wealthy.
—*Webster's Ninth New Collegiate Dictionary* (1990)

Welfare

Private beneficence is totally inadequate to deal with the vast numbers of the city's disinherited.
—Jane Addams, *Twenty Years at Hull House* (1910)

To his eternal dishonor . . . Clinton signed a welfare bill that ends the federal responsibility to children in poverty.
—Barbara Ehrenreich, "Sex Happens," *Progressive* (March 1998)

We are in a national state of overwork, but the welfare debate now hinges on getting the poorest mothers of young children to work longer hours.
—Ellen Goodman, "Does Mother's Day Help Mothers?" *Boston Globe* (May 8, 2005)

The public sector that was a support system and safety net for millions of Americans across three generations is in tatters.
—Bill Moyers, "For America's Sake," *Nation* (January 22, 2007)

Work

The Republican Party is good for . . . people who don't work but inherit money and live off of dividends and capital gains while they sip daiquiris in Palm Beach.
—Larry Beinhart, "A Manifesto (for Democrats & Liberals)," *Common Dreams* (December 15, 2005)

Suppose that humans happen to be so constructed that they desire the opportunity for freely undertaken productive work. Suppose that they want to be free from the meddling of technocrats and commissars, bankers and tycoons.
—Noam Chomsky, *For Reasons of State* (1973)

America's industrial workers face deadly labor conditions due to anemic—and politically hogtied—government safety enforcement. Each year, more than 6,000 workers die and 4.5 million are injured on the job.
—Christopher D. Cook, "Coal Miners' Slaughter," *In These Times* (January 25, 2006)

It's clear that the rigid, workaholic rules of the American workplace were not written by people who put a high priority on children or family life.
—Ann Crittenden, "The Friedan Mystique," *American Prospect* (February 10, 2006)

Nobody who works full-time should have to raise children in poverty, or in fear that one health emergency or pink slip will drive them over the cliff.
—John Edwards, quoted in *StraightTalk: Common Sense for the Common Good*, 2006)

Something has really changed. Something has changed in the corporate world—that really seismic change away from any kind of sense of loyalty to employees.
—Barbara Ehrenreich, in an interview entitled "Barbara Ehrenreich's *Bait and Switch* Gives the Lie to America's Most Powerful Myth," *BuzzFlash* (September 19, 2005)

We are a nation of unhappy people consuming miles of aisles of cheap consumer goods, hoping to dull the pain of unfulfilling work. Is this who we want to be?
—Robert Jensen, "Anti-Capitalism in Five Minutes or Less," *Common Dreams* (April 30, 2007)

We need an economy that values work fairly, that puts the needs of families ahead of excessive profits—an economy whose goal is growth with full employment and good jobs with good benefits for all.
—Edward M. Kennedy, address to the National Press Club, "A Democratic Blueprint for America's Future," (January 12, 2005)

Where the private sector fails to provide jobs, the public sector has a moral responsibility to do so. People want work, not welfare.
—Dennis Kucinich, "A New Horizon for the Democratic Party," *Nation* (June 3, 2002)

This is the new metaphysics of work. Companies are portable, workers are throwaway.
—Lance Morrow, "The Temping of America," *Time* (March 29, 1993)

Too many employers don't believe they have any moral obligation to pay their workers a living wage.
—Ted Rall, *Wake Up, You're Liberal!"* (2004)

A job should keep you out of poverty, not keep you poor.
—Rev. Paul Sherry, quoted in "High Wages, Low Wages, and Morality," *Christian Science Monitor* (January 30, 2006)

Our country is filled with people who do things at work that they would never do at home.
—Jane Smiley, "Is There Something Wrong with the System?" *Huffington Post* (January 23, 2007)

I want to look back on my career and be proud of the work, and be proud that I tried everything. Yes, I want to look back and know that I was terrible at a variety of things.
—Jon Stewart, quoted in the *Orange County Register* (July 9, 1999)

Every adult who needs it shall be given meaningful work to do, at a living wage.
—Kurt Vonnegut, proposed amendment to the U.S. Constitution, *Timequake* (1997)

Worker Rights

Why should workers agree to be slaves in a basically authoritarian structure? They should have control over it themselves. Why shouldn't the communities have a dominant voice in running the institutions that affect their lives?
—Noam Chomsky, "One Man's View," *Business Today* (May 1973)

Every man has the inalienable right to work.
—Eugene Debs, from a 1908 speech quoted in *Debs: His Life, Writings and Speeches* (2002)

If anyone is "ruining" the American family, it's all the employers who refuse to recognize that their employees have family responsibilities, as well as jobs.
—Barbara Ehrenreich, "Corporate Home Wreckers," *Progressive* (March 2006)

What corporations call "flexibility"—the right to dispose of workers at will—is what workers experience as disposability, not to mention insecurity and poverty.
—Barbara Ehrenreich, "Kleenex Workers," *Progressive* (May 2006)

For an unnecessarily large number of Americans, the workplace has become a hub of anxiety and fear, an essential but capricious environment in which you might be shown the door at any moment.
—Bob Herbert, "Laid Off and Left Out," *New York Times* (May 25, 2006)

What we're seeing is people throughout the entire world, without rights and without unions, working long hours for poverty wages, all in harness to increase the wealth of corporate honchos.
—Marty Jezer, "Economic Recovery: Losers and Winners," *Common Dreams* (April 9, 2004)

A living wage should be the right of all working Americans.
—Rev. Martin Luther King, Jr. (March 18, 1966)

Firing employees for endeavoring to form unions has been illegal since 1935 under the National Labor Relations Act, but beginning in the 1970s, employers have preferred to violate the law—the penalties are negligible—rather than have their workers unionize.
—Harold Meyerson, "Card Check's Reality Check," *American Prospect* (June 21, 2007)

The Democrats should stand for fundamental tax and labor law reforms to make the tax system less rigged and to give workers in companies like Wal-Mart a chance to establish trade unions.
—Ralph Nader, "Go On Offensive Against the Republicans," *Common Dreams* (May 21, 2005)

No one should have to lose a job because they get ill. But across this land, hardworking people are getting fired simply because their company offers no sick days and they got sick.
—Joe Robinson, "Trouble in Cubicle Nation" (January 30, 2006)

No business which depends for existence by paying less than living wages to its workers has any right to continue in this country.
—Franklin D. Roosevelt, statement on the National Industrial Recovery Act (June 16, 1933)

Workers are entitled to participate fully in the decisions that affect their work lives and their work responsibilities.
—John Sweeney, quoted in *One Electorate Under God?* (2004)

If working class people are ever to receive their fair share of the wealth they produce for their employers, they must organize on a grand scale.
—Charles Sullivan, "Squeezing the Work Force," OpEdNews (January 19, 2006)

Workplaces

Our workplaces, where many spend most of their waking hours, are cradles of authoritarianism.
—John Buell, "The Importance of Labor Day," *Progressive Populist* (October 1, 2000)

A corporation or an industry is, if we were to think of it in political terms, fascist; that is, it has tight control at the top and strict obedience has to be established at every level.
—Noam Chomsky, quoted in "One Man's View," *Business Today* (May 1973)

The interior landscape of most corporations is authoritarian, often exploitative.
—Julian Edney, "How Capitalism Threatens Your Health," *CounterPunch* (April 3, 2006)

Orwell's fascist "1984" is already here and it's called the American workplace.
—Barbara Ehrenreich, "Challenging the Workplace Dictatorship," *Huffington Post* (March 8, 2007)

It is the insecurity of white-collar employment that makes the demand for passion so cruel and perverse . . . Not even prostitutes are expected to perform "passionately" time after time.
—Barbara Ehrenreich, *Bait and Switch* (2005)

The whole relationship between corporations and their white-collar employees has broken down since the beginning of the nineties. Now people are tossed off, out of their jobs for the slightest reason.
—Barbara Ehrenreich, in an interview entitled "Barbara Ehrenreich's *Bait and Switch* Gives the Lie to America's Most Powerful Myth," *BuzzFlash* (September 19, 2005)

We can hardly pride ourselves on being the world's preeminent democracy, after all, if large numbers of citizens spend half their waking hours in what amounts, in plain terms, to a dictatorship.
—Barbara Ehrenreich, "On the Outside Looking In: How Low-Wage Workers Get Squeezed," *Record* (Bergen County, New Jersey)(September 2, 2001)

Workplaces are not democracies—in the United States they're run more like kingdoms.
—Thom Hartmann, *Screwed: The Undeclared War Against the Middle Class* (2006)

While there may be more talk in boardrooms these days about teamwork, it is usually situated in the context of competitiveness—that is, working together so we can defeat another group of people working together.
—Alfie Kohn, "The 500-Pound Gorilla," *Phi Delta Kappan* (October 2002)

When [an individual] merges his person into an organizational structure, a new creature replaces autonomous man, unhindered by the limitations of individual morality, freed of humane inhibition, mindful only of the sanctions of authority.
—Stanley Milgram, *Obedience to Authority* (1974)

Organizations that used to see people as long-term assets to be nurtured and developed now see people as short-term costs to be reduced.
—David Noer, *Healing and Wounds* (1993)

For four decades, working women have poured into the paid labor force. Yet American society has done precious little to restructure the workplace or family life. The result? Working mothers are burdened and exhausted, families are fractured and children are often neglected.
—Ruth Rosen, "What Women Talk About When Men Are Not Listening," *TMP Cafe* (April 27, 2006)

For at least half their waking hours, the American people live in a dictatorship. At home or in public places, Americans enjoy a measure of freedom and liberty envied by most people around the world: freedom of speech, freedom of assembly and freedom of association. But, the moment Americans walk through the doors of their workplace, they enter into a world that strips away all their basic rights.
—Jonathan Tasini, "A 10-Step Program for Democrats," *TomPaine.com* (January 2, 2007)

THE STRUGGLE FOR EQUALITY

African–Americans

To be black and conscious in America is to be in a constant state of rage.
—James Baldwin, quoted in "Negro Leaders on Violence," *Time* (August 20, 1965)

Black pastors who have aligned themselves with white Christian evangelicals and Conservatives are the ideological descendents of the same people who opposed Dr. King in the fifties . . . giving new meaning to the name "Uncle Tom."
—Jasmyne Cannick, "Purchased Pulpits and Spiritual Exploitations," *Black Commentator* (March 3, 2005)

One out of three black men in their twenties is out on bail, probation, court supervision, community service or parole—or behind bars.
—Bruce Dixon, "A Leaderless Community," *TomPaine.com* (May 29, 2007)

You have seen how a man was made a slave; you shall see how a slave was made a man.
—Frederick Douglass, *Narrative of the Life of Frederick Douglass* (1845)

The problem of the twentieth century is the problem of the color line.
—W. E. B. DuBois, *The Souls of Black Folk* (1905)

The Republican Party has a multi-generational history of purging, demonizing, and opposing African American political empowerment.
—Michael K. Fauntroy, "Republicans and the Black Vote," *Huffington Post* (January 4, 2007)

African Americans make up an estimated 15 percent of drug users, but they account for 37 percent of those arrested on drug charges.
—Arianna Huffington, citing an ACLU report, "The War on Drugs' War on Minorities," *Los Angeles Times* (March 24, 2007)

Not all Black skin is kin.
—Zora Neal Hurston, quoted in "Purchased Pulpits and Spiritual Exploitations," *Black Commentator* (March 3, 2005)

Black men are criminalized to the point where one out of every three African-American boys faces the prospect of jail at some point in his life. Black men can't even drive without facing a significantly higher chance of being stopped by police.
—Derrick Z. Jackson, "U.S. Abuse of Black Men a Prelude to Scandal," *Boston Globe* (May 12, 2004)

I have a dream that one day even the state of Mississippi . . . sweltering with the heat of injustice and oppression, will be transformed into an oasis of freedom and justice.
—Rev. Martin Luther King, Jr., in his address delivered on the steps of the Lincoln Memorial in Washington, D.C. (August 28, 1963)

This modern house Negro loves his master. He wants to live near him. He'll pay three times as much as the house is worth just to live near his master, and then brag about "I'm the only Negro out here."
—Malcolm X, quoted in *Malcolm X Speaks* (1965)

Although black men are about 6 percent of the U.S. population, they make up about half of the nation's prisoners. Study after study has provided statistics that confirm how racial injustices corrupt and corrode the criminal justice system.
—Salim Muwakkil, "So Very Sorry," *In These Times* (July 21, 2005)

I want to be remembered as a person who stood up to injustice, who wanted a better world for young people; and most of all, I want to be remembered as a person who wanted to be free and wanted others to be free.
—Rosa Parks, *Quiet Strength* (1994)

The sellout of progressive politics has been a total disgrace for the Democratic Party. Not only is it morally wrong and politically cheap, but it doesn't even work.
—Rev. Al Sharpton, quoted in "Muzzling the African–American Agenda with Black Help," *Black Commentator* (June 12, 2003)

Bigotry and Ignorance

There are two things which cannot be attacked in front: ignorance and narrow-mindedness. They can only be shaken by the simple development of the contrary qualities. They will not bear discussion.
—John Acton, quoted in *Lord Acton and His Circle* (1906)

The Scout Law declares that all Boy Scouts should be trustworthy, loyal, helpful, friendly, courteous, kind, obedient, cheerful, thrifty, brave, clean, and reverent. But how does discrimination against boys and men who are gay uphold the Scout Law? What is loyal or helpful or friendly or courteous or kind or brave about prejudice?
—Frank Edward Allen, "Boy Scouts of America: A Symbol of Prejudice," *San Francisco Chronicle* (September 24, 2000)

The man who never alters his opinion is like standing water, and breeds reptiles of the mind.
—William Blake, *The Marriage of Heaven and Hell* (1790)

If ignorance were truly bliss, Americans would be ecstatic.
—Bumper sticker

The enemy is our urgent need to stereotype and close off people, places, and events into isolated categories.
—Andrea Canaan, quoted in *This Bridge Called My Back* (1981)

We hold that all human life is valuable, and that the view that some nationalities, races, religions, sexual orientations and genders are more valuable than others disgraces the notion of democracy.
—Martin Duberman, quoted in "What Is Patriotism?" *Nation* (July 15, 2001)

Fear and ignorance about AIDS can so weaken people's senses as to make them susceptible to an equally virulent threat: bigotry.
—Editorial, "AIDS and the New Apartheid," *New York Times* (October 7, 1985)

The Republicans today are the party of anti-intellectualism, of rough frontier contempt for sophisticated ideas and pantywaist book-learning.
—Thomas Frank, *What's the Matter with Kansas?* (2005)

In communist countries, where capitalism was the Enemy, Jews were said to be the Leading Capitalists. In capitalist countries, where communism is the Enemy, Jews are smeared as leaders of the Communist Conspiracy.
—Miriam Greenspan, "The New Anti-Semitism," *Tikkun* (November/December 2003)

Unreason is now ascendant in the United States—in our schools, in our courts, and in each branch of the federal government. Only 28 percent of Americans believe in evolution; 68 percent believe in Satan.
—Sam Harris, *The End of Faith* (2005)

You have attributed conditions to villainy that result from stupidity.
—Robert Heinlein, *Logic of Empire* (1941)

The true test of intelligence is not how much we know how to do, but how to behave when we don't know what to do.
—John Holt, *How Children Fail* (1964)

The ignorant are not satisfied with what can be demonstrated. Science is too slow for them, and so they invent creeds.
—Robert Ingersoll, quoted in *What's God Got to Do with It?* (2005)

If a nation expects to be ignorant and free, in a state of civilization, it expects what never was and will never be.
—Thomas Jefferson, in a letter to Charles Yancey (January 6, 1816)

The signs proclaiming "whites only" may be gone, but we know that discrimination and bigotry in countless other manifestations still blight our society.
—Edward M. Kennedy, "No to Alito," *Working For Change* (January 20, 2006)

Nothing in all the world is more dangerous than sincere ignorance and conscientious stupidity.
—Rev. Martin Luther King, Jr., *Strength to Love* (1963)

Too many progressives think that people who vote conservative are just stupid.
—George Lakoff, *Thinking Points: Communicating Our Values and Vision* (2006)

The next reality show must be called "America's Stupidest State." We'll start at fifty, and each week, if your state does something really stupid with, say, evolution or images of the Virgin Mary, you'll move on to the next round.
—Bill Maher, *New Rules* (2005)

The purpose of the Right in America is to keep the majority here as stupid as possible.
—Norman Mailer, *The Big Empty* (2006)

Although it is not true that all conservatives are stupid people . . . it is true that most stupid people are conservative.
—John Stuart Mill, quoted in "Dark of Heartness," *Common Dreams* (April 13, 2007)

The parallel between antifeminism and race prejudice is striking. The same underlying motives appear to be at work, namely fear, jealousy, feelings of insecurity, fear of economic competition, guilt feelings, and the like.
—Ashley Montagu, *Man in Process* (1961)

The prejudice surrounding AIDS exacts a social death which precedes the actual physical one.
—Ron Nyswaner, spoken by the character Andrew Beckett in the film *Philadelphia* (1993)

Demonizing our fellow Americans by using constitutions to deny rights rather than protect them is antithetical to our American values.
—People for the American Way, in an e-mail urging opposition to the so-called Marriage Protection Amendment (May 31, 2006)

Discrimination—whether it's racial resegregation or denial of reproductive healthcare or antigay legislation—is not some touchy-feely issue of "identity politics." It's a central feature of the social injustice we all claim to be fighting.
—Katha Pollitt, "Happy New Year!" *Nation* (January 22, 2007)

The error that progressives have consistently committed over the years is to underestimate the vitality of ignorance in America.
—Jane Smiley, "The Unteachable Ignorance of the Red States," *Slate* (November 4, 2004)

Appalling moral blindness, a sort of high-functioning, sociopathic stupidity, has been a consistent characteristic of the numerous Republicans indicted during the Bush era.
—Matt Taibbi, "Time to Go! Inside the Worst Congress Ever," *Rolling Stone* (November 2006)

It is never too late to give up your prejudices.
—Henry David Thoreau, *Walden* (1854)

The GOP is addicted to the bigot vote, addicted to suppressing the votes of people whose skin is not white. Like every addict, they tell themselves they can stop whenever they want—I'll kick next year, I just need it one more time to get me through this election.
—Paul Waldman, "Courting the Bigot Vote," *TomPaine.com* (November 1, 2006)

What could be more bigoted than to claim that you have a monopoly on God?
—Rabbi Eric Yoffie, quoted in "Jewish Leader Blasts 'Religious Right'," the Associated Press (AP) (November 19, 2005)

Civil Rights

There are those who say to you—we are rushing this issue of civil rights. I say we are 172 years late.
—Hubert H. Humphrey, in his speech to the Democratic National Convention (1948)

The Christian right would like today's public to forget exactly where religious conservatives stood on civil-rights legislation forty years ago.
—Susan Jacoby, *Freethinkers* (2004)

Our civil rights have no dependence on our religious opinions, any more than our opinions in physics or geometry.
—Thomas Jefferson, quoted in "Why We Are Infidels," *Nation* (May 8, 2003)

All Americans just must have the right to vote. And we are going to give them that right. All Americans must have the privileges of citizenship regardless of race.
—Lyndon B. Johnson, *Public Papers of the Presidents of the United States: Lyndon B. Johnson* (1965)

If you look at who's being denied the right to vote, on absentee ballots, on provisional ballots, it's Hispanics, it's Blacks and it's Native Americans, and the Democratic Party ought to be touting this as the biggest civil-rights issue of our time. But they are ignoring it.
—Robert F. Kennedy, Jr., "Democracy in Crisis—Interview with Robert F. Kennedy, Jr.," Bradblog (July 18, 2006)

I have a dream that my four little children will one day live in a nation where they will not be judged by the color of their skin, but by the content of their character.
—Rev. Martin Luther King, Jr., in his address delivered on the steps at the Lincoln Memorial in Washington, D.C. (August 28, 1963)

The civil rights of none shall be abridged on account of religious belief or worship, nor shall any national religion be established, nor shall the full and equal rights of conscience be in any manner, or on any pretext, infringed.
—James Madison, *The Papers of James Madison* (1962–1991)

To our everlasting shame America nurtured slavery in the cradle of liberty.
—Bill Moyers, "America 101," *TomPaine.com* (November 1, 2006)

The Democratic Party became an ally of civil rights during the '60s, but has been in slow retreat ever since.
—Salim Muwakkil, "The Persistent Taint," *In These Times* (February 2, 2005)

Our mistreatment was not right, and I was tired of it.
—Rosa Parks, on her historic refusal to give up her seat to a white man on a segregated bus, *Quiet Strength* (1994)

Disabilities

The world is not made for me, so I must be made for the world.
—Comment overheard from disabled man struggling with crutches to walk down the basement hall of the State Health and Welfare Building, Harrisburg, Pennsylvania (January 26, 2006)

Someday our grandchildren will look up at us and say, "Where were you, Grandma, and what were you doing when you first realized that President Reagan was, er, not playing with a full deck?"
—Barbara Ehrenreich, *The Worst Years of Our Lives* (1991)

The moral test of government is how it treats those who are in the dawn of life, children; those who are in the twilight of life, the aged; and those who are in the shadows of life, the sick, the needy, and the handicapped.
—Hubert H. Humphrey, *Congressional Record* (November 4, 1977)

All of us do not have equal talent, but all of us should have an equal opportunity to develop our talents.
—John F. Kennedy, in his address to San Diego State College (June 6, 1963)

We live in a country filled with people who are sick and disabled, people who are imprisoned, and people who hunger and thirst for justice.
—Fran Quigley, "How the ACLU Didn't Steal Christmas," *Common Dreams* (December 6, 2005)

Any one of us could get hurt at any moment. . . . We should never walk by somebody who's in a wheelchair and be afraid of them or think of them as a stranger. It could be us—in fact, it is us.
—Christopher Reeve, television interview, ABC (May 4, 1998)

There are two kinds of "disabled" persons: those who dwell on what they have lost and those who concentrate on what they have left.
—Thomas S. Szasz, *The Untamed Tongue* (1990)

Diversity

What we have to do . . . is to find a way to celebrate our diversity and debate our differences without fracturing our communities.
—Hillary Rodham Clinton, in her University of Pennsylvania commencement speech, *New York Times* (May 18, 1993)

Fortunately, the time has long passed when people liked to regard the United States as some kind of melting pot, taking men and women from every part of the world and converting them into standardized, homogenized Americans.
—Hubert H. Humphrey, in his speech in Chicago (January 15, 1967)

The white, the Hispanic, the black, the Arab, the Jew, the woman, the Native American, the small farmer, the businessperson, the environmentalist, the peace activist, the young, the old, the lesbian, the gay, and the disabled make up the American quilt.
—Rev. Jesse Jackson, in his address to the Democratic National Convention in San Francisco (July 17, 1984)

If we cannot end now our differences, at least we can help make the world safe for diversity.
—John F. Kennedy, in his American University commencement address (June 10, 1963)

Our liberalism has its roots in our diverse origins.
—John F. Kennedy, accepting the New York Liberal Party nomination (September 14, 1960)

Ultimately, America's answer to the intolerant man is diversity, the very diversity which our heritage of religious freedom has inspired.
—Robert F. Kennedy, "Extremism, Left and Right," *The Pursuit of Justice* (1964)

As long as the differences and diversities of mankind exist, democracy must allow for compromise, for accommodation, and for the recognition of differences.
—Eugene McCarthy, quoted in the *Culver Daily Bulletin* (October 6, 2004)

The great strength of America lies in its pluralistic nature with its respect for diversity of viewpoints, whether liberal or conservative, Christian, Jewish, or any other.
—Resolution of the Union of American Hebrew Congregations (November 22, 1980)

A clash of doctrines is not a disaster—it is an opportunity.
—Alfred North Whitehead, *Science and the Modern World* (1925)

If you look at history from the point of view of black people, of Native Americans, of women, of working people, everything looks different. A lot of the heroes suddenly are not heroes anymore.
—Howard Zinn, quoted in an interview with Terrence McNally in "Howard Zinn: Vision and Voice," AlterNet (October 21, 2005)

Equality

We reaffirm the great principle of liberalism: that every citizen is entitled by right to the elementary means to a good life. We believe passionately that societies should afford their citizens equal treatment under the law—regardless of accidents of birth, race, sex, property, religion, ethnic identification, or sexual disposition.
—Bruce Ackerman and Todd Gitlin, "We Answer to the Name of Liberals," *American Prospect* (October 18, 2006)

We need women's constitutional equality in this country. . . . The United States must declare that women are equal under the law, no matter which state we live in, without reservation.
—Martha Burk and Eleanor Smeal, "Why We Need an ERA," *Washington Post* (April 27, 2007)

What if the playing field really was level? I'd love to see how far I could go.
—Margaret Cho, *I Have Chosen to Stay and Fight* (2005)

Widening disparities in the U.S. are the result of three decades of bipartisan public policies that have tilted the rules of the economy to the benefit of major corporations.
—Chuck Collins and Felice Yeskel, "Inequality in America: Version 2.0," *Common Dreams* (October 21, 2005)

We hold these truths to be self-evident, that all men are created equal, that they are endowed by their Creator with certain Unalienable Rights, that among these are Life, Liberty, and the pursuit of Happiness.
—Declaration of Independence of the United States of America (July 4, 1776)

There are very few jobs that actually require a penis or a vagina. All other jobs should be open to everybody.
—Florynce Kennedy, "Freelancer with No Time to Write," *Writer's Digest* (February 1974)

Unequal societies tend to be corrupt societies. When there are huge disparities in wealth, the rich have both the motive and the means to corrupt the system on their behalf.
—Paul Krugman, "The Great Wealth Transfer," *Rolling Stone* (November 30, 2006)

We are all children of one and the same God and, therefore, absolutely equal.
—Mahatma Gandhi, in *Harijan* (February 2, 1934)

I have a dream that one day this nation will rise up and live out the true meaning of its creed: "We hold these truths to be self-evident: that all men are created equal."
—Rev. Martin Luther King, Jr., in his speech delivered on the steps of the Lincoln Memorial in Washington, D.C. (August 28, 1963)

Women, like men, have a duty to their minds and talents and selves that cannot be fulfilled by living vicariously through husbands and children. An equal cannot live a happy subordinate life.
—Katha Pollitt, "Betty Friedan, 1921–2006," *Nation* (February 2006)

Equality of rights under the law shall not be denied or abridged by the United States or by any state on account of sex.
—Proposed Equal Rights Amendment, defeated in 1982

Each person is to have an equal right to the most extensive basic liberty compatible with a similar liberty for others.
—John Rawls, *A Theory of Justice* (1971)

No one can make you feel inferior without your consent.
—Eleanor Roosevelt, *This Is My Story* (1937)

This nation is dedicated to the proposition that we are all "created equal" . . . and that we are all deserving of equal dignity and respect.
—Geoffrey R. Stone, opining against discrimination in the military based on sexual orientation, "The Wrong Side of History," *Huffington Post* (June 10, 2007)

Feminism

Feminism has given me a powerful lens with which to view the world.
—Jennifer Baumgardner, "Feminism Is a Failure, and Other Myths," AlterNet (November 17, 2005)

The logic of the raunch culture is eerily similar to that Christian ideal of femininity, the Surrendered Wife. Both preach empowerment through acquiescence, promising greater happiness through the fulfillment of archetypal female roles.
—Lakshmi Chaudhry, "Babes in BushWorld: Raunch Culture Offers Good Old-Fashioned Pleasure, Republican Style," *In These Times* (October 28, 2005)

Maybe we should have known that . . . the triumph of feminism would last a nanosecond while the backlash lasted forty years.
—Maureen Dowd, *Are Men Necessary?* (2005)

We need a kind of feminism that aims not just to assimilate into the institutions that men have created over the centuries, but to infiltrate and subvert them.
—Barbara Ehrenreich, "Feminism's Assumptions Upended," *Los Angeles Times* (May 16, 2004)

Eliminating the patriarchal and racist base of the existing social system requires a revolution, not a reform.
—First issue of *Ms.* magazine (1971)

The opposite of patriarchy is not matriarchy, but democracy.
—Jane Fonda, "A Powerful Media Can Stop a War," Women's Media Center (January 16, 2007)

The labor of women in the house, certainly, enables men to produce more wealth than they otherwise could; and in this way women are economic factors in society. But so are horses.
—Charlotte Perkins Gilman, quoted in *Women and Economics* (1898)

True emancipation begins neither at the polls nor in courts. It begins in woman's soul.
—Emma Goldman, *Anarchism and Other Essays* (1917)

What would they make of a holiday that began with feminism and pacifism and ended up with perfume and flowers?
—Ellen Goodman, on what the founding mothers would think of Mother's Day, "Does Mother's Day Help Mothers?" *Boston Globe* (May 8, 2005)

For me, to be a feminist is to answer the question: "Are women human?" with a yes.
—Katha Pollitt, *Introduction to Reasonable Creatures* (1994)

Before feminism, stifling your personal ambitions in favor of doting on your husband was just a drawback to being a woman.
—Christopher Hayes, "How to Turn Your Red State Blue," *In These Times* (March 22, 2005)

Feminist solidarity rooted in a commitment to progressive politics must include a space for rigorous critique, for dissent, or we are doomed to reproduce in progressive communities the very forms of domination we seek to oppose.
—bell hooks, *Outlaw Culture* (1994)

My only hope is that, one day soon, women—who have all earned the right to their opinions—instead of being labeled opinionated, will be called smart or well-informed, just as men are.
—Teresa Heinz Kerry, "Remarks at the Democratic National Convention," *USA Today* (July 27, 2004)

Any woman that tells the truth about herself is a feminist.
—Alice Munro, quoted in the *Toronto Star* (May 6, 1979)

Trying to be a perfect feminist . . . is not really a big improvement on trying to be a perfect wife, mother, and lady.
—Jane O'Reilly, *The Girl I Left Behind* (1980)

Sometimes, we act as if feminism were about women. It isn't. It is, inevitably, about women and men. . . . One side cannot change without requiring the other to do the same.
—Leonard Pitts, Jr., "Response to Show [Commander in Chief] Off Mark," *Detroit Free Press* (November 2, 2005)

Women have learned to describe everything they do, no matter how apparently conformist, submissive, self-destructive or humiliating, as a personal choice that cannot be criticized because personal choice is what feminism is all about.
—Katha Pollitt, *Virginity or Death!* (2006)

The great accomplishment of the modern women's movement was to name such private experiences—domestic violence, sexual harassment, economic discrimination, date rape—and turn them into public problems that could be debated, changed by new laws and policies, or altered by social customs. That is how the personal became political.
—Ruth Rosen, "The Care Crisis," *Nation* (March 12, 2007)

Can man be free if woman be a slave?
—Percy B. Shelley, *The Revolt of Islam* (1871)

Feminism has fought no wars. It has killed no opponents. It has set up no concentration camps, starved no enemies, practiced no cruelties. Its battles have been for education, for the vote, for better working conditions . . . for safety on the streets . . . for child care, for social welfare . . . for rape crisis centers, women's refuges, reforms in the law. If someone says, "Oh, I'm not a feminist" I ask, "Why? What's your problem?"
—Dale Spender, *For the Record: The Making & Meaning of Feminist Knowledge* (1985)

If you say, "I'm for equal pay," that's a reform. But if you say, "I'm a feminist," that's . . . a transformation of society.
—Gloria Steinem, quoted in "How to Survive a Revolution," *Time* (March 9, 1992)

I myself have never been able to find out precisely what feminism is: I only know that people call me a feminist whenever I express sentiments that differentiate me from a doormat or a prostitute.
—Rebecca West, quoted in *The Clarion* (November 14, 1913)

I'm amazed, actually, that feminism is still around, given the press it gets.
—Katha Pollitt, "The World According to Dowd," *Nation* (November 28, 2005)

I do not wish them [women] to have power over men; but only over themselves.
—Mary Wollstonecraft, *A Vindication of the Rights of Woman* (1792)

Gays and Lesbians

Best I can tell, God has been creating gay and lesbian people for a long time and my guess is that trend will continue in the future.
—Rev. Chris Ayers, "Gay Marriage Not Defeated," The Center for Progressive Christianity Newsletter (December 2004)

I believe God's creation is marked by diversity rather than conformity. I believe homosexual orientation and responsible homosexual expression are just as much a part of the will of God as heterosexual orientation and heterosexual expression.
—Rev. Howard Bess, from his book *Pastor, I Am Gay*, quoted in "No Christian Left Behind," *Anchorage Press* (November 18, 2004)

If Michelangelo were a heterosexual, the Sistine Chapel would have been painted basic white and with a roller.
—Rita Mae Brown, quoted in the *New York Times* (May 15, 1988)

My lesbianism is an act of Christian charity. All those women out there praying for a man, and I'm giving them my share.
—Rita Mae Brown, *Venus Envy* (1993)

Jesse Helms and Newt Gingrich were shaking hands congratulating themselves on the introduction of an anti-gay bill in Congress. If it passes, they won't be able to shake hands, because it will then be illegal for a prick to touch an asshole.
—Judy Carter, quoted in "Editor's Bit," *BC Magazine* (June 16, 2005)

The gay issue has taken the place of the race issue for the Republican right.
—Richard Cohen, "The Politics of Fear," *Rolling Stone* (June 29, 2006)

The outright bigotry of demonizing gays and lesbians to gain a few votes ranks right up there on my personal list of what's not decent and right and moral.
—Anita Creamer, "Call for 'Moral Values' Badly Misses the Point," *Sacramento Bee* (November 26, 2004)

Over the past four years, our nation has taken on many of the same characteristics of an unsupervised schoolyard, where the majority rules and that group often is controlled by a bully. As a gay American, I have been waiting and praying for the bell to ring.
—John Crabtree-Ireland, "The Bullies Win," *Baltimore Sun* (November 9, 2004)

What do you mean, you "don't believe in homosexuality"? It's not like the Easter Bunny, your belief isn't necessary.
—Lea DeLaria, quoted in the *University of California–San Diego Rainbow* Newsletter (August 28, 2006)

The Democrats' response to gay issues over the last few years has been incoherent and spineless.
—Matt Foreman, quoted in "Gays Push to Recast Marriage on Morals," Reuters (November 12, 2005)

America I'm putting my queer shoulder to the wheel.
—Allen Ginsberg, from the poem "America" (1956)

You don't have a choice when the other side continually invokes religion and acts as if they have a monopoly on faith. One can't remain silent in the face of that. Not all people of faith believe gay marriage is against the Bible or that all communities of faith are opponents of justice for the gay community.
—Charles Keener, quoted in "Religious Gays Press Case for Equal Rights," *Washington Blade* (November 12, 2004)

The fact that I am gay is certainly one of the characteristics with which I have been endowed by my creator and it is an important part of who I am as a human being. But it is certainly not the only characteristic that defines me.
—Scott McCoy, "Gay Activist Appointed to Utah Senate," the Associated Press (AP) (February 7, 2005)

At a point in every person's life, one has to look deeply into the mirror of one's soul and decide one's unique truth in the world, not as we may want to see it or hope to see it, but as it is. And so my truth is that I am a gay American.
—James McGreevey, "McGreevey: 'I Am a Gay American,'" CNN (August 13, 2004)

Human beings do not choose their sexual orientation; they discover it as something given. To pray for a change in sexual orientation is about as meaningful as to pray for a change from blue eyes to brown.
—John J. McNeill, quoted in *Voices of the Religious Left* (2000)

It is one thing to have gay friends and espouse messages of diversity but, when the going gets rough, few liberals will stand with gay people on principle, regardless the cost.
—Patrick Moore, "The Best Response to Religious Groups' SpongeBob-Is-Gay Complaint Would Have Been, 'So What?'" *Newsday* (January 25, 2005)

There are certain principles in life that transcend patience, and one of them to me is the obligation not to discriminate against people.
—Gavin Newsom, quoted in "San Francisco Mayor Becomes Hero of Equal Rights Movement After Allowing Gay Marriages," *City Mayors* (February 2004)

What is the gay life style? Short hair? Minimalist decor? We can't simply be talking sex acts here, can we? Because if we are, that would mean that the heterosexual lifestyle would consist largely of the missionary position.
—Anna Quindlen, *New York Times* (October 15, 1994)

I decided to talk to a couple of gay people myself to see if they'd reveal to me the Gay Agenda. I confess I did not speak directly to the Head Homosexual, but I did have a chat with some average, everyday queers.
—Beth Quinn, "Gay Agenda Revealed Here for First Time!" *Middletown Times Herald-Record* (February 20, 2006)

I'm not embarrassed about being a gay man.
—Bishop Gene Robinson, quoted in "Gay Bishop: Being Honest," CBS News (August 1, 2004)

Gays and lesbians are our neighbors, our co-workers, our friends. They serve as firefighters, police, doctors and professional athletes. They laugh at the same jokes and worry about car payments and credit card debt. Amending the Constitution to deny them the same rights we all take for granted just isn't very American.
—Anthony D. Romero, "Same-Sex Marriage Ban of 'National Importance,'" *San Francisco Chronicle* (February 25, 2004)

We need to club Republican ideas back under the rock where they belong. We need to make "faggot" as morally repugnant an epithet as "nigger."
—Terry Sawyer, "Mind Over Matters: Smear the Queer," *PopMatters* (November 10, 2004)

The Gay Republican: Oxymoron, or Just Moron?
—Gene Stone, title of post, *Huffington Post* (April 24, 2006)

Do you think homosexuals are revolting? You bet your sweet ass we are.
—Stonewall documents, quoted in *The Gay Militants* (1971)

Perhaps the most striking difference between progressive believers and their socially conservative counterparts is that they don't see a direct relationship between sexual orientation and religion. In other words, they don't see being gay and being Christian as mutually exclusive identities.
—Keila Szpaller, "New Time Religion," *Missoula Independent* (January 6, 2005)

Despite what you might have read, heard, or been taught throughout your churchgoing life, homosexuality is, in fact, determined at birth and is not to be condemned by God's followers.
—Rev. Oliver "Buzz" Thomas, "When Religion Loses Its Credibility," *USA Today* (November 20, 2006)

Immigration

If someone breaks into my property for the purpose of trashing and looting, I would be hell-bent on restitution. But if they break in for the purpose of cleaning it—scrubbing the bathroom, mowing the lawn—then, in my way of thinking anyway, the debt goes in the other direction.
—Barbara Ehrenreich, "What America Owes Its 'Illegals,'" *Huffington Post* (June 5, 2007)

We'll Lock Up Your Tired, Your Poor, Your Huddled Masses Yearning to Breathe Free
—Amy Goodman, title of article regarding the U.S. imprisonment of immigrant children, Truthdig (February 27, 2007)

We don't have an "illegal immigration" problem in America. We have an "illegal employer" problem.
—Thom Hartmann, "Reclaiming the Issues: It's an Illegal Employer Problem," *Common Dreams* (July 5, 2006)

The best way to increase border security is to narrow the gap between rich and poor nations. The more we help the countries from which economic refugees flee, the less reason they have to leave.
—David Howard, "Eight Steps to Create Sensible Immigration," *Ventura County Star* (September 2, 2005)

Do not build a fence. It will not work. They will come anyway. Over, under, or through.
—Molly Ivins, "Immigration 101," AlterNet (March 30, 2006)

We need comprehensive immigration reform—reform that removes the discrimination that embraces Europeans and excludes Africans, or hunts Mexicans and hugs Canadians.
—Rev. Jesse Jackson, "Let's Deport Immigration Myths," *Chicago Sun-Times* (May 9, 2006)

The immigration problem was one of our own making, initiated by corporate agribusiness's decades-old mania for a slave-labor force.
—A. V. Krebs, "Dems: Lost in the Political Desert," *Progressive Populist* (June 15, 2006)

The immigration issue is mainly hurting the Republican Party, which is divided between those who want to expel immigrants and those who want to exploit them.
—Paul Krugman, "The Road to Dubai," *New York Times* (March 31, 2006)

If capital is going to freely cross borders, should people and labor be able to do so as well, going where globalization takes the jobs?
—George Lakoff, "The Framing of Immigration," Rockridge Institute (May 25, 2006)

If you want to stop illegal immigrants, stop the people who hire them—quit punishing people who come because there are jobs.
—Molly Ivins, "White House Whopper Becomes Instant Classic," Truthdig (April 13, 2006)

So long as the global economy is designed, as NAFTA was, to keep workers powerless, Mexican desperation and American anger will only grow. Forget the fence. We need a new rule book for the world.
—Harold Meyerson, "NAFTA and Nativism," *American Prospect* (February 9, 2006)

I AM A WORKER, NOT A CRIMINAL
—Protest sign seen at a march of undocumented immigrants

Millions of undocumented immigrants pay income taxes. . . . They pay into the Social Security system, too, even though they're not eligible to collect benefits.
—Anna Quindlen, "Undocumented, Indispensable," *Newsweek* (May 15, 2006)

The last "reform" corporate America wants is a genuine crackdown on illegal immigration.
—Ted Rall, "Legal, Safe and Common," *Common Dreams* (January 19, 2005)

One of the main reasons employers hire undocumented immigrants is that people who are here illegally don't complain when they're paid below the minimum wage or forced to work in unsafe and unhealthy conditions.
—Robert Reich, "Immigration Follies," *American Prospect* (March 29, 2006)

For decades, the United States has pursued a de facto policy of exploiting and abusing immigrant labor, mostly from Mexico. It is hypocritical and un-American.
—Cynthia Tucker, "A Rational Approach to Immigration," *Baltimore Sun* (April 18, 2005)

The only ones I want to hear speaking up and complaining about immigration are the Native Americans who we screwed.
—Edward Rendell, "Rendell Says Hazleton Ordinance Feeds Off Hatred," the Associated Press (AP) (July 21, 2006)

It is time we acknowledged that we need the immigrant workers as much as they need us and began to treat them with the respect they deserve.
—Robert Scheer, "An Old Story: Scapegoat Immigrants," *San Francisco Chronicle* (March 29, 2006)

Immigrants want the same things most Americans do: decent jobs, basic rights, and a life free of violence and coercion.
—David Segal and Miguel Luna, "U.S. Shares Blame For Immigration Woes," *Providence Journal* (March 31, 2007)

America without immigration is an oxymoron. . . . It lies at the heart of what it means to be American.
—Philip Slater, "The Heart Is at the Periphery," *Huffington Post* (April 19, 2006)

As long as there is no system that allows them to migrate legally, undocumented immigrants will continue to find ways to enter the country illegally.
—Hilda Solis, "Realistic Immigration," *Nation* (February 6, 2006)

Because employers threaten undocumented immigrants with deportation, these workers cannot effectively assert their rights in the workplace by, for example, asking for raises, complaining about violations of wage and hour or workplace safety laws, or by supporting union organizing drives.
—Amy M. Traub, "Principles for an Immigration Policy to Strengthen and Expand the American Middle Class," Drum Major Institute for Public Policy (December 8, 2005)

Immigrants are not the threat—corporate power is. People are flowing into the country because they are economic refugees, battered at home by, among other things, our country's insistence on shoving so-called "free trade" down their throats.
—Jonathan Tasini, "Democrats: Get a Real Economic Agenda or Become the Minority Party Again," *Huffington Post* (December 5, 2006)

When immigrants lack rights in the workplace, labor standards are driven down, and all working people have less opportunity to enter or remain part of the middle class.
—Amy M. Traub, "Principles for an Immigration Policy to Strengthen and Expand the American Middle Class," Drum Major Institute for Public Policy (December 8, 2005)

Illegal immigration is one of those complex problems—like crime, poverty and terrorism—that demand thoughtful and courageous leaders, not demagogues who pander to our basest instincts.
—Cynthia Tucker, "Behind Immigration Rhetoric Is Complex Set of Problems," Universal Press Syndicate (October 3, 2005)

I'm sick of all this illegal immigration into this country. I think we ought to send every illegal back. But instead of starting with the newest arrivals, I think we should start with the ones that have been here illegally the longest. . . . So, it's about time we threw those English bastards out.
—Cenk Uygur, "Nativists for Native Americans," AlterNet (April 12, 2006)

Inclusion

My house shall be called a house of prayer for all peoples.
—Isaiah 56:7

Jesus' treatment of the outcasts of his time—tax collectors, lepers, the mentally ill, prostitutes—ought to inform our attitudes toward those on the margins today, including those who are homosexual.
—Rev. David C. Bloom and Patrick Higgins, "The Perfect Time to Talk About Our Moral Values," *Seattle Times* (December 24, 2004)

We ought not turn our back on pro-life people, even though the vast majority of people in this party are pro-choice.
—Howard Dean, quoted in "Democrats Weigh De-emphasizing Abortion as an Issue," *New York Times* (December 24, 2004)

There are people in this nation who aren't affiliated religiously but who care deeply about moral values and about the moral crisis of the country, and they need to be part of this conversation too.
—Rev. Jim Wallis, "Rescuing Religion from the Right," *Beliefnet* (January 26, 2005)

God doesn't reject people. Neither do we.
—United Church of Christ advertising message rejected NBC, CBS, ABC, and FOX, quoted in "Divine Denial," *American Prospect* (May 5, 2006)

Intolerance

The core claim of every creed is that it, alone, is true.
—Sam Harris, interviewed by Blair Golson, Truthdig (April 3, 2006)

Would God give a bird wings and make it a crime to fly?
—Robert G. Ingersoll, in his speech on religious intolerance, Pittsburgh Opera House (October 14, 1879)

There is a growing movement within this country of people who are convinced that God is only on their side and the rest of us are going to Hell.
—W. David Jenkins III, "The Seeds of the American Taliban," *Counterbias* (December 10, 2004)

The core problem is not intolerance but white supremacy—and the way in which, day in and day out, white people accept white supremacy and the unearned privileges it brings.
—Robert Jensen and Robert Wosnitzer, "Crash and the Self-Indulgence of White America," *Working for Change* (March 22, 2006)

The stronger the belief, the greater its intolerance. Men dominated by a certitude cannot tolerate those who do not accept it.
—Gustave Le Bon, *Opinions and Beliefs* (1911)

From the trials of witches in Salem to the talking-head evangelists of the present day, we have a rich tradition of faith-based bullying in this country.
—Anna Quindlen, "The Spirit of the Season," *Newsweek* (December 27, 2004)

This religious debate is fuelling a new kind of intolerance in the U.S. It is not, notably, an intolerance of any religious minority, but an intolerance of secularism.
—Natasha Walter, "U.S. Presidential Campaign: It's Policies, Not Prayers, That We Want," *Independent (UK)* (September 4, 2000)

Latinos

Over the last decade Latino workers' fatality rates have soared, outstripping their share of the workforce.
—Stephen Franklin and Darnell Little, "Fear of Retaliation Trumps Pain," *Chicago Tribune* (September 3, 2006)

The new immigrants seek precisely what has made our country great: They thirst for democracy and freedom, a job and security for their families, for citizenship rights and to leave repression and poverty behind.
—Rev. Jesse Jackson, "Are Immigrants Putting Justice on Parade?" *Chicago Sun-Times* (May 2, 2006)

The sleeping Latino giant has finally awakened.
—Felix Ortiz, on the nationwide protests against criminalizing immigrant workers, quoted in "Latino Giant Awakens: Demonstrations Gaining Strength," *New York Daily News* (March 28, 2006)

Decades ago the Republican Party built its "solid South" with thinly disguised, and sometimes blatant, appeals to white racist voters who felt threatened by blacks. Now Republicans seem to have decided to paint Latinos as the new menace.
—Eugene Robinson, "Bigotry Beneath the Fog," *Washington Post* (June 23, 2006)

Racism

Racism . . . is America's original sin and, as it is institutionalized at all levels of society, it is its most persistent and intractable evil.
—James H. Cone, quoted in *Soul Work: Anti-Racist Theologies in Dialogue* (2003)

The percentage of black Americans living in poverty is 24.7, almost twice as high as the overall rate for all races.
—Bernd Debusmann, "U.S. Poverty: Chronic Ill, Little Hope for Cure" Reuters (October 5, 2005)

What, to the American slave, is your Fourth of July? I answer: A day that reveals to him, more than all other days in the year, the gross injustice and cruelty to which he is the constant victim. To him your celebration is a sham.
—Frederick Douglass, in his speech delivered to the Rochester, New York Ladies' Anti-Slavery Society (July 5, 1852)

Racism is a serious offense against God precisely because it violates the innate dignity of the human person. . . . Since we cannot claim to love God unless we love our neighbor, we can only be one with God if we reject racism and work aggressively to remove it from our personal lives, our church, and our society.
—Archbishop Harry J. Flynn, *In God's Image: Pastoral Letter on Racism* (September 12, 2003)

For most of the time between the Revolutionary War and the Civil War, the United States was governed by presidents who owned slaves.
—Bob Herbert, "Slavery Is Not Dead. It's Not Even Past," *New York Times* (March 1, 2007)

Racists seem obsessed by the idea that illegal workers—the hardest-working, poorest people in America—are somehow getting away with something, sneaking goodies that should be for Americans.
—Molly Ivins, "Immigration 101," AlterNet (March 30, 2006)

What happened in Iraq is a natural extension of the humiliation that has gone on for two decades in this country.
—Derrick Z. Jackson, "U.S. Abuse of Black Men a Prelude to Scandal," *Boston Globe* (May 12, 2004)

In the political realignment that resulted from the Democrat's embrace of the civil rights movement, the racist right wing migrated to the Republican Party.
—Marty Jezer, "Capture the Flag," *Common Dreams* (August 6, 2004)

Until justice is blind to color, until education is unaware of race, until opportunity is unconcerned with the color of men's skins, emancipation will be a proclamation but not a fact.
—Lyndon B. Johnson, in his Memorial Day speech in Gettysburg, Pennsylvania (May 30, 1963)

Hypersegregated inner-city schools . . . are the norm, not the exception, in most northern urban areas today.
—Jonathan Kozol, "Overcoming Apartheid," *Nation* (December 19, 2005)

If current trends continue, one of every three black males and one of every six Latino males born today can expect to go to prison at some point in his lifetime.
—Marc Mauer, "America Has Become Incarceration Nation," AlterNet (December 22, 2006)

There are those who would keep us slipping back into the darkness of division, into the snake pit of racial hatred, of racial antagonism, and of support for symbols of the struggle to keep African-Americans in bondage.
—Carol Moseley-Braun, referring to the continued use of the Confederate flag, quoted in *Newsweek* (December 16, 1991)

We are racially segregated in every meaningful sense except the letter of the law.
—Bill Moyers, "Life on the Plantation," *Common Dreams* (January 17, 2006)

In 1865, shortly after Lincoln signed the Emancipation Proclamation freeing the slaves, blacks owned 0.5 percent of the nation's net wealth. Today . . . the percentage of the nation's net worth owned by blacks totals just 1 percent.
—John Robbins, "Is Racism Real?" *Common Dreams* (December 23, 2006)

The insult of segregation was searing and unforgettable. It has left a great scar, and will be with me for the rest of my life.
—Randall Robinson, interviewed by Amitabh Pal, *Progressive* (October 2005)

This country has used a prison-based apartheid system as an alternative to truly integrating its largest racial minorities into the mainstream of educational and economic opportunity.
—Robert Scheer, "What Does It Say About Us That We've Imprisoned So Many of Our Minorities?" *Los Angeles Times* (March 7, 2000)

We don't want apartheid liberalized. We want it dismantled. You can't improve something that is intrinsically evil.
—Bishop Desmond Tutu, quoted in the *Observer (UK)* (March 10, 1985)

I hate the way they portray us in the media. You see a black family, it says, "They're looting." You see a white family, it says, "They're looking for food."
—Kanye West, on the Bush administration's attitude toward victims of Hurricane Katrina, on NBC (September 2, 2005)

Race is a manufactured thing, an artificial thing, and . . . it matters only because certain people want it to matter.
—Howard Zinn, *Original Zinn* (2006)

Sexism

Let me say here and now that the black woman in America can justly be described as a "slave of a slave."
—Frances M. Beal, quoted in *Sisterhood Is Powerful* (1970)

This religion and the Bible require of woman everything, and give her nothing. They ask her support and her love, and repay her with contempt and oppression.
—Helen H. Gardener, *Men, Women and Gods* (2001)

Progressive male Christian leaders say that if the Democratic Party opened its doors and welcomed pro-life Democrats, it would work wonders among centrist evangelicals and Catholics. . . . If the nearly all-male club of progressive clerical leaders welcomed women into their leadership, they might learn something about life and choice.
—Frances Kissling, in a letter to the editor, "Courting the Values Voters," *Washington Post* (November 17, 2004)

Women are a colonized people.
—Robin Morgan, *The Word of a Woman* (1992)

The absence of feminine symbolism for God marks Judaism, Christianity, and Islam in striking contrast to the world's other religious traditions.
—Elaine Pagels, *The Gnostic Gospels* (1979)

Our religion, laws, and customs, are all founded on the belief that woman was made for man.
—Elizabeth Cady Stanton, in a letter to Susan B. Anthony (June 14, 1860)

The simplistic labels of "feminine" and "masculine" are mostly about what society wants us to do: submerge our unique humanity in care giving and reproducing if we're women, and trade our unique humanity for power if we're men.
—Gloria Steinem, "Why Being a Feminist Does Not Mean Backing All Women," Women's Media Center (January 11, 2007)

The ownership of women begins in the lower barbaric stages of culture, apparently with the seizure of female captives.
—Thorstein Veblen, *The Theory of the Leisure Class* (1899)

THE CORRUPTION OF PUBLIC SERVICE

Checks and Balances

If we are to preserve freedom and keep constitutional government alive in America, it cannot be left to a President and his agents alone to decide what must be kept secret.
—Frank Church, quoted in the *Washington Post* (February 17, 1976)

Unregulated capitalism is not a pretty sight, which is why we have labor laws, environmental regulations, health and safety standards, unions, much-eroded consumer-protection laws, and other checks on the system.
—Molly Ivins, "Capitalism Doesn't Do Squat for Social Justice," *Miami Herald* (April 12, 2000)

The great security against a gradual concentration of the several powers in the same department consists in giving to those who administer each department the necessary constitutional means, and personal motives, to resist encroachments of the others.
—James Madison, *The Federalist*, No. 51 (February 6, 1788)

Checks and balances never looked so thoroughly unchecked and unbalanced.
—J. R. Norton, *Saving General Washington* (2006)

It's a virulent animosity toward gay people that really unites the leaders of the anti-"activist" judiciary crusade. . . . Their campaign . . . uses gay people as cannon fodder on the way to its greater goal of taking down a branch of government that is crucial to the constitutional checks and balances.
—Frank Rich, "Just How Gay Is the Right?" *New York Times* (May 15, 2005)

I know that corporations exist for one reason and one reason only: the relentless, single-minded pursuit of profit, no matter who gets shafted. . . . But in our country, corporations aren't supposed to pursue this purpose in a vacuum, unchecked, unregulated, unopposed.
—David Sirota, "Careless Industry," *In These Times* (May 1, 2006)

Congress

Rich white men still compose about 80 percent of the Senate, their average age is sixty-two, and even those who call themselves Democrats often think and act like Republicans.
—Medea Benjamin, "Have You Called Your Senator Today?" *Common Dreams* (May 21, 2007)

Congress seems drugged and inert most of the time. . . . Its idea of meeting a problem is to hold hearings or, in extreme cases, to appoint a commission.
—Shirley Chisholm, *Unbought and Unbossed* (1970)

The scandal of a Congress for Sale is the most urgent domestic problem in America today.
—Mark Green, "Ms. Speaker, After 100 Hours, Let's Enact 'Democracy Funding' of Campaigns," *Huffington Post* (January 5, 2007)

Modest Proposal: Waterboard Congress: Maybe White House–Favored Interrogation Techniques Would Coax Lawmakers to Tell the Truth about U.S. Anti-Terror Policies
—Headline introducing article by James Bovard, *Los Angeles Times* (August 27, 2006)

Congress is furious. They want to know how oil company profits are so high, but their money under the table has remained the same.
—Jay Leno, quoted in "Jay Leno, Conan O'Brien and Stephen Colbert," *Washington Post* (April 30, 2006)

Corporations' wish list is now Congress's to-do list.
—Ralph Nader, "How to Curb Corporate Power," *Nation* (October 10, 2005)

These past six years were more than just the most shameful, corrupt and incompetent period in the history of the American legislative branch. . . . Its whole history is one long love letter to sleaze, idiocy, and pigheaded, glacial conservatism.
—Matt Taibbi, "Time to Go! Inside the Worst Congress Ever," *Rolling Stone* (November 2006)

It could probably be shown by facts and figures that there is no distinctly native American criminal class except Congress.
—Mark Twain, *Following the Equator* (1897)

Suppose I am a crook, and suppose I am a congressman, but I repeat myself.
—Mark Twain, quoted in *Restoration: Congress, Term Limits, and the Recovery of Deliberative Democracy* (1992)

The level of discourse in the House and the Senate is so low that there are parents who, instead of grounding their teenage children for infractions of the family's rules, make them listen to three hours of floor discussion in Congress as a punishment.
—Nicholas von Hoffman, "America's Idiotic Political Debates," *Nation* (May 4, 2007)

Corruption

Virtually every federal agency is now captive to the corporate interests it is supposed to regulate.
—Russ Baker, "Crashing Watergate Gate," *TomPaine.com* (May 8, 2006)

The real scandals in Washington don't make the press and aren't even against the law. Washington has been taken over by lobbyists and campaign contributors who get paid back in special interest favors.
—Robert L. Borosage and Robert Loper, eds., *StraightTalk: Common Sense for the Common Good* (2006)

When conservatism was a movement of ideas, it attracted oddballs; now that it's a movement with power, it attracts sleazeballs.
—David Brooks, quoted in "The Rise of the Rebels," *Nation* (December 24, 2005)

It's one kind of scandal when a president cannot control a need for sexual satisfaction. . . . It's another kind of scandal when a president cannot control a need for power.
—Joan Chittister, "Monica, We Need You Now," *National Catholic Reporter* (December 31, 2005)

Corruption involves more than bribe-taking and jet-setting junkets. It is also the hijacking of the legislative process for narrow partisan purposes rather than the public good.
—Marie Cocco, "As DeLay Leaves, Shoddy Culture Lingers," *Boulder Daily Camera* (June 12, 2006)

As long as a relatively few men own the railroads, the telegraph, the telephone, own the oil fields and the gas fields and the steel mills and the sugar refineries and the leather tanneries—own, in short, the sources and means of life—they will corrupt our politics; they will enslave the working class; they will impoverish and debase society.
—Eugene Debs, from a 1908 speech quoted in *Debs: His Life, Writings and Speeches* (2002)

Washington under Republican rule is defined by a culture of corruption.
—Editorial, "Kickback Mountain," *Nation* (January 30, 2006)

Sell not virtue to purchase wealth, nor Liberty to purchase power.
—Benjamin Franklin, *Poor Richard's Almanack* (May 1738)

Gerrymandering of district boundaries has reached such absurd limits that more than 99 percent of congressional seats have been safe for the incumbent party in the past few election cycles.
—Andrew Gumbel, "George Bush's *Annus Horribilis*," *Los Angeles CityBeat* (December 30, 2005)

We all know what has happened to politics in America. It is corrupt. It is corrupted by money, interest groups, and mass media.
—Gary Hart, "Where the Little Guy Can Win" (December 9, 2005)

History tells us that when corporate power is unrestrained, and corporations grow so large that the largest among them come to control and then stifle the marketplace, the result is the corruption of democracy.
—Thom Hartmann, "Is Wal-Mart a Person?" *BuzzFlash* (January 28, 2005)

Mired in the sickening muck of corrupt corporate money and right-wing ideology, our so-called leaders continue to divert our public treasury and our nation's unlimited potential for good into war, into the pockets of the superrich.
—Jim Hightower, "Forget Washington, All Good Politics Is Local," *Hightower Lowdown* (February 2006)

The big-money corruption that rampages throughout our political system touches and taints practically every issue we care about—health care, pollution, war, jobs and wages, pure food, education. . . . This is the defining battle of our times.
—Jim Hightower, "Candidates Who Shun Corporate Cash Are Winning," AlterNet (February 26, 2007)

Here we sit, watching a great, stinking skein of corruption being fished to the surface of Washington, while the town is simultaneously filled with a great babble about God, prayer, and morality.
—Molly Ivins, "Let God Speak for Himself," *Boulder Daily Camera* (December 2, 2005)

It has always been those seeking wealth who were the source of corruption in government.
—Thomas Jefferson, quoted in "There's Nothing 'Normal' About a Middle Class," *Huffington Post* (October 26, 2006)

I believe there is now a professional, well-trained elite, supported by large institutions, that is adept and willing to use corrupt practices to accumulate wealth. . . . There is no way the counter-class made up of regulators, watchdogs, and do-gooders and hack columnists can match wits with the predator class.
—Dick Meyer, "The Predator Class," CBS News (November 19, 2003)

If the corporate, political, and religious right have their way, we will go back to the first Gilded Age, when privilege controlled politics, votes were purchased, legislatures were bribed, bills were bought, and laws flagrantly disregarded—all as God's will.
—Bill Moyers, "A Time for Heresy," AlterNet (March 24, 2006)

There are no victimless crimes in politics. The price of corruption is passed on to you.
—Bill Moyers, "Saving Democracy," *Common Dreams* (February 24, 2006)

The Republicans have turned Congress into an auction house for sale to the highest bidder.
—Nancy Pelosi, "Democrats Answer GOP with Own Ethics Plan," MSNBC (January 18, 2006)

America is clearly sick of pay-to-play politics.
—David Sirota, "On the Verge of Political Reform," *San Francisco Chronicle* (January 5, 2006)

Our government has been the victim of a hostile takeover. Over the last thirty years, Corporate America has applied its most effective business tactics to the task of purchasing the one commodity that's not supposed to be for sale: American democracy.
—David Sirota, "Careless Industry," *In These Times* (May 1, 2006)

The campaign financing system really is at the root of corruption. We have a system that is legalized bribery—legal campaign contributions go in, and legal legislative favors go out.
—David Sirota, "Dems Must End Legalized Bribery of Campaign Finance," AlterNet (November 23, 2006)

A progressive agenda has no hope, long-term, without cutting off the mountains of campaign cash that keep legislators on the hook to corporate interests.
—Jonathan Tasini, "A 10-Step Program for Democrats," *TomPaine.com* (January 2, 2007)

Courts

Conservatives have been mad at the Supreme Court since it decided to desegregate the schools in 1954 and seen fit to blame the federal bench for everything that has happened since then that they don't like.
—Molly Ivins, "The New 'Activist' Judges," AlterNet (August 24, 2006)

This President is in the midst of a radical realignment of the powers of the government and its intrusiveness into the private lives of Americans. This nomination is part of that plan.
—Patrick Leahy, on President Bush's nomination of Samuel Alito to the Supreme Court, "Alito a Threat to Our Fundamental Rights," Truthout (January 26, 2006)

In our country our courts are the great levelers, and in our courts all men are created equal.
—Atticus Finch, *To Kill a Mockingbird* (1960)

There is no liberty, if the power of judging be not separated from the legislative and executive powers.
—Montesquieu, *The Spirit of the Laws* (1748)

We must be ever-vigilant against those who would strong-arm the judiciary.
—Sandra Day O'Connor, on Republican efforts at intimidation, quoted in "Former Top Judge Says U.S. Risks Edging Near to Dictatorship," *Guardian (UK)* (March 13, 2006)

We need to know that presidents and paupers will receive equal justice in your courtroom.
—Chuck Schumer, to Judge Alito, quoted in "Alito Sounds Death Knell for Individual Rights," Truthout (January 10, 2006)

The court's role in settling the 2000 presidential election seemed to shatter once and for all any notion that it occupied some antiseptic zone untouched by politics.
—Scott Shane, "Ideology Serves as a Wild Card in Senate Debate on Court Pick," *New York Times* (November 4, 2005)

[Judicial] fundamentalists believe that the Constitution must be interpreted according to the "original understanding." . . . If the Constitution did not originally ban the federal government from discriminating on the basis of race, then the federal government is permitted to discriminate on that basis.
—Cass R. Sunstein, *Radical in Robes* (2005)

Democracy

The cure for the illness of democracy is more democracy.
—Jane Addams, *Democracy and Social Ethics* (1902)

Corporations are not democratic institutions—their directors and managers own no accountability to anyone but the shareholders that employ them.
—Joel Bakan, *The Corporation: The Pathological Pursuit of Profit and Power* (2004)

Capitalism is not too strong; democracy is too weak. . . . We have grown too timid as citizens, acquiescing to deregulation and privatization . . . and a growing tyranny of money over politics.
—Benjamin R. Barber, "A Failure of Democracy, Not Capitalism," *New York Times* (July 29, 2002)

Democracy cannot be imposed; it has to be nurtured.
—Bob Burnett, "A Liberal Foreign Policy: Ten Maxims," *Huffington Post* (March 1, 2007)

Personally I'm in favor of democracy, which means that the central institutions in the society have to be under popular control. Now, under capitalism we can't have democracy by definition. Capitalism is a system in which the central institutions of society are in principle under autocratic control.
—Noam Chomsky, "One Man's View," *Business Today* (May 1973)

A democracy is more than a form of government; it is primarily a mode of associated living.
—John Dewey, *Democracy and Education* (1916)

Democracy is not a spectator sport.
—Marian Wright Edelman, *Families in Peril* (1987)

The secular democratic state is the surest protector of religious and intellectual liberty ever crafted by human ingenuity.
—Edward L. Ericson, *American Freedom and the Radical Right* (1982)

We are on the brink of losing our democracy for the sake of keeping our empire.
—Chalmers Johnson, "Empire vs. Democracy," *TomPaine.com* (January 31, 2007)

America's corporate and political elites now form a regime of their own and they're privatizing democracy. All the benefits—the tax cuts, policies and rewards—flow in one direction: up.
—Bill Moyers, "Now," PBS (April 18, 2003)

Jesus drove the money changers from the temple. We must drive them from the temples of democracy.
—Bill Moyers, "Democracy in the Balance," *Sojourners* (August 2004)

A strong democracy is good for good business and bad for bad business.
—Ralph Nader, "I Will Work As President for Need, Not Greed," *London Daily Telegraph* (October 31, 2000)

In no other Western democracy do third-party or independent candidates confront more obstacles and exclusions from contributing to a competitive democratic process than in the United States.
—Ralph Nader, "Break Down Barriers to Minority Parties," *Baltimore Sun* (July 9, 2006)

Man's capacity for justice makes democracy possible, but man's inclination to injustice makes democracy necessary.
—Reinhold Neibuhr, foreword to *The Children of Light and the Children of Darkness* (1944)

Democracies decay when one segment of society flourishes at another's expense, when fortunes—and power—concentrate at the top.
—Sam Pizzigati, ed. *Executive Excess 2006* (August 30, 2006)

Democracy, the modern world's holy cow, is in crisis. And the crisis is a profound one. Every kind of outrage is being committed in the name of democracy.
—Arundhati Roy, *An Ordinary Person's Guide to Empire* (2004)

When we talk of the American democratic faith, we must understand it in its true dimensions. It is not an impervious, final, and complacent orthodoxy, intolerant of deviation and dissent, fulfilled in flag salutes, oaths of allegiance, and hands over the heart. It is an ever-evolving philosophy, fulfilling its ideals through debate, self-criticism, protest, disrespect, and irreverence.
—Arthur M. Schlesinger, Jr., *The Disuniting of America* (1991)

We cannot bring democracy to any nation, to any people, until we demand it here.
—Charles Sullivan, "The Great Perversion," OpEdNews (December 13, 2005)

We're spreading democracy, are we? Same way European explorers brought Christianity to the Indians.
—Kurt Vonnegut, "Cold Turkey," *In These Times* (May 10, 2004)

Given the ambiguity of religious texts and teachings, the mixed historical record, and the empirical evidence, it would be foolhardy to assert that religious faith necessarily upholds democratic values.
—Kenneth D. Wald, *Religion and Politics in the United States* (2003)

Democracy can come undone. It's not something that's necessarily going to last forever once it's been established.
—Sean Wilentz, *The Rise of American Democracy* (2005)

I believe in democracy because it releases the energies of every human being.
—Woodrow Wilson, quoted in "A Time for Anger, A Call to Action," *Common Dreams* (March 22, 2007)

Government

Corporations now govern society, perhaps more than governments themselves do.
—Joel Bakan, *The Corporation: The Pathological Pursuit of Profit and Power* (2004)

A simple and proper function of government is to make it easy for us to do good and difficult for us to do wrong.
—Jimmy Carter, in his acceptance of his presidential nomination (July 15, 1976)

Opposition to the death penalty is widely misunderstood to be only a liberal cause. It is odd that many conservatives who advocate limited government are willing to give government the power to kill its prisoners.
—Mary Catherine Cassidy, "Capital Punishment Is Killing in Your Name," *Corpus Christi Caller-Times* (December 13, 2004)

I believe the government that governs best is the government that governs least. And by these standards, we have set up a fabulous government in Iraq.
—Stephen Colbert, quoted in "Did Media Miss Real Colbert Story?" *Chicago Sun-Times* (May 7, 2006)

Government's basic purpose is to allow those blessed with talent to go as far as they can—on their own merits. But . . . government also has an obligation to assist those who, for whatever reason, have been left out by fate: the homeless, the infirm, the destitute.
—Mario Cuomo, in his first inaugural address as New York governor (January 1, 1983)

Government succeeds more than we want to acknowledge. Ask any elderly person if he or she would prefer to live without Social Security and Medicare. Ask parents in a good school district if they would like to abolish the public schools.
—E. J. Dionne, Jr., "The Risk-Aversion Spiral," Truthdig (December 22, 2006)

Government exists to defend the weak and poor and the injured party; the rich and strong can take care of themselves.
—Ralph Waldo Emerson, in his speech delivered in Concord, Massachusetts, on the anniversary of the emancipation of the slaves from the British West Indies (August 1, 1844)

Government is not a necessary evil but a necessary good.
—Gerald R. Ford, in his speech for the U.S. Bicentennial in Philadelphia (July 4, 1976)

In their breathtaking incompetence and comprehensive failure in government, Republicans have undermined Americans' confidence in the ability of government to play a role in solving America's problems.
—Stanley B. Greenberg, "Democrats Are Back—But . . . " *American Prospect* (June 18, 2007)

The failure to govern well is a natural and a predictable result of disbelief in government.
—Gary Hart, "The Art of Caring for Souls," *Huffington Post* (October 14, 2005)

According to hard-right Republicans, killing off government to make way for corporate rule is truly at the core of the so-called "conservative agenda."
—Thom Hartmann, "Healthcare Reveals Real 'Conservative' Agenda," *Common Dreams* (February 25, 2003)

The boneheaded, shortsighted, self-aggrandizing, "kill government" ideologues of today are enemies of history, common sense, progress, and America's public welfare.
—Jim Hightower, "Blasting American Infrastructure Away," AlterNet (November 29, 2006)

Governments are instituted among men, deriving their just powers from the consent of the governed. That whenever any form of government becomes destructive of these ends, it is the right of the people to alter or to abolish it, and to institute new government.
—Thomas Jefferson, Declaration of Independence (July 4, 1776)

I believe in a government which acts, which exercises its full powers and full responsibilities. Government is an art and a precious obligation; and when it has a job to do, I believe it should do it.
—John F. Kennedy, accepting the New York Liberal Party nomination (September 14, 1960)

In the end, Republicans didn't shrink the government. But they did degrade it.
—Paul Krugman, "A Failed Revolution," *New York Times* (December 29, 2006)

The conservatives who run today's Republican Party are devoted, above all, to the proposition that government is always the problem, never the solution.
—Paul Krugman, "Emerging Republican Minority," *New York Times* (March 26, 2007)

Smaller government is, in conservative propaganda, supposed to eliminate waste. It is really about eliminating social programs.
—George Lakoff, *Don't Think Like an Elephant* (2004)

The legitimate object of government, is to do for a community of people, whatever they need to have done, but can not do . . . for themselves.
—Abraham Lincoln, *The Collected Works of Abraham Lincoln* (1953)

Since the election of Ronald Reagan . . . we've gone from the idea of a government in service to the public interests to a government in service to the wealthy interests.
—Joyce Marcel, "Two Capitalisms," *Common Dreams* (March 2, 2006)

Conservative rhetoric has succeeded in denigrating government even as conservative politicians plunder it.
—Bill Moyers, "For America's Sake," *Nation* (January 22, 2007)

We long to join the government in working for a healthy environment, peace, and adequate health care even as we want government to stay out of our bedrooms, our doctors' offices, and our churches.
—Rev. Katherine Hancock Ragsdale, "Defining 'Moral Values' for the Next Four Years," Religious Coalition for Reproductive Choice (2004)

Bad administration, to be sure, can destroy good policy, but good administration can never save bad policy.
—Adlai E. Stevenson, *Speeches of Adlai Stevenson* (1952)

Government has been shirking its basic responsibilities since the eighties, when Ronald Reagan sold us his belief that the sick, poor and unlucky should no longer count on "big government" to help them, but should rather live and die at the whim of contributors to private charities.
—Ted Rall, "Leave Katrina Relief Efforts to Government," uExpress (September 15, 2005)

Government's size isn't the issue. It's what it does, and for whom.
—Robert Reich, *Reason: Why Liberals Will Win the Battle for America* (2004)

The issue of government has always been whether individual men and women will have to serve some system of government of economics—or whether a system of government and economics exists to serve individual men and women.
—Franklin D. Roosevelt, in his 1932 speech to the Commonwealth Club of San Francisco, quoted in "Vision Check for the Democrats," *Washington Post* (November 8, 2005)

For half a century, free-market purists have to great effect denigrated the essential role that modern government performs as some terrible liberal plot.
—Robert Scheer, "The Real Costs of a Culture of Greed," *Nation* (September 6, 2005)

Government is not the enemy.
—Paul Simon, quoted in "Editorial: Paul Simon," *Nation* (December 11, 2003)

The Right has thoroughly brainwashed an entire American generation against believing that such a thing as good government is even possible. All government aid recipients are depicted as cheats, all government workers are slackers, all taxation is wasteful.
—Robert Steinback, "Reviving Faith in Role of Government," *Miami Herald* (November 9, 2005)

The government must be the trustee for the little man because no one else will be. The powerful can usually help themselves—and frequently do.
—Adlai E. Stevenson, quoted in *Peter's Principle* (1979)

Government and Corporations

Corporations have overwhelmed government in the borderless global economy.
—Lou Dobbs, *Exporting America: Why Corporate Greed Is Shipping American Jobs Overseas* (2004)

The search of the youth today is for ways and means to make the machine—and the vast bureaucracy of the corporation state and of government that runs that machine—the servant of man.
—William O. Douglas, *Points of Rebellion* (1970)

Unfettered capitalism leads invariably to corporate control of government.
—Robert F. Kennedy, Jr., "Crimes Against Nature," *Rolling Stone* (December 11, 2003)

Corporations aren't used to public officials who say no.
—Dennis Kucinich, interviewed by Joshua Scheer, "The Charge of the Muny Light Brigade," Truthdig (December 14, 2006)

We need a new relationship between corporations and our society. Just as our founders understood the need for separation of church and state, we need to institutionalize the separation of corporations and the state.
—Dennis Kucinich, "A New Horizon for the Democratic Party," *Nation* (June 3, 2002)

Instead of trying to keep a level playing field, government now favors the rich, powerful, and privileged.
—Bill Moyers, "America 101," *TomPaine.com* (November 1, 2006)

The two major parties are rapidly morphing into corporate power, where corporate money produces a permanent corporate government.
—Ralph Nader, "I Will Work As President for Need, Not Greed," *London Daily Telegraph* (October 31, 2000)

The legacy of the Bush administration may well be that government can no longer be entrusted to business people.
—David Olive, "He's No Warren Buffett," *Toronto Star* (September 25, 2005)

I want to preach a new doctrine. A complete separation of business and government.
—Franklin D. Roosevelt, quoted in *F.D.R.: An Intimate History* (1983)

It was natural and perhaps human that the privileged princes of these new economic dynasties, thirsting for power, reached out for control over government itself. . . . And as a result the average man once more confronts the problem that faced the Minute Man.
—Franklin D. Roosevelt, in his speech to the Democratic National Convention, Philadelphia, Pennsylvania (June 27, 1936)

Behind the ostensible Government sits enthroned an invisible Government, owing no allegiance and acknowledging no responsibility to the people. To destroy this invisible Government, to dissolve the unholy alliance between corrupt business and corrupt politics, is the first task of the statesmanship of the day.
—Theodore Roosevelt, *The Progressive Party Platform, An Autobiography* (1913)

There once was a time in history when the limitation of governmental power meant increasing liberty for the people. In the present day the limitation of governmental power, of governmental action, means the enslavement of the people by the great corporations.
—Theodore Roosevelt, *Progressive Principles: Selections from Addresses Made During the Presidential Campaign of 1912* (1913)

This is what happens when you deregulate industry. People die. This is what happens when you let companies act as their own watchdogs. People die.
—Matthew Rothschild, "Sago Mine Disaster Indicts Deregulation," *Progressive* (January 5, 2006)

We live in an era where our government has been the victim of a hostile takeover by Big Money interests.
—David Sirota, "Rick Santorum's Hostile Takeover," *Philadelphia Inquirer* (May 5, 2006)

The power of government and the power of corporations, instead of being set against each other, are actually becoming aligned.
—Jay Stanley, *The Surveillance-Industrial Complex*, American Civil Liberties Union (August 2004)

Hurricane Katrina

Katrina was not "unforeseeable," the loss of life and suffering was not "unavoidable." It was the result of a political authority that sub-contracts its responsibility to the private sector and abdicates responsibility altogether when it comes to housing, health care, education and even evacuation.
—Harry Belafonte, in a speech made during the PBS/BET-televised Higher Ground Hurricane Relief Benefit concert (September 17, 2005)

We only have to recall the color of the faces of those in Louisiana, Alabama and Mississippi who are most devastated by Katrina to know that there are not yet equal opportunities for all Americans.
—Jimmy Carter, remarks at the memorial service for Coretta Scott King, quoted in "A Healthy Dose of Reality for Mr. Bush," *Nation* (February 9, 2006)

The corruption of politics by big money might explain why for the last five years the President and Congress have been more interested in repealing the federal estate tax, paid only by multi-millionaires, than on reinforcing levees along the Gulf Coast.
—Chuck Collins and Felice Yeskel, "Inequality in America: Version 2.0," *Common Dreams* (October 21, 2005)

Republicans have cut and run when it comes to rebuilding the Gulf Coast.
—Howard Dean, "Dean Says Bush 'Cut and Run' on Katrina," Reuters (April 22, 2006)

Hurricane Katrina has created the moment for a true paradigm shift in American politics, because many Americans have actually become scared about what it means to have an eviscerated, dysfunctional federal government.
—Susan J. Douglas, "Missing Their Moment," *In These Times* (October 26, 2005)

New Orleans is our Gettysburg.
—Glen Ford and Peter Gamble, on the elections being held while 300,000 displaced African– Americans were in exile, "New Orleans Is Our Gettysburg, a Generation's Defining Event," *Black Commentator* (April 22, 2006)

Our society still remains segregated in many ways, from where we live and where we worship, to who survives a hurricane.
—Paul Halley, "Who Needs Black History Month?" *Pop and Politics* (January 31, 2006)

Whatever you've heard about New Orleans, the reality is much worse. Think of it as a vast open wound, this once-great American city that is still largely in ruins, with many of its people still writhing in agony more than a year after the catastrophic flood that followed Hurricane Katrina. . . . The recovery in New Orleans has gone about as well as the war in Iraq.
—Bob Herbert, "America's Open Wound," *New York Times* (December 21, 2006)

We now know that the ghastly drowning of New Orleans was not the result of Hurricane Katrina, but the failure of presidents, Congress, and the Army Corps of Engineers to fortify the levees—a disaster that had been predicted and was preventable.
—Jim Hightower, "Blasting American Infrastructure Away," AlterNet (November 29, 2006)

[Bush] sat and was briefed on the danger of a hurricane wiping out a major American city, and without asking a single question, he got up from the table and walked away and resumed his vacation.
—Garrison Keillor, "Only the GOP Can Save Us," *Salon* (March 15, 2006)

Unless a radical change of course is demanded, New Orleans will prove to be a glimpse of a dystopic future, a future of disaster apartheid in which the wealthy are saved and everyone else is left behind.
—Naomi Klein, "Pay to Be Saved: The Future of Disaster Response," *Common Dreams* (August 28, 2006)

In the aftermath of Hurricane Katrina, we have an opportunity to construct something far more important than higher levees—a national health care system that looks less like a tightrope and more like a safety net.
—Nicholas D. Kristof, "Medicine's Sticker Shock," *New York Times* (October 2, 2005)

The Katrina Tragedy should become a watershed in American politics.
—George Lakoff, "The Post-Katrina Era," *Huffington Post* (September 8, 2005)

Katrina raises the fact there are consequences for our actions—that there's a heavy price to pay for destroying wetlands, subjugating rivers, ignoring global warming.
—Carl Pope, "Ideologues vs. Environmentalists," *Miami Herald* (September 29, 2005)

I hope we realize that the people of New Orleans weren't just abandoned during the Hurricane. They were abandoned long ago—to murder and mayhem in their streets, to substandard schools, to dilapidated housing, to inadequate health care, to a pervasive sense of hopelessness.
—Barack Obama, statement released by the senator's office (September 6, 2005)

The people left behind in the evacuation of New Orleans after Katrina are the same people left behind in rebuilding of New Orleans—the poor, the sick, the elderly, the disabled, and children, mostly African-American.
—Bill Quigley, "Six Months After Katrina: Who Was Left Behind—Then and Now," *Common Dreams* (February 21, 2006)

When we look back at Katrina, we may see that the greatest savagery was that of our public officials.
—Rebecca Solnit, "The Uses of Disaster: Notes on Bad Weather and Good Government," *Harper's* (September 9, 2005)

Hurricane Katrina is George Bush's Monica Lewinsky. The only difference is that tens of thousands of people weren't stranded in Monica Lewinsky's vagina.
—Jon Stewart, on "The Daily Show," Comedy Central (September 7, 2005)

Katrina remains a stain on our nation, not only because it exposes for all the depth of our racial and class divide, but the hollowness of our promises to right these wrongs.
—James J. Zogby, "The Shame of Katrina Is Still With Us," *Huffington Post* (April 21, 2006)

Impeachment

There can be no serious question that warrantless wiretapping, in violation of the law, is impeachable.
—John W. Dean, "George W. Bush as the New Richard M. Nixon: Both Wiretapped Illegally, and Impeachably," FindLaw (December 30, 2005)

Willful disregard of a law . . . is at least as impeachable as having a sexual escapade under the Oval Office desk and lying about it later.
—Thomas G. Donlan, "Unwarranted Executive Power," *Barron's Online* (December 26, 2005)

These are not grounds for impeachment. These are grounds for divorce.
—Maureen Dowd, on Bill Clinton's affair with Monica Lewinsky, quoted in the *Guardian (UK)* (September 14, 1998)

Bush is lucky that he had a Republican Congress, or he almost certainly would have been impeached and imprisoned.
—Al Franken, *The Truth (With Jokes)* (2005)

Any President who maintains that he is above the law—and repeatedly violates the law—thereby commits high crimes and misdemeanors, the constitutional standard for impeachment and removal of office.
—Elizabeth Holtzman, "The Impeachment of George W. Bush," *Nation* (January 30, 2006). Former Congresswoman Holtzman served on the House Judiciary Committee during the impeachment proceeding against Richard Nixon.

Leaking the names of CIA agents is not politics; it is a crime.
—James Moore, "The Criminalization of Criminals," *Huffington Post* (October 28, 2005)

121 to 29.
—Outcome of a Newfane, Vermont, town meeting vote in which residents said George W. Bush should be impeached, "Small Town Provokes Big Outrage," *Boston Globe* (March 18, 2006)

Two words: Dick Cheney.
—Harry Reid, on why incoming Democrats were unlikely to impeach Bush, quoted in "Washington Whispers," *U.S. News & World Report* (November 19, 2006)

Resolved, that the Democratic Party of New Mexico supports the impeachment of President George Bush and his lawful removal from office.
—Resolution passed by delegates to state party convention, quoted in "New Mexico Democrats call for Bush impeachment," *Santa Fe New Mexican* (March 21, 2006)

Corporations took over America using politicians as sock puppets. It certainly makes a difference who sits in office, but we have not solved our problems if we impeach one of the socks.
—Rev. Jim Rigby, "Progressives: Stop Waiting for a Hero," *Huffington Post* (July 4, 2006)

Clinton lied about a blow job, and got impeached by the media and Congress. [Bush] got us into [the Iraq] war based on lies . . . yet no one in the media is calling for impeachment.
—Tim Robbins, "Hollywood Star Robbins Blasts U.S. Media Ignorance of 'High Crimes' in Iraq," *Agence France Presse* (May 2, 2006)

The framers of our Constitution feared executive power run amok and provided the remedy of impeachment to protect against it.
—Elizabeth Holtzman, "The Impeachment of George W. Bush," *Nation* (January 30, 2006)

Jail to the Chief
—T-shirt

Law

No community suffers from too much rule of law.
—Kofi A. Annan, "What I've Learned," *Washington Post* (December 11, 2006)

No free man shall be seized or imprisoned, or stripped of his rights or posses-sions, or outlawed or exiled, or deprived of his standing in any other way, nor will we proceed with force against him, or send others to do so, except by the lawful judgment of his equals or by the law of the land.
—Article 39, Magna Carta (1215)

For a corporation, compliance with law, like everything else, is a matter of costs and benefits.
—Joel Bakan, *The Corporation: The Pathological Pursuit of Profit and Power* (2004)

Law is a bit like a printing press—it's kind of neutral, you can make it do anything.
—Noam Chomsky, *Understanding Power* (2002)

We must be governed by the force of law, not by the law of force.
—Rev. William Sloane Coffin, quoted in "A Genius of a Man, He Believed in Hope," *Boston Globe* (April 24, 2006)

What does it say about our nation's commitment to the rule of law that this nominee will not say that torture is against the law?
—Christopher Dodd, voting against the nomination of Albert Gonzales to be attorney general, quoted in "Disunited Opposition to Gonzales," *Nation* (February 2, 2005)

Bush has issued more signing statements . . . more provisions of more laws than all forty-two of America's previous presidents combined. He has used these statements not merely to express his opinions regarding legislation pre-sented to him for his signature, but also to suggest that he does not feel bound to obey the bills he has just signed into law.
—Mickey Edwards, "The Erosion of American Constitutional Principle," *Huffington Post* (July 18, 2006)

I was taught that it was the Congress that makes the laws, and the president's supposed to sign them, and he's supposed to enforce them. He's not just supposed to make them up.
—Russ Feingold, interviewed on "The Daily Show," quoted in "Jon Stewart Plugs Feingold's Censure Call," the Associated Press (AP) (March 23, 2006)

An unjust law is itself a species of violence. Arrest for its breach is more so.
—Mahatma Gandhi, *Non-Violence in Peace and War* (1949)

We have made a mockery of the very international laws that we once used to protect our prisoners, and we lost an opportunity to distinguish our democratic values from the authoritarian impulses of our adversaries.
—James S. Hirsch, "America has Lost Its Moral Authority on POWs," *Boston Globe* (May 22, 2004)

The vast majority still believe in strong laws to keep our air and water clean, our families healthy and our beautiful landscapes preserved.
—Robert F. Kennedy, Jr., "Nature: A Real Moral Value," AlterNet (January 11, 2005)

It may be true that the law cannot make a man love me, but it can keep him from lynching me, and I think that's pretty important.
—Rev. Martin Luther King, Jr., *Wall Street Journal* (November 13, 1962)

State laws that create corporations promote behavior which managers and shareholders do not condone in their personal lives. Those laws encourage managers to act as if shareholders are psychopaths—concerned only that their company makes more and more money without regard for the human or environmental costs.
—Lois A. Levin and Robert C. Hinkley, "Is Corporate Social Responsibility an Oxymoron?" *Common Dreams* (July 26, 2004)

No one is above the law.
—George Lakoff, *Thinking Points: Communicating Our American Values and Vision* (2006)

You must remember that that some things that are legally right are not morally right.
—Abraham Lincoln, letter to John J. Crittenden (December 22, 1859)

We . . . have, at least as a matter of political language, internalized the fiction that liberal judges "make" law, while conservative judges "interpret" it.
—Dahlia Lithwick, "Of Judicial Activism and 'Re-activism,'" *St. Paul Pioneer Press* (August 18, 2004)

Those less favored in life should be more favored in law.
—Thomas Reed Powell, quoted in *Losing Our Democracy* (2006)

The real scandal in Washington is the everyday bribery that remains legal.
—Robert B. Reich, "Keeping Up Appearances," *American Prospect* (January 17, 2007)

Laws are like cobwebs, which may catch small flies, but let wasps and hornets break through.
—Jonathan Swift, *Gulliver's Travels* (1726)

It is the spirit and not the form of the law that keeps justice alive.
—Earl Warren, "The Law and the Future," *Fortune* (November 1955)

Lobbying

Corporate interests spend more money on lobbying than the federal government spends on the staff of Congress.
—Lou Dobbs, interviewed by Bill Moyers, "Outsourcing and Patriotism," Alternet (August 21, 2004)

Corporate lobbyists . . . have developed a "corporate state" where government lavishes subsidies, inflated contracts, guarantees, and research and development and natural resources giveaways on big business—while denying comparable benefits to individuals and family businesses.
—Ralph Nader, "Corporate Socialism," *Washington Post* (July 18, 2002)

Lobbying today is essentially legalized bribery.
—Press release for Public Citizen, a nonprofit public interest organization (January 6, 2006)

The number of lobbyists in Washington has doubled over the past ten years. Now, there are sixty of them for every single member of Congress.
—Robert Reich, "Keeping Up Appearances," *American Prospect* (January 17, 2007)

When it comes to social issues like gay marriage and a woman's right to choose, give me a Democrat any day; but when it comes to issues of war and peace, I am afraid the Democrats are getting their strings pulled by the same greed-infected puppeteers that are pulling the strings of the Republicans.
—Cindy Sheehan, "Cure the Disease," *Common Dreams* (June 13, 2006)

Average Americans who get up and go to work every day, raise their kids the best they can, and play by the rules don't have the high-paid lobbyists jamming the halls of the Senate . . . rigging the tax system in their favor.
—Paul Wellstone, news release, "Wellstone Ups the Ante on Marriage Penalty Tax Relief" (July 29, 1999)

Both parties are parasitic on corporate interests and powerful lobbyists. They are both part of a government that can be characterized at least in part as legalized bribery, normalized corruption, and institutionalized graft.
—Cornel West, interviewed by Terrence McNally, "Matters of Justice," AlterNet (September 29, 2004)

Corporate lobbyists are why one in six Americans has no health insurance even though almost two-thirds want a universal government healthcare system that would provide coverage to everyone.
—Gary Younge, "Like Arsenic in the Water Supply, Lobbyists Have Poisoned Washington," *Guardian (UK)* (January 9, 2006)

Power

Power abdicates only under stress of counter-power.
—Martin Buber, *Paths in Utopia* (1946)

If you lessen your anger at the structures of power you lower your love for the victims of power.
—Rev. William Sloane Coffin, address at Ripon College, "The Spiritual and the Secular: Can They Meet?" (September 29, 1996)

Our whole system is rigged to keep the incumbents in office.
—Mario Cuomo, quoted in *The Great Incumbency Machine, New York Times magazine* (September 27, 1992)

Power concedes nothing without a demand. It never did, and it never will.
—Frederick Douglass, in a letter to Gerrit Smith (March 30, 1849)

Christ's birth is not a silent night—it's the beginning of a revolution that threatened to undermine the whole basis of Roman power.
—Rev. Giles Fraser, "Empires Prefer a Baby and the Cross to the Adult Jesus," *Guardian (UK)* (December 24, 2004)

Media monopoly and militarism go hand-in-hand.
—Amy Goodman, quoted in "Voice of America," AlterNet (February 14, 2005)

The kiss-ass media, the revolving-door congressmen, the sycophant lobbyists and congressional staffers, the greedy media consultants—all are dependent on and addicted to the trappings of power.
—Don Hazen, "Stephen Colbert: New American Hero," AlterNet (May 9, 2006)

There are two types of power: Organized money and organized people.
—Linda Jeffers, New Orleans mayoral candidate, quoted in "Big Business Sees A Chance For Ethnic and Class Cleansing," *Guardian (UK)* (April 20, 2006)

Everyone lines up in some relationship to power, either in defense of, or resistance to. Claims of taking a neutral stance—especially when made by privileged professionals—are illusory; neutrality is simply another way of supporting the existing distribution of power.
—Robert Jensen, "September 11 and the Politics of University Teaching," *Common Dreams* (December 6, 2001)

The concentration of wealth and power in the hands of the few is the death knell of democracy. No republic in the history of humanity has survived this.
—Garrison Keillor, "We're Not in Lake Wobegon Anymore," *In These Times* (August 26, 2004)

Men who create power make an indispensable contribution to the nation's greatness—but men who question power make a contribution just as indispensable—for they determine whether we use power, or power uses us.
—John F. Kennedy, in honor of Robert Frost, quoted in "Galbraith Remembered," *Nation* (June 1, 2006)

Power at its best is love implementing the demands of justice, and justice at its best is power correcting everything that stands against love.
—Rev. Martin Luther King, Jr., in an address to the Southern Christian Leadership Conference, "Where Do We Go from Here?" (August 16, 1967)

Just speaking truth to power doesn't work. You need to frame the truths from your perspective.
—George Lakoff, *Don't Think Like an Elephant* (2004)

Power-worship blurs political judgment because it leads, almost unavoidably, to the belief that present trends will continue. Whoever is winning at the moment will always seem to be invincible.
—George Orwell, *Shooting an Elephant* (1950)

Fortunately, power has a shelf life.
—Arundhati Roy, quoted in *The Impossible Will Take a Little While Longer* (2003)

All over the world, autocratic-minded rulers . . . have learned that de facto control of the political content of television is perhaps the most important lever of power in our day.
—Jonathan Schell, "Too Late for Empire," *Nation* (August 14, 2006)

The powerful used to just take what they wanted by the sword. The rise of democracy required the powerful to trade in the sword for the con job: Just manipulate the people into choosing against their true interests.
—Andrew Bard Schmookler, "A Nation Deceived," *Baltimore Sun* (October 27, 2004)

Power, like a desolating pestilence, pollutes whate'er it touches.
—Percy Bysshe Shelley, "Queen Mab" (1813)

We must never delude ourselves into thinking that physical power is a substitute for moral power, which is the true sign of national greatness.
—Adlai Stevenson, in a speech in Hartford, Connecticut (September 18, 1952)

Be neither a hammer nor a nail.
—Anonymous

The question is, how great an imbalance in the possession of power, as represented by money, can a democratic society take?
—Nicholas von Hoffman, "Here's a Capital Idea: Make the Rich Pay Taxes!" *New York Observer* (March 26, 2001)

The right has a different attitude toward power than the left does—they know what power is, they know they want to get it, and they know they want to keep it. The left are much more suspicious of power. Their heroes are the outsiders.
—Paul Waldman, in an interview with Mark Karlin, "Paul Waldman Knows Progressives Can Win—and Here's How," *BuzzFlash* (May 25, 2006)

People who seem to have no power, whether working people, people of color, or women—once they organize and protest and create movements—have a voice no government can suppress.
—Howard Zinn, quoted in an interview with Terrence McNally in "Howard Zinn: Vision and Voice," AlterNet (October 21, 2005)

Privatization

Governments have abdicated much of their control over the corporation, despite its flawed character, by freeing it from legal constraints through deregulation and by granting it ever greater authority over society through privatization.
—Joel Bakan, *The Corporation: The Pathological Pursuit of Profit and Power* (2004)

Privatization is not about limiting government; it is about terminating democracy.
—Benjamin Barber, quoted in "The 500-Pound Gorilla," *Phi Delta Kappan* (October 2002)

When the government privatizes the disaster planning, abatement, and relief efforts, it puts your life in the hands of the lowest bidder.
—Charlie Demerjian, "New Orleans Catastrophe Down to Privatization," *Inquirer (UK)* (September 6, 2005)

Government offices are filled with private contractors, doing roughly the same work as the government employees sitting next to them—but frequently getting paid far more, often for inferior performance and without the commitment to their agencies' mission.
—Editorial, "The State of Corporate Welfare," *Multinational Monitor* (September/October 2006)

Privatization means corporate control of our schools.
—Robert Freeman, "Are We Buying Our 'McStudent' Lie?" *San Francisco Chronicle* (January 18, 2005)

Look at how many times the Republicans have said, over and over and over again, starting back in the sixties, that government is bad. . . . "Therefore, let's replace government with corporate governance. Instead of the people's elected officials, let's replace government answerable to the people with corporate boards of directors."
—Thom Hartmann, "Thom Hartmann Brings Context to Today's Political Frays," *BuzzFlash* (February 7, 2006)

For all of their pretensions about being self-made, self-reliant entities, the corporate powers could not function without the public infrastructure that so many of them scorn, try to privatize, and seek to defund.
—Jim Hightower, "Blasting American Infrastructure Away," AlterNet (November 29, 2006)

There are now more people doing federal jobs under corporate contract than there are people employed directly by the federal government.
—Jim Hightower, "The Bushites Have Outsourced Our Government to Their Pals," *Hightower Lowdown* (June 2007)

Whatever its form, privatization is based on the general concept that business is good, government is bad.
—Susan Jhirad, "The Public Cost of Privatization," *Boston Globe* (December 3, 2004)

Privatizing education is predicated on an almost childlike faith in competition: let self-interested people struggle against one another, and somehow all of them—even their children, presumably—will benefit.
—Alfie Kohn, *What Does It Mean To Be Educated* (2004)

Privatization . . . means policy is driven by profit-seeking.
—Robert Koulish, "A Corporate Takeover of American Borders," *Baltimore Sun* (August 21, 2006)

America is ruled by conservatives, and they have a private obsession: they believe that more privatization, not less, is always the answer. And their faith persists even when the evidence clearly points to a private sector gone bad.
—Paul Krugman, "A Private Obsession," *New York Times* (April 29, 2005)

Every other wealthy nation manages to provide almost all its citizens with guaranteed health insurance, while spending less on health care than we do. And there's no mystery why: we're paying the price for pointless, destructive reliance on private insurers.
—Paul Krugman, "Insurance Horror Stories," *New York Times* (September 22, 2006)

The real beneficiaries of Bush's plan to privatize Social Security are in the financial industry . . . Big campaign donors.
—Floyd J. McKay, "Bush Erasing FDR's Legacy While Waging Class Warfare," *Seattle Times* (February 16, 2005)

What all forms of privatization hold in common is a pulling back from concern for our shared public fate.
—Deborah Meier, *The Power of Their Ideas* (2002)

Without letting the American people know what is going on in recent years, the corporatists, who fund both major Parties, have been turning more and more essential governmental functions into business deals.
—Ralph Nader, "Outsourcing Democracy at Taxpayers' Expense," *Common Dreams* (May 10, 2004)

Governors and lawmakers, unwilling to tax the rich to maintain America's roads, are now taking bids to sell these roads to the rich.
—Sam Pizzigati, "Coming Soon to A Toll Booth Near You," *TomPaine.com* (May 8, 2007)

All that privatization typically gets us is a private worker with worse wages and benefits than the public one who was displaced.
—Joel Rogers, "'Privatize' Equals 'Redistribute,'" *Capital Times* (Madison, Wisconson) (August 26, 2002)

Government is different from making and selling stuff. A citizen is different from a consumer. Not every human need and every human desire has to do with getting and spending.
—Jane Smiley, "Marxism through the Looking Glass," *Huffington Post* (February 26, 2006)

Privatizing is the central theme of our times. . . . And our religious institutions have jumped on board, promoting a kind of privatized ambition and morality that works against the common good.
—Kathleen Kennedy Townsend, *Failing America's Faithful* (2007)

Secrecy

Information is the oxygen of democracy.
—Steven Aftergood, quoted in "Spying and Lying," *Nation* (December 21, 2005)

Sunlight is said to be the best of disinfectants.
—Louis Brandeis, *Other People's Money* (1932)

Secret detentions have no place in a democracy.
—Jamie Fellner, quoted in "New U.S. Court Ruling Sanctions Secret Arrests," OneWorld.net (June 18, 2003)

The people in government work for us. What they do is our responsibility because they do it in our name and with our money—that's why we have a right to know about it.
—Molly Ivins, "The Great Bush Reclassification Project," Truthdig (April 26, 2006)

Democracies die behind closed doors.
—Damon J. Keith, U.S. Court of Appeals judge, quoted in "Secrecy Is Our Enemy," *New York Times* (September 2, 2002)

Since 9/11, the country has seen a historic, regressive shift in public accountability. Open-records laws nationwide have been rolled back more than three hundred times—all in the name of national security.
—Charles Lewis, "A Culture of Secrecy," Center for Public Integrity (February 8, 2005)

It's an old story: the greater the secrecy, the deeper the corruption.
—Bill Moyers, "There Has Been Nothing in Our Time Like the Bush Administration's Obsession with Secrecy," *Huffington Post* (December 15, 2005)

Secrecy is contagious, scandalous—and toxic.
—Bill Moyers, "Journalism Under Fire," AlterNet (September 18, 2004)

In a nation where free speech is the last line of defense against absolute power, they don't want you to know, because the more you know, the worse they look.
—Jim McDermott, "The Big Chill," *Huffington Post* (May 10, 2006)

Media reports about secret prisons are not "shameless acts." The secret prisons themselves are shameless acts. Stories about NSA spying are not shameless act. Spying on Americans is a shameless act.
—Bill Press, "The War on Journalists," *Huffington Post* (March 6, 2006)

The Bush administration has quietly but efficiently dropped a shroud of secrecy across many critical operations of the federal government. . . . The result has been a reversal of a decades-long trend of openness in government.
—Christopher H. Schmitt and Edward T. Pound, "Keeping Secrets," *U.S. News & World Report* (December 22, 2003)

Under a veil of secrecy, government failings not only go unaddressed, they can fester and worsen.
—Nick Schwellenbach and Peter Brand, "Government Secrecy Oaths Imperil Public," *Springfield News-Leader* (December 8, 2004)

A government of the people and for the people must be visible to the people.
—Steven Shapiro, quoted in "New U.S. Court Ruling Sanctions Secret Arrests," OneWorld.net (June 18, 2003)

Secrecy and a free, democratic government don't exist.
—Harry S. Truman, quoted in "Secrecy and a Free, Democratic Government Don't Exist," *Common Dreams* (September 3, 2006)

Treason

There is no graver crime than to mislead a country into war, and then lie to cover it up.
—Petition, "President Bush: No Pardons for Treason," *Act for Change* (November 2005)

Bad as he was, Nixon didn't jeopardize national security for political revenge.
—Ted Rall, "Bush-Cheney Traitors Deserve Prison, Impeachment," uExpress (November 1, 2005)

It's the recklessness at the top of our government, not the press's exposure of it, that has truly aided the enemy, put American lives at risk and potentially sabotaged national security. That's where the buck stops, and if there's to be a witch hunt for traitors, that's where it should begin.
—Frank Rich, "Will the Real Traitors Please Stand Up?" *New York Times* (May 14, 2006)

Watergate's dirty tricks were mainly prompted by the ruthless desire to crush the political competition at any cost . . . but this [Bush] administration has upped the ante by playing dirty tricks with war.
—Frank Rich, "One Step Closer to the Big Enchilada," *New York Times* (October 30, 2005)

Did the Bush administration manipulate intelligence about Saddam Hussein's weapons programs to justify an invasion of Iraq? . . . I have little choice but to conclude that some of the intelligence related to Iraq's nuclear weapons program was twisted to exaggerate the Iraqi threat.
—Joseph C. Wilson, from the op-ed piece that prompted the Bush Administration to retaliate by outing Wilson's wife, a covert C.I.A. agent, "What I Didn't Find in Africa," *New York Times* (July 6, 2003)

Tyranny

The worst tyrants are those which establish themselves in our own breasts.
—Rev. William Ellery Channing, in a sermon entitled "Spiritual Freedom" (May 26, 1830)

Tyrants have known forever that first you make the people afraid.
—Alice Daly, "Antiwar Protester Draws Inspiration from Thoreau's Call for Civil Disobedience," *Globe & Mail* (Canada) (March 26, 2003)

I have sworn upon the altar of God, eternal hostility against every form of tyranny over the mind of man.
—Thomas Jefferson, in a letter to Benjamin Rush (September 23, 1800)

Of all tyrannies a tyranny exercised for the good of its victims may be the most oppressive. It may be better to live under robber barons than under omnipotent moral busybodies.
—C. S. Lewis, *God in the Dock: Essays on Theology and Ethics* (1994)

The accumulation of all powers, legislative, executive, and judiciary, in the same hands . . . may justly be pronounced the very definition of tyranny.
—James Madison, *The Federalist*, No. 47 (January 30, 1788)

Tyranny is always better organized than freedom.
—Charles Peguy, in *Basic Truths* (1943)

THE COMMITMENT TO EDUCATION

Creationism and Intelligent Design

Whatever their motives, they're giving the rest of us a bad name. We all get lumped into the stereotype that we're a bunch of yahoos and slack-jawed yokels who have no need for fancy book-learning and such.
—Mike Arento, central Pennsylvania resident on the Dover Area School District mandate that intelligent design be taught as science, "Intelligent Design Flap Makes York Look Foolish Again," *York Sunday News* (December 19, 2004)

Creationists make it sound as though a "theory" is something you dreamt up after being drunk all night.
—Isaac Asimov, in his address to the National Coalition Against Censorship (1980)

Paradoxically, when the Religious Right asserts intelligent design is science, it implies that faith in God is . . . inadequate, that it needs the imprimatur of the scientific method.
—Randall Balmer, quoted in "The Bible vs. Science," *USA Today* (February 5, 2007)

Why just one designer?
—Ian Bell, on the possibility of a committee of intelligent designers, "Whoever Designed the Universe Made a Right Mess of Religion," *Sunday Herald* (Scotland) (September 17, 2006)

The proper place for the study of religious beliefs is in a church or temple, at home, or in a course on comparative religions, but not in a biology class.
—Tim Berra, *Evolution and the Myth of Creationism* (1990)

I would defend the liberty of consenting adult creationists to practice whatever intellectual perversions they like in the privacy of their own homes; but it is also necessary to protect the young and innocent.
—Arthur C. Clarke, *1984: Spring; A Choice of Futures* (1984)

There is no "Complete Idiot's Guide to Creationism," but perhaps one is not needed.
—Andrei Codrescu, National Public Radio (August 25, 1999)

Accepting creationism, intelligent design, and other scientific-sounding hokum opens the door to a narrow religious reevaluation of nearly every observed truth of the last five hundred years.
—Editorial, "Unintelligent Design: The Loony Right is Hammering Science Harder Than Ever," *New York Daily News* (December 30, 2004)

Most scientists believe that teaching "intelligent design" as an alternative to evolution is like teaching the flat-Earth theory as an alternative to the round.
—Ellen Goodman, "The Pseudo and the Science," *Working For Change* (October 13, 2005)

Belief in "intelligent design" is completely compatible with scientific acceptance of evolution.
—Father Andrew Greeley, "Creationists Still Fighting Evolution," *Chicago Sun-Times* (February 11, 2005)

How much reverence can you have for a Supreme Being who finds it necessary to include such phenomena as phlegm and tooth decay in His divine system of Creation?
—Joseph Heller, *Catch-22* (1961)

Not only is Intelligent Design poor science, it is poor theology. It reduces God to a magic word to use whenever we are stymied by a lack of information.
—Todd Huffman, "Teach Our Children Well," *Common Dreams* (November 21, 2005)

Those who purge Darwin from America's schools must yell in order to drown out their own misgivings, the inchoate realization that they are barking at the moon.
—Russell Jacoby, "The New PC: Crybaby Conservatives," *Nation* (March 16, 2005)

The overwhelming evidence at trial established that ID [Intelligent Design] is a religious view, a mere relabeling of creationism and not a scientific theory.
—John E. Jones, judge who struck down the Dover, Pennsylvania anti-evolution policy, "Judge Rules Against Intelligent Design," *Washington Post* (December 21, 2005)

Creationism, intelligent design, and other claims of supernatural intervention in the origin of life or of species are not science because they are not testable by the methods of science.
—National Academy of Sciences, "Bush Endorses Teaching 'Intelligent Design' Theory in Schools," Knight Ridder (August 2, 2005)

Why don't we talk about astrology in astronomy class, why don't we talk about the Christian Science theory of medicine in medical class? . . . The point is, it's not science.
—Sarah Pallas, quoted in "Creationists Try to Edge around Ban," *Richmond Times-Dispatch* (December 5, 2004)

The foremost advocates of intelligent design are silent on whether that intelligent hand belongs to God or some other intelligent force, even including a space alien.
—Michael Powell, "Pa. Case Is Newest Round in Evolution Debate," *Washington Post* (September 27, 2005)

We should not give an inch in fighting to make sure our children are not taught nonsense.
—Robert M. Sapolsky, "Controversy over Life's Origins," *San Francisco Examiner* (December 10, 2004)

We're becoming a laughingstock, not only of the nation, but of the world.
—Janet Waugh, Kansas Board of Education member, on the state's decision to undercut the teaching of evolution, "Kansas Education Board First to Back 'Intelligent Design,'" *Washington Post* (November 9, 2005)

Any possible universe could be explained as the work of some sort of designer. Even a universe that is completely chaotic . . . could be supposed to have been designed by an idiot.
—Steven Weinberg, *Facing Up: Science and Its Cultural Adversaries* (2001)

Education

Public schools, like all public institutions, have come under an insistent ideological attack by those who are hostile to any tax-supported endeavor. If it's public, and if taxes support it, then by definition it must be bad.
—Jay Bookman, "Vouchers Sure to Hurt Those Most in Need," *Atlanta Journal-Constitution* (October 6, 2003)

Critical thought . . . the other national deficit.
—Bumper sticker

It will be a great day when our schools get all the money they need and the Air Force has to hold a bake sale to buy a bomber.
—Bumper sticker

We don't need elaborate testing to find failing schools. As one critic has quipped, zip codes would do just fine.
—John Buell, "Poverty and Educational Opportunity," *Common Dreams* (November 16, 2005)

It's revolting to me that students are being trained to work in corporations. It's obscene to me that the corporations are running the world.
—Helen Caldicott, quoted in "'Green' Means 'Black,'" *HopeDance* magazine (May 2006)

American public education is really composed of two systems—an excellent one that serves the children of the already comfortable and a wretched one that barely serves the rest.
—Mario Cuomo, *Reason to Believe* (1996)

What the best and wisest parent wants for his own child, that must the community want for all its children. Any other ideal for our schools is narrow and unlovely; acted upon, it destroys our democracy.
—John Dewey, *The School and Society* (1900)

Our standardized-test-driven schools reward the right answer, not the unsettling question.
—Barbara Ehrenreich, "All Together Now," *New York Times* (July 15, 2004)

We can continue to mass produce cookie-cutter students on the cheap and we will reap a generational whirlwind of well-regimented, intellectually impotent dullards.
—Robert Freeman, "Getting Our Money's Worth in Public Education," *San Francisco Chronicle* (January 18, 2005)

The Republican Party has become the stronghold of men who fundamentally oppose public education because they think women should school their kids themselves.
—Michelle Goldberg, "Saving Secular Society," *In These Times* (May 16, 2006)

Education begins by teaching children to read and ends by making most of them hate reading.
—Holbrook Jackson, *Maxims of Books and Reading* (1934)

Measuring failure doesn't mean anything if you don't have a reform plan to fix what isn't working.
—Rev. Jesse Jackson, on the so-called "No Child Left Behind" law, "Young African-American Boys Are in Crisis—And Nation Is Silent," *Chicago Sun-Times* (March 27, 2007)

Every child must be encouraged to get as much education as he has the ability to take. We want this not only for his sake—but for the nation's sake.
—Lyndon B. Johnson, *Public Papers of the Presidents of the United States: Lyndon B. Johnson (1965)*

Intelligence plus character—that is the goal of true education.
—Rev. Martin Luther King, Jr., in his speech in Washington, D.C. (March 26, 1964)

"Back to basics"? When did we ever leave?
—Alfie Kohn, "Feel-Bad Education," *Education Week* (September 15, 2004)

Don't let anyone tell you that standardized tests are not accurate measures . . . . They offer a remarkably precise method for gauging the size of the houses near the school where the test was administered.
—Alfie Kohn, "Fighting the Tests," *Phi Delta Kappan* (January 2001)

[No Child Left Behind] . . . is not about discovering which schools need help; we already know. This law is not about narrowing the achievement gap; its main effect has been to sentence poor children to an endless regimen of test-preparation drills.
—Alfie Kohn, "NCLB: Too Destructive to Salvage," *USA Today* (May 31, 2007)

Channel One, an advertiser-sponsored school television program, beams its news and ads for candy bars, fast food, and sneakers directly into the class-room for twelve minutes a day in more than twelve thousand schools. . . . Teachers are not allowed to interrupt the show or turn it off.
—David C. Korten, *When Corporations Rule the World* (2001)

Schooling is what happens inside the walls of the school, some of which is educational.
—Sara Lawrence Lightfoot, quoted in *A World of Ideas* (1989)

Education . . . is the great equalizer of the conditions of men—the balance wheel of society.
—Horace Mann, from his report as Secretary of the Massachusetts Board of Education (1848)

Even prisons and army units aren't as huge, impersonal, and anonymous as many schools are for children.
—Deborah Meier, *The Power of Their Ideas* (2002)

When Congress passes No Child Left Unfed, No Child Without Health Care and No Child Left Homeless, then we can talk seriously about No Child Left Behind.
—Susan Ohanian, quoted in "American Education: No Child Left Behind?" AlterNet (December 15, 2006)

The United States spends a far smaller percentage of its national budget on education than other developed—and developing—nations. Not only do we lack the skilled workforce we need; we are accumulating masses of dysfunctional citizens who imperil our society.
—Major Owens, "Education Mobilization," *Nation* (February 6, 2006)

Why, at the very moment that we are talking obsessively about academic "excellence" and leaving no child behind, are we turning our public schools into factories of rote learning and multiple-choice testing?
—Katha Pollitt, "Intelligible Design," *Nation* (October 3, 2005)

Public education is the single most important public institution in a democratic society.
—Wendy Puriefoy, quoted in *StraightTalk: Common Sense for the Common Good* (2006)

Constant testing will no more address the problems with our educational system than constantly putting an overweight person on the scale will cure obesity.
—Anna Quindlen, "Testing: One, Two, Three," *Newsweek* (June 19, 2005)

To educate a person in mind but not in morals is to educate a menace to society.
—Theodore Roosevelt, quoted in "A Textbook of Virtues," *New York Times* (January 8, 1995)

The question of what deserves to be taught—and what gets forgotten—is a political matter.
—Anneli Rufus, "New Battlefront Opens in the Textbook Wars," AlterNet (September 28, 2006)

If the object [of education] were to make pupils think, rather than accept certain conclusions, education would be conducted quite differently; there would be less . . . instruction and more discussion.
—Bertrand Russell, *Principles of Social Reconstruction* (1916)

Politicians scramble to build more prisons than schools and pay guards more than teachers.
—Robert Scheer, What Does It Say About Us That We've Imprisoned So Many of Our Minorities?" *Los Angeles Times* (March 7, 2000)

Do we want our kids to have the best education possible, or do we want millionaires and Wall Street speculators to have enough money to buy another yacht?
—Jonathan Tasini, "Democrats: Get a Real Economic Agenda or Become the Minority Party Again," *Huffington Post* (December 5, 2006)

In the field of public education, the doctrine of "separate but equal" has no place. Separate educational facilities are inherently unequal.
—Earl Warren, *Brown v. Board of Education of Topeka, Kansas* (May 17, 1954)

Education for Profit

Kids are not a captive audience for sale, our children are in school to learn, not watch commercials.
—John F. Borowski, "Pupils, Pawns, Profit and Pornography," *Common Dreams* (May 9, 2003)

How many parents are willing to turn their children over to companies whose principal goal is to make a profit off them? How many want them taught by the cheapest teachers, crammed into the largest classrooms, reciting only the most rote repetition?
—Robert Freeman, "Getting Our Money's Worth in Public Education," *San Francisco Chronicle* (January 18, 2005)

Most of the calls for "educational reform" today would have us do what we intuitively recoil from: make our schools even more machine-like, even more relentlessly mechanical. The "reformers" want to make schools into business-es, profit-making educational factories.
—Robert Freeman, "Competing Models for Public Education," *Common Dreams* (February 26, 2005)

What happens to schools when they are plunged into the marketplace? To begin with, they must shift much of their time and resources to, well, mar-keting.
—Alfie Kohn, *What Does It Mean To Be Educated?* (2004)

When business thinks about schools, its agenda is driven by what will maxi-mize its profitability, not necessarily by what is in the best interest of students.
—Alfie Kohn, "The 500-Pound Gorilla," *Phi Delta Kappan* (October 2002)

You leave things to the free market and the rich will go to college and the poor will go to work.
—Howard Zinn, quoted in an interview with Terrence McNally in "Howard Zinn: Vision and Voice," AlterNet (October 21, 2005)

WHAT LIBERALS BELIEVE *273*

Higher Education

The Greek system is founded on discriminations of race, class, and family—sugar-coated over the years as a "way to make friends."
—Susie Bright, "Delta Dawn, What's That Frat Pin You Have On?" AlterNet (February 28, 2007)

American opinion on the whole has shifted so far to the right as compared with, say, Western Europe, that by the general standards of the Western European democracies, the faculties in American universities are really quite conservative.
—Noam Chomsky, "One Man's View," *Business Today* (May 1973)

Never forget that Yale University and the Harvard Business School gave our nation the worst president and manager of civic affairs we have ever had. That's a stigma those otherwise respected institutions must bear. They helped create this monster.
—Bill Gallagher, "Treasonous Bush Fostering Fascism," *Niagara Falls Reporter* (January 31, 2006)

More and more, universities are influenced by the wealthy donors and corporations that exercise increasing power as public funding for higher education shrinks . . . That means that people doing work that critiques the fundamental assumptions of powerful institutions in this culture (one reasonable definition of a "leftist") are becoming even more marginalized.
—Robert Jensen, "Horowitz and the Myth of the Radical University," *Common Dreams* (March 24, 2001)

The typical American university is dominated by centrist to moderately conservative faculty members and administrators, with steady movement to the right in the past two decades.
—Robert Jensen, "Horowitz and the Myth of the Radical University," *Common Dreams* (March 24, 2001)

The Right's immoral fiscal policies are bankrupting the very principles we claim to cherish like access to public education and the possibility of upward mobility for lower and middle-class Americans.
—Katrina vanden Heuvel, "The Plight of Public Universities," *Nation* (November 27, 2005)

There is social control in loading young people up with financial obligations . . . . Would there have been a civil rights movement? Would there have been an antiwar movement if those collegians had been saddled with the debts our present-day young people carry?
—Nicholas von Hoffman, "Student Debts, Stunted Lives," *Nation* (March 13, 2006)

Only eight of the 30 fastest-growing jobs in America require a college education.
—Andy Stern, "Changing How America Works," AlterNet (November 2, 2006)

Learning

They know enough who know how to learn.
—Henry Adams, *The Education of Henry Adams* (1906)

There is, I think, no point in the philosophy of progressive education which is sounder than its emphasis upon the importance of the participation of the learner in the formation of the purposes which direct his activities in the learning process.
—John Dewey, *Experience and Education* (1938)

The logic [of the Bush administration] is impeccable. No child will be left behind, because no children are going anywhere.
—Percival Everett, quoted in *What Do We Do Now?* (2004)

The anxiety children feel at constantly being tested . . . drives them away from the material being studied into strategies for fooling teachers into thinking they know what they really don't know.
—John Holt, *How Children Learn* (1967)

Poverty must not be a bar to learning and learning must offer an escape from poverty.
—Lyndon B. Johnson, in a commencement address at the University of Michigan (May 22, 1964)

The Western arrogance of feeling that it has everything to teach others and nothing to learn from them is not just.
—Rev. Martin Luther King, Jr., in his speech delivered at Riverside Church in New York City, "A Time to Break Silence" (April 4, 1967)

The intellectual life is being squeezed out of classrooms, schools are being turned into giant test-prep centers, and many students—as well as some of our finest educators—are being forced out.
—Alfie Kohn, "Confusing Harder with Better," *Education Week* (September 15, 1999)

Knowledge will forever govern ignorance: And a people who mean to be their own Governors must arm themselves with the power which knowledge gives.
—James Madison, quoted in *The Mind of the Founder: Sources of the Political Thought of James Madison* (1973)

Everybody is ignorant, only on different subjects.
—Will Rogers, quoted in *The Will Rogers Book* (1972)

It is difficult to get a man to understand something when his salary depends upon his not understanding it.
—Upton Sinclair

What's needed are a million personal conversations between ordinary Americans. The complexities and nuances of color and culture, the disparities of wealth and education are best understood by learning the stories of each others' lives.
—Maria Luisa Tucker, "Finding Words to Talk About Race," AlterNet (January 16, 2006)

Dogmatism is the anti-Christ of learning.
—Alfred North Whitehead, *Modes of Thought* (1938)

Educators and politicians may say that students ought to learn pure facts, innocent of interpretation, but there's no such thing!
—Howard Zinn, quoted in an interview with Terrence McNally in "Howard Zinn: Vision and Voice," AlterNet (October 21, 2005)

Liberal Education

I don't believe that scholarship within the university attempts to come to grips with the real structure of the society.
—Noam Chomsky, "One Man's View," *Business Today* (May 1973)

The intellectual tradition is one of servility to power, and if I didn't betray it I'd be ashamed of myself.
—Noam Chomsky, quoted in the *Guardian (UK)* (November 23, 1992)

The case against the university is that it is chiefly a handmaiden of the state or of industry or, worse yet, of the military-industrial complex.
—William O. Douglas, *Points of Rebellion* (1969)

The surest path to wisdom is a liberal education.
—A. Whitney Griswold, "A Little Learning," *Atlantic Monthly* (November 1952)

Higher education stands as the only institution in American life today with a significant progressive presence.
—Christopher Hayes, "How to Turn Your Red State Blue," *In These Times* (March 22, 2005)

Education is a kind of continuing dialogue, and a dialogue assumes . . . different points of view.
—Robert Maynard Hutchins, quoted in *Time* (December 8, 1952)

Universities, by their nature, tend to be liberal institutions . . . Conservatives may bemoan the social forces behind this phenomenon, but there is nothing sinister about it.
—Steven Lubet, "Nothing Sinister About Liberal Campuses," *Minneapolis Star Tribune* (December 1, 2004)

America is rapidly privatizing its public colleges and universities, whose mission used to be to serve the public good.
—Katharine C. Lyall, quoted in "At Public Universities, Warnings of Privatization," *New York Times* (October 16, 2005)

Leftists in the academy have permitted cultural politics to supplant real politics, and have collaborated with the Right in making cultural issues central to public debate.
—Richard Rorty, *Achieving Our Country: Leftist Thought in Twentieth-Century America* (1998)

We seem to have forgotten that the expression "a liberal education" originally meant among the Romans one worthy of free men.
—Henry David Thoreau, quoted in *The Writings of Henry David Thoreau* (1906)

School Prayer

The State must be steadfastly neutral in all matters of faith, and neither favor nor inhibit religion . . . Government cannot sponsor religious exercises in the public schools without jeopardizing this neutrality.
—*Abington School District v. Schempp* (1963)

The answer to disputes over religion in public schools is simple: Keep the government out of the private religious lives of students. Leave decisions about when and how to pray (or whether to pray at all) to the home.
—Brochure entitled "Religion, Education, and Your Rights," Americans United for Separation of Church and State

The mindless notion that serious social problems can be solved by prayer in schoolrooms, instead of by thoughtful analysis and sufficient resources, appeals to no one but the radical religious right.
—Constitutional Amendment on School Prayer, American Civil Liberties Union (March 11, 2002)

Children in public schools are a captive audience. Making prayer an official part of the school day is coercive and invasive. What five-, eight-, or ten-year-old could view prayers recited as part of class routine as "voluntary"?
—Annie Laurie Gaylor, brochure entitled "The Case Against School Prayer," Freedom from Religion Foundation (1995)

I'm not making light of prayers here, but of so-called school prayer, which bears as much resemblance to real spiritual experience as that freeze-dried astronaut food bears to a nice standing rib roast. From what I remember of praying in school, it was almost an insult to God, a rote exercise in moving your mouth.
—Anna Quindlen, *New York Times* (December 7, 1994)

School Vouchers

If vouchers are ever widely adopted, they would further fragment a nation that is already struggling to define a common future.
—Jay Bookman, "Vouchers Sure to Hurt Those Most in Need," *Atlanta Journal-Constitution* (October 6, 2003)

Americans want to improve our public school system, not divert taxpayer funds to religious schooling.
—Rev. Barry Lynn, in a news release entitled "U.S. Senate Rejects School Voucher Proposal," Americans United for Separation of Church and State (June 13, 2001)

Vouchers would not be an issue if we properly funded public schools.
—Derrick Z. Jackson, "The Realities of School Vouchers," *Boston Globe* (July 10, 2002)

Sex Education

The Religious Right doesn't care about reducing abortions. If they did, their focus would be on reducing unintended pregnancies by providing sex education and contraception.
—Bob Burnett, "Why Don't Men Write About Abortion?" *Common Dreams* (March 29, 2006)

Abstinence-only advocates confuse education with endorsement. They are wrong, and their narrow-minded alternative to comprehensive sex education is hurting the very children they're trying to help.
—Editorial, *Oregon Register Guard* (June 14, 2005)

The burgeoning abstinence-only industry reflects a moral agenda that's not grounded in fact, science or reality. Yes, teens ought to be encouraged to postpone sex because it's better for their health and their well-being. But if they choose not to . . . they need to know how to protect themselves from pregnancy and disease.
—Editorial, *Atlanta Journal-Constitution* (December 9, 2004)

It is inexcusably lazy to let Hollywood and prime-time television stand in for an accurate education about sex and sexual assault.
—Courtney E. Martin, "Willful Ignorance," *American Prospect* (January 17, 2007)

Teenagers deserve sex education from teachers who are comfortable and experienced talking about sex, not just a randomly assigned wrestling coach.
—Courtney E. Martin, "Willful Ignorance," *American Prospect* (January 17, 2007)

Whether we see ourselves as traditional or progressive in our views about sexuality, we may not, in the end, have very much of a say over how our children will handle this aspect of their lives. . . . In the end they choose.
—Jean Jacobs Speizer, *Ourselves and Our Children* (1978)

The religious right has managed to manipulate the sex education curriculum to its own disadvantage—that is, increasing the number of unwanted pregnancies in this country.
—Rev. Tim Simpson, quoted in "The Left Reclaims Religion," *Choice!* magazine (September 9, 2005)

Teaching

Rigorous, creative teaching, not kill-and-drill test-driven instruction, fosters students' development into critically minded democratic citizens.
—Ross Collin, "We Must Challenge Bush Over Schools," *Capital Times* (Madison,Wisconson) (January 22, 2005)

I want students to be able to learn in ways that are meaningful to them and teachers to feel like they have the freedom to teach their kids. I want to stop . . . offering services only to those that can make a difference on school scores.
—Katie Martin, quoted in "Middle School Literacy Coach Reflects on NCLB," *The Message from the Middle*, Hawai'i Association of Middle Schools (August 2007)

Caring and compassion are not soft, mushy goals. They are part of the hard core of subjects we are responsible for teaching.
—Deborah Meier, *The Power of Their Ideas* (2002)

For the life of me I cannot fathom why we expect so much from teachers and provide them so little in return.
—Bill Moyers, "America 101," *TomPaine.com* (November 1, 2006)

Teachers now are expected to staff the permanent emergency rooms of our country's dysfunctional social order. They are expected to compensate for what families, communities, and culture fail to do.
—Bill Moyers, "America 101," *TomPaine.com* (November 1, 2006)

The task of thinking and teaching, especially in an age of emergent fundamentalisms, is to cultivate a faith in doubt that calls into question every certainty.
—Mark C. Taylor, "The Devoted Student," *New York Times* (December 21, 2006)

THE HUMAN CONDITION

Alienation

What truly alienates voters is a politician who won't stand up for what s/he believes in.
—Andrew Foster Altschul, "The Myth of the Moderate Republican," *Huffington Post* (January 26, 2006)

We are imprisoned in life in the company of persons powerfully unlike us.
—Ralph Waldo Emerson, quoted in *Emerson: The Mind on Fire* (1995)

The alienation I have felt comes from living in a country in which one segment of the population is drunk on triumphalism and another is hiding from the pressing issues.
—Robert Jensen, "Fighting Alienation in the USA," *Common Dreams* (April 30, 2003)

We are bemused and crazed creatures, strangers to our true selves, to one another, and to the spiritual and material world.
—R. D. Laing, *The Politics of Experience* (1967)

Without alienation, there can be no politics.
—Arthur Miller, *Marxism Today* (January 1988)

Children

Children have never been very good at listening to their elders, but they have never failed to imitate them.
—James A. Baldwin, "The Precarious Vogue of Ingmar Bergman," *Esquire* (April 1960)

Sociologists have spent decades comparing the kids of working moms with those of full-time homemakers, consistently failing to prove that the latter do better.
—Leslie Bennetts, "The Feminine Mistake," *Huffington Post* (March 31, 2007)

Children are being violated today less by sexually explicit rock lyrics than they are by shoddy schools, poor diets, and endemic poverty.
—Rev. F. Forrester Church, *God and Other Famous Liberals* (1991)

The future which we hold in trust for our own children will be shaped by our fairness to other people's children.
—Marian Wright Edelman, quoted in "Our Future Depends on How We Treat America's Children," *Money* (May 1995)

Children cannot eat rhetoric and they cannot be sheltered by commissions. I don't want to see another commission that studies the needs of kids. We need to help them.
—Marian Wright Edelman, quoted in *I Dream a World* (1989)

The U.S. locks up more juveniles for life without parole than all nations combined.
—Earl Ofari Hutchinson, "No-Parole Sentences Hurt Black Teens," AlterNet (November 16, 2005)

No day can be so sacred but that the laugh of a little child will make it holier still.
—Robert G. Ingersoll, *The Lectures of Col. R.G. Ingersoll: Latest* (1898)

The agenda for poor children isn't a mystery: prenatal care, adequate nutrition, decent housing, early education, smaller classes with skilled teachers, safe streets.
—Rev. Jesse Jackson, "Time to Push New Congress to Revive U.S.," *Chicago Sun-Times* (January 2, 2007)

This country is squashing its young. We're sending them to die in a war we don't believe in anymore. We're cheating them so we can offer tax relief to the rich.
—Garrison Keillor, "A Plan to Save the Country," *Baltimore Sun* (August 31, 2006)

I don't think there is any such thing as Republican children or Democratic children.
—Robert F. Kennedy, Jr., "Those of Us Who Know That America's Worth Fighting for Have to Take It Back Now from Those Who Don't," in his speech at the Sierra Summit in San Francisco (September 10, 2005)

Insecure kids look for the reassurance provided by tradition and authority, and find it in conservative politics.
—Kurt Kleiner, from a study in the *Journal of Research into Personality*, "How to Spot a Baby Conservative," *Toronto Star* (March 19, 2006)

All our children ought to be allowed a stake in the enormous richness of America.
—Jonathan Kozol, *Savage Inequalities* (1991)

The best reason to give a child a good school . . . is so that child will have a happy childhood, and not so that it will help IBM in competing with Sony.
—Jonathan Kozol, quoted in "The 500-Pound Gorilla," *Phi Delta Kappan* (October 2002)

Children are the prime casualties of modern war.
—Daniel C. Maguire, "The 'Pro-Life' Lie," *Common Dreams* (February 2, 2005)

Child-care workers are pretty much the lowest paid workers in America.
—Terrence McNally, "The Mommy Wage Gap," AlterNet (June 12, 2006)

Baby-happy conservatives are out-breeding liberals by a margin of some 20 to 40 percent. It's a fact. It's a trend. It's an onslaught.
—Mark Morford, "Attention Liberals: Please Breed," *San Francisco Chronicle* (September 29, 2006)

We in the developed world hold the key to ending child labor and sweatshop abuses.
—Anita Roddick, "The Price of Dignity," *Guardian (UK)* (September 22, 2003)

In terms of infant mortality rates, the U.S. tied for thirty-eighth in the world with Estonia, Poland, Slovakia, and the United Arab Emirates.
—Kristin Rowe-Finkbeiner and Joan Blades, *The Motherhood Manifesto: What America's Moms Want—And What to Do about It* (2006)

There are forty thousand kindergarteners home alone every day after school because we don't offer enough quality, affordable after-school programs.
—Kristin Rowe-Finkbeiner, interviewed by Celina R. De Leon, "The State of the American Mom," AlterNet (September 14, 2006)

How we care for our children speaks volumes about our society.
—Edward G. Rendell, quoted in press release "Governor Rendell Delivers 2006–07 Budget," (February 8, 2006)

Whatever is done to children, they are likely to do to society.
—Gloria Steinem, "I'm a Hopeaholic. There's Nothing George Bush Can Do About It," *Guardian (UK)* (September 13, 2005)

Not every child is a dominator or competitor designed to be a gladiator in the American cultural marketplace.
—Rebecca Walker, quoted in "Reimagining Boyhood," *New York Times Magazine* (June 13, 2004)

Children begin by loving their parents; as they grow older they judge them; sometimes they forgive them.
—Oscar Wilde, *The Picture of Dorian Gray* (1891)

Which scenario should provoke more panic: the possibility that your child may become one of the approximately one hundred children who are kidnapped by strangers each year, or one of the country's fifty-eight million overweight adults?
—L. J. Williamson, "Let Kids Outdoors: Crime Is Down, But Parents Shelter Their Children as If There's a Child Predator on Every Corner," *Los Angeles Times* (March 29, 2007)

Cowardice

What did acquiescing on Iraq get the Democrats? Substantively, they are complicit in the misadventure and will be part of the political generation that must spend the next decade or two digging out from the rubble.
—Marie Cocco, "Democrats' Fury, and Values, Go AWOL," *Newsday* (January 11, 2005)

Any coward can fight a battle when he's sure of winning, but give me the man who has pluck to fight when he's sure of losing. That's my way, sir; and there are many victories worse than a defeat.
—George Eliot, quoted in *Blackwood's* magazine (1857)

When cowardice is made respectable, its followers are without number both from among the weak and the strong; it easily becomes a fashion.
—Eric Hoffer, *The Passionate State of Mind* (1955)

"Vote for us—we kinda, sorta disagree." The [Democratic] Party leaders are so timid, spineless, and lacking in confidence that to compare them to jellyfish would be an insult to invertebrates.
—Arianna Huffington, "Democrats: Profiles in Spinelessness," *Arianna Online* (May 28, 2003)

We will have to repent in this generation not merely for the hateful words and actions of the bad people but for the appalling silence of the good people.
—Rev. Martin Luther King, Jr., "Letter from Birmingham Jail" (April 16, 1963)

Members of both parties voted like clapping seals for the Iraq war.
—Eric Margolis, "The Final Say," *Toronto Sun* (October 29, 2006)

To what level of cowardliness will this castrated Democratic Party descend?
—Ralph Nader, quoted in "Scorn, Anger, and Resolve Sustain Nader," *Portland Press Herald* (October 6, 2004)

We lose jobs, we lose medical care, we lose sons and daughters. Because . . . when the other side starts shooting, Democrats hoist the white flag of surrender and political cowardice.
—Stephen Pizzo, "The 'Retreat and Defeat' Dems," *News for Real* (December 14, 2005)

It's always easier to bully someone smaller than you. It would require too much courage and energy, for example, to challenge corporations for downsizing their work force while paying astronomical sums to their CEOs. It's much easier to blame Mexican immigrants, and put up fences to keep them from stealing our toilet-cleaning and berry-picking jobs.
—Philip Slater, "Why Americans Get Surly," *Huffington Post* (June 14, 2006)

There are young men coming home now without arms and legs because the Wolf Blitzers of the world were too afraid to lose their jobs or piss off advertisers bucking the war hysteria of the times.
—Matt Taibbi, "Blame for Iraq Extends Far Beyond the GOP," *Rolling Stone* (November 5, 2006)

Conservatives are cowards, and they hope you are, too. We're afraid, they shout. We're so afraid of terrorists, we have to become more like the things we hate. We're so afraid, we have to let our government sanction torture. We're so afraid, we have to let the government spy on us.
—Paul Waldman, "It's the Conservatism, Stupid," *TomPaine.com* (July 12, 2006)

Families

The religious right . . . espouses the values of patriarchy. They imagine a world of families with men as heads of household and women taking the role of their "helpers."
—Rebecca T. Alpert, *Voices of the Religious Left* (2000)

A democratic home is the foundation of a democratic state.
—Agnes E. Benedict, *The Happy Home* (1948)

Honor thy father and thy mother.
—Exodus 20:12

One's family is the most important thing in life. I look at it this way: One of these days I'll be over in a hospital somewhere with four walls around me. And the only people who'll be with me will be my family.
—Robert C. Byrd, *New York Times* (March 27, 1977)

I'm so sick of hearing about family values. Most of us are in therapy because of our families.
—Judy Carter, quoted in *Wild Words from Wild Women* (1999)

We define the family descriptively rather than prescriptively.
—Rev. F. Forrester Church, *God and Other Famous Liberals* (1991)

We need a sense that children are a shared responsibility for mothers and fathers.
—Karen DeCrow, quoted in "NOW at 40: What's Left to Do?" *Christian Science Monitor* (July 19, 2006)

At best the family teaches the finest things human beings can learn from one another—generosity and love. But it is also, all too often, where we learn nasty things like hate, rage, and shame.
—Barbara Ehrenreich, *The Snarling Citizen* (1995)

The family . . . is a necessary part of life, but it allows fewer opportunities for full human flourishing than public spheres like the market or the government. This less-flourishing sphere is not the natural or moral responsibility only of women.
—Linda R. Hirshman, "America's Stay-at-Home Feminists," *American Prospect* (November 24, 2005)

Moral values at the national level are idealized family values projected onto the nation.
—George Lakoff, "Our Moral Values," *Nation* (November 18, 2004)

The greatly expanded childless segment of contemporary society, whose members are drawn disproportionately from the feminist and countercultural movements of the 1960s and '70s, will leave no genetic legacy. Nor will their emotional or psychological influence on the next generation compare with that of people who did raise children.
—Phillip Longman, "The Liberal Baby Bust," *USA Today* (March 13, 2006)

There's a lot of talk about family values in this country. Yet in most states women with children can be denied jobs or given less pay, just because they are mothers.
—Terrence McNally, "The Mommy Wage Gap," AlterNet (June 12, 2006)

The right-wing ideologues who have championed outsourcing, offshoring, and union-busting, who have celebrated the same changes that have condemned American workers to lives of financial instability, piously lament the decline of family stability that has followed these economic changes as the night the day.
—Harold Meyerson, "'Family Values' Chutzpah," *Washington Post* (March 7, 2007)

When . . . the larger culture aggrandizes wife beaters, degrades women, or nods approvingly at child slappers, the family gets a little more dangerous for everyone, and so, inevitably, does the larger world.
—Barbara Ehrenreich, *The Snarling Citizen* (1995)

Patriarchy's chief institution is the family. It is both a mirror of and a connection with the larger society.
—Kate Millet, *Sexual Politics* (1969)

The politics of the family are the politics of a nation.
—Letty Cottin Pogrebin, *Family and Politics* (1983)

Narcissistic absorption in one's family is almost as morally unattractive as narcissistic absorption in oneself.
—Judith R. Shapiro, "Why Women Still Feel Persecuted," *USA Today magazine* (January 2006)

What makes the Iraqi babies and families less precious than ours?
—Cindy Sheehan, "War-Hawk Republicans and Anti-War Democrats: What's the Difference?" *Common Dreams* (October 4, 2005)

The religious right finds threats to the family pretty much everywhere it finds difference. To them, "family values" are rules that require everyone's family to look like their families, love like their families, and believe in the same things as their families.
—Rev. William G. Sinkford, "Family Values for Diverse Families," *UU World* (December 6, 2005)

Most American children suffer from too much mother and too little father.
—Gloria Steinem, quoted in the *New York Times* (August 26, 1971)

Happiness

Happiness depends more on the inward Disposition of Mind than on outward Circumstances.
—Benjamin Franklin, *Poor Richard's Almanac* (November 1757)

America is not a happy place. A generation of increasingly conservative policies has shrunk the American middle and induced not just fantastic inequality but a sharp decline in social mobility and opportunity.
—Will Hutton, "A Dark Week for Democracy," *Observer (UK)* (November 10, 2002)

My creed is this. Happiness is the only good. The time to be happy is now. The place to be happy is here. The way to be happy is to make others so.
—Robert G. Ingersoll, quoted in *What's God Got to Do with It?* (2005)

We hold these truths to be self-evident, that all men are created equal, that they are endowed by their Creator with certain unalienable rights, that among these are life, liberty, and the pursuit of happiness.
—Thomas Jefferson, *Declaration of Independence of the United States of America* (1776)

The ancient Greek definition of happiness was the full use of your powers along the lines of excellence.
—John F. Kennedy, to a group of foreign students (May 8, 1963)

Real fulfillment in your life will come from striving with all of your physical and spiritual might for a worthwhile objective that helps others and is larger than your self-interest.
—George J. Mitchell, in a commencement speech at Susquehanna University, *New York Times* (June 1, 2003)

I have never felt that anything really mattered but the satisfaction of knowing that you stood for the things in which you believed and had done the very best you could.
—Eleanor Roosevelt, in her syndicated newspaper column, "My Day," *United Feature Syndicate* (November 8, 1944)

Paradise is not the place in which you arrive but the journey toward it.
—Rebecca Solnit, *Hope in the Dark* (2004)

I hypothesize that Republicans, as a group, may be happier because, on average, they prioritize personal goals and largely identify with people similar to them. Compared with Democrats and Independents, their main goals are narrower and more selfish, and thus more easily obtained.
—Matt Vidal, "Republican Bliss: The Selfish Road to Happiness," *Common Dreams* (April 6, 2006). The Pew Research Center conducted a study that found that Republicans said they were happier more often than did Democrats or independents.

Those who are happiest are those who do the most for others.
—Booker T. Washington, *Up from Slavery* (1901)

Human Nature

Self-interest and materialistic desire are part of who we are, but not all.
—Joel Bakan, *The Corporation: The Pathological Pursuit of Profit and Power* (2004)

Man is fundamentally a creative, searching, self-perfecting being.
—Noam Chomsky, quoted in *The Chomsky Reader* (1987)

Without bonds of solidarity, sympathy, and concern for others, a socialist society is unthinkable. We may only hope that human nature is so constituted that these elements of our essential nature may flourish and enrich our lives, once the social conditions that suppress them are overcome.
—Noam Chomsky, quoted in "Utopianism, Human Nature, and the Left," *Dissent* (Winter 2001)

In spite of everything I still believe that people are really good at heart.
—Anne Frank, in her diary entry dated July 15, 1944, *The Diary of a Young Girl* (1952)

I believe that humankind is improvable, and that you can take common action for the common good.
—Joe Klein, in an interview with Onnesha Roychoudhuri, "Faking It: How America Lost Politics," AlterNet (May 2, 2006)

Someone who thinks well of himself is said to have a healthy self-concept and is envied. Someone who thinks well of his country is called a patriot and is applauded. But someone who thinks well of his species is regarded as hopelessly naïve and is dismissed.
—Alfie Kohn, *The Brighter Side of Human Nature* (1990)

The old notion with which I grew up was that human nature could be seen as progressive in its essence. That happy assumption is now in disrepute. It is as if we are coming to the end of the Enlightenment.
—Norman Mailer, *The Big Empty* (2006)

There is no original corruption in the human heart.
—Jean-Jacques Rousseau, *Emile* (1762)

Existence precedes and rules essence.
—Jean-Paul Sartre, *Being and Nothingness* (1943)

Neither brute nor angel.
—Arthur M. Schlesinger, Jr., on human nature, quoted in "Kennedy Insider Schlesinger Dies at 89," *San Francisco Chronicle* (March 1, 2007)

The blue state citizens make the Rousseauvian mistake of thinking humans are essentially good, and so they never realize when they are about to be slugged from behind.
—Jane Smiley, "The Unteachable Ignorance of the Red States," *Slate* (November 4, 2004)

Maybe each of us has the capacity to be a saint or a sinner, altruistic or selfish, gentle or cruel, dominator or submissive, perpetrator or victim, prisoner or guard. Maybe it is our social circumstances that determine which of our many mental templates, our potentials, we develop.
—Philip Zimbardo, *The Lucifer Effect: Understanding How Good People Turn Evil* (2007)

Humanity

Human beings may be the only species whose elimination would benefit all other species.
—John K. Bullard, "Heading for a Roasted World," *Boston Globe* (March 6, 2006)

We need to accept and apply this basic truth: that we're all in this together, like a family, interconnected and interdependent, and that we cannot afford to revert to a world of "us against them."
—Mario Cuomo, *Reason to Believe* (1996)

No man is an island, entire of itself; every man is a piece of the continent, a part of the main. . . . Any man's death diminishes me because I am involved in mankind; and therefore never send to know for whom the bell tolls; it tolls for thee.
—John Donne, *Devotions upon Emergent Occasions* (1624)

My country is the world; my countrymen are mankind.
—William Lloyd Garrison, *Prospectus of the Public Liberator* (1830)

Even in a time of elephantine vanity and greed, one never has to look far to see the campfires of gentle people.
—Garrison Keillor, *We Are Still Married* (1989)

We are all much more alike than not, and we are all loved and welcome here, exactly as we are right now, despite all evidence to the contrary.
—Anne Lamott, "Anne Lamott on God, Politics, and Parenting," *Press Democrat* (Santa Rosa) (March 13, 2005)

The goodness of humanity is always just a few inches from the surface, on the verge of being released.
—Rabbi Michael Lerner, "The Neverending Story," *Tikkun* (January 5, 2005)

Men's propensity to injustice is not a permanent aspect of community life; it is greater or less depending in large part on social institutions, and in particular on whether these are just or unjust.
—John Rawls, *A Theory of Justice* (1971)

What type of humanity would survive paradise . . . for paradise does not require of us courage, selflessness, creativity, passion: paradise in all accounts is passive, is sedative, and if you read carefully, soulless.
—Rebecca Solnit, *Hope in the Dark* (2004)

To be a moral human being is to pay, be obliged to pay, certain kinds of attention.
—Susan Sontag, in her speech at the Los Angeles Public Library on April 7, 2004, "Essay: The Truth of Fiction Evokes Our Common Humanity," *Newsday* (December 29, 2004)

It is through the truthful exercising of the best of human qualities—respect for others, honesty about ourselves, faith in our ideals—that we come to life in God's eyes. It is how our soul, as a nation and as individuals, is revealed.
—Bruce Springsteen, "Chords for Change," *New York Times* (August 5, 2004)

Human beings are chimpanzees who get crazy drunk on power.
—Kurt Vonnegut, "Cold Turkey," *In These Times* (May 10, 2004)

We need to assert our allegiance to the human race, and not to any one nation.
—Howard Zinn, "Put Away the Flags," *Progressive* (July 2006)

Life

Life is a long lesson in humility.
—James M. Barrie, *The Little Minister*, 1891.

Life is a tragedy for those who feel and a comedy for those who think.
—Margaret Cho, *I Have Chosen to Stay and Fight* (2005)

Life is precious. We're never going to get another one.
—Richard Dawkins, "Atheist Richard Dawkins on 'The God Delusion,'" interviewed by Terrence McNally, AlterNet (January 18, 2007)

My church teaches life begins at conception. It used to teach something else. Thomas Aquinas believed something else. Augustine believed something else. Now, it says it begins at conception.
—Mario Cuomo, on the Catholic Church's changing ideas on when life begins, "Meet the Press," NBC (August 7, 2005)

It's one of the great privileges of middle-class American life that we typically navigate our days in flight from boredom rather than murder, starvation, disease, or rape.
—Phyllis Eckhaus, "Terrornomics," *In These Times* (June 28, 2005)

Our way of life—our gas-guzzling, tree-destroying, extinction-producing way of life—is finished. We have to find a new way of life.
—Barbara Ehrenreich, in her Haverford College commencement speech, "The Apocalypse Is Yours Now," *Huffington Post* (May 21, 2007)

The corporate takeover of life in fact has already happened, but one of the most salient characteristics of our emerging corporocracy—this Republic of Business—is that it doesn't demand order, conformity, gray clothes, and Muzak; it presents itself as an opponent to those very things.
—Thomas Frank, quoted in *Conglomerates and the Media* (1997)

Man is the only animal who finds his own existence a problem which he has to solve and from which he cannot escape.
—Erich Fromm, *The Sane Society* (1955)

Life is about living, and about helping other real people get through this world with a minimum of pain and a maximum of human dignity.
—Doris "Granny D" Haddock, quoted in "Looking at Life at 75 Years and Counting," *Common Dreams* (February 12, 2006)

I have ever judged of the religion of others by their lives. It is in our lives, and not from our words, that our religion must be read.
—Thomas Jefferson, in a letter to Mrs. Harrison Smith (August 6, 1816)

The more appliances that middle-class existence requires, the more influence their producers have over the texture of our lives.
—Robert D. Kaplan, "Was Democracy Just a Moment?" *Atlantic Monthly* (December 1997)

An individual has not started to live until he can rise above the narrow confines of his individualistic concerns to the broader concerns of humanity.
—Rev. Martin Luther King, Jr., quoted in "Streets and Dreams: Martin Luther King, Jr. Roadways," *Seattle Times* (1998)

Our lives begin to end the day we become silent about things that matter.
—Rev. Martin Luther King, Jr., quoted in "Making Noise on Global Warming," *Boston Globe* (December 21, 2006)

We're bugs struggling in the river, brightly visible to the trout below.
—Anne Lamott, *Bird by Bird* (1994)

Life, liberals believe, is meant to be pleasurable, God is forgiving if He exists at all, and it's important to think about others' feelings and motivations as well as your own.
—Roland Merullo, "A Puzzling America," *Boston Globe* (September 20, 2004)

The conservative mindset springs from what, for lack of a better term, might best be described as an Old Testament world view: Life is harsh, God is angry, enemies ought to be treated without mercy.
—Roland Merullo, "A Puzzling America," *Boston Globe* (September 20, 2004)

For 1,400 years the Catholic Church did not teach that life begins at conception. It embraced the view that a fetus is first endowed with a vegetative soul; then an animal soul; and when its body is fully developed, a rational, human soul.
—David Morris, "The Pro-Life Continuum," AlterNet (December 19, 2005)

If life is to be fully human it must serve some end which is, in some sense, outside human life, some end which is impersonal and above mankind, such as God or truth or beauty.
—Bertrand Russell, *Principles of Social Reconstruction* (1916)

The unexamined life is not worth living.
—Socrates, quoted in Plato's *Apology* (4th century B.C.)

The art of life is not controlling what happens to us, but using what happens to us.
—Gloria Steinem, *Revolution from Within* (1992)

An aim in life is the only fortune worth finding.
—Robert Louis Stevenson, quoted in *Author 101* (2005)

This is how we got where we are. You get a whole nation full of people who spend 99 percent of their free time worrying about their lawns or their short iron game, you convince them that they know something about something they actually know nothing about, and next thing you know, they're blundering into a 1000-year blood feud between rival Islamic groups.
—Matt Taibbi, "Saddam's Execution Was a Gargantuan PR Disaster," AlterNet (January 7, 2007)

The mass of men lead lives of quiet desperation.
—Henry David Thoreau, *Walden* (1854)

We are here to help each other get through this thing, whatever it is.
—Mark Vonnegut, to his famous father "Kurt," quoted in "Cold Turkey," *In These Times* (May 10, 2004)

Marriage

Whilst you are proclaiming peace and good will to men, emancipating all nations, you insist upon retaining absolute power over wives.
—Abigail Adams, in a letter to John Adams (May 7, 1776)

The only people who count in any marriage are the two that are in it.
—Hillary Rodham Clinton, quoted from interview on NBC's *Today* show, "Excerpts of Mrs. Clinton Interview," *Washington Post* (January 27, 1998)

Marriage is socialism among two people.
—Barbara Ehrenreich, *The Worst Years of Our Lives* (1991)

The married are those who have taken the terrible risk of intimacy and, having taken it, know life without intimacy to be impossible.
—Carolyn Heilbrun, "Marriage Is the Message," *Ms.* magazine (August 1974)

The notion that there is a fixed, unchanging standard of traditional marriage is itself a fallacy.
—Brian Holmes, "The Language of American Values," *Cornell Daily Sun* (January 26, 2005)

Divorce is as common among Evangelical Christians as among other faith groups.
—Jane Lampman, "A 'Moral Voter' Majority? The Culture Wars Are Back," *Christian Science Monitor* (November 8, 2004)

Marrying a divorced man is ecologically responsible. In a world where there are more women than men, it pays to recycle.
—Rita Rudner, *Rita Rudner's Guide to Men* (1994)

Well then what's to be the reason for becoming man and wife?
Is it love that brings you here or love that brings you life?
And if loving is the answer, then who's the giving for?
Do you believe in something that you've never seen before?
Oh there's love, there is love.
—Paul Stooky, of Peter, Paul & Mary, "Wedding Song" (1971)

Those who call themselves defenders of marriage . . . as only a union between man and woman—imply that anything different demeans marriage. But that's like saying that giving women the right to vote demeaned men's vote or that extending freedom to blacks demeaned the freedom of whites.
—Pierre Tristam, "Piety's Ruse: Invoking Sanctity to Label Different as Second Class," *Daytona Beach News-Journal* (November 25, 2003)

Meaning

We are meaning-seeking creatures. Dogs, as far as I know, do not agonize about the canine condition.
—Karen Armstrong, *A Short History of Myth* (2005)

The secular Left has virtually ceded the field of "values" to the Right, preferring mind-numbing social programs and plans without addressing the core emptiness that vast numbers of people are feeling.
—Brent Borgeois, "The Network of Spiritual Progressives," *Common Dreams* (May 23, 2006)

We religious liberals and progressive people too often simply cede our power to opponents when we leave interpretation of our religious heritage—or the meaning of our nation, or authentic "family values"—to the reactionaries, the chauvinists, and the bigots.
—Rev. John Buehrens, "Why Bother With the Bible?" *UU World* (July/August 2003)

I cannot imagine living without a purpose of changing the world for the better. It gives life meaning.
—Sheila Jeffreys, quoted in "The Ugly Side of Beauty," *Guardian (UK)* (July 2, 2005)

The meaning of life is not . . . explained by one's business life, nor is the deep desire of the human heart answered by a bank account.
—Carl Gustav Jung, *Man and His Symbols* (1964)

The meaning of life is what we choose to give it.
—Paul Kurtz, *Exuberance: A Philosophy of Happiness* (1977)

People have a need for a meaning to their lives that transcends the narrow utilitarian logic of the competitive marketplace and its materialist assumptions about what is important in human life.
—Rabbi Michael Lerner, "Tikkun at Eighteen: The Voice of Radical Hope and Practical Utopianism," *Tikkun* (November/December 2004)

He who has a why to live for can bear with almost any how.
—Friedrich Nietzsche, quoted in *Man's Search for Meaning* (1997)

People are looking for something to believe in. They're looking for meaning in life.
—Adam Werbach, quoted in "Is Liberalism Dead?" AlterNet (December 8, 2004)

Men

Do not put such unlimited power into the hands of husbands. Remember all men would be tyrants if they could.
—Abigail Adams, in a letter to John Adams (March 31, 1776)

There are a lot of men out there who need to stop acting like boys; who need to realize that responsibility does not end at conception; who need to know that what makes you a man is not the ability to have a child but the courage to raise one.
—Barack Obama, "Obama's Father's Day Sermon," Truthdig (June 19, 2007)

The human male has become the most predatory animal on our planet.
—Deepak Chopra, quoted in "10 Questions for Deepak Chopra," *Time* (January 24, 2005)

Men are now the weaker sex, geneticists say, and could soon disappear altogether.
—Maureen Dowd, *Are Men Necessary?* (2005)

I don't think the planet can long survive if the current conception of masculinity endures.
—Robert Jensen, "The High Cost of Manliness," AlterNet (September 8, 2006)

Steroid use in sports is a . . . window on Jock Culture, on its connection to the complicated, dangerous, exhilarating way manhood is measured in America from the field house to the White House.
—Robert Lipsyte, "Shooting Up on Jock Culture," *TomDispatch.com* (September 17, 2006)

We have reached the end of the road that is built on the set of traits held out for male identity—advance at any cost, pay any price, drive out all competitors, and kill them if necessary.
—Jean Baker Miller, *Toward a New Psychology of Women* (1976)

Don't accept rides from strange men, and remember that all men are as strange as hell.
—Robin Morgan, *Sisterhood Is Powerful* (1970)

There are millions of men who actually feel confident that women's freedom doesn't erode their own strength and sexuality and humanity. To those men, I say this: We like you the best.
—Beth Quinn, "Report: Men Are Reining in Those Uppity U.S. Girls," *Middletown Times Herald-Record* (March 13, 2006)

We are in our sixth year of government by gonads.
—Francis Wilkinson, "Who's Your Daddy Party?" *American Prospect* (June 1, 2006)

The world of men is dividing into egalitarian and patriarchalists—those men who are trying to learn the language and customs of the new emerging world, and those who are determined to keep that new order from taking root.
—Naomi Wolf, *Fire with Fire* (1993)

A real man is not threatened by the way other people live, be they gay, straight, atheist, Zen Buddhist—he is content to live and let live—and support laws that broaden human freedom, not limit it.
—Sherman Yellen, "Can a Man Become President?" *Huffington Post* (October 11, 2005)

Parenting

In my experience, there's not a dime's worth of difference between my morally conservative friends and neighbors and me in our attitudes toward the obligations of parenthood.
—E. J. Dionne, Jr. "'Family Values' for All of Us," *Washington Post* (October 7, 2006)

Americans once expected parents to raise their children in accordance with the dominant cultural messages. Today they are expected to raise their children in opposition to them. . . . Parents are considered "responsible" only if they are successful in their resistance.
—Ellen Goodman, "Battling Our Culture Is Parents' Task," *Chicago Tribune* (August 18, 1993)

In this vulgar age of war and institutionalized greed, let's resist the "kid-centered" parenting advice that so temptingly invites us to ignore the real world, and implies that our job as parents is to forever fine-tune our interactions with our own private offspring.
—Cynthia Peters, "Parenting in a Vulgar Age/Happy Mothers Day," ZNET (May 11, 2002)

All parents should be aware that when they mock or curse gay people, they may be mocking or cursing their own child.
—Anna Quindlen, "No Closet Space," *New York Times* (May 27, 1992)

Halloween is fast approaching and retailers across America are stocking up on slutty costumes for your daughters. . . . Our daughters are being pimped out and sexualized well before their time.
—Erin Kotecki Vest, "Pimping Out Your Daughter Made Easy!" *Huffington Post* (September 14, 2006)

It is the content of adult-child interactions, not the structure of families, that most strongly determines the shape of children's ethical development. That's what makes parenting a profoundly moral act, and learning to parent well a profound moral achievement.
—Richard Weissbourd, "Moral Parent, Moral Child," *American Prospect* (July 15, 2002)

Pregnancy

Half of the six million pregnancies each year in this country are unintended, and nearly half of these unplanned pregnancies end in abortion. . . . Most of these unintended pregnancies—and the resulting abortions—can be prevented if we eliminate the barriers that prevent women from having access to affordable and effective contraception.
—Hillary Rodham Clinton and Harry Reid, quoted in "Clinton and Reid Co-Author 'Common Ground' Abortion Piece," the Associated Press (AP) (April 18, 2006)

Our teen pregnancy rate is almost twice that of the next-highest industrialized nation. Yet we're wasting hundreds of millions on abstinence programs that have been shown never to work.
—Brian Dixon, quoted in "How Many People Is Too Many?" AlterNet (August 10, 2006)

My only regret about Mary Cheney's pregnancy is that it didn't happen earlier—say, during the 2004 presidential race, when Cheney was working for her father's campaign and his running mate was busy trying to write discrimination against people like her into the Constitution.
—Ruth Marcus, "It's a Cheney!" *Washington Post* (December 8, 2006)

Only four countries in the world—Lesotho, Swaziland, Papua New Guinea, and the United States—fail to provide paid maternity leave to all workers.
—Courtney E. Martin, "Wake Up, Employers: Working Moms Are Giving Up," AlterNet (December 20, 2006)

One of the most tragic stories that we've heard about is a survivor of a sexual assault who's been to the emergency room, been given the prescription, goes and tries to get it filled, and is obviously in an emotionally distressed situation already, and then denied access to the medication that can prevent an unintended pregnancy.
—Susanne Martinez, on refusals by some pharmacists to dispense emergency contraception, *Voice of America News* (November 17, 2004)

It is now quite lawful for a Catholic woman to avoid pregnancy by a resort to mathematics, though she is still forbidden to resort to physics and chemistry.
—H. L. Mencken, *Minority Report* (1956)

Pregnancy is different from any other state of being. The situation in which an embryo is permitted to grow over time into an independent human in the body of another is just not comparable to anything else.
—Anna Quindlen, "Bedroom v. Courtroom," *Newsweek* (November 14, 2005)

If women cannot plan their pregnancies, they can plan little else in their lives.
—Alice Rossi, "The Right to One's Body," *The Feminist Papers* (1973)

Life is tough enough without having someone kick you from the inside.
—Rita Rudner, on pregnancy, *Naked Beneath My Clothes* (2001)

Relationships

A fundamentalist mind sees the world simplistically. Such a mind cannot see the world in terms of fluid relationships and reciprocities, but only as a stand-off between the forces struggling for preeminence.
—Nick Bromell, "Scooter Libby and Me," *American Scholar* (Winter 2007)

People who have spent all day learning how to sell themselves and to manipulate others are in no position to form lasting friendships or intimate relationships.
—Rabbi Michael Lerner, quoted in "Bind Us Together!" *New American* (March 21, 1994)

We are so often wide awake about the decisions our elected officials make in the political, public realm and so asleep about our private choices.
—Courtney E. Martin, "Love Is Our Most Powerful, Lasting Form of Activism," AlterNet (February 14, 2007)

What kind of relationship do you want to be in? What sort of partnership will push you to be your best, freest, happiest self?
—Courtney E. Martin, "Love Is Our Most Powerful, Lasting Form of Activism," AlterNet (February 14, 2007)

The most important thing in any relationship is not what you get but what you give.
—Eleanor Roosevelt, *This Is My Story* (1937)

We consume too much when market relationships displace the bonds of community, compassion, culture, and place. We consume too much when consumption becomes an end in itself.
—Mark Sagoff, "Do We Consume Too Much?" *Atlantic Monthly* (June 1997)

Sex

Is sex dirty? Only if it's done right.
—Woody Allen, from the film *Everything You Wanted to Know About Sex* (1972)

I have looked on a lot of women with lust. I've committed adultery in my heart many times. God recognizes I will do this and forgives me.
—Jimmy Carter, in an interview in *Playboy* magazine (November 1976)

In a Bush World where commerce is king, it is all but inevitable that the dominant image of sexuality is that of a woman on sale.
—Lakshmi Chaudhry, "Babes in BushWorld: Raunch Culture Offers Good Old-Fashioned Pleasure, Republican Style," *In These Times* (October 28, 2005)

A hard dog to keep on the porch.
—Hillary Rodham Clinton, "Hillary Explains Away Clinton's Infidelity," *Guardian (UK)* (August 2, 1999)

The current morals/values debate, let's face it, is centered on sex and who gets to have it. We can broaden that debate.
—John Fairbanks, "A Real Discussion of Moral Values," *Barre-Montpelier Times Argus* (November 21, 2004)

Despite a lifetime of service to the cause of sexual liberation, I have never caught venereal disease, which makes me feel rather like an Arctic explorer who has never had frostbite.
—Germaine Greer, *Observer (UK)* (March 4, 1973)

George W is an absolute corporate wet dream.
—Jim Hightower, "What I Want for Christmas," *Hightower Lowdown* (December 2005)

No one has ever had a fantasy about being tied to a bed and sexually ravished by someone dressed up as a liberal.
—P. J. O'Rourke, *Give War a Chance* (1992)

The only aspect of sexual behavior that is subject to moral judgment is consent.
—Cameron Scott, "Queer 101: A Guide for Heteros," AlterNet (March 1, 2007)

Sexuality is not a choice—it is a natural, immutable orientation.
—Michelangelo Signorile, *Queer in America: Sex, the Media and the Closets of Power* (1993)

We should be afraid of government forces interested in repressing sexual expression. But we also should be afraid of the influence of misogynist pornography. These two fears are not mutually exclusive and can co-exist. Our fear of the former shouldn't stop us from critiquing the latter.
—Chyng Sun, "Revisiting the Porn Debate," *Common Dreams* (January 31, 2005)

Suffering

Suffering does not ennoble. It destroys.
—Dorothy Allison, *Skin* (1994)

Morality becomes hypocrisy if it means accepting mothers' suffering or dying in connection with unwanted pregnancies and illegal abortions and unwanted children.
—Gro Harlem Brundtland, quoted in the *New York Times* (September 6, 1994)

Why should any man, woman or child suffer for food, clothing, or shelter?
—Eugene Debs, from a 1908 speech quoted in *Debs: His Life, Writings and Speeches* (2002)

It's easy enough to decry the actions of world leaders and corporate CEOs, but some of the blame must be directed at each and every citizen who benefits from someone else's poverty and suffering, whether by purchasing affordable goods made by almost-slave labor or food farmed by malnourished migrant workers.
—Rachel Giese, "Our Greed Causes Third World Suffering," *Toronto Star* (July 19, 2001)

We become fully human when we are aware of another's suffering as if it were our own.
—D'vorah Kost, "Compassion Is the Only Way to Peace," *Seattle Post-Intelligencer* (September 1, 2006)

A genuine Left doesn't consider anyone's suffering irrelevant or titillating; nor does it function as a microcosm of capitalist economy, with men competing for power and status at the top, and women doing all the work at the bottom. . . . Goodbye to all that.
—Robin Morgan, *Goodbye to All That* (1970)

The world was but an inn at which humans spent a night on their voyage to eternity, so what difference could it make if the food were disgusting or the innkeeper a brute?
—Arthur M. Schlesinger, Jr., describing early Christians' indifference to human suffering, *War and the American Presidency* (2005)

Women

Woman must not depend upon the protection of a man, but must be taught to protect herself.
—Susan B. Anthony, speech (July 1871)

Women who abandon their careers and become financially dependent on their husbands often look back on that decision as the biggest mistake of their lives.
—Leslie Bennetts, "The Feminine Mistake," *Huffington Post* (March 31, 2007)

Issues affecting women are not soft or marginal, but are central to decisions involving all nations.
—Hillary Rodham Clinton, *It Takes a Village* (1996)

Take motherhood: nobody ever thought of putting it on a moral pedestal until some brash feminists pointed out, about a century ago, that the pay is lousy and the career ladder nonexistent.
—Barbara Ehrenreich, *The Worst Years of Our Lives* (1991)

I belong to a generation of working mothers who traded depression for stress.
—Ellen Goodman, "Mommy Wars Continue," *Washington Post* Writers Group (January 5, 2006)

Our lives are littered with mid-course corrections. Fully half of us are divorced . . . many of our career paths look like games of Chutes and Ladders. We have changed directions and priorities again and again. But our "mistakes" became crucial parts, sometimes the best parts, of the lives we have made.
—Ellen Goodman, "Reunion of the Ungeneration," *Washington Post* (June 1988)

Social conservatives have built their movement on hostility to women and women's rights . . . Many progressive religionists think they can build a movement of people of faith that ignores those issues and concentrates on the 1960s agenda of antimilitarism and the eradication of poverty.
—Frances Kissling, "Sex and the Clergy," *Nation* (November 24, 2004)

A generation of women insisted that the personal was the political, that they would only be in relationship with those who respected their full humanity, and we—their daughters and sons—are engaged in far more fair partnerships as a result.
—Courtney E. Martin, "Love Is Our Most Powerful, Lasting Form of Activism," AlterNet (February 14, 2007)

At this time in our history, for the first time ever, there are more women living that are single than are married.
—Joslyn Matthews, "Is Open Marriage the Modern Couple's Answer to Infidelity?" AlterNet (June 14, 2007)

Women have child-bearing equipment. For them to choose not to use the equipment is no more blocking what is instinctive than it is for a man who, muscles or no, chooses not to be a weightlifter.
—Betty Rollin, "Motherhood: Who Needs It?" Look (May 16, 1971)

We hold these truths to be self-evident, that all men and women are created equal.
—Elizabeth Cady Stanton, first women's rights convention (July 19, 1848)

Women become more radical as they get older. The pattern is that women are conservative when they're young. That's when there's the most pressure on us to conform, when we're potential child bearers and sex objects.
—Gloria Steinem, "Gloria Steinem," *New York Observer* (December 19, 2005)

THE PUBLIC'S RIGHT TO KNOW

Blogosphere

America is going to hell in a hand basket under a morally and economically bankrupt Republican leadership. We need an authentic and populist democratic movement to crash the gate and save our nation.
—Jerome Armstrong and Markos Moulitsas Zúniga, *Crashing the Gate: Netroots, Grassroots, and the Rise of People-Powered Politics* (2006)

I have a real sense of optimism that we are revolutionizing the way we do politics in this country. Through our site [MoveOn.org], ordinary citizens who once felt powerless are much more involved in the democratic process in a direct and meaningful way.
—Joan Blades, "Women of the Year 2003," *Ms.* magazine (Winter 2003)

The blossoming of the web has turned the Democratic Party on its head.
—Julian Borger, "U.S. Primaries: How a Coalition of Bloggers is Turning the Democratic Donkey," *Guardian (UK)* (June 22, 2006)

We don't want Democrats who can break bread with Republicans, we need Democrats who will cut their opponents' balls off and serve them back to them on a platter.
—James Boyce, "Lamont's Campaign," *Huffington Post* (August 8, 2008)

Internet engagement of a base of support does more than bring financial support. It gives leaders another channel for engaging with real people and to understand their issues and concerns.
—Wes Boyd, interviewed by Don Hazen, "MoveOn Muscles Up," AlterNet (April 26, 2005)

We are passionate about politics, and in this era of Republican corruption, excess and failure, that passion sometimes manifests itself as anger. But how can you not be angry? So many institutions have failed us in the last decade that being vitriolic seems the only sane response.
—Digby (pseudonym for a blogger) accepting the Paul Wellstone Citizen Leadership Award, "Digby Speaks: The Netroots Revolution," *Nation* (June 20, 2007)

Few liberal bloggers would dispute the notion that the national Democratic Party is a clueless, witless beast, profoundly disconnected from the views of its adherents.
—John Heilemann, "The Kos Campaign," *New York* (July 17, 2006)

On the left, the rise of the blogosphere has as much to do with the weakness of the Democratic Party as with the intrinsic power of the Web.
—John Heilemann, "The Kos Campaign," *New York* (July 17, 2006)

Blogging has empowered the little guy—leveling the playing field between the media haves and the media have-only-a-laptop-and-an-internet connection.
—Arianna Huffington, "Now the Little Guy Is the True Pit Bull of Journalism," *Guardian (UK)* (March 14, 2006)

The blogosphere is now the most vital news source in America.
—Arianna Huffington, "Now the Little Guy Is the True Pit Bull of Journalism," *Guardian (UK)* (March 14, 2006)

We have no interest in being anti-establishment. We're going to be the establishment.
—Matt Stoller, a blogger for MyDD, quoted in "Can Blogs Revolutionize Progressive Politics?" *In These Times* (February 6, 2006)

It's our responsibility to demand accountability from the Democratic Party and allied organizations that claim to represent our interests. If they refuse to reform, if they refuse to be more accountable, if they refuse to join this people-powered movement as it seeks to move our country forward, well, then they'll be relegated to the dustbin of history.
—Markos Moulitsas Zuniga, quoted in "Democrats Link with Blogosphere," *Knight Ridder Tribune Business News* (June 11, 2006)

The media elite has failed us. The political elite has failed us. . . . Republicans failed us because they can't govern. Democrats failed us because they can't get elected.
—Markos Moulitsas Zuniga, quoted in "Dems attest to growing clout of bloggers," *Seattle Times* (June 11, 2006)

Censorship

We, in America, have given over control of the media almost entirely to commercial interests in the belief that this free-market system works. . . . But what if someone gets control of the market and won't let certain ideas in?
—Larry Beinhart, "Censorship Isn't Mickey Mouse Stuff," *Newsday* (June 1, 2004)

Some of America's biggest technology companies have cooperated with the Chinese authorities to censor Web sites and curb dissent or free speech online as they seek access to China's booming Internet marketplace.
—David Barboza and Tom Zeller, "Microsoft Shuts Blog's Site After Complaints by Beijing," *New York Times* (January 6, 2006)

I'm tired of all the Bushit
—Bumper sticker, for which police gave a Georgia nurse a $100 ticket for displaying, "'Bushit' Bumper Sticker Owner Files Lawsuit," *Progressive* (October 17, 2006)

The voices of proud Americans on the left side of the political spectrum are muted. Occasionally, they will appear on Fox and other stations as guests, but they are like the dolls in the carnival booth on the midway. They are there to have objects thrown at them for the amusement of the onlookers.
—Phil Donahue, "Out in Left Field," interviewed by Bruce Kluger in *Time Out New York* (November 24-30, 2005)

The voices and stories of gays and lesbians cannot be silenced in our culture or on our bookshelves.
—Michael Gorman, quoted in a press release from the America Library Association (August 2005)

Books won't stay banned. They won't burn. Ideas won't go to jail. In the long run of history, the censor and the inquisitor have always lost.
—A. Whitney Griswold, "A Little Learning," *Atlantic Monthly* (November 1952)

In my more than three decades in government, I have never seen anything approaching the degree to which information flow from scientists to the public has been screened and controlled as it has now.
—James E. Hansen, NASA's top climate scientist on government, attempting to repress his views on the dangers of global warming, quoted in "Putting Some Heat on Bush," *Washington Post* (January 19, 2006)

We need more new ideas for more wise men reading more good books in more public libraries. These libraries should be open to all—except the censor.
—John F. Kennedy, *Saturday Review* (October 29, 1960)

There can be no real democracy if information is controlled, manipulated and censored. The corporate decision to censor critical reporting is pushing millions of viewers off their TVs and on to their computers.
—Jacqueline Marcus, "TV News Viewership Declines, Internet Use Rises," *Common Dreams* (January 21, 2005)

Virtually everything the average person sees or hears outside of her own personal communications is determined by the interests of private, unaccountable executives and investors whose primary goal is increasing profits. . . . More insidiously, this small group of elites determines what ordinary people do not see or hear.
—Bill Moyers, "Life on the Plantation," *Common Dreams* (January 17, 2006)

Scrotum.
—Susan Patron used this word in her Newbery Medal–winning *The Higher Power of Lucky* (2007), leading some school libraries to ban the book.

Corporate media censorship is an attack on democracy itself. It undermines the very fabric of our society by creating a highly entertained but poorly informed electorate.
—Peter Phillips, "American Censorship," *Common Dreams* (May 1, 2001)

Day by day, conservatives come closer to securing practically a monopoly on the mass dissemination of political ideas in America.
—James Ridgeway, "Reading From Left to Right," *Village Voice* (July 16, 2003)

The problem has not been censorship but something very nearly censorship's opposite: the deafening noise of the official megaphone and its echoes. . . . If you whisper something to your friend in the front row of a rock concert, you have not been censored, but neither will you be heard.
—Jonathan Schell, "Too Late for Empire," *Nation* (August 14, 2006)

Corporate Media

What I found inside cable news was a drunken exuberance for sex, crime, and celebrity stories. . . . The biggest fear is of doing anything that could get you, or your network, accused of being liberal.
—Jeff Cohen, *Cable News Confidential: My Misadventures in Corporate Media* (2006)

It may be decades before we see a single corporation controlling the entire flow of information, but we are certainly on that path.
—Flavia Colgan, "The Media Monster That's Eating the Dems," *Common Dreams* (November 17, 2005)

Corporate consolidation corrupts the nation's politics and marketplace, especially in the media industry.
—Chuck Collins, "Oversight Hearings: What Should Congress Do?" *Nation* (January 4, 2007)

This is the state of corporate media today . . . journalists trading truth for access.
—Amy Goodman and David Goodman, *Static* (2006)

Our very lives and liberty are at unprecedented risk because our press has long since disappeared into "the media"—a mammoth antidemocratic oligopoly that is far more responsive to its owners, big shareholders and good buddies in the government than it is to the rest of us, the people of this country.
—Mark Crispin Miller, "The Death of News," *Nation* (June 20, 2006)

American media have become a cesspool of political spin, product placement, and celebrity gossip. Popular information that matters, and the means of acquiring it, is being choked off by the handful of corporations that have come to control the vast majority of American broadcast and print communications.
—Editorial, "Media and Democracy," *Capital Times (Madison, Wisconson)* (March 5, 2005)

Television is driven not by the creative people who have something to tell, but by global conglomerates that have something to sell.
—George Gerbner, quoted in "Is Media Violence Free Speech?" Hot Wired (June 1997)

Of all the forms of concentrated corporate power in America that are harming our citizens, concentrated corporate media power is the most pernicious.
—Thom Hartmann, "Why Wal-Mart Is Not a Person," *BuzzFlash* (January 28, 2005)

Corporate media will serve corporate interests.
—Don Hazen, "Does Media Reform Have a Chance in the Digital Age?" AlterNet (January 11, 2007)

Democracy is premised on a free press, and freedom of the press is premised on the absence of public or private gatekeepers with monopolistic power.
—Robert W. McChesney, "Fight for a Free Press," *Nation* (June 15, 2006)

Corporate media pollutes the meaning of "fair and balanced" with the pretense that two well-rehearsed sound bites by representatives of self-serving interests constitute "analysis" of the news.
—Bill Moyers, "Address to PBS Annual Meeting," *Working for Change* (May 31, 2006)

We in the United States must try to reclaim our democracy from the accelerating grip of big-money politics and concentrated corporate media.
—Ralph Nader, press release "On Media Concentration and Bias" (October 30, 2000)

Whether it is television, radio, newspapers, magazines, books, or the Internet, a few giant conglomerates are determining what we see, hear, and read.
—Bernie Sanders, "Congress Can No Longer Ignore Corporate Control of the Media," *The Hill* (June 12, 2002)

The people who run our media are . . . promoting a culture of consumption, not of engaged citizenship. They want eyeballs for advertisers, not activists to promote change.
—Danny Schechter, "Manufacturing Indifference," *Common Dreams* (May 19, 2007)

We need to confront the roles of the corporate media in helping to drag the United States into one war after another.
—Norman Solomon, "Iraq Is Not Vietnam. But . . . ," *Common Dreams* (October 24, 2005)

The corporate grip on opinion in the United States is one of the wonders of the Western World. No First World country has ever managed to eliminate so entirely from its media all objectivity—much less dissent.
—Gore Vidal, *A View from the Diner's Club* (1991)

Journalism

American journalism is not represented by the media establishment, which has essentially been co-opted into an extension of government-sponsored propaganda, or else has demeaned itself into a Vanna White–style superficiality.
—Larisa Alexandrovna, "The Most Trusted Names in News (Really!)" AlterNet (August 25, 2006)

Given the many obvious and quite consequential differences between a blow job and a botched war effort, the Washington press corps appears to have reached a consensus that the former is a far more serious matter.
—Eric Alterman, "Lies about Blowjobs, Bad. Wars? Not So Much," *Nation* (February 20, 2006)

I do not remember a time I felt as unhopeful about politics and journalism as I do now.
—Carl Bernstein, in a speech at Auburn University, *Montgomery Advertiser* (September 22, 2004)

The president makes decisions; he's the decider. The press secretary announces those decisions, and you people of the press type those decisions down. Make, announce, type. Put them through a spell check and go home.
—Stephen Colbert, parodying the White House correspondents at their annual dinner, "Stephen Colbert's Remarks to the President," AlterNet (May 3, 2006)

The people who own and manage the great networks of America today are—and I choose this word thoughtfully—frightened of the word "liberal."
—Phil Donahue, "Out in Left Field," in an interview with Bruce Kluger in *Time Out New York* (November 24–30, 2005)

The once sacrosanct wall between editorial and advertising in TV newsrooms has all but crumbled to dust. . . . Local TV news is no longer in the business of shedding light on our social ills. It's in the business of keeping the viewer's hand off the remote.
—Kevin Foley, *O'Dwyer's PR Report* (April 2006)

Go to where the silence is. That is the responsibility of a journalist: giving a voice to those who have been forgotten, forsaken, and beaten down by the powerful.
—Amy Goodman and David Goodman, *The Exception to the Rulers* (2004)

The media have a responsibility to show the true face of war. But many corporate journalists, so accustomed by now to trading truth for access . . . can no longer grasp what's missing from their coverage.
—Amy Goodman and David Goodman, "Americans Deserve Media That Won't Bow to Bush," *Baltimore Sun* (April 7, 2005)

There's a reason why our profession, journalism, is the only one explicitly protected by the U.S. Constitution. Because we are the check and balances on government, we are supposed to hold those in power accountable, not cozy up to them.
—Amy Goodman, quoted in "Voice of America," AlterNet (February 14, 2005)

Over the last decade reporters have lost sight of the fact that their mission is to uncover the truth—not slip between the covers with the powers-that-be.
—Arianna Huffington, "On Awards, the Spineless Press, and Ann Coulter's Legs," *Huffington Post* (April 5, 2006)

The popular illusion that television journalists are liberals does them too much honor. Like all mercenaries they fight for money, not ideology.
—Ted Koppel, "And Now, a Word for Our Demographic," *New York Times* (January 29, 2006)

The press in this country will studiously ignore any story that too violently rocks the boat, whose implications are too shattering.
—Mark Crispin Miller, interviewed by Terrence McNally, "Election Theft Emergency," AlterNet (January 27, 2006)

The fundamental reason for the disappearance of the news . . . is the media cartel itself. Fixated on the bottom line, it cuts the costs of real reporting while overplaying cheap crapola.
—Mark Crispin Miller, "The Death of News," *Nation* (June 20, 2006)

The greatest moments in the history of the press came not when journalists made common cause with the state, but when they stood fearlessly independent of it.
—Bill Moyers, "Keynote Address to the National Conference on Media Reform," *Common Dreams* (November 12, 2003)

The quality of democracy and the quality of journalism are deeply entwined.
—Bill Moyers, quoted in "A Powerful Media Can Stop a War," Women's Media Center (January 16, 2007)

On the eve of his recent sojourn in Europe, President Bush had an unpleasant run-in with a species of creature he had not previously encountered often: a journalist.
—John Nichols, "Pampered Bush Meets a Real Reporter," *Capital Times (Madison, Wisconson)* (June 29, 2004)

Real news speaks truth to power and challenges the hegemonic top-down corporate entertainment news systems.
—Peter Phillips, *Censored* (2006)

Journalistic courage should include the refusal to publish . . . any statements made by the President or any other government official that are designed solely as a public relations tool, offering no new or valuable information to the public.
—Walter Pincus, "Fighting Back Against the PR Presidency," Nieman Foundation for Journalism at Harvard University (July 13, 2006)

Always fight for progress and reform, never tolerate injustice and corruption, always fight demagogues of all parties, never belong to any party, always oppose privileged classes and public plunderers, never lack sympathy with the poor, always remain devoted to the public welfare.
—Joseph Pulitzer, a formula for journalists, quoted in "Behind the Curtain," AlterNet (February 21, 2006)

What we're really looking at is the criminalization of investigative reporting in this country, and we're on a very slippery slope that we're already starting to slide down.
—Brian Ross, ABC investigative reporter, quoted in "The Enemy Within," *Village Voice* (January 22, 2007)

Skepticism and freedom are indissolubly linked, and it is the skepticism of journalists, their show-me, prove-it unwillingness to be impressed . . . [their] disrespect for power, for orthodoxies, for party lines, for theologies, for vanity, for arrogance, for folly, for pretension, for corruption, for stupidity, maybe even for editors . . . that is perhaps their most important contribution to the free world.
—Salman Rushdie, speech to the American Society of Newspaper Editors, quoted by Bill Moyers in "Address to PBS Annual Meeting," *Working For Change* (May 31, 2006)

Newspapers are unable, seemingly, to discriminate between a bicycle accident and the collapse of civilization.
—George Bernard Shaw, quoted in "Stop It Now," *Common Dreams* (February 12, 2007)

Why Doesn't Presidential Dismantling of the Constitution Get the Same Intense Scrutiny as Presidential Adultery?
—Andrew Bard Schmookler, article title, OpEdNews (January 17, 2006)

The incentive system in journalism today is to reward not the people who challenge power, but the people who worship it.
—David Sirota, "When Journalism Became Transcription and Reporting Disappeared," *Working for Change* (April 26, 2007)

There aren't necessarily two sides to a story if only one side has all the verifiable facts on their side.
—David Sirota, "They Didn't Jump the Shark—They Are the Shark," *Working For Change* (September 27, 2006)

It's very important to assess whether a journalist has been serving as a watchdog or a flunky for powerful government officials.
—Norman Solomon, "Other Shoe Dropping on Classified Leaks and Journalists," *Common Dreams* (January 23, 2006)

There is no such thing as Objective Journalism. The phrase itself is a pompous contradiction in terms.
—Hunter S. Thompson, *Fear and Loathing: On the Campaign Trail '72* (1985)

The balance fallacy is hurting the country. Presenting every issue as a he said/she said dispute, an unending, irresolvable argument, sounds fair, but what happens when one side really is wrong?
—Allan Uthman, "Bias, Balance, and Bullshit: 'Balanced' News Is Making You Stupid," *Buffalo Beast* (February 1–15, 2006)

Media

The left need to recognize this new paradigm. The media is no longer in the business of truth, or advocacy of the public good.
—Steve Almond, quoted in *What Do We Do Now?* (2004)

I think the press in general is a failed institution in this country. . . . The biggest problem with the media is first that 90 percent of Americans get their news from eleven corporations . . . And the second problem is that entertainment has supplanted news value.
—Howard Dean, in an interview with Matthew Rothschild, *Progressive* (May 2004)

The reduction of politics to a spectator sport . . . has been one of the more malign accomplishments of television. Television newsmen are breathless on how the game is being played, largely silent on what the game is all about.
—John Kenneth Galbraith, *A Life in Our Times* (1981)

Instead of learning from the media what is actually going on in the world, we get static—a veil of distortion, lies, omissions, and half-truths that obscure reality.
—Amy Goodman and David Goodman, *Static* (2006)

When the press acts as a conveyor belt for the lies of government, the lies take lives.
—Amy Goodman, "A Liberal Voice Shares Her Views, Trumpets Alternative Media," *San Luis Obispo Tribune* (November 13, 2006)

I want the American people to see where media takes politics in this country. We start talking about endorsements, now we're talking about polls and then talking about money. When you do that you don't have to talk about what's important to the American people.
—Dennis Kucinich, quoted in "Kucinich Makes Media an Issue," *Nation* (December 16, 2003)

Why have the media been so laid back, so unconcerned or even unaware that a corporate coup is happening in plain sight? An obvious reason is that the owners controlling today's conglomerated, centralized media are part of the coup.
—Jim Hightower, *Thieves in High Places* (2003)

We need a vigorous and an independent press that is willing to speak truth to power. And we no longer have that in the United States of America.
—Robert F. Kennedy, Jr., in his speech at the Sierra Summit in San Francisco, "Those of Us Who Know That America's Worth Fighting for Have to Take It Back Now from Those Who Don't," (September 10, 2005)

While various studies have debunked the myth of the liberal media, none has debunked the reality of the sleaze-hounding media and the journalism of trivial pursuit.
—Susan Lenfestey, "Public Scrutiny—of the Trivial," *Common Dreams* (November 5, 2006)

President Bush invaded Iraq on false pretenses, and many in the news media not only didn't question his assertions but served to legitimize them.
—Lois Melina, "Compliant News Media Have Failed the American People," *Baltimore Sun* (December 23, 2004)

You don't get rewarded in commercial broadcasting for trying to tell the truth about the institutions of power in this country.
—Bill Moyers, quoted in "Bill Moyers Retiring from TV Journalism," the Associated Press (AP) (December 10, 2004)

If you keep serving people crap and telling them it's a meal, they're eventually going to think it is a meal.
—Rosie O'Donnell, regarding the popular TV show *American Idol*, quoted in "Fox: 'Idol' Not Cruel to Contestants," the Associated Press (AP) (January 20, 2007)

The days of the "liberal" press are long gone. . . . This is a national media that will be suspicious at best and hostile at worst toward any broad-ranging progressive political program.
—Wayne M. O'Leary, "Controlling the Narrative," *Progressive Populist* (January 1–15, 2007)

We have a media that cared more about Bill Clinton's willingness to lie about fellatio than about President Bush's willingness to lie us into a war that has killed thousands, seriously endangered U.S. national security, and generally destabilized the Planet Earth.
—David Sirota, "They Didn't Jump the Shark—They Are the Shark," *Working for Change* (September 27, 2006)

What has become rewarded in political discourse is the extremity of viewpoint. People like the conflict. Conflict, baby! It sells. Crossfire! Hardball! "Shut up! You shut up!"
—Jon Stewart, "Jon Stewart Roasts Real News," CBS News (October 24, 2004)

A free and independent press is essential to the health of a functioning democracy. It serves to inform the voting public on matters relevant to its well-being. Why they've stopped doing this is a mystery.
—Jon Stewart and the writers of *The Daily Show*, *America (The Book): A Citizen's Guide to Democracy Inaction* (2004)

No matter who you are, or where you are on life's journey, you are welcome here.
—United Church of Christ message that CBS and NBC considered too controversial to air, quoted in "Love One Another? Not on NBC, CBS," *Nation* (December 1, 2004)

A flawed media leads to a flawed democracy.
—Katrina vanden Heuvel, "It's Not About Dan and Katie," *Nation* (June 13, 2007)

Propaganda

When some community group wants to force their local industry to take PCBs [cancer-causing toxin] out of the river, the corporations will form a group called Citizens for Healthy Rivers.
—Larry Beinhart, on the evils of corporate public relations, interviewed by Joshua Holland, "Reality and Spin in the Media," AlterNet (December 13, 2005)

Propaganda is to democracy what violence is to totalitarianism.
—Noam Chomsky, quoted in *The Chomsky Reader* (1987)

It's time for the American media to un-embed themselves from the U.S. government. We need media that are fiercely independent, that ask the hard questions and hold those in power accountable. Only then will government propaganda be seen for what it is.
—Amy Goodman and David Goodman, "Americans Deserve Media That Won't Bow to Bush," *Baltimore Sun* (April 7, 2005)

Propaganda does not deceive people; it merely helps them to deceive themselves.
—Eric Hoffer, *The Passionate State of Mind* (1955)

On one side there are puppies and rainbows and steaming casseroles of perfectly delicious homemade macaroni-and-cheese with that delightful crust on top. They're with us. On the other side are panting, foul-smelling, cross-eyed Islamofascists intent on gang-raping those puppies.
—Joshua Holland, parodying Bush's crude propagandizing, "Highlights from the Wingnut-in-Chief," AlterNet (January 11, 2007)

History does matter, which is why people in power put so much energy into controlling it.
—Robert Jensen, "No Thanks to Thanksgiving," AlterNet (November 23, 2006)

We ask you to publicly renounce the use of covert propaganda to influence public opinion . . . whether through contracts with commentators, the distribution of video news releases, or other means.
—Nancy Pelosi, in a letter to Bush co-signed by other Democratic leaders (January 7, 2005)

The forces now ruling America have already taught their followers to discredit all the possible alternative sources of thought. Not only have "liberals" been demonized . . . but also discredited are all media that are not propaganda mouthpieces of the regime.
—Andrew Bard Schmookler, "Field Notes from Bush Country," *Common Dreams* (January 31, 2006)

Those who corrupt the public mind are just as evil as those who steal from the public purse.
—Adlai Stevenson, in his speech in Albuquerque, New Mexico (September 12, 1952)

At phony town hall meetings, Bush's audiences are hand-picked to prevent any possibility of spontaneous challenge. At fake forums . . . new initiatives are unveiled on platforms festooned with meaningless slogans, mindlessly repeated.
—Jacob Weisberg, "Beyond Spin: The Propaganda Presidency of George W. Bush," *Slate* (December 7, 2005)

Propaganda is . . . a calculated and systematic effort to manage public opinion; it transcends mere lying and routine political dishonesty.
—Jacob Weisberg, "Beyond Spin: The Propaganda Presidency of George W. Bush," *Slate* (December 7, 2005)

Right-Wing Media

The conscious effort by the right wing to misinform the American citizenry—to collapse the distinction between journalism and propaganda—is . . . an assault on democracy itself.
—David Brock, *The Republican Noise Machine: Right-Wing Media and How it Corrupts Democracy* (2004)

You'd have to be blind to miss the pattern. Every prominent progressive leader who comes along is openly derided in the media as fake, dishonest, conniving, out-of-the-mainstream, and weak.
—Jamison Foser, "Media Matters," *Media Matters for America* (May 26, 2006)

Every day, there's labor news happening all over this country. None of it is getting reported in the mainstream media any longer. So workers don't identify with themselves.
—Thom Hartmann, interviewed by Mark Karlin, "Thom Hartmann Comes to the Defense of the Embattled, and Shrinking, Middle Class," *BuzzFlash* (September 25, 2006)

The biggest political joke in America is that we have a liberal press.
—Mark Hertzgaard, *The Eagle's Shadow* (2002)

If Bush said the earth was flat, the mainstream media would have stories with the headline: "Shape of the Earth—Views Differ." Then they'd quote some Democrats saying that it was round.
—Paul Krugman, interviewed by Terrence McNally, "The Professor Takes the Gloves Off," AlterNet (November 12, 2003)

Democratic victories are understood as a product of the Democrats moving to the right, while Republican victories are the product of a conservative electorate.
—Media Matters/Campaign for America's Future report, quoted in "Will the Progressive Majority Emerge?" *Nation* (July 9, 2007)

The Communists had PRAVDA. The Republicans have FOX.
—MoveOn.org, full-page ad in the *New York Times* (July 21, 2004)

I'm going out telling the story that I think is the biggest story of our time: how the right-wing media has become a partisan propaganda arm of the Republican National Committee.
—Bill Moyers, quoted in "Bill Moyers Retiring from TV Journalism," the Associated Press (AP) (December 10, 2004)

Right-wing partisans . . . have always attacked aggressive reporting as liberal. We were biased, all right—in favor of uncovering the news that powerful people wanted to keep hidden.
—Bill Moyers, former host of PBS's "Now," in an interview with John Eggerton, "Moyers Has His Say," Broadcasting & Cable (November 28, 2005)

The Right has created such a powerful media apparatus that it can virtually create its own reality.
—Robert Parry, "America's Slide to Totalitarianism," *Consortium News* (November 6, 2006)

Women audacious enough to seek political office are routinely dogged by double-standard-laced news coverage that focuses on their looks, fashion sense, familial relationships, and other feminizing details that have nothing to do with their ability to lead.
—Jennifer L. Pozner, "Why Fixing the Media System Should Be on the Feminist Agenda," AlterNet (January 11, 2007)

Whenever Republicans win an election, mainstream pundits cite the results as prima facie proof that the American people have handed them a mandate to do whatever they want. . . . When a majority of Americans cast votes for the Dems, the results are invariably interpreted by the media as a public desire for moderation and bipartisanship.
—Ted Rall, "When It's Democratic," uExpress (November 14, 2006)

Large corporations are not going to launch publishing imprints that consistently argue a liberal viewpoint. They won't do it. In the end, the owners are conservative.
—Colin Robinson, publisher of the New Press, quoted in "Making Books: The Politics of Publishing," *Washington Post* (November 6, 2005)

FOX is not per se a "right-wing" network devoted to conservative principles. It is a soulless propaganda network devoted to keeping the Republican Party in power.
—Michael Tomasky, "Switching Channels," *American Prospect* (April 13, 2007)

If you listen to the media, you'd think that conservatives have values and progressives have positions.
—Paul Waldman, interviewed by Mark Karlin, "Paul Waldman Knows Progressives Can Win—and Here's How," *BuzzFlash* (May 25, 2006)

Democracy is meaningless if the public cannot get accurate information.
—Howard Zinn, *Original Zinn* (2006)

THE NATURE OF RIGHT AND WRONG

Ethics

A man's ethical behavior should be based effectually on sympathy, education, and social ties and needs; no religious basis is necessary. Man would indeed be in a poor way if he had to be restrained by fear of punishment and hope of reward after death.
—Albert Einstein, "Religion and Science," *New York Times* Magazine (November 9, 1930)

The only angels we need to invoke are those of our better nature: reason, honesty, and love.
—Sam Harris, *The End of Faith* (2005)

Is turning food into fuel as millions starve to death really the ethical answer to our oil addiction?
—Headline regarding the push for corn-based ethanol, Stephen Pizzo's "Fill 'er Up—With Food," AlterNet (June 24, 2006)

There has got to be a very special place in hell for corporations willing to sacrifice the health of their customers on the altar of increased profits.
—Arianna Huffington, "Capitalism Without Conscience," *Huffington Post* (July 23, 2002)

It is an open question whether any behavior based on fear of eternal punishment can be regarded as ethical or should be regarded as merely cowardly.
—Margaret Mead, *Redbook* (February 1971)

It's not enough to just change the players. We have to change the game.
—Barack Obama, "A Chance to Change the Game," *Washington Post* (January 4, 2007)

Ethical achievement is measured by the degree in which our actions are governed by compassion and love, not by greed and aggressiveness.
—Arnold J. Toynbee, *The Toynbee-Ikeda Dialog* (1976)

Evil

Silence in the face of evil is itself evil: God will not hold us guiltless. Not to speak is to speak. Not to act is to act.
—Dietrich Bonhoeffer, quoted in *Soul Work: Anti-Racist Theologies in Dialogue* (2003)

Presidents, politicized clerics and suicide bombers claim the stamp of divine endorsement. They're all fighting "evil" and they're all claiming the guarantee of ultimate victory.
—Will Braun, "The Super-Powered Gospel," *Winnipeg Free Press* (Canada) (October 21, 2006)

Every generation or so an evil arises which is so monstrous, so degrading to the human spirit, so morally bankrupt that even to debate it is a sign of moral corruption. . . . Today, torture, a practice far more degrading to us than to our victims, represents such an evil.
—Fred Branfman, "On Torture and Being Good Americans," *Tikkun* (March/ April 2006)

Evil so perplexes people that attributing it to a cosmic Prince of Darkness provides some explanation at least. It saves the trouble of taking responsibility for it ourselves.
—Deepak Chopra, "Satan Leaves the Scene," *Huffington Post* (January 20, 2006)

The nature of evil is to dominate, control, and possess. There is the test for exposing the evil nature of the abusive spouse as well as abusive national leaders.
—Karen Horst Cobb, "WWIII: Whose Side Are You On?" *Common Dreams* (August 1, 2006)

A belief in a supernatural source of evil is not necessary; men alone are quite capable of every wickedness.
—Joseph Conrad, *Under Western Eyes* (1911)

As soon as men decide that all means are permitted to fight an evil, then their good becomes indistinguishable from the evil that they set out to destroy.
—Christopher Dawson, *The Judgment of the Nations* (1942)

In my humble opinion, non-cooperation with evil is as much a duty as cooperation with good.
—Mahatma Gandhi, *Nonviolence in Peace and War* (1942)

The real "axis of evil" is fascism, whether it is dressed in native or foreign garb.
—Elizabeth Hartmann, "America's Climate of Fear and Loathing," *Boston Globe* (April 19, 2002)

To ignore evil is to be an accomplice to it.
—Rev. Martin Luther King, Jr., *"Where Do We Go From Here?"* (1967)

In the past, there was a tendency for liberals to see evil as something out in the world that we are called to stop, such as poverty or oppression. Today there is a growing sense that part of the work of countering evil and building up our world is done through self-awareness and personal transformation.
—Rev. Marlin Lavanhar, quoted in "From 'Liberal' Pews, a Rising Thirst for Personal Moral Code," *Christian Science Monitor* (December 8, 2004)

Let us not become the evil we deplore.
—Barbara Lee, the only member of congress who voted against giving Bush authority to go to war against Afghanistan, quoted in "White House Snow Globe," *Common Dreams* (December 2, 2005)

The Religious Right saw the evil in the world as ontological, built into the very structure of reality and humankind. . . . Life is fundamentally scary because people are likely to hurt us as they seek to dominate and control us unless we can dominate and control them first.
—Rabbi Michael Lerner, "Hostile Takeover: Theocracy in America," *Tikkun* (January/February 2006)

Americans are not immune from evil; no people are.
—Anthony Lewis, "The Torture Administration," *Nation* (December 26, 2005)

Evil is always the assertion of some self-interest without regard to the whole, whether the whole be conceived as the immediate community or the total community of humanity.
—Reinhold Niebuhr, quoted in "Confronting Evil," *UU World* (January/February 2002)

He who fights against monsters should see to it that he does not become a monster in the process. And when you stare persistently into an abyss, the abyss also stares into you.
—Friedrich Nietzsche, *Beyond Good and Evil* (1886)

Men never do evil so completely and cheerfully as when they do it from religious conviction.
—Blaise Pascal, quoted in *Preserving the Constitution* (1984)

The devil can cite Scripture for his purpose.
—William Shakespeare, from the play The *Merchant of Venice*

If only there were evil people somewhere insidiously committing evil deeds, and it were necessary only to separate them from the rest of us and destroy them. But the line dividing good and evil cuts through the heart of every human being.
—Alexander Solzhenitsyn, *The Gulag Archipelago* (1973)

There are a thousand hacking at the branches of evil to one who is striking at the root.
—Henry David Thoreau, *Walden* (1854)

The liberal sees outer, removable institutions as the ultimate source of evil, sees man's social task as creating a world in which evil will disappear. . . . The conservative sees the inner unremovable nature of man as the ultimate source of evil.
—Peter Viereck, *The Unadjusted Man: A New Hero for Americans* (1956)

If evil in this world is deeply human and very real . . . it just doesn't make spiritual sense to suggest that the evil all lies "out there" with our adversaries and enemies, and none of it "in here" with us—embedded in our own attitudes, behaviors, and policies.
—Rev. Jim Wallis, *God's Politics: Why the Right Gets It Wrong and the Left Doesn't Get It* (2005)

Our usual take on evil focuses on the violent, destructive actions of perpetrators, but the failure to act can also be a form of evil, when helping, dissent, disobedience, or whistle-blowing are required.
—Philip Zimbardo, *The Lucifer Effect: Understanding How Good People Turn Evil* (2007)

Golden Rule

Unless we look out for everyone, no one is secure.
—Ronald Aronson, "The Left Needs More Socialism," *Nation* (March 31, 2006)

What you do not want done to yourself do not do to others.
—Confucius, Quoted in *Confucian Analects* (1930)

Whatever you wish that men would do to you, do so to them.
—Jesus, in Matthew 7:12

The heart of the [moral] question is whether all Americans are to be afforded equal rights and equal opportunities, whether we are going to treat our fellow Americans as we want to be treated.
—John F. Kennedy, in a broadcast on civil rights (June 11, 1963)

To do on to all men as you would wish to have done to you, and to reject for others what you would reject for yourself.
—Muhammad, *The Sayings of Muhammad* (1941)

There are some things that I'm absolutely certain about—the Golden Rule, the need to battle cruelty in all its forms, the value of love and charity, humility, and grace.
—Barack Obama, *The Audacity of Hope* (2006)

Goodness

What does God want? Does God want goodness or the choice of goodness? Is a man who chooses the bad perhaps in some way better than a man who has the good imposed upon him?
—Anthony Burgess, *A Clockwork Orange* (1962)

Waste no more time arguing what a good man should be. Be one.
—Marcus Aurelius, *Meditations* (A.D. 167)

No good comes fully fashioned out of God's hand, but has to be carved out through repeated experiments and repeated failures by ourselves.
—Mahatma Gandhi, *M.K. Gandhi: Speeches and Writings* (1918)

Belief in God alone does not guarantee goodness.
—Jeff Jacoby, "Atheists' Bleak Alternative," *Boston Globe* (December 13, 2006)

The kingdom of God is within you.
—Jesus, Matthew 18:3

It is the time for this land to become again a witness to the world for what is just and noble in human affairs.
—George McGovern, from his 1972 speech accepting the Democratic nomination for president, quoted in "Come Home Again, America," AlterNet (November 21, 2005)

All God's creatures are His family; and he is the most beloved of God who does the most good to God's creatures.
—Muhammad, *The Sayings of Muhammad* (1941)

Problems will always torment us because all important problems are insoluble: that is why they are important. The good comes from the continuing struggle to try and solve them, not from the vain hope of their solution.
—Arthur M. Schlesinger, Jr., *The Vital Center: The Politics of Freedom* (1949)

The struggle that now must urgently be waged is not that of liberal values against conservative values, but of those who really care about goodness against those in power who only pretend to.
—Andrew Bard Schmookler, "What America Needs Now: A Prophetic Social Movement That Speaks Moral Truth to Amoral Power," *Common Dreams* (October 19, 2005)

Everything that exalts and expands consciousness is good, while that which depresses and diminishes it is evil.
—Miguel de Unamuno, *Tragic Sense of Life* (1913)

The perfect is the enemy of the good.
—Voltaire, *Dictionnaire Philosophique* (1764)

There is no reason good can't triumph over evil, if only angels will get organized along the lines of the Mafia.
—Kurt Vonnegut, *A Man without a Country* (2005)

Moral Values

Not only do water-boarding and the other types of torture . . . put us in company with the most vile regimes of the past half century; they're also designed specifically to generate a (usually false) confession, not to obtain genuinely actionable intel. This isn't a matter of sacrificing moral values to keep us safe; it's sacrificing moral values for no purpose whatsoever.
—Jonah Blank, quoted in "Good People—Bad Government?" *Common Dreams* (October 16, 2006)

Why is a nation consumed with moral values so blind to state-sanctioned immorality?
—Marie Cocco, "Moral Values Apply to Torture, Too," *Newsday* (December 16, 2004)

There's not the slightest evidence that religious people in a given society are any more moral than non-religious people.
—Richard Dawkins, "Atheist Richard Dawkins on 'The God Delusion,'" interviewed by Terrence McNally, AlterNet (January 18, 2007)

The moral values debate is precisely the one Democrats need to be having right now. Because if they don't capture the moral high ground back from the Republicans, they'll never be able to capture the hearts and votes of Red America.
—Arianna Huffington, "Real Moral Values," AlterNet (November 10, 2004)

Nothing less is at stake in the torture crisis than the soul of our nation. What does it profit us if we proclaim high moral values but fail to reject torture?
—George Hunsinger, "American Scar," *Baltimore Sun* (January 31, 2005)

Advocates of religiosity extol the virtues or moral habits that religion is supposed to instill in us. But we should be equally concerned with the intellectual habits it discourages.
—Wendy Kaminer, "The Last Taboo," *New Republic* (October 14, 1996)

Morals cannot be legislated.
—Rev. Martin Luther King, Jr., *Stride Toward Freedom* (1958)

[Americans] want their lives to have meaning—and they respond to candidates who seem to care about values and some sense of transcendent purpose.
—Rabbi Michael Lerner, "The Democrats Need a Spiritual Left," *Common Dreams* (November 4, 2004)

I believe in moral coherence. . . . You cannot assert your own humanity, then turn right around and deny someone else's.
—Leonard Pitts, Jr., "Coming Out of the Closet to Declare My Humanity," *Seattle Times* (December 17, 2006)

Essential to conservative moral systems is the existence of rules. . . . Any challenge to the rules leads inevitably to chaos and immorality. It is always a slippery slope. Rules represent the natural order, the way things are. This emphasis on rules leads to either/or thinking. . . . Those who break the rules must be punished.
—Bernard Brandon Scott, quoted in "Strict Father, Metaphors, and Fundamentalism," *Timeline* (November/December 2004)

Morality

No moral system can rest solely on authority.
—A. J. Ayer, *The Humanist Outlook* (1968)

The people who run corporations are, for the most part, good people, moral people. . . . Despite their personal qualities and ambitions, however, their duty as corporate executives is clear: they must always put their corporation's best interests first and not act out of concern for anyone or anything else.
—Joel Bakan, *The Corporation: The Pathological Pursuit of Profit and Power* (2004)

Whoever wishes to become a truly moral being . . . must first divorce himself from all the prohibitions, crimes and hypocrisies of the Christian Church.
—James Baldwin, *The Fire Next Time* (1963)

Every liberal thinks he's intellectually superior to conservatives; every conservative I know wants to think of himself as morally superior.
—Paul Begala, quoted in "Aphorisms 2006," *Yahoo! News* (December 25, 2005)

We hope to challenge the fallacies that "conservative equals moral" and "Christian equals Republican."
—Rev. Allen Brill, "Liberal Get Cross-Wise," *Progressive Populist* (May 15, 2004)

When morality comes up against profit, it is seldom that profit loses.
—Shirley Chisholm, *Unbought and Unbossed* (1970)

The lust for money, dominance, and military power is at the core of America's moral decline.
—Karen Horst Cobb, "America's Moral Decline and the Rise of False Christianity," *Common Dreams* (February 16, 2006)

I've been on the losing side before, but it never felt like this, and I've grappled with why this loss is harder to swallow. I think it has something to do with the attempted theft of the word "morality" and the claim that the Bush victory was a triumph for righteous people.
—Judy Emerson, "Morality Can Come in More Than One Color," *Rockford Register Star* (November 5, 2004)

The truth is that virtually everything we humans do has a moral dimension.
—Herb Field, "Selective Horizon," *Harrisburg Patriot-News* (November 10, 2004)

True morality consists, not in following the beaten track, but in finding out the true path for ourselves and in fearlessly following it.
—Mahatma Gandhi, *Ethical Religion* (1930)

Too many liberals identify all talk of morality with bigoted, self-righteous Puritanism. They miss the boat.
—Harold Gilliam, "Poetry Can Get Outside the Box of Politics," *San Francisco Examiner* (January 9, 2005)

Humans grow in virtue not by being forced to repeat virtuous actions but by freely choosing such actions.
—Father Andrew Greeley, "Moral Health Tip to America: Stay out of the Draft," *Chicago Sun-Times* (December 1, 2006)

The notion that morality is safe only in the hands of the religions does not stand in the face of historical evidence.
—Arthur Hertzberg, quoted in "Bully in the Pulpit?" *Nation* (February 22, 2001)

A nation that increases spending on war and reduces investment in education, a nation that rolls back taxes on the wealthy and cuts back help for the elderly, the disabled, the impoverished, is a nation that has lost its way.
—Rev. Jesse Jackson, "Poor Get Cuts as Rich Get Tax Cuts," *Chicago Sun-Times* (June 6, 2006)

If we are soon to die, or if we believe the Day of Judgment to be near at hand, how quickly do we put our moral house in order?
—William James, *The Varieties of Religious Experience* (1902)

A man does what he must—in spite of personal consequences, in spite of obstacles and dangers and pressures—and that is the basis of all human morality.
—John F. Kennedy, *Profiles in Courage* (1956)

The word "moral" has such bad associations: with fundamentalism, stiff-necked preachers, priggishness. We have to get past that.
—Anne Lamott, *Bird by Bird* (1994)

Morality is found within the heart and soul of each human being, and is not equated with any one religious faith.
—Floyd J. McKay, "Christians and Karl Rove hold no monopoly on values," *Seattle Times* (November 10, 2004)

The scale of the disorder in our national priorities right now is truly stagger-ing; it approaches moral anarchy.
—Bill Moyers, "A Parable For Our Times," *TomPaine.com* (December 22, 2006)

It took me years to realize that you don't need to be Christian to be a good moral person.
—Julia Scheeres, "On the 'Jesus Land' of Her Youth," *BuzzFlash* (November 28, 2005)

The art of acting morally is behaving as if everything we do matters.
—Gloria Steinem, "The Birth of *Ms.*" *New York Times* (April 19, 1993)

Aim above morality. Be not simply good, be good for something.
—Henry David Thoreau, in a letter to Harrison Blake (March 27, 1848)

We don't think religious people have a monopoly on morality. There are peo-ple in this country who have deeply held moral values who aren't affiliated in any religion.
—Rev. Jim Wallis, *Meet the Press*, NBC (November 28, 2004)

Morality and Government

Conservatives have taken the word "moral" for themselves and liberals have let them keep it! It is time to take it back.
—George Lakoff, *Moral Politics* (1996)

What we need . . . is to moralize politics, and not to politicize morals.
—Karl R. Popper, *The Open Society and Its Enemies* (1945)

There is no morality in the government forcing the victim of rape or incest to bear the fruit of that horror or to dismiss the health of the mother in abortion decisions. There is no morality in the denial of legal rights based solely on whom one chooses to love.
—Editorial, "Whose Morality?" *Seattle Post-Intelligencer* (November 7, 2004)

I'd think red-staters would have confidence in their faith and the strength of their convictions to persuade people to make the right moral choices—and do everything in their power to keep government emphatically secular and out of the morality business. Yet it seems to be just the opposite.
—Robert Steinback, "'Red' Reasoning on Morality Is Confusing," *Miami Herald* (November 24, 2004)

We need to get our legislators and policymakers to understand that there's more to morality than who you have sex with and whether or not you have an abortion.
—Rev. Leslie Tune, quoted in "Pushing Poverty into 'Moral-Values' Debate," *San Francisco Examiner* (December 12, 2004)

Sin

Hell is nothing more than separation from God.
—Nicolas Berdyaev, *The Destiny of Man* (1931)

Jesus preached and talked against a whole gamut of sins. He never mentioned homosexuality at all.
—Jimmy Carter, in an interview with the *San Francisco Chronicle* (January 10, 1997)

For conservatives, the sins that matter are personal irresponsibility, the flight from family life, sexual permissiveness, the failure of individuals to work hard. For liberals, the gravest sins are intolerance, a lack of generosity toward the needy, narrow-mindedness toward social and racial minorities.
—E. J. Dionne, Jr., *The War Against Public Life: Why Americans Hate Politics* (1991)

The seven social sins: . . . politics without principle, pleasure without conscience, wealth without work, knowledge without character, business without morality, science without humanity, and worship without sacrifice.
—Mahatma Gandhi, quoted in *Christian Science Monitor* (February 1, 1995)

The most unpardonable sin in society is independence of thought.
—Emma Goldman, *Anarchism and Other Essays* (1910)

There is objective sin in the Iraq war, and our country as a country is guilty of sin.
—Father Andrew Greeley, "How Many More Iraqis Must Die for Our Revenge?" *Chicago Sun-Times* (November 12, 2004)

Fashions in sin change.
—Lillian Hellman, *Watch on the Rhine* (1941)

Let him who is without sin cast the first stone.
—Jesus, John 8:7

We Americans have become accustomed to letting our institutions do our sinning for us.
—Ray McGovern, in a letter from a former CIA agent, "I Do Not Wish to Be Associated with Torture," *Common Dreams* (March 3, 2006)

Soul

What does it profit a man, if he shall gain the whole world, and lose his soul?
—Mark 8:36

Growth of the soul is our goal, and there are many ways to encourage that growth, such as through love, nature, healing our wounds, forgiveness, and service.
—Joan Borysenko, quoted in *Handbook for the Soul* (1996)

Because the soul is progressive, it never quite repeats itself, but in every act attempts the production of a new and fairer whole.
—Ralph Waldo Emerson, *Essays, First Series* (1841)

What profit a party if it gain a majority and lose its soul?
—Christopher Hayes, "How to Turn Your Red State Blue," *In These Times* (March 22, 2005)

To dispose a soul to action we must upset its equilibrium.
—Eric Hoffer, *The Ordeal of Change* (1964)

All emotions, all human activities, and all spheres of life have deep roots in the mysteries of the soul, and therefore are holy.
—Thomas Moore, *Care of the Soul* (1993)

America is continuously struggling for its soul.
—Gunnar Myrdal, quoted in "The American Creed," *Nation* (August 29, 2002)

These are the times that try men's souls.
—Thomas Paine, quoted in *The Writings of Thomas Paine* (1894)

The happiest people I have known have been those who gave themselves no concern about their own souls, but did their uttermost to mitigate the miseries of others.
—Elizabeth Cady Stanton, quoted in *Women Without Superstition* (1997)

There is a little conservatism in everyone's soul—even those who proudly call themselves liberals. No one is untouched by loss. We all grow old. We watch ourselves age and decline; we see new generations supplant and outrun us.
—Andrew Sullivan, *The Conservative Soul* (2006)

To practice any art, no matter how well or badly, is a way to make your soul grow.
—Kurt Vonnegut, "Knowing What's Nice," *In These Times* (November 6, 2003)

Spirituality

Those of us who exercise our spirituality by attempting to follow in the footsteps of Jesus are very much aware that when Jesus was around religious people it made him nauseated. I believe that is why Jesus always enjoyed eating with sinners.
—Rev. Kenneth W. Chalker, "Praying for the Demise of Religion," *Cleveland Plain Dealer* (December 12, 2005)

If the secular elites believe that happiness and well-being can be established without a spiritual basis entirely, they are fooling themselves.
—Deepak Chopra, "Atheists for God," *Huffington Post* (July 17, 2006)

I believe that divinity exists in all of us and that if we eliminate some of the chatter in our lives, the voice of compassion will have a chance to be heard.
—Sheryl Crow, "On Deception, Spin, and Losing Our Way," *Huffington Post* (May 4, 2007)

I believe politics must arise from a spiritual source as well as an ideological one.
—Tom Hayden, quoted in "Bully in the Pulpit?" *Nation* (February 22, 2001)

This nation cannot afford to be materially rich and spiritually poor.
—John F. Kennedy, in his State of the Union address (January 14, 1963)

Will faith and spirituality be a path to liberation for all, the window through which we see our commonality with all beings and join together to pursue fairness and equality? Or will religion divide us, emphasizing our differences more than our similarities and privileging certain religious "truths" over others?
—Sally Kohn, "Ding, Dong, Falwell's Dead," *Common Dreams* (May 16, 2007)

People not only have material needs, but spiritual needs . . . They hunger for a framework of purpose for their lives that transcends the values of the capitalist marketplace and the accumulation of money and power.
—Rabbi Michael Lerner, quoted in interview "Finding Spirit Among the Dems," AlterNet (February 10, 2006)

Speaking to spiritual needs actually leads to a more radical critique of the dynamics of corporate capitalism and corporate globalization, not to a mimicking of right-wing policies.
—Rabbi Michael Lerner, "The Democrats Need a Spiritual Left," *Common Dreams* (November 4, 2004)

In the end, we are spiritual creatures, generators of meaning, beings who must not and cannot live by bread alone.
—Glenn C. Loury, quoted in *One Electorate Under God?* (2004)

Americans, finding no spiritual vision on the left, have become vulnerable to a spiritual con job from the right.
—Andrew Bard Schmookler, "Lack of Vision in Presenting Spiritual Side of Liberalism," *Baltimore Sun* (July 14, 2005)

I hope that spirituality overwhelms religion. I say this because spirituality links, religion ranks; spirituality sees God in all living things, religion rations out God to some more than others; spirituality celebrates life, religion celebrates life after death.
—Gloria Steinem, "I'm a Hopeaholic. There's Nothing George Bush Can Do About It," *Guardian (UK)* (September 13, 2005)

There is no spirit in the absence of justice, and no justice that is not first spiritual.
—Curtis White, *The Spirit of Disobedience* (2006)

Values

That word "values" has lately become a codeword for appeasement of the right-wing fringe. But when political calculations make us soften our opposition to bigotry, or sign on to policies that add to the burden of ordinary Americans, we have abandoned our true values.
—Howard Dean, announcing his candidacy for the Democratic Party Chair, quoted in "Dr. Dean Calling," *Nation* (January 12, 2005)

What do gay activists and homophobic fundamentalists, liberal feminists and right-to-life fanatics, Green defenders of the natural environment and those who see the planet as a resource to be used by humans have in common? . . . The fact is that contemporary democratic societies lack any deep consensus on values.
—John Gray, "In Theory," *Nation* (June 5, 2006)

That scraping noise you hear? It's the sound of sheepish voters creeping out to the garage late at night, furtively removing "Bush-Cheney 2004" bumper stickers from the back of their SUVs.
—David Michael Green, "George Bush in Hell," *Common Dreams* (September 27, 2005)

The average person is uncertain of Democratic and liberal values. They have a sense of the Republicans as a repository of values, and that the Democrats aren't, because they don't fight every fight, and use each one—even the losing ones . . . as a venue to get their values out there.
—Thom Hartmann, in an interview entitled "Thom Hartmann Brings Context to Today's Political Frays," *BuzzFlash* (February 7, 2006)

"Values" need not be the anti-choice, anti-gay, anti-science mores of the right wing.
—Bernie Horn, "How Progressives Can Win," *TomPaine.com* (June 22, 2006)

I don't care who anyone in politics is screwing in private, as long as they're not screwing the public.
—Molly Ivins, "The Best Little Whorehouse in Washington," Truthdig (May 8, 2006)

This country was founded on a whole new set of values never seen before—it was founded on American Values . . . not born-again Christian values.
—Tim Keane, "Redefining 'Values,'" Democratic Underground (November 9, 2004)

The "values vote" has always been something of a chimera, part niche-marketing to white evangelicals and part clever branding designed to exaggerate the Christian right's power at the polls.
—Richard Kim, "Haggard Values," *Nation* (November 27, 2006)

My values are my own business.
—Michael Kinsley, "To Hell with Values," *Los Angeles Times* (November 28, 2004)

Trying to govern with your finger in the air, instead of true convictions and moral leadership, means that political winds can blow Democrats into dangerous waters.
—Sally Kohn, "Abandoning the See Saw of Centrism," *Common Dreams* (October 31, 2006)

Never answer a question framed from your opponent's point of view. Always reframe the question to fit your values.
—George Lakoff, *Don't Think Like an Elephant* (2004)

Progressive values are the best of traditional American values. Stand up for your values with dignity and strength.
—George Lakoff, *Don't Think Like an Elephant* (2004)

Progressives have been under the illusion that if only people understood the facts, we'd be fine. Wrong. The facts alone will not set us free. People make decisions about politics and candidates based on their value systems, and the language and frames that invoke those values.
—George Lakoff, *Don't Think Like an Elephant* (2004)

The profiteering motive is driven and single-minded. When unconstrained, it can override or erode community, health, safety, parental nurturing, due process, clean politics, and many other basic social values that hold together a society.
—Ralph Nader, quoted in *The Ralph Nader Reader* (2000)

The pundits like to slice and dice our country into red states and blue states . . . But I've got news for them, too. We worship an awesome God in the blue states, and we don't like federal agents poking around our libraries in the red states.
—Barack Obama, in his keynote address to the Democratic National Convention (July 27, 2004)

Maybe this time the voters chose what they actually want: nationalism, pre-emptive war, order not justice, "safety" through torture, backlash against women and gays, a gulf between haves and have-nots . . . Where, I wonder, does that leave us?
—Katha Pollitt, "Mourn," *Nation* (November 5, 2004)

Fairness is a liberal value. Equality is a liberal value. Education is a liberal value. Honesty in government, public service for modest remuneration, safe-guarding public resources and the land—these are all values we share.
—Katha Pollitt, "Let's Not Devalue Ourselves," *Nation* (July 29, 2004)

The world of right and wrong is much larger than the world of profit and loss.
—Jane Bryant Quinn, quoted in "What Numbers Aren't Saying About the Economy Most Live In," *Daytona Beach News-Journal* (January 10, 2006)

All Americans, not just social conservatives, are "values" voters.
—Ted Rall, "What's the Matter with Manhattan?" Universal Press Syndicate (January 5, 2005)

Deep down, under layers of commercially sustained coarseness, religious fak-ery, and politically inspired meanness, we are, I believe, the most open and charitable people on God's Earth when we manage to get around to it.
—Robert Scheer, "Homophobia and Apple Pie," *Los Angeles Times* (July 20, 2004)

America would be fine in the hands of people devoted to real conservative values. But this is something different, something dangerous. For America is now ruled by forces apparently not guided by any genuine values at all. One can look in vain for any juncture where they've made a decision that sacrificed any of their power or wealth in favor of some larger good.
—Andrew Bard Schmookler, "What America Needs Now: A Prophetic Social Movement that Speaks Moral Truth to Amoral Power," *Common Dreams* (October 19, 2005)

Religious people turn out to vote more than nonreligious people.
—Julie A. Segal, quoted in *One Electorate Under God?* (2004)

Robust moral values look at a range of "public" issues, about which the Religious Right has been strangely silent.
—Jim Seeber, "Where Is Our Public Moral Courage?" *Aberdeen News* (December 19, 2004)

Liberal values represent the essence of the world's great religions. At the root of all of the great faiths are fundamental beliefs in compassion, justice, love, and charity.
—Adele M. Stan, "A Canterbury Tale," *American Prospect* (July 11, 2006)

The liberal project was largely an economic project. It said people are rational economic actors and if you give them survival-based services, they will vote for you. Most Americans today are not survival-oriented; they're fulfillment-oriented.
—Adam Werbach, quoted in "Is Liberalism Dead?" AlterNet (December 8, 2004)

There are profoundly important and precious values that liberals stand for that are central to the founding of this country—liberty, human rights, and human dignity.
—Alan Wolfe, quoted in "The Culture Wars Are Back," *Green Bay News-Chronicle* (November 8, 2004)

What ordinary people want is a good family, a good job, and a chance for a better life.
—Adrian Wooldridge, quoted in "The Problem(s) with Democrats," AlterNet (November 22, 2004)

We must have a way by which the pursuit of profit does not trump all other values of the society.
—Cornel West, *Washington Journal,* C-SPAN (February 3, 2001)

THE MEANING OF PATRIOTISM

America

We are a republic, not a monarchy. We believe in the rule of law, not secret prisons. We insist on justice for all, not privilege for the few.
—Bruce Ackerman and Todd Gitlin, "We Answer to the Name of Liberals," *American Prospect* (October 18, 2006)

America! America!
God mend thine every flaw,
Confirm thy soul in self-control,
Thy liberty in law!
—Katharine Lee Bates, from the second verse of "America the Beautiful" (1913)

Liberals sought and achieved independence from Great Britain with the Revolutionary War. Conservatives, then known as Tories, opposed independence and fought against it.
—Thomas Bonsell, "Differences Between Liberal and Conservative," OpEdNews (December 31, 2006)

I remember an America that used to feel more like one country—an America that shared the sacrifice of war, and tightened its belt so we could pay for it. Now we borrow to go to war, and cut taxes to spare those in high brackets from sacrifice.
—Robert Byrd, in his speech delivered to the U.S. Senate, "A Call for Debate on National Priorities" (September 13, 2005)

We Americans have never outgrown the narcissistic notion that the rest of the world wants (or should want) to emulate us.
—Chalmers Johnson, "Exporting the American Model: Markets and Democracy," *TomDispatch.com* (May 3, 2006)

For revolting barbarity and shameless hypocrisy, America reigns without a rival.
—Frederick Douglass, quoted in "The Fear of the Liberals," *Nation* (September 8, 2005)

We Are All Americans.
—French editorial following 9/11, *Le Monde* (September 12, 2001). American conservatives ultimately reciprocated by calling the French "cheese-eating surrender monkeys" and changing the name of "French fries" to "freedom fries."

America and the Christian religions have no monopoly on goodness or saintliness. God has not chosen Americans as people above others.
—Chris Hedges, *American Fascists* (2006)

We now live in a nation where the top 1 percent control more wealth than the bottom 90 percent combined, where we have legalized torture and can lock up citizens without trial.
—Chris Hedges, "Christianists on the March," *Truthdig* (January 28, 2007)

America is a liberal idea. Give me your tired, your poor, your huddled masses—not your rich and your elite and your aristocrats.
—Rev. Jesse Jackson, "Jesus, we learn, was a liberal," *San Diego Union-Tribune* (July 30, 2004)

Will America police the world while cutting support for police on its own streets? Will it build schools in Baghdad and not in Baltimore?
—Rev. Jesse Jackson, "Poor Get Cuts as Rich Get Tax Cuts," *Chicago Sun-Times* (June 6, 2006)

I tremble for my country when I reflect that God is just.
—Thomas Jefferson, *Notes on the State of Virginia* (1785)

America is not a melting pot. It is a sizzling cauldron.
—Barbara Mikulski, quoted in *The Decade of Women* (1980)

Americans like backbone.
—David Morris, "Minority Retort," AlterNet (February 15, 2005)

America is a broken promise, and we are called to do what we can to fix it—
to get America back on the track.
—Bill Moyers, "Democracy in the Balance," *Sojourners* (August 2004)

The United States government has lost its moral authority. It has no soul. It
is too big, too centralized, too powerful, too materialistic, too intrusive, too
militarist and too unresponsive to the needs of Vermont citizens and communities.
—Thomas Naylor, leading a movement to have the state secede from the
union, quoted in "Please Throw Vermont Out," *Common Dreams* (January 25,
2006)

There's not a liberal America and a conservative America; there's the United
States of America.
—Barack Obama, in his keynote address to the Democratic National
Convention (July 27, 2004)

My country is the world and my religion is to do good.
—Thomas Paine, *The Rights of Man* (1792)

Canada . . . is an exemplar of the kind of free, just and prosperous country
that the United States once was and which, through the determined and courageous resistance of its people, the United States can become once again.
—Ernest Partridge, "O Canada!" OpEdNews (August 2, 2006)

America is said to be the arena on which the battle of freedom is to be fought;
but surely it cannot be freedom in a merely political sense that is meant. Even
if we grant that the American has freed himself from a political tyrant, he is
still the slave of an economical and moral tyrant.
—Henry David Thoreau, *The Writings of Henry David Thoreau* (1906)

America is great because America is good, and if America ever ceases to be
good, America will cease to be great.
—Alexis de Tocqueville, *Democracy in America* (1835)

America, the first real democracy in history, was a product of Enlightenment values—critical intelligence, tolerance, respect for evidence, a regard for the secular sciences.
—Garry Wills, "The Day the Enlightenment Went Out" (November 4, 2004)

We have had repressive governments before, but none has legislated the end of *habeas corpus*, nor openly supported torture, nor declared the possibility of war without end.
—Howard Zinn, "Impeachment by the People," *Progressive* (January 31, 2007)

The American Dream

Everywhere you go, you hear, "What has happened to the United States of America? We thought you used to be the champion of human rights. We thought you used to protect the environment. We thought you used to believe in the separation of church and state."
—Jimmy Carter, quoted in "Carter 'Disturbed' by Direction of U.S.," the Associated Press (AP) (November 12, 2005)

The amount of racism, sexism, homophobia, and hatred in general that lies beneath the surface of the American Dream is astounding.
—Margaret Cho, *I Have Chosen to Stay and Fight* (2005)

The problem with the American Dream is that it offers no explanation for failure other than that you deserve your lot in life, and that if you fail there must be something wrong with you.
—Lani Guinier, interviewed by Rebecca Parrish, "The Meritocracy Myth," *Dollars & Sense* (January/February 2006)

Our country now appears, as at no time in her history, like a lumbering, bellicose, dimwitted giant.
—Sam Harris, *Letter to a Christian Nation* (2006)

Whenever I think of the American dream, I think in terms of tolerance. I think in terms of making an attempt, even if it's not always successful, to reach out to disparate groups, and try to find a common ground and bring them together.
—Bob Herbert, quoted in interview "*Times* Columnist Bob Herbert Views the American Dream: But Can It Still Be Found?" *BuzzFlash* (May 3, 2005)

The American Dream is not dead. True, it is gasping for breath, but it is not dead.
—Barbara Jordan, in her keynote address to the Democratic National Convention (July 13, 1992)

The American Dream has had its heart cut out, and is on life support.
—Bill Moyers, "America 101," *TomPaine.com* (November 1, 2006)

We need the American dream to add up to something beyond the Target receipts and HDTV.
—Jill Raymond, "Let New American Dream End Our Listless Slumber," *Baltimore Sun* (October 10, 2002)

What do I believe? As an American I believe in generosity, in liberty, in the rights of man.
—Adlai Stevenson, in his speech in Libertyville, Illinois (May 21, 1954)

What the hell is going on here? How could this once proud nation have changed so much, so drastically, in only a little more than two years? In what seems like the blink of an eye, this George Bush has brought us from a prosperous nation at peace to a broke nation at war.
—Hunter S. Thompson, "Hunter S. Thompson, George W. Bush and the Free Republic," *BuzzFlash* (June 16, 2004)

America lives in the heart of every man everywhere who wishes to find a region where he will be free to work out his destiny as he chooses.
—Woodrow Wilson, in a speech in Chicago, Illinois (April 6, 1912)

The American Flag

It is against the law to let the flag touch the ground or to leave the flag flying when the weather is bad. The flag has to be treated with respect. You can tell just how important this cloth is because when you compare it to people, it gets much better treatment. Nobody cares if a homeless person touches the ground.
—Charlotte Aldebron, in an essay written for her sixth-grade competition, "What the American Flag Stands For," *Common Dreams* (April 3, 2002)

Whenever an election draws near, lawmakers trot out a constitutional amendment to ban "flag desecration." . . . This is a solution to a problem that doesn't exist.
—Editorial, "Shielding the Flag, Shattering Liberty," *Minneapolis Star Tribune* (June 22, 2006)

Our flag is red, white and blue, but our nation is a rainbow—red, yellow, brown, black and white—and we're all precious in God's sight.
—Rev. Jesse Jackson, in his speech at the Democratic National Convention in San Francisco (July 16, 1984)

It occurs to me that my patriotic duty is to recapture my flag from the men now waving it in the name of jingoism and censorship.
—Barbara Kingsolver, "And Our Flag Was Still There," *San Francisco Chronicle* (September 25, 2001)

When liberals burned the U.S. flag during the Vietnam War rather than waving it and insisting that America live up to its great tradition, they lost the most powerful territorial symbol in our culture.
—Rev. Davidson Loehr, "The Fundamentalist Agenda," *UU World* (January/ February 2004)

I think it's time for those of us who love this country—and everything it should stand for—to reclaim our flag from those who would use it to crush rights and freedoms, both here at home and overseas. We need to redefine what it means to be a proud American.
—Michael Moore, "The Patriot's Act," *Los Angeles Times* (July 4, 2004)

The flag's been hijacked and turned into a logo—the trademark of a monopoly on patriotism.
—Bill Moyers, "The Battle for PBS," *In These Times* (May 31, 2005)

If the flag needs protection at all, it needs protection from members of Congress who value the symbol more than the freedoms that the flag represents.
—Jerrold Nadler, "Flag Proposal Threatens First Amendment," *Cranbury Press* (June 25, 2005)

The liberties of the freest people are in danger when they set up symbols of liberty as fetishes, worshipping the symbol instead of the principle it represents.
—Wendell Phillips, quoted in *Liberty and the Great Libertarian* (1995)

Americans are the planet's biggest flag wavers. They are reared on the conceit that theirs is the world's best and most enviable country. . . . But events have revealed a creeping mildew of pain and privation, graft and injustice and much incompetence lurking beneath the glow of star-spangled superiority.
—Dermot Purgavie, "Is This the Death of America?" *Daily Mirror (UK)* (October 8, 2005)

The true beauty of our flag comes not from its design but from its representation of a free society that tolerates all manner of peaceful dissent.
—Terri Ann Schroeder, news release, "ACLU Warns against Flag 'Protection' Amendment to Constitution" (May 7, 2003)

You want to claim this land as the land of the free, then the symbol of your country can't just be a flag; the symbol also has to be one of its citizens exercising his right to burn that flag in protest. Show me that, defend that, celebrate that in your classrooms. Then you can stand up and sing about the land of the free.
—Aaron Sorkin, spoken by the character Andrew Shepherd in the film *The American President* (1995)

I keep another flag, one that more accurately portrays the truth about America . . . In place of the fifty stars there are corporate symbols that depict the corporate states of America.
—Charles Sullivan, "The Flag of the Corporate States of America," *Information Clearing House* (June 14, 2006)

If you want a symbolic gesture, don't burn the flag, wash it.
—Norman Thomas, quoted in *50 Simple Things You Can Do To Fight the Right* (2006)

If one pays attention to modern politics, one realizes that most of it has to do with parading around with banners, and most of them have almost nothing to do with education, health care, highways, drinking water and jobs.
—John Young, "Governance? Just Rally 'Round the Flag," *Boulder Daily Camera* (May 7, 2006)

It was always absurd for giant American flags to fly over our most visible wastelands, car dealerships strewn with gargantuan gas guzzlers.
—Derrick Z. Jackson, "Bah, Hummerbug," *Boston Globe* (December 5, 2005)

There is no flag large enough to cover the shame of killing innocent people.
—Howard Zinn, quoted in "The Flag of the Corporate States of America," *Information Clearing House* (June 14, 2006)

Citizenship

Back in the late '70s, the Republicans learned that if you hailed people as "taxpayers" rather than citizens, and appealed to their meaner instincts, you could convince many that they were downright righteous to withhold their money from supporting the common good.
—Susan J. Douglas, "The Immoral Majority," *In These Times* (July 18, 2005)

Big corporations should not be able to tell citizens how to live their lives and run their communities.
—Lee Drutman and Charlie Cray, "The People's Business," *In These Times* (February 18, 2005)

Citizenship in the United States shall be conferred only on human beings. Neither this Constitution nor the constitution of any State, nor state or federal law, shall be construed to require that citizenship or the legal incidents thereof be granted to corporations, partnerships, proprietorships or trusts.
—Joshua Holland, proposed Defense of Human Citizenship Amendment, "Corporations Aren't People," AlterNet (July 3, 2006)

Our most fundamental responsibility as citizens is to love not only our own children, but other people's as well—including children we will never meet, who grow up in situations we'd prefer to ignore.
—Paul Rogat Loeb, *Soul of a Citizen* (1999)

No society, no matter how tolerant, can expect to thrive if its citizens don't prize what their citizenship means.
—Salman Rushdie, "What This Cultural Debate Needs Is More Dirt, Less Pure Stupidity," *London Times* (December 10, 2005)

Civil Disobedience

The defiance of established authority, religious and secular, social and political, as a worldwide phenomenon may well one day be accounted the outstanding event of the last decade.
—Hannah Arendt, "Civil Disobedience," *Crises of the Republic* (1972)

Good men must not obey the laws too well.
—Ralph Waldo Emerson, *Essays, Second Series* (1844)

Civil disobedience is the assertion of a right which law should give but which it denies.
—Mahatma Gandhi, quoted in *Mahatma* (1960)

Wars will be stopped only when soldiers refuse to fight, when workers refuse to load weapons onto ships and aircrafts, when people boycott the economic outposts of Empire that are strung across the globe.
—Arundhati Roy, *Public Power in the Age of Empire* (2004)

My hope is that you will not be content just to be successful in the way that our society measures success, that you will not obey the rules when the rules are unjust, that you will act out the courage that I know is in you.
—Howard Zinn, *Original Zinn* (2006)

Dissent

The dissent we witness is a reaffirmation of faith in man; it is protest against living under rules and prejudices and attitudes that produce the extremes of wealth and poverty and that make us dedicated to the destruction of people through arms, bombs, and gases, and that prepare us to think alike and be submissive objects.
—William O. Douglas, *Points of Rebellion* (1969)

A free society doesn't just accommodate dissenters; it thrives on them.
—Editorial, "Up with Dissent," *Boston Globe* (November 20, 2001)

May we never confuse honest dissent with disloyal subversion.
—Dwight D. Eisenhower, in his speech at Columbia University (May 31, 1954)

I think we Americans tend to put too high a price on unanimity . . . as if there were something dangerous and illegitimate about honest differences of opinion honestly expressed by honest men.
—J. William Fulbright, in his speech to the U.S. Senate (October 22, 1965)

In a democracy, dissent is an act of faith.
—J. William Fulbright, in his speech to the U.S. Senate (April 21, 1966)

True patriots must defend the right of dissent and listen to the dissenters.
—John F. Kerry, "Patriotism Is Truth, Today as in Vietnam," *Boston Globe* (April 22, 2006)

Have we become so complacent, so cowardly and intimidated by this government that we have forgotten our own revolutionary birthright of rebellion and dissent?
—Ron Kovic, "Breaking the Silence of the Night," Truthdig (October 10, 2006)

The dissenter is every human being at those moments of his life when he resigns momentarily from the herd and thinks for himself.
—Archibald MacLeish, "In Praise of Dissent," *New York Times* (December 16, 1956)

There is one tradition in America I am proud to inherit. It is our first freedom and the truest expression of our Americanism: the ability to dissent without fear.
—Natalie Merchant, quoted in "What Is Patriotism?" *Nation* (July 15, 2001)

No one who truly cares about democracy favors punishing critics and demonizing dissenters.
—Robert Parry, "Dixie Chicks, Valerie Plame and Bush," *Consortium News* (May 16, 2006)

Free speech can cost you if you're out there protesting in today's chilly climate, where the forecast for dissent is cloudy with a chance of consequences.
—Susan Paynter, "A Sister of Conscience Confronts a Lack of Tolerance for Dissent," *Seattle Post-Intelligencer* (January 15, 2003)

Mass resistance movements, individual activists, journalists, artists, and film makers have come together to strip Empire of its sheen. . . . This was the beginning of real globalization. The globalization of dissent.
—Arundhati Roy, *Public Power in the Age of Empire* (2004)

I'm tired of being labeled anti-American because I ask questions.
—Susan Sarandon, on her opposition to the Iraq War, *Time* (Asia Edition) (February 3, 2003)

Let's not underestimate the force of what we oppose. Let's not underestimate the retaliation that may be visited on those who dare to dissent from the brutalities and repressions thought justified by the fears of the majority.
—Susan Sontag, "Of Courage and Resistance," *Nation* (May 5, 2003)

Foreign Policy

We may look up to armies for our defense, but virtue is our best security.
—Samuel Adams, quoted in "An Interview with Rev. William Sloane Coffin," *Common Dreams* (October 22, 2005)

Until recently, the "soft power" of our human and civil rights record was admired—and sometimes envied—around the world. People wanted to be like us, and that gave us a power we have squandered.
—Tom Blackburn, "Danger of Imperious Presidency," *Palm Beach Post* (February 2, 2004)

America needs to lead by example, rather than by force.
—Bob Burnett, "A Liberal Foreign Policy: Ten Maxims," *Huffington Post* (March 1, 2007)

Conservatives believe that because America is big and powerful we can do whatever we want in the world.
—Bob Burnett, "Killing Conservatism," Smirking Chimp (December 7, 2006)

Human rights is the soul of our foreign policy, because human rights is the very soul of our sense of nationhood.
—Jimmy Carter, commemorating the thirtieth anniversary of the UN Declaration of Human Rights (December 6, 1978)

Corporate Power is the Driving Force Behind U. S. Foreign Policy—and the Slaughter in Iraq
—John Kenneth Galbraith, article title, *Guardian (UK)* (July 15, 2004)

It is precisely our moral authority that is our greatest source of strength, and it is precisely our moral authority that has been recklessly put at risk by the cheap calculations and mean compromises of conscience wagered with history by this willful president [George W. Bush].
—Al Gore, remarks at New York University (May 26, 2004)

Progressives must articulate a coherent foreign policy that is non-imperialist, non-militaristic, and non-corporatist.
—Christopher Hayes, "How to Turn Your Red State Blue," *In These Times* (March 22, 2005)

People in places many of us never heard of . . . want human dignity and a voice in their own futures. They want their children to grow up strong and healthy and free.
—Hubert H. Humphrey, in his speech in Faribault, Minnesota (June 4, 1966)

America is strongest in the world when we use our superpower status to join with other nations to achieve great goals, instead of bullying them to salute us.
—Edward M. Kennedy, in his address to the National Press Club, "A Democratic Blueprint for America's Future" (January 12, 2005)

Acting on our own, by ourselves, we cannot establish justice throughout the world.
—John F. Kennedy, in his speech in Philadelphia (July 4, 1962)

The reason that Woodrow Wilson and Franklin Roosevelt and Harry Truman and Adlai Stevenson had influence abroad, and the United States in their time had it, was because they moved this country here at home, because they stood for something here in the United States, for expanding the benefits of our society to our own people, and the people around the world looked to us as a symbol of hope.
—John F. Kennedy, accepting the New York Liberal Party nomination (September 14, 1960)

We are reduced from a beacon of hope to a saber-rattling thug.
—Jerry Landay, "What Happens When the Dream Dies?" *Providence Journal* (August 3, 2006)

No more bitching about the French. At least they're standing up to the Bush administration, which is more than I can say for the Democrats.
—Bill Maher, *New Rules* (2005)

Both Osama bin Laden and Saddam Hussein were groomed and armed by the United States.
—George Monbiot, "America's War on Itself," *Guardian (UK)* (December 21, 2004)

Far from being the most beloved country on earth, today the U.S. is the most thoroughly detested.
—Jan Morris, "Once the Most Beloved Country in the World, the U.S. Is Now the Most Hated," *Guardian (UK)* (February 14, 2007)

The crimes of the United States have been systematic, constant, vicious, re-morseless . . . while masquerading as a force for universal good.
—Harold Pinter, "Playwright Takes a Prize and a Jab at U.S.," *New York Times* (December 8, 2005)

If we fail to meet our problems here, no one else in the world will do so. If we fail, the heart goes out of progressives throughout the world.
—Eleanor Roosevelt, in a 1947 address to the founding of Americans for Democratic Action, quoted in *Eleanor: The Years Alone* (1972)

We cannot exist as a little island of well-being in a world where two-thirds of the people go to bed hungry every night.
—Eleanor Roosevelt, in her speech at a Democratic Party dinner (December 8, 1959)

Never before in American history has the United States been so feared and hated by the rest of the world.
—Arthur M. Schlesinger, Jr., *War and the American Presidency* (2005)

We were world leaders once—helping found the United Nations, the Marshall Plan, NATO, and programs like Food for Peace, international human rights, and international environmental standards. The world admired not only the bravery of our Marine Corps but also the idealism of our Peace Corps.
—Theodore C. Sorensen, in his commencement speech at the New School University in New York (May 21, 2004)

We now present ourselves to the rest of the world as proud, grinning, jut-jawed, pitiless war lovers, with appallingly powerful weaponry.
—Kurt Vonnegut, "I Love You, Madame Librarian," *In These Times* (August 6, 2004)

The United States now presents itself as what amounts to the globe's largest and most powerful rogue state—a nuclear-armed superpower capable of projecting military force to the furthest corners of the earth, acting utterly without legal or moral constraint whenever the president proclaims it necessary.
—Matthew Yglesias, "Rogue State," *American Prospect* (September 26, 2006)

I wonder how the foreign policies of the United States would look if we wiped out the national boundaries of the world . . . and thought of all the children everywhere as our own.
—Howard Zinn, *A People's History of the United States* (2003)

Do we want to be reviled by the rest of the world? Do we have a right to invade and bomb other countries, pretending we are saving them from tyranny and in the process killing them in huge numbers?
—Howard Zinn, "Harness That Anger," *Progressive* (January 2005)

Idealism

The America we long for is still out there, somewhere ahead of us, waiting for us to find her.
—Jimmy Carter, in his speech in Los Angeles (June 1, 1976)

This, then, is the test we must set for ourselves; not to march alone but to march in such a way that others will wish to join us.
—Hubert H. Humphrey, in his speech in Buffalo, New York (January 6, 1967)

I'm not arguing for a holier-than-thou purism on all doctrine at all times; we have to be strategic in offering support to politicians with whom we inevitably will have some disagreements.
—Robert Jensen, "The Bipartisan Empire," *TomPaine.com* (February 27, 2007)

I am going to build the kind of nation that President Roosevelt hoped for, President Truman worked for, and President Kennedy died for.
—Lyndon B. Johnson, in a speech quoted in the *Sunday Times (UK)* (December 27, 1964)

I would rather have a party that loses now, but believes in the moral value of treating all citizens with respect, than a party that appeals to people's worst fears and intolerance.
—Mike Koehler, in a letter to the editor, *Newsweek* (November 29, 2004)

Ideas are great arrows, but there has to be a bow. And politics is the bow of idealism.
—Bill Moyers, quoted in "LBJ's Young Man in Charge of Everything," *Time* (October 29, 1965)

The extraordinary thing about this new consciousness is that it has emerged out of the wasteland of the Corporate State, like flowers pushing up through the concrete pavement. . . . For one who thought the world was irretrievably encased in metal and plastic and sterile stone, it seems a veritable greening of America.
—Charles A. Reich, *The Greening of America* (1970)

Many in the Democratic Party elite fear, if not outright despise, idealism.
—Tim Robbins, "What I Voted For," *Nation* (August 6, 2001)

What America is looking for is authentic people who want to go into public service because they strongly believe in something, not people who are [just] trying to get elected.
—Susan Sarandon, on her disappointment with Hillary Clinton, quoted in "Leftist Lament," *New York Post* (March 17, 2006)

Now it is our turn to prove that the New Frontier was not a place in time but a timeless call.
—Caroline Kennedy Schlossberg, quoted from her speech to the Democratic National Convention, "Kennedys Deliver Family Values," *Guardian (UK)* (August 17, 2000)

Patriotism

A patriot does not tell people who are intensely concerned about their country to just sit down and be quiet . . . to show slavish, blind obedience, and deference to a dishonest, war-mongering, human-rights-violating president.
—Rocky Anderson, quoted in "A Demand for Truth: Mayor's Blunt Criticisms Focus War Debate," *Salt Lake Tribune* (August 30, 2006)

You make men love their government and their country by giving them the kind of government and the kind of country that inspire respect and love: a country that is free and unafraid.
—Zechariah Chafee, Jr., *Free Speech in the United States* (1942)

I like to believe that I am an American patriot who loves his country enough to address her flaws.
—Rev. William Sloane Coffin, *Credo* (2003)

No matter that patriotism is too often the refuge of scoundrels. Dissent, rebellion, and all-around hell-raising remain the true duty of patriots.
—Barbara Ehrenreich, *The Worst Years of Our Lives* (1991)

When the whole nation is roaring patriotism at the top of its voice, I am fain to explore the cleanness of its hands and purity of its heart.
—Ralph Waldo Emerson, *Journal* (December 10, 1824)

Patriotism strikes me as divisive, a kind of misplaced pride based on the geographic fluke of where one happened to be born. . . . I don't ask "God" to bless America—I wish good things to all peace-loving people throughout the world.
—Laura Kaminker, "Patriotism? Or Just Conformity?" *Common Dreams* (October 27, 2003)

Real patriotism cannot be coerced.
—Bob Kerrey, "Our Flag and Our Freedom," *Washington Post* (June 15, 2006)

In America, the true patriots are those who dare speak truth to power.
—Teresa Heinz Kerry, "Remarks at the Democratic Convention," *USA Today* (July 27, 2004)

Each of us who is female, nonwhite or without land would have been guaranteed in 1776 the same voting rights as a horse. We owe a precious debt to Americans before us who refused to believe patriotism just meant going with the crowd.
—Barbara Kingsolver, "It's My Flag, Too," *San Francisco Chronicle* (January 13, 2002)

There are as many ways to love America as there are Americans.
—Barbara Kingsolver, "It's My Flag, Too," *San Francisco Chronicle* (January 13, 2002)

The greatest testament to one's love of country is when one works to improve it.
—George Lakoff, *Thinking Points: Communicating Our American Values and Vision* (2006)

It's been over a year since they graduated, but neither of the Bush twins has been able to find work. Why don't they sign up [for the army]? Do they hate America or just freedom in general?
—Bill Maher, "Real Time with Bill Maher," HBO (May 13, 2005)

So many challenges face us at home and abroad that we should not waste time, tolerance and good will debating which politician loves America most ardently, which one is most devoted to marriage and the family and which one is closest to the Almighty.
—George McGovern, "Patriotism Is Nonpartisan," *Nation* (March 24, 2005)

What, exactly, is patriotism? Is it a yellow car ribbon or is it calling for truth and dignity in the conduct of this nation?
—Floyd J. McKay, "Calling for Truth and Dignity in the Nation's Conduct," *Seattle Times* (November 16, 2005)

Not every patriot thinks we should do to the people of Baghdad what Bin Laden did to us.
—Bill Moyers, "The Battle for PBS," *In These Times* (May 31, 2005)

[The corporations] are counting on your patriotism to distract you from their plunder. They're counting on you to stand at attention with your hand over your heart, pledging allegiance to the flag, while they pick your pocket.
—Bill Moyers, quoted in "Corporate Patriotism," *Common Dreams* (November 10, 2001)

Patriotism is modeled on the mentality of the sports fan.
—Martha Nussbaum, quoted in *What Do We Do Now?* (2004)

One of the greatest attractions of patriotism—it fulfills our worst wishes. In the person of the nation we are able, vicariously, to bully and cheat . . . with a feeling that we are profoundly virtuous.
—George Orwell, *Eyeglasses in Gaza* (1936)

I worry that patriotism run amok will trample the very values that the country seeks to defend.
—Dan Rather, "Veteran CBS News Anchor Dan Rather Speaks Out on BBC Newsnight Tonight," BBC News (May 16, 2002)

For some, patriotism means giving unflagging support to our military, regardless of whether we agree or disagree with their current mission. . . . But is that really patriotism?
—Reggie Rivers, "Waving a Flag is the Easy Part," *Denver Post* (October 4, 2001)

I feel this do-or-die, my-country-right-or-wrong kind of patriotism is not merely out of place in a nuclear armed world, it is criminal egotism on a monstrous scale.
—Benjamin Spock, *Decent and Indecent* (1968)

Most conservatives are tremendously patriotic, but their patriotism is largely symbolic. It isn't about making sacrifices for their country. . . . Ask not what you can do for your country, they say, ask whether you can tape a flag to your car.
—Paul Waldman, *Being Right Is Not Enough* (2006)

Patriotism means loving your country and its best ideals, enough even to oppose it when it is grievously wrong.
—Rev. Jim Wallis, *God's Politics: Why the Right Gets It Wrong and the Left Doesn't Get It* (2005)

Yellow ribbon patriots finally have an opportunity to support our troops in a meaningful way. They can begin by removing their magnetic yellow ribbon bumper stickers, by listening to the troops and helping to get them home.
—Robert Weitzel, "Cure for Yellow Ribbon Patriotism," *Common Dreams* (January 8, 2007)

Is not nationalism—that devotion to a flag, an anthem, a boundary so fierce it engenders mass murder—one of the great evils of our time, along with racism, along with religious hatred?
—Howard Zinn, "Put Away the Flags," *Progressive* (July 2006)

Protest

In the sixties, when I was growing up, one of the great elements of American culture was the protest song. There were songs about the civil rights movement, the women's rights movement, the antiwar movement . . . Now you can find only two or three bands that'll do that. I think it's just part of the corporate world.
—George Clooney, interviewed by Rob Nelson, *Mother Jones* (November/December 2005)

I do not know of any salvation for society except through eccentrics, misfits, dissenters, people who protest.
—William O. Douglas, quoted in *The Power of Reason* (1964)

Where the hell is our outrage? We should be screaming bloody murder. We've got a gang of clueless bozos steering our ship of state right over a cliff, we've got corporate gangsters stealing us blind, and we can't even clean up after a hurricane much less build a hybrid car.
—Lee Iacocca, *Where Have All the Leaders Gone?* (2007)

Freedom of assembly? Welcome to your first "First Amendment zone" experience and be careful not to step beyond the yellow police tape unless you want to discover what the verb "tazered" means.
—Mike Malloy and Kathy Bay, quoted in *Air America: The Playbook* (2006)

To sin by silence, when we should protest, makes cowards out of men.
—Ella Wheeler Wilcox, "Protest," *Poems of Problems* (1914)

THE POLITICAL PARTIES

Activism

Organize, agitate, educate, must be our war cry.
—Susan B. Anthony, quoted in *The Life and Work of Susan B. Anthony* (1898)

The day you realize you're a grownup is the day you realize that you have to do something.
—Barbara Boxer, in an interview with Ruth Conniff, *Progressive* (July 2005)

Being part of a progressive religious community means that we are called to be active in the world.
—Rev. Clare Butterfield, "Religious Left Needn't Be Ashamed to Speak Up," *Chicago Sun-Times* (November 24, 2004)

It is in organization for action that liberals are weak, and without this organization there is danger that democratic ideals may go by default.
—John Dewey, *Liberalism and Social Action* (1935)

Religious progressives must now learn the lesson evangelicals learned long ago: the key to organizing people of faith is not through celebrity clergy but through congregations. Congregations are where the rubber hits the road. This is where the faithful meet, greet, eat and mobilize.
—Rev. David Dyson, in his speech delivered December 2, 2004, "Playing Catch-Up with the Evangelicals," *Nation* (January 1, 2005)

Why are American students sucking their thumbs while the Bush Administration proposes a $12.7 billion cut in student loans?
—Barbara Ehrenreich, "Kleenex Workers," *Progressive* (May 2006)

Our deeds determine us . . . as much as we determine our deeds.
—George Eliot, *Adam Bede* (1859)

The biggest sin is sitting on your ass.
—Florynce Kennedy, quoted in *Ms.* magazine (March 1973)

Organized people have always had to take on organized money. If they had not, blacks would still be three-fifths of a person, women wouldn't have the vote, workers couldn't organize, and children would still be working in the mines.
—Bill Moyers, "Saving Democracy," *Common Dreams* (February 24, 2006)

Conservatives look like activists flogging new ideas because they are; they're forever presenting new ways of attacking the prevailing social and political structure.
—Ted Rall, *Wake Up, You're Liberal!* (2004)

No grassroots movement ever got anywhere compromising its ideals.
—Tim Robbins, "What I Voted For," *Nation* (August 6, 2001)

In the long run there is no more liberating, no more exhilarating experience than to determine one's position, state it bravely, and then act boldly.
—Eleanor Roosevelt, quoted in *Eleanor Roosevelt: 1884–1933* (1992)

Try something. If it doesn't work, try something else. But for God's sake— try something.
—Franklin D. Roosevelt, to his cabinet when he took office in 1933

It is not the critic who counts; not the man who points out how the strong man stumbles, or where the doer of deeds could have done them better. The credit belongs to the man who is actually in the arena, whose face is marred by dust and sweat and blood; who strives valiantly . . . if he fails, at least fails while daring greatly, so that his place shall never be with those cold and timid souls who know neither victory nor defeat.
—Theodore Roosevelt, in his address in Paris on April 23, 1910, *The Works of Theodore Roosevelt* (1926)

Moral action is the meeting-place between the human and divine.
—Leon Roth, *Jewish Thought as a Factor in Civilization* (1954)

Pray to God, but row for the shore.
—Russian proverb

A grassroots base that is organized around hollow partisan labels rather than an overarching belief system—no matter how seemingly energized—will never defeat an opponent that puts ideological warriors ready to walk through fire on the political battlefield.
—David Sirota, "Partisan War Syndrome," *In These Times* (October 17, 2005)

Action is impossible without hope.
—Rebecca Solnit, *Hope in the Dark* (2004)

I use the term activist to mean . . . one that seeks to democratize the word, to share power, to protect differences and complexity, human and otherwise.
—Rebecca Solnit, *Hope in the Dark* (2004)

Who will get to heaven first—the man who talks or the man who acts?
—Melvin B. Tolson, "The Death of an Infidel," *Washington Tribune* (April 2, 1938)

You have to be willing to fight. You don't have to be unethical, but you have to be willing to hit your opponents and hit them hard. Otherwise, you're just going to keep losing.
—Paul Waldman, in an interview with Mark Karlin, "Paul Waldman Knows Progressives Can Win—and Here's How," *BuzzFlash* (May 25, 2006)

If we don't fight hard enough for the things we stand for, at some point we have to recognize that we don't really stand for them.
—Paul Wellstone, quoted in *Politics the Wellstone Way* (2005)

Small acts, when multiplied by millions of people, can transform the world.
—Howard Zinn, "The Optimism of Uncertainty," *Nation* (September 2, 2004)

When a social movement adopts the compromises of legislators, it has forgotten its role, which is to push and challenge the politicians, not to fall in meekly behind them.
—Howard Zinn, "Are We Politicians or Citizens?" *Progressive* (May 2007)

Apathy

When historians look back on the years 2001 to 2006, they will be astonished at how easily fundamental American traditions were violated and how casually fundamental American rights were not only taken away, but surrendered.
—Brent Budowsky, "New Congress: Americanism Means No Torture, Eavesdropping with Warrants, Honest Elections, *Habeas Corpus*," *Huffington Post* (November 13, 2006)

Too many in this country today are . . . indifferent to politics. Tyrannized by their overscheduled lives, distracted by money and possessions, celebrity and sport, or preoccupied with simply keeping their heads and those of their children above water, too many Americans live believing the state of the world does not concern them.
—Todd Huffman, "The Politics of Hope," *Common Dreams* (November 7, 2006)

We may have found a cure for most evils; but it has found no remedy for the worst of them all—the apathy of human beings.
—Helen Keller, *My Religion* (1927)

Men are accomplices to that which leaves them indifferent.
—George Steiner, *Language and Silence* (1967)

The sad fact is that we have been turned into complacent consumeroids. We are now the beneficiaries of a material comfort that has succeeded in making us overwhelmingly passive with regard to what goes on in our government, not to mention what is going on in the rest of the world.
—J. D. Suss, "The Real Culprit: Corpocracy," *Information Clearing House* (December 16, 2006)

Campaign Finance

Will the centrist Democratic Party face up to the responsibility for its failure to mold public opinion in resistance to big money?
—Warren Beatty, "Why Not Now?" *New York Times* (August 22, 1999)

Poor people do not make campaign contributions.
—Jason DeParlem, "Liberal Hopes Ebb in Post-Storm Poverty Debate," *New York Times* (October 11, 2005)

Money buys access; access buys influence.
—Elizabeth Drew, KQED (San Francisco) (May 15, 1997)

We are the only people in the world required by law to take large amounts of money from strangers and then act as if it has no effect on our behavior.
—Barney Frank, quoted in "Saving Democracy," *Common Dreams* (February 24, 2006)

What politician in this success-worshiping country really wants to be the voice of poor people? Where's the soft money in that?
—Thomas Frank, "Red-State America Against Itself," *TomDispatch.com* (July 16, 2004)

What has happened is that a democracy has been turned into a dollar-ocracy, or into a lobby-ocracy.
—Richard Gwyn, "DeLay Downfall Reflects Poorly on Democracy," *Toronto Star* (April 7, 2006)

If we could slap corporate logos on politicians, like NASCAR drivers do with their cars, we could get to the bottom of where they really stand on the issues.
—Headline, introducing an article by Stephen Pizzo, "Campaign Finance Reform, NASCAR-style," AlterNet (April 27, 2006)

The relentless pursuit of corporate dollars by practically all of our political leaders shows that we no longer have elections—we have auctions.
—Jim Hightower, "Forget Washington, All Good Politics Is Local," *Hightower Lowdown* (February 2006)

Congressional incumbents raise ten times more money than challengers, giving them a virtually insurmountable advantage at election time.
—Mark Hertzgaard, *The Eagle's Shadow* (2002)

The corporate owned congress continues to feed its contributors and give the bill to the American people.
—John M. Kelley, "Watch That Pea," Truthout (November 2005)

Our democracy is broken because of our campaign finance system, which is just a system of legalized bribery, which has allowed corporations and the very wealthy to control the electoral results.
—Robert F. Kennedy, Jr., "Democracy in Crisis—Interview with Robert F. Kennedy, Jr.," Bradblog (July 18, 2006)

The soul of democracy has been dying, drowning in a rising tide of big money contributed by a narrow, unrepresentative elite.
—Bill Moyers, "Which America Will We Be Now?" *Nation* (November 1, 2001)

Until we offer qualified candidates a different source of funding for their campaigns—"clean," disinterested, accountable public money—the selling of America will go on. From scandal to scandal.
—Bill Moyers, "Saving Democracy," *Common Dreams* (February 24, 2006)

Corporations are legal entities, not human beings; as such they should be prohibited from contributing to campaigns, sponsoring PACs or lobbying.
—Ralph Nader, "How to Curb Corporate Power," *Nation* (October 10, 2005)

The only way to stop the system of legalized bribery is to cut it off at its roots. Require television and radio networks that use the public airwaves to offer candidates free time.
—Robert Reich, "Keeping Up Appearances," *American Prospect* (January 17, 2007)

Government by organized money is just as dangerous as Government by organized mob.
—Franklin D. Roosevelt, quoted in "Time Machine," *American Heritage* (October/November 1986)

Full public financing must be the ultimate goal. . . . By cutting off the demand for private money, we will cut off the special-interest influence that comes with it.
—Eliot Spitzer, quoted in "Lobbyists: 'I'm Going to Be Hugged & Kissed as Long as I'm Giving Them a Check,'" AlterNet (January 4, 2007)

The flood of money that gushes into politics today is a pollution of democracy.
—Theodore H. White, *Time* (November 19, 1984)

Large campaign contributions are like addictive narcotics. They create a help-less dependency in lawmakers seeking reelection.
—Jim Wright, "Big Money Contributors Defeat Public Interest," *Miami Herald* (July 3, 2001)

George W. Bush

Bush Had an Exit Strategy for Vietnam
—Bumper sticker

This administration has been the worst in history.
—Jimmy Carter, quoted in "Jimmy Carter Slams Bush Administration," the Associated Press (AP) (May 19, 2007)

[Bush is] strangely resentful about the actual core of his job. Even after the debacles of Iraq and Katrina, he continues to treat the presidency as a colossal interference with his desire to mountain bike and clear brush.
—Maureen Dowd, "Animal House Summit," *New York Times* (July 19, 2006)

Bush's animating idea has been that the peoples of the Middle East can be bombed into democracy and terrorized into moderation.
—Jonathan Freedland, "At the Heart of the Lebanon Crisis Lie the Lethal Mistakes of George Bush," *Guardian (UK)* (July 26, 2006)

The country club culture and the Ivy League affirmative action his family sta-tus guaranteed assured this manifestly mediocre man his richly undeserved academic opportunities, business "successes," personal wealth and the powers of high public office.
—Bill Gallagher, "Treasonous Bush Fostering Fascism," *Niagara Falls Reporter* (January 31, 2006)

I think [Bush's] weakness is a moral weakness. I think he is a bully, and like all bullies, he's a coward when confronted with a force that he's fearful of. His reaction to the extravagant and unbelievably selfish wish list of the wealthy interest groups that put him in the White House . . . can only come from genuine moral cowardice.
—Al Gore, quoted in "The Wilderness Campaign," *New Yorker* (September 13, 2004)

The essential cruelty of Bush's game is that he takes an astonishingly selfish and greedy collection of economic and political proposals and then cloaks them with a phony moral authority, thus misleading many Americans who have a deep and genuine desire to do good in the world.
—Al Gore, *The Assault on Reason* (2007)

[Bush's] breathtaking arrogance is exceeded only by his incompetence. And that's the real problem. That's where you'll find the mind-boggling destructiveness of this regime, in its incompetence.
—Bob Herbert, "A President Who Can Do No Right," *New York Times* (January 26, 2006)

Here we have a slacker son of a powerful patrician father who resolves unconscious Oedipal issues through inappropriate acting-out in foreign countries . . . . We've all had issues with our dads. But do we need this many people to die so that one dude can look like a leader?
—Garrison Keillor, "Time for the Father to Chat with the Son," *Baltimore Sun* (January 4, 2007)

This is the worst environmental president we've had in American history.
—Robert F. Kennedy, Jr., in his speech at the Sierra Summit in San Francisco, "Those of Us Who Know That America's Worth Fighting for Have to Take It Back Now from Those Who Don't" (September 10, 2005)

You might say that the Bush administration favors people who live off their wealth over people who have a job.
—Paul Krugman, "The Great Wealth Transfer," *Rolling Stone* (November 30, 2006)

I would like to apologize for referring to George W. Bush as a "deserter." What I meant to say is that George W. Bush is a deserter, an election thief, a drunk driver, a WMD liar, and a functional illiterate.
—Michael Moore, open letter posted at MichaelMoore.com (January 27, 2004)

I'm not anti-Bush; I'm anti-Bush behavior. In other words, I'm against cheating, greed, cruelty, racism, imperialism, religious fundamentalism, treason, and the seemingly limitless capacity for hypocrisy.
—Viggo Mortensen, in an interview with Nina Siegal, *Progressive* (November 2005)

Mr. Bush's peculiar combination of zealotry and utter incompetence constitutes a clear and present danger to national security. . . . Small wonder that
everywhere I go, people are talking about moving to Canada.
—Leonard Pitts, Jr., "Is This the Beginning of the End for America?" *Baltimore Sun*
(November 8, 2004)

Despite the trappings of his office he is still the intellectually and ethically
challenged frat boy he was forty years ago, a world-class embarrassment.
—David Rossie, "President Doing Harm to Nation," *Binghamton Press & Sun
Bulletin* (July 30, 2006)

Bush will never be absolved of sending young people to kill and be killed in a
war without moral justification.
—Robert Scheer, "Pomp and Improper Circumstance," *Nation* (January 18,
2005)

The priorities of the Bush White House are clear. For killing in Iraq, they
spare no expense. For protecting and sustaining life, the cupboards go bare.
—Norman Solomon, "Ending the Impunity of the Bush White House,"
Common Dreams (September 2, 2005)

While I listen to you talk about freedom, I see you assert your right to tap
my telephone, to arrest me and hold me without charges, to try to preclude
me from breathing clean air and drinking clean water. I have never felt more
ashamed of or more frightened by my leadership in Washington.
—Harry Taylor, to President Bush at a town hall meeting, quoted in
"Questioner Sharply Criticizes President Bush at Appearance," Knight Ridder
(April 7, 2006)

The president who started out by claiming to be a compassionate conservative
will go down in history as The Torture President.
—Cenk Uygur, "Maverick Senators Cave in to the Torture President,"
Huffington Post (September 22, 2006)

We've had idiots as presidents before. He's not unique. But he's certainly the
most active idiot that we have ever had.
—Gore Vidal, to President Bush in "Gore Vidal's State of the Union,"
Democracy Now! radio (January 31, 2006)

Centrism

When . . . pundits call for Democrats to move toward the center, what they're really saying is that they need to become more conservative.
—Eric Alterman, "Think Again: The Viral Center," *Huffington Post* (January 18, 2007)

Governing "from the center"—simply reflecting public opinion—is relatively easy, but it is neither good policy nor good politics. It doesn't produce the reforms needed to make America better.
—Robert L. Borosage, "Passion or Positioning," *Huffington Post* (January 16, 2007)

It's silly to try to move to the center. There is no center.
—Wes Boyd, interviewed by Don Hazen, "MoveOn Muscles Up," AlterNet (April 26, 2005)

You never will see the right move to some theoretical center, because they understand that their power stems from projecting a coherent story about the problems we face and where we need to go. They are wrong, but they're coherent. They don't mumble.
—Wes Boyd, interviewed by Don Hazen, "MoveOn Muscles Up," AlterNet (April 26, 2005)

The Clinton era did not produce a stronger Democratic Party. To the contrary, its legacy is the philosophy that principles don't matter, that what counts is reading the mood of the electorate and being nimble enough to adjust to changing voter preferences.
—Bob Burnett, "Busting the Clinton Ghost," *Common Dreams* (March 8, 2006)

Sooner or later you figure out that pragmatism and compromise are principles in a democracy. It's not selling out your convictions.
—Bill Clinton, the quintessential centrist strategist, quoted in "Clinton Calls for Kinder, Gentler Political Talk," *USA Today* (November 21, 2005)

It seems that after every losing election, there's a consensus reached among decision-makers in the Democratic Party is that the way to win is to be more like Republicans.
—Howard Dean, "The Future of the Democratic Party," remarks at George Washington University (December 8, 2004)

Hand-wringing over extreme partisanship has become a popular cause among learned analysts. They operate from Olympian heights and strain for even-handedness by issuing tut-tuts to all sides, Democrats and Republicans, liberals and conservatives.
—E. J. Dionne, Jr., "Who's Hyperpartisan?" *Washington Post* (March 9, 2007)

The Washington conventional wisdom machine always defines "fairness" as a carefully calibrated point exactly between the positions of the two parties, no matter how outrageous one of the positions might be.
—E. J. Dionne, Jr., "I Was Against Presidential Privilege Before I Was for It," Truthdig (March 23, 2007)

For God's sake, act like Democrats.
—Editorial, "Do the Right Thing: Where Hillary Clinton and Joe Biden Fail—and Gene McCarthy Succeeded," *Boston Phoenix* (December 16–22, 2005)

Centrist Democrats should not be flirting with faith but re-examining their affinity for candidates too mumble-mouthed and compromised to articulate poverty and war as the urgent moral issues they are.
—Barbara Ehrenreich, "Act Like Christians," *Nation* (November 11, 2004)

Centrism and bipartisanship are euphemisms for the mutual interests of Washington party insiders.
—R. J. Eskow, "Centrism and Bipartisanship: For Democrats Only," *Huffington Post* (December 2, 2006)

If you are a progressive, a populist Democrat, someone who thinks moving the party to the center is a dead end in this political debate, then it may be time to step up and make yourself heard.
—Don Hazen, "Power Play," AlterNet (January 7, 2005)

The Democratic policy of trying to reach out to a movement that attacks whole segments of the society as worthy only of conversion or eradication is frightening.
—Chris Hedges, interviewed by Michelle Goldberg, "The Holy Blitz Rolls On," *Salon* (January 8, 2007)

There's Nothing in the Middle of the Road but Yellow Stripes and Dead Armadillos
—The title of Jim Hightower's 1997 book

Today, politicians are proud to pronounce that we have abolished slavery. But in its time, slavery was the political center, and abolitionists were punished for their moral strength. Today, politicians hold up the gains of women. Yet in its time, denial of the vote to women was the political center.
—Rev. Jesse Jackson, quoted in "What Is Patriotism?" *Nation* (July 15, 2001)

The political center has disappeared.
—Jim Kelley, "Democrats Must Reclaim Moral Ground," *Atlanta Journal-Constitution* (March 9, 2005)

Centrism is not a "third way," it's their way—taking right-wing ideas and trying to pass them off as enlightened Democratic compromise.
—Sally Kohn, "Abandoning the See Saw of Centrism," *Common Dreams* (October 31, 2006)

Right-wing ideology has become so influential in our society that Democrats, who once sought power to enact a progressive agenda for the future, now seek power at any cost, even if it means jumping on the conservative bandwagon.
—Sally Kohn, "The Victory That Masks Defeat: Democrats Right-Leaning Win," *Common Dreams* (November 28, 2006)

By moving to the right, progressives actually help activate the right's values and give up on their own.
—George Lakoff, *Thinking Points: Communicating Our Values and Vision* (2006)

Democrats moving to the middle is a double disaster that alienates the party's progressive base while simultaneously sending a message to swing voters that the other side is where the good ideas are.
—George Lakoff, quoted in "The Next DNC Chair: Why You Should Care," AlterNet (December 8, 2004)

Too often during the [2006] campaign, I couldn't tell the difference between the Democratic and the Republican positions on Iraq.
—John R. MacArthur, "'Centrist' Democrats Want It Both Ways," *Providence Journal* (December 6, 2006)

The days of trying to move the Democratic Party to the right are over.
—Michael Moore, "It's Time to Stop Being Hit," YubaNet (December 13, 2004)

The process of moving the Democrats rightward has no end point, because every time the Democrats shift rightward the Republicans respond by shifting a little further rightward so they can continue to denounce the Democratic position as radical leftism.
—Timothy Noah, "Whither Liberalism? Again?" *Slate* (November 3, 2004)

Centrism is bogus. The "center" keeps shifting further right because Radcons [Radical Conservatives] stay put while Democrats keep meeting them halfway.
—Robert Reich, *Reason: Why Liberal Will Win the Battle for America* (2004)

There's a sick collusion going on in Washington. And I'm not talking about the corporate lobbyists and the elected officials who represent them. No, I'm talking about centrist Democrats and the hack journalists who cover them.
—Matthew Rothschild, "A Journalistic Bias Toward Acquiescence," *Progressive* (January 5, 2007)

When enough people self-consciously move to the political "center," it ceases to be the center and becomes a new pole.
—Julian Sanchez, "Is There a 'Middle Ground' on Choice?" *Campus Progress* (November 14, 2006)

The "centrists" tell Democrats not to hammer corporations for their misbehavior and not to push for a serious crackdown on corporate excess, for fear the party will be hurt by an "anti-business" image.
—David Sirota, "Debunking 'Centrism,'" *Nation* (January 3, 2005)

Washington's definition of "centrism" is not just about promoting those who capitulate to Republicans, but more broadly, those who genuflect to the Establishment and support the hostile takeover of our government.
—David Sirota, "Joe Lieberman & the Hostile Takeover of 'Centrism'," *Working For Change* (May 30, 2006)

The real responsibility for the Iraq war lay not with Bush but with . . . the malleable middle of the American political establishment who three years ago made a conscious moral choice to support a military action that even a three-year-old could have seen made no fucking sense at all.
—Matt Taibbi, "Blame for Iraq Extends Far Beyond the GOP," *Rolling Stone* (November 5, 2006)

When given the choice, people will vote for the real Republican over the fake one every time.
—Harry S. Truman, quoted in "Power Play," AlterNet (January 7, 2005)

When religion defines morality, the wall between church and state comes to be seen as immoral. This is what we're facing now—not only from Bush and the Christian right, but from the earnest centrists and liberals who are doing their dirty work.
—Ellen Willis, "Freedom from Religion," *Nation* (February 1, 2001)

Things fall apart; the centre cannot hold.
—William Butler Yeats, "The Second Coming," *The Collected Poems of W. B. Yeats* (1989)

Scholars, who pride themselves on speaking their minds, often engage in a form of self-censorship which is called "realism." To be "realistic" in dealing with a problem is to work only among the alternatives which the most powerful in society put forth.
—Howard Zinn, *Howard Zinn on War* (2000)

Democratic Luminaries

He was right on Iraq. He was right on global warming.
—Lawrence Bender, producer of *An Inconvenient Truth*, on Al Gore, "Could Gore's Road to the Oval Office Begin in Hollywood?" CNN (February 23, 2007)

We don't want the first female president to be Joe Lieberman in drag, pushing Bush-lite politics. We expect something better.
—Susan J. Douglas, "Why Women Hate Hillary," *In These Times* (April 26, 2007)

He transplanted a spine into the presidential campaign.
—Editorial, on Howard Dean's departure from the presidential race, *New York Times* (February 19, 2004)

He had a knack for convincing people on both sides of an issue that he agreed with them.
—Ron Fournier, on consummate centrist Bill Clinton, "Sen. Hillary Clinton an Artful Dodger," the Associated Press (AP) (June 20, 2007)

It was an incompetent, corporatized Democratic Party, along with the orchestrated fraud by the Republican Party, that threw the 2000 election to Bush, not Ralph Nader. . . . What about Gore, whose campaign was so timid and empty—he never mentioned global warming—that he could not carry his home state of Tennessee?
—Chris Hedges, "Pariah or Prophet?" Truthdig (February 26, 2007)

My brother need not be idealized, or enlarged in death beyond what he was in life, to be remembered simply as a good decent man, who saw wrong and tried to right it, saw suffering and tried to heal it, saw war and tried to stop it.
—Edward Kennedy, eulogizing Bobby Kennedy (June 8, 1968)

He's the only decent man in the Senate.
—Robert F. Kennedy, regarding George McGovern, "Rallying the Kennedy Vote," *Time* (August 16, 1968). After RFK's assassination, McGovern became the unofficial leader of Democrats opposed to the Vietnam War.

He is trying to be both a progressive and someone beyond conventional categories. Alas, there's no such thing.
—Robert Kuttner on Barack Obama, "Third Time's the Charm?" *American Prospect* (April 17, 2007)

For most of his career, the knock on the state's junior senator has been that he was too cautious, always carefully calculating the angles as he looked ahead for a chance to run nationally. Long on ambition, he's seemed short on conviction.
—Scot Lehigh, on John Kerry's decision to not run for president again, "For [John] Kerry, a New Mission," *Boston Globe* (January 25, 2007)

Lieberman . . . has been such an enthusiastic booster of the occupation that Bush actually kissed the Connecticut senator at the 2005 State of the Union.
—John Nichols, "Joe Lieberman's Connecticut Problem," *Nation* (July 4, 2006)

I find Hillary Clinton to be a great disappointment. . . . What America is looking for is authentic people who want to go into public service because they believe strongly in something, not people who are trying to get elected.
—Susan Sarandon, "Sarandon Unhappy with Centrist Hillary," *Washington Times* (March 21, 2006)

Underneath his joy in combat, he was a do-gooder in the dark of night.
—Arthur M. Schlesinger, Jr., on the death of John Kenneth Galbraith, quoted in "Arthur M. Schlesinger, Jr., Historian of Power, Dies at 89," *New York Times* (March 1, 2007)

[Joe] Lieberman has built his career by serving the interests of the rich.
—Norman Solomon, "Holy Smoke and Mirrors: The Rise of Centrist Theocrats," *Progress Report* (August 10, 2000)

He transformed our government into an active instrument of social justice.
—William J. vanden Heuvel, regarding Franklin D. Roosevelt on the occasion of the International Disability Award Presentation to Canada (March 2, 1998)

I am a proud liberal senator. I am a labor senator. I am an environmentalist senator. I am an education senator. I am a civil rights senator. And that's how we win this election.
—Paul Wellstone, quoted in "Paul Wellstone, Fighter," *Nation* (May 27, 2002)

The Democratic Party

Is it our party's position that we're rich enough to police the world but not rich enough to take care of our own?
—Warren Beatty, "Why Not Now?" *New York Times* (August 22, 1999)

Democrats would be well advised to stop bragging about their clever positioning, and stay focused on what they are prepared to fight for with a passion.
—Robert L. Borosage, "Passion or Positioning," *Huffington Post* (January 16, 2007)

Upon which side will the Democratic party fight; upon the side of "the idle holders of idle capital" or upon the side of "the struggling masses"?
—William Jennings Bryan, from his famous "Cross of Gold" speech in 1896, quoted in *Three Centuries of American Rhetorical Discourse* (1988)

I'm here to represent the Democratic wing of the Democratic Party.
—Howard Dean, "The Democratic Wing of the Democratic Party," *Guardian (UK)* (January 20, 2004). This expression was coined by Paul Wellstone and popularized by Howard Dean.

The [Bush] administration's assault on some of the nation's founding principles continues unabated. If the Democrats were to shirk their responsibility to stop it, that would make them no better than the Republicans who formed and enabled these policies in the first place.
—Editorial, "The Imperial Presidency," *New York Times* (January 7, 2007)

I'm a Democrat because our party gives voice to people who don't have a voice. It's why I've always been a Democrat; it's why I am one today.
—John Edwards, quoted in *Air America: The Playbook* (2006)

The Democratic establishment has a problem. It doesn't like its foot soldiers much.
—Laura Flanders, *Blue Grit* (2007)

Democratic political strategy simply assumes that people know where their economic interest lies and that they will act on it by instinct.
—Thomas Frank, "Red-State America Against Itself," *TomDispatch.com* (July 16, 2004)

Today that's the battle that's being played out for the heart and soul of the Democratic Party—between the DLC [Democratic Leadership Council] and their front groups, who are basically Republican lite—and the progressives within the Democratic Party.
—Thom Hartmann, interview entitled "Thom Hartmann Brings Context to Today's Political Frays," *BuzzFlash* (February 7, 2006)

The challenge for Democrats will be to find a resonant voice on populist and class issues or drift further toward becoming the liberal wing of an ascendant Republican majority.
—Tom Hayden and Lori M. Wallach, "Kerry's Trade Winds," *Nation* (September 30, 2004)

I have no more patience with this perennially pathetic patient, this terminally timid Democrat who continues to lie cowering and trembling on the analyst's couch, wondering why the Demolition Derby Republicans control virtually all of the levers of power in the United States.
—Bob Herbert, "Where's the Beef?" *New York Times* (May 11, 2006)

Democrats can't get to the Promised Land by treating moral values as just another tactic their pollsters tell them they need to pursue, as something "we" need to figure out so we can convince "them" to vote for us.
—Arianna Huffington, "Real Moral Values," AlterNet (November 10, 2004)

I am proud to be a member of a party that opens its doors to all men—and closes its hearts to none.
—Lyndon B. Johnson, *Congressional Record* (January 7, 1960)

The last thing this country needs is two Republican parties.
—Edward M. Kennedy, urging Democrats to oppose privatizing Social Security, *Time* (January 24, 2005)

This is a struggle for the soul of the Democratic Party, which in too many cases has become so corporate and identified with corporate interests that you can't tell the difference between Democrats and Republicans.
—Dennis Kucinich, quoted in "Ohio Rep. Kucinich: 'I'm Ready to Run for President,'" CNN (February 18, 2003)

They are gutless, clueless and spineless. The Democratic Party is a shell of its former self.
—Ralph Nader, quoted in "Why Nader Could Be the Nail in Democrats' Coffin," *Observer (UK)* (October 3, 2004)

Democrats have to become a genuine opposition party before they can ever again hope to become a majority party.
—John Nichols, "The Boxer Rebellion," *Nation* (February 10, 2005)

In many religious circles, Democrats are seen as scornful, secular, urban lite-
rati who do not understand or appreciate traditional lifestyles.
—Laura R. Olson, "Religious Left Faces Tough Challenge," *Newsday*
(November 22, 2004)

America could use a Democratic Party again and there's a rumor it's alive—
somewhere.
—Greg Palast, "Bush Strafes New Orleans, Where's Huey Long?" *Common
Dreams* (September 2, 2005)

The Democrats, if they ever find their spine, have to also find their base. That
won't be hard. Just stop by any picket line, union hall, emergency room,
former factory town, foreclosed family farm, soup line, church, anywhere
working people gather.
—Nick Parker, "The Democrats Lost This Election Twenty Years Ago,"
Common Dreams (November 20, 2004)

Democrats have generally opposed efforts by social conservatives to impose
their religious beliefs on other Americans, a stance that often leaves them
open to attack as "antireligious."
—Eyal Press, "God and the Blue States," *Nation* (August 12, 2004)

The Democratic Party has repeatedly sold out its core values. It has frequently
failed to look out for ordinary citizens.
—Ted Rall, *Wake Up, You're Liberal!* (2004)

My recommendation to Democrats is not to become more religious. Religion
is a personal matter. But perhaps Democrats need somewhat fewer plans and
policies, and a bit more moral conviction.
—Robert Reich, "The Moral Agenda," *American Prospect* (November 4, 2004)

You've got to be [an] optimist to be a Democrat, and you've got to be a humorist to stay one.
—Will Rogers, quoted in *Radio Broadcasts of Will Rogers* (1983)

Herein lies the real political crisis in this country: the Democrats are not an
opposition party. . . . The Democrats ran a pro-war campaign in 2004 with
Kerry struggling to convince people that Dems do occupation and war better.
—Jeremy Scahill, "Vegetarians Between Meals: This War Cannot Be Stopped
by a Loyal Opposition," *Common Dreams* (November 18, 2005)

It used to be George Bush's war. You could have ended it honorably. Now it is yours. . . . You betrayed us.
—Cindy Sheehan, letter to Democrats following their vote to continue funding the Iraq War, quoted in "Cindy Sheehan Quits Anti-War Activism," ABC News (May 29, 2007)

We don't know if the source of [Democratic] weakness is fear or corruption. If it is fear, they might wake up, enforce the Constitutional checks and balances, and lead the country out of the dangerous mess we are in, but if it is corruption, if they are only just Big Corporation suck-ups, then there is no hope at all.
—Jane Smiley, "Is There Something Wrong with the System?" *Huffington Post* (January 23, 2007)

The Democratic Party should disband if it ever stops being the party that stands by the little guy, leads the fight against racial and economic disadvantage, sticks by working families when times are tough, and takes on those with privilege who don't play by the rules.
—Gene Sperling, *The Pro-Growth Progressive: An Economic Strategy for Shared Prosperity* (2005)

I'm no big fan of the Democratic party. I think they pussyfoot about key issues like the war and they whore for their campaign donors almost as much as the Republicans.
—Matt Taibbi, "Unhinged Republicans Can't Even Get Their Insults Straight," AlterNet (March 21, 2007)

The United States has only one party—the property party. It's the party of big corporations, the party of money. It has two right wings; one is Democrat and the other is Republican.
—Gore Vidal, interviewed by David Barsamian, *Progressive* (August 2006)

If the heart of the Democratic Party is not liberal, then what the hell is it?
—Nicholas von Hoffman, "Now Is Not the Time for National Unity!" *New York Observer* (November 22, 2004)

Fear

Totalitarianism is never content to rule by external means, namely, through the state and a machinery of violence . . . [it] has discovered a means of dominating and terrorizing human beings from within.
—Hannah Arendt, *The Origins of Totalitarianism* (1951)

Biblical fundamentalism and literalism are not authentic faith, but disguised fear, reactions against modernity.
—Rev. John Buehrens, "Why Bother with the Bible?" *UU World* (July/August 2003)

There is something that this administration and the Republican Party are very afraid of. It is that we may actually begin fighting for what we believe.
—Howard Dean, quoted in "The Fighting Moderates," *New York Times* (February 15, 2005)

The party that once galvanized a nation by declaring that there is nothing to fear but fear itself has become afraid—afraid of being too liberal, afraid of being weak on defense, afraid of being culturally permissive, afraid of being seen as apologizing for big government. Democrats are obsessed with telling people who they are not. As a result, no one knows who they are.
—E. J. Dionne, Jr., *Stand Up, Fight Back: Republican Toughs, Democratic Wimps, and the Politics of Revenge* (2004)

No national party, least of all the Democratic Party, can survive by trying to flee its own base.
—Laura Flanders, *Blue Grit* (2007)

The values that were promoted most within the conservative religious community were almost always tied to a fear factor.
—Rev. Welton Gaddy, quoted in "Liberal Christians Challenge 'Values Vote,'" *Washington Post* (November 10, 2004)

The Democrats have become an opposition party too fractured to generate daring, forward, progressive policies and too frightened to embrace them when they do come along.
—Joshua Holland, "Stolen Society," AlterNet (February 28, 2005)

Fearlessness is not the absence of fear. Rather, it's the mastery of fear. It's getting to the point where our fears do not stop us from daring to think new thoughts, try new things, take risks, fail, and start again.
—Arianna Huffington, *On Becoming Fearless: . . . in Love, Work, and Life* (2006)

Our history is rank with these fits of fear. We get so afraid of some dreadful menace, so afraid of anarchists, Reds, crime or drugs or communism or illegal aliens or terrorists that we think we can make ourselves safer by making ourselves less free.
—Molly Ivins, "24/7 Coverage Doesn't Cover It," Truthdig (July 27, 2006)

For too much of my life, I was too afraid, too frightened by it all. That fear is one of my biggest regrets. I wish I had put myself out there a little bit more and experienced people more instead of protecting myself.
—Diane Keaton, "The Upside of Turning 60," *Huffington Post* (January 20, 2006)

Living in fear of our government is a new experience for Americans.
—Hubert G. Locke, "Hard to be Optimistic about New Year," *Seattle Post-Intelligencer* (December 30, 2005)

We will not be driven by fear into an age of unreason.
—Edward R. Murrow, in his report on Senator Joseph R. McCarthy, "See It Now," CBS (March 9, 1954)

The Democrats' phobia about the liberal label has given the right free rein to define the word in its own terms.
—Geoffrey Nunberg, *Talking Right: How Conservatives Turned Liberalism into a Tax-Raising, Latte-Drinking, Sushi-Eating, Volvo-Driving,* New York Times-*Reading, Body-Piercing, Hollywood-Loving, Left-Wing Freak Show* (2006)

No one ever does the right thing from fear, and so many of the wrong things are done in its shadow: homophobia, sexism, racism, religious bigotry.
—Anna Quindlen, in her commencement address at Colby College (May 28, 2006)

The only thing we have to fear is fear itself.
—Franklin D. Roosevelt, in his first inaugural address (March 4, 1933)

Fear is the main source of superstition, and one of the main sources of cruelty. To conquer fear is the beginning of wisdom.
—Bertrand Russell, *Unpopular Essays* (1950)

People would likely rather have a corrupt party running the show than one that is so weak, so indecisive, and so needlessly frightened of its own shadow that it can't take the most basic stands.
—David Sirota, "GOP's Culture of Corruption vs. Democrat's Culture of Weakness," *Working For Change* (March 14, 2006)

I love the color-coded concept of homeland security. I like to wear clothes that match my level of dread.
—Jon Stewart in an interview with Larry King, CNN (March 22, 2002)

Our deepest fear is not that we are inadequate. Our deepest fear is that we are powerful beyond measure.
—Marianne Williamson, *A Return to Love* (1992)

Green Party

Greens don't only oppose corporate giveaways. We challenge the status corporations enjoy as "persons" according to a misinterpretation of the 14th Amendment, which has allowed corporations to escape public accountability and to dominate our political system.
—Marnie Glickman, press release, "Say No to Bush's Reckless Budget Plan" (January 30, 2004)

Human societies must operate with the understanding that we are part of nature, not separate from nature.
—Green Party Platform of 2000, quoted in *Dissent in America* (2007)

The federal minimum wage was meant to provide workers with an income floor, but it has become a pathetic sub-basement. Working full-time should afford the dignity of being able to support your loved ones.
—Kevin McKeown, quoted in Green Party press release, "Greens Demand Preservation of Overtime, Urge Reversal Of Policies That Hurt U.S. Workers" (July 8, 2003)

The Green Party, whose nomination I seek, stands for the regeneration of American politics. The new populism which the Green Party represents involves motivated, informed voters who comprehend that "freedom is participation in power."
—Ralph Nader, "Statement of Ralph Nader, Announcing His Candidacy for the Green Party's Nomination for President" (February 21, 2000)

The tired whine of "but the Republicans are worse" will fall flat as more young Americans take charge of their future and move, with their reenergized elders, toward the Green Party and parallel civic and political movements.
—Ralph Nader, *Crashing the Party* (2002)

Fueled by idealistic fervor for its social-change program . . . the Green Party has become an odd sort of counterpoint to the liberals who have allowed pro-corporate centrists to dominate the Democratic Party for a dozen years now. Those liberal Democrats routinely sacrifice principles and idealism in the name of electoral strategy.
—Norman Solomon, "Green Party Taking the Plunge for 2004," *Common Dreams* (July 24, 2003)

Ideology

The problem with ideology is . . . you've already got your mind made up. You know all the answers and that makes evidence irrelevant and arguments a waste of time. You tend to govern by assertion and attacks.
—Bill Clinton, quoted in "Clinton Urges Dems to Question Criticism," the Associated Press (AP) (October 18, 2006)

Ideas are what men and women live by, and will occasionally die for.
—Terry Eagleton, *Ideology* (1991)

It is part of the ideology of the center to deny that it has an ideology.
—Vic Navasky, *A Matter of Opinion* (2005)

It has not always been the pragmatist, the voice of reason, or the force of compromise that has created the conditions for liberty.
—Barack Obama, *The Audacity of Hope* (2006)

Democratic politicians have always said that "ideological diversity is the Democrats strength," but that refrain is now being shamelessly used as a way to obscure the fact that the Democratic Party is ideologically rudderless.
—David Sirota, "The Resurgence of Movement Politics," *Nation* (August 12, 2005)

Movements based on ideology and ideas are far more powerful than loyalties to any political party.
—David Sirota, "The Resurgence of Movement Politics," *Nation* (August 12, 2005)

The people who shun the concept of "ideology" aren't anti-ideological—they are quietly pushing an elitist ideology they know that most of America doesn't support.
—David Sirota, "The Rise of Seinfeld Politics and the End of Principles," AlterNet (April 2, 2007)

Insults

[Scott] McClellan is a flea on the windshield of history. . . . He was a vessel for his masters, did whatever he was told, put out disinformation without objection, and was willing to defend any travesty. He is the ultimate dispensable man.
—Sidney Blumenthal, on the resignation of Bush's press secretary, "Walking the White House Plank," *Common Dreams* (April 20, 2006)

Jesus loves you . . . but everyone else thinks you are an ass.
—Bumper sticker

Jon Stewart: "You [the news media] have a responsibility to the public discourse, and you fail miserably."
Tucker Carlson: "You need to get a job at a journalism school."
Jon Stewart: "You need to go to one."
—Exchange on the program "Crossfire" (October 15, 2004)

As his B-actor career faded, Reagan became a mouthpiece for General Electric, one of the world's largest arms manufacturers. Reagan's one clear talent was the ability to read a Teleprompter or memorize his lines on the glories of free enterprise.
—Bob Fitrakis, "Ronald Reagan: A Legacy of Crack and Cheese," Free Press (Columbus, Ohio) (June 16, 2004)

Bill O'Reilly always talks about his "traditional values"—as opposed to "the far left's secular humanist values." I didn't realize phone sex was a traditional value. I didn't think the phone had been around long enough. Maybe telegraph sex.
—Al Franken, from his debate with Ann Coulter sponsored by the University of Judaism, Gibson Amphitheatre at Universal City Walk, Los Angeles (March 27, 2006)

If you cut out every passage in the New Testament where Jesus talks about helping the poor, or helping the least among us—if you cut out each one of those passages, you'd have the perfect box to smuggle Rush Limbaugh's drugs.
—Al Franken, *BuzzFlash* interview, *Working for Change* (March 10, 2006)

Evidence God Exists; Ralph Reed Concedes Defeat in Primary
—Headline, former head of the so-called Christian Coalition rejected in his bid for Georgia Lieutenant Governor, OpEdNews (July 19, 2006)

Do you ever wake up in the middle of the night and think to yourself, "I am just full of hot gas"?
—David Letterman, to Rush Limbaugh, a guest on "The Late Show," CBS (December 17, 1993)

I have the feeling about 60 percent of what you say is crap.
—David Letterman, to Fox News's Bill O'Reilly when he was a guest on "The Late Show," CBS (January 3, 2006)

Don't call everyone you don't like "Hitler." Bush is not Hitler. For one thing, Hitler was a decorated frontline combat veteran. Also, in the election that brought him to power in 1933, Hitler got more votes than the other candidates.
—Bill Maher, *New Rules* (2005)

People like James Dobson spend more time thinking about gay sex than any ten gay people I know put together.
—Paul Waldman, "Why Rudy Giuliani Is Destined to Fall," *TomPaine.com* (March 1, 2007)

Phyllis Schlafly, right-wing hit woman and dogged defeater of the Equal Rights Amendment, spent most of her high-powered career traveling the country spreading the good word of stay-at-home motherhood while her young children were at home without her.
—Kirsten A. Powers, "Feminist Mystique," *American Prospect* (May 4, 2006)

Poor George, he can't help it. He was born with a silver foot in his mouth.
—Ann Richards, on former President George G. W. Bush, quoted in "Former Governor of Texas, Dies at 73," *New York Times* (September 14, 2006)

You have always occupied a special place as one of the most pompous and grandiloquent horse's asses in all of American pop culture—and, I know, that's saying a lot in the era of Sean Hannity, Bill O'Reilly, and David Brooks.
—David Sirota, "Another Open Letter to Thomas Friedman," *Working For Change* (October 6, 2006)

I have sympathy for you because you're the guy who has to spray perfume on these turds.
—Jon Stewart, to Republican National Chairman Ken Mehlman on his responsibility to defend his party leaders, "The Daily Show," Comedy Central (June 13, 2006)

John McCain is just another go-along-to-get-along bullshit artist—in other words, a senator.
—Allan Uthman, "John McCain's Shameless Call for Escalation in Iraq," AlterNet (December 15, 2006)

Well, I really think he shatters the myth of white supremacy once and for all.
—Charles Rangel, regarding President Bush, quoted in "In the Loop," *Washington Post* (April 4, 2005)

Politics

Politics: A strife of interests masquerading as a contest of principles.
—Ambrose Bierce, *The Devil's Dictionary* (1911)

Politics is driven by passion—by people passionate about causes. The passionate provide the volunteers, the energy, the emotion to engage citizens. That was true when unions were organizing, when the civil rights and women's movements were mobilizing. It is true on the right and on the left.
—Robert L. Borosage, "Passion or Positioning," *Huffington Post* (January 16, 2007)

Every American at some point has got to make the connection between their own hopes and dreams and who is elected to office.
—Barbara Boxer, interviewed by Ruth Conniff, *Progressive* (July 2005)

I believe 9/11 truly distorted our politics . . . it gave the president and his advisers an opening to take a far hard right agenda.
—Tom Friedman, "Meet the Press," NBC (September 25, 2005)

There are times in politics when you must be on the right side and lose.
—John Kenneth Galbraith, *Observer (UK)* (February 11, 1968)

If a political party's job is to win elections by doing what is politically expedient, the activist's job is to make doing the right thing politically expedient.
—Christopher Hayes, "How to Turn Your Red State Blue," *In These Times* (March 22, 2005)

American politics is broken—under the thumb of a small corporate elite using its financial clout to control both parties' political agendas.
—Arianna Huffington, *How to Overthrow the Government* (2000)

That's the mission of politics: to give our kids as good a chance as we had.
—Garrison Keillor, "Our Magnificent Isolation," *Salon* (September 6, 2006)

We're living in an age of one-letter politics, in which a politician's partisan affiliation is almost always far more important than his or her personal beliefs. And those who refuse to recognize this reality end up being useful idiots.
—Paul Krugman, "Centrism Is for Suckers," *New York Times* (August 4, 2006)

You can ignore politics, but you can't escape it.
—Robert Kuttner, "Another Year, Another Wage Loss," *Boston Globe* (September 2, 2006)

Our politics are organized around two opposite and idealized models of the family: the strict father and the nurturant parent.
—George Lakoff, *Don't Think Like an Elephant* (2004)

A politics that takes seriously both working on our inner lives and working on our social healing is the only politics that is sustainable, and it is the only politics that can win.
—Rabbi Michael Lerner, quoted in "Finding Spirit among the Dems," AlterNet (February 10, 2006)

No individual, party or ideology has cornered the market on truth or God's blessing.
—Stuart S. Light, "Some Meditations Before You Vote," *Los Angeles Times* (October 30, 2004)

These bastards who run our country are a bunch of conniving, thieving, smug pricks who need to be brought down and removed and replaced with a whole new system that we control.
—Michael Moore, *Dude, Where's My Country?* (2003)

Politics is principally about who decides, who pays and who is held accountable.
—Ralph Nader, "I Will Work as President for Need, Not Greed," *London Daily Telegraph* (October 31, 2000)

In our age, there is no such thing as "keeping out of politics." All issues are political issues, and politics itself is a mass of lies, evasions, folly, hatred, and schizophrenia.
—George Orwell, "Politics and the English Language," *Shooting an Elephant* (1950)

It's an article of faith among progressives that moving to the left wins votes. . . . But what if it isn't true? What if it wins fewer votes than being a liar and a bigot?
—Katha Pollitt, "Mourn," *Nation* (November 5, 2004

Before Bush came along, it was hard for Americans to tell the two parties apart.
—Ted Rall, *Wake Up, You're Liberal!* (2004)

Politics is a bar brawl, not a tea party. When one is engaged in battle with an unprincipled adversary, taking the high road is more counterproductive than noble.
—Ted Rall, *Wake Up! You're Liberal!* (2004)

Whereas Republicans see politics as war, strategists for the Democratic Party tend to see politics as debate.
—Sheldon Rampton and John Stauber, *Banana Republicans: How the Right Wing is Turning America into a One-Party State* (2004)

This is the real divide that matters in politics—not Republicans and Democrats, but Money vs. People.
—David Sirota, "The Money Party vs. The People Party," *Huffington Post* (November 24, 2006)

We live in a two-party system where both parties are pro-war.
—Matt Taibbi, "Don't Let Hillary's Dems Cash in on Iraq," *Rolling Stone* (August 10, 2006)

If there's one thing Republicans have understood and Democrats haven't, it is that politics is not about issues. Politics is about identity. . . . The winners are those who form a positive image in the public mind of who they are (and a negative image of who their opponents are).
—Paul Waldman, "Elections Aren't About Issues," *Boston Globe* (September 6, 2006)

Politics is what we create out of what we do, what we hope for, what we dare to imagine.
—Paul Wellstone, quoted in "Radical Realist; Bill Clinton Wasn't the Only Comeback Story of 1996," *Washington Post* (January 19, 1997)

Presidential Elections

2008: The End of an Error
—Bumper sticker

Every presidential election since 1980 has had a Bush or a Clinton on a major party ticket.
—Jeff Cohen, "I'm Tired of Bushes and Clintons," *Common Dreams* (May 3, 2006)

If [the 2004] election had been decided on moral values, Democrats would have won.
—Howard Dean, "Democratic Moral Values," YubaNet (December 13, 2004)

The president got re-elected by dividing the country along fault lines of fear, intolerance, ignorance, and religious rule.
—Maureen Dowd, "The Red Zone," *New York Times* (November 4, 2004)

I don't think Bush was legitimately elected President.
—Roger Ebert, in an interview with Matthew Rothschild, *Progressive* (August 2003)

I find myself speculating on what might have been if the man who got the most votes in 2000 had actually become president. It's like imagining an alternate universe.
—Bob Herbert, "The Passion of Al Gore," *New York Times* (June 5, 2007)

I am Al Gore. I used to be the next president of the United States of America.
—Al Gore, from the film *An Inconvenient Truth* (2006)

We would not have invaded a country that didn't attack us. We would not have taken money from the working families and given it to the most wealthy families. We would not be trying to control and intimidate the news media. We would not be routinely torturing people.
—Al Gore, on how the U.S. would have been different if the Supreme Court had not given 2000 election to Bush, the Associated Press (AP) (October 12, 2005)

I'm damned if I want to go through another presidential primary with everyone trying to figure out who has the best chance to win instead of who's right.
—Molly Ivins, "Run Bill Moyers for President, Seriously," Truthdig (July 24, 2006)

For the second election in a row, the president of the United States was select-
ed not by the uncontested will of the people but under a cloud of dirty tricks.
—Robert F. Kennedy, Jr., "Was the 2004 Election Stolen?" *Rolling Stone*
(June 1, 2006)

The idea that a presidential election can be stolen was the stuff of airport fiction
until someone did it.
—Michael Kinsley, regarding the 2000 race, "Election Day," *New York Times
Book Review* (November 5, 2006)

I thought the decision of the Kerry campaign to back off any real criticism
of Bush was one of the biggest acts of political malpractice in the history of
American politics.
—Terry McAuliffe, quoted in "Ex-Dem. Party Boss Blasts Kerry in Book,"
the Associated Press (AP) (January 5, 2007)

The Republicans' campaign is . . . about exploiting homophobia, provincial-
ism and cultural insecurity. Or, as they put it, values.
—Harold Meyerson, "With Values Like These," *Washington Post* (July 14,
2004)

I know you are dismayed at the results of last week's election. You've got to
be freaking out about what this bunch of tree-hugging, latte-sipping, men-
kissing-men advocates will do now that the country is in our hands.
—Michael Moore, "Let's Extend an Olive Branch to Disheartened
Conservatives," *Los Angeles Times* (November 17, 2006)

When historians sort out what happened to the United States at the start of
the twenty-first century, one of the mysteries may be why the national press
corps ganged up like school-yard bullies against a well-qualified Democratic
presidential candidate while giving his dimwitted Republican opponent virtually a free pass.
—Robert Parry, "U.S. News Media's 'War on Gore,'" *Consortium News*
(March 22, 2007)

Re-Elect Gore 2008
—Political button

They lost because they were mean and let it show. They lost because they were bullies and kicked sand in too many faces.
—Katha Pollitt, on the Republicans' loss in the 2006 elections, "Why They Lost," *Nation* (December 4, 2006)

If Democrats want to hold a governing majority, they must see the [2006] election for what it was: a mandate for economic populism and a battle cry against Big Money's war on middle-class Americans.
—David Sirota, "Embracing Populism," *In These Times* (November 28, 2006)

How Can 59,054,087 People Be So DUMB?
—Tabloid headline in the *Daily Mirror (UK)* regarding the U.S. election results (November 3, 2004)

The 2004 election panned out as a choice between committed evangelicals and committed secularists. Evangelicals won.
—Pierre Tristam, "Subordinating Nation's Secular Values to Zealots' Will," *Daytona Beach News-Journal* (November 9, 2004)

All the Democratic Presidents since Lincoln owe their election, in no small measure, to something the Republicans did wrong.
—Nicholas von Hoffman, "Timid Democrats Fail to Pin Blame on Bush," *New York Observer* (July 26, 2006)

Presidential politics is not designed to support progressive candidates; indeed, it is set up to exclude them.
—Gary Younge, "Their Opportunism, Our Opportunity," *Nation* (November 26, 2006)

Republican Luminaries

The fortieth president was indeed a clear-eyed visionary: He envisioned a world where women would never be granted equality in the U.S. constitution, abortion was illegal, and equal employment laws were a thing of the past.
—Martha Burk, "Re-Electing Ronald Reagan," *TomPaine.com* (March 6, 2007)

Be honest. Who would you rather share a foxhole with: a gay soldier or Mitt Romney? A gay soldier, of course. In a dicey situation like that, you need someone steadfast who knows who he is and what he believes, even if he's not allowed to say it out loud.
—Maureen Dowd, "Outing the Out of Touch," *New York Times* (June 10, 2007)

We will always remember [Rev. Falwell] as a founder and leader of America's anti-gay industry . . . someone who demonized and vilified us for political gain and someone who used religion to divide rather than unite our nation.
—Matt Foreman, executive director of the National Gay and Lesbian Task Force, quoted in "TV Evangelist Jerry Falwell Dies at 73," the Associated Press (AP) (May 15, 2007)

I was just talking to Newt Gingrich the other day. And I said to him, "Don't you want for a gay couple what you had with your first wife? Don't you want that bond that comes with the pledge of fidelity that you had with your second wife? Don't you want what comes with that lifelong bond that you may or may not have with your third wife?"
—Al Franken, in his debate with Ann Coulter, sponsored by the University of Judaism, Gibson Amphitheatre at Universal City Walk, Los Angeles (March 27, 2006)

Richard Cheney is a vile, indeed evil, influence in American political life.
—Father Andrew Greeley, "Cheney Really Wants U.S. Dictator," *Chicago Sun-Times* (July 7, 2006)

Two of the most admired political figures among Christian conservatives— Rush Limbaugh and Newt Gingrich—have the most shameful, tawdry and degenerate personal lives . . . Yet the gross disparity between their personal conduct and the religious and moral values they espouse has not injured their standing in the slightest among the "values voters."
—Glenn Greenwald, quoted in "Why Rudy Giuliani Is Destined to Fall," *TomPaine.com* (March 1, 2007)

Watching a true American hero hang a "For Sale" sign on his principles is a profoundly sad thing.
—Arianna Huffington, on John McCain's "cheerleading" for President Bush, "The Tragic Irony of John McCain's Faustian Bargain," *Huffington Post* (April 3, 2006)

I've learned one thing in listening to all the debates and reading about all these people running for office, and the one fact I've learned . . . is that Rudy Giuliani has been married more times than Mitt Romney's been hunting.
—Harry Reid, quoted in "Senator Reid on a Few Choice G.O.P. Candidates," *New York Times* (June 11, 2007)

He shot his friend in the face.
—Alex Rossmiller, "Wanted: A Liberal Dick Cheney," *American Prospect* (May 23, 2007)

While the man has been associated with a pernicious assault on our freedoms, he has never been the independent actor, but rather a dutiful toady.
—Robert Scheer, on U.S. Attorney General Albert Gonzales, "Gonzales: The Dutiful Toady," *Nation* (May 23, 2007)

Who's the girlie-man now?
—Robert Scheer, to Arnold Schwarzenegger on the defeat of Schwarzenegger's anti-union referenda, *Huffington Post* (November 9, 2005)

He has decided that life begins not at conception, not at birth, but when you de-cide to run for president.
—Jon Stewart, on pro-choice Republican Governor Mitt Romney's new anti-choice position, *The Daily Show*, Comedy Central (August 8, 2005)

The entirety of Giuliani's appeal, of course, is built on the fact that on the day of 9/11, he managed to hold a series of press conferences without wetting his pants.
—Paul Waldman, "Why Rudy Giuliani Is Destined to Fall," *TomPaine.com* (March 1, 2007)

The Republican Party

My question for today is: Why are contemporary Republicans so full of shit?
—Alec Baldwin, "What Happened to the Party of Lincoln?" *Huffington Post* (October 24, 2005)

The Republicans deny that they are the electoral refuge for America's bigots. But whenever an ex-Klansman, decrying the mongrelization of the white race, enters a primary election somewhere in Louisiana or Texas, it's always a Republican primary.
—David Benjamin, "America's Journey From 'Dixiecrats' to 'Rednecklicans,'" *Common Dreams* (March 13, 2005)

When [Republicans] shift from propaganda to policy, their proposals are inadequate and in some cases demonstrably harmful.
—Mario Cuomo, *Reason to Believe* (1996)

In my view, Republicans use politics to push religion. I don't believe we ought to emulate that. But what we ought to do is reflect our values in the work that we do. And we ought to say it.
—Rosa Delauro, quoted in "Democrats and Religion," *Religion & Ethics Newsweekly* (July 23, 2004)

Moral values? How in God's name (and I use the phrase sincerely) did the Republicans become the party of moral values? I am terrified for the future of this country precisely because of moral issues.
—Vivian Dent, "From the Heart," AlterNet (November 11, 2004)

The spotted owl is in good shape compared with liberal Republicans.
—E. J. Dionne, Jr., "The GOP's Shrinking Middle," *Washington Post* (March 21, 2006)

I saw the Republican National Convention as essentially a hyper-masculine strut-fest. The real point of the convention was to make John Kerry their woman.
—Stephen J. Ducat, quoted in interview "Stephen J. Ducat Dissects 'Anxious Masculinity,' Making Sense of America's Strutting, in a Psychoanalytic Kind of Way," *BuzzFlash* (March 2, 2005)

"It's easier for a camel to pass through the eye of a needle than for a rich man to enter Heaven." If that's true—literally true—where do you think the leadership of the Republican Party will be spending eternity?
—R. J. Eskow, "Celebrate Christmas the Old-Fashioned Way: Defy Authority!" *Yahoo! News* (December 24, 2006)

I love Republican conventions. In America, celebrity trumps ideology, so people in the hall will say, "I hate everything you stand for. Would you sign my credentials?"
—Al Franken, "Franken Brings a Message to NYC—and to the Media," *USA Today* (August 30, 2004)

Americans are not getting screwed by the Republican Party. They are getting screwed by Large Corporations that bought and own the Republican Party.
—Molly Ivins, "Now They're All for Bipartisanship," Truthdig (November 14, 2006)

Republicans have no monopoly on religion or on faith. And Republican policies often seem divorced from the teachings of the Bible.
—Rev. Jesse Jackson, "No GOP Monopoly on God," *Chicago Sun-Times* (November 9, 2004)

Republicans: The No. 1 reason the rest of the world thinks we're deaf, dumb and dangerous.
—Garrison Keillor, "We're Not in Lake Wobegon Anymore," *In These Times* (August 26, 2004)

[The Republicans] are a party that is all about perceptions, the Christian party that conceals enormous glittering malice.
—Garrison Keillor, *Homegrown Democrat* (2004)

The Republican Party is now controlled by ideological extremists who reject any meaningful role for government in expanding economic opportunity or preventing the abuses of private economic power.
—Edward M. Kennedy, quoted in "Kennedy's Other Speech," *Nation* (March 10, 2004)

I made the conclusion many years ago that there's not a huge values difference between Red State Republicans and Blue State Democrats. The distinction is really informational. 80 percent of Republicans are just Democrats who don't know what's going on.
—Robert F. Kennedy, Jr., "Democracy in Crisis—Interview with Robert F. Kennedy, Jr.," Bradblog (July 18, 2006)

The Bush administration has stolen the soul of the Republican Party. . . . They talk about law and order while encouraging corporate polluters to violate the law. They proclaim free markets while advocating corporate welfare.
—Robert F. Kennedy, Jr., *Crimes Against Nature* (2004)

The dictionary definition of the word "terrorize" is simple and not open to misinterpretation: "To fill or overpower with terror; terrify. To coerce by intimidation or fear." . . . By this definition . . . the leading terrorist group in this country right now is the Republican Party.
—Keith Olbermann, "Olbermann: GOP Is 'Leading Terrorist Group in This Country,'" *USA Today* (October 24, 2006)

The Republican Party has always been the party of business and it was once the party of law, fiscal conservatism, probity, and small government as well . . . . The Party of Lincoln has become a gang of thieves given to cutting taxes for the wealthy and willing to "do whatever it takes" to stay in power.
—David W. Orr, "The Imminent Demise of the Republican Party: Part Two," *Common Dreams* (November 2, 2005)

Republicans are people, too. Mean, selfish, greedy people.
—Political button

The Republican Party is mired in corruption and cronyism.
—Katha Pollitt, "It Wasn't All Bad," *Nation* (January 9, 2006)

I couldn't join a party that, frankly, tolerates members who are bigots for one thing. Homophobes, racists. You know, there's no way I could be a part of a party like that.
—Ron Reagan, Jr., in an interview, explaining why he's not a Republican, "Ron Reagan Calls Iraq War Unnecessary and Optional," CNN (June 24, 2004)

Theirs is a greedy, small-minded conservatism. In their policies, they seek not to improve government, and certainly not to shrink it, but to ruin it—to starve the regulatory agencies with tax cuts, then spend so wildly on pork that there's nothing left to pay for actual government work.
—Eugene Robinson, "Immoral Majority," *Washington Post* (September 30, 2005)

The Republicans believe that moneyed "aristocracy," the few great financial minds, should rule the Government; the Democrats believe that the whole people should govern.
—Eleanor Roosevelt, "Jeffersonian Principles the Issue in 1928," *Current History* (June 1928)

For years we were told how terrible communism was and how we had to be anti-communist. But now these guys love China! They love authoritarianism. They love the reality that they can pay desperate workers in China thirty cents an hour and send them to jail if they stand up for a union.
—Bernie Sanders, quoted in "Sanders Steps Up," *In These Times* (May 24, 2005)

The aim of Republican strategy has been a Republican Party that permanently runs the United States and a United States that permanently runs the world.
—Jonathan Schell, "The Fall of the One-Party Empire," *TomDispatch.com* (November 24, 2005)

The Grand Old Party is now hostage to a group of flat-earthers who deny evolution, mock gays, denounce stem cell research, suspect contraceptives, and believe all Muslims are going to hell.
—Cynthia Tucker, "Values Promoted by Falwell Are Dangerous to Democracy," *Yahoo! News* (May 20, 2007)

The Republican Party is driven by an ideological value that is primarily de-signed to help the wealthy to stay that way.
—Gary Vance, "Wasn't Jesus a Liberal? Part Two," *Common Dreams* (October 9, 2005)

The Religious Right has been institutionalized within the Republican Party.
—Kenneth Wald, quoted in "The Right Stuff," *Sojourners* (July 2004)

What GOP voters want to know is, are you one of us or not? And what makes a candidate "one of us"? That tribal identity is formed by one thing above all else: Do you hate the right people?
—Paul Waldman, "Why Rudy Giuliani Is Destined to Fall," *TomPaine.com* (March 1, 2007)

Moral outrage all too quickly becomes self-righteous authoritarianism.
—Ellen Willis, quoted in "Bully in the Pulpit?" *Nation* (February 22, 2001)

Over the past thirty years, as the Republican agenda of unrestricted corporate power has come increasingly to dominate this country, workers' living standards have declined in well-documented ways—lower pay, longer hours, less health care, ruined pensions, more insecurity.
—Michael Zweig, "Stand up For Moral Value of Economic Justice," *Baltimore Sun* (November 19, 2004)

Vision

Eventually, the Democrats have to be the party of something more than "we're not them."
—Dante Chinni, "Republican Woes Won't Rescue Democrats from Their Confusion," *Christian Science Monitor* (November 29, 2005)

Stand for something.
—E. J. Dionne, Jr., "Lessons for Democrats," *Washington Post* (December 31, 2004)

We believe in hope over despair, we believe in possibilities over problems, we believe in optimism over cynicism. We believe in doing what's right even when others say it can't be done. And we believe in fighting desperately for those who have no voice in America.
—John Edwards, "Back in N.H., Edwards Is Mum on 2008 Run," *Washington Post* (February 6, 2005)

Our country needs something much bigger to strive for than mere possessions.
—Jim Hightower, "What I Want for Christmas," *Hightower Lowdown* (December 2005)

I believe that this nation should commit itself, before this decade is out, to the goal of landing a man on the Moon and returning him safely to Earth.
—John F. Kennedy, in his address to a joint session of Congress (May 25, 1961)

Like anybody, I would like to live a long life. Longevity has its place. But I'm not concerned about that now. I just want to do God's will. And He's allowed me to go up to the mountain. And I've looked over, and I've seen the Promised Land. I may not get there with you, but I want you to know tonight that we as a people will get to the Promised Land.
—Rev. Martin Luther King, Jr., the day before he was assassinated, quoted in the *New York Times* (April 5, 1968)

It is the glory and the greatness of our tradition to speak for those who have no voice.
—Edward M. Kennedy, in his speech to the Democratic National Convention (August 12, 1980)

The basic progressive vision is of community—of America as family, a caring, responsible family.
—George Lakoff, *Don't Think Like an Elephant* (2004)

The conservative movement stands intellectually and morally bankrupt while Democrats talk about a "new direction" without convincing us they know the difference between a weather vane and a compass.
—Bill Moyers, "For America's Sake," *Nation* (January 22, 2007)

If there's a child on the south side of Chicago who can't read, that matters to me, even if it's not my child. If there's a senior citizen somewhere who can't pay for her prescription and has to choose between medicine and the rent that makes my life poorer, even if it's not my grandmother. It's that fundamental belief—I am my brother's keeper, I am my sister's keeper—that makes this country work.
—Barack Obama, in his keynote address to the Democratic National Convention (July 27, 2004)

Instead of playing desperate defense, the Democrats might try searching their souls, asking themselves simple questions with complex answers. What really matters to me? What are the principles on which I will not compromise?
—Anna Quindlen, "The Ghost of Politics Past," *Newsweek* (January 3, 2005)

WHAT LIBERALS BELIEVE *411*

I'm not saying Democrats have to adopt my particular moral positions. But unless or until Democrats return to larger questions of public morality, they won't inspire the American public. Plans and policies are important, of course. But there's no substitute for offering a vision of what we can become as a nation—and giving citizens the faith we can get there.
—Robert Reich, "The Moral Agenda," *American Prospect* (November 4, 2004)

Many of the issues for which Democrats stand are highly divisive—stem-cell research, gay rights, abortion—and in their attempts to finesse that divisiveness, they often seem to stand for nothing at all.
—Tom Tomorrow, "The Party's Message Is Low Risk, Low Reward," *Slate* (November 3, 2004)

History has decreed that the Democrats . . . have been deprived of a bundled center of belief or a fixed point to steer by. They are forever a congress or confederation of groups that must negotiate out a programmatic hodgepodge that each can live with.
—Nicholas von Hoffman, "Timid Democrats Fail to Pin Blame on Bush," *New York Observer* (July 26, 2006)

The Democratic Party is today in the hands of people who have failed to articulate a moral-intellectual vision for America and the world, and you can't win the confidence of the electorate without a vision.
—Adam Werbach, "November Third Theses," *Common Dreams* (November 12, 2004)

Voting

When your vote doesn't count, neither do you.
—Missy Comley Beattie, OpEdNews (December 17, 2005)

There is no place in our democracy for faulty voting equipment, long lines at the polls, untrained poll workers, and any forms of chads. It's time we erase the vast disparities between poor and affluent communities with respect to reliable voting systems.
—Donna Brazile, quoted in "Democratic Party Searches for Leader Again," *Guardian (UK)* (December 11, 2004)

How is it possible that a woman who is unfit to vote should be the mother of, and bring up, a man who is?
—Carrie Chapman Catt, president of the National American Woman Suffrage Association in 1920, quoted in "She Stood Up for Disenfranchised," *Investor's Business Daily* (March 26, 2007)

It is better to vote for what you want and not get it than to vote for what you don't want and get it.
—Eugene Debs, quoted in "Looking for Lefty," *Village Voice* (September 13-19, 2000)

Our votes must be counted by a nonpartisan public agency dedicated to accuracy, not by a private corporation dedicated to its bottom line.
—Allegra Dengler, letter to the editor, "Trust and the Voting Machine," *New York Times* (December 25, 2005)

The American way of electing presidents is antiquated, impractical and dangerous. It is odd indeed that in 2000, a nation devoted to spreading democracy throughout the world gave power to a man who received 543,895 fewer votes than his opponent.
—E. J. Dionne, Jr., "Bypassing the Electoral College," *Washington Post* (April 2, 2007)

The American election system needs significant improvement, starting with voter-verified paper trails for every vote cast electronically.
—Editorial, "Count Every Vote," *New York Times* (December 20, 2004)

Election reform has been framed principally as a technology issue. . . . But they overlooked one thing: The most crucial element of fair and glitch- free elections is the people who run them.
—Editorial, "Electability Tops Ideology," *USA Today* (September 14, 2006)

Why are we the people allowing private, for-profit corporations, answerable only to their officers and boards of directors, and loyal only to agendas and politicians that will enhance their profitability, to handle our votes?
—Thom Hartmann, "The Ultimate Felony Against Democracy," *Common Dreams* (November 4, 2004)

You vote not for the perfect but for the best.
—John Kenneth Galbraith, quoted in "John Kenneth Galbraith Interview," *Progressive* (October 2000)

The lesson out of Ohio (and Florida before it) is that the integrity of the election process needs to be more fiercely defended in the face of outrageous Republican assaults.
—Bob Herbert, "Those Pesky Voters," *New York Times* (June 12, 2006)

The winners will always believe the results of elections. But it eats away at democracy if the loser thinks that something went wrong, for accidental or malicious reasons.
—Rush Holt, on the need for a paper trail, quoted in "The Paranoids Are Right," *Working for Change* (October 10, 2006)

When your house is on fire, you need to put the fire out, not talk about re-modeling.
—Arianna Huffington, on why she voted for Kerry rather than Nader in 2004, quoted by Cornel West in "Matters of Justice," AlterNet (September 29, 2004)

Unlike the First Amendment's guarantee of freedom of religion, press, and assembly, the individual right to vote is not guaranteed in our Constitution!
—Congressman Jesse L. Jackson, Jr., "Do Americans Have the Right to Vote?" PBS (September 1, 2004)

The American people are gradually losing confidence in the credibility, fair-ness, effectiveness and efficiency of our voting system. . . . We need to build our democracy and our voting system on a rock, the rock of adding a Voting Rights Amendment to the U.S. Constitution that applies to all states and all citizens.
—Congressman Jesse L. Jackson, Jr., "Our Voting System Needs a New Constitutional Foundation," *Common Dreams* (January 6, 2005)

We can live with winning and losing. We cannot live with fraud and stealing.
—Rev. Jesse Jackson, "One Month Later, Fight over Ohio Continues," *Guardian (UK)* (November 29, 2004)

The single greatest threat to our democracy is the insecurity of our voting system. If people lose faith that their votes are accurately and faithfully recorded, they will abandon the ballot box. Nothing less is at stake here than the entire idea of a government by the people.
—Robert F. Kennedy, Jr., "Was the 2004 Election Stolen?" *Rolling Stone* (June 1, 2006)

In four states today, if you're a convicted felon, you can lose the right to vote forever.
—Ankush Khardori, "Prisons, Democracy, and Political Opportunism," *Huffington Post* (March 25, 2007). The states are Florida, Iowa, Kentucky, and Virginia.

How can we call ourselves a beacon of democracy abroad when the right to vote hasn't been secured in free and fair elections at home?
—Dennis Kucinich, quoted in "Was the 2004 Election Stolen?" *Rolling Stone* (June 1, 2006)

It's a very, very common liberal mistake to assume that people just vote on the basis of their economic self-interest and that you can appeal to them that way.
—George Lakoff, "The F Word," *American Prospect* (July 10, 2006)

People do not necessarily vote in their own self interest. They vote their values. They vote for who they identify with.
—George Lakoff, *Don't Think Like an Elephant* (2004)

Every state in our nation has different laws for voting, and the imperfect (even defective) technologies voters use to cast their ballots can vary from county to county—even from one polling location to the next.
—Sharon J. Lettman, e-mail from "People for the American Way" (April 28, 2006)

The only time you waste a vote is when you vote for someone you don't believe in.
—Ralph Nader, quoted in "Nader Wraps Up His Campaign," *Chicago Tribune* (November 2, 2004)

A nasty little secret of American democracy is that, in every national election, ballots cast are simply thrown in the garbage. Most are called "spoiled," supposedly unreadable, damaged, invalid . . . In the 2004 election, for example, more than three million ballots were never counted.
—Greg Palast, "Recipe for a Cooked Election," *Yes!* magazine (October 21, 2006)

There is an overwhelming accumulation of statistical, anecdotal, and circumstantial evidence that paperless, secretly coded voting machines are facilitators of massive fraud.
—Ernest Partridge, "In 2006, Voting Fraud Is the Keystone Issue," *Crisis Papers* (January 3, 2006)

All computer systems can be rigged or manipulated.
—John Schneider, "Touch-Screen Voting Isn't the Right Answer," *Baltimore Sun* (March 31, 2006)

The process by which our votes are cast and counted is controlled by private corporations to an extent that threatens the foundations of democracy.
—Warren Stewart, "Do You Know How Your Vote Will Be Counted?" *Washington Spectator* (March 2, 2006)

The essence of the marketplace is the unequal power of money. In the market, the woman with one dollar has one vote, the billionaire has a billion votes, and the man outside the market, with no money in his pocket, has no vote at all.
—George H. Rosen, "Democracy, Charity, and the Market," *Boston Globe* (April 2, 2004)

Imagine walking into the ballot booth and casting your vote without having to hold your nose. Imagine being able to vote for what you really believe, instead of telling yourself (yet again) that the best you can do is pick the lesser of two evils.
—Jonathan Tasini, "Why I'm Taking on Hillary Clinton," AlterNet (December 5, 2005)

Who really picks our nation's leaders today? Is it the people? Or the contributors?
—Jim Wright, "Big Money Contributors Defeat Public Interest," *Miami Herald* (July 3, 2001)

THE THREAT OF RELIGIOUS EXTREMISM

Agnosticism

To admit to theological skepticism is political suicide.
—Brooke Allen, "Our Godless Constitution," *Nation* (February 3, 2005)

I do not consider it an insult, but rather a compliment to be called an agnostic. I do not pretend to know where many ignorant men are sure—that is all that agnosticism means.
—Clarence Darrow, in his speech defending John Scopes who was accused of teaching evolution (1925)

Do not pretend that conclusions are certain which are not demonstrated or demonstrable. That I take to be the agnostic faith.
—Thomas H. Huxley, *Aphorisms and Reflections* (1907)

Question with boldness even the existence of a God; because, if there be one, he must more approve of the homage of reason, than that of blindfolded fear.
—Thomas Jefferson, in his letter to Peter Carr (1787)

An agnostic position is one that leaves open the question whether there exists a god or gods, professing to find such a question unanswered or unanswerable.
—Jaroslav Pelikan, quoted in *The Melody of Theology: A Philosophical Dictionary* (1988)

An atheist, like a Christian, holds that we can know whether or not there is a God. . . . The Agnostic suspends judgment, saying that there are not sufficient grounds either for affirmation or for denial.
—Bertrand Russell, "What Is an Agnostic?" quoted in the *Basic Writings of Bertrand Russell* (2001)

Atheism

It was easier for me to think of a world without a creator than of a creator loaded with all the contradictions of the world.
—Simone de Beauvoir, quoted in "Toward a Hidden God," *Time* (April 8, 1966)

There can be no Creator, simply because his grief at the fate of his creation would be inconceivable and unendurable.
—Elias Canetti, *The Human Province* (1978)

"Thou shalt not kill" loses much of its force when reduced from a commandment to a suggestion.
—Don Feder, "Atheism Isn't The Final Word," *USA Today* (April 16, 2007)

When was the last atheist riot? Is there a newspaper anywhere on this earth that would hesitate to print cartoons about atheism for fear that its editors would be kidnapped or killed in reprisal?
—Sam Harris, *Letter to a Christian Nation* (2006)

There is no more evidence to justify a belief in the literal existence of Yahweh and Satan than there was to keep Zeus perched upon his mountain throne or Poseidon churning the seas.
—Sam Harris, *The End of Faith* (2005)

We are all atheists with respect to Zeus and Thor.
—Sam Harris, "An Atheist Manifesto," Truthdig (February 8, 2006)

What can be asserted without proof can be dismissed without proof.
—Christopher Hitchens, "Less than Miraculous," *Free Inquiry* (February/ March 2004)

In a pluralistic search for truth and meaning . . . a belief in God is one belief among many. The government has no place promoting any religious point of view.
—Rev. Jeffrey Jones, "Are atheists, agnostics, non-Christians part of Scalia's America?" *Fredericksburg Free Lance-Star* (January 31, 2003)

God, once imagined to be an omnipresent force throughout the whole world of nature and man, has been increasingly tending to seem omniabsent.
—Corliss Lamont, *The Philosophy of Humanism* (1988)

I have friends who don't believe in God, and don't believe in an afterlife, and, strangely enough, they are some of the best people I know.
—Roland Merullo, "Of God, and Men," *Boston Globe* (September 5, 2006)

There is a difference between true atheism and anti-theism. Atheism can be the naked pursuit of truth, but anti-theism is more often the adolescent joy of upsetting and mocking religious people.
—Rev. Jim Rigby, "Why We Let an Atheist Join Our Church," AlterNet (April 1, 2006)

No Gods—No Masters.
—Margaret Sanger, her motto, quoted in *Women Without Superstition* (1997)

A world absent monsters, ghosts, demons, and gods unfetters the mind to soar to new heights, to think unthinkable thoughts, to imagine the unimaginable, to contemplate infinity and eternity knowing that no one is looking back.
—Michael Shermer, *How We Believe* (1999)

An atheist may be simply one whose faith and love are concentrated on the impersonal aspects of God.
—Simone Weil, quoted in *A Certain World* (1970)

The Bible

I am halfway through Genesis, and quite appalled by the disgraceful behavior of all the characters involved, including God.
—J. R. Ackerley, quoted in the essay "Evil," *Time* (June 10, 1991)

We know that religious truth did not appear all in the past, that it did not all get sealed between the covers of the Bible.
—Rev. John Buehrens, "Why bother with the Bible?" *UU World* (July/August 2003)

The Bible may be the truth, but it is not the whole truth, nor is it nothing but the truth.
—Samuel Butler, quoted in *Further Extracts from the Note-Books of Samuel Butler* (1934)

There are two major biblical imperatives: pursue justice and seek peace.
—Rev. William Sloane Coffin, quoted in "In Pursuit of Justice, in Search of Peace," *Nation* (April 16, 2006)

If we went by the Bible, we'd still be taking slaves.
—Richard Dawkins, "Atheist Richard Dawkins on 'The God Delusion,'" interviewed by Terrence McNally, AlterNet (January 18, 2007)

Progressives, liberals and leftists . . . have allowed their fear and ignorance of the Bible to prevent them from seeing that it contains some of the most radically egalitarian, progressive ideals in Western civilization.
—Sean Gonsalves, "What It Means to be 'Evangelical,'" AlterNet (November 9, 2004)

Any Christian who believes that homosexuality is a more important issue than justice for the poor just hasn't read his Bible straight.
—David Hilfiker, "Onward Christian Organizers," *TomDispatch.com* (March 1, 2006)

The Bible isn't America's holiest book. America doesn't have a holy book. It does have two holy documents, however. One is called the Constitution. The other is known as the Declaration of Independence.
—David Kuo, "America's 'Holiest Book'?" *Huffington Post* (December 3, 2006)

Scripture neither condemns nor prohibits abortion.
—Letter to Religious Leaders, Religious Institute on Sexual Morality, Justice, and Healing (2005)

The Bible doesn't "say" anything. Every translation is an interpretation and every preacher is an interpreter of that interpretation.
—Rev. Jan Linn et al., "Falwell and His 'Christian Right' Have It Wrong," *Minneapolis Star Tribune* (October 19, 2002)

It ain't those parts of the Bible that I can't understand that bother me, it is the parts that I do understand.
—Mark Twain, quoted in *The Wit and Wisdom of Mark Twain* (1987)

When the missionaries came to Africa they had the Bible and we had the land. They said "Let us pray." We closed our eyes. When we opened them we had the Bible and they had the land.
—Bishop Desmond Tutu, quoted in *Observer* (December 16, 1984)

"God bless America" is found nowhere in the Bible.
—Rev. Jim Wallis, quoted in "I Want My Faith Back," *Arkansas Times* (December 23, 2004)

Christianity

Those who currently exhort their listeners to support American crusades, demean gays and lesbians, and ignore the needs of the hungry and sick on the basis of "Christianity" do so based upon a foundation of sand.
—Rev. Allen Brill, "Liberals Get Cross-Wise," *Progressive Populist* (May 15, 2004)

We should live our lives as though Christ were coming this afternoon
—Jimmy Carter, in a Bible-class speech quoted in *Boston Sunday Herald Advertiser* (April 11, 1976)

The Christian ideal has not been tried and found wanting. It has been found difficult; and left untried.
—G. K. Chesterton, *What's Wrong With the World?* (1910)

The only test of a Christian is this: How does he treat the poor? How does he treat the lame, the halt, and the blind?
—Melvin B. Tolson, "The Death of an Infidel," *Washington Tribune* (April 2, 1938)

Christianity . . . is simply a faith. Christianism is an ideology. . . . It is the belief that religion dictates politics and that politics should dictate the laws for everyone, Christian and non-Christian alike.
—Andrew Sullivan, "My Problem with Christianism," *Time* (May 15, 2006)

How did the faith of Jesus come to be known as pro-rich, pro-war, and pro-American?
—Rev. Jim Wallis, "Hearts & Minds," *Sojourners* (September 2004)

You can't reduce Christian ethics down to one or two hot-button issues like abortion or same-sex marriage. Poverty is a moral issue. So are truth-telling and the ethics of war.
—Rev. Jim Wallis, quoted in "Christian Strategy: Go Beyond 2004 Election's Hot-Button Issues," *San Francisco Chronicle* (November 7, 2004)

Christians

History is shamefully littered with the moral bankruptcy of people who were Christian in name but not behavior.
—Rev. Ed Bacon, Jr., in a sermon at the All Saints Church in Pasadena, California, after being targeted by the IRS for anti-war sermon, "Neighbor Love is Never Neutral," *Common Dreams* (September 18, 2006)

I am no longer a Christian, but just a person who continues trying to follow the example of Christ.
—Karen Horst Cobb, "No Longer a Christian," *Common Dreams* (October 25, 2004)

For the next four years and well beyond, liberals and progressives will need to emulate these original Christians, who stood against imperial Rome with their bodies, their hearts and their souls.
—Barbara Ehrenreich, "Act Like Christians," *Nation* (November 11, 2004)

By "Christian," I don't mean true Christians. I mean those right-wing politicized clergymen who profess Christian beliefs in order to gain wealth and political power by allying themselves with the GOP.
—R. J. Eskow, "Burn That Yellow Ribbon! Our 'Republichristian' Leaders Have Dishonored Memorial Day," *Huffington Post* (May 29, 2006)

Secular moderates, liberals and progressives don't need to fear authentic Bible-believing Christians.
—Sean Gonsalves, "Charity Is Not Enough," *AlterNet* (December 7, 2004)

Christians generally imagine that no faith imparts the virtues of love and forgiveness more effectively than their own. The truth is that many who claim to be transformed by Christ's love are deeply, even murderously, intolerant of criticism.
—Sam Harris, *Letter to a Christian Nation* (2006)

The Christians I know do not promote hatred against other people. They don't oppose medical research that could save millions of lives. They don't want ignorance taught in our schools.
—Joel McNally, "Far-Right Politicians Give Christians a Bad Name," *Capital Times (Madison, Wisconson)* (October 9, 2005)

If Christ were here now, there is one thing he would not be—a Christian.
—Mark Twain, quoted in *Mark Twain's Notebook* (1935)

Where are the sincere Christians for whom torture and internment camps and tax cuts for the rich are emphatically not WJWD [What Jesus Would Do]?
—Ellis Weiner, "A Public Presentation of My New Theory," *Huffington Post* (April 19, 2006)

Churchgoing

It is not my duty . . . to attend the churches. My own spirit preaches sounder doctrine than I there hear, and I must listen to its divine teachings.
—Bronson Alcott, in his journal (December 20, 1835)

We remember Christians who would own slaves, expecting them to have the Sunday meal prepared when they returned from church.
—Rev. Ed Bacon, Jr., in a sermon at the All Saints Church in Pasadena, California after being targeted by the IRS for anti-war sermon, "Neighbor Love is Never Neutral," *Common Dreams* (September 18, 2006)

Every day people are straying away from the church and going back to God.
—Lenny Bruce, *The Essential Lenny Bruce* (1967)

A new poll shows that 66 percent of Americans think President Bush is doing a poor job of handling the war in Iraq, and the remaining 34 percent think Adam and Eve rode dinosaurs to church.
—Tina Fey, on *Saturday Night Live*, quoted in "Punchlines," *Newsday* (November 3, 2005)

I have found Christian dogma unintelligible. Early in life I absented myself from Christian assemblies.
—Benjamin Franklin, quoted in *Has Science Found God?* (2001)

We know the values of a politician not by the public prayers he or she attends, but by the priorities supported in his or her budget vote. . . . A nation's budget is a moral document.
—Rev. Jesse Jackson, "False Piety Is Wrong Cure for Dems," *Chicago Sun-Times* (July 18, 2006)

I believe in an America where religious intolerance will someday end—where all men and all churches are treated as equals—where every man has the same right to attend or not attend the church of his choice.
—John F. Kennedy, in his address to the Houston Ministerial Association (September 12, 1960)

We used to be Catholics. Now, as Confucian-Druid-Nietzscheian-Pan worshipers, Sunday mornings are pretty much our own.
—Jerry and Joe Long, "Thoughts on the Religious Season," *Huffington Post* (April 13, 2006)

I do think that there's a strain of the Democratic Party—it's not uniform—that is somewhat patronizing towards people who go to church.
—Barack Obama, quoted in "Great Expectations," *American Prospect* (February 2006)

My mind is my own church.
—Thomas Paine, *The Age of Reason* (1794)

Church attendance is not the only indicator of living out your faith.
—Rev. Brenda Bartella Peterson, quoted in "Politics in America: Religious Left Seeks Center of Political Debate," *Washington Post* (June 10, 2004)

The churches must learn humility as well as teach it.
—George Bernard Shaw, in the preface to *Saint Joan* (1923)

Lincoln, widely considered the most spiritual United States president, admitted during his campaign that he'd never joined a church.
—Sankara Saranam, interview regarding his book *God Without Religion*, godwithoutreligion.com (2005)

I have been into many of the ancient cathedrals—grand, wonderful, mysterious. But I always leave them with a feeling of indignation because of the generations of human beings who have struggled in poverty to build these altars to the unknown god.
—Elizabeth Cady Stanton, *Elizabeth Cady Stanton, Vol. II* (1922)

People don't come to church for preachments, of course, but to daydream about God.
—Kurt Vonnegut, Jr., quoted in the *New York Times* (April 30, 1980)

Evangelism

Forget about being apologetic about preaching to the choir. It's called energizing the base, and it's just as important for progressives as for right-wing nuts.
—Robert Abian, quoted in *The Bush Survival Bible* (2004)

Had Howard Dean been an evangelical Christian with an evangelical Christian base, would his followers have deserted him because his Iowa holler made him "unelectable"?
—Joel Bleifuss, "Face the Facts," *In These Times* (March 22, 2005)

The obsession of the evangelical community over "values" is never centered on the true evils of the world: poverty, overpopulation, crime and cruelty, war and persecution, the ruination of the planet through environmental poisoning, and the indiscriminate rape of the world's resources.
—Earl Doherty, "Invasion of the Mind Snatchers: What is Happening to America?" *Axis of Logic* (November 22, 2004)

The evangelical right doesn't have a monopoly on "moral values," nor do they have a monopoly on proper and rigorous biblical interpretation. . . . I'll go so far as to say that these Bible-thumpers are just that—people who thump on the Bible without bothering to open it up and wrestle with the prophetic tradition contained within.
—Sean Gonsalves, "What it Means to be 'Evangelical,'" AlterNet (November 9, 2004)

As the right has actively pursued a program of evangelization, it has simultaneously sought to infiltrate, discredit or destroy any institution that exposes people to progressive thought.
—Christopher Hayes, "How to Turn Your Red State Blue," *In These Times* (March 22, 2005)

If belief in heaven was private, like the tooth fairy, I'd say fine. But tooth fairy supporters don't come around to your house and try to convert you.
—Christopher Hitchens, in an interview with Jon Wiener, "Religion Poisons Everything," Truthdig (June 6, 2007)

Here's the problem: religious liberals don't wear their faith on their sleeves. We don't evangelize; we consider it disrespectful to shove our spiritual views down other people's throats.
—Susanna Rodell, "Religious Liberals Must Take Off Kid Gloves & Fight the Right," *Charleston Gazette* (November 5, 2004)

The evangelical social agenda is now much broader and deeper, engaging issues like poverty and economic justice, global warming, HIV/AIDS, sex trafficking, genocide in Darfur, and the ethics of the war in Iraq.
—Rev. Jim Wallis, "The Religious Right's Era Is Over," *Time* (February 16, 2006)

Extremism

The greatest dangers to liberty lurk in insidious encroachment by men of zeal, well-meaning but without understanding.
—Louis D. Brandeis, *Olmstead v. United States* (1928)

Religious fanatics are scary in any country
—Bumper sticker

Imagine for a moment the risks America would face if all three branches of our government were controlled by these right-wing extremists.
—Al Gore, "Gore Lambastes GOP Leaders as Right-Wing Extremists," *Seattle Post-Intelligencer* (October 3, 1995)

The extent to which the dominant factions of the Republican Party are hostile to our most basic constitutional traditions and defining political principles really cannot be overstated. They simply do not believe in them.
—Glenn Greenwald, "Your Modern-Day Republican Party," *Salon* (April 1, 2007)

Proselytizing is . . . a search for a final and irrefutable demonstration that our absolute truth is indeed the one and only truth. The proselytizing fanatic strengthens his own faith by converting others.
—Eric Hoffer, *The True Believer* (1951)

The fanatic cannot be away weaned from his cause by an appeal to his reason or moral sense. . . . He cannot be convinced, but only converted.
—Eric Hoffer, *The True Believer* (1951)

The defining trait of the fanatic . . . is the utter refusal to allow anything as piddling as evidence to get in the way of an unshakable belief.
—Arianna Huffington, "A White House Fluent in Language of Fanatics" (May 21, 2003)

The question is not whether we will be extremist but what kind of extremist will we be.
—Rev. Martin Luther King, Jr., "Letter from Birmingham Jail," *Why We Can't Wait* (1964)

Opposition to abortion has now become the spearhead of political fanaticism.
—Lawrence Lader, *New York Times* (January 11, 1978)

Domestic terrorists of the radical right will never realize their fantasies of "Aryan Revolution." But they do remain ready, willing, and able to kill for their causes. As we saw in Oklahoma City and on 9/11, it takes only a handful of committed zealots to wreak havoc.
—Daniel Levitas, "Our Enemies at Home," *New York Times* (December 13, 2003)

The race to be most pious ultimately moves a nation to extremism, a path all of us should hope to avoid.
—Floyd J. McKay, "Christians and Karl Rove Hold No Monopoly on Values," *Seattle Times* (November 10, 2004)

America's religious extremists are as dangerous as those in the Middle East and around the globe.
—Jason Miller, "The Iron Fist of Jesus," OpEdNews (December 8, 2005)

The hardening of lines, the embrace of fundamentalism and tribe, doom us all.
—Barack Obama, quoted in "The Audacity of Hope," *Newsweek* (December 27, 2004)

Extremists of the right and of the left have long attacked liberalism as their greatest enemy. In our own time liberal democracies have been crushed by such extremists.
—Full-page advertisement entitled "A Reaffirmation of Principle," *New York Times* (October 26, 1988)

Extremism means that someone's going to get hurt. It's a complete lack of compassion and feeling for people.
—Julia Scheeres, in an interview about her fundamentalist upbringing, *BuzzFlash* (November 28, 2005)

Political commentators at this point are mostly rewarded by the extremity of their viewpoint.
—Jon Stewart, interviewed by Lev Grossman, "10 Questions for Jon Stewart," *Time* (September 27, 2004)

The religious right has opened up a new battlefield, and, like it or not, we have to play on it. And the way to begin is by understanding clearly the difference between religious extremists and religious people.
—Michael Tomasky, "The Gettables," *American Prospect* (November 8, 2004)

While Christian extremists usually don't practice violence, but merely threaten it . . . they share with extremist Muslims the belief that all people should be forced to live according to their views. That's about as un-American as it gets.
—Cynthia Tucker, "Right-Wing Jihadists Chip Away at Americans' Liberty," *Cleveland Call & Post* (April 28, 2005)

The best lack all conviction, while the worst are full of passionate intensity.
—William Butler Yeats, "The Second Coming," *The Collected Poems of W. B. Yeats* (1989)

Faith

Never place a period where God has placed a comma.
—Gracie Allen, quote adopted by the United Church of Christ in its "God Is Still Speaking" campaign, "Divine Denial," *American Prospect* (May 5, 2006)

Faith is the substance of things hoped for, the evidence of things not seen.
—Hebrews 11:1

Faith without works is dead.
—James 2:26

Church doctrines are not immune to error.
—Rev. William Sloane Coffin, interviewed by Or N. Rose, "Righteous Indignation," *Tikkun* (March/April 2006)

God may have a future, but it is probably going to be very different from the picture painted by fundamentalists, the mass media, and divinity schools. Each of us now has to decide in private who to worship and pray to, whether the soul is real, what happens after we die.
—Deepak Chopra, "Does God Have a Future?" *Huffington Post* (March 10, 2006)

We liberals need to make a distinction between attacking politicians who see their faith as a necessary part of them and those who want to see that their faith becomes a necessary part of us.
—Andrew Hammond, "Religious Rhetoric Isn't Bad; Hypocrisy Is," *Chicago Maroon* (January 20, 2005)

Faith presupposes that we cannot know. We can never know.
—Chris Hedges, *American Fascists* (2006)

Absolute faith corrupts as absolutely as absolute power.
—Eric Hoffer, "Thoughts of Eric Hoffer," *New York Times* Magazine (April 25, 1971)

Faith is not a political posture. True faith isn't exhibited by symbolic acts, but by substance.
—Rev. Jesse Jackson, "False Piety Is Wrong Cure for Dems," *Chicago Sun-Times* (July 18, 2006)

Gentleness is everywhere in daily life, a sign that faith rules through ordinary things: through cooking and small talk, through storytelling, making love, fishing, tending animals and sweet corn and flowers, through sports, music and books, raising kids—all the places where the gravy soaks in and grace shines through.
—Garrison Keillor, *We Are Still Married* (1989)

It is, I believe, the faith in our fellow citizens as individuals and as people that lies at the heart of the liberal faith.
—John F. Kennedy, accepting the New York Liberal Party nomination (September 14, 1960)

I think that everything you do in public life has to be guided by your faith, affected by your faith, but without transferring it in any official way to other people. That's why I fight against poverty. That's why I fight to clean up the environment and protect this Earth. That's why I fight for equality and justice.
—John Kerry, in the third and final presidential debate with George W. Bush, Tempe, Arizona (October 13, 2004)

Faith is taking the first step even when you don't see the whole staircase.
—Rev. Martin Luther King, Jr., quoted in *Pocket Patriot* (2005)

Let us have faith that right makes might.
—Abraham Lincoln, in his address in New York City (February 27, 1860)

There's a Buddhist metaphor that says all religions, gods, saviors, sages, and teachings are so many fingers pointing to the moon. The object, of course, is to see where they're pointing, not to worship the finger.
—Rev. Davidson Loehr, "The New F-Word?" *UU World* (October 21, 2005)

Faith is not just something you have, it's something you do.
—Barack Obama at the 2006 Global Summit on AIDS and the Church, Lake Forest, California, "Race Against Time" (December 1, 2006)

God has not abandoned us.
—Martin Sheen, interviewed by David Kupfer, *Progressive* (July 2003)

I dissent from the political pollution of sincere, personal faith. I dissent most strongly from the attempt to argue that one party represents God and that the other doesn't.
—Andrew Sullivan, "My Problem with Christianism," *Time* (May 15, 2006)

There lives more faith in honest doubt, believe me, than in half the creeds.
—Alfred Lord Tennyson, quoted in *The Poetic and Dramatic Work of Alfred Lord Tennyson* (1899)

Instead of emphasizing the fact that we are all children of God, faith in America now divides communities.
—Kathleen Kennedy Townsend, *Failing America's Faithful* (2007)

Faith is, before all and above all, wishing God may exist.
—Miguel De Unamuno, *Tragic Sense of Life* (1913)

The life of faith is the inward and outward journey, contemplation, and action.
—Rev. Jim Wallis, quoted in *Voices of the Religious Left* (2000)

With the advent of television preachers, faith . . . became another commodity: "I have it, and you don't." Or worse, "Here's how to get it too. Our operators are standing by!"
—Rev. Jim Wallis, quoted in *The Impossible Will Take a Little While Longer* (2003)

I have ever thought religion a concern between God and our consciences, for which we were accountable to Him, and not the priests.
—George Washington, quoted in *Saving General Washington* (2006)

Faith is not finite and fragile, and never requires "cultural wars" to protect it.
—Kay Whitlock, news release, American Friends Service Committee (February 27, 2004)

As history shows . . . you can't fight America's profound social inequalities without appealing to Americans' profound religious faith.
—Jonathan Zimmerman, "Who Would Jesus Tax?" *Christian Science Monitor* (September 15, 2003)

Fundamentalism

Fundamentalists have gained so much power that the rest of us can't really afford to separate ourselves from politics anymore.
—Rev. Bruce Bjork, quoted in "Christianity in Chains?" *Pulse of the Twin Cities* (January 20, 2005)

Would anyone who turned over the money-changers tables in the temple have had anything nice to say about today's televangelists?
—Rev. F. Forrester Church, *God and Other Famous Liberals* (1991)

Fundamentalism really cannot help itself—it is absolutist and can compromise with nothing, not even democracy.
—E. L. Doctorow, "Why We Are Infidels," *Nation* (May 8, 2003)

It's a particular kind of religiosity. It's the American version of the same fundamentalist impulse that we see in Saudi Arabia, in Kashmir, in religions around the world: Hindu, Jewish, Christian, Muslim. . . . It's the vengeance, the brimstone.
—Al Gore, on George W. Bush's fundamentalism, quoted in "The Wilderness Campaign," *New Yorker* (September 13, 2004)

Fundamentalist movements often seek the restoration of a golden age . . . though a politics of nostalgia leads fundamentalists to wish for a return to a world they believe they have lost, that world—while rooted in historical reality—is also a mythical construction.
—Rev. Martin Marty, *Politics, Religion and the Common Good* (2000)

The South especially cherished the most literal readings [of the Bible], because on these terms it could find biblical passages in support of slavery.
—Rev. Martin Marty, *Pilgrims in Their Own Land: 500 Years of Religion in America* (1985)

Christianity and Islam have been hijacked by fundamentalists who have made religion the language of power, the excuse for violence, and the alibi for empire.
—Bill Moyers, "A Time for Heresy," AlterNet (March 24, 2006)

The only way to cooperate with fundamentalists, it has been said, is to obey them.
—Bill Moyers, "A Time for Heresy," AlterNet (March 24, 2006)

Intellectually, scientifically, even artistically, fundamentalism—biblical literalism—is a road to nowhere, because it insists on fidelity to revealed truths that are not true.
—Katha Pollitt, "Intelligible Design," *Nation* (October 3, 2005)

The rapture, end-times, and Armageddon hucksters in the United States rank with any Shiite ayatollahs.
—Kevin Phillips, *American Theocracy* (2006)

This mass movement, composed of highly charged biblical literalists, represents an in-your-face, we are the only way, absolutely true, old time religion.
—Allan Powell, "Fundamentalism: A Return to Dark Ages," *Hagerstown Herald-Mail* (January 23, 2005)

If we can get past various fundamentalist attitudes about the spiritual life, such as attachment to a too simple code of morality, fixed interpretations of stories, and a community in which individual thinking is not prized, then many different ways of being spiritual come into view.
—Thomas Moore, *Care of the Soul* (1993)

I define fundamentalism as the attempt to impose a single truth on a plural world.
—Rabbi Jonathan Sacks, quoted in *Religion Gone Bad* (2006)

It was a very closed, suspicious subculture that I grew up in. You didn't trust people if they didn't believe exactly the same thing you did. They were out to get you. They were going to lead you astray, lead you to the devil.
—Julia Scheeres, in an interview about her fundamentalist upbringing, *BuzzFlash* (November 28, 2005)

The most dangerous people in the world today are those who persuade themselves that they are executing the will of the Almighty.
—Arthur M. Schlesinger, Jr., "Bush's Faith-Based Presidency Crosses the Line," Tribune Media Service, *New Perspectives Quarterly* (Fall 2004)

Where else do we find fundamentalist zeal, a rage at secularity, religious intolerance, fear of and hatred for modernity? Not in France or Britain or Germany or Italy or Spain. We find it in the Muslim world, in Al Qaeda, in Saddam Hussein's Sunni loyalists.
—Gary Wills, "The Day the Enlightenment Went Out," *New York Times* (November 4, 2004)

There are two visions of America. One . . . is very suspicious of freedom, uncomfortable with diversity, hostile to science, unfriendly to reason, contemptuous of personal autonomy. It sees America as a religious nation. It views patriotism as allegiance to God. It secretly adores coercion and conformity.
—Rabbi Sherwin T. Wine, at an Independence Day celebration in Farmington Hills, Michigan (July 4, 1985)

God

Most of the people throughout history who claim to know God's will have tended to get a lot of the rest of us killed, burnt, raped, tortured, pillaged, thrown out of planes.
—Eric Alterman, "God Is a Concept," *Media Matters for America* (December 19, 2006)

The blessing of a bigoted, political God isn't worth having.
—Deepak Chopra, "Winning God's Blessing," *Huffington Post* (January 6, 2006)

We have squeezed God into the volume of a body and the span of a lifetime; given God a male identity, an ethnic background; made him a tribal chief and gone to war.
—Deepak Chopra, quoted in "10 Questions for Deepak Chopra," *Time* (January 24, 2005)

The mind alone cannot discover God.
—Rev. William Sloane Coffin, interviewed by Or N. Rose, "Righteous Indignation," *Tikkun* (March/April 2006)

I cannot imagine a God who rewards and punishes the objects of his creation, whose purposes are modeled after our own—a God, in short, who is but a reflection of human frailty.
—Albert Einstein, obituary in the *New York Times* (April 19, 1955)

God is the name we give to our belief that life has meaning, one that transcends the world's chaos, randomness and cruelty . . . which works upon us and through us to seek and achieve truth, beauty and goodness.
—Chris Hedges, "I Don't Believe in Atheists," Truthdig (May 23, 2007)

God does not send us despair in order to kill us; he sends it in order to awaken us to new life.
—Hermann Hesse, *Reflections* (1974)

Here on earth, God's work must truly be our own.
—John F. Kennedy, in his inaugural address (January 20, 1961)

God talks to human beings through many vectors: through each other, through organized religion, through the great books of those religions, through wise people, through art, literature, music, and poetry—but nowhere with such clarity, texture, grace, and joy as through Creation.
—Robert F. Kennedy, Jr., "For the Sake of Our Children," EarthLight (Winter 2005)

God seems to have left the receiver off the hook, and time is running out.
—Arthur Koestler, *The Ghost in the Machine* (1967)

I am so abjectly grateful, to have a God in my life, a God of mercy and forgiveness and patience, who I believe rolls exasperated eyes at my spiritual ineptness but lets me try again.
—Anne Lamott, "Word by Word," *Salon* (October 23, 1997)

Oh for the days of the Greek gods! They didn't imbue their followers with crazed infallibility. They didn't decree eternal rights and wrongs. They simply took human form and humped their brains out.
—Jerry and Joe Long, "Thoughts on the Religious Season," *Huffington Post* (April 13, 2006)

How to reconcile a God who creates homosexuals with a God who condemns practicing homosexuals to hell? A mysterious God may be well and good, but a capricious or contradictory God can inspire so much doubt that He threatens the credibility of the entire religious enterprise.
—Harold Meyerson, "God and His Gays," *Washington Post* (March 21, 2007)

Although He's regularly asked to do so, God does not take sides in American politics.
—George Mitchell, Iran-Contra hearings (July 13, 1987)

There is a very good saying that if triangles invented a god, they would make him three-sided.
—Montesquieu, *Persian Letters* (1721)

The last thing that the Almighty needs is a wackjob calling down the wrath of, er, well, God on communities that fail to follow the instructions in the "Christian Coalition Voter Guide."
—John Nichols, on Pat Robertson's condemnation of Dover, Pennsylvania, for ousting its "intelligent design" school board, "God's Pat Problem," *Nation* (November 13, 2005)

It is incomprehensible that God should exist and it is incomprehensible that He should not exist.
—Blaise Pascal, *Pensées* (1670)

Trust in God. She will provide.
—Emmeline Pankhurst, quoted in *Time* (November 21, 1969)

"God" is a symbol of the reality deeper than our ultimate concern. . . . The point is not to affirm the reality of the symbol itself, but to affirm the reality to which the symbol points.
—Rev. Jim Rigby, "Why We Let an Atheist Join Our Church," AlterNet (April 1, 2006)

God is not a Republican. Or a Democrat. Tell America the Religious Right doesn't speak for you.
—Sojourners Christian Ministry advertisement, *New York Times* (August 30, 2004)

If God is ultimately unknowable, then how can we be so certain of what God's real position is on, say . . . the morality of contraception? Or the role of women? Or the love of a gay couple?
—Andrew Sullivan, "My Problem with Christianism," *Time* (May 15, 2006)

It is a mistake to suppose that God is only, or even chiefly, concerned with religion.
—William Temple, *In Search of Serenity* (1955)

The only proof he ever needed of the existence of God was music.
—Kurt Vonnegut, Jr., "Knowing What's Nice," *In These Times* (November 6, 2003)

Who speaks for God? God speaks for God. And it is the voiceless and power-less for whom the voice of God has always been authentically raised.
—Rev. Jim Wallis, *Who Speaks for God?* (1996)

Government and Religion

The government of the United States is not, in any sense, founded on the Christian religion.
—John Adams, 1797 treaty with Tripoli, *The Works of John Adams* (1856)

Politics is not religion, and we should govern on the basis of evidence, not theology.
—Bill Clinton, quoted in "Bill Clinton, Candidate for the Bestseller List," *Washington Post* (June 4, 2004)

The powerbrokers in the Christian right have moved from the fringes of soci-ety to the floor of the House of Representatives and the Senate.
—Chris Hedges, "Christianists on the March," Truthdig (January 28, 2007)

The church must be reminded that it is not the master or the servant of the state, but rather the conscience of the state.
—Rev. Martin Luther King, Jr., *Strength to Love* (1963)

A politically enforced or supported religious faith becomes corrupt, dead, and oppressive, encouraging inevitably in reaction a deep personal distaste and moral distain at such spiritual imperialism.
—Gilkey Langdon, *Creationism on Trial* (1985)

This is an age of religion. Allah is busily assembling nukes. . . . And Jesus, as we all know, lives in the White House and brings freedom to the world one air strike at a time.
—Jerry and Joe Long, "Thoughts on the Religious Season," *Huffington Post* (April 13, 2006)

It is a reproach to religion and government to suffer so much poverty and excess.
—William Penn, *Some Fruits of Solitude* (1693)

Jesus

Who would Jesus torture?
—David Batstone, "Who Would Jesus Torture?" *Sojourners* (November 10, 2005)

Jesus stood with everybody who was nobody. He made a beeline (always) to stand with those on the margins, those whose dignity had been denied, the poor and excluded, the easily despised, the demonized, and those whose burdens were more than they could bear. And they killed him for it.
—Father Gregory Boyle, quoted in "Learning from the Loss," AlterNet (November 8, 2004)

We are furious that the religious right has made Jesus into a Republican. That's idolatry. To recreate Jesus in your own image rather than allowing yourself to be created in Jesus' image is what's wrong with politics.
—Rev. Tony Campolo, quoted in "Religion Taking a Left Turn?" CBS News (July 10, 2006)

I want Jesus to come back and say, "That's not what I meant!" Where's the kindness? Where's the compassion? Where's the charity?
—Margaret Cho, *I Have Chosen to Stay and Fight* (2005)

Jesus never said one word about homosexuality, never said one word about civil marriage or abortion.
—Rev. Bob Edgar, quoted in "Religion Taking a Left Turn?" CBS News (July 10, 2006)

I think the religious right is making Jesus into some kind of Old Testament wrathful prophet who is judgmental, divisive, and opposed to any notion of liberalism, whereas the teachings of Jesus tell quite a different story. He was tolerant. He was forgiving. He preached love, not hate.

—Gary Hart, interviewed by Mark Karlin, *BuzzFlash* (December 21, 2005)

The Jesus I believe in was born of the most humble beginnings and raised in poverty. Throughout his life, Jesus was concerned with the poor, the power-less, and the oppressed. He was the friend of sinners, of the undesirables, and of the outcasts.

—Todd Huffman, "How the Christian Left Can Get It Right," *Common Dreams* (November 10, 2005)

Those of us who are Christians must take back Jesus. . . . The Jesus I am talk-ing about is the one who turned over the tables of the moneychangers right inside the temple. . . . The Jesus I am talking about never said one word about homosexuality.

—Rev. Bernice Powell Jackson, "On Moral Values," *People's Weekly World* (December 4, 2004)

Jesus was born in a manger, not in a mansion.

—Rev. Jesse Jackson, "No GOP Monopoly on God," *Chicago Sun-Times* (November 9, 2004)

Jesus was quite a troublemaker. In fact, I'm thinking the Bush administration would have a special place for Jesus were the swarthy Nazarene to take up his ministry today in the U. S. of A.—in a cell with other Middle Eastern men awaiting deportation.

—Rick Mercier, "If You Read the Gospels, the Religious Right is Most Often Wrong," *Free-Lance Star* (November 29, 2004)

Jesus has been hijacked and turned into a guardian of privilege instead of a cham-pion of the dispossessed.

—Bill Moyers, "Democracy in the Balance," *Sojourners* (August 2004)

The real Jesus was an anarchist. He spent his life refusing to claim power over anyone. He said that God is understood in terms of love not power.

—Rev. Jim Rigby, "Christians Who Want Democracy Must Stop Bowing to a Dictator Christ," *Huffington Post* (June 13, 2006)

I still believe in the nonviolent Jesus and the basic human goodness present in all of us.
—Martin Sheen, interviewed by David Kupfer, *Progressive* (July 2003)

Here is what my great grandfather Clemens Vonnegut said one time about Jesus, "If what he said was good, and it was marvelous, what did it matter if he was god or not?"
—Kurt Vonnegut, Jr.,"Kurt Vonnegut's Last Interview," *In These Times* (May 9, 2007)

Jesus Christ is the Prince of Peace, not the Prince of War.
—Anthony Wade, OpEdNews (2004)

Pluralism

In a pluralistic society a fundamental assumption of public policy is the recognition that everything immoral need not be declared illegal. . . . Citizens who come to different conclusions are not necessarily immoral or un-Christian. The tendency to so brand one's political opponents suggests a kind of moral fascism.
—Editorial, *America: The National Catholic Weekly* (September 13, 1980)

Our pluralism has to be a profound offense to the fundamentalist, who by definition is an absolutist intolerant of all forms of belief but his own, all stories but his own.
—E. L. Doctorow, "Why We Are Infidels," *Nation* (May 8, 2003)

We today cannot help being conscious of the wider realms of man's relationship to the divine, within which Christianity represents one major historical strand among others.
—John Hicks, quoted in "Bring Back Old-Time Religion," AlterNet (December 13, 2005)

Difference of opinion is advantageous in religion.
—Thomas Jefferson, *Notes on the State of Virginia* (1787)

The foundation of our pluralism is that the government will never determine which religion is right, and religion will not put its imprimatur on some politicians while damning others.
—Edward M. Kennedy, in his speech at Liberty University (October 3, 1983)

The tradition I cherish is the ideal this country was built upon, the concept of religious pluralism, of a plethora of opinions, of tolerance and not the jihad.
—Anna Quindlen, "Thinking Out Loud," *New York Times* (September 6, 1992)

Something is very wrong when a single ideology, regardless of what that dogma is, dominates a society.
—Ted Rall, *Wake Up, You're Liberal!* (2004)

This is the question of our time: how does a fractured community of multiple cultures decide what values it must share in order to cohere?
—Salman Rushdie, "What This Cultural Debate Needs Is More Dirt, Less Pure Stupidity," *London Times* (December 10, 2005)

The present trend to repudiate the concept of America as a secular state and officially identify this nation with God and certain sectarian religious views does not bode well for religious pluralism in the United States, in which virtually all of the world's religions are represented among its citizens.
—James E. Wood, quoted in *Ecumenical Perspectives on Church and State* (1988)

Politics and Religion

It is always a mistake, in my view, for people of faith to think their religious and moral insights necessarily give them policy insights. . . . Your faith and moral understanding can motivate you to help the poor, but it will not tell you whether a given welfare program does that or actually hurts the poor.
—Jay Ambrose, "Religion and the presidency," *Naples Daily News* (June 21, 2004)

Religion is too important an aspect of human life to be prostituted to politics, just as politics is too important a part of human life to be enslaved to religion.
—Joseph L. Blau, quoted in "The Wall of Separation," *Union Seminary Quarterly Review* (1984)

You can't divorce religious belief and public service.
—Jimmy Carter, to the National Conference of Baptist Men (June 16, 1978)

Political involvement dictated by faith is not the exclusive province of the right wing.
—Bill Clinton, quoted in "Clintons Say Re-election of Bush Would Be 'a Disaster,'" MSNBC (August 29, 2004)

To most of us, the manipulative invoking of religion to advance a politician or a party is frightening and divisive.
—Mario Cuomo, in a speech at the University of Notre Dame (September 13, 1984)

The best way to ruin religion is to politicize it.
—Chet Edwards, in his address to the U.S. House of Representatives (June 4, 1998)

When religion is too organized, it gets bound up with politics and power and loses sight of the sacred.
—R. J. Eskow, "Celebrate Christmas the Old-Fashioned Way: Defy Authority!" *Yahoo! News* (December 24, 2006)

Those who say religion has nothing to do with politics do not know what religion is.
—Mahatma Gandhi, *An Autobiography or The Story of My Experiments with Truth* (1927)

The reason you can't mix religion and politics is, religion is about absolutes, right and wrong, good and evil. Politics is about compromise.
—Gary Hart, in an interview with Mark Karlin, *BuzzFlash* (December 21, 2005)

Instead of "Jesus Saves," we need to save Jesus. This is no time for the Democrats to begin pandering to any on the Christian Right who have turned Jesus into a symbol for a vast and potentially illegal political network of tax-exempt, church-based, right wing partisan activism.
—Tom Hayden, "Learning from the Loss," AlterNet (November 8, 2004)

The founders of this nation would regard the mixing of religion and politics in the ways now being engineered by the religious right as part of the problem of public morality, rather than as the answer.
—Isaac Kramnick, *The Godless Constitution* (1996)

Like history, religion is written by the victors.
—Mark Morford, "Slyboots Judas Is Winking in Your Direction," *San Francisco Chronicle* (April 14, 2006)

How do we nurture the healing side of religion over the killing side? How do we protect the soul of democracy against the contagion of a triumphalist theology in the service of an imperial state?
—Bill Moyers, "Democracy in the Balance," *Sojourners* (August 2004)

The new wedge issue is religiosity, not to be confused with faith.
—Anna Quindlen, "At the Left Hand of God," *Newsweek* (March 8, 2004)

I can think of no greater disaster to this country than to have the voters of it divide upon religious lines.
—Alfred E. Smith, in an Oklahoma City address (September 20, 1928)

The religion that politicians practice in public blurs the distinction between piety and nationalism; it smells of self-idolatry. Its symbolic gestures make for bad religion and bad politics.
—Jeffrey Stout, quoted in *One Electorate Under God?* (2004)

Many of us who are Christians and not supportive of the religious right are not on the left either. In fact, we are opposed to any politicization of the Gospels by any party.
—Andrew Sullivan, "My Problem with Christianism," *Time* (May 15, 2006)

Religion is not a two-party system.
—Keila Szpaller, "New Time Religion," *Missoula Independent* (January 6, 2005)

Will the Church continue to be the lap dog of one political party or will it assume the position of becoming the watchdog of both?
—Gary Vance, "Wasn't Jesus a Liberal? Part Two," *Common Dreams* (October 9, 2005)

Corporations are making space available and sweetly pressuring their employees into religious groups.
—Nicholas von Hoffman, "Democrats Should Oppose Empowering the Pious," *New York Observer* (December 1, 2004)

The best contribution of religion is precisely not to be ideologically predictable or loyally partisan but to maintain the moral independence to critique both the left and the right.
—Rev. Jim Wallis, "Progressive Faith Did Not Lose This Election," *Sojourners* (November 2004)

When either party tries to politicize God or co-opt religious communities to further political agendas, it makes a terrible mistake.
—Rev. Jim Wallis, "God's Politics: A Better Option," *Sojourners* (February 2005)

Among politicians, the esteem of religion is profitable, the principles of it are troublesome.
—Benjamin Whichcote, *Moral and Religious Aphorisms* (1703)

For some of the most visible leaders in the religious right, politics trumps religion every time.
—Alan Wolfe, "With God on Their Side?" *Guardian (UK)* (October 16, 2006)

Prayer

God bless everyone. No exceptions.
—Bumper sticker

The government ought to stay out of the prayer business.
—Jimmy Carter, in a Washington, D.C., press conference (1979)

Do you find more grace in the search for meaning than in absolute certainty, in the questions rather than in the answers?
—Center for Progressive Christianity Web site (2004)

My prayer is that those of faith would flee the churches that do not preach love.
—Karen Horst Cobb, "No Longer a Christian—Part II," *Common Dreams* (November 30, 2004)

It is while praying that I experience my greatest doubts about God, and it is while looking at the stars that I make the leap of faith.
—Alan Dershowitz, "Taking Disbelief Out of the Closet," *Free Inquiry* (Summer 1999)

Though we travel the world over to find the beautiful, we must carry it with us, or we find it not.
—Ralph Waldo Emerson, *Essays: First Series* (1841)

Prayer is not asking. It is a longing of the soul.
—Mahatma Gandhi, *Young India* (1930)

Do not pray for easy lives. Pray to be stronger men.
—John F. Kennedy, at a prayer breakfast (February 7, 1963)

In liberal Christianity, you can't earn grace—you are given grace unconditionally by God.
—George Lakoff, *Don't Think Like an Elephant* (2004)

Grace . . . is that force that infuses our lives, that keeps letting us off the hook. It is unearned and gratuitous love; the love that goes before, that greets us on the way.
—Anne Lamott, "Word by Word," *Salon* (December 4, 1997)

Dear Lord, please grant me strength, patience, wisdom, and humility. Help me always to search for the truth, but spare me the company of those who have found it. Amen.
—Norman Lear, "Letter to God," *Huffington Post* (December 16, 2005)

The breeze of God's grace is blowing continually. You have to set your sail to catch that breeze.
—Swami Prabhavananda, quoted in *Vedanta for The Western World* (1945)

When you find your voice, your life takes on grace.
—M. Night Shyamalan, "M. Night Shyamalan's Scary Future," *Time* (July 24, 2006)

Religion

The religious perspective must be that of a persuasive outsider rather than an authoritarian insider.
—Rebecca T. Alpert, *Voices of the Religious Left* (2000)

Joy in the universe, and keen curiosity about it all—that has been my religion.
—John Burroughs, journal entry (February 18, 1910)

Religion is bad for American politics when it undermines the civil religion: when it speaks of political matters with the certitude of faith . . . when it treats opponents as agents of Satan.
—Jim Castelli, *A Plea for Common Sense* (1988)

What do we want the Church to do? We don't ask for more cathedrals. We don't ask for bigger churches of fine gifts. We ask for its presence with us, beside us, as Christ among us. We ask the Church to sacrifice with the people for social change, for justice, and for love of brother.
—Cesar E. Chavez, "The Mexican-American and the Church," presented at the Second Annual

Mexican Conference in Sacramento, California (March 8-10, 1968)
There is so much religion in the world, but only enough to make us fight over who is right, not enough to make us love one another.
—Margaret Cho, *I Have Chosen to Stay and Fight* (2005)

Almost every Protestant denomination has lost its secure core and given in to the fundamentalist fringe.
—Deepak Chopra, "Winning God's Blessing," *Huffington Post* (January 6, 2006)

The slave auctioneer's bell and the church-going bell chime in with each other, and the bitter cries of the heart-broken slave are drowned in the religious shouts of his pious master. Revivals of religion and revivals in the slave trade go hand in hand.
—Frederick Douglass, quoted in "Ammunition for Atheists," AlterNet (February 8, 2007)

The religion of one age is the literary entertainment of the next.
—Ralph Waldo Emerson, *Lectures and Biographical Sketches* (1883)

Keep in mind that religion is always a product of somebody's selection and interpretation.
—Roger Gottlieb, interviewed by Nelson Harvey, "Not Just For Hippies," *American Prospect* (April 19, 2006)

Religion is a part of America, but it should not be a part of our law.
—Andrew Hammond, "Religious Rhetoric Isn't Bad; Hypocrisy Is," *Chicago Maroon* (January 20, 2005)

The point of religion, authentic religion, is that it is not, in the end, about us. It is about the other, about the stranger lying beaten and robbed on the side of the road, about the poor, the outcasts, the marginalized, the sick, the destitute, about those who are being abused and beaten in cells in Guantanamo.
—Chris Hedges, "I Don't Believe in Atheists," Truthdig (May 23, 2007)

Let us remember that there is no one religion.
—Holiday Message, *BuzzFlash* (December 25, 2005)

The dangers posed by people and groups inspired by or operating under the guise of religion have never been clearer.
—Charles Kimball, *When Religion Becomes Evil* (2002)

Any religion that professes to be concerned about the souls of men and is not concerned about the slums that damn them, the economic conditions that strangle them, and the social conditions that cripple them is a spiritually moribund religion awaiting burial.
—Rev. Martin Luther King, Jr., "Pilgrimage to Nonviolence," *Christian Century* (April 13, 1960)

My religion is very simple. My religion is kindness.
—The Fourteenth Dalai Lama, *My Tibet* (1995)

The liberal world has developed such a knee-jerk hostility to religion that it has both marginalized those many people on the Left who actually do have spiritual yearnings and simultaneously refused to acknowledge that many who move to the Right have legitimate complaints about the ethos of selfishness in American life.
—Rabbi Michael Lerner, "The Democrats Need a Spiritual Left," *Common Dreams* (November 4, 2004)

I certainly remember the days when being religious meant fighting for civil rights and social justice.
—Frank Newport, quoted in "Religious Left Seeks Center of Political Debate," *Washington Post* (June 10, 2004)

Sound religion and sound science need not be in conflict.
—John Nichols, "God's Pat Problem," *Nation* (November 13, 2005)

Religion is about accepting, unquestioningly, what some father figure tells you is true. To be religious is to be the ultimate ditto-head.
—David Horton, "Religion Bad for People and Countries?" *Huffington Post* (November 27, 2006)

Homo sapiens is the species that invents symbols in which to invest passion and authority, then forgets that symbols are inventions.
—Joyce Carol Oates, "The Calendar's New Clothes," *New York Times* (December 30, 1999)

All national institutions of churches, whether Jewish, Christian, or Turkish, appear to me no other than human inventions, set up to terrify and enslave mankind, and monopolize power and profit.
—Thomas Paine, *The Age of Reason* (1794)

I believe that religious duties consist in doing justice, loving mercy, and endeavoring to make our fellow-creatures happy.
—Thomas Paine, *The Age of Reason* (1794)

Religion is most essentially a decision to be engaged in a world that cannot be understood and offers no guarantees.
—Rev. Jim Rigby, "Why We Let an Atheist Join Our Church," AlterNet (April 1, 2006)

Being religious means asking passionately the question of the meaning of our existence and being willing to receive answers, even if the answers hurt.
—Paul Tillich, *Saturday Evening Post* (June 14, 1958)

I do not believe that, on . . . balance, religious belief has been a force for good.
—Bertrand Russell, *Sceptical Essays* (1928)

You may go over the world and you will find that every form of religion which has breathed upon this earth has degraded women.
—Elizabeth Cady Stanton, in a speech to the National Suffrage Association (January 1885)

History teaches that the one thing religions hate more than secularism is other religions.
—Nicholas von Hoffman, "Democrats Should Oppose Empowering the Pious," *New York Observer* (November 29, 2004)

Religion, left or right, center, across the spectrum, ought to agree that torture is simply morally unacceptable.
—Rev. Jim Wallis, "Rescuing Religion from the Right," Beliefnet (January 26, 2005)

Religion is what the individual does with his own solitariness.
—Alfred North Whitehead, *Religion in the Making* (1926)

Religious Freedom

What is threatened today is moral liberty, conscience, respect for the soul, the very nobility of man.
—Henri Amiel, *Journal* (June 17, 1852)

Religious liberty in a nation is as real as the liberty of its least popular religious minority.
—Paul Blanshard, Orlando, in a Florida address (February 1974)

Congress shall make no law respecting an establishment of religion, or prohibiting the free exercise thereof; or abridging the freedom of speech, or of the press; or the right of the people peaceably to assemble, and to petition the Government for a redress of grievances.
—First Amendment to the U.S. Constitution (1791)

Nothing is more fallacious, or inimical to genuine religious liberty, than the seductive notion that the state should "favor" or "foster" religion. All history testifies that such practices inevitably result in favoring one religion over less powerful minorities and secular opinion.
—Edward L. Ericson, *American Freedom and the Radical Right* (1982)

In a nation committed to religious liberty, public schools are neither the local church nor religion-free zones.
—Charles C. Haynes, "The Truth About God in Public Schools," *USA Today* (November 21, 2005)

The Religious Left

How does the religious left invite itself back into the public conversation? And how do we claim our own ground of hopefulness—and move the public conversation away from fear, where it currently resides?
—Rev. Clare Butterfield, "Religious Left Needn't Be Ashamed to Speak Up," *Chicago Sun-Times* (November 24, 2004)

I call that mind free, which resists the bondage of habit, which does not mechanically repeat itself and copy the past, which does not live on old virtue, which does not enslave itself to precise rules, but forgets what is behind, [and] listens for new and higher monitions of conscience.
—William Ellery Channing, in a sermon entitled "Spiritual Freedom" (1830)

The religious right has been effectively organizing for thirty-five years, and as I always say, it took Moses forty years to lead his people out of the wilderness, and it's going to take us a few years more to catch up.
—Rev. Bob Edgar, quoted in "FOCUS: Liberal Theology," *Newsdesk* (December 9, 2004)

The early Christian church was a model of revolutionary inspiration before the Powers That Be got hold of it. There was no priestly class. Communion was celebrated, well, communally. Women as well as men led worship services.
—R. J. Eskow, "Celebrate Christmas the Old-Fashioned Way: Defy Authority!" *Yahoo! News* (December 24, 2006)

If we insist that we know the one way to God, we've put God in a very small box.
—Bishop Katharine Jefferts-Schori, "[Pat] Robertson Unhinged over New Female Bishop," AlterNet (November 2, 2006)

Our mother Jesus gives birth to a new creation—and you and I are His children.
—Bishop Katharine Jefferts-Schori, "Episcopalians to Consecrate Female Bishop," *Washington Times* (November 2, 2006)

Liberal Christianity sees God as essentially beneficent, as wanting to help people.
—George Lakoff, *Don't Think Like an Elephant* (2004)

If the Democrats were to foster a religious/spiritual Left, they would no longer pick candidates who support preemptive wars or who appease corporate power.
—Rabbi Michael Lerner, "The Democrats Need a Spiritual Left," *Common Dreams* (November 4, 2004)

The greatest heretic of all is Jesus of Nazareth, who drove the money changers from the temple in Jerusalem as we must now drive the money changers from the temples of democracy.
—Bill Moyers, "A Time for Heresy," AlterNet (March 24, 2006)

Unlike evangelicals, religious progressives encourage a wide range of scriptural interpretations. Thus it becomes challenging for clergy and other elites on the left to be viewed as authoritative . . . and to mobilize anyone for political action.
—Laura R. Olson, "Religious Left faces tough challenge," *Newsday* (November 22, 2004)

Religious-left progressives, so prominent in the civil rights, anti-poverty and anti-war movements of the 1960s, somehow lost their mojo in the eighties.
—Clarence Page, "Running with Religion in 2004," *Chicago Tribune* (March 21, 2004)

At the heart of the beliefs of the liberal Christians who make up the hunger coalitions and peace movements throughout this country is the conviction that Christ blesses those who feed the hungry and clothe the naked.
—Rosa Maria Pegueros, "Charity Begins at Home," *Common Dreams* (January 5, 2005)

Where are the people who preach—and live—the biblical values of inclusion, service, humility, sacrifice, and why haven't they coalesced into an alternative political force?
—Leonard Pitts, "Where's the Morality in Bush's Policy?" *Miami Herald* (November 8, 2004)

The word "Christian" has come to be so strongly associated with beliefs that are the polar opposite of mine. It's frankly embarrassing to share a label with Pat Robertson and Jerry Falwell.
—Jennifer Barnett Reed, "I Want My Faith Back," *Arkansas Times* (December 23, 2004)

The moderate mainstream church is helpless against fundamentalism because it is built on a nuanced version of the same cracked foundation of a theology of power.
—Rev. Jim Rigby, "Christians Who Want Democracy Must Stop Bowing to a Dictator Christ," *Huffington Post* (June 13, 2006)

Until very recently, our silence has been deafening.
—Rev. William G. Sinkford, quoted in "Our Power Problem," *UU World* (January/February 2005)

Those of the religious left, who care about social justice, are doing the hands-on work that Jesus advocated.
—Bev Smith, in a letter to the editor, "Trib watching," *Pittsburgh Tribune-Review* (December 24, 2004)

Whenever anyone speaks out defending Christianity, they are immediately lumped into the category of some right-winged, conservative, Super-Christian Republican. They are typecast as some Bible-belt, scripture-throwing, holier-than-thou hypocrite who uses and pan handles Christianity for political gain. Please do not lump me with them.
—Etan Thomas, "My Christmas Story," *Huffington Post* (December 21, 2006)

The Christian clergy of the United States was either pro-Bush or silent. . . . Organized Christian religion is either controlled by the other side, or indifferent, or too weak and spineless to defy Republican godliness.
—Nicholas von Hoffman, "Now Is Not the Time for National Unity!" *New York Observer* (November 22, 2004)

Conventional wisdom suggests that the antidote to religious fundamentalism is more secularism. That's a very big mistake. The best response to bad religion is better religion.
—Rev. Jim Wallis, quoted in "Fundamentalism and the Modern World," *Sojourners* (March/April 2002)

We seek a prophetic biblical perspective that is progressive rather than repressive; inclusive and respectful of pluralism instead of exclusive and sectarian.
—Rev. Jim Wallis, quoted in *Voices of the Religious Left* (2000)

We are indeed motivated by our faith to seek justice and peace. But in the public arena, we don't make arguments based on others' accepting the "absolute truth" of our faith.
—Rev. Jim Wallis, quoted in "Bully in the Pulpit?" *Nation* (February 22, 2001)

The Religious Right

The success of televangelists lies largely in their being parasites on family culture and morality. Far from providing a foundation for morality, they have gained for their religion a free ride on the back of the family culture that most Americans embrace.
—Joe L. Barnhart, *Jim and Tammy* (1990)

"Religious Right" . . . summons images of God-fearing rednecks from backwoods Kentucky who hunt down gays, see blacks as savages, and who generally have lost all capacity for rational thought.
—Ross Clark, "What is . . . 'The Religious Right'?" *London Times* (October 8, 2005)

The great story here . . . is the vast right-wing conspiracy that has been conspiring against my husband since the day he announced for president.
—Hillary Rodham Clinton, quoted from interview on NBC's *Today* show, "Excerpts of Mrs. Clinton Interview," *Washington Post* (January 27, 1998)

There is perhaps no phenomenon which contains so much destructive feeling as "moral indignation," which permits envy or hate to be acted out under the guise of virtue.
—Eric Fromm, *Man for Himself* (1974)

While I support liberal struggles for economic justice—higher wages, universal health care, affordable education, and retirement security—I don't think economic populism will do much to neutralize the religious right. Cultural interests are real interests, and many drives are stronger than material ones.
—Michelle Goldberg, "Saving Secular Society," *In These Times* (May 16, 2006)

The religious right in America . . . is seeking a dictatorship of the minority.
—Gary Hart, *God and Caesar in America* (2005)

For some conservative Christians, neither the Crusades nor the Confederacy are over.
—Tom Hayden, "Learning from the Loss," AlterNet (November 8, 2004)

The Christian right has lured tens of millions of Americans, who rightly feel abandoned and betrayed by the political system, from the reality-based world to one of magic—to fantastic visions of angels and miracles, to a childlike belief that God has a plan for them and Jesus will guide and protect them.
—Chris Hedges, "Christianists on the March," Truthdig (January 28, 2007)

The engine that drives the radical Christian Right in the United States, the most dangerous mass movement in American history, is not religiosity, but despair.
—Chris Hedges, "The Radical Christian Right Is Built on Suburban Despair," AlterNet (January 19, 2007)

These corporations, and their enraged and manipulated followers in the Christian right, tens of millions of them, if left unchecked will propel us into despotism.
—Chris Hedges, "Pariah or Prophet?" Truthdig (February 26, 2007)

It is far, far easier to be on the right than in the middle or on the left, because everything is already determined for you.
—Rev. Randy Hyde, quoted in "I Want My Faith Back," *Arkansas Times* (December 23, 2004)

The religious right—not to be confused with religious Americans in general—isn't a majority, or even a dominant minority. It's just one bloc of voters, whom the Republican Party has learned to mobilize with wedge issues.
—Paul Krugman, "No Surrender," *New York Times* (November 5, 2004)

The power and seduction of [the Bush] administration emerges from its dia-
bolical manipulation of Christian rhetoric.
—Rev. Rich Lang, quoted in "Is Bush the Antichrist?" *Seattle Weekly*
(December 8, 2004)

The Christian Right is unwilling to challenge the capitalist marketplace. . . .
Their loyalty to conservative capitalist economics trumps for them their com-
mitment to serving God.
—Rabbi Michael Lerner, "How the Jews and Secularists Did Not Steal
Christmas," *San Francisco Chronicle* (December 17, 2006)

Instead of blaming the absence of values and the prevalence of narcissism and
materialism on the dynamics of the marketplace, Americans are taught by the
Religious Right that the problem is a militant secular Left.
—Rabbi Michael Lerner, "Hostile Takeover: Theocracy in America," *Tikkun*
(January/February 2006)

For a good chunk of the GOP base, the Democrats are literally in league with
the Devil, so any means of keeping them out of power is legitimate.
—Bill Maher, "Republicans = Scientologists," *Huffington Post* (November 9,
2006)

These people draw near to me with their mouth, and honor me with their
lips; but their heart is far from me. And in vain do they worship me, teaching
as doctrine rules made by men.
—Matthew 15:8-9

Believing in divine power should not make you a blind lockstep jingoist zealot
right-wing homophobe drone, bowing and kneeling and feeling unworthy
and sinful and then changing the channel to ESPN2 and watching log-rolling.
—Mark Morford, "Pat Robertson, God's Simp," *San Francisco Chronicle* (July
18, 2003)

It was inevitable that the opposite of the religious right would become the ir-
religious left. It just doesn't happen to be accurate.
—Anna Quindlen, "At the Left Hand of God," *Newsweek* (March 8, 2004)

Real conservatives are cautious. . . . But radical conservatives are revolution-
aries, for them, ends justify means.
—Robert Reich, *Reason: Why Liberal Will Win the Battle for America* (2004)

A specter is haunting America. . . . It is the specter of Americans kneeling in submission to a particular interpretation of a religion that has become an ideology, an all-encompassing way of life. It is the specter of our nation ruled by the extreme Christian right.
—Rabbi James Rudin, *The Baptizing of America: The Religious Right's Plans for the Rest of Us* (2006)

Conservative American Christians are very concerned about the need to restore what they say is a biblical view of the family: a male-dominated nuclear family consisting of a working husband, a nonworking wife who is a full-time mother, and several dependent children.
—Rosemary Radford Ruether, quoted in *Voices of the Religious Left* (2000)

How can America accept the religious right's reduction of morality to issues like homosexuality and abortion, which are scarcely mentioned in the Bible?
—David Saperstein, "Three Challenges for Mainstream Jewry," *Haaretz* (Israel) (December 25, 2005)

One of the great problems with the extreme religious right is that it is so difficult to tell where they think the Republican Party platform stops and Christianity begins, because they've confused the two.
—Rev. Tim Simpson, quoted in "The Left Reclaims Religion," *Choice!* Magazine (September 9, 2005)

The essence of true religiosity—kindness, humility, love, tolerance—means nothing to these people.
—Gene Stone, on the Christian Right, "What Would Jesus Boo?" *Huffington Post* (May 1, 2006)

There's the religious right, and then there are voters who are religious. They are not the same thing. The former are not persuadable; they want to extinguish modernity, they privilege mystical belief over physical evidence, and they will never vote Democratic.
—Michael Tomasky, "The Gettables," *American Prospect* (November 8, 2004)

Like right-wing Muslims, [right-wing Christians] rage against modernity itself.
—Cynthia Tucker, "Religious Extremists Have Powerful Political Allies," *Yahoo! News* (July 22, 2006)

What remains the best-kept secret from the Second World War, because it is so embarrassing, is that Hitler was a Christian.
—Kurt Vonnegut, "Dear Mr. Vonnegut," *In These Times* (February 28, 2003)

The core of the Christian Right . . . is about legislating morality.
—Clyde Wilcox, *Onward Christian Soldiers? The Religious Right in American Politics* (1997)

The Separation of Church and State

No religious test shall ever be required as a qualification to any office or public trust under the United States.
—Article VI, Section 3 of the United States Constitution

Render therefore unto Caesar the things which are Caesar's, and unto God the things that are God's.
—Matthew 22:21

I am extremely concerned by a fundamentalist shift in many houses of worship and in government, as church and state have become increasingly intertwined in ways previously thought unimaginable.
—Jimmy Carter, "This Isn't the Real America," *Los Angeles Times* (November 14, 2005)

The god whom I worship and serve has a perfect attendance record and has never been tardy.
—James Dunn, in his reply to fundamentalists who said God had been expelled from the classroom, quoted in "A Time for Heresy," AlterNet (March 24, 2006)

America is . . . an amalgam of different races, cultures, nationalities, religions. In these conditions Americans can only be grateful for the Constitution's wisdom of erecting a wall of separation between church and state and leaving religious practice to individual conscience.
—Editorial, *Christian Science Monitor* (October 27, 1980)

Americans have every right, of course, to seek for their children a religiously oriented education and to send their children to private schools which provide the sort of religious orientation they want. But they have no more right to ask the general public to pay for such schools . . . than to ask the general public to pay for the churches.
—Editorial, *Washington Post* (March 3, 1971)

The religion that has to be supported by law is not only without value, but a fraud and a curse. The religious argument that has to be supported by musket is hardly worth making.
—Robert Ingersoll, quoted in *What's God Got to Do with It?* (2005)

What the Christian right says today is that the founding fathers were only concerned about religious freedom from government interference. They weren't concerned about government freedom from religious interference. That is the big lie of the religious right.
—Susan Jacoby, quoted in *BuzzFlash* interview (February 14, 2005)

[Congress] should make no law respecting an establishment of religion, or prohibiting the free exercise thereof, thus building a wall of separation between church and state.
—Thomas Jefferson, in his letter to the committee of the Danbury Connecticut Baptist Association (January 1, 1802)

I believe in an America where the separation between church and state is absolute.
—John F. Kennedy, in his address to the Houston Ministerial Association (September 12, 1960)

God belongs in the churches, not in the schools.
—Jim Logan, "They're Baaack! Intelligent Design Resurrected, This Time as Philosophy," *Huffington Post* (January 11, 2006)

It was to keep the people's freedom thus preserved from the oppressive troops of any faith—and thereby keep religious liberty itself alive—that Jefferson and his associates deliberately conceived our godless Constitution.
—Mark Crispin Miller, *Cruel and Unusual* (2004)

We will be a better country when each religious group can trust its members to obey the dictates of their own religious faith without assistance from the legal structure of the country.
—Margaret Mead, *Redbook* (February 1963)

The Constitution contains no reference to a deity. The Declaration of Independence contains not one word on religion.
—Robin Morgan, quoted in *What Do We Do Now?* (2004)

If I am opposed to abortion for religious reasons but seek to pass a law banning the practice, I cannot simply point to the teachings of my church. I have to explain why abortion violates some principle that is accessible to people of all faiths, including those with no faith at all.
—Barack Obama, "Politicians Need Not Abandon Religion," *USA Today* (July 9, 2006)

The great religious ages were notable for their indifference to human rights in the contemporary sense—not only for their acquiescence in poverty, inequality and oppression, but for their enthusiastic justification of slavery, persecution, torture and genocide.
—Arthur M. Schlesinger, Jr., *The Cycles of American History* (1999)

We criticize that in most Islamic states the role of religion in society and the secular character of the legal system are not clearly separated. But we haven't taken note as readily of the U.S. Christian fundamentalists and their interpretation of the Bible that show similar tendencies.
—Gerhard Schroeder, former German chancellor, quoted in "Schroeder says Bush's religious talk worried him," Reuters (October 22, 2006)

The separation of church and state does not mean the separation of values from our public life.
—Rev. Jim Wallis, *Meet the Press*, NBC (November 28, 2004)

Tax-Subsidized Religion

Forcing taxpayers to subsidize religious institutions they may or not believe in is no different from forcing them to put money in the collection plates of churches, synagogues, and mosques.
—Americans United for Separation of Church and State, press release (February 20, 2001)

Once we've got politicians dangling million-dollar grants in front of cooperative ministers, and ministers free to pledge their flock's support to politicians who send money their way, oh what a lovely mess it's gonna be.
—Jay Bookman, "A Theocracy Won't Forgive Our Trespasses," *Atlanta Journal-Constitution* (November 18, 2004)

Government is contemptuous of true religion when it confiscates the taxes of Caesar to finance the things of God.
—Samuel J. Ervin, in a letter to Ronald Reagan, *Congressional Record* (April 29, 1982)

What religious groups do with their own money is their business. But when they use our tax dollars and then say they won't hire us for jobs that we help fund, that is unacceptable.
—Matt Foreman, news release, "Bush Administration's Orwellian Logic," National Gay and Lesbian Task Force (June 25, 2003)

It's not a coincidence that the most "faith-based" government we've had in over a century is also the most corrupt, secretive, murderous, lying, and law breaking in history.
—Tom Gilroy, "Bush's Trojan Christ," *Huffington Post* (May 3, 2006)

Bringing the disposed to Jesus Christ has become something very close to a domestic policy goal of the United States government.
—Michelle Goldberg, *Kingdom Coming: The Rise of Christian Nationalism* (2006)

The diversion of billions of taxpayer dollars from secular social service organizations to . . . sectarian religious outfits has been one of the most underreported stories of the Bush presidency.
—Michelle Goldberg, *Kingdom Coming: The Rise of Christian Nationalism*, (2006)

If American faith-based charities receive funding from the federal government, how will they dare to criticize that government? . . . Will their faith become Americanized, their scriptures revised, in accord with prevailing political winds?
—Susannah Heschel, quoted in *One Electorate Under God?* (2004)

Faith-based social policy, faith-based war, faith-based science, faith-based education, and faith-based medicine, all are leading our nation down a road to ruin.
—Todd Huffman, "If You Don't Mind, Why Don't You Mind?" *Common Dreams* (April 8, 2006)

Faith-based funding is a fig leaf for a strategy of abandoning the most needy, and religious people should not be part of that.
—Rabbi Michael Lerner, "Faith-Based Defunding of the Public Sector," *Tikkun* (May/June 2001)

Christianity has sufficient inner strength to survive and flourish on its own. It does not need state subsides, nor state privileges, nor state prestige.
—William O. Douglas, *The Bible and the Schools* (1966)

Under Bush's "faith-based initiatives," taxpayer dollars already are flowing into coffers of right-wing religious groups, which, in turn, turn out their followers as Republican foot soldiers.
—Robert Parry, "Bush and the Rise of 'Managed-Democracy,'" *Consortium News* (February 13, 2005)

Theocracy

I think that having any religious group dominate the government is dangerous. In my opinion, our focus must be on the transformation of ourselves, our churches, and our society—in that order.
—Rev. James R. Adams, "President's Report," The Center for Progressive Christianity Newsletter (December 2004)

Religious leaders are even daring to instruct us in how to vote, and in some cases are suggesting that those who dare to vote contrary to their leaders' wishes risk their soul and standing with God. This is America?
—Jay Bookman, "A Theocracy Won't Forgive Our Trespasses," *Atlanta Journal-Constitution* (November 18, 2004)

The original colonies were mostly Christian theocracies. It was precisely this 150 years of experience that the Framers of the Constitution specifically rejected when they voted unanimously to pass Article VI of the Constitution, which abolished religious tests for public office.
—Frederick Clarkson, "The Rise of Christian Nationalism in the U.S.: What Do We Do Now?" *Free Inquiry* (Fall 1996)

Why is it so important for some Americans to insist this is a Christian nation? Are they so insecure in their beliefs that they need government sanction for their faith?
—Alan Colmes, *Red, White, & Liberal* (2003)

Let there be no mistake about the ultimate goal of the Christian right: to turn the United States into a theocracy, ruled by Christian evangelicals . . . and to establish Christianity as the official state religion.
—Alan Dershowitz, *The Vanishing Jew* (1996)

Bush's faith-based social welfare strategy only accelerates the downward spiral toward theocracy. . . . The evangelical church-based welfare system is being fed by the deliberate destruction of the secular welfare state.
—Barbara Ehrenreich, "The Faith Factor," *Nation* (November 11, 2004)

The drive by the Christian right to take control of military chaplaincies, which now sees radical Christians holding roughly 50 percent of chaplaincy appointments in the armed services and service academies, is part of a much larger effort to politicize the military and law enforcement. This effort signals the final and perhaps most deadly stage in the long campaign by the radical Christian right to dismantle America's open society and build a theocratic state.
—Chris Hedges, "America's Holy Warriors," Truthdig (December 31, 2006)

This nation is lurching toward theocracy and we need to understand what happens when church and state become one.
—Randolph T. Holhut, "It's Time to Start Taking Theocrats Seriously," OpEdNews (November 2, 2005)

We have tried the government of priests, and we know that such governments are without mercy. In the administration of theocracy, all the instruments of torture have been invented.
—Robert Ingersoll, quoted in *What's God Got to Do with It?* (2005)

The Republican Party has become the first religious party in U.S. history.
—Kevin Phillips, "How the GOP Became God's Own Party," *Anniston Star* (April 10, 2006)

For the first time in our history, ideology and theology hold a monopoly of power in Washington.
—Bill Moyers, "Battlefield Earth," *Axis of Logic* (January 8, 2005)

In my view, Al Qaeda, the Taliban, and American fundamentalists like Jerry Falwell and Pat Robertson are indeed theocrats asking that their religious agenda be enforced by the power of the state.
—Rev. Jim Wallis, quoted in "Fundamentalism and the Modern World," *Sojourners* (March-April 2002)

THE ASSAULT ON SCIENCE AND THE ENVIRONMENT

Commons

The idea of the commons helps us identify and describe the common values that lie beyond the marketplace. . . . A language of the commons also serves to restore humanistic, democratic concerns to their proper place in public policymaking. It insists that citizenship trumps ownership.
—David Bollier, quoted in "The People's Business," *In These Times* (February 18, 2005)

Either the general population will take control of its own destiny and will concern itself with community interests, guided by values of solidarity, sympathy, and concern for others, or alternatively there will be no destiny for anyone to control.
—Noam Chomsky, quoted in the film *Manufacturing Consent: Noam Chomsky and the Media* (1992)

This land is your land,
This land is my land,
From California to the New York Island,
From the redwood forest to the Gulf Stream waters,
This land was made for you and me.
—Woody Guthrie, "This Land Is Your Land" (1956)

In a democracy there are some things we all own together. Often referred to as "the commons," they include the necessities and commonalities of life: our air, water, septic systems, transportation routes, educational systems, radio and TV spectrums, and, in every developed nation in the world except America, the nation's health-care system.
—Thom Hartmann, "Healthcare Reveals Real 'Conservative' Agenda," *Common Dreams* (February 25, 2003)

Our government has abandoned its duty to safeguard our health and steward our national treasures, eroding not just our land, but our nation's moral authority.
—Robert F. Kennedy, Jr., *Crimes Against Nature* (2004)

The best way to judge the effectiveness of a democracy is to measure how it allocates the goods of the land: Does the government protect the commonwealth on behalf of all the community members, or does it allow wealth and political clout to steal the commons from the people?
—Robert F. Kennedy, Jr., "Crimes Against Nature," *Rolling Stone* (December 11, 2003)

The earth is our common wealth, on loan from God. Instead of trying to find new ways to patent it and make profit from it, we need to put our energies into preserving it as the shared inheritance of humanity, our commons.
—Rabbi Michael Lerner, *The Left Hand of God* (2006)

The appetite of Big Business for the appropriation of public resources is limitless.
—Ralph Nader, "Reclaiming Our Commons," *Common Dreams* (June 27, 2002)

We need a government that connects us and cares for us, that protects and promotes the common good and our commons—the lands and waters we all share and that humble us equally.
—Carl Pope, "Ideologues vs. Environmentalists," *Miami Herald* (September 29, 2005)

The commons is the part of life that is neither the market nor the state, but rather is the shared property and heritage of us all. It includes the gifts of nature, such as oceans and atmosphere, wilderness areas, and the quiet of the night. . . . They are open and free to all.
—Jonathan Rowe, "Our Neglected Wealth," *Christian Science Monitor* (April 30, 2002)

Conservation

Ours is the most wasteful nation on Earth.
—Jimmy Carter, quoted in "Carter Was Right on Energy All Along," *Capital Times (Madison, Wisconson)* (February 8, 2006)

We are entering the last few decades of the oil era, with ominous consequences for the future of a global economy that is utterly dependent on fossil fuels.
—Jeremy Rifkin, "Sorry, Mr. President, Homilies Won't Stop the Hurricanes," *Guardian (UK)* (September 23, 2005)

The movement for the conservation of wildlife, and the larger movement for the conservation of all our natural resources, are essentially democratic in spirit, purpose, and method.
—Theodore Roosevelt, quoted in "Conservation: Our Leaders Fiddle While the Public Turns," *Arianna Online* (July 9, 2001)

While we account for less than 5 percent of the world's people, we use up about a quarter of the world's energy. And we Americans apparently think we have the God-given right to do so.
—Cynthia Tucker, "Oiloholic Nation Has No Business Lecturing China," *Baltimore Sun* (April 24, 2006)

We live in a land of vanishing beauty, of increasing ugliness, of shrinking open space, and of an overall environment that is diminished daily by pollution and noise and blight. This, in brief, is the quiet conservation crisis.
—Stewart L. Udall, *The Quiet Crisis* (1963)

Energy

Each person in the U.S. consumes as much energy as 2.1 Germans, 12.1 Columbians, 28.9 citizens of India, 127 Haitians and 395 Ethiopians.
—Alan Bisbort, "Overcoming American Gluttony," AlterNet (June 5, 2007)

Why do we need so many vehicles with seven seats? Look around you. How many minivans, SUVs, station wagons, and large sedans are carrying more people than the driver?
—Warren Brown, "Energy Policy Without the Fear Factor," *Washington Post* (June 11, 2006)

No blood for oil.
—Protest sign

We simply must balance our demand for energy with our rapidly shrinking resources. Only by saving energy can we maintain our standard of living and keep our people at work.
—Jimmy Carter, quoted in "Carter Was Right on Energy All Along," *Capital Times (Madison, Wisconson)* (February 8, 2006)

If we remain dependent on fossil fuels, then we remain dependent on the countries that produce them.
—Jonathan Freedland, "When It Comes to Global Warming, Market Rule Poses a Mortal Danger," *Guardian (UK)* (October 25, 2006)

The entire design of the U.S. economy—from the size of its cars, the expanse of its highways, to the very fact of suburbia—is an artifact of cheap, plentiful oil.
—Robert Freeman, "Bush's Economic Policies: Don't Look Behind the Curtain," *Common Dreams* (October 29, 2006)

American suburbia represents the greatest misallocation of resources in the history of the world. The far-flung housing subdivisions, commercial highway strips, big-box stores, and all the other furnishings and accessories of extreme car dependence will function poorly, if at all, in an oil-scarce future.
—James Howard Kunstler, "Finding Hope in a Post-Oil Society," *Orion* (January/February 2007)

The fact that Iraq is the last unharvested oil bonanza on earth, in an era of increasingly fierce global competition for dwindling oil reserves, only makes U. S. motives all the more suspect.
—Linda McQuaig, "The Real Problem Is That It Is Illegal for One Country to Invade Another Country," *Toronto Star* (October 29, 2006)

Four years ago, gasoline was $1.36 a gallon.
—Ralph Nader, "Stop ExxonMobil from Squeezing Us Dry," *Common Dreams* (July 29, 2006)

There's much talk of wind and solar power. But how about the oceans and their massive tidal and current patterns? Driven by the gravitational force of the sun and the moon, tides and currents represent a source that's as infinite and everlasting as any force on Earth.
—Neal Peirce, "Tapping Into Tidal Power," *Seattle Times* (August 1, 2006)

Environment

We are far more concerned with the desecration of our flag than the desecration of our land.
—Wendell Berry, *What Are People For?: Essays* (1990)

Over increasingly large areas of the United States spring now comes unheralded by the return of birds, and the early mornings are strangely silent where once they were filled with the beauty of bird song.
—Rachel Carson, *Silent Spring* (1962)

We have trampled most corners of the earth, and when the wild lands are gone, they are just that—gone.
—Catharine Cooper, "Driving Wilderness to Extinction," *Laguna Beach Coastline Pilot* (November 4, 2005)

I'm appalled that we'd risk not just the beauty, but the very stability of our planet for the sake of short-term profit.
—Vivian Dent, "From the Heart," AlterNet (November 11, 2004)

The interests of the corporation state are to convert all the riches of the earth into dollars.
—William O. Douglas, *Points of Rebellion* (1969)

The "control of nature" is a phrase conceived in arrogance, born of the Neanderthal age of biology and the convenience of man.
—Rachel Carson, *The Silent Spring* (1962)

The fast-food chain that helped make our kids the fattest on Earth is now selling future car buyers on the fun of driving a super-sized, smog-spewing, gas-guzzling SUV originally built for the military.
—Environmental Working Group newsletter, on McDonald's use of Happy Meals toys to promote Hummers, "Ronald McHummer" (2006)

Jesus said, "Blessed are the meek, for they shall inherit the Earth." We haven't seen much meekness in Washington lately, except from Democrats. The question is, "Will the Earth be worth inheriting after the oil companies and polluters trash it?"
—Brett Hulsey, "Bush and His Cohorts Would Be Wise to Implement Jesus Agenda," *Capital Times (Madison, Wisconson)* (December 18, 2004)

The planet's resources do not belong to the United States. The century is not America's. We own neither the world nor time. And if we don't give up the quest—if we don't find our place in the world instead of on top of the world—there is little hope for a safe, sane and sustainable future.
—Robert Jensen, "A Defeat for an Empire," *Fort Worth Star-Telegram* (December 9, 2004)

Corporate polluters, their phony think tanks, and political toadies like to marginalize environmentalists as tree huggers, or radicals. But there is nothing radical about clean air or water.
—Robert F. Kennedy, Jr., "Redefining the Environmental Debate," Truthout (April 4, 2006)

We are called to assist the Earth to heal her wounds and in the process heal our own.
—Wangari Maathai, "Nobel Winner Maathai Sounds Alarm Over Planet," Reuters (December 10, 2004)

The earth we abuse and the living things we kill will, in the end, take their revenge.
—Marya Mannes, *More in Anger* (1958)

Homegrown ayatollahs are more set on savaging gay people than saving the green earth.
—Bill Moyers, in his speech to the Society of Environmental Journalists Convention in Austin, Texas, "A Question for Journalists: How Do We Cover Penguins and the Politics of Denial?" (October 1, 2005)

The Earth does not belong to us. We belong to the Earth.
—Chief Seattle, quoted in "Poetry Can Get Outside the Box of Politics," *San Francisco Examiner* (January 9, 2005)

Evolution

There is no law that mandates the teaching of evolution, and there should not be, yet it is practically universally taught in universities and colleges around the world.
—Tim Berra, *Evolution and the Myth of Creationism* (1990)

There is nothing wrong with the idea of a creator, but teaching it as [a part of science] leads to detriment of both religion and science.
—Andrew Buncombe, "The School of Creationism," *Independent (UK)* (December 20, 2004)

Evolution and the literally exhaustive geologic records that establish the Earth's multibillion-year age remain the most solid, well-proved science ever developed.
—Editorial, "Unintelligent Design: The Loony Right Is Hammering Science Harder Than Ever," *New York Daily News* (December 30, 2004)

This week, Georgia's board of education approved the plan that allows teachers to keep using the word "evolution" when teaching biology. Though, as a compromise, dinosaurs are now called "Jesus Horses."
—Jimmy Fallon, *Saturday Night Live*, NBC (February 21, 2004)

An epoch will come when people will disclaim kinship with us as we disclaim kinship with the monkeys.
—Kahlil Gibran, quoted in *Spiritual Sayings of Kahlil Gibran* (1962)

Man as we know him is a poor creature, but he is halfway between ape and god, and he is traveling in the right direction.
—Julian Huxley, *New Bottles for New Wine* (1957)

I would rather be the offspring of two apes than be a man and afraid to face the truth.
—Thomas Huxley, quoted in *T. H. Huxley: Scientist, Humanist and Educator* (1959)

Man is not God's last word: God can still create. If you cannot do His work, He will produce some being who can.
—George Bernard Shaw, *Back to Methuselah* (1921)

For most of our evolutionary history we were a prey species—a scruffy primate just recently evolved from a rodent. . . . In the future, if we want to survive, we will become symbionts—life forms that live in partnership with others.
—Kelpie Wilson, "Climate Shock: We're on Thin Ice," Truthout (December 30, 2005)

Global Warming

It's easy to write off Republicans as mindless lemmings. But why do so many otherwise rational Democrats and Independents disregard the dire warnings about global climate change?
—Bob Burnett, "Global Warming? Not in My Backyard," *Common Dreams* (April 19, 2006)

The Kyoto Protocol, the landmark treaty requiring cuts in gas emissions which cause global warming, is now in effect with the support of 141 nations but not of the world's biggest polluter, the United States.
—Agence France Presse, "Historic Kyoto Treaty Inked Without the World's Biggest Polluter, the U.S." (February 16, 2005)

I think it's crazy for us to play games with our children's future. We know what's happening to the climate, we have a highly predictable set of consequences if we continue to pour greenhouse gases into the atmosphere.
—Bill Clinton, "U.S., Under Fire, Eases Its Stance in Climate Talks," *New York Times* (December 10, 2005)

Global warming is real and rapidly altering our weather, our economy and our world. The 1990s were the hottest decade in the last 1,000 years.
—Laurie David, "Snubbing Kyoto: Our Monumental Shame," *Los Angeles Times* (February 11, 2005)

Humanity cannot avoid a warmer Earth and some rise in sea level, largely because of the gases we have already deposited in the atmosphere. But the worst outcomes may be avoided if the world takes concerted action to stabilize industrial emissions of greenhouse gases.
—Editorial, "Time to Connect the Dots," *New York Times* (September 28, 2005)

If humans pursue a business-as-usual course for the first half of this century, I believe the collapse of civilization due to climate change becomes inevitable.
—Tim Flannery, quoted in "Heat Wave," *Nation* (June 12, 2006)

Climate change is too big a problem to be solved simply by virtuous individuals hopping on a bus instead of taking the car. . . . This is a job for government.
—Jonathan Freedland, "When It Comes to Global Warming, Market Rule Poses a Mortal Danger," *Guardian (UK)* (October 25, 2006)

Global warming is a deadly threat precisely because it fails to trip the brain's alarm, leaving us soundly asleep in a burning bed.
—Daniel Gilbert, "If Only Gay Sex Caused Global Warming," *Los Angeles Times* (July 2, 2006)

Ten of the hottest years in recorded history have occurred in the past twelve years.
—Amy Goodman, "Global Warming, Warring and Warning," *Seattle Post-Intelligencer* (January 11, 2007)

The people who still say that global warming isn't real are actually in the same boat with the flat earth society. They get together and party on Saturday nights with the folks that believe the moon landing was in a movie lot in Arizona.
—Al Gore, "Countdown with Keith Olbermann," MSNBC (June 19, 2006)

"Global warming" is the name it was given a long time ago. But it should be understood for what it is: a planetary emergency that now threatens human civilization on multiple fronts.
—Al Gore, "The Time to Act Is Now," *Salon* (November 4, 2005)

Climate change is the most critical problem the Earth has ever faced.
—Tony Haymet et al.n, "The Planet NASA Needs to Explore," *Washington Post* (May 10, 2007)

The failure of the United States to get serious about climate change is unforgivable, a human folly beyond imagining.
—David Ignatius, "Is It Warm in Here? We Could Be Ignoring the Biggest Story in Our History," *Washington Post* (January 18, 2006)

America is a decade late in addressing the serious threat from global warming largely due to ExxonMobil's campaign of deliberate deception. ExxonMobil's conduct amounts to a war on civilization.
—Robert F. Kennedy, Jr., on the company's multimillion-dollar propaganda campaign, "Exposing ExxonMobil," *Huffington Post* (January 28, 2007)

We know more about Tom [Cruise] and Katie [Holmes] than we do about global warming. We're the most entertained, least informed people in the world."
—Robert F. Kennedy, Jr., "Robert Kennedy Jr.: 'We Have a Negligent Press in This Country,'" FishbowlNY (October 24, 2006)

Climate change is the most severe problem that we are facing today—more serious even than the threat of terrorism.
—David King, "Climate Change Science: Adapt, Mitigate, or Ignore?" *Science* (January 9, 2004)

Whether humanity can move toward a global civilization will depend by and large on how it can act collectively deal with what's arguably the central issue of our time: global warming.
—Andrew Lam, "The Politics of Climate Change: It Will Happen and They Will Come," *San Francisco Chronicle* (November 15, 2005)

The truth about the climate crisis may be inconvenient for some of the biggest polluters who want us to think it's not real. It may be inconvenient for all of us to think about changing long-established patterns. But the truth is that we have to change and we have to do so fairly rapidly in order to meet our moral obligation to our children and grandchildren.
—Al Gore, "Countdown with Keith Olbermann," MSNBC (June 19, 2006)

We should be the heart and mind of the Earth, not its malady.
—James Lovelock, "The Earth Is About to Catch a Morbid Fever That May Last as Long as 100,000 Years," *Independent (UK)* (January 16, 2006)

The science tells us clearly we need to act now to reduce inputs of greenhouse gases, but unless all countries act in equitable proportions, the virtuous will be economically disadvantaged while all suffer the consequences of the sinners' inaction.
—Lord May, "Impact of Climate Change Can Be Likened to WMD," *Independent (UK)* (November 29, 2005)

A century's carelessness is now melting away the world's storehouses of ice, a melting whose momentum may be nearing the irreversible.
—Bill McKibben, "The Coming Meltdown," *New York Review of Books* (January 12, 2006)

The United States is, by far, the world's worst contributor to the root causes of global warming, and yet we are the least concerned about it.
—Mark Morford, "Behold, the Lost Americans," *San Francisco Chronicle* (February 23, 2007)

The average American generates more than ten times the greenhouse gas emissions as does the average Chinese, and perhaps thirty times more than the average citizen of Bangladesh.
—David Morris, "What Al Gore Hasn't Told You About Global Warming," AlterNet (January 9, 2007)

Climate change is for real. We have just a small window of opportunity and it is closing rather rapidly. . . . We are risking the ability of the human race to survive.
—Rajendra Pachauri, quoted in "Global Warming Approaching Point of No Return, Warns Leading Climate Expert," *Independent (UK)* (January 23, 2005)

Those most vulnerable to climate change are not the ones responsible for causing it. Our energy-consumptive lifestyles are having lethal impacts on other people around the world, especially the poor.
—Jonathan Patz, quoted in "Climate Shift Tied to 150,000 Fatalities," *Washington Post* (November 17, 2005)

Global climate change and the ripples of that change will affect every aspect of life, from municipal budgets for snowplowing to the spread of disease.
—Report by the Center for Health and the Global Environment at Harvard Medical School and other groups, quoted in "Ripples of Global Warming Spread Outward," Inter Press Service (November 4, 2005)

Human life still entirely depends on the health of the larger biosphere. But America's present rulers act as if they either do not understand, or do not care about, this basic reality.
—Andrew Bard Schmookler, "The Bushite Regime and the Collapse of Civilizations," *Common Dreams* (June 5, 2006)

Exxon has reportedly been funding so-called think tanks to undermine confidence in the science of global warming, just as the tobacco industry funded "research" to question the validity of statistical findings showing the link between smoking and cancer.
—Joseph Stiglitz, "Global Warming: Don't Ignore the Risks," *Miami Herald* (November 15, 2006)

Here's what I think the truth is: We are all addicts of fossil fuels in a state of denial, about to face cold turkey.
—Kurt Vonnegut, Jr., "Cold Turkey," *In These Times* (May 10, 2004)

Nature

Nature, to be commanded, must be obeyed.
—Francis Bacon, *Novum Organum* (1620)

In the developed world . . . we speak of nature as if we are not part of it.
—James Carroll, "Disease Takes Wing," *Boston Globe* (February 20, 2006)

It's clear from the Bible that the Earth belongs to God, not Exxon.
—Roger Gottlieb, in an interview with Nelson Harvey, "Not Just for Hippies," *American Prospect* (April 19, 2006)

The Powers That Be have turned the production of our edibles away from the high art of cooperating with nature into a high-cost system of always trying to overwhelm nature.
—Jim Hightower, quoted in "Slow Food Nation," *Nation* (September 11, 2006)

Teach your children to regard the land as a living thing, an ecosystem of which we are a part, not a commodity that belongs to us.
—Rev. Robin Myers, *Why the Christian Right Is Wrong* (2006)

Nature in America has always been suspect, on the defensive, cannibalized by progress.
—Susan Sontag, *On Photography* (1977)

Pollution

Our government should be taking the lead in reducing greenhouse gases, recognizing our responsibilities as the world's leading polluter.
—Bruce Ackerman and Todd Gitlin, "We Answer to the Name of Liberals," *American Prospect* (October 18, 2006)

Experience has shown time and again that polluters can easily dominate state political landscapes, and that state governments are generally willing to abandon enforcement of their own environmental laws in order to recruit polluting industries.
—Robert F. Kennedy, Jr., "Destroying the Clean Water Act" (February 23, 2006)

Polluters spend hundreds of millions every election cycle on lobbying and campaign contributions to control the political process, and billions more on phony think tanks and deceptive advertising. . . . Industry outspends environmental groups 1,000 to 1 on political campaigning and advertising.
—Robert F. Kennedy, Jr., "Attack Polluters, Not Environmental Leaders," *San Francisco Chronicle* (January 11, 2006)

A free market should not include the right to pollute the environment.
—George McGovern, PBS television interview (September 13, 1989)

The cancer of water pollution was engendered by our abuse of our lakes, streams, rivers, and oceans; it has thrived on our half-hearted attempts to control it; and like any other disease, it can kill us.
—Edmund Muskie, Congressional Research Service Reports (1972)

The nation that destroys its soil destroys itself.
—Franklin D. Roosevelt, in a letter to state governors (February 26, 1937)

Through a few chairmen of the board in jail for polluting the air and water, and you'll see pollution disappear quite rapidly.
—Fortney H. Stark, Jr., quoted in "Tumult & Shouting," San Francisco Sunday Examiner & Chronicle (January 2, 1972)

We cannot allow the continued rape of the land by polluters who would deplete our forests, scar our public lands, pollute our air and water, and then have the tax code subsidize their destruction.
—Pete Stark, quoted in news release, "Tax Breaks for Polluters Growing More Expensive," Friends of the Earth (December 15, 1998)

Polluters are not paying the full costs of the damage they cause.
—Joseph Stiglitz, "Global Warming: Don't Ignore the Risks," Miami Herald (November 15, 2006)

Science

In our post-factual world . . . conclusions have become immune to facts; for too many, the only facts that are valid are those that confirm what they already "know" to be true.
—Jay Bookman, "When Facts Collide with Beliefs," Atlanta Journal-Constitution (April 4, 2005)

If science proves some belief of Buddhism wrong, then Buddhism will have to change.
—Dalai Lama, "Our Faith in Science," New York Times (November 14, 2005)

I shall never believe that God plays dice with the world.
—Albert Einstein, quoted in Einstein: His Life and Times (1947)

By now you may be forgiven for suspecting that science is tinted—if not entirely tainted—by politics. The arguments over evolution and global warming alone are enough to make anyone believe that we have red and blue science as well as red and blue states.
—Ellen Goodman, "Science Progresses Despite Politics," Truthdig (June 14, 2007)

From environmental hazards to sex education, the federal government in the past several years has been twisting science to political ends. The ends are sometimes ideological—as in the suppression of information about condoms and sexual safety—and sometimes simply take the form of favors to business interests.
—Marjorie Heins, "The Attack on Science," *Common Dreams* (December 21, 2004)

Science is based not on claims of absolute truth, but on evidence marshaled to support a theory. . . . Ideas must be capable of being proven false to be scientifically valid. Rather than saying something is TRUE, we can only say that to date it has not been proven false.
—Robert Jensen, "ID debate reveals limits of religion and science," *Working for Change* (December 21, 2005)

Over the past two decades, industry and conservative think tanks have invested millions of dollars to corrupt science. They distort the truth about everything from tobacco, pesticides, and dioxin to ozone depletion, acid rain, and global warming.
—Robert F. Kennedy, Jr., quoted in *Air America: The Playbook* (2006)

For fifty years, tobacco companies employed a stable of scientists to challenge the evidence that cigarettes caused lung cancer.
—David Michaels, "Science-for-Hire Hazardous to Health," *Baltimore Sun* (April 17, 2006)

Science politicization succeeds, at least in part, because it confuses the public and policymakers, leading them to believe that a scientific "controversy" exists where one actually does not.
—Chris Mooney, *The Republican War on Science* (2005)

I don't think it is a coincidence . . . that in a nation where nearly half our people believe in creationism, much of the populace also doubts the certainty of climate change science.
—Bill Moyers, in his speech to the Society of Environmental Journalists Convention in Austin, Texas, "A Question for Journalists: How Do We Cover Penguins and the Politics of Denial?" (October 1, 2005)

Religion and science conflict only when one or both forget their proper bounds. . . . The proper concern of religion is not declarations of truth, but the search for meaning.
—Rev. Jim Rigby, quoted in "ID Debate Reveals Limits of Religion and Science," *Working For Change* (December 21, 2005)

I don't think we ought to lie to our children about science.
—Henry Waxman, quoted in "Some Abstinence Programs Mislead Teens, Report Says," *Washington Post* (December 2, 2004)

Stem Cell Research

Some of the most fervent protectors of microscopic stem cells are the most ardent proponents of the death penalty.
—Jimmy Carter, *Our Endangered Values* (2005)

There is no morality in rejecting the promise of a cure to those who suffer from a terrible disease.
—Editorial Board, regarding embryonic stem cell research, "Whose Morality?" *Seattle Post-Intelligencer* (November 7, 2004)

It is immoral to allow your sectarian beliefs to stop research which can save lives.
—Terry Curtis Fox, "The Immoral Veto," *Huffington Post* (July 20, 2006)

Suppose there is a fire at a fertility clinic. In one room is a freezer with a hundred embryos. In another room is a baby. Now, suppose you have only enough time to enter ONE room. Do you save the baby, or the freezer? The Republican case is that you must save the freezer, not the baby.
—Dave Johnson, "Save the Baby or the Freezer?" *Huffington Post* (July 27, 2006)

Promoting life means . . . fulfilling the promise of stem cell research, rather than destroying the hopes of millions of suffering Americans for the sake of a tiny cluster of undifferentiated cells that will otherwise be discarded.
—George Lakoff, *Thinking Points: Communicating Our American Values and Vision*, 2006)

Stem cell lines in a Petri dish are not human life. They will never become human life. On behalf of the most virulent religious extremists, politicians are still trying to shut down this life-saving research.
—Joel McNally, "Far-Right Politicians Give Christians a Bad Name," *Capital Times (Madison, Wisconson)* (October 9, 2005)

The ethical and moral obligation lies with saving lives, not saving potential lives.
—JoAnne Gatti-Petito, in a letter to the editor, "Stem Cells and the President's Veto," *New York Times* (July 21 2006)

How is it that an embryo cannot be used for research because it is human life and yet it can be discarded?
—Kathleen Reardon, "Stem Cell Hypocrisy—Having It Both Ways," *Huffington Post* (July 23, 2006)

THE INSANITY OF WAR AND VIOLENCE

Child Molestation

By many estimates, over 100,000 people were molested by priests over the last few decades.
—Amy Berg, "The Sins of Our Fathers," *Huffington Post* (October 12, 2006)

In a culture in which the sexualization of childhood is big business . . . is it any wonder that pedophiles feel emboldened to claim that they shouldn't be ostracized for wanting sex with children?
—Rosa Brooks, "No Escaping Sexualization of Young Girls," *Los Angeles Times* (August 25, 2006)

If any one group "caused" the priest sex-abuse scandal, it was not gays, but rather the bishops themselves, who now scapegoat gays. . . . While a small percentage of priests abused children, the overwhelming majority of bishops knowingly protected the abusers instead of the abused.
—James Carroll, "The Basilica of Denial," *Boston Globe* (December 5, 2005)

[Republican Congressman] Mark Foley was chairman of a House caucus on missing and exploited children. This was a party that literally put a pedophile in charge of pedophilia.
—Robert Kuttner, "Same Song, Different Scandal," *Boston Globe* (October 7, 2006)

Why did the hierarchy cling to the perfidious priests whom one cardinal called "moral monsters"? Was it because there are so few priests that they felt they had to hang on to the perverts and protect them. . . . Or was it because they did not regard molestation of children as that serious?
—Mary McGrory, "Church Still Defensive, Not Penitent," *Boston Globe* (April 27, 2002)

Churches must break the dynamics of silence surrounding rape, battering, and sexual abuse of children.
—Mary Pellauer, quoted in *Voices of the Religious Left* (2000)

Pedophilia is a serious crime, irrevocably damaging young lives. The problem here is not that the church had sick priests but rather that their evil ways were permitted to fester by the indifference of corrupt cardinals and bishops who then and now blame everyone but themselves for the terrible harm that has been done.
—Robert Scheer, "Blame Church Arrogance, Not Oversexed Society," *Los Angeles Times* (April 30, 2002)

What would happen if every minute and every dollar spent limiting the rights of gays and lesbians was instead spent on prosecuting sexual harassment, rape, and child molestation?
—Cameron Scott, "Queer 101: A Guide for Heteros," AlterNet (March 1, 2007)

I know that it's a tough situation for the Catholic Church and I do understand. What I'd like to propose to them is, just give up the molestation for Lent. Just try it for forty days. See how that goes. A trial period, if you will.
—Jon Stewart, interviewed by Judy Woodruff, "Inside Politics," CNN (May 3, 2002)

It's the Catholic Church that has given gays a bad name, not the other way around.
—Pierre Tristam, "Homophobia as National Sport: Marriage by Constitutional Writ," *Daytona Beach News Journal* (July 15, 2003)

Pedophilia is as much a heterosexual illness as a homosexual one. . . . The real problem here is a lack of accountability.
—Rev. Jim Wallis, "What Must Be Done," *Sojourners* (July/August 2002)

Cruelty

Nearly seventy thousand women and girls died last year because they went to back-street abortionists. . . . Critics of America's aid policy say some might have lived if the U.S. had not withdrawn funding from clinics that provide safe services—or that simply tell women where to find them.
—Sarah Boseley, "Britain Defies U.S. with Funding to Boost Safe Abortion Services," *Guardian (UK)* (February 6, 2006). The global gag rule imposed in 2001 requires any organization applying for U.S. funds to be anti-abortion.

Cruelty is, perhaps, the worst kid of sin.
—G. K. Chesterton, *All Things Considered* (1908)

Cruelty disfigures our national character. It is incompatible with our constitutional order, with our laws, and with our most prized values.
—Alberto Mora, former navy general counsel who warned against the use of torture, quoted in "Ugly Portrait Emerges Dot by Dot," *Vermont Times Argus* (June 18, 2006)

There is no hope in Guantanamo. The only thing that goes through your mind day after day is how to get justice or how to kill yourself. It is the despair—not the thought of martyrdom—that consumes you there.
—Shafiq Rasul, quoted in "Former Guantanamo Detainees Recall Despair," the Associated Press (AP) (June 12, 2006)

The infliction of cruelty with good conscience is a delight to moralists. That is why they invented Hell.
—Bertrand Russell, *Sceptical Essays* (1929)

The creepy thing about the far-right Republicans . . . is not that they are dismantling government because they won't raise taxes, [but that] they're dismantling government because they think it shouldn't help people. They really think health and human services should not be provided.
—Molly Ivins, "Putting the Legislature Out of Our Misery," *Star-Telegram* (Fort Worth) (May 15, 2003)

It is hard to overstate the cruelty of the corporate schemes used to undermine loyal workers' pension benefits. Workers who have relied in good faith on company pension promises are left helpless in the face of cutbacks that deprive them of expected payments that will support them in retirement and old age.
—Ralph Nader, "Pension Takeaway," *San Francisco Bay Guardian* (September 26, 2000)

When people torture and humiliate . . . they are denying that their victims have a fully human status, a dignity that demands respect, a soul.
—Martha Nussbaum, quoted in *What Do We Do Now?* (2004)

No one shall be subject to torture or cruel, inhuman, or degrading treatment or punishment.
—Universal Declaration of Human Rights (1948)

Cruelty to Animals

Animal liberation movements are being demonized not just as whacko or extremist, but also as terrorist.
—Steven Best, quoted in "Stepping Up the Attack on Green Activists," AlterNet (September 30, 2005)

Detested sport,
That owes its pleasures to another's pain;
That feeds upon the sobs and dying shrieks
Of harmless nature.
—William Cowper, *The Task* (1785)

The lower animals are our brethren. I include among them the lion and the tiger. We do not know how to live with these carnivorous beasts and poisonous reptiles because of our ignorance. When man learns better, he will learn to befriend even these.
—Mahatma Gandhi, quoted in *Explorations in Psychohistory* (1974)

There is simply no spiritual defense in either the Western or Eastern religious traditions for eating meat. . . . Animals are sentient beings and their deaths, particularly in the grotesquery of what is euphemistically called food processing, causes them great pain and suffering.
—Rabbi Marc Gellman, quoted in "The Pretzel Logic of Vegetarianism," *Yahoo! News* (March 1, 2007)

To kill for recreation living creatures who bond and mate, who give birth and nurture their young, who experience happiness, pain, fear and grief is quite simply barbaric. In some measure, I feel that killing animals for sport can desensitize the individual to the value of life in general.
—Paul M. Howey, "If We Won't Ban Hunting, at Least Let Animals Have the Sabbath as a Day of Rest," *Asheville Citizens-Times* (North Carolina) (February 4, 2007)

A sportsman is a man who, every now and then, simply has to go out and kill something.
—Stephen Leacock, *My Remarkable Uncle, and Other Sketches* (1942)

The link between cruelty to animals and violence toward people has been well established.
—Colleen Patrick-Goudreau, "From Cradle to Grave," *Common Dreams* (October 31, 2006)

Factory farming is . . . the biggest system of cruelty to animals ever devised. In the United States alone, every year nearly ten billion animals live out their entire lives confined indoors.
—Peter Singer, quoted in "Slow Food Nation," *Nation* (September 11, 2006)

The Death Penalty

The U.S. has a homicide rate that is five times greater than European countries which do not have the death penalty.
—Bob Burnett, "Tookie Williams—On the Killing Floor," *Common Dreams* (December 12, 2005)

Ninety percent of all executions are carried out in just four countries: China, Iran, Saudi Arabia, and the United States.
—Jimmy Carter, *Our Endangered Values* (2005)

The question for society is not whether the criminal deserves to die, but does government deserve the right to kill?
—Mary Catherine Cassidy, "Capital Punishment Is Killing in Your Name," *Corpus Christi Caller-Times* (December 13, 2004)

The United States is the only Western democracy that still executes its citizens.
—Marjorie Cohn, "The Death Penalty Is Not Pro-Life," Truthout (December 12, 2005)

There remains no evidence that the death penalty is a deterrent to crime and plenty of evidence that it is invoked arbitrarily—and often mistakenly.
—Andrew Cuomo, "Don't Revive the Death Penalty," *New York Times* (December 12, 2004)

I am against the death penalty because I think it is bad and unfair. It is debasing. It is degenerate. It kills people. It eclipses other more significant issues that we should be addressing when we talk about murder.
—Mario Cuomo, quoted in *One Electorate Under God?* (2004)

There is no more decisive issue than the death penalty . . . separating Europe from the United States. Even more than the use of torture or preventive war.
—Editorial, *La Repubblica* (Rome) (December 14, 2005)

The deliberate institutionalized taking of human life by the state is the greatest conceivable degradation to the dignity of the human personality.
—Arthur L. Goldberg, Supreme Court Justice, quoted in "The Death Penalty Is Not Pro-Life," Truthout (December 12, 2005)

Many countries reject the death penalty as unworthy of humans. They are right, and the United States is wrong.
—Father Andrew Greeley, "Saddam Execution Is Stain on America," *Chicago Sun-Times* (January 5, 2007)

The essential case for the abolition of capital punishment has long been complete, whether it is argued as an overdue penal reform, as a shield against the arbitrary and the irreparable or as part of the case against "big government."
—Christopher Hitchens, "Tinkering with the Death Machine," *Nation* (July 3, 2002)

Defendants are sentenced to death not for committing the worst crimes, but for having the worst lawyers.
—Bianca Jagger, from the speech given at Stanley Tookie Williams's memorial service, "Saying Goodbye to Tookie," AlterNet (December 24, 2005)

The death penalty is the ultimate, irreversible denial of human rights.
—Irene Khan, quoted in "China, Iran, Saudi, U.S. Main Executioners: Amnesty," Reuters (April 20, 2006)

Justice is never advanced in the taking of a human life. Morality is never upheld by a legalized murder.
—Coretta Scott King, quoted in "Murder Is Murder," *Capital Times (Madison, Wisconson)* (December 14, 2005)

I shall ask for the abolition of the death penalty until I have the infallibility of human judgment demonstrated to me.
—Marquis de Lafayette, quoted in a speech by Senator Russ Feingold in "A New Millennium: Time to Stop Tinkering with the Machinery of Death," Columbia University School of Law (April 10, 2000)

What about the death penalty? How can it be that there isn't yet, within the political parties, especially the Democratic Party . . . a trend of opinion calling for the abolition of this civilized barbarity?
—Bernard-Henri Lévy, "A Letter to the American Left," *Nation* (February 8, 2006)

Can the death penalty ever be justified as public policy when it inherently necessitates the occasional taking of wrongly convicted, innocent life?
—Martin O'Malley, "Why I Oppose the Death Penalty," *Washington Post* (February 21, 2007)

Allowing our government to kill citizens compromises the deepest moral values upon which this country was conceived: the inviolable dignity of human persons.
—Sister Helen Prejean, *Dead Man Walking* (1993)

Stop State Killing
—Protest banner outside the death chamber in Huntsville, Texas

We have prisons and laws that guarantee permanent removal from society of our most dangerous criminals. We no longer need to kill them to keep them out of our communities.
—Joan Ryan, "The Decision/Society: Values Should Preclude Legal Killing as an Act of Revenge," *San Francisco Chronicle* (December 14, 2004)

Liberals often wonder how conservatives can claim to be pro-life and pro-death penalty.
—Bernard Brandon Scott, "Father Knows Best: Where Is Fundamentalism Taking Us?" SnowStar Institute of Religion (2003)

It is the deed that teaches, not the name we give it. Murder and capital punishment are not opposites that cancel one another, but similars that breed their kind.
—George Bernard Shaw, quoted in "Dispatches: 'Evolving Standards of Decency,'" *South Brunswick Post* (January 4, 2007)

When a corporation is convicted of repeated felonies that harm or endanger the lives of human beings or destroy our environment, the corporation should be put to death, its corporate existence ended, and its assets taken and sold at public auction.
—Eliot Spitzer, quoted in "Fixing the Rotten Corporate Barrel," *Nation* (December 23, 2002)

Corporate leaders kill people regularly, often consciously, with personal impunity. Why not hold the individuals behind corporations that poison, harm and kill people accountable the same way we do for individuals who commit murder.
—Karyn Strickler, "Is It Time For a Corporate Death Penalty Act?" *Common Dreams* (January 28, 2005)

Isn't capital punishment always more about revenge than justice?
—Rev. Jim Wallis, "More Revenge Than Justice," Beliefnet (January 4, 2007)

It is morally reprehensible to take a life, and it is especially reprehensible for the state to do so.
—Lisa Weinert, "Death Penalty Talking Points," *Nation* (December 18, 2002)

The death penalty has always been applied disproportionately against poor people—especially black poor people.
—Cornel West, C-SPAN's *Washington Journal* (February 3, 2001)

Domestic Terror

It is only a small minority of fundamentalists who commit acts of terror, but even the most peaceful and law-abiding are perplexing, because they seem so adamantly opposed to many of the most positive values of modern society.
—Karen Armstrong, *The Battle for God* (2000)

Terrorism is not a foreign concept to the thousands of women and men who put themselves at risk daily to ensure a woman's right to choose. Abortion clinics were the target of terrorist activity long before anyone had heard of Timothy McVeigh or Osama bin Laden.
—Allison Brewer, "The Deadly Risks of Being Pro-Choice," *Globe & Mail* (Toronto) (November 8, 2001)

Terrorism against women's health clinics has been a fact of life for years, but our government hardly investigates let alone jails all "pro life" sympathizers.
—John Buell, "Civil Liberties and the Fear of Freedom," *Common Dreams* (December 12, 2001)

80 percent of facilities that provide abortion services experience some form of harassment or violence, including arson and death threats.
—Gloria Feldt, "Planned Parenthood Urges Law Enforcement to Bring All Anti-Choice Terrorists to Justice," U.S. Newswire (May 9, 2003)

It is time for anti-choice leaders to spend as much energy lobbying the extremists among their movement as they do lobbying Congress to outlaw abortion.
—Gloria Feldt, in a press release, "A Call to End Domestic Terrorism," Planned Parenthood (October 24, 1998)

For the terrorist believer—Christian, Muslim, or otherwise—it's a sacramental act, almost transcendental. It's nearly incomprehensible to the non-fanatic.
—Bruce Hoffman, quoted in "Religious Views of Some Extremists May Fuel More Violence Terrorism," *Los Angeles Times* (April 29, 1995)

The clinic protests have gone too far. As long as the right to abortion and reproductive services is legal in this country, we must support the right of men
and women to seek such services without fear of being killed.
—Elenora Giddings Ivory, Washington director of the Presbyterian Church,
quoted in "Discord over Clinic Slayings," *Christian Century* (January 25, 1995)

Because of anti-choice terrorism and political action, thousands of doctors
have stopped providing abortions and thousands of towns have stopped leas-
ing space to abortion providers. . . . Without access, legal abortion is meaningless.
—Laura Kaminker, "For Millions of American Women, Roe Is Already
History," *Common Dreams* (January 24, 2005)

Americans should question whether the Justice Department is making
America's far-right fanatics a serious priority.
—Daniel Levitas, "Our Enemies at Home," *New York Times* (December 13,
2003)

Years ago, the anti-choice movement decided doctors were the Achilles' heel
of the abortion rights movement. Get rid of the doctors who perform abortions, and it becomes a right in name only. Every day, doctors work behind
bulletproof glass, wearing bulletproof vests.
—Kate Michelman, quoted in "When Anti-Choice Becomes Anti-Life,"
Washington Post (October 28, 1998)

Muslims have no monopoly on holy violence.
—Bill Moyers, "Reckoning with the God Squad," *In These Times* (September
24, 2005)

Every fresh incident of anti-abortion terrorism is a reminder that women's
health supporters are not safe in a country where abortion is legal but mo-
bilized zealots believe Jesus has empowered them to kill to prevent women
from choosing it.
—Jennifer L. Pozner, "The Terrorists Who Aren't in the News," AlterNet
(November 11, 2006)

Abortion providers have been the targets of anti-choice terrorism for over
twenty-five years.
—Vicki Saporta, in a news release from the National Abortion Federation
(December 6, 2001)

Domestic Violence

Domestic violence is not a women's issue, and it's not a private matter that belongs behind closed doors.
—Editorial, "Domestic Violence Is Men's Issue, Too," *Knight Ridder Tribune Business News* (April 16, 2006)

The federal government can tell you how many women dye their hair each year but can't tell you how many women are killed by guns in domestic violence situations.
—Stephen Hargarten, quoted in "Focus on the Real Terror—Gun Violence," *San Francisco Chronicle* (November 6, 2001)

On average, more than three women are murdered by their husbands or boyfriends in this country every day.
—Judith Siers-Poisson, "Domestic Violence Must End," *York Daily Record* (October 19, 2003)

Victims of domestic violence who receive welfare need help achieving the economic independence that will allow them to escape abuse and live in dignity. They do not need programs that coerce them to stay in abusive relationships.
—Kiersten Stewart, "GOP to Poor Women: Get Hitched," Gadflyer (September 20, 2004)

A woman's home can be the most violent, dangerous, and deadliest place she can be.
—Sheila Wellstone, "This Is Not Right: Sheila Wellstone Presses the Cause Against Domestic Violence," *Minneapolis Star Tribune* (October 27, 1993)

Gun Violence

Except for lawful police and military purposes, the possession of weapons by individuals is not constitutionally protected.
—American Civil Liberties Union, Policy #47 (March 4, 2002)

Gunplay in our nation is almost as much a national pastime as baseball. And, with the never-ending, inadequately controlled abundant supply of firearms, we're killing ourselves more effectively than any terrorist organization could.
—Monroe Anderson, "We're Killing Ourselves More Effectively than Terrorists," *Chicago Sun-Times* (July 30, 2006)

The National Rifle Association are the gun nuts of the world.
—Cecil D. Andrus, quoted in the *New York Times* (April 2, 1990)

Most guns used in crime come from a small percent of licensed gun dealers, with the rest coming from gun shows and flea markets. Only a small amount comes from theft from gun owners.
—Michael Barnes, "Realistic Solutions to Gun Violence," *Boston Globe* (December 29, 2000)

What civilian need is there for an AK-47?
—Michael Barnes, "Realistic Solutions to Gun Violence," *Boston Globe* (December 29, 2000)

We live in a country where in some places it is easier to buy a gun than to vote.
—David Barsamian, *Original Zinn* (2006)

Law enforcement officials describe the United States as a one-stop shop for the guns sought by terrorists, mercenaries and international criminals of all stripes.
—Jake Bergman and Julia Reynolds, "How U.S. Dealers Arm the World," *Nation* (November 14, 2002)

Actually, guns do kill people.
—Bumper sticker, quoted in "Moms to NRA: Grow Up!" *Nation* (May 25, 2000)

Handguns . . . are not hunting weapons—unless human beings are the prey.
—Richard Cohen, "Heaven Help the Gun Nuts," *Washington Post* (March 23, 2000)

We're losing eight children and teenagers a day to gun violence. As far as young people are concerned, we lose the equivalent of the massacre at Virginia Tech about every four days.
—Marian Wright Edelman, quoted in "Hooked on Violence," *New York Times* (April 26, 2007)

Guns most often kill the people who own them or people the owners know well.
—Editorial, *Time* (July 17, 1989)

Handguns are a public health issue.
—Joycelyn Elders, *USA Today* (November 9, 1993)

No true hunter goes looking for deer with an assault weapon. No hunter shoots at doves with a handgun. Those guns are made and sold by the gun industry to kill people.
—Gun Guys, Freedom States Alliance (July 20, 2006)

In the U.S., there are roughly 17,000 murders a year, of which about 15,000 are committed with firearms. By contrast, Britain, Australia, and Canada combined see fewer than three hundred and fifty gun-related murders each year.
—Andrew Gumbel, "The Big Question: Can America Ever Be Weaned off Its Love Affair with Guns?" *Independent (UK)* (October 4, 2006)

NRA Works for Gun Industry, Not Hunters
—Headline in "Gun Guys," Freedom States Alliance (July 20, 2006)

In almost every state there is no limit on the number of guns you can buy in a single purchase. . . . Isn't it obvious why it is so easy for gang members to get guns on the street?
—Paul Helmke, "Gun Violence: What Are We Going to Do About It?" *Huffington Post* (May 1, 2007)

It makes no sense for the police of this country to be outgunned by criminals or for our citizens to live in fear of criminals . . . armed with assault rifles.
—William J. Hughes, House Judiciary Committee hearings (June 12, 1990)

Guns are not intended just for target practice or sport.
—George Lakoff, *Moral Politics* (1996)

How about this: You can own any gun you want, as long as it works on technology developed before 1787. This is what conservatives call "original intent."
—Bill Maher, "A Re-Look-See at the Constitution," *Boston Globe* (November 17, 2006)

Politically, it's always been advantageous to divide people, to make America a place of warmongers versus wimps, elitists versus morons, gun nuts versus people with normal-size penises.
—Bill Maher, *Real Time with Bill Maher*, HBO (February 25, 2005)

The gun lobby promotes a vision of a future American society in which gun violence is answered by still more guns.
—Ralph C. Martin, II, "As You Were Saying . . . Gun Violence in America Challenges Our Next Leaders," *Boston Herald* (October 14, 2000)

Terrorists and gun smugglers like to buy guns in America because of the abundant inventory at gun shops and gun shows, and the laxity of U.S. gun-law enforcement.
—David Montero, "Guns 'R' U.S.," *Nation* (December 2, 2002)

If you need an automatic weapon or a handgun to kill a bird or a deer, then you really aren't much of a hunter and you should, perhaps, take up another sport.
—Michael Moore, "Let's Extend an Olive Branch to Disheartened Conservatives," *Los Angeles Times* (November 17, 2006)

We should protect children, not the National Rifle Association.
—John Podesta, interviewed on *ABC This Week* (July 23, 2000)

The gun culture is a highly masculine preserve, and so is most gun violence—drive-by shootings, mass murders by school kids, racist killing sprees, domestic murder-suicides.
—Katha Pollitt, "Moms to NRA: Grow Up!" *Nation* (May 25, 2000)

There is a lot of talk now about metal detectors and gun control. Both are good things. But they are no more a solution than forks and spoons are a solution to world hunger.
—Anna Quindlen, regarding school violence, *Thinking Out Loud* (1993)

Every year, small arms alone kill more people than the atomic bombs dropped on Hiroshima and Nagasaki put together.
—Bishop Desmond Tutu, "The Modern Successor to the Slave Trade: No Longer Should the Peace Business Be Undermined by the Arms Business," *Independent (UK)* (September 13, 2006)

Toy guns and teddy bears have more federal manufacturing regulations than real guns.
—Web site for the organization Stop Hand Gun Violence

Hand gun control is a must. . . . We can no longer allow criminals to buy truckloads of guns in our state and resell them at will.
—Douglas Wilder, quoted on *CBS Sunday Morning*, CBS (February 21, 1993)

There was no history of discussion of the private right to own guns when the Second Amendment was passed. The right to bear arms was for the militias.
—Gary Wills, interview on CNN (November 8, 1999)

Iraq War and Occupation

Every day in Iraq we lose three to four U.S. soldiers, with another seven to ten seriously wounded . . . Every day, the stay-the-course proponents have more blood on their hands. Every day, the rest of us, but especially those elected to bring this to an end, are guilty of creeping complicity.
—Paul Abrams, "Growing Immorality, Creeping Complicity," *Huffington Post* (November 19, 2006)

As a patriotic American proud to serve the nation in uniform, I respectfully urge my political leaders in Congress to support the prompt withdrawal of all American military forces and bases from Iraq. Staying in Iraq will not work and is not worth the price.
—Appeal for Redress, signed by hundreds of active-duty soldiers, quoted in "Resistance to War Cannot Be Jailed," *Seattle Post-Intelligencer* (February 1, 2007)

I wonder sometimes what galvanizing event will bring Americans out of the malls. When will the body count of dead Iraqis, dead Americans and wasted treasure supersede basketball and football scores and the latest Hummer?
—Jane Bright, "When Will We Know That Enough Americans Have Died?" *Common Dreams* (January 23, 2007)

We invaded Iraq for reasons quite unrelated to the welfare of the Iraqi people (and, it turned out, for reasons unrelated to the welfare of the American people as well).
—Rosa Brooks, "Those Ungrateful Iraqis!" *Los Angeles Times* (April 7, 2006)

The war in Iraq has backfired, producing more recruits for terrorism, and deep divisions within our own country. It is a war we should never have begun.
—Robert C. Byrd, remarks on the floor of the U.S. Senate, "I Hope That We May Find the Courage," *Common Dreams* (September 13, 2006)

Be nice to America. Or we'll bring democracy to your country.
—Bumper sticker

The debate over Iranian interference in Iraq proceeds without ridicule on the assumption that the United States owns the world.
—Noam Chomsky, "What If Iran Had Invaded Mexico?" *TomDispatch.com* (April 6, 2007)

How can you bomb people into democracy?
—Alice Daly, "Antiwar Protester Draws Inspiration From Thoreau's Call for Civil Disobedience," *Globe & Mail* (Canada) (March 26, 2003)

Every day the U.S. occupation [in Iraq] continues and deepens the very problems it was supposed to solve.
—Editorial, "Democrats and the War," *Nation* (November 10, 2005)

Bush . . . sold the American people on a quick, clean war of necessity. What they got instead was a dirty, protracted war of convenience that day by day is bleeding the American people of both the blood of their sons and daughters and the money from their billfolds.
—Editorial, "Iraq: No WMD, No Reason for War," *Minneapolis Star Tribune* (January 14, 2005)

It is time to face facts. The invasion was illegal and foolish in the first place. And the occupation has failed. . . . Bring the troops home.
—Editorial, *Progressive* (February 2005)

If Congress doesn't stop this war, it's not because it doesn't have the power. It's because it doesn't have the will.
—Russ Feingold, "How to End the War," *TomPaine.com* (February 2, 2007)

A new study suggests that middle-aged adults who go on periodic drinking binges may face a heightened sense of dementia later in life. The study is entitled "National Strategy for Victory in Iraq."
—Tina Fey on *Saturday Night Live*, quoted in "Punchlines," *Newsday* (December 8, 2005)

George W. Bush believes that he can buy another couple of years of violent stalemate so he can hand off the disaster to whoever succeeds him in the White House on January 20, 2009.
—Joseph L. Galloway, on Bush's escalation of the Iraq War, "Continuing the Flight from Reality," *Miami Herald* (January 10, 2007)

The only thing worse than soldiers dying in vain are more soldiers dying in vain.
—Mike Gravel, former U.S. senator from Alaska on the Iraq War, quoted in "Democratic Presidential Debate Amazingly Maintains Status Quo," *Huffington Post* (April 27, 2007)

All of the tortured, twisted rationales for this war—all of the fatuous intellectual pyrotechnics dreamed up to justify it—have vaporized, and we're left with just the mad, mindless, meaningless, and apparently endless slaughter.
—Bob Herbert, "Another Thousand Lives," *New York Times* (January 4, 2007)

The war was a botch from the beginning. Mr. Bush never sent enough troops to get the job done, and he never provided enough armor to protect the troops that he did send.
—Bob Herbert, "Voters' Remorse on Bush," *New York Times* (September 22, 2005)

What about all those men and women, some of them barely out of childhood, who are lying awake nights, hardly able to move their broken, burned and paralyzed bodies? . . . What do we tell them about this war that their country inflicted on them for no good reason whatsoever?
—Bob Herbert, "For No Good Reason," *New York Times* (October 3, 2005)

The countless Iraqi dead are only countless because America does not bother to count them.
—Todd Huffman, "Time To Bring Our Troops Home," *Common Dreams* (September 25, 2005)

I have a suggestion for a withdrawal deadline: Let's leave Iraq before we've killed more Iraqis than Saddam Hussein did.
—Molly Ivins, quoted in "Molly Ivins, In Memoriam," *Progressive* (February 1, 2007)

There's no war in Iraq. It's an ugly, failing, incompetently planned occupation.
—Rob Kall, "It's the Occupation, Stupid; Dem Language Lesson Desperately Needed," OpEdNews (June 20, 2006)

No matter how many battles we win, the war can't be won because it's based on false premises. How can we win a war that we're fighting on behalf of people who hate us and who want us to leave their country?
—Dan Kennedy, "Faces of Death," *Boston Phoenix* (December 7, 2004)

Iraq is George Bush's Vietnam.
—Edward M. Kennedy, in his address to the National Press Club, "A Democratic Blueprint for America's Future" (January 12, 2005)

Fury is an entirely appropriate response to a system that sends young people to kill other young people in a war that never should have been waged.
—Naomi Klein, "The Grieving Parents Who Might Yet Bring Bush Down," *Guardian (UK)* (July 10, 2004)

You cannot "win" an occupation. . . . Occupiers have to leave; the only question is when and how.
—George Lakoff, "Occupation: The Inconvenient Truth About Iraq," Rockridge Institute (July 2, 2006)

Sending 140,000 predominantly Christian troops into the heart of Islam and expecting them to be greeted as liberators—that is a faith-based initiative.
—Ned Lamont, "Iraq: One Way or the Other," *Hartford Courant* (December 20, 2006)

The war begun by President Bush with such bravado and so little braino . . . has been lost.
—Dave Lindorff, "Murtha and the L Word," CounterPunch (November 19, 2005)

Car decals admonish us to "support our troops"; the support they really need is from those who sent them into Iraq in the first place.
—Hubert G. Locke, "Despite Despair, a New Year Brings Hope," *Seattle Post-Intelligencer* (January 1, 2005)

To an extent, we got suckered into Vietnam. We can't make that claim about Iraq. Iraq was the premeditated, willful invasion of a sovereign nation that was threatening nobody.
—Tony Long, "What If They Gave a War . . . ?" *Wired News* (May 25, 2006)

The New York/Washington power elite, dominated by Bush and the Clintons, doesn't have the guts or the honesty to admit that Iraq is hopeless.
—John R. MacArthur, "'Centrist' Democrats Want It Both Ways," *Providence Journal* (December 6, 2006)

It is immoral to invade a comparatively defenseless country and kill its people because they have the misfortune to be ruled by a ruthless dictator who our war strategists speculate might someday be a threat to us.
—George McGovern, *The Essential America: Our Founders and the Liberal Tradition* (2004)

It is a lost war, lost because it never had a right to be won, lost because it was started by men who have never been to war.
—Michael Moore, "Quitting Iraq Is the Only Brave Thing to Do," AlterNet (November 27, 2006)

Iraq is not overwhelmed by foreign terrorists. It is overwhelmed by Iraqis fighting Iraqis.
—John Murtha, quoted in "Donald Rumsfeld's Dance with the Nazis," *New York Times* (September 3, 2006)

The only people who want us in Iraq are Iran and Al Qaeda.
—John Murtha, quoted in "So Far, No Good," AlterNet (March 16, 2006)

"Support Our Troops" is a wonderful patriotic slogan. But the best way to support troops thrust by unwise commanders in chief into ill-advised adventures like Vietnam and Iraq is to bring them home.
—Al Neuharth, "They Can Only Dream of Holidays at Home," *USA Today* (December 24, 2004)

I don't oppose all wars. What I am opposed to is a dumb war. What I am opposed to is a rash war. What I am opposed to is the cynical attempt by . . . armchair, weekend warriors in this administration to shove their own ideological agendas down our throats.
—Barack Obama, September 2002 remarks, quoted in "They Told You So," *New York Times* (December 8, 2006)

The invasion of Iraq, I believe, will turn out to be the greatest strategic disaster in U.S. history.
—William Odom, quoted in "Retired General: Iraq Invasion Was 'Strategic Disaster,'" *Lowell Sun* (September 30, 2005). Odom is the former director of the National Security Agency, the largest intelligence agency in the U.S.

This is what George W. Bush's war comes down to: The death of innocents for a senseless war, led by a man who shirked his own duty during a time of war.
—Rosa Maria Pegueros, "Where Have All the Young Ones Gone?" *Common Dreams* (June 18, 2007)

This war is going to be more of a lingering disease than Vietnam.
—Morley Safer, quoted in "Two Veteran Journalists Critical of Today's Media Coverage," *The Day* (December 6, 2004)

I think if one is not speaking out right now against the killing in Iraq, one is supporting it.
—Cindy Sheehan, "War-Hawk Republicans and Anti-War Democrats: What's the Difference?" *Common Dreams* (October 4, 2005)

The problem isn't that this war may not be winnable. The problem is the war was and is and always will be wrong, and must be stopped.
—Norman Solomon, "Why Are We Here?" AlterNet (March 20, 2006)

No Democratic Party candidate can expect the fervor of the party's progressive base if he or she doesn't acknowledge the evil the Bush administration has done in Iraq.
—John Richard Starkey, "Hillary, You've Got Some 'Fessing Up To Do," *Newsday* (December 9, 2004)

Remember that dire threat posed by Saddam Hussein's possession of weapons of mass destruction? The peril that required us to send hundreds of thousands of soldiers to invade a foreign land to "pre-empt" a looming danger?
—Robert Steinback, "Drop the 'Bush Doctrine,'" *Miami Herald* (January 19, 2005)

Any normal human being ought to be feeling considerable outrage and deep, deep, deep hurt for so-called ordinary Iraqi people. . . . How I wish that politicians could have the courage and the humility to admit that they have made mistakes.
—Archbishop Desmond Tutu, "Q&A: Desmond Tutu," *Newsweek* (January 10, 2005)

My son, Casey, was in the first thousand to be killed in Iraq.
—Cindy Sheehan, "The Opposite of Good is Apathy," *Common Dreams* (January 6, 2006)

The notion that our problem in Iraq is a resource deficit is pure, unadulterated madness. Our enemies don't have airplanes or armor. They are fighting us with garage-door openers and fifty-year-old artillery shells.
—Matt Taibbi, "NYT's Tom Friedman and the Pundits Will Blame Us for Iraq," AlterNet (March 7, 2007)

Thousands of lives have been lost and hundreds of billions of dollars wasted in a war the United States initiated and should never have fought.
—United Methodist Church, quoted in "Sweet Victory: United Methodist Church Calls for Withdrawal," *Nation* (November 1, 2005)

The president took us into this war recklessly. . . . We are now, as a nation, held hostage to the predictable—and predicted—disarray that has followed.
—Jim Webb, quoted in "A Reagan Democrat," Truthdig (January 25, 2007)

Some 100,000 civilians have died in Iraq—that's a profound moral crisis involving religious values. That this doesn't register with so many Americans is disturbing and difficult to understand.
—Alan Wolfe, quoted in "The Culture Wars Are Back," *Green Bay News-Chronicle* (November 8, 2004)

It has never been clearer that the war in Iraq is a moral and functional failure. Human decency, fiscal sanity and national security demand that we move quickly to bring our soldiers home.
—Lynn Woolsey and Barbara Lee, "Out of Iraq," *Nation* (February 6, 2006)

The real question, the moral question [in Iraq] is not "are we losing or are we winning?" The question is, "why are we there?"
—Howard Zinn, quoted in an interview with Terrence McNally in "Howard Zinn: Vision and Voice," AlterNet (October 21, 2005)

Support our troops in the only way that word support can have real meaning—by saving their lives, their limbs, their sanity. By bringing them home.
—Howard Zinn, "Support Our Troops: Bring Them Home," *Miami Herald* (January 22, 2005)

Military

Six in ten women who have served in the National Guard and Reserves say they were sexually harassed or assaulted . . . One in ten said she was raped.
—Lolita C. Baldor, "Survey: 6 in 10 Military Women Harassed," the Associated Press (AP) (September 29, 2005)

A politicized military presents a threat to democratic ideals of civilian control.
—Rosa Brooks, "Weaning the military from the GOP," *Los Angeles Times* (January 5, 2007)

Politicians used to kiss babies, but in these days of terrorism and war, babies have gone out of style. Today's most coveted political accessory? An active-duty member of the American military.
—Rosa Brooks, "Kiss a Baby Then, Support Our Troops Now," *Los Angeles Times* (February 9, 2007)

The Abu Ghraib portraits of sexual humiliation and submission have exposed the unbelievably tangled strands of racism, misogyny, homophobia, national arrogance, and hyper-masculinity that characterize the U.S. military.
—Linda Burnham, "Sexual Domination in Uniform: An American Value," *Common Dreams* (May 19, 2004)

We have never done this before. Never in the history of our republic have we ever financed a conflict, military conflict, by borrowing money from somewhere else.
—Bill Clinton, quoted in "Clinton Launches Withering Attack on Bush on Iraq, Katrina, Budget," Agence France Presse (September 19, 2005)

More than a decade ago, the Pentagon set out on the path of outsourcing some of its operations. What began as a small experiment has now morphed out of control.
—Editorial, "Outsourcing Common Sense," *Multinational Monitor* (March 2004)

When was the last time we witnessed a senior military officer willingly accept blame for a catastrophe that occurred on his watch?
—Gregory D. Foster, "Detainee Deaths: The Failure of a Society," *International Herald Tribune* (March 10, 2006)

To many Muslims young and old, democracy and liberty have become synonymous with military occupation, the physical and sexual abuse of prisoners, and the death of civilians. . . . How does this make us more secure?
—Todd Huffman, "*Time* to Bring Our Troops Home," *Common Dreams* (September 25, 2005)

We have military forces in over seven hundred bases located in over one hundred and thirty nations across the globe. Our fleets patrol the world's seas. . . . Our military budget is nearly half the military budget of the entire world.
—Rev. Jesse Jackson, "Challenge Our Violent Culture," *Chicago Sun-Times* (June 26, 2007)

We spend more than $500 billion a year on the mightiest military that the world has ever known, but we are more insecure than ever.
—Rev. Jesse Jackson, "Peace Is at the Heart of the Christmas Story," *Chicago Sun-Times* (December 19, 2006)

We now station over half a million U.S. troops, spies, contractors, dependents, and others on military bases located in more than 130 countries, many of them presided over by dictatorial regimes that have given their citizens no say in the decision to let us in.
—Chalmers Johnson, "Empire vs. Democracy," *TomPaine.com* (January 31, 2007)

There are currently over seven hundred U.S. military bases spread around the globe, a modern equivalent of the Roman legions.
—Gilbert Jordan, "War: A Theft from Those Who Hunger," *Common Dreams* (April 3, 2006)

The whole U.S. military . . . is coming to be dominated by members of a small, characteristically intolerant sliver of Christianity who truly regard themselves as Christian soldiers, on a God-appointed mission to harvest souls and battle evil.
—Robert Koehler, "The Crusaders," *Huffington Post* (May 3, 2007)

How can it be that hundreds of Americans, at a modest estimate, have been involved in the tormenting of prisoners, using the "waterboard" technique to bring them to the brink of drowning, beating them, or worse?
—Anthony Lewis, "The Torture Administration," *Nation* (December 26, 2005)

Let's be frank, shall we? Republicans always prefer tax cuts to funding veteran's benefits. They also ignore the health care reality of our returning soldiers, leaving tens of thousands of veterans fending for themselves.
—Taylor Marsh, "Who Really Supports the Troops?" *Huffington Post* (February 19, 2007)

Military justice is to justice what military music is to music.
—Groucho Marx, quoted in "Military Injustice," *Salon* (June 7, 2005)

What happened in Haditha [Iraq] can best be described as deliberate homicide committed by soldiers of the U.S. Marine Corps, making them in a sense no different from the al-Qaeda insurgents they are combating.
—Sami Moubayed, "My Lai to Haditha, Wars' Turning Points," *Asia Times* (June 5, 2006)

There's no question in my mind that this president and this administration would never have invaded Iraq . . . if indeed we had a draft and members of Congress and the administration thought that their kids from their communities would be placed in harm's way.
—Charles Rangel, quoted in "Rep. Rangel will seek to reinstate draft," the Associated Press (AP) (November 19, 2006)

People join the military to defend their country, not lies.
—Adam Reuter, veteran of the Iraq War, quoted in "End This War: Hundreds of Thousands Protest Iraq War," Reuters (September 24, 2005)

The U.S. political system has been carefully crafted to ensure that no one who questions the natural goodness of the military-industrial-corporate power structure will be allowed through the portals of power.
—Arundhati Roy, quoted in "Narcissists 'R' Us?" *In These Times* (August 14, 2006)

Jenna and Barbara are able-bodied citizens well within the age of enlistment. Yet they have conspicuously not followed their father's leadership on this urgent life-and-death matter. Why the silence about the twins' not volunteering for military service?
—John Seery, "Bush Family AWOLism," *Huffington Post* (July 28, 2006)

Being against the war and saying you support the troops is one of the wussiest positions. . . . I'm not advocating that we spit on returning veterans like they did after the Vietnam War, but we shouldn't be celebrating people for doing something we don't think was a good idea.
—Joel Stein, "Warriors and Wusses," *Los Angeles Times* (January 24, 2006)

This year, we will spend more on the military than the rest of the world combined—more than six hundred billion dollars.
—Matt Taibbi, "NYT's Tom Friedman and the Pundits Will Blame Us for Iraq," AlterNet (March 7, 2007)

Support the troops. . . . But don't force them to fight an immoral fight. That's like swearing allegiance to a gun without caring where it's aimed.
—Steven Weber, "Sorry, Johnny," *Huffington Post* (May 14, 2007)

Why do we soldiers have to dig through local landfills for pieces of scrap metal and compromised ballistic glass to uparmor our vehicles?
—Thomas Wilson, soldier at an Iraq "town meeting" to Defense Secretary Donald Rumsfeld, CNN (December 9, 2004). Rumsfeld replied, "You can have all the armor in the world on a tank, and it can [still] be blown up."

Recruiters take advantage of the inequality and segregation of this country . . . and hold up joining the military as a way out.
—Elizabeth Wrigley-Field, quoted in "Counter-Recruitment Day Sweeps U.S. Colleges," *Common Dreams* (December 5, 2005)

The best thing I did in my life was join the military, and the second best thing I did was get out. . . . I was a Republican going into the army and I came out a Democrat.
—Markos Moulitsas Zuniga, quoted in "When It Comes to Liberal Blogs, Daily Kos Leads the Pack," *Allentown Morning Call* (September 9, 2005)

Nuclear Weapons

The first line of defense against the spread of nuclear weapons is to make states feel that they don't need them.
—Hans Blix, former U.N. chief weapons inspector, quoted in "Study Wants

Nuclear Weapons Outlawed," the Associated Press (AP) (June 1, 2006)
The world has achieved brilliance without wisdom, power without conscience. Ours is a world of nuclear giants and ethical infants.
—Omar Bradley, speech delivered on Armistice Day (1948)

The real "rogue" nations that continue to hold the world at nuclear ransom are Russia and the United States. . . . Of the thirty thousand nuclear weapons in the world today, the United States and Russia possess 96 percent of them.
—Helen Caldicott, "The Way the World Ends," *Ottawa Citizen* (October 21, 2006)

For this generation, ours, life is nuclear survival, liberty is human rights, the pursuit of happiness is a planet whose resources are devoted to the physical and spiritual nourishment of its inhabitants.
—Jimmy Carter, in his farewell address (January 14, 1981)

We have now become a prime culprit in global nuclear proliferation. America also has abandoned the prohibition of "first use" of nuclear weapons against nonnuclear nations, and is contemplating the previously condemned deployment of weapons in space.
—Jimmy Carter, "This Isn't the Real America," *Los Angeles Times* (November 14, 2005)

Nuclear war is an issue of species survival.
—Noam Chomsky, "Nuclear Terror at Home," AlterNet (February 26, 2005)

The U.S. invasion of Iraq virtually instructed Iran to develop a nuclear deterrent. The message was that the U.S. attacks at will, as long as the target is defenseless.
—Noam Chomsky, "A Predator Becomes More Dangerous When Wounded," *Guardian (UK)* (March 9, 2007)

There are presently thirty thousand nuclear arms around the world. Nuclear powers must do more than simply condemn non-nuclear states for attempting to acquire or develop weapons of mass destruction; they must themselves disarm.
—Rev. William Sloane Coffin, interviewed by Or N. Rose, "Righteous Indignation," *Tikkun* (March/April 2006)

The best security, perhaps the only security, against nuclear weapons being used again, or getting into the hands of terrorists, is to eliminate them.
—Walter Cronkite, "Hiroshima's Lessons Loom Large 60 Years Later," *Capital Times (Madison, Wisconson)* (August 6, 2005)

The unleashed power of the atom has changed everything save our modes of thinking and we thus drift toward unparalleled catastrophe.
—Albert Einstein, quoted in "The Einstein Letter That Started It All," *New York Times Magazine* (August 2, 1964)

The Japanese were ready to surrender and it wasn't necessary to hit them with that awful thing.
—Dwight D. Eisenhower, quoted in "Hiroshima, Rewritten," *New York Times* (January 31, 1995)

Nukes breed nukes. As long as some nations continue to insist that nuclear weapons are essential to their security, other nations will want them.
—Mohammed ElBaradei, 2005 Nobel Peace Prize winner, "'Nukes Breed Nukes,' ElBaradei Warns," Reuters (May 26, 2006)

I regard the employment of the atom bomb for the wholesale destruction of men, women, and children as the most diabolical use of science.
—Mahatma Gandhi, 1946 comment quoted in "Gandhi, Bush, and the Bomb," *Common Dreams* (February 27, 2006)

Mankind must put an end to war or war will put an end to mankind.
—John F. Kennedy, in his U.N. address, New York City (September 25, 1961)

In our days of space vehicles and guided ballistic missiles, the choice is either nonviolence or nonexistence.
—Rev. Martin Luther King, Jr., *Strength to Love* (1963)

Countries that have nukes teach other countries to have nukes.
—Sally Kohn, "I Learned It by Watching You," *Common Dreams* (October 23, 2006)

We spend on nuclear weapons and their delivery systems what it would cost to feed the world's hungry, shelter the world's homeless, care for the world's sick and infirm, and educate the world's children.
—David Krieger, "Awakening America—Before It's Too Late," *Common Dreams* (October 21, 2005)

Never again can the U.S. use nuclear weapons on another nation's children.
—Anne Miller, "Yes, Hillary, We Do Need Moral Leadership," *Common Dreams* (February 14, 2007)

There's blood on my hands.
—Robert Oppenheimer, father of the atomic bomb, to Harry S. Truman, quoted in *Roots of War* (1971)

The whole world must summon the moral courage and technical means to say "no" to nuclear conflict; "no" to weapons of mass destruction; "no" to an arms race which robs the poor and the vulnerable.
—Pope John Paul II, quoted in *The Challenge of Peace: God's Promise and Our Response* (1983)

The nuclear bomb launched from a Minuteman silo produces uncontrollable radiation, massive heat and a blast capable of vaporizing and leveling everything within a fifty-mile radius. Outside the fifty square miles—extending into hundreds of miles—the blast [is] intended to kill, severely wound and poison every living thing.
—Bill Quigley, "No Clowning Around Weapons of Mass Destruction!" *Common Dreams* (September 9, 2006)

Nuclear weapons can't be controlled by saying, in effect, "Do as we say, not as we do."
—Norman Solomon, "Welcome to the Nuclear Club," *Common Dreams* (October 9, 2006)

While Uncle Sam continues to maintain a nuclear arsenal capable of destroying life on Earth, the American finger-wagging at Iran is something righteous to behold.
—Norman Solomon, "News Media in the 60th Year of the Nuclear Age," *Common Dreams* (November 29, 2004)

Pornography

We are unalterably opposed to the presentation of the female body being stripped, bound, raped, tortured, mutilated and murdered in the name of commercial entertainment and free speech.
—Susan Brownmiller, *Against Our Will: Men, Women and Rape* (1993)

Raunch is Republican. The sexuality that reigns supreme in Bush World bears the basic imprimaturs of right-wing ideology: gross materialism, sexual hypocrisy, and acquiescence in the name of empowerment. It is in every sense a conservative wet dream come true.
—Lakshmi Chaudhry, "Babes in BushWorld: Raunch Culture Offers Good Old-Fashioned Pleasure, Republican Style," *In These Times* (October 28, 2005)

I have to admit that watching porn is not unlike eating a McDonald's value meal—it seems like a really good idea at the time, but when it's all over you feel pretty unsatisfied and sometimes even disgusting.
—Dave Hill, "The History of Pornography," *Huffington Post* (April 13, 2006)

I think if a woman has a right to an abortion and to control her body, then she has the right to exploit her body and make money from it.
—Kathy Keeton, quoted in *Newsweek* (December 16, 1991)

Pornography is free speech applied to the sexual realm.
—Wendy McElroy, "A Feminist Defense of Pornography," Free Inquiry (Fall 1997)

Commercial sex tends to be viewed as enslavement in America—by moral conservatives as enslavement to sin, by feminists as enslavement to men.
—Alastair McKay, "Continental Drift," Nerve (January 3, 2006)

Pornography is the theory, and rape is the practice.
—Robin Morgan, *Going Too Far* (1977)

It's almost impossible to get a handle on how much money corporate America is reaping by peddling smut.
—Terry M. Neal, "GOP Corporate Donors Cash In on Smut," *Washington Post* (December 21, 2004)

Pornography is about dominance. Erotica is about mutuality.
—Gloria Steinem, *Outrageous Acts and Everyday Rebellions* (1983)

Pornography tells lies about women. But pornography tells the truth about men.
—John Stoltenberg, *Refusing to Be a Man: Essays on Sex and Justice* (1989)

It is typical that liberal-minded people, when facing censorship, would rush to defend pornographers' right to produce whatever they want, even if the products objectify, humiliate and violate women. But shouldn't we ponder what we are defending and what kind of value system supports that defense?
—Chyng Sun, "Revisiting the Porn Debate," *Common Dreams* (January 31, 2005)

While the corporations generate millions in profits from providing adult content, their political contributions are often given to those elected, in no small part, because of their stance on "moral values."
—Jake Tapper and Avery Miller, "Cable Companies Provide Porn While Funding Politicians," ABC News (February 9, 2005)

Private Armies

War outsourcing is creating the corporate equivalent of Guantanamo Bay—a virtual rules-free zone in which perpetrators are not likely to be held accountable for breaking the law.
—Larry Cox, quoted in "War Outsourcing Could Lead to Abuses, Says Amnesty Group," *Houston Chronicle* (May 24, 2006)

The second-biggest army in Iraq consists of armed security forces supplied by private contractors. They act above the law. . . . When the Abu Ghraib prison torture scandals were revealed, private security forces and interrogators were at the center of it. But none was held accountable.
—Rev. Jesse Jackson, "War Privatization Is Public Scandal," *Chicago Sun-Times* (February 6, 2007)

[Blackwater USA] has secured a status as the elite Praetorian Guard for the global war on terror, with the largest private military base in the world, a fleet of twenty aircraft and twenty thousand soldiers at the ready.
—Jeremy Scahill, "Our Mercenaries in Iraq," *Los Angeles Times* (January 25, 2007)

Is the day coming where corporate armies will dominate the battlefield of international politics and eliminate all other contenders?
—Peter W. Singer, quoted in "The Privatized Military: The Unmonitored, Unregulated and Unchecked Global Growth of Private Military Firms," *Multinational Monitor* (March 2004)

Private corporations have penetrated western warfare so deeply that they are now the second biggest contributor to coalition forces in Iraq after the Pentagon.
—Ian Traynor, "The Privatization of War," *Guardian (UK)* (December 10, 2003). There were roughly 9,900 British troops compared to 10,000 private military contractors.

Soldiers who disobey orders or violate standards of conduct can be court-martialed and incarcerated. . . . Private companies, by contrast, are able to operate in almost complete secrecy, with little accountability to civilian or military authorities.
—Barry Yeoman, "Soldiers of Good Fortune," *Mother Jones* (May/June 2003)

Sexual Assault and Harassment

It is little wonder that rape is one of the least-reported crimes. Perhaps it is the only crime in which the victim becomes the accused.
—Freda Adler, *Sisters in Crime* (1975)

No one has the right to force sex. This is a crime of violence, not sex.
—Susan Estrich, "Male-on-Male Rape," Truthdig (December 20, 2006)

What does it tell us that men's most terrified reaction to the idea of prison is the fear that women experience all the time?
—Stan Goff, "[Prison] Rape," *Huffington Post* (May 15, 2006)

Sexual harassment and sexual assault is an epidemic in the [U.S.] army.
—Larry Hildes, quoted in "Woman Soldier Refuses Return to Iraq, Claiming Sexual Harassment," *Guardian (UK)* (June 21, 2006)

One of the oddest episodes I remember was an occasion in which [Clarence] Thomas was drinking a Coke in his office. He got up from the table, at which we were working, went over to his desk to get the Coke, looked at the can and asked, "Who has put pubic hair on my coke?"
—Anita Hill, quoted in *The Real Anita Hill* (1991). Despite Hill's claims of sexual harassment, Thomas's appointment to the Supreme Court was approved.

Every girl should be able to go to school without being groped or jeered.
—Patricia Ireland, in a press release entitled "NOW President Patricia Ireland Applauds High Court's Important First Step on School Sexual Harassment" (May 24, 1999)

Every two-and-a-half minutes, someone is sexually assaulted in America.
—Courtney E. Martin, "Willful Ignorance," *American Prospect* (January 17, 2007)

One woman in three will be raped, beaten, coerced into sex, or otherwise abused in her lifetime.
—Anne Penketh, "International Women's Day: Struggle for Equality and Freedom In Developing Countries," *Independent (UK)* (March 8, 2007)

I learned that if I ever claim sexual harassment, I will be confronted with every bozo I once dated, every women I once impressed as snotty and superior, and together they will provide a convenient excuse to disbelieve me.
—Anna Quindlen, *Thinking Out Loud* (1993)

Across the country, lesbian, gay, bisexual, and transgender people endure the injustices of discrimination, entrapment, and verbal abuse as well as brutal beatings and sexual assault at the hands of those responsible for protecting them—the police.
—William F. Schulz, quoted in a press release from Amnesty International USA (September 22, 2005)

Terrorism

History is chock full of examples where brutal and prejudicial anti-terror policies have done more to propel the cause of terrorism than to quell it.
—Abhinav Aima, "Justified Murder: Don't Ever Become a Terror Suspect!" *Common Dreams* (July 25, 2005)

The "war on terror" is more a metaphor than a fact. Terrorism is a method, not an ideology; terrorists are criminals, not warriors.
—Joyce Appleby and Gary Hart, "The Founders Never Imagined a Bush Administration," *History News Network* (March 27, 2006)

The best way for the United States to combat the religious fundamentalism that underwrites terrorism is to remain a liberal state guided by liberal principles.
—Nick Bromell, "Scooter Libby and Me," *American Scholar* (Winter 2007)

The war in Iraq created a hotbed of terrorism where none existed before.
—Robert Byrd, in a speech delivered to the U.S. Senate, "A Call for Debate on National Priorities" (September 13 2005)

Bush created a cohesive enemy where it did not really exist before. So-called jihadists have been rallied, strengthened, and made lethal by Iraq. They will haunt the world for years, in a global war unlike anything ever seen before. All of it unnecessary. Foolishness worthy of a stupid child.
—James Carroll, "An Enemy and War Born from Ignorance," *Boston Globe* (October 2, 2006)

We have to make a world where there are fewer potential terrorists and more partners. And that responsibility falls primarily upon the wealthy nations to spread the benefits and shrink the burdens.
—Bill Clinton, Institute of Education lecture in London (December 18, 2001)

There is no military solution to terrorism.
—Marc Cooper, "Liberals Stuck in Scold Mode," *Los Angeles Times* (October 14, 2001)

I am not sure which is more frightening, another major terror attack or the response of authoritarian conservatives to that attack.
—John Dean, "John Dean Knocks Imperial Presidency," the Associated Press (AP) (July 26, 2006)

The terrorists moved into George Bush's Iraq, not Saddam Hussein's.
—Maureen Dowd, "Bush's *Fleurs du Mal*," *New York Times* (May 27, 2007)

We could have cracked the 9/11 plot if the FBI wasn't run by dunces.
—Maureen Dowd, "Fly Into a Building? Who Could Imagine?" *New York Times* (March 22, 2006) The FBI officer who arrested a 9/11 conspirator before the event told his superiors that the man might be plotting to hijack an airplane.

The war on terror is a slogan designed only for politics, not a strategy to make America safe. It's a bumper sticker, not a plan.
—John Edwards, quoted in "The War Over 'War on Terror,'" *Nation* (June 4, 2007)

Let's stop calling the enemy "terrorism," which is like saying we're fighting "bombings." Terrorism is only a method; the enemy is an extremist Islamic insurgency whose appeal lies in its claim to represent the Muslim masses against a bullying superpower.
—Barbara Ehrenreich, "To Defeat Terrorists, Try Listening to Feminists," *Baltimore Sun* (August 3, 2004)

There are many reasons why human beings turn to terrorism, but high among them is humiliation.
—H. D. S. Greenway, "The Humiliation Bomb," *Boston Globe* (May 14, 2004)

Being against the war in Iraq doesn't mean you are against fighting the war on terror. It means you are against a failed policy that has created more terrorists than it has killed . . . that has thrown Iraq into a bloody sectarian civil war.
—Arianna Huffington, "Beyond Chutzpah: Cheney Implies Terrorists Are Happy Lieberman Lost," *Huffington Post* (August 10, 2006)

Our problem now is that we're not fighting the people who attacked us— they're still running around on the Afghan-Pakistan border while we battle Iraqis who don't like us occupying their country.
—Molly Ivins, "So Far, No Good," AlterNet (March 16, 2006)

We would be safer, as the 9/11 commission has so recently reminded us, if some obvious and necessary precautions were taken at both nuclear and chemical plants—but that is not happening because those industries contribute to Republican candidates.
—Molly Ivins, "Big Brother Bush," AlterNet (December 29, 2005)

We have failed to grasp that nuclear weapons are a far more powerful tool in the hands of the weak than in the hands of the strong.
—David Krieger, "Awakening America—Before It's Too Late," *Common Dreams* (October 21, 2005)

Our leaders would like the FBI to have the right to know what books we're reading, check out our medical records without our knowledge, monitor our telephone calls and e-mails, and continue to imprison anyone suspected of terrorism and hold them for indeterminate amounts of time without charging them with a crime. At the same time, cargo ships are still entering our harbors with unchecked cargo.
—Norman Lear, "Letter to God," *Huffington Post* (December 16, 2005)

Mr. President, after the 9/11 hit against the Twin Towers in New York, which gained us the sympathy and support of the entire world, why did you then order the invasion of Iraq, which had nothing to do with 9/11?
—George McGovern, "An Impartial Interrogation of George W. Bush," *Nation* (January 17, 2007)

The pre-emptors are every bit as dangerous as the terrorists because they both react to and feed off each other's fantasies of total victory.
—Henry Porter, "True Democrats Uphold Our Liberties—Not Destroy Them," *Guardian (UK)* (September 3, 2006)

Even if you include the 9/11 casualties, the number of Americans killed by international terrorists since the late 1960s . . . is about the same as that killed by lightning—or by accident-causing deer, or by severe allergic reactions to peanuts.
—William Pfaff, "A 'Long War' Designed to Perpetuate Itself," *International Herald Tribune* (February 10, 2006)

The answer to terrorism must be found in redressing the wrongs that breed violence between nations.
—Rev. Konrad Raiser, in a letter to the U.N. Secretary-General (October 2, 2001)

Disaffection is the root cause of terrorism; a political system that allows no legitimate outlet for those with grievances to express themselves and drives those not vested in their system to pursue eradication of that system.
—Ted Rall, *Wake Up, You're Liberal!* (2004)

If you want to eliminate terrorism, you have to address the political problems that gave it birth.
—Charley Reese, "Terrorism Is a Tactic," *Information Clearing House* (June 13, 2006)

You can tighten security all you want, but if you keep manufacturing terrorists, at some point they're going to succeed.
—Matthew Rothschild, "When Threats Are Real, Why Multiply Them?" *Progressive* (August 11, 2006)

There is an alternative to terrorism. It's called justice.
—Arundhati Roy, *Public Power in the Age of Empire* (2004)

[Terrorist] feelings towards the individual are abolished by his loathing of the group, and it is this—rather than his cowardice, cruelty, or intemperate hate—that constitutes his true moral corruption.
—Roger Scruton, *Untimely Tracts* (1987)

Our declared doctrine of preemptive strikes, without legal justification or evidence, is music to the ears of terrorist organizations that specialize in such strikes.
—Theodore C. Sorensen, quoted in "Former Writer for Kennedy Laments Hawkish Strategy," *New York Times* (May 12, 2003)

The fact that the terrorists are manifestly evil does not make whatever counter-actions we take automatically good.
—George Soros, in his speech at the National Press Club (September 28, 2004)

America's response to 9/11 was basically to blow off the entire question of why it happened.
—Matt Taibbi, "Americans in Denial about 9/11," AlterNet (September 14, 2006)

Bin Laden Determined to Strike Inside United States.
—Title of a declassified intelligence document submitted to President Bush on August 6, 2001, warning that Al-Qaeda terrorists could be planning airplane hijackings.

What the terrorists did to us, what they want to do to us, revealed who they are. The ways we choose to deal with it reveals who we are.
—Tommy Tomlinson, "For Foes of Bush Plan, Values Win," *Charlotte Observer* (September 17, 2006)

The War on Terror will never end, nor is it meant to end. . . . The Long War will eternally justify what are ostensibly temporary measures: suspension of civil liberties, military expansion, domestic spying, massive deficit spending, and the like.
—Allan Uthman, "Top 10 Signs of the Impending U.S. Police State," *Buffalo Beast* (May 26, 2006)

How come the people in countries we invade can't fight like ladies and gentlemen, in uniform and with tanks and helicopter gunships?
—Kurt Vonnegut, Jr., "Vonnegut's Blues for America," *Sunday Herald* (Scotland) (February 5, 2006)

Nothing can, nothing will justify the murder of innocent people and helpless children.
—Elie Wiesel, "Hope, Despair, and Memory," Nobel Peace Lecture (December 11, 1986)

Terrorism is ugly, wrong, and vicious, but you don't want to get in the same gutter as the terrorist to simply reinforce the same cycle of killing innocent people, demonizing others, losing sight of the humanity of others.
—Cornel West, in an interview with Terrence McNally, "Matters of Justice," AlterNet (September 29, 2004)

Torture

SILENCE + TORTURE = COMPLICITY
—Advertisement condemning torture appearing in *New York Times* (October 4, 2006)

Nothing could be less American than a government that can indefinitely hold people in secret torture cells, take away their protections against horrific and cruel abuse, put them on trial based on evidence that they cannot see, sentence them to death based on testimony literally beaten out of witnesses, and then slam shut the courthouse door for any habeas petition. But that's exactly what Congress just approved.
—Christopher Anders, ACLU Legislative Counsel, press release, "Senate Passes Dangerous Bush Military Commissions Bill" (September 28, 2006)

Today's joke:
Q: What do Americans do after they commit war crimes?
A: They pass a law that says they can't be prosecuted for committing war crimes.
—Larry Beinhart, "Fear the Penis," *BuzzFlash* (October 6, 2006)

We have adopted the tactics of those authoritarian regimes we used to revile. As a Christian and a patriot, I am deeply saddened that this great nation no longer has the moral fiber to be different from its enemies.
—Charles C. Bonwell, retired captain in the U.S. Naval Reserve, "Alternative interrogation tools ring of torture," *USA Today* (September 14, 2006)

Whatever a movement to abolish torture will achieve for society, it is clear what participating in it means for each of us as individuals. It means above all that our children and grandchildren will not remember us with shame.
—Fred Branfman, "On Torture and Being Good Americans," *Tikkun* (March/April 2006)

If you need any more evidence that the American public has gotten blasé about torture, consider the hit Fox action drama "24." The show featured sixty-seven torture scenes during its first five seasons, and most of those depicted torture being used by "heroic" U.S. counter-terror agents.
—Rosa Brooks, "America Tortures (yawn)," *Los Angeles Times* (February 23, 2007)

The Military Commissions Act provided congressional approval of the Bush administration's malfeasance. It wiped out any chance for non-citizens held by the U.S. anywhere in the world to challenge their detentions or demand evidence for them.
—Marie Cocco, "Our Most Vulgar Instinct," Truthdig (December 7, 2006)

This is the year we condoned torture. . . . We re-elected a president who abandoned the Geneva Conventions; who constructed a gulag at Guantánamo Bay, Cuba.
—Marie Cocco, "Moral Values Apply to Torture, Too," *Newsday* (December 16, 2004)

If the events I am about to describe were taking place in a movie or novel, I would lose my ability to suspend disbelief: Who could conceive of an American President and Vice President demanding that Congress give them authority to torture anyone, under any circumstances?
—John W. Dean, "Shocking the Conscience of America," FindLaw (December 16, 2005)

Ban Torture. Period.
—Editorial, *New York Times* (December 16, 2005)

This vice president has become an open advocate of torture.
—Editorial on Dick Cheney, "Vice President for Torture," *Washington Post* (October 26, 2005)

If we cloak cruel or degrading interrogations done in the name of American safety with euphemisms like "alternative techniques" . . . we will have betrayed our principles and ourselves.
—Russ Feingold, in a statement in Opposition of the Military Commissions Act (September 28, 2006)

On a couple of occasions I entered interview rooms to find a detainee chained hand and foot in a fetal position to the floor, with no chair, food, or water. Most times they had urinated or defecated on themselves, and had been left there for eighteen to twenty-four hours or more.
—FBI memo on treatment of Islamic prisoners at Guantanamo Bay (August 2, 2004)

What did you feel after the invasion of Iraq when you saw American soldiers holding dog leashes attached to helpless prisoners, 99 percent of whom, by the way, were innocent of any connection to violence against our troops, much less terrorism—innocent prisoners who were being tortured in our name—what did you feel?
—Al Gore, in his speech given at the National Sierra Club Convention in San Francisco (September 9, 2005)

Their souvenir photographs [at Abu Ghraib] are reminiscent of the smiling lynch mobs who took each other's photographs under the hanging trees of the American South or the German soldiers who took out their cameras when the Jews were being shot in pits. This is what happens when the system allows people to be dehumanized and degraded.
—HDS Greenway, "The Humiliation Bomb," *Boston Globe* (May 14, 2004)

Under the new [Military Commissions Act], the United States can snatch a person anywhere in the world, declare him an enemy combatant, and imprison him indefinitely without due process or trial on the grounds that he "supported" a terrorist organization, possibly by making donations to a charity he may not realize is a front for a terrorist group.
—Jonathan Hafetz, "Power Strip," *American Prospect* (October 5, 2006)

The only reason anyone tortures is because they like to do it. It's about vengeance, it's about revenge, or it's about cover-up. You don't gain intelligence that way.
—Eric Haney, founding member of Delta Force, the military's elite covert counter-terrorist unit, quoted in "Unit's Military Expert Has Fighting Words for Bush," *L.A. Daily News* (March 26, 2006)

Any government that commits, condones, promotes, or fosters torture is a malignant force in the world. And those who refuse to raise their voices against something as clearly evil as torture are enablers, if not collaborators.
—Bob Herbert, "Torture, American Style," *New York Times* (February 11, 2005)

It is both peculiar and chilling to find oneself discussing the problem of American torture. . . . Is this American? Is it Christian? What are our moral values?
—Molly Ivins, "Is This American?" AlterNet (December 2, 2004)

The construction of such a system [at Guantanamo], whose stated purpose is the production of intelligence, cannot be considered other than an intentional system of cruel, unusual, and degrading treatment, and a form of torture.
—International Red Cross report, quoted in "Is This American?" AlterNet (December 2, 2004)

Abuse of detainees was not aberrational. The Defense Department adopted extreme interrogation techniques as a matter of policy.
—Jameel Jaffer, quoted in "Detainee Abuse by Marines Is Detailed," *Washington Post* (December 14, 2004)

President Lincoln instituted the first formal code of conduct for the humane treatment of prisoners of war in 1863. Lincoln's order forbade any form of torture or cruelty, and it became the model for the 1929 Geneva Convention.
—Robert F. Kennedy, Jr., "America's Anti-Torture Tradition," *Los Angeles Times* (December 17, 2005)

It's frightening that, at this time and in this nation, torture must be discussed as if it were a legitimate issue. What's next—the pros and cons of child molestation?
—Ed Kinane, "On Torture," *Common Dreams* (September 30, 2006)

Torture continues to be debated in the United States as if it were merely a morally questionable way to extract information, not an instrument of state terror.
—Naomi Klein, "Torture's Dirty Secret: It Works," *Peacework* (November 2005)

If the United States of America . . . grants itself the right to abuse prisoners, not only are our soldiers at greater risk, but our national soul.
—Robert Kuttner, "Rebelling against torture and Bush," *Boston Globe* (September 16, 2006)

The Bush administration's torture policy seems to have been created through spontaneous combustion. No one will take responsibility for it.
—Patrick J. Leahy, "Senators Quiz Gonzales on Torture Policy," *Los Angeles Times* (January 7, 2005)

If a CIA operative is doing the dirty work, and you support his interrogation methods, then you are committing the act of torture as well.
—Jacqueline Marcus, "If You're for Torture, You Are a Torturer," *Common Dreams* (November 17, 2005)

Abhorring torture, in deed as well as word, is a moral principle in a world yearning for moral footing.
—Edward J. Markey, "U.S. Must Stop 'Outsourcing' Torture," *Boston Globe* (March 12, 2005)

There were times when he rolled about the floor, as shameless as an animal, writhing his body this way and that in an endless, hopeless effort to dodge the kicks, and simply inviting more and yet more kicks, in his ribs, in his belly, on his elbows, on his shins, in his groin, in his testicles, on the bone at the base of his spine.
—George Orwell, *1984* (1949)

Rotten food crawling with bugs, traces of rats and dirt. Rancid meats and spoiled food resulting in diarrhea and food poisoning. This is what detainees at the Abu Ghraib prison near Baghdad were regularly given to eat.
—David Phinney, "Insult to Injury," *CorpWatch* (December 9, 2004)

The United States has never before officially practiced torture. It was not deemed necessary in order to defeat Nazi Germany or Imperial Japan.
—William Pfaff, "Torture: Shock, Awe, and the Human Body," *International Herald Tribune* (December 21, 2004)

Destroying cities and torturing prisoners are things you do when you are losing the real war, the war your enemies are fighting. They are signals of moral
bankruptcy.
—William Pfaff, "Torture: Shock, Awe, and the Human Body," *International
Herald Tribune* (December 21, 2004)

Consider the breezy way we Americans—Americans!—are debating the
pros and cons of torture. Marvel at our moral bankruptcy.
—Ted Rall, "The Normalization of Horror: American Gulags Become
Permanent, Universal Press Syndicate (January 12, 2005)

The recently passed Military Commissions Act removes the United States
from the ranks of civilized nations. It codifies racial and political discrimination, legalizes kidnapping and torture of those the government deems its
political enemies, and eliminates *habeas corpus*—the ancient precept that pre-
vents the police from arresting and holding you without cause.
—Ted Rall, "America's Nuremberg Laws: The End of the U.S. as a Civilized
Nation," *Common Dreams* (October 12, 2006)

The practice of torture is a moral horror that only a morally compromised
and corrupt American body politic can remain indifferent about.
—Carl Raschke, "Many Are Hypocrites on Torture," *Denver Post* (January
16, 2005)

Civilized nations do not debate slavery or genocide, and they don't debate
torture, either.
—Eugene Robinson, "Torture Is Torture: Bush's 'Program' Disgraces All
Americans," *Washington Post* (September 19, 2006)

The more the government is forced to reveal, the more we learn that individ-
uals in U.S. custody, many of whom have not been accused of wrongdoing,
were tortured and abused.
—Anthony D. Romero, ACLU press release, "Iraqi Detainees Had Burn
Marks and Bruises; Harsh Techniques Appear to Have Continued Even After
Abu Ghraib Scandal" (December 7, 2004)

Torture destroys the soul of the torturer even as it destroys the body of his
victim.
—Jonathan Schell, "What Is Wrong with Torture," *TomDispatch.com* (January
20, 2005)

What has happened to our country? We have been in wars before, without resorting to sexual humiliation as torture.
—Theodore C. Sorensen, in his commencement speech at the New School University in New York entitled "A Time to Weep" (May 21, 2004)

[The Military Commissions Act is] a law even Stalin would admire . . . a potentially disastrous step toward authoritarianism.
—Matt Taibbi, "Time to Go! Inside the Worst Congress Ever," *Rolling Stone* (November 2006)

Treat them with humanity.
—George Washington, on how to treat prisoners of war, quoted in "America's Anti-Torture Tradition," *Los Angeles Times* (December 17, 2005)

Violence

Exploitation is the essence of violence.
—Mahatma Gandhi, quoted in *Harijan* (November 4, 1939)

I am an uncompromising opponent of violent methods even to serve the noblest of causes.
—Mahatma Gandhi, *Young India* (December 11, 1924)

The ultimate weakness of violence is that it is a descending spiral, begetting the very thing it seeks to destroy. . . . Returning violence for violence multiplies violence, adding deeper darkness to a night already devoid of stars.
—Rev. Martin Luther King, Jr., *Where Do We Go from Here: Chaos or Community?* (1967)

What could be worse, for kids who desperately desire a feeling of connection, than to plop them in a giant factory of a school, a huge, seemingly uncaring place where they feel invisible, anonymous, lost?
—Alfie Kohn, "Constant Frustration and Occasional Violence," *American School Board Journal* (September 1999)

Half of all murdered women are killed by their current or former husbands or partners.
—Anne Penketh, "International Women's Day: Struggle for Equality and Freedom in Developing Countries," *Independent (UK)* (March 8, 2007)

America, today, spends more on armaments and military than all the other nations of the world, combined.
—James Wallerstedt, "We Face a Fork in the Road," *Common Dreams* (May 14, 2004)

Violence is not the problem; it is a consequence of the problem.
—Rev. Jim Wallis, *The Soul of Politics* (1994)

Violence is readily deployed by those who cloak themselves in innocence—those unwilling to examine themselves and uninterested in counting the number of innocent victims they kill.
—Cornel West, "Democracy Matters Are Frightening in Our Time," *Logos* (Summer 2004)

War

After each war there is a little less democracy to save.
—Brooks Atkinson, *Once Around the Sun* (1951)

I am already against the next war.
—Bumper sticker

White people sending black people to make war on yellow people in order to defend land they stole from red people.
—Stokely Carmichael, on the Vietnam War draft in April 1967, quoted in *An Ordinary Person's Guide to Empire* (2004)

War may sometimes be a necessary evil. But no matter how necessary, it is always an evil, never a good. We will not learn how to live together in peace by killing each other's children.
—Jimmy Carter, in his acceptance speech for the Nobel Peace Prize (December 10, 2002)

War is a coward's escape from the problems of peace.
—Rev. William Sloane Coffin, quoted in "In Pursuit of Justice, In Search of Peace," *Nation* (April 16, 2006)

What we have to end is the idea of war, which has turned into the habit of war, and then into the numbing constancy of war. The last time the U.S. wasn't on a war footing was December 6, 1941.
—Deepak Chopra, *Peace Is the Way* (2005)

War destroys environments, rips apart families, spreads disease, and creates poverty and starvation. Women are left to fend for themselves and their children in extremely fragile situations. They are raped and forced into sexual slavery.
—Myrna Cunningham, "'Every War Is a War on Women'," *Miami Herald* (December 10, 2004)

The answer to mass murder is not mass murder.
—Ronnie Dugger, "What Are We In?" *Progressive Populist* (November 15, 2001)

What difference does it make to the dead, the orphans, and the homeless, whether the mad destruction is brought under the name of totalitarianism or the holy name of liberty or democracy?
—Mahatma Gandhi, *Nonviolence in Peace and War* (1942)

How we can ask a man to be the last man to die for a mistake?
—John Kerry, to a Senate committee about ending the Vietnam War, (1971)

War without ethics leads to victory without honor, or defeat without dignity.
—Liz Larocca, "The Good Soldier," *Intervention* magazine (February 13, 2005)

War is essentially an evil thing.
—Nuremberg Tribunal, quoted in "The Real Problem Is That It Is Illegal for One Country to Invade Another Country," *Toronto Star* (October 29, 2006)

War against a foreign country only happens when the moneyed classes think they are going to profit from it.
—George Orwell, *The Collected Essays, Journalism, and Letters* (2000)

The public policies that would have us spend all of our money on defense while impoverishing our society must be stopped before there is nothing left to save.
—Rosa Maria Pegueros, "Charity Begins at Home," *Common Dreams* (January 5, 2005)

There will be no veterans of World War III.
—Walter Mondale, in a speech (September 5, 1984)

He who is the author of a war lets loose the whole contagion of hell and opens a vein that bleeds the nation to death.
—Thomas Paine, "The American Crisis" (1778)

You can't politicize a war—because wars are political to begin with. Political leaders decide to fight them; elections determine what course they take or if they are fought at all.
—James Poniewozik, "You Can't Bury the Truth," *Time* (July 16, 2006)

It is in the interest of the Republican Party . . . to make sure that the country thinks of itself as "at war" for as long as possible.
—Richard Rorty, "Fighting Terrorism with Democracy," *Nation* (October 3, 2002)

War is not an adventure. It is a disease.
—Antoine De Saint-Exupery, *Flight to Arras* (1942)

Sometime they'll give a war and nobody will come.
—Carl Sandburg, from the poem "The People, Yes" (1936)

When the rich wage war, it is the poor who die.
—Jean-Paul Sartre, *The Devil and the Good Lord* (1951)

War is not healthy for children and other living things.
—Lorraine Schneider, 1960s protest poster, quoted in "War Is Not Healthy: The True Story," AIGA (September 20, 2005)

In the name of freedom, America is mutilating Vietnam. . . . And in the name of democracy, America is burying its own dreams.
—Students for a Democratic Society, 1965 leaflet, quoted in *Events That Shaped the Century* (1998)

For a certain kind of conservative, the life lived in anything other than a state of war is hardly worth living. War clarifies things. War divides the world neatly between us and our enemies. War offers a kind of moral cleansing that makes one's own transgressions meaningless in the face of the other side's abominations against all that is right and good.
—Paul Waldman, "Boor War," *Washington Monthly* (December 2006)

The act of war is the last option of a democracy, taken when there is a grave threat to our national security.
—Joseph C. Wilson, "What I Didn't Find in Africa," *New York Times* (July 6, 2003)

In all wars, at all times, in every country, wars transform ordinary, even good men into killers.
—Philip Zimbardo, *The Lucifer Effect: Understanding How Good People Turn Evil,* (2007)

Most Americans do not want war. Most want the wealth of this country to be used for human needs—health, work, schools, children, decent housing, a clean environment—rather than for billion dollar nuclear submarines and four billion dollar aircraft carriers.
—Howard Zinn, "Harness That Anger," *Progressive* (December 2, 2004)

War kills more children than soldiers.
—Howard Zinn, in a speech at Carleton College, PBS American Perspectives (March 16, 1997)

War for Profit

Law enforcement officials describe the United States as a one-stop shop for the guns sought by terrorists, mercenaries and international criminals of all stripes.
—Jake Bergman and Julia Reynolds, "How U.S. Dealers Arm the World," *Nation* (December 2, 2002)

War is a racket. It always has been. It is possibly the oldest, easily the most profitable, surely the most vicious . . . It is the only one in which the profits are reckoned in dollars and the losses in lives.
—Smedley Butler, quoted in "Mamas Don't Let Your Babies Grow Up to Be Soldiers," *Common Dreams* (July 11, 2006)

In the councils of government, we must guard against the acquisition of un-warranted influence, whether sought or unsought, by the military-industrial complex. The potential for the disastrous rise of misplaced power exists and will persist. We must never let the weight of this combination endanger our liberties or democratic processes.
—Dwight D. Eisenhower, in his farewell address on January 17, 1961, *Public Papers of the Presidents of the United States: Dwight D. Eisenhower* (1960–61)

The military system is, to a substantial extent, a method whereby the popula-tion provides a subsidy to the high technology industry.
—Noam Chomsky, interviewed by Bill Moyers, PBS (November 4, 1988)

Defense firms create the demand for weaponry, prescribe the technological development of our defense system, and supply the needed funds—the de-fense budget . . . . This is the military-industrial complex, a characterization that goes safely back to Dwight D. Eisenhower.
—John Kenneth Galbraith, "Free Market Fraud," *Progressive* (January 1999)

There are certain things that are too important to leave to hired guns.
—William D. Hartung, on privatizing the military, "Outsourcing Is Hell," *Nation* (June 7, 2004)

The official number of 3,400 troops killed in Iraq does not include any from Bush's contract army. How many have been killed? No one knows. [Bush has over 100,000 military contractors in Iraq, compared to approximately 140,000 U.S. troops.]
—Jim Hightower, "The Bushites Have Outsourced Our Government to Their Pals," *Hightower Lowdown* (June 2007)

The global arms trade is enormous . . . From 1998 to 2001 the U.S., Britain and France earned more from arms sales to the developing world than they gave in aid.
—Bianca Jagger, "One Death Every Minute," *Guardian (UK)* (January 25, 2006)

These growing military theatre contractors are now forming their own lobby to represent their interests before Congress. Their interests are clearly not Peace. The profits are in War, and the more War, the more profits.
—Ralph Nader, "Outsourcing Democracy at Taxpayers' Expense," *Common Dreams* (May 10, 2004)

Our present emergency and a common sense of decency make it imperative that no new group of war millionaires shall come into being in this nation as a result of the struggles abroad. The American people will not relish the idea of any American citizen growing rich and fat in an emergency of blood and slaughter and human suffering.
—Franklin D. Roosevelt, *The Fireside Chats of Franklin Delano Roosevelt* (May 1940)

The U.S. political system has been carefully crafted to ensure that no one who questions the natural goodness of the military-industrial-corporate power structure will be allowed through the portals of power.
—Arundhati Roy, *Public Power in the Age of Empire* (2004)

The U.S. military no longer cooks its own food, washes its own laundry, repairs its own vehicles, or guards its own VIPs. We've privatized everything, right down to the shooting—mercenaries make up the second largest contingent in the Coalition of the Killing.
—David Swanson, "The Industrial Services Complex Formerly Known as the Military," Truthout (October 21, 2006)

Defense contractors cannot make billions by waging peace.
—Charles Sullivan, "War Is Still a Racket," *Information Clearing House* (June 26, 2006)

[The Vietnam] war only made billionaires out of millionaires. Today's war is making trillionaires out of billionaires. Now I call that progress.
—Kurt Vonnegut, Jr., on the Iraq War, "Vonnegut's Blues for America," *Sunday Herald* (Scotland) (February 5, 2006)

Tough-talking cowboys and weapons manufacturers have little value in times of peace, so it's in their interest to foment never-ending strife.
—Heather Wokusch, "It's Not Just Bush: We're Accountable Too." *Common Dreams* (December 15, 2006)

The Pentagon has become so dependent on private military companies that it literally cannot wage war without them.
—Barry Yeoman, "Soldiers of Good Fortune," *Mother Jones* (May/June 2003)

THE BETTER ANGELS OF OUR NATURE

Character

Character and empathy are what matter. Being gay or straight is not a measure of a person's worth.
—Frank Edward Allen, "Boy Scouts of America: A Symbol of Prejudice," *San Francisco Chronicle* (September 24, 2000)

For Republicans, "character" mostly consists of having a penis placed securely inside the confines of a heterosexual marriage.
—Larry Beinhart, *Fog Facts* (2005)

I did like President Bush's celebration of National Character Counts Week. He went to Pennsylvania to support Rep. Don Sherwood, who is being sued for repeatedly beating his mistress.
—Molly Ivins, "A Campaign of Sleaze," Truthdig (October 26, 2006)

Character is much easier kept than recovered.
—Thomas Paine, *The American Crisis* (1783)

In the long run, the best proof of character is good actions.
—John Stuart Mill, *Utilitarianism* (1863)

Character is congruence between the inner and the outer person, the private and the public being. . . . Character, at least sometimes, means choosing what is difficult rather than what is convenient.
—Anthony B. Robinson, "Nation Has Cause for Moral Reflection," *Seattle Post-Intelligencer* (February 26, 2003)

Moral character is determined, not so much from the values we espouse, as from the choices we make, particularly those choices we make when our values and our self-interests conflict.
—Larry Robinson, "The Soul of a Nation," *Common Dreams* (January 10, 2003)

Standing for right when it is unpopular is a true test of moral character.
—Margaret Chase Smith, in her speech to Westbrook Junior College (June 7, 1953)

Civility

Lately, the claims about civility that come from the political right seem to mask an unstated and troubling assertion: Never, ever, challenge anyone in power.
—Rosa Brooks, "When Crass Is Called For," *Los Angeles Times* (February 10, 2006)

The civility which money will purchase is rarely extended to those who have none.
—Charles Dickens, *Sketches by Boz* (1836)

Civility must be subordinate to the larger goal of justice.
—Paul Rogat Loeb, "The Perils of Civility," *Christian Science Monitor* (February 15, 2001)

I think that people are very hungry for something new. I think they are interested in being called to be part of something larger than the kind of small, petty, slash-and-burn politics that we have been seeing over the last several years.
—Barack Obama, "Obama Says N.H. Will Help Him Make Decision on Seeking the Presidency," *Boston Globe* (December 10, 2006)

Don't let the pledges of "civility" from politicians divert your attention. There is too much bipartisanship in pursuit of selling out, and too much civility that hides a very uncivil class war.
—David Sirota, "The Money Party vs. the People Party," *Huffington Post* (November 24, 2006)

The bullies and braggarts might appear to win in the short term, but over the long haul nice guys finish first.
—Linda Kaplan Thaler and Robin Koval, "How We Discovered the Power of Nice," *Huffington Post* (September 26, 2006)

Here's a modest proposal for improving national political discussion. Let's stop equating our opponents with famous dictators, their chief executioners, police apparatus, or ideologies.
—Katrina vanden Heuvel, "Don't We Need a New Political Language?" *Nation* (March 28, 2006)

Cooperation

There is no defect in traditional education greater than its failure to secure the active cooperation of the pupil in construction of the purposes involved in his studying.
—John Dewey, *Experience and Education* (1938)

We must learn to live together as brothers, or perish together as fools.
—Rev. Martin Luther King, Jr., quoted in "The Politics of Pronouns," *Common Dreams* (June 11, 2006)

Kindness and cooperation underpin much of human society. From the Kyoto agreement to arms controls or the state of public toilets, they all depend on individual willingness to commit resources to a common good.
—Johnjoe McFadden, "The Unselfish Gene," *Guardian* (UK) (December 18, 2003)

I want to live in a world that values cooperation over competition, compassion over punishment, respect over control, and the dazzling diversity of creation over conformity.
—Rev. Katherine Hancock Ragsdale, "Defining 'Moral Values' for the Next Four Years," Religious Coalition for Reproductive Choice (2004)

Competition has been shown to be useful up to a certain point and no further, but cooperation, which is the thing we must strive for today, begins where competition leaves off.
—Franklin D. Roosevelt, quoted in *An Intimate History* (1983)

Both political parties now compete to sound more hawkish, to criticize as naïve or even unpatriotic those who favor peaceful world cooperation.
—Theodore C. Sorensen, quoted in "Former Writer for Kennedy Laments Hawkish Strategy," *New York Times* (May 12, 2003)

Enlightenment

Philosophers since the Enlightenment . . . have warned of the dangers of forcing religion into the public square.
—Russell Cobb, "Dems Need Reasonable Leaders, Not Progressive Christian Rhetoric," *Daily Texan* (February 9, 2005)

America's side must be the side of freedom and Enlightenment, of liberation from stale constricting dogmas. It must be the side that elevates reason above the commands of holy books and human solidarity above religious supremacism. Otherwise, God help us all.
—Michelle Goldberg, "Saving Secular Society, *In These Times* (May 16, 2006)

If you go back in history, you'll discover that democracy came out of the liberals of the Enlightenment. The early liberal movement was the Enlightenment, Rousseau and John Locke, and Jefferson, and George Washington, Franklin, Paine, and Madison. They defined themselves as liberals.
—Thom Hartmann, *BuzzFlash* (February 7, 2006)

This battle over scientific integrity in government is part of a longer-term struggle for Enlightenment values and against theocratic yearnings in America.
—Marjorie Heins, "The Attack on Science," *Common Dreams* (December 21, 2004)

The candle of enlightenment is in danger of flickering out, and the dark ages again loom large on the horizon.
—John M. Kelley, "The End of the Enlightenment," *Common Dreams* (May 3, 2005)

Americans hold dear their articles of faith, and no one but the purest Enlightenment liberal truly welcomes having his belief system challenged.
—John R. MacArthur, "Religion's Kidnapping of the Campaign," *Providence Journal* (November 2, 2004)

The re-election of a president such as George W. Bush . . . is a culminating event in the political retreat of modernity, a condition of existence whose fundamental tenet was the triumph of scientific skepticism over what used to be called "blind" faith.
—Michael Tomasky, "The Gettables," *American Prospect* (November 8, 2004)

Democracy . . . depends on the Enlightenment values of freedom and equality, which are essential to genuine self-government. In a democracy, truths are provisional and subject to debate—which doesn't mean arbitrary, only arguable.
—Ellen Willis, "Freedom from Religion," *Nation* (February 1, 2001)

Can a people that believes more fervently in the Virgin Birth than in evolution still be called an enlightened nation?
—Garry Wills, "The Day the Enlightenment Went Out" source? (November 4, 2004)

The children of the new enlightenment rose up to defy the tyranny of arrogant clergy and the censorship of pious bureaucrats. They boldly proclaimed that the state must be free from religious coercion and that religion must be free from state control.
—Rabbi Sherwin T. Wine, in a service in Farmington Hills, Michigan (October 21, 1988)

Forgiveness

Injuries too well remembered cannot heal.
—Benjamin R. Barber, *Jihad vs. McWorld: Terrorism's Challenge to Democracy* (1996)

I've been thinking a lot recently about forgiveness, which is at the very heart of Christian morality. Has this country forgiven anyone recently? Or have we turned into a society of perpetual blame and punishment?
—Deepak Chopra, "What Does Jesus Mean by 'Resist Not Evil'?" *Huffington Post* (December 16, 2005)

I believe any person who asks for forgiveness has to be prepared to give it.
—Bill Clinton, in his statement following acquittal by the U.S. Senate in his impeachment trial (February 12, 1999)

I have had the privilege to stand in the presence of forgiveness in situations of incalculable loss and have been awed by its transforming power.
—Mike Miles, "Forgiveness: The Harsh and Dreadful Precursor to Justice," *Common Dreams* (December 20, 2001)

Christian nations consider it a duty to be suspicious of disreputable notions like mercy and forgiveness when the eye-for-an-eye ethic has worked so well for thousands of years in the Holy Land.
—Tony Norman, "Has this Christian Nation Forgotten Jesus' Teachings?" *Pittsburgh Post-Gazette* (September 5, 2003)

How shalt thou hope for mercy, rendering none?
—William Shakespeare, *The Merchant of Venice*

I believe in the forgiveness of sin and the redemption of ignorance.
—Adlai Stevenson, UN Day address in Dallas, *Time* (November 1, 1963)

Forgiving means abandoning your right to pay back the perpetrator in his own coin, but it is a loss that liberates the victim.
—Bishop Desmond Tutu, *No Future Without Forgiveness* (2000)

Love is an act of endless forgiveness, a tender look which becomes a habit.
—Peter Ustinov, quoted in the *Christian Science Monitor* (December 9, 1958)

Generosity

The best way to teach a child restraint and generosity is to be a model of those qualities yourself.
—Lawrence Balter, *Who's In Control?* (1989)

Give to another human being without the expectation of a return.
—Bill Bradley, in his speech at the "Call to Renewal" conference, C-SPAN (September 1996)

We are, in fact, the stingiest of all industrialized nations.
—Jimmy Carter, *Our Endangered Values: America's Moral Crisis* (2005)

Liberalism . . . is the supreme form of generosity; it is the right which the majority concedes to minorities and hence it is the noblest cry that has ever resounded in this planet.
—José Ortega Y Gasset, *The Revolt of the Masses* (1930)

[Democrats] must reclaim the party's true identity and return to the idealism, boldness, generosity of spirit, and core values that marked the presidencies of FDR and JFK.
—Arianna Huffington, in an interview with Don Hazen, AlterNet (April 20, 2005)

Imagine a Democratic Party that could call for schools to teach gratitude, generosity, caring for others, and celebration of the wonders that daily surround us!
—Rabbi Michael Lerner, "The Democrats Need a Spiritual Left," *Common Dreams* (November 4, 2004)

Gratitude

Gratitude suggests that no matter how proud we are of our own accomplishments, we know they would have been impossible without the help of others.
—E. J. Dionne, Jr., "The Politics of Gratitude," *Washington Post* (November 26, 2004)

One looks back with appreciation to the brilliant teachers, but with gratitude to those who touched our human feelings.
—Carl Jung, *The Gifted Child* (1943)

I celebrated Thanksgiving in an old-fashioned way. I invited everyone in my neighborhood to my house, we had an enormous feast, and then I killed them and took their land.
—Jon Stewart, "75 Funniest Jokes of All Time," *GQ* (June 1999)

No one is as capable of gratitude as one who has emerged from the kingdom of night.
—Elie Wiesel, in his speech on receiving the Nobel Peace Prize, "Hope, Despair, and Memory" (December 11, 1986)

When a person doesn't have gratitude, something is missing in his or her humanity. A person can almost be defined by his or her attitude toward gratitude.
—Elie Wiesel, interview in *O: The Oprah Magazine* (November 2000)

Honesty

I personally believe that your loyalty to the mission you were given overwhelmed your respect for the truth.
—Barbara Boxer, to Condoleezza Rice regarding her justification for the Iraq War, quoted in "Boxer Rebellion Spreads," *Nation* (January 26, 2005)

Honesty is a moral value.
—Howard Dean, "The Future of the Democratic Party," *Common Dreams* (December 8, 2004)

Matters of state and the heart that start with a lie rarely end well.
—Maureen Dowd, on Bush's mishandling of the Iraq War, "Defining Victory Down," *New York Times* (January 9, 2005)

The Democrats . . . soft-pedal what they really think about things like the separation of church and state. And it doesn't work to pretend to be something you're not.
—Susan Jacoby, quoted in *BuzzFlash* interview (February 14, 2005)

It is necessary to the happiness of man that he be mentally faithful to himself.
—Thomas Paine, *The Age of Reason* (1794)

Let's be clear. We've always had gay bishops. All I'm doing is being honest about it.
—Bishop Gene Robinson, the Episcopal Church's first openly gay bishop, quoted in "Gay Bishop: Being Honest," CBS News (August 1, 2004)

People . . . appreciate candor. They do appreciate someone who is going to say really what they think and not filter it through to the point where it's mush.
—Barbara Boxer, quoted in "The Boxer Rebellion," *Nation* (February 10, 2005)

Hope

You've got to keep selling yourself a bill of goods.
—Woody Allen, "Cloud in the Silver Lining," *Washington Post* (July 26, 2006)

The hope of the world lies in what one demands, not of others, but of oneself.
—James Baldwin, "Malcolm and Martin," *Esquire* (April 1972)

When hope is taken away from people, moral degeneration follows shortly after.
—Pearl S. Buck, in a letter to the *New York Times* (November 15, 1941)

Hope arouses, as nothing else can arouse, a passion for the possible.
—William Sloane Coffin, Jr., quoted in *Christian Science Monitor* (January 5, 1978)

The citizen who criticizes his country is paying it an implied tribute. . . . It means that he has not given up hope for his country.
—J. William Fulbright, in his speech to the American Newspaper Publishers Association (April 28, 1966)

Political will is a renewable resource.
—Al Gore, "The Time to Act Is Now," *Salon* (November 4, 2005)

A little patience, and we shall see the reign of witches pass over, their spells dissolve, and the people, recovering their true sight, restore their government to its true principles.
—Thomas Jefferson, in a letter to John Taylor in 1798, quoted in *Saving General Washington* (2006)

Real hope . . . is radical. A belief that people are not evil and stupid, not consigned merely to live out pre-determined roles in illegitimate structures of authority, is radical.
—Robert Jensen, "Critical Hope: Radical Citizenship in Reactionary Times," *Common Dreams* (December 17, 2001)

For all those whose cares have been our concern, the work goes on, the cause endures, the hope still lives, and the dream shall never die.
—Edward M. Kennedy, in his speech at the Democratic National Convention (August 12, 1980)

The defining aspect of our country is opportunity—the hope that you can do better, that your children can do better. But you need an even playing field.
—Edward M. Kennedy, quoted in "At 74, Sen. Edward Kennedy Still Roars," Reuters (April 22, 2006)

Hope is not a consumer product. You have to generate your own hope.
—James Howard Kunstler, "Finding Hope in a Post-Oil Society," *Orion* (January/February 2007)

Hope begins in the dark, the stubborn hope that if you just show up and try to do the right thing, the dawn will come.
—Anne Lamott, *Bird by Bird* (1995)

Hope is not for wimps; it is for the strong-hearted who can recognize how bad things are and yet not be deterred, not be paralyzed.
—Frances Moore Lappé, quoted in "The Politics of Hope," *Common Dreams* (November 7, 2006)

The audacity of hope! In the end, that is God's greatest gift to us, the bedrock of this nation. A belief in things not seen. A belief that there are better days ahead.
—Barack Obama, in his keynote address in to the Democratic National Convention in Boston (July 27, 2004)

We have it in our power to begin the world over again.
—Thomas Paine, *Common Sense* (1776)

Another world is not only possible, she is on her way. On a quiet day, I can hear her breathing.
—Arundhati Roy, quoted in "We Need to Share our Stories of Hope," *Common Dreams* (January 14, 2005)

A good world . . . needs a fearless outlook and a free intelligence. It needs hope for the future, not looking back all the time toward a past that is dead.
—Bertrand Russell, delivered in a lecture in London to the National Secular Society, "Why I Am Not a Christian" (March 6, 1927)

I want to live in a country that gives hope to the world. . . . I want to live in a country that listens to its citizens and not the lobbyists of the war profiteers.
—Cindy Sheehan, "Vermont: The Land of Hope," *Common Dreams* (March 6, 2007)

Threats to democracy from the right always collapse. Whatever their short-term appeal, they are borne of hubris and hatred, and will destroy their purveyors in the end.
—Jane Smiley, "The Unteachable Ignorance of the Red States," *Slate* (November 4, 2004)

Hope is believing in spite of the evidence, then watching the evidence change.
—Rev. Jim Wallis, quoted in *The Impossible Will Take a Little While Longer* (2003)

We have to remain prisoners of hope, no matter what.
—Cornel West, interviewed by Terrence McNally, "Matters of Justice," AlterNet (September 29, 2004)

I do feel hopeful: everywhere I go, I hear disgust at our long drunken lurch through recent history give way to a renewed interest among ordinary people in activism, in justice, in what we used to understand as citizenship.
—Naomi Wolf, "We Americans Are Like Recovering Addicts after a Four-Year Bender," *Guardian* (UK) (November 7, 2005)

History is full of instances where people, against enormous odds, have come together to struggle for liberty and justice, and won.
—Howard Zinn, *You Can't Be Neutral on a Moving Train* (1995)

Humility

The foundation of humility is truth. The humble man sees himself as he is.
—Henry Fairlie, *The Seven Deadly Sins Today* (1979)

The cosmos isn't designed with you in mind.
—Christopher Hitchens, quoted in "Hitchens Book Debunking the Deity Is Surprise Hit," *Wall Street Journal* (June 22, 2007)

It is my humble opinion that some folks should do a lot more listening to God and a lot less talking for Him.
—Molly Ivins, "Let God Speak for Himself," *Boulder Daily Camera* (December 2, 2005)

Be patient. God is not finished with me yet.
—Rev. Jesse Jackson, in his speech at the Democratic National Convention (July 17, 1984)

We should practice the virtue of humility and avoid the excessive pride that can, when combined with great power, lead to great abuses of power.
—Robert Jensen, "No Thanks to Thanksgiving," AlterNet (November 23, 2006)

I think this is the most extraordinary collection of talent, of human knowledge, that has ever been gathered at the White House, with the possible exception of when Thomas Jefferson dined alone.
—John F. Kennedy, in his speech at a dinner honoring 49 Nobel Prize winners, quoted in the *New York Times* (April 30, 1962)

I don't want to claim that God is on our side. As Abraham Lincoln told us, I want to pray humbly that we are on God's side.
—John Kerry, in his acceptance speech at the Democratic National Convention (July 29, 2004)

In pluralistic America, what faith requires is humility. Your neighbor's faith in democracy (not his religion) is paramount.
—Bill Moyers, "Faith in Democracy Is Crucial, Moyers Says," *Austin American-Statesman* (January 5, 2002)

The president who promised us humility has instead given us humiliation.
—Richard Reeves, "From Humility in 2000 to Humiliation in 2006," *Yahoo! News* (November 6, 2006)

The very scale of the universe—more than a hundred billion galaxies, each containing more than a hundred billion stars—speaks to us of the inconsequentiality of human events in the cosmic context.
—Carl Sagan, "Broca's Brain: Reflections on the Romance of Science," *Science* (1979)

Independence

Independent journalists, independent judges, independent filmmakers, independent professors—all are anathema to the radical right.
—Michael Berube, quoted in "When Teaching the Liberal Arts Becomes an Un-American Activity," *Daytona Beach News Journal* (March 6, 2007)

It is easy in the world to live after the world's opinion; it is easy in solitude after our own; but the great man is he who in the midst of the crowd keeps with perfect sweetness the independence of solitude.
—Ralph Waldo Emerson, *Essays: First Series* (1841)

Authoritarian methods do not produce independence: they reinforce dependence. Independent functioning is not simply the ability to do something, but also the ability to decide what to do.
—Elaine Heffner, *Mothering* (1978)

We hold these truths to be sacred and undeniable; that all men are created equal and independent, that from that equal creation they derive rights inherent and inalienable, among which are the preservation of life, and liberty, and the pursuit of happiness.
—Thomas Jefferson, original draft of the Declaration of Independence (1776)

Independence I have long considered as the grand blessing of life, the basis of every virtue.
—Mary Wollstonecraft, *A Vindication of the Rights of Women* (1792)

Individuality

Individuality is the aim of political liberty.
—James Fenimore Cooper, *The American Democrat* (1838)

All that is valuable in human society depends upon the opportunity for development accorded the individual.
—Albert Einstein (September 15, 1933)

The individual is the true reality in life. A cosmos in himself, he does not exist for the State, nor for that abstraction called "society," or the "nation."
—Emma Goldman, *The Individual, Society, and the State* (1936)

The great challenge which faces us is to assure that . . . the grand orchestration of society leaves ample room for the man who marches to the music of another drummer.
—Hubert H. Humphrey, in his address to the U.S. Junior Chamber of Commerce (June 29, 1966)

The infidels have been the brave and thoughtful men; the flower of all the world; the pioneers and heralds of the blessed day of liberty and love; the generous spirits of the unworthy past.
—Robert G. Ingersoll, *The Great Infidels* (1881)

That so few dare to be eccentric marks the chief danger of the time.
—John Stuart Mill, *On Liberty* (1859)

The liberal insists that the individual must remain so supreme as to make the State his servant.
—Wayne Morse, quoted in *New Republic* (July 22, 1946)

Men are created different; they lose their social freedom and their individual autonomy in seeking to become like each other.
—David Riesman, *The Lonely Crowd* (1950)

We only become what we are by the radical and deep-seated refusal of that which others have made of us.
—Jean-Paul Sartre, in his preface to Frantz Fanon's *Wretched of the Earth* (1961)

There will never be a really free and enlightened State until the State comes to recognize the individual as a higher and independent power, from which all its own power and authority are derived.
—Henry David Thoreau, "Civil Disobedience," *The Writings of Henry David Thoreau* (1906)

Why should we be in such desperate haste to succeed, and in such desperate enterprises? If a man does not keep pace with his companions, perhaps it is because he hears a different drummer.
—Henry David Thoreau, *Walden* (1854)

Integrity

For what profit has a country if it shall control the whole world and lose its democratic soul?
—Jack M. Balkin, "Using Our Fears to Justify a Power Grab," *Los Angeles Times* (November 29, 2001)

A dysfunctional division of labor exists between Democratic politicians and the progressive base, in which the base spends much of its energy attempting to stop Democratic politicians from selling out core progressive principles
—Christopher Hayes, "How to Turn Your Red State Blue," *In These Times* (March 22, 2005)

Democrats have to appeal to Red State voters—not by aping conservatives but by standing up for progressive values.
—Arianna Huffington, "Before the Polls Close," AlterNet (November 7, 2006)

You might as well speak your mind and do what is in your heart because you never know what waits around the corner—what unforeseen forces are headed your way.
—Arianna Huffington, "Obama Happens: A Cautionary Tale for Perfect Little Hillarys Everywhere," *Huffington Post* (December 4, 2006)

A time comes when silence is betrayal.
—Rev. Martin Luther King, Jr., in his speech delivered at a meeting of clergy and laity at Riverside Church in New York City (April 4, 1967)

I wouldn't feel that I was living up to . . . my faith if I were not speaking out about things that are hurting people and killing people and destroying nations.
—Rev. Joyce Myers-Brown, quoted in "Religious Left Finds Its Voice," *Atlanta Journal-Constitution* (August 14, 2004)

Democrats have to say to themselves, "What are the values we care most deeply about?" then do the hard spiritual work ahead of time. You can't every once in a while just throw in the word "God."
—Barack Obama, quoted in "The Audacity of Hope," *Newsweek* (December 27, 2004)

Did the Democrats learn nothing from that war resolution, on which most of them played possum, trading human life and political principle for poll numbers?
—Anna Quindlen, "The Ghost of Politics Past," *Newsweek* (January 3, 2005)

What does the Democratic Party win if it loses its historic principles as the party of working people and the downtrodden?
—Ralph Nader, *In Pursuit of Justice: Collected Writings 2000–2003* (2004)

Never separate the lives you live from the words you speak.
—Paul Wellstone, quoted in a tribute to Paul and Sheila Wellstone, *Common Dreams* (November 15, 2002)

Leadership

Good leaders reach out to our common humanity and our better instincts. They don't pander.
—Wes Boyd, interviewed by Don Hazen, "MoveOn Muscles Up," AlterNet (April 26, 2005)

The most important virtue lacking in the Democratic leadership today is passion. . . . Dems—decide what you stand for, and stand by your decision.
—Katherine Brengle, "Passion: The Missing Democratic Party Variable; The Ineffective Centrist-Democrat Movement," OpEdNews (December 2004)

Divorced from ethics, leadership is reduced to management and politics to mere technique.
—James MacGregor Burns, *Leadership* (1978)

Rather than worry about the top of the next Democratic ticket, progressives and liberals need to work from the bottom to make their ideas and values trickle up.
—Christopher D. Cook, "The Next Campaign: Ideas," *In These Times* (January 2005)

Perhaps the most central characteristic of authentic leadership is the relinquishing of the impulse to dominate others.
—David Cooper, *Psychiatry and Anti-Psychiatry* (1967)

I'm sick and tired of being sick and tired. We crave leaders who will take positions because they are right and damn the consequences.
—Ed Garvey, "Dems Must Do What's Right, Not What's Safe," *Capital Times (Madison, Wisconson)* (September 27, 2005)

The ability to just take a stand and know that you can move the country to that stand is a lost art we need to recapture.
—Doris Kearns Goodwin, quoted in "FDR and Eleanor: Profiles in Leadership—and Transformation," *Huffington Post* (May 10, 2006)

Accept no leaders who would lead you with fear or anger—who are forever dividing and punishing the people instead of uniting, encouraging and empowering them.
—Doris "Granny D" Haddock, in a commencement address at Hampshire College, "Great Leaders Lead from a Better Vision of a Possible Future" (May 21, 2005)

There's a hole in the American system where the leadership used to be. The country that led the miraculous rebuilding effort in the aftermath of World War II can't even build an adequate system of levees on its own Gulf Coast.
—Bob Herbert, "Long on Rhetoric, Short on Sorrow," *New York Times* (January 25, 2007)

We all may be passengers in a vehicle that has made a radically wrong turn and is barreling along a dark road, with its headlights off and with someone behind the wheel who may not know how to drive.
—Bob Herbert, "Did Somebody Say War?" *New York Times* (May 24, 2004)

Today's corporate leadership is playing with fire. The elites are so focused on enriching themselves—knocking down the workaday majority's wages and benefits in order to grab more of the nation's wealth . . . that they have become blind to the looming threat that their avarice poses to the social order and to their own well-being.
—Jim Hightower, "How the Social Glue of America Is Being Dissolved," *Hightower Lowdown* (January 2006)

I am utterly uninterested in the marital fidelity of our politicians. "Does not stray" might be a wonderful attribute in a husband—or a dog—but history has clearly shown that it says nothing about what kind of leader a person will be.
—Arianna Huffington, "By What Definition Is Gavin Newsom's Sex Life 'Breaking News'?" *Huffington Post* (February 1, 2007)

The good news of having spineless leaders is that they scare easily. When the public is outraged and shows it, you'll be amazed how quickly these leaders will get in the front of the parade.
—Arianna Huffington, interview entitled "Who Are the Pigs at the Trough?" *BuzzFlash* (March 6, 2003)

The prevailing models of leadership today have been the leader as panderer or the leader as fear monger.
—Arianna Huffington, *On Becoming Fearless . . . In Love, Work and Life* (2006)

Leadership has a harder job than just to choose sides. It must bring sides together.
—Rev. Jesse Jackson, "Face the Nation" (April 9, 1988)

A president's hardest task is not to do what is right but to know what is right.
—Lyndon B. Johnson, in his State of the Union address (1965)

Our nation is led by . . . men devoid of a sense of the nation's and their own moral fallibility. By men who have led us into a moral desert and aren't even looking for a way back home.
—Harold Meyerson, "Into a Moral Desert," *Washington Post* (September 20, 2006)

While the Democratic base sees a life-or-death battle over the future of democracy, the Democratic leadership generally favors a business-as-usual approach that requires little more than tweaking the party's rhetoric.
—Robert Parry, "Bush and the Rise of 'Managed-Democracy,'" *Consortium News* (February 13, 2005)

The greatest politicians create their own issues, ones that no one knew existed.
—Rick Perlstein, on not being poll-driven, "Will the Progressive Majority Emerge?" *Nation* (July 9, 2007)

Leaders can only take you so far. At some point it's up to the people to govern themselves.
—Rev. Jim Rigby, "Progressives: Stop Waiting for a Hero," *Huffington Post* (July 4, 2006)

We need people who don't stick their finger up to see which way the wind is blowing but work to change the way the wind is blowing.
—Jonathan Tasini, "Democrats: Get a Real Economic Agenda or Become the Minority Party Again," *Huffington Post* (December 5, 2006)

The buck stops here.
—Harry S. Truman, sign on his White House desk.

There are plenty of social and economic goods for everybody if our leaders call us to a vision of love and justice rather than one of fear and resentment.
—Kay Whitlock, in a news release, American Friends Service Committee (February 27, 2004)

Love

How do I love thee? Let me count the ways.
I love thee to the depth and breadth and height
My soul can reach.
—Elizabeth Barrett Browning, *Sonnets from the Portuguese* (1850)

I call that mind free, which sets no bounds to its love, which is not imprisoned in itself or in a sect, which recognizes in all human beings the image of God.
—William Ellery Channing, in his sermon entitled "Spiritual Freedom" (1830)

Did Christ teach love or is that just a liberal bias?
—Deepak Chopra, "Who Owns Christianity?" *San Francisco Chronicle* (July 17, 2006)

We need to love one another, to come together to create a good society, and use that mutuality discretely in order to gain the benefits of community without sacrificing individual freedom and responsibility.
—Mario Cuomo, quoted in *One Electorate Under God?* (2004)

If you would be loved, love and be lovable.
—Benjamin Franklin, *Poor Richard's Almanack* (February 1755)

High on a throne, with all the splendor and pomp his gold can command, man is yet poor and desolate, if love passes him by.
—Emma Goldman, *Anarchism and Other Essays* (1911)

Love, the strongest and deepest element in all life, the harbinger of hope, of joy, of ecstasy; love, the defier of all laws, of all conventions; love, the freest, the most powerful molder of human destiny; how can such an all-compelling force be synonymous with that poor little State and Church-begotten weed, marriage?
—Emma Goldman, *Anarchism and Other Essays* (1911)

Love is a snowmobile racing across the tundra and then suddenly it flips over, pinning you underneath. At night, the ice weasels come.
—Matt Groening, quoted in the *Los Angeles Times* (February 14, 1991)

Mankind must evolve for all human conflict a method which rejects revenge, aggression, and retaliation. The foundation of such a method is love.
—Rev. Martin Luther King, Jr., in his Nobel Prize acceptance speech, Stockholm, Sweden (December 11, 1964)

Love doesn't just sit there, like a stone, it has to be made, like bread; remade all the time, made new.
—Ursula Le Guin, *The Lathe of Heaven* (1971)

Love is an instinct, an accident, an epiphany, a stomach ache. It can feel like incarceration and pardon, alienation and intimacy, tragedy and comedy.
—Courtney E. Martin, "Love Is Our Most Powerful, Lasting Form of Activism," AlterNet (February 14, 2007)

True love begins when nothing is looked for in return.
—Antoine De Saint-Exupery, quoted in *Love* (2007)

Moderation

There are no moderate Republicans . . . only administration patsies, sent out to reassure the public that not all Republicans are knuckle-draggers, war-mongers, and plutocrats.
—Andrew Foster Altschul, "The Myth of the Moderate Republican," *Huffington Post* (January 26, 2006)

Cautious, careful people, always casting about to preserve their reputation and social standing, never can bring about a reform.
—Susan B. Anthony, quoted in *Dissent in America* (2006)

The hottest places in hell are reserved for those who in times of great moral crisis maintain their neutrality.
—Dante, paraphrased by John F. Kennedy at the establishment of a peace corps in West Germany (June 24, 1963)

Tell a man whose house is on fire to give a moderate alarm; tell him to moder-ately rescue his wife from the hands of the ravisher; tell the mother to gradu-ally extricate her babe from the fire into which it has fallen; but urge me not to use moderation in a case like the present.
—William Lloyd Garrison, antislavery editorial, *The Liberator* (January 1, 1831)

It's usually moderates who want Democrats to be less elitist, less negative, more respectful of red-state values, more . . . moderate. It's usually liberals who want Democrats to be less apologetic, less wishy-washy, more willing to speak truth to power, more . . . liberal.
—Michael Grunwald, "How to Reconnect with Voters and Realize Your Dreams of Victory," *Washington Post* (June 11, 2006)

I would simply say that we've got to get back to the kind of moderate consen-sus which prevailed up until, let's say, the age of Reagan, and the period in which the religious right began to assert itself through the Republican Party.
—Gary Hart, interviewed by Mark Karlin, *BuzzFlash* (December 21, 2005)

History will have to record that the greatest tragedy of this period of social transition was not the strident clamor of the bad people, but the appalling silence of the good people.
—Rev. Martin Luther King, Jr., quoted in "Demand Peace: Vote in the Streets This Martin Luther King Weekend," *Working for Change* (January 16, 2003)

The Negro's great stumbling block in the drive toward freedom is not the White Citizens Councilor or the Ku Klux Klanner but the white moderate who is more devoted to order than to justice.
—Rev. Martin Luther King, Jr., in a letter from the Birmingham jail (April 16, 1963)

Moderation in temper is always a virtue; but moderation in principle is a species of vice.
—Thomas Paine, quoted in *The Writings of Thomas Paine* (1895)

It is not moderation that redresses the great injustices.
—Anna Quindlen, "A Leap into the Possible," *Newsweek* (August 9, 2004)

The culture of wimpiness may be so ingrained into the liberal mindset that its ideals are doomed, as right-wingers claim, to the ash heap of history.
—Ted Rall, *Wake Up, You're Liberal!* (2004)

The current administration could turn the most milquetoast moderate into a radical.
—Dana Spiotta, interviewed Astra Taylor, "Don't Steal This Book, Read It," AlterNet (June 8, 2006)

It's very hard to organize reasonable people with moderate views. Reasonable people with moderate views don't usually light their torches and head out to town with pitchforks shouting, "Be reasonable."
—Jon Stewart, quoted in "Such a tease," *Guardian (UK)* (October 1, 2005)

In their eagerness to appear reasonable and moderate—and to avoid at all costs being tarred with the dread epithet "liberal"—[Democrats] become the enablers, the loyal opposition seeking common ground (even as the opposition is doing its best to destroy them and scorch the very earth where they once stood).
—Tom Tomorrow, "The Party's Message Is Low Risk, Low Reward," *Slate* (November 3, 2004)

People who call themselves "moderate" aren't midway between the parties. When you examine what they believe, you find that they look much more like liberals than conservatives.
—Paul Waldman, *Being Right Is Not Enough* (2006)

Peace

There will be no peace and no security, even for the most privileged amongst us, in a world that remains divided between extremes of wealth and poverty, health and disease, knowledge and ignorance, freedom and oppression.
—Kofi Annan, quoted in "A War to End All Wars," *Common Dreams* (January 17, 2005)

Blessed are the peacemakers, for they shall be called the children of God.
—Matthew 5:3-9

They shall beat their swords into plowshares, and their spears into pruning forks: nation shall not lift up sword against nation, neither shall they learn war any more.
—Isaiah 2:4

Fighting for peace is like screwing for virginity.
—Bumper sticker

Because of the destructiveness of modern weapons, there will be no distant future unless humans, having seen through the congenital illusion of justice-and-peace through violence, come to the rejection of war.
—James Carroll, "Reject the War," *Boston Globe* (December 18, 2006)

The rage against peace is irrational and venomous.
—Deepak Chopra, "Rage, Rage Against the Peace," *Huffington Post* (November 9, 2005)

Nothing can bring you peace but yourself.
—Ralph Waldo Emerson, *Essays: First Series* (1841)

There never was a good war or a bad peace.
—Benjamin Franklin, in a letter to Josiah Quincy (September 11, 1783)

Nonviolence is a powerful and just weapon. . . . It is a sword that heals.
—Rev. Martin Luther King, Jr., *Why We Can't Wait* (1964)

One day we must come to see that peace is not merely a distant goal we seek, but a means by which we arrive at that goal.
—Rev. Martin Luther King, Jr., quoted in *The Left Hand of God* (2006)

Leave mass destruction to nature. Our job should be to protect and preserve life.
—Jonathan Schell, "Letter from Ground Zero," *Nation* (January 6, 2005)

Make levees, not war.
—T-shirt message, quoted in "Speaking Truth to Power in Washington, DC," Columbus Free Press (September 26, 2005)

Independent thought, intelligence, and moral clarity are the enemies of dictators, torturers and warmongers everywhere.
—Teresa Whitehurst, "Do You Feel Guilty for the Sins of Bush and Blair? Should You?" *Common Dreams* (January 28, 2005)

Peace hath higher tests of manhood
Than battle ever knew.
—John Greenleaf Whittier, from the poem "The Hero" (1853)

I have come to the conclusion that war solves no fundamental problems and leads only to more wars.
—Howard Zinn, *Original Zinn* (2006)

Trust

Liberals need to find a means to bridge the gap between Americans' belief in liberal solutions and their willingness to trust liberals to enact them.
—Eric Alterman, "Can We Talk?" *Nation* (November 21, 2005)

The central tenet of every democracy in the end is trust.
—Bill Clinton, quoted in "Bill and Al's Traveling Medicine Show," *New York Times* (September 9, 1993)

Trust of government cannot be demanded, or asserted, or assumed; it must be earned. And this government has not earned our trust. It has fought reasonable safeguards for constitutional freedoms every step of the way.
—Russ Feingold, quoted in "Feingold Beats Bush in Patriot Act Fight," *Nation* (December 16, 2005)

Love all, trust a few,
Do wrong to none.
—William Shakespeare, *All's Well That Ends Well* (1604)

Trust the people. Trust their good sense, their decency, their fortitude, their faith. Trust them with the facts. Trust them with the great decisions. And fix as our guiding star the passion to create a society where people can fulfill their own best selves.
—Adlai E. Stevenson, in a speech in Harrisburg, Pennsylvania, *The New America* (1957)

Trust is based upon the belief that we are all in this together, part of a moral community.
—Eric Uslaner, quoted in "The Great Wealth Transfer," *Rolling Stone* (November 30, 2006)

Truth

The United States government is currently run by a group of people for whom verifiable truth holds no particular privilege over ideologically inspired nonsense.
—Eric Alterman, "Better Red than Dead?" *Nation* (February 12, 2005)

We accept our understandings of truth as incomplete and have faith that new perceptions of truth will continue to be revealed both to us and to others.
—American Friends Service Committee (Quakers), adopted by the Board of Directors (June 19, 1994)

Truth no longer matters in the context of politics and, sadly, in the context of cable news.
—Aaron Brown, former CNN anchor, quoted in "Broadcaster Says Serious News at Risk," *Palm Beach Daily News* (January 26, 2006)

There is a need to resurrect a concern for what's true—to draw clearer distinctions between fact and opinion, between information and mere assertion.
—E. J. Dionne, Jr., "The Making of Democracy 2006: How the New Media and the Old Media Could Live Together Happily and Enhance Public Life," *Huffington Post* (December 19, 2006)

Truth matters.
—Patrick J. Fitzgerald, commenting on the prison term given Dick Cheney's chief of staff for lying to a grand jury, quoted in "Libby Gets 30 Months in Prison in CIA Leak Case," *New York Times* (June 5, 2007)

Truth never damages a cause that is just.
—Mahatma Gandhi, *Non-Violence in Peace and War* (1949)

Some truths are hard to hear, because if you really hear them—and understand that they are in fact true—then you have to change.
—Al Gore, from his film *An Inconvenient Truth* (2006)

Truth, Torture, and the American Way
—Jennifer Harbury, title of her book documenting the CIA's decades-long involvement in torture (2005)

Political truth is libel—religious truth, blasphemy.
—William Hazlitt, *Commonplaces in the Roundtable* (1817)

Live truth instead of professing it.
—Elbert Hubbard, *The Roycroft Dictionary and Book of Epigrams* (1923)

Veracity is the heart of morality.
—Thomas H. Huxley, *Universities Actual and Ideal* (1874)

There are times when regular politics will not do, and this is one of those times. There are times a country is so tired of bull that only the truth can provide relief.
—Molly Ivins, "I Will Not Support Hillary Clinton for President," Columbus Free Press (January 20, 2006)

It is error alone that needs the support of government. Truth can stand by itself.
—Thomas Jefferson, in a letter to William Roscoe (December 27, 1820)

The great enemy of the truth is very often not the lie—deliberate, contrived, and dishonest—but the myth—persistent, persuasive, and unrealistic.
—John F. Kennedy, in his commencement address at Yale University (June 11, 1962)

We live in a culture that would absolutely fall apart if the truth were told.
—R. D. Laing, quoted in *East-West Journal* (September 1987)

Tell the truth as you understand it. If you are a writer, you have a moral obligation to do this. And it is a revolutionary act—truth is always subversive.
—Anne Lamott, *Bird by Bird* (1994)

Where do left and right meet? At the truth.
—Bill Maher, "When Can We Finally Be Funny Again?" *Los Angeles Times* (September 10, 2006)

Democracy doesn't live by bread alone; it lives on ideas, too, and occasionally it needs a full-course banquet of truth.
—Bill Moyers, "Address to PBS Annual Meeting," *Working For Change* (May 31, 2006)

We arrive at truth, not by reason only, but also by the heart.
—Pascal, *Pensées* (1670)

Truth is the only safe ground to stand upon.
—Elizabeth Cady Stanton, *The Women's Bible* (1865)

The truth will set you free, but first it will piss you off.
—Gloria Steinem, "Steinem Still Waging Battle against Discrimination," *Telegram & Gazette* (Worcester, Massachusettes) (November 15, 2006)

I never give them hell. I just tell the truth and they think its hell.
—Harry S. Truman, remark during his 1948 presidential campaign

The truth is not partisan. But sometimes it reflects poorly on one party more than the other. That's not bias; that's reality.
—Allan Uthman, "Bias, Balance, and Bullshit: 'Balanced' News Is Making You Stupid," *Buffalo Beast* (February 1–15, 2006)

Wisdom

The world is too dangerous for anything but truth and too small for anything but love.
—Rev. William Sloane Coffin, quoted in "Where Are All the Leaders of Faith?" *San Francisco Chronicle* (May 4, 2006)

Wisdom lies in being tolerant of your own complexity and then extending that tolerance to everyone else.
—Deepak Chopra, "Why Did I Do That?" *Huffington Post* (February 23, 2007)

We estimate the wisdom of nations by seeing what they did with their surplus capital.
—Ralph Waldo Emerson, *English Traits* (1856)

I hope our wisdom will grow with our power, and teach us, that the less we use our power the greater it will be.
—Thomas Jefferson, letter (June 12, 1815)

Beware when you fight a dragon, lest you become a dragon.
—Friedrich Nietzsche, quoted in "Is Christianity a Casualty of War?" *Huffington Post* (January 5, 2006)

Wisdom lies neither in fixity nor in change, but in the dialectic between the two.
—Octavio Paz, *London Times* (June 8, 1989)

With wisdom we shall learn liberality.
—Henry David Thoreau, *The Writings of Henry David Thoreau* (1906)

In dwelling, live close to the ground. In thinking, keep to the simple. In conflict, be fair and generous. In governing, don't try to control. In work, do what you enjoy. In family life, be completely present.
—Lao Tzu, *Tao Te Ching* (6th century BC)

CALLOUS AND CLUELESS QUOTES FROM THE RIGHT

Anti-LGBT

The sudden change in military structure would add distractions from worrying about accidentally contracting AIDS by sharing showers and quarters to unwanted sexual advances and flamboyant displays of homosexual pride.
—Eugene Delgaudio, executive director of the conservative organization Public Advocate of the U.S., quoted in "Super Loon Eugene Delgaudio: Repeal Of DADT Means Soldiers Will Get AIDS From Sharing Showers With Homos," Joe. My. God. blog (September 15, 2010)

Don't Say Gay
—Informal name of a bill passed by the Republican-controlled Tennessee Senate that would prohibit teachers from acknowledging any sexuality other than heterosexuality to students between kindergarten and eighth grade, "'Don't Say Gay' Bill Troubles Tenn. School Counselors," USA Today (February 21, 2012)

It will lead to alcohol use, adultery, fraternization, and body art.
—Republican Senator's Saxby Chambliss, his dire warning about the repeal of "Don't Ask, Don't Tell," because soldiers don't currently drink or commit adultery or get tattoos, quoted in "Chambliss: If Gays Serve, There'll Be, OMG, Tattoos," Atlanta Journal-Constitution (February 2, 2010)

There is nothing to be proud of in being a dysfunctional homosexual. That's not how God created us.
—New York GOP gubernatorial candidate Carl Paladino, quoted in "Paladino Goes on Anti-gay Rant, Warns against 'Brainwashing,'" New York Post (October 10, 2010)

Attacks on Barack Obama

This president I think has exposed himself over and over again as a guy who has a deep-seated hatred for white people or the white culture.
—Glenn Beck, "Glenn Beck: Obama Is a Racist," CBS News (July 29, 2009)

The Antichrist
—Glenn Beck, regarding President Obama, quoted in *Tears of a Clown* (2010)

A little boy said to his mother; "Mommy, how come I'm black and you're white?" His mother replied, "Don't even go there, Barack! From what I can remember about that party, you're lucky you don't bark!"
—U.S. District Judge Richard Cebull, appointed by George W. Bush, email to friends from his official court account, "Federal Judge Who Sent Racist Obama E-mail Requests Review," *USA Today* (March 3, 2012)

Tar baby.
—Congressman Doug Lamborn, "Republican Racism: Rep. Lamborn Calls Obama 'Tar Baby'," *Democrat Examiner* (August 1, 2011)

Barack the Magic Negro
—Rush Limbaugh, "G.O.P. Receives Obama Parody to Mixed Reviews," *New York Times* (December 27, 2008)

Michele Bachmann

Carbon dioxide is portrayed as harmful. But there isn't even one study that can be produced that shows that carbon dioxide is a harmful gas.
—Michele Bachmann, quoted in "Top Ten Michele Bachmann Moments," *This Week* (October 27, 2009)

I find it interesting that it was back in the 1970s that the swine flu broke out then under another Democrat (sic) president Jimmy Carter. And I'm not blaming this on President Obama, I just think it's an interesting coincidence.
—Michele Bachmann, although the flu began in February 1976 when Republican Gerald Ford was president, quoted in "Michele Bachmann Links Swine Flu to Democrats, Gets History Wrong," *Huffington Post* (May 29, 2009)

But we also know that the very founders that wrote those documents worked tirelessly until slavery was no more in the United States.
—Michele Bachmann, except the founders virtually ignored the issue of slavery and many of them owned slaves, quoted in "Michele Bachmann's Historical Blunder," ABC News (March 14, 2011)

I will tell you that I had a mother last night come up to me here in Tampa, Florida, after the debate and tell me that her little daughter took that vaccine, that injection, and she suffered from mental retardation thereafter.
—Michele Bachmann, on the HPV vaccine, which does not cause mental retardation, but does protect girls from cervical cancer, "Bachmann Questions Safety of HPV Vaccine for Girls," *Washington Post* (September 13, 2011)

Birthers

A 6-month-long investigation conducted by my cold case posse has led me to believe there is probably cause to believe that President Barack Obama's long-form birth certificate . . . is a computer-generated fraud.
—Sheriff Joe Arpaio, Tea-Party Republican at a news conference, quoted in "Arizona Sheriff Claims 'Proof' Obama Faked Birth Certificate," Capitol Hill Blue (March 2, 2012)

I was in Kenya a year and a half ago and everybody said, "You know, [Obama] was born here."
—Pat Boone, celebrity member of the Beverly Hills Tea Party, "50's Heartthrob Pat Boone Revives Golden Oldie: Obama Born in Kenya, a 'Photoshopping Fraud,'" *San Francisco Chronicle* (September 16, 2011)

I have doubts that it is really his real birth certificate.
—Rep. Vicky Hartzler, not the first Congressional Republican to don a tin foil hat on this issue, quoted in "GOP Rep. Vicky Hartzler: 'I Have Doubts That It Is Really His Real Birth Certificate,'" Think Progress (April 8, 2012)

I do know that the man in the White House now is an imposter. The only question is which kind of an imposter: an incompetent "pretender" or a genuine phony, a "Manchurian candidate," who is a liberal, ½ black and ½ white, and an obvious Muslim sympathizer.
—D. M. Lukas and John L. Mariotti, *Hope Is Not a Strategy* (2012)

I haven't a clue where Obama was born . . . . But the point is, is what he has done on the White House website is he has put up a document which he [sic] is plainly a forgery.
—Lord Christopher Monckton, former advisor to Margaret Thatcher, "'I'm No Birther,' but Obama Birth Certificate 'Plainly a Forgery,'" Daily Caller (March 22, 2011)

I have people that have been studying [Obama's birth certificate] and they cannot believe what they're finding . . . I would like to have him show his birth certificate, and can I be honest with you, I hope he can. Because if he can't, if he can't, if he wasn't born in this country, which is a real possibility . . . then he has pulled one of the great cons in the history of politics.
—Donald Trump, quoted in "Trump: I Have 'Real Doubts' Obama Was Born in U.S.," MSNBC (April 7, 2011)

George W. Bush

Go shopping.
—George W. Bush, when asked what Americans could do for their country after 9/11, quoted in "Our Leaders Have Led the Nation Adrift," Chicago Sun-Times (June 13, 2006)

I think I may need a bathroom break. Is this possible?
—George W. Bush, in a note to Condoleezza Rice during a UN Security Council meeting, quoted in "President Bush's 'Brownie' Quote Wins Award," Reuters (December 30, 2005)

Our enemies are innovative and resourceful, and so are we. They never stop thinking about new ways to harm our country and our people, and neither do we.
—George W. Bush, at the signing of the Defense Appropriations Act (August 5, 2004)

President Bush: "You work three jobs?"
Ms. Mornin: "Three jobs, yes."
President Bush: "Uniquely American, isn't it? I mean, that is fantastic that you're doing that."
—Conversation with a divorced mother of three, Omaha, Nebraska (February 4, 2005)

Herman Cain

They [China] have indicated that they're trying to develop nuclear capability and they want to develop more aircraft carriers like we have. So yes, we have to consider them a military threat.
—Republican presidential candidate Herman Cain, issuing a warning against nuclear proliferation about a country that has had nuclear weapons for over 50 years, "Herman Cain Incorrectly Suggests China Doesn't Have Nuclear Capability," *PBS NewsHour* (October 31, 2011)

OK, Libya. [pause] President Obama supported the uprising, correct? President Obama called for the removal of Gadhafi. I just wanted to make sure we're talking about the same thing before I say, "Yes, I agreed" or "No I didn't agree." I do not agree with the way he handled it for the following reason—nope, that's a different one. [pause] I gotta go back and see. I got all this stuff twirling around in my head. Specifically, what are you asking me that I agree or not disagree with Obama?
—Herman Cain, in a painful brain freeze before the *Milwaukee Journal Sentinel* editorial board, quoted in "9 Most Ridiculed Herman Cain Quotes," *The Week* (November 18, 2011)

I'm ready for the "gotcha" questions and they're already starting to come. And when they ask me who is the president of Ubeki-beki-beki-beki-stan-stan I'm going to say, you know, I don't know. Do you know?
—Herman Cain, acting almost boastfully ignorant of foreign policy, quoted in "Exclusive: Herman Cain Feeling 'Like Moses' and Ready for Media 'Gotcha' Questions," CBN News (October 8, 2011)

I believe these words came from the Pokémon movie. Life can be a challenge. Life can seem impossible. It's never easy when there's so much on the line.
—Herman Cain, final words of wisdom exiting the presidential race, "Cain Quotes 'Pokémon' Movie in Final Speech," Daily Beast (December 3, 2011)

Dick Cheney

Conservation may be a sign of personal virtue, but it is not a sufficient basis for a sound, comprehensive energy policy.
—Dick Cheney, in a Toronto speech, quoted in "Going Backwards: Cheney Promises Big U.S. Nuclear Power Expansion," *Guardian (UK)* (May 2, 2001)

Go fuck yourself.
—Dick Cheney, to Senator Patrick Leahy on the senate floor about war profiteering by Cheney's company, quoted in "Sources: Cheney Curses Senator over Halliburton Criticism," CNN (June 25, 2004)

I had other priorities in the sixties than military service.
—Dick Cheney, pro-war vice president and secretary of defense who dodged personal military service in Vietnam five times by obtaining determents, quoted in the *Washington Post* (April 5, 1989)

My belief is we will, in fact, be greeted as liberators.
—Dick Cheney on how U.S. forces would fare in Iraq, quoted in "Notable Quotes on Iraq War," *San Diego Union-Tribune* (March 7, 2007)

Christian Nationalism

Blow them all away in the name of the Lord.
—Rev. Jerry Falwell, quoted in "Call to Kill Terrorists 'in the Name of the Lord' Sparks Outcry," Associated Baptist Press (November 5, 2005)

God is pro-war.
—Rev. Jerry Falwell, quoted in "Wayward Christian Soldiers," *New York Times* (January 20, 2006)

Christians have an obligation, a mandate, a commission, a holy responsibility to reclaim the land for Jesus Christ . . . But it is dominion we are after. Not just a voice.
—George Grant, former executive director of Coral Ridge Ministries, *The Changing of the Guard: Biblical Principles for Political Action* (1987)

If you're not electing Christians, then in essence you are going to legislate sin.
—Rep. Katherine Harris, former Florida secretary of state, "Congresswoman: Elect Christians or Legislate Sin," *Seattle Times* (August 26, 2006)

This is our land. This is our world. This is our heritage, and with God's help, we shall reclaim this nation for Jesus Christ.
—Rev. D. James Kennedy, *Character & Destiny: A Nation in Search of Its Soul* (1997)

We must use the doctrine of religious liberty . . . until we train up a genera-tion of people who know that there is no religious neutrality, no neutral law, no neutral education, and no neutral civil government. Then they will get busy constructing a Bible-based social, political, and religious order which finally denies the religious liberty of the enemies of God.
—Gary North, quoted in "A Nation Under God," *Mother Jones* (December/ January 2006)

I believe homosexual acts between two individuals are immoral and that we should not condone immoral acts. I do not believe the United States is well served by a policy that says it is okay to be immoral in any way.
—General Peter Pace, chairman of the Joint Chiefs of Staff, quoted in "Pentagon Homophobia Now Out of the Closet," *Yahoo! News* (March 16, 2007)

The [Supreme] Court has become increasingly hostile to Christianity. It represents more of a threat to representative government than any other force—more than budget deficits, more than terrorism.
—Tony Perkins, President and CEO of the Family Research Council, quoted in "The Top 10 Power Brokers of the Religious Right," *Church and State* (July 7, 2006)

Our Party pledges to do everything within its power to dispel the myth of separation of church and state.
—Texas Republican Party Platform, quoted in *Religion Gone Bad* (2006)

Contraception

Viagra actually answers a medical problem. . . . Contraception is a choice that somebody will make, but it doesn't answer a particular healthcare need.
—Helen Alvare, spokesperson for the National Conference of Catholic Bishops, on how erections are medically necessary, but avoiding pregnancies are not, quoted on *The Daily Show with Jon Stewart* (February 16, 2012)

You know, back in my days, they used Bayer aspirin for contraception. The gals put it between their knees, and it wasn't that costly.
—Foster Friess, the mega donor behind the pro-Rick Santorum Super PAC, "In My Day, 'Gals' Put Aspirin 'Between Their Knees' for Contraception," Politico (February 16, 2012)

Women don't care about contraception.
—Republican Governor Nikki Haley, quoted in "Gov. Nikki Haley Mixes It Up on 'The View,'" Politico (April 4, 2010)

I think contraception is disgusting—people using each other for pleasure.
—Joseph M. Scheidler, the National Director of the Pro-Life Action League, quoted in "Pro-Life or Just Pro-Sperm?" Common Dreams (March 15, 2012)

Corporate Irresponsibility

If you find an executive who wants to take on social responsibilities, fire him. Fast.
—Peter Drucker, quoted in "Corporation as Psychopath," *Common Dreams* (February 18, 2004)

When a good is produced more cheaply abroad, it makes more sense to import it than make it domestically.
—Greg Mankiw, chairman of George W Bush's Council of Economic Advisers, quoted in "Top White House Aide Defends Outsourcing," *Business Times/Singapore* (January 24, 2004)

Wal-Mart is opposed to unionization. You, as a manager, are expected to support the company's position. . . . This may mean walking a tightrope between legitimate campaigning and improper conduct.
—Wal-Mart guidebook, quoted in "Wal-Mart: The World's Biggest Corporation," *CorpWatch* (May 8, 2002)

I apologize. I do not want to live in a country where anytime a citizen or a corporation does something that is legitimately wrong, [it is] subject to some sort of political pressure that . . . amounts to a shakedown.
—Republican Rep. Joe Barton, the House's biggest recipient of oil and gas industry campaign contributions, publicly apologizing to BP's CEO for expecting the company to pay for the clean-up of its Gulf oil disaster, "Rep. Joe Barton Apologizes to BP's Tony Hayward for White House 'Shakedown,'" CBS News (June 17, 2010)

Ann Coulter

We just want Jews to be perfected, as they say.
—Ann Coulter, on why it would be better if everyone were Christian, "Coulter: We Want Jews to Be 'Perfected,'" CBS News (February 11, 2009)

If we took away women's right to vote, we'd never have to worry about another Democrat [sic] president. It's kind of a pipe dream, it's a personal fantasy of mine.
—Ann Coulter, "If We Took Away Women's Right to Vote, We'd Never Have to Worry about Another Democrat President," Media Matters for America (October 4, 2007)

You're either a liberal or you're a conservative if you have an IQ above a toaster.
—Ann Coulter, on independent voters, "Ann Coulter and Lady Gaga," *Kansas City Star* (Undated)

Cruelty and Bigotry

Sir, prove to me that you are not working with our enemies.
—CNN news person Glenn Beck to Congressman Keith Ellison, the first Muslim ever elected to Congress, CNN Headline News (November 14, 2006)

It's a no-brainer for me.
—Dick Cheney on the use of water-boarding as a torture technique, Office of the Vice President (October 24, 2006)

Hey, hey, ho, ho, Social Security has got to go!
—College Republicans chanting at a campaign event for Senator Rick Santorum, quoted in *Crashing the Gate: Netroots, Grassroots, and the Rise of People-Powered Politics* (2006).

I've never seen people enjoying their husbands' deaths so much.
—Ann Coulter on women widowed by 9/11, *Godless: The Church of Liberalism* (2006). Coulter also called the widows "witches and harpies."

I was going to have a few comments on the other Democratic presidential candidate, John Edwards, but it turns out that you have to go into rehab if you use the word "faggot."
—Ann Coulter, to a meeting of the Conservative Political Action Conference, quoted in "Coulter Under Fire for Anti-Gay Slur," CNN (March 4, 2007). Coulter's comment was followed by applause.

Gays can't have kids—other than going to the abandoned kids store and getting one or two, or borrowing sperm from someone with more sperm than brains—so by definition they're out of the marriage game.
—John Gibson, host of *The Big Story*, Fox News (March 16, 2005)

Certainly is a good PR move.
—Colleen Graffy, Bush's deputy assistant secretary of state, on the Guantánamo Bay suicides, quoted in "Spinning Suicide," Truthout (June 12, 2006)

If an individual wants to discriminate against Negroes or others in selling or renting his house, he has a right to do so.
—Ronald Reagan, opposing the Fair Housing Act, quoted in "Reagan, White as Snow," *TomPaine.com* (May 8, 2007). Reagan also opposed the Civil Rights Act and the Voting Rights Act.

The Church, while profoundly respecting the persons in question, cannot admit to the seminary or to holy orders those who practice homosexuality, present deep-seated homosexual tendencies or support the so-called "gay culture."
—Vatican edict, scapegoating gays for the Catholic Church's pedophilia scandals, quoted in "Bishop Says Edict Allows Some Gay Priests," *Washington Post* (November 30, 2005)

Individual of great courage.
—Former Republican presidential candidate Pat Buchanan, on Adolf Hitler, "MSNBC's Pat Buchanan Defends Hitler. Again," Media Matters for America (September 2, 2009)

[Registering the poor] to vote is like handing out burglary tools to criminals.
—Matthew Vadum, conservative columnist quoted in "Voter Suppression 101: How Conservatives Are Conspiring to Disenfranchise Millions of Americans," Center for American Progress (April 4, 2012)

Drill Baby Drill

What better way to head off more oil drilling, nuclear plants, than by blowing up a rig?
—Rush Limbaugh, accusing environmentalists, "Left Wing: Oil Spill Should Take Drilling off the Table for Good," Daily Beast (April 30, 2010)

Drill Baby Drill
—Sarah Palin, promoting offshore drilling as the massive oil disaster continued, "The 7 Stupidest Statements Made about the BP Gulf Oil Spill," AlterNet (May 3, 2010)

There's no one who wants this over more than I do. I would like my life back.
—British Petroleum CEO Tony Hayward, on his personal hardship regarding the oil disaster that claimed 11 lives and has spewed million gallons of toxic oil into the Gulf of Mexico, "BP CEO Tony Hayward: 'I'd Like My Life Back,'" *Huffington Post* (June 1, 2010)

Fearmongering

We don't want the smoking gun to be a mushroom cloud.
—Condoleeza Rice, on the need to attack Iraq because of its nuclear weapons, quoted in "Top Bush Officials Push Case against Saddam," September 8, 2002)

I'd like to say to the good citizens of Dover: if there is a disaster in your area, don't turn to God, you just rejected Him from your city.
—Rev. Pat Robertson, on the school's rejection of teaching intelligent design in biology classes, quoted in "Pat Robertson Warns Pa. Town of Disaster," The Associated Press (AP) (November 10, 2005)

The atomic bomb is a marvelous gift that was given to our country by a wise God.
—Phyllis Schlafly, quoted in "A Guide to the Religious Right," *Mother Jones* (November/December 1995)

Fundamentalism

Ninety-six percent of Americans celebrate Christmas. Spare me the diversity lecture.
—William Donohue, president of the Catholic League, quoted in "Holiday Cards Ring Hollow for Some on Bushes' List," *Washington Post* (December 7, 2005)

IRAN BANS FILMS PROMOTING LIBERALISM, FEMINISM, OR SECULARISM
—Headline, Iran Press Service (October 24, 2005)

Believers, make war on the infidels who dwell around you. Deal harshly with them.
—Koran 9:123.

Most of the evils in the world today can be traced to humanism, which has taken over our government, the UN, education, TV, and most of the other influential things of life.
—Tim LaHaye, *The Battle for the Mind* (1980)

Newt Gingrich

I think one of the great problems we have in the Republican Party is that we don't encourage you to be nasty.
—Newt Gingrich, in his first successful run for Congress, *Frontline*, PBS (Undated)

Cheerful
—Newt Gingrich, how the usually dour politician replied when asked to a describe himself in a single word, "Romney Jabs at Santorum's Record in CNN Debate," CNN (February 23, 2012)

I believe the kids could mop the floor and clean up the bathroom and get paid for it, and it would be OK.
—Newt Gingrich, doubling down on his proposal to have children as young as nine years old replace the janitors in schools, "Newt Gingrich Expands on His Support for Child Labor," *Los Angeles Times* (December 1, 2011)

There's no question at times of my life, partially driven by how passionately I felt about this country, that I worked far too hard and things happened in my life that were not appropriate.
—Newt Gingrich, explaining why he cheated on his first two wives. He had the first affair while his wife was suffering from cancer, and the second while he was impeaching Bill Clinton for adultery, quoted in "Newt Gingrich Cheated on His Wives for America" *New York Magazine* (March 9, 2011)

Global Warming

There's no scientific proof that global warming even exists. To be honest, it's a bogus consensus dreamed up by Greens because they hate industry. They hate advancement. They hate technology.
—Jonathan Hoenig, "Fox Analyst: Global Warming is Bogus . . . Dreamed Up by The Greens Because They Hate Industry,'" quoted in Think Progress (May 29, 2006)

The greatest hoax ever perpetrated on the American people.
—Republican Senator James Inhofe, on the notion of man-made global warming, quoted in "Gore Steals the Scene in Global Warming Stop on Capitol Hill," *Dallas Morning News* (March 22, 2007)

If the world is warming, I say "bravo."
—James S. Robbins, *National Review* (August 8, 2006)

There's much we know and can agree on around the climate change issue, and there's much that we just don't believe we do know . . . and we want to have a debate about the things we know and understand, the things we know about that we don't understand very well, and the things we don't even know about around this very complex issue of climate science. So that is what will continue to be our position.
—ExxonMobil CEO Rex Tillerson, quoted in "On Global Warming, ExxonMobil's CEO Channels Rumsfeld," *Huffington Post* (June 1, 2007)

Greed

Nothing is more important in the face of a war than cutting taxes.
—Republican Majority Leader Tom DeLay, quoted in "The DeLay Principle," *New York Times* (June 9, 2006)

Oil companies are enjoying record profits. That's fine. This is America.
—Denny Hastert, Republican House Speaker discounting the effects on families who can no longer afford to heat their homes, the Associated Press (AP) (October 25, 2005)

I don't want to abolish government. My goal is to cut government in half in twenty-five years, to get it down to the size where we can drown it in the bathtub.
—Grover Norquist, expressing his conservative philosophy to National Public Radio's Mara Liasson in a *Morning Edition* interview (May 25, 2001)

Guns

It seems that people, and politically speaking on the left, have this misconception about weapons being something dangerous. They're only dangerous in the hands of a criminal.
—Sean Hannity, *Hannity & Colmes*, Fox News (March 15, 2005). Each year in the U.S. there are about 15,000 unintentional gun-related injuries and 800 accidental firearm-related fatalities.

I was the first governor in America to have a concealed carry permit, so don't mess with me.
—Republican presidential aspirant Governor Mike Huckabee, quoted in "Romney and Giuliani Make Pitch to Conservatives," *New York Times* (March 3, 2007)

Hunting uniquely provides self-actualization, completeness, and expression, which are complex, higher-order needs.
—International Council for Game and Wildlife Conservation, quoted in "If We Won't Ban Hunting, at Least Let Animals Have the Sabbath as a Day of Rest," *Asheville Citizens-Times* (North Carolina) (February 4, 2007)

To make our schools safe for our students to learn, all options should be on the table. Israel and Thailand have well-trained teachers carrying weapons and keeping their children safe from harm. It can work in Wisconsin.
—Republican Representative Frank Lasee, "Wis. Lawmaker Wants Teachers to Carry Guns," MSNBC (October 5, 2006)

[A gun] is a recreational tool, like a golf club or a tennis racket. You can kill someone with a golf club, you know.
—Martel Lovelace, official of the National Rifle Association, quoted in *No Comment* (1984)

Guns cause crime like flies cause garbage.
—Anonymous

I'm actually for gun control—use both hands.
—Rick Perry, quoted in "Egghead and Blockheads," *New York Times* (September 17, 2011

Hatred

I wonder if I'm alone in this—you know it took me about a year to start hating the 9/11 victims' families?
—Glenn Beck, Clear Channel radio host later hired by CNN, *The Glenn Beck Program* (September 9, 2005)

You know, I hate gay people, so I let it be known. I don't like gay people and I don't like to be around gay people. I'm homophobic.
—NBA player Tim Hardaway, quoted in "Ex-NBA star's Anti-Gay Remarks a Disgrace," *Delaware County Daily Times* (February 18, 2007)

What we'll do is randomly pick one night—every week—where we will kill whoever crosses the border. Step over there and you die.
—Brian James, conservative radio host advocating murder of undocumented immigrants, KFYI (March 8, 2006)

AIDS cures fags.
—Rev. Fred Phelps of the Westboro Baptist Church in Topeka, Kansas, quoted in "What Has Happened to Jesus?" *USA Today* (February 13, 2006)

Hurricane Katrina

If you'll look at my lovely FEMA attire, you'll really vomit. I am a fashion god.
—Disgraced FEMA Director Michael Brown discussing his wardrobe during the Hurricane Katrina crisis, quoted in "Brown Discussed Wardrobe During Katrina," *Washington Post* (November 3, 2005)

So I guess you want me to be the superhero that is going to step in there and suddenly take everybody out of New Orleans.
—Michael Brown, on FEMA's response to Hurricane Katrina, "Verbatim 2005," *Time* (December 19, 2005)

So many of the people in the arena here, you know, were underprivileged anyway, so this is working very well for them.
—Barbara Bush, after touring the Hurricane Katrina refugee camp at the Houston Astrodome, American Public Media (September 5, 2005)

Brownie, You're Doing a Heckuva Job!
—George W. Bush, to his FEMA director, Michael Brown (September 2, 2005)

Now tell me the truth, boys, is this kind of fun?
—Tom DeLay, House Republican leader, to Hurricane Katrina refugees living in a shelter, quoted in "FEMA Says Debit Card Distribution at Reliant Park Complete," *Houston Chronicle* (September 9, 2005)

When 75 percent of New Orleans residents had left the city, it was primarily immoral, welfare-pampered blacks that stayed behind and waited for the government to bail them out.
—Rev. Jesse Lee Peterson, "Moral Poverty Cost Blacks in New Orleans," WorldNetDaily (September 21, 2005)

Iraq

Why should we hear about body bags and death and how many? . . . Oh, I mean, it's not relevant. So why should I waste my beautiful mind on something like that.
—Barbara Bush, regarding her son's pending war on Iraq, *Good Morning America*, ABC (March 18, 2003)

I think the Iraqi people owe the American people a huge debt of gratitude.
—George Bush, in an interview on CBS's *60 Minutes*, quoted in "Bush: Troop Level up to Me," *Newsday* (January 15, 2007)

Major combat operations in Iraq have ended.
—George W. Bush, from the deck of the aircraft carrier USS Abraham Lincoln on May 1, 2003, quoted in "Notable Quotes on Iraq War," *San Diego Union-Tribune* (March 7, 2007)

One of the hardest parts of my job is to connect Iraq to the war on terror.
—George W. Bush, interviewed by Katie Couric, *CBS Evening News* (September 6, 2006)

There's been a certain amount of . . . pop sociology in America that, you know, the Shia can't get along with the Sunni and the Shia in Iraq just want to establish some kind of Islamic fundamentalist regime. There's almost no evidence of that at all.
—William Kristol, renowned neoconservative thinker, *Fresh Air*, National Public Radio (April 1, 2003)

It's time for Democrats who distrust President Bush to acknowledge that he will be the commander in chief for three more critical years, and that in matters of war, we undermine presidential credibility at our nation's peril.
—Joe Lieberman, quoted in "A Primary Lesson for Lieberman," *Washington Post* (August 1, 2006)

I would call the French scumbags, but that, of course, would be a disservice to bags filled with scum. I say we invade Iraq, then invade Chirac.
—Dennis Miller, on the audacity of French President Jacques Chirac to question U.S invasion plans, quoted in "Four Years and a Weak Punch Line Later, the Joke's on Us," *Daytona Beach News-Journal* (March 20, 2007)

We're not at war. War ended a long time ago.
—Military recruiter, quoted in "Army Recruiters Accused of Misleading Students to Get Them to Enlist," AMC News (November 3, 2006)

I will bet you the best dinner in the gaslight district of San Diego that military action will not last more than a week. Are you willing to take that wager?
—Bill O'Reilly, Iraq War prediction made on January 3, 2003, quoted in "Words for Right Wing Pundits to Choke On," *Capital Times (Madison, Wisconson)* (April 5, 2006)

Enhanced interrogation techniques.
—Republican weasel words for torture.

As you know, you go to war with the Army you have. They're not the Army you might want or wish to have at a later time. You can have all the armor in the world on a tank, and it can [still] be blown up.
—Defense Secretary Donald Rumsfeld, responding to soldiers who needed to go to Iraq garbage dumps to armor their military vehicles, CNN (December 9, 2004)

The Gulf War in the 1990s lasted five days on the ground. I can't tell you if the use of force in Iraq today would last five days, or five weeks or five months. But it certainly isn't going to last any longer than that.
—Donald Rumsfeld, quoted in "Notable Quotes on Iraq War," *San Diego Union-Tribune* (March 7, 2007)

I think that there are ethnic differences in Iraq, but they are exaggerated.
—Paul Wolfowitz on Islam's ancient Sunni-Shiite animosities, quoted in "Dehumanizing Others Is No Virtue," *Chicago Sun-Times* (August 4, 2006)

Liberals

Our job is to remove liberals from power permanently.
—Jack Abramoff, former chairman of the College Republican National Committee, who pled guilty to charges of bribery, embezzlement, and corruption, quoted in "A Culture of Corruption," *Washington Spectator* (April 6, 2006)

They [liberals] hate the idea of Christmas with a deep abiding hate.
—Pat Buchanan, "Do They Know It's Christmas?" *American Conservative* (January 17, 2005)

American conservatives should join Muslims and others in condemning the global moral degeneracy that is produced by liberal values.
—Dinesh D'Souza, quoted in "Ayatollah D'Souza," *Nation* (February 5, 2007)

You owe liberals nothing. They despise you because they despise your Christ.
—Bob Jones III, president of Bob Jones University, in his post-election letter to Bush, *Newsweek* (November 22, 2004)

This guy had to be a liberal. . . . He was turned into a liberal somewhere along the line. So it's a liberal that committed this act.
—Rush Limbaugh, on Seung-Hui Cho's massacre of thirty-two people at Virginia Tech, quoted in "Limbaugh Said Virginia Tech Shooter 'Had to Be a Liberal,'" Media Matters (April 19, 2007)

The Liberal State is a mask behind which there is no face; it is a scaffolding behind which there is no building.
—Benito Mussolini, speech (October 6, 1922, Milan, Italy)

God Almighty . . . The day will come when unpleasant things are going to happen to a bunch of stupid liberals. It's going to be amusing to watch, it's going to be very amusing to watch.
—Radio talk show host Lee Rodgers, on Disney-owned station KSFO, quoted in "Electrocute Bill Keller! No, Hang Him!" Salon (July 14, 2006). (Co-host Melanie Morgan called for New York Times editor Bill Keller to be sent to the gas chamber.)

Liberals saw the savagery of 9/11 attacks and wanted to prepare indictments and offer therapy and understanding to our attackers.
—Karl Rove, Inside Politics, CNN (June 23, 2005)

Priests, like all of us, are affected by culture. When the culture is sick, every element in it becomes infected. While it is no excuse for this scandal, it is no surprise that Boston, a seat of academic, political and cultural liberalism in America, lies at the center of the storm.
—Rick Santorum's for the Catholic Church's national child molestation scandal, "Fishers of Men," Catholic Online (July 12, 2002)

To fight only the Al Qaeda scum is to miss the terrorist network operating within our own borders . . . Who are these traitors? Every rotten radical left-winger in this country, that's who.
—Michael Savage, Savage Nation (2003)

I never use the words Democrats and Republicans. It's liberals and Americans.
—James G. Watt, George H. W. Bush's secretary of the interior, quoted in the Washington Post (May 4, 1989)

Lies

I don't think anybody anticipated the breach of the levees.
—George W. Bush, four days after being warned, on tape, that the levees were a "very, very grave concern," *Good Morning America*, ABC (September 1, 2005)

We are doing everything we can to avoid war in Iraq.
—George W. Bush, radio address (March 8, 2003)

We do not torture.
—George W. Bush, quoted in "We Do Not Torture and Other Funny Stories," *New York Times* (November 13, 2005)

I think they're in the last throes, if you will, of the insurgency.
—Dick Cheney, quoted in "Iraq Insurgency in 'Last Throes,' Cheney Says," CNN (June 20, 2005)

The President of the United States and the Secretary of Defense would not assert as plainly and bluntly as they have that Iraq has weapons of mass destruction if it was not true.
—Ari Fleischer, Bush's press secretary, NewsMax Wires (December 6, 2002)

I was buying it for me, but I never used it.
—Rev. Ted Haggard, president of the National Association of Evangelicals, on buying methamphetamines and getting a massage from a gay prostitute, quoted in "Perspectives," *Newsweek* (January 8, 2007)

[Guantanamo] is essentially a model facility.
—General Richard Myers, chairman of the Joint Chiefs, FOX News Sunday (May 29, 2005)

Fascism was really the basis for the New Deal.
—Ronald Reagan, *Time* (May 1976)

I think Mr. Bush is going to go down in history as one of the great peacemakers and democracy-builders in the history of the world.
—Ben Stein, television personality and former Nixon speechwriter, quoted on "Your World with Neil Cavuto," Fox News (December 15, 2005)

Rush Limbaugh

Let the unskilled jobs that take absolutely no knowledge whatsoever to do—
let stupid and unskilled Mexicans do that work.
—Rush Limbaugh, quoted in "Sparring in Spanish," FactCheck.org (September
19, 2008)

What does it say about the college co-ed Susan Fluke [sic] who goes before
a congressional committee and essentially says that she must be paid to have
sex—what does that make her? It makes her a slut, right? It makes her a prostitute.
—Rush Limbaugh, quoted in "Sandra Fluke: Obama 'Was So Kind,'" *Los Angeles
Times* (March 02, 2012)

You know who deserves a posthumous Medal of Honor? James Earl Ray [the
confessed assassin of Martin Luther King]. We miss you, James. Godspeed.
—Rush Limbaugh, quoted in "Choice Quotes from GOP Boss Limbaugh,"
Daily Kos (March 04, 2009)

Take that bone out of your nose and call me back.
—Rush Limbaugh, in response to a caller, quoted in "Limbaugh: A Color Man
Who Has a Problem with Color?" FAIR (June 7, 2000)

Nature-Deficit Disorder

The difference between animals and humans is that animals change themselves
for the environment, but humans change the environment for themselves.
—Ayn Rand, quoted in "Ayn Rand's Case for Human Liberty," Daily Bell
(April 2, 2012)

We don't know what those other cycles were caused by in the past. Could be
dinosaur flatulence, you know, or who knows?
—Republican Rep. Dana Rohrabacher, "Gop Rep. Suggests 'Flatulence' Killed
Dinosaurs, Caused Global Warming," *Huffington Post* (May 25, 2011)

Environmentalists are a socialist group of individuals that are the tool of the
Democrat [sic] Party. I'm proud to say that they are my enemy. They are not
Americans, never have been Americans, never will be Americans.
—Republican Rep. Don Young, quoted in "Stupid Republican and Religious
Right Comments," America For Purchase (November 5, 2009)

Sarah Palin

All of 'em, any of 'em that have been in front of me over all these years.
—Sarah Palin, in an interview with Katie Couric, not able to name a single newspaper or magazine she reads, CBS News (October 1, 2008)

The America I know and love is not one in which my parents or my baby with Down syndrome will have to stand in front of Obama's death panel.
—Sarah Palin, Facebook posting making her most preposterous claim about Obamacare, (August 7, 2009)

We used to hustle over the border for health care we received in Canada. And I think now, isn't that ironic?
—Sarah Palin, admitting how her family preferred Canada's single-payer health care system, an approach she now criticizes as socialized medicine, "Palin Crossed Border for Canadian Health Care," *Huffington Post* (March 8, 2010)

He who warned, uh, the British that they weren't gonna be takin' away our arms, uh, by ringing those bells, and um, makin' sure as he's riding his horse through town to send those warning shots and bells that we were going to be sure and we were going to be free, and we were going to be armed.
—Sarah Palin, her embarrassingly inaccurate attempt to explain who Paul Revere was, quoted in "Sarah Palin Claims Paul Revere Warned the British," *Los Angeles Times* (June 3, 2011)

Paranoia and Conspiracy

Do you have a professor who just can't stop talking about President Bush, about the war in Iraq, about the Republican Party, or any other ideological issue that has nothing to do with the class subject matter? If you help . . . expose the professor, we'll pay you for your work.
—Bruin [UCLA] Alumni Association, quoted in "Rightwing Group Offers Students $100 to Spy on Professors," *Guardian* (UK) (January 19, 2006)

Hollywood is controlled by secular Jews who hate Christianity.
—William Donahue, president of the Catholic League, appearing on *Scarborough Country*, MSNBC (December 8, 2004)

The cultural left in this country is responsible for causing 9/11.
—Dinesh D'Souza, *The Enemy at Home: The Cultural Left and Its Responsibility for 9/11*, (2007)

The War on Christmas: How the Liberal Plot to Ban the Sacred Christian Holiday is Worse Than You Thought
—Title of Fox News reporter John Gibson's book (2005)

The Jews are responsible for all the wars in the world.
—Mel Gibson, quoted in "Crossing This Line Could Cost Him Deals," *Los Angeles Times* (July 31, 2006)

They are racists, murderers, sexual deviants, and supporters of Al Qaeda—and they could be teaching your kids!
—Rev. Pat Robertson on college professors, 700 Club, CBN (March 21, 2006) Later in the broadcast, he described professors as "killers."

They want to permeate sperm banks with gay semen to perpetuate the gay gene.
—Laura Schlessinger, quoted in "Gay Agenda Revealed Here for First Time!" *Middletown Times Herald-Record* (February 20, 2006)

A dangerous Marxist/Leftist/Homosexual/Islamic coalition has formed—and we'd better be willing to fight it with everything in our power.
—Rev. Louis P. Sheldon, founder of the Traditional Values Coalition, quoted in "The Top 10 Power Brokers of the Religious Right," *Church and State* (July 7, 2006)

Power

I'm the decider and I decide what's best.
—George W. Bush to reporters in the White House rose garden, quoted in "Tide Turns on Dubya's Wreck," *Sydney Morning Herald* (April 22, 2006)

There is no express grant of *habeas* in the Constitution.
—Attorney General Alberto Gonzales, denying the fundamental right of prisoners to be protected from illegal imprisonment, quoted in "Oh Boy, Alberto," *American Spectator* (January 22, 2007)

When the President does it, that means that it is not illegal.
—Richard M. Nixon in a television interview with David Frost (May 19, 1977)

Publicly, we say one thing. Actually, we do another.
—Richard Nixon, in a letter to aides regarding his secret war in Cambodia, quoted in "Documents Show Nixon Deception on Cambodia," *Washington Post* (November 17, 2005)

Propaganda and the Media

We paid $3 billion for these television stations. We will decide what the news is. The news is what we tell you it is.
—David Boylan, station manager of Fox's WTVT in Tampa, Florida, quoted in "The People's Media Reaches More People Than FOX Does," *Common Dreams* (June 15, 2004)

See, in my line of work you got to keep repeating things over and over and over again for the truth to sink in, to kind of catapult the propaganda.
—George W. Bush, quoted in "President Bush's 'Brownie' Quote Wins Award," Reuters (December 30, 2005)

The great mass of people . . . will more easily fall victim to a big lie than to a small one.
—Adolf Hitler, *Mein Kampf* (1925)

Racial and Ethnic Slurs

Macaca . . . welcome to America.
—Republican U.S. Senator George Allen, to an American of Indian descent. The word *macaca* is a racial slur derived from "macacque," a type of monkey. Quoted in "Gaffes Put Presidential Hopeful Allen in Trouble," Reuters (October 2, 2006)

It's true that if you wanted to reduce crime, you could—if that were your sole purpose, you could abort every black baby in this country, and your crime rate would go down.
—William Bennett, Ronald Reagan's Secretary of Education, on his talk show *Morning in America* (September 29, 2005)

So many minority youths had volunteered . . . that there was literally no room for patriotic folks like myself.
—Tom Delay, explaining why he didn't enlist during Vietnam, quoted in "The BEAST 50 Most Loathsome People in America, 2005," *Buffalo Beast* (June 21–July 12, 2006)

Why do Sunnis kill Shiites? How do they tell the difference? They all look the same to me.
—Trent Lott, quoted in "Lott: Bush Barely Mentioned Iraq in Meeting with Senate Republicans," CNN (September 28, 2006)

With the [Latino] population that has emerged, since they breed like rabbits, in many cases the whites will become a minority in their own nation . . . The white people don't breed as often for whatever reason. I guess many homosexuals are involved.
—Michael Savage, *San Francisco Bay Guardian* (September 9, 2000)

There is another way, or other ways, to look at the race issue in America. Africa at the time of slavery was still primarily a jungle. . . . Life there was savage . . . and those brought to America, and other countries, were in many ways better off.
—Gerald Schoenewolf, member of anti-gay research organization, quoted in "Essay by Promoter of 'Ex-Gay' Movement Sparks Racism Charges," Intelligence Report (Southern Poverty Law Center) (October 6, 2006)

Our blacks are better than theirs.
—Ann Coulter, a comment that could have come from a slave owner, "Top 10 Racist Quotes of 2011," News One (December 29, 2011)

Stay out of heavily black neighborhoods . . . . Do not attend events likely to draw a lot of blacks . . . . If you are at some public event at which the number of blacks suddenly swells, leave as quickly as possible.
—John Derbyshire, writer for the flagship conservative magazine, "National Review's John Derbyshire Pens Racist Screed: 'Avoid Concentrations of Blacks,' 'Stay Out Of' Their Neighborhoods,' *Huffington Post* (April 6, 2012)

Teabaggers Chant "Nigger" at John Lewis; Scream "Faggot" at Barney Frank; Spit on Emanuel Cleaver; Mock Anthony "Schlomo Weiner"
—Headline, as congressmen exited the Capitol, Joshua Blog (March 21, 2010)

They are 12 percent of the population. Who the hell cares?
—Rush Limbaugh, in response to a caller arguing that black people need to be heard, quoted in "Limbaugh: A Color Man Who Has a Problem with Color?" FAIR (June 7, 2000)

Niggerhead
—Name of Rick Perry's family campground, "At Rick Perry's Texas Hunting Spot, Camp's Old Racially Charged Name Lingered," *Washington Post* (October 1, 2011)

There are times when an abortion is necessary. I know that. When you have a black and a white. Or a rape.
—Richard Nixon, quoted in "On Nixon Tapes, Ambivalence Over Abortion, Not Watergate," *New York Times* (June 23, 2009)

Darkies are wonderful people, and they have their place in our Church.
—Joseph Fielding Smith, former president of The Church of Jesus Christ of Latter-day Saints (Mormons), quoted in *Look Magazine* (October 1963)

I have a great relationship with the blacks.
—Donald Trump, "Donald Trump: 'Great relationship with the Blacks,'" *USA Today* (April 4, 2011)

Right-Wing Bumper Stickers

Don't Re-Nig in 2012
—Bumper sticker, subtitle states "Stop repeat offenders. Don't reelect Obama!" "'Don't Re-Nig,' the Racist Anti-Obama Bumper Sticker, Appears Real," Yahoo News (March 16, 2012)

Save Water. Water Board Two Together.
—Bumper sticker

If You Can Read This You're In Range.
—Bumper Sticker

My wife says life is what you make of it. So I let her make dinner, make the bed, make the payments . . .
—Bumper sticker

Some Common Parasites: Leeches, Worms, Lice, Public Sector Unions
—Bumper sticker

Mitt Romney

Mornin' y'all! Good to be with ya. I got started right this morning with a biscuit and some cheesy grits.
—Mitt Romney, quoted in "Jon Stewart Rips Mitt Romney's Southern Pandering," *Huffington Post* (March 13, 2012)

I'm not concerned about the very poor.
—Mitt Romney, quoted in "Mitt Romney: Middle Income Americans Are Focus, Not Very Poor," CNN (February 1, 2012)

I like being able to fire people who provide services to me.
—Mitt Romney, quoted in "Mitt Romney: 'I Like Being Able to Fire People' for Bad Service," CBS News (January 9, 2012)

I love this state. The trees are the right height.
—Mitt Romney, quoted in "Mitt Romney Repeatedly References Height of Trees in Michigan," *Huffington Post*, (February 24, 2012)

I'm not a big-game hunter. I've made that very clear. I've always been a rodent and rabbit hunter. Small varmints, if you will.
—Mitt Romney, quoted in "Desperately Seeking Dalrymple," *New York Times* (October 5, 2011)

Corporations are people, my friend . . . of course they are. Everything corporations earn ultimately goes to the people. Where do you think it goes? Whose pockets? Whose pockets? People's pockets. Human beings, my friend.
—Mitt Romney, to a member of the audience who said that taxes should be raised on corporations, "Mitt Romney at Iowa State Fair: 'Corporations Are People, My Friend,'" ABC News (August 11, 2011)

I was a severely conservative Republican governor.
—Mitt Romney, formerly a pro-choice, pro-gay rights, pro-government health care governor of Massachusetts, "Romney Makes an Appeal to the Right," ABC News (February 10, 2012)

Planned Parenthood, we're going to get rid of that.
—Mitt Romney, promising to eliminate the largest provider of maternal, child health, and reproductive health services in the United States, "Mitt Romney's Plan to 'Get Rid of Us' Won't Balance Budget," *Huffington Post* (March 14, 2012)

I should tell my story. I'm also unemployed.
—Mitt Romney, who is worth more than 200 million dollars, speaking to unemployed workers, quoted in "Romney: 'I'm Also Unemployed,'" *New York Times* (June 16, 2011)

Resolute
—Mitt Romney, what the legendary flip-flopper said when asked to describe himself in a single word, "Romney Is 'Resolute' in Arizona Debate, but Will That Be Good Enough?" *National Journal* (February 23, 2012)

Rick Santorum

I don't care what the unemployment rate is going to be. It doesn't matter to me.
—Rick Santorum, "Oops! Candidates' Gaffes Can Cost Them Votes," *The Patriot-News* (March 23, 2012)

Phony theology
—Rick Santorum, decidedly un-Christian characterization of President Obama's religion, "Santorum's 'Satan' Comments & More of His Outlandish Statements," Daily Beast (February 22, 2012)

That makes me want to throw up.
—Rick Santorum's reaction to JFK's historic speech pledging to keep the Pope and American politics separate, *New York Daily News* (February 26, 2012)

What a snob!
—Rick Santorum, how the former Pennsylvania senator characterized President Obama's hope that every American should be able to go to college, ABC News (February 25, 2012)

Many of the Christian faith have said . . . contraception is okay. It's not okay. It's a license to do things in a sexual realm that is counter to how things are supposed to be.
—Rick Santorum, "Rick Santorum Fine with Shaming Women in Certain Situations," *New York Magazine* (February 15, 2012)

If the Supreme Court says that you have the right to consensual [gay] sex within your home, then you have the right to bigamy, you have the right to polygamy, you have the right to incest, you have the right to adultery. You have the right to anything . . . That's not to pick on homosexuality. It's not, you know, man on child, man on dog, or whatever the case may be.
—Rick Santorum, "Santorum under Fire for Comments on Homosexuality," CNN (April 22, 2003)

There is income inequality in America. There always has been and, hopefully . . . there always will be.
—Rick Santorum, pandering to an audience of fat cats at the Detroit Economic Club, quoted in "A Drunkard in the Gutter Is Just Where He Ought to Be," *Slate* (March 29, 2012)

I would advocate that any doctor that performs an abortion, should be criminally charged for doing so.
—Rick Santorum, "Santorum: Abortion Because of Rape or Incest?—Dr. Should be Criminally Charged," Democratic Underground (June 12, 2011)

Sexual Harassment and Violence

Foley: "What are ya wearing?"
Teenage boy: "T-shirts and shorts."
Foley: "Love to slip them off of you."
—Republican Congressman Mark Foley's text messages to a teenage boy, quoted in "How Mark Foley Represents the Entire Republican Party," *Huffington Post* (October 1, 2006)

We track library books better than we track pedophiles.
—Mark Foley, on *Huffington Post* (October 1, 2006). Foley cochaired the U.S. House Caucus on Missing and Exploited Children, and had sponsored numerous bills aimed at protecting children from predators.

So anyway I'd be rubbing your big boobs and getting your nipples really hard.
—Bill O'Reilly, talk show host for Fox News, as he is quoted in a sexual harassment suit filed against him by a Fox News producer, *FrontPageMagazine* (October 16, 2004)

If it's inevitable, just relax and enjoy it.
—Clayton Williams, Republican candidate for Texas governor, on rape (April 1990)

Stupidity

Stephan Colbert: "What are the Ten Commandments?"
Republican Congressman Lynn Westmoreland: "You mean all of them? Um . . . Don't murder. Don't lie. Don't steal. Um . . . I can't name them all."
—Interview on *The Colbert Report*, Comedy Central (June 16, 2006). Westmoreland co-sponsored bills mandating the display of the Ten Commandments in the U.S. House and Senate.

Jesus was no sissy. He was tough, he was a he-man. If he played football, you'd be slow getting up after he tackled you.
—Rev. Jerry Falwell, quoted in "The Church of Football," *Nation* (January 29, 2007)

May our nation continue to be the beakon of hope to the world.
—Dan Quayle's family's 1989 Christmas card

Republicans understand the importance of bondage between a mother and child.
—Dan Quayle, quoted in *U.S. News and World Report* (October 10, 1988)

Show me just what Muhammad brought that was new, and there you will find things only evil and inhuman, such as his command to spread by the sword the faith he preached.
—Pope Benedict XVI, "The Pope's Words," *New York Times* (September 16, 2006)

It's not something you call, I mean, rape or penetration or anything like that, you know. It was just fondling.
—Roman Catholic priest Anthony Mercieca, who also admitted massaging GOP Rep. Tom Foley in the nude when Foley was thirteen years old, quoted in "Diocese Opens Inquest of Foley Priest," the Associated Press (AP) (October 20, 2006)

A tree is a tree—how many do you need to look at?
—Ronald Reagan in a speech to the Western Wood Products Association (September 12, 1965)

As we know, there are known knowns. There are things we know we know. We also know there are known unknowns. That is to say we know there are some things we do not know. But there are also unknown unknowns, the ones we don't know we don't know.
—Donald Rumsfeld, quoted in "Farewell, Rummy," Truthdig (November 16, 2006)

It's a slam-dunk.
—George Tenet, Bush's CIA chief, on the likelihood of finding weapons of mass destruction in Iraq, quoted in *Plan of Attack* (2004)

It's three agencies of government, when I get there, that are gone: Commerce, Education and the—what's the third one there? Let's see. . . . OK. So Commerce, Education and the— . . . The third agency of government I would—I would do away with the Education, the . . . Commerce and—let's see—I can't. The third one, I can't. Sorry. Oops.
—Rick Perry, during a GOP debate, forgetting his plan to cut the Department of Energy, "Top Ten: 2011 Political Fumbles, Gaffes, and Scandals," *Washington Times* (December 10, 2011)

An Internet was sent by my staff at 10 o'clock in the morning on Friday; I just got it yesterday.
—Republican Senator Ted Stevens, who on another occasion said the Internet was "a series of tubes," "Senator's Slip of the Tongue Keeps on Truckin'" over the Web," *New York Times* (July 17, 2006)

I guess we better unzip him and let the real Mitt Romney out.
—Ann Romney, insisting her husband is not "too stiff," "Ann Romney Says Campaign Will 'Unzip' Real Mitt," ABC News (April 2, 2012)

Public Education

Both sides ought to be properly taught.
—George W. Bush on whether intelligent design should be taught along side evolution in science classes, quoted in "Culture of Intellectual Corruption," *Washington Post* (March 9, 2006)

The problem with public schools is that they must take whoever walks in the door.
—John Chubb, privatization advocate, quoted in "The 500-Pound Gorilla," *Phi Delta Kappan* (October 2002)

America's public education is purposely designed to eradicate Jesus from the scene and replace Him with the likes of John Dewey, Sigmund Freud, Wilhelm Wundt, Friedrich Nietzsche, Karl Marx, Charles Darwin, and many more.
—Tim LaHaye, coauthor of the Left Behind series, *Mind Siege: The Battle for Truth in the New Millennium* (2001)

Threats and Thuggery

I think the government should be spying on all Arabs, engaging in torture as a televised spectator sport, dropping daisy cutters wantonly throughout the Middle East and sending liberals to Guantanamo.
—Ann Coulter, "Live and Let Spy," *Yahoo! News* (December 21, 2005)

We need somebody to put rat poisoning in Justice Stevens' crème brûlée.
—Ann Coulter, who added that her death wish for Supreme Court Justice John Paul Stevens was "just a joke," quoted in "Ann Coulter 'Jokes' That a Supreme Court Justice Should Be Poisoned," *Editor & Publisher* (January 27, 2006)

Today, it is not about guilt or innocence. It's about unlawful enemy combatants.
—Rear Admiral Harry B. Harris, Jr., commanding officer of Guantanamo Bay Prison, quoted in "Guantanamo Is Not a Prison: 11 Ways to Report on Gitmo without Upsetting the Pentagon," *TomDispatch.com* (March 9, 2007)

Mr. Clinton better watch out if he comes down here. He'd better have a bodyguard.

—Jesse Helms, Republican U.S. senator threatening the president of the United States in 1994, quoted in "Fear, Loathing and the GOP," *In These Times* (April 18, 2005)

We don't need another $200 billion war to get rid of one, you know, strong-arm dictator. It's a whole lot easier to have some of the covert operatives do the job and then get it over with.

—Rev. Pat Robertson, calling for the assassination of Hugo Chavez, democratically elected president of Venezuela, quoted in "Why They Hate Us," *Capital Times (Madison, Wisconson)* (August 28, 2005)

When abortion is made illegal again, you will be hunted down and tried for genocide.

—Randall A. Terry, founder of Operation Rescue, in a letter to doctors sent to the *New England Journal of Medicine*, quoted in *Time* (September 11, 1995)

Any member of Congress who introduces, co-sponsors or votes in favor of . . . amnesty [for undocumented immigrants] will be declared a domestic enemy and will be considered a legitimate target for assassination.

—Conservative radio talk-show host Hal Turner, quoted in "Assassination Schedule Announced for Congress," World Net Daily (December 6, 2006)

As far as I'm concerned, it wouldn't bother me a bit to pull the trigger on one of 'em.

—John Wayne, who was a World War II draft dodger, commenting on Vietnam War protesters, quoted in "Memorializing the Deadly Myth of John Wayne," Truthdig (May 26, 2007)

I'm thinking about killing Michael Moore, and I'm wondering if I could kill him myself, or if I would need to hire somebody to do it.

—Glenn Beck, *Glenn Beck Program* (May 17, 2005)

If this guy prints more money between now and the election, I don't know what y'all would do to him in Iowa, but we—we would treat him pretty ugly down in Texas. Printing more money to play politics at this particular time in American history is almost treacherous, err, treasonous in my opinion.

—Rick Perry, on what he would do to Ben S. Bernanke, the Federal Reserve chairman, quoted in "Off the Cuff, Into the Headlines," *New York Times* (August 19, 2011)

Women

I am particularly proud of my contributions in recent cases in which the government has argued in the Supreme Court that . . . the Constitution does not protect a right to an abortion.
—Supreme Court Justice Samuel A. Alito, in his application to become deputy assistant attorney general in 1985, quoted in "Court Pick Described View on Abortion in '85 Document," *New York Times* (November 14, 2005)

I am outraged that it is viewed through the perspective of the woman.
—Republican Majority Leader Dick Armey, his view of abortion (May 1994)

Bitch
—Conservative CNN commentator Glenn Beck, referring to Hillary Clinton, quoted in "Rosie the Riveter," *American Prospect* (May 1, 2007)

The women are the problem in history. Women who don't want to have children should cut away their breasts, bottoms, and love organ because the purpose for those was first for the children. If they don't fulfill that purpose, then they are not needed.
—Rev. Sun Myung Moon, conservative owner of the *Washington Times*, quoted in "Rev. Moon's Conjugal Visitations," AlterNet (April 17, 2006)

A real-life description to me would be a rape victim, brutally raped, savaged. The girl was a virgin. She was religious. She planned on saving her virginity until she was married.
—Republican State Senator Bill Napoli, when asked about any possible exception to the South Dakota law that would have virtually outlawed abortion, Online News Hour, PBS (March 3, 2006)

I know this is painful for the ladies to hear, but if you get married, you have accepted the headship of a man, your husband. Christ is the head of the household and the husband is the head of the wife, and that's the way it is, period.
—Rev. Pat Robertson, *The 700 Club*, CBN (January 8, 1992)

The purported need to provide things for their children simply provides a convenient rationalization for pursuing a gratifying career outside the home.
—U.S. Senator Rick Santorum on working mothers, *It Takes a Family: Conservatism and the Common Good* (2005)

You just have to close your eyes.

—Pennsylvania Governor Tom Corbett, advice to women on an intrusive, trans-vaginal ultrasound procedure he wants to mandate for women seeking an abortion, *Huffington Post* (March 15, 2012.)

THE BEST OF THE OBAMA YEARS AND MORE

2012 Elections

Every week Republicans are excited about a new candidate because the one they liked last week turned out to be a moron.
—Andy Borowitz, Borowitz Report (December 28, 2011)

Every major contender for the 2012 Republican presidential nomination who isn't currently holding office and isn't named Mitt Romney is now a paid contributor to Fox News.
—Paul Krugman, "Fear and Favor," *New York Times* (October 3, 2010)

Romney: Oh Right, Like You're Gonna Vote for the Black Guy.
—Bill Maher, on Romney's probable fall campaign slogan to finally make inroads in the South, "Heard on Late Night Last Week," PhillyBurbs (March 25, 2012)

Romney, Santorum Supporters to Beat Living Shit Out Of Each Other at Montana Primary
—Satirical headline regarding the state's unique primary process, in which the state's delegates are awarded to the winner of a no-holds-barred street fight, *Onion* (March 15, 2012)

About Barack Obama

I suspect the unvarnished hate directed toward Obama, the radical rhetoric behind it . . . is unprecedented for our modern politics.
—Eric Boehlert, "Unhinged in 30 Days: The Right-Wing Media's Obama Era Implosion," Media Matters for America (February 23, 2009)

Whatever policy differences people may have with him, we can all agree that he exemplifies reticence, dispassion and the other traits associated with dignity.
—David Brooks, conservative columnist who treats Obama fairly, "In Search of Dignity," *New York Times* (July 6, 2009)

If Hillary gave up one of her balls and gave it to Obama, he'd have two.
—James Carville, "Obama Needs a Pair," Politico (November 18, 2010)

Obama came to power in circumstances as grim as those that greeted Roosevelt in 1932. But he . . . did not challenge Wall Street's power.
—Nick Cohen, "Pity the Billionaire: The Hard-Times Swindle and the Unlikely Comeback of the Right by Thomas Frank—Review," *Telegraph* (UK) (January 5, 2012)

Obama is head of the dysfunctional family that is America—a rational man running a most irrational nation, a high-minded man in a low-minded age.
—Maureen Dowd, "Going Mad in Herds," *New York Times* (August 21, 2010)

If Barack Obama loses this fall, he will forever seem a disappointment: a symbolically important but accidental figure who raised hopes he could not fulfill and met difficulties he did not know how to surmount.
—James Fallows, "Obama Explained," *Atlantic* (March 2012)

Sometimes it takes a while to recognize that someone has a special ability to get us to believe in ourselves, to tie that belief to our highest ideals, and to imagine that together we can do great things. In those rare moments, when such a person comes along, we need to put aside our plans and reach for what we know is possible.
—Caroline Kennedy, regarding Barack Obama, "A President Like My Father," *New York Times* (January 28, 2008)

His opponents remain filled with a passionate intensity, while his supporters, having received no respect, lack all conviction.
—Paul Krugman, "Krugman: Progressives Wondering, with Friends Like Obama . . ." *Statesman* (July 30, 2010)

Muhammad Ali also had a way with words, but it helped enormously that he could also punch guys in the face.
—Bill Maher, on President Obama's speech-making ability, "New Rule: Float Like Obama, Sting Like Ali," *Huffington Post* (September 11, 2009)

I am proud of you.
—Signed to the president by Stephon Williams, a 26-year-old deaf college student on a rope line at Prince George's Community College in Maryland. Obama reflexively signed back "thank you." "Obama Signs 'Thank You' to Deaf Supporter," ABC News (March 21, 2012)

From his personal life, who he married, how he treats his daughters, he understands that women are absolutely full human beings. He has a good heart, a good mind, treats people with dignity, doesn't court conflict and represents I think the best in this country.
—Gloria Steinem, "Gloria Steinem, In Pro-Obama Video: This Election Is a 'Turning Point,'" *Huffington Post* (March 25, 2012)

The president begins by extending a hand to his opponents; when they respond by raising a fist, he demonstrates that they are the source of the problem; then, finally, he moves to his preferred position of moderate liberalism and fights for it without being effectively tarred as an ideologue or a divider.
—Andrew Sullivan, on Obama's recurring pattern, "Why Are Obama's Critics So Dumb?" *Newsweek* (January 23, 2012)

About Donald Trump

"Trump is a racist": Bob Schieffer Attacks *The Apprentice* Host . . . as Liberals Desert Reality Show in Protest at Anti-Obama Campaign
—Headline, about CBS newsman's reaction to Donald Trump's accusations that Obama could be not qualified to be admitted to Harvard, *Daily Mail* (UK) (April 29, 2011)

Donald Trump is attacking President Obama's background. And I said, "Wait a minute, Trump also is from a mixed background. He's half jack and half ass."
—David Letterman, "Late Night Humor," *Fort Wayne Journal Gazette* (April 23, 2011)

Donald Trump has been saying that he's going to run for president as a Republican—which is surprising, since I just assumed he was running as a joke.
—Seth Myers, at the White House Correspondence Dinner, "Obama Roasts Trump," Daily Beast (May 1, 2011)

Donald Trump is here tonight! Now, I know that he's taken some flak lately, but no one is happier, no one is prouder to put this birth certificate matter to rest than the Donald. And that's because he can finally get back to focusing on the issues that matter—like, did we fake the moon landing?
—Barack Obama at the White House Correspondence Dinner, White House press release (May 1, 2011)

About Mitt Romney

Mitt Romney's campaign might take solace in the fact that "Mormon" is no longer the single most frequently mentioned one-word descriptor for the former Massachusetts governor, but they may bemoan its replacements atop the list: "no" and "rich."
—Peyton M. Craighill and Jon Cohen, "One Word Impressions of GOP Candidates," *Washington Post* (March 22, 2012)

Why do you have Swiss bank account? . . . You want to hide something.
—Sen. Dick Durbin, asking what Romney is concealing in his secret fund, "Barack Obama Campaign Attacks Mitt Romney over Swiss Bank Account," *Huffington Post* (April 9, 2012)

I think you hit a reset button for the fall campaign. Everything changes. It's almost like an Etch a Sketch. You can kind of shake it up and we start all over again.
—Eric Fehrnstrom, Romney advisor inadvertently shedding light on his candidate's lack of core principles, "Mitt Romney Platform 'Like an Etch A Sketch,'" Top Spokesman Says," *Huffington Post* (March 21, 2012)

More than a decade into the war in Afghanistan, GOP presidential candidate Mitt Romney does not have enough information to "take a stand" on whether troops should remain or continue to withdraw on the timetable set by President Obama.
—Ryan Grim, "Mitt Romney Doesn't Have Enough Information to 'Take a Stand' on Afghanistan," *Huffington Post* (March 18, 2012)

Romney Tells "Humorous" Story about Closing a Factory
—Headline, Taegan Goddard's Political Wire (March 28, 2012)

It's a question that has dogged him for years. Why did Mitt Romney once strap the family dog in its carrier to the roof of the car and then set off on a summer vacation to Canada?
—Neil King, "Romney and Seamus the Dog," *Wall Street Journal* (December 21, 2011)

How about Mitt Romney? Now there's a guy who looks like you would see his picture on a package of men's briefs.
—David Letterman, quoted in "Jokes about Willard Romney," Boise Weekly Forum (March 7, 2012)

There are a lot of other people out there that some of us wish had run for president—but they didn't.
—U.S. Senator Marco Rubio, ringing endorsement of Mitt Romney, "Rubio: Obama's Open Mic Gaffe Prompted Timing of Romney Endorsement," Daily Caller (March 29, 2012)

Rick Santorum is the actual guy Romney's pretending to be.
—Jon Stewart, quoted in "Late Night: Jon Stewart Vows to Stop Making 'Santorum' Jokes," *Los Angeles Times* (January 5, 2012)

Happy birthday to Mitt Romney, he's 65 years old. At his party, he didn't blow out the candles. He gave a speech and the candles just flickered and died.
—Jay Leno, *The Tonight Show with Jay Leno*, NBC (March 12, 2012)

Romney is the most radically anti-women candidate in a generation. He supports banning all abortions, backed a so-called "personhood" amendment that could make certain forms of birth control illegal, and says he would "get rid of" federal funding for Planned Parenthood that provides preventive services like cancer screenings for millions of women.
—Jim Messina, campaign letter, Obama for America (April12, 2012)

Republican voters are now the political equivalent of Mitt Romney's famously abused dog Seamus. Mitt has put voters on the roof of his car, and he's driving for the nomination whether they like it or not.
—Robert Shrum, "Mitt Romney Has the GOP Strapped to the Roof of His Car," *This Week* (March 15, 2012)

Mitt Romney is corporate America's 2012 presidential candidate. He's reaped a personal fortune from downsizing U.S. businesses by laying off American workers and outsourcing jobs to third world and other low wage, low labor-standards, low environmental-standards countries.
—Deborah White, "Liberal Guide to Rick Santorum in 2012 Election," About .com (Undated)

About Newt Gingrich

Serial adulterer Newt Gingrich, the former Speaker of the House who openly cheated on his first and second wives, has promised to be faithful to his current wife, a former House committee staff member who slept with him while he was married and criticizing a sitting President for adultery.
—Staff reports, "Serial Adulterer Newt Gingrich Promises, Again, to Not Cheat on His Wife," agreeing for the fourth time in his career to a no-adultery pledge, Capitol Hill Blue (December 13, 2011)

[He is] one of the nastiest, most malignant pieces of work ever to grace American politics. Newt Gingrich extolling the virtues of bipartisanship is like Hannibal Lecter promoting the value of good nutrition.
—Kevin Drum, quoted in "The Wrong Spokesperson for 'Bipartisanship,'" *Washington Monthly* (December 5, 2011)

He's a stupid man's idea of what a smart person sounds like.
—Paul Krugman, *ThisWeek* with Christiane Amanpour, ABC News (November 20, 2011),

6. Do I have to touch him?
5. Is this how Newt met his three wives?
4. Seriously, have I lost my mind?
3. Does Newt have to be in the photo?
2. What would Rick Santorum think of this idea?
1. Will Rush Limbaugh think I'm a slut?
—David Letterman, selected from "Top Ten Questions to Ask Yourself Before Spending $50 on a Photo with Newt Gingrich," quoted in Liberal Values blog (April 3, 2012)

I love people who have three of "the one true faith"!
—Bill Maher, on Newt Gingrich's evolution from Lutheran to Baptist to Catholic, quoted in "Bill Maher Compares Newt Gingrich to 'A Batman Villain' on *Late Late Show*," *Huffington Post* (February 22, 2012)

About Rick Santorum

Giving conservative activists everything they want in a presidential nominee would ultimately be clarifying for the Republican Party . . . There's nothing like losing 40 states to refocus the mind.
—John Avalon, "The Case for Crazy: What the GOP Would Learn by Picking Rick Santorum," The Daily Beast (March 16, 2012)

A new study has confirmed what many in the lesbian, gay, bisexual and transgender (LGBT) community have suspected for some time: that homophobic attitudes are likely to be more pronounced among those who've experienced unacknowledged attraction towards members of the same sex.
—"Homophobic Attitudes Likely to Be Stronger among Those Who Have Repressed Same-Sex Attraction: Report," a likely personality profile of Rick Santorum, *Huffington Post* (April 9, 2012)

Yeah, what a snob. Obama thinks everybody should go to college like he did. Some of us weren't handed a ticket to Harvard by being the biracial son of a single mother on food stamps. Must be nice.
—Stephen Colbert, regarding Rick Santorum calling the president a "snob" for his hope that kids should be able to attend some type of post-secondary institution, "Heard on Late Night," Phillyburbs (March 2, 2012)

Rick Santorum nearly won Ohio, despite a flood of ads that said that Rick Santorum is a creepy, far-right, socially backward extremist—and those were his ads. That's how he sells himself.
—Bill Maher, *Real Time with Bill Maher*, HBO (March 11, 2012)

[Santorum's] so conservative, he won't even shop at a store that has parking in the rear.
—Jay Leno, *The Tonight Show with Jay Leno*, NBC (March 1, 2012)

He's grotesquely self-righteous and humorless . . . [and] is famed for his freakishly extreme feelings on the gay community.
—Deborah White, "Liberal Guide to Rick Santorum in 2012 Election," About. com (Undated)

About Rush Limbaugh

She and I have something in common. We both have been attacked by Rush Limbaugh. She was 30, I was 13.
—Chelsea Clinton, quoted in "Chelsea Clinton, Sandra Fluke Unite over Rush Limbaugh Attacks," ABC News (April 2, 2012). Limbaugh once hosted a television show and said, "Socks is the White House cat. But did you know there is also a White House dog?" He showed a picture of Chelsea. Sandra Fluke is the woman he called a "slut."

Rush Limbaugh Is a Big Fat Idiot and Other Observations
—Al Franken, title of his book (1996)

I would argue that Rush is the leader of the conservative movement in the country.
—Sean Hannity, quoted in "Colbert Calls Hannity's Praise for Rush 'Obsequious Crack-Licking,'" Raw Story (March 6, 2009)

About Sarah Palin

Caribou Barbie is one nutty puppy.
—Maureen Dowd, on Sarah Palin's quitting as governor of Alaska before finishing her first term, "Now, Sarah's Folly," *New York Times* (July 4, 2009)

Sarah Palin is . . . the mother of stupid conservatism.
—Maureen Dowd, "Egghead and Blockheads," *New York Times* (September 17, 2011)

I can see Russia from my house!
—Tina Fey, impersonating Sarah Palin, *Saturday Night Live*, NBC (September 13, 2008)

And, you know, politics aside, the success of Sarah Palin and women like her is good for all women—except, of course—those who will end up, you know, like, paying for their own rape kit 'n' stuff, But for everybody else, it's a win-win. Unless you're a gay woman who wants to marry your partner of 20 years—whatever. But for most women, the success of conservative women is good for all of us. Unless you believe in evolution. You know—actually, I take it back. The whole thing's a disaster.
—Tina Fey, accepting the Mark Twain Award, "Tina Fey's Controversial Speech Edited by PBS," *Hollywood Reporter* (November 16, 2010)

According to expense reports, Sarah Palin charged the state of Alaska over $21,000 for her children to travel with her on official business. In fairness to Gov. Palin, when she leaves them home alone, they get pregnant.
—Seth Meyers, quoted in "Top 10 Reasons Sarah Palin's Outrage is a Little Late . . ." *Alaska Report* (June 14, 2009)

He was a great man and you are a nincompoop.
—Peggy Noonan, Reagan's speechwriter on Sarah Palin's claim that she's modeled herself in Ronald Reagan's image, "Peggy Noonan: Sarah Palin a 'Nincompoop' for Reagan Reduction," *Huffington Post* (May 25, 2011)

I will show you President Obama's birth certificate when you show me Sarah Palin's high school diploma.
—Bill Maher, quoted in "Best Bill Maher Quotes Ever," About.com (January 20, 2011)

America

America! America! God shed His grace on thee,
And crown thy good with brotherhood
From sea to shining sea!
—Katharine Lee Bates, feminist and lesbian poet, "America the Beautiful," *The Congregationalist* (1895)

Oh Beautiful for smoggy skies, insecticided grain,
For strip-mined mountain's majesty above the asphalt plain.
America, America, man sheds his waste on thee,
And hides the pines with billboard signs, from sea to oily sea.
—George Carlin, parody of "America the Beautiful" quoted in *Food, Inc.: The Silence of the Yams*, *Huffington Post* (June 10, 2009)

As nightfall does not come all at once, neither does oppression.
—Supreme Court Justice William O. Douglas, quoted in *The End of America* (2007)

America has core values. Those core values include helping others in need, caring for the sick, making sure that everyone is equal under the law, fairness, and making sure everyone has the right to privacy and personal liberty.
—Stephen D. Foster, Jr., liberal preamble to "40 Quotes Demonstrating the Conservative Values Republicans Want to Destroy America with," Addicting Info (April 3, 2012)

We have become a society that can't self-correct, that can't address its obvious problems, that can't pull out of its nosedive . . . We have entered an age of folly.
—Thomas Frank, "How Americans Have Gotten Played—Over and Over and Over Again," AlterNet (March 28, 2012)

New Rule: America must stop bragging it's the greatest country on earth, and start acting like it.
—Bill Maher, *The New New Rules: A Funny Look at How Everybody But Me Has Their Head Up Their Ass* (2011)

We do have two Americas. We have the America that's living in reality. The people who understand that Obama is a centrist liberal from Hawaii who is trying to dig us out of the hole we're in. And then we have this other FOX/ Matt Drudge/Rush Limbaugh reality where he is a Muslim sleeper cell, Manchurian candidate who was sent over by his Kenyan father.
—Bill Maher, interviewed on *Larry King Live* (September 14, 2010)

In this country, broad-based prosperity has never trickled down from the success of a wealthy few. It has always come from the success of a strong and growing middle class.
—Barack Obama, "Obama Takes on Republicans over Tax Fairness," Reuters (UK) (April 3, 2012)

We live in the middle of an American paradox. We can put a black man in the White House, but we can't walk a black child through a gated neighborhood.
—Reverend Al Sharpton, on the shooting of unarmed Trayvon Martin, "This Is Not about a Hoodie," *The Patriot-News* (April 1, 2012)

Big Banks

Bankers Form Super PAC: A New Vortex of Evil Opens in Fabric of the Universe
—Headline, AlterNet (April 5, 2012)

The captains of high finance are demanding that we reduce public debt, which we ran up to bail them out . . . That takes a lot of nerve. First they crash the system and run away with a fat pocket of cash. Then they demand that we clean up our financial act or they won't loan out any money.
—Les Leopold, "Why the Wall Street-BP Double Standard?" *Huffington Post* (June 25, 2010)

If enough people who have money in one of the Big Six banks—that is, JP Morgan/Chase, Citi, Wells Fargo, Bank of America, Morgan Stanley, and Goldman Sachs—move it into a local community bank or credit union, then collectively we, the people, will have taken a big step toward fixing our broken financial system.
—Bill Maher, "Stop the Abuse: It's Time to Break Up with Your Big Bank," *Huffington Post* (January 13, 2010)

Pull your money out of one of the big, risk-taking, profit-driven corporate banks whose speculation helped ruin our economy, and put it in a nonprofit, community-minded credit union. No outrageous debit fees. No sneaky other fees inserted insidiously into the fine print.
—Will Oremus, on the national movement started by Kristen Christian, "Should You Transfer Your Money to a Credit Union?" *Slate* (November 7, 2011)

In a year's time, we may look back at Bank Transfer Day [November 5th] as a landmark event.
—Justine Rivero, a call to action for consumers to switch from large banks to not-for-profit credit unions, "Will Bank Transfer Day Really Change Anything?" *Forbes* (November 4, 2011)

Incredibly, three out of the four largest financial institutions are bigger today than before the financial crisis started. Today, the four largest banks in America issue two-thirds of all credit cards and about half of all mortgages.
—U.S. Sen. Bernie Sanders, why we must break up "too-big-to-fail" financial institutions, "Time to Save the Middle Class," *In These Times* (May 18, 2010)

Birth Control

Religious freedom means I get to chose whether or not to be religious and if so, how. It does not mean that I get to impose my religion on others.
—Soraya Chemaly, on banning insurance for contraceptives for religious reasons, "10 Reasons the Rest of the World Thinks the U.S. Is Nuts," *Huffington Post* (March15, 2012)

This is America. We must defend the principles symbolized by Lady Liberty—unless she's on the pill, in which case, she is a giant green tramp.
—Stephen Colbert, quoted in the Liberal Values blog (March 19, 2012)

The attacks on birth control are demonstrable proof that the religious right, including the Republican presidential candidates, intends, at root, to re-impose archaic sexual mores and roll back the clock on women's equality.
—Emily Douglas, "Women's Rights, Another Round of Defensive Victories," *The Nation* (March 16, 2012)

Attacking me and women who use contraception by calling us prostitutes and worse cannot silence us.
—Sandra Fluke, in an opinion piece responding to Rush Limbaugh, "Sandra Fluke: Slurs Won't Silence Women," CNN (March 14, 2012)

More and more American pharmacists are refusing to fill prescriptions for birth control because of their personal moral objections. Hey, you know what would really teach us a lesson? If you took off your pretend doctor jacket and got another job.
—Bill Maher, quoted in "Bill Maher Takes Down Fundie Pharmacists," Democratic Underground (April 2004)

Keep Your Mitt(s) Off My Birth Control!
—National Abortion Rights Action League protest sign outside a hotel in Washington, D.C., where Mitt Romney was holding a fundraiser, photo in *In These Times* (March 22, 2012)

A photo of a shirtless Rick Santorum lounging in a pool is circulating on the Internet. Ironically, the photo has proven to be a very effective form of birth control.
—Conan O'Brien, "Heard on Late Night Last Week," PhillyBurbs (March 25, 2012)

Birther Conspiracy

Here's how transparently loony the whole thing is. There's not only the Hawaii birth certificate that marks Obama's birth (although birthers claim it's a forgery). There are also the real-time, 1961 birth announcements printed up in *The Honolulu Advertiser* and the *Honolulu Star-Bulletin*.
—Eric Boehlert, Obama's family presumably planted these announcements just in case he was to someday run for president, "Crazy 'Birther' Conspiracy Theories Get Boost in Mainstream Media," AlterNet (July 24, 2009)

Obama Gives Hanukkah Wishes in Hebrew; Birthers Now Claim He Was Born in Israel
—Andy Borowitz, satirical headline, *Huffington Post* (December 11, 2009)

These people could have personally witnessed Obama being born out of an apple pie, in the middle of a Kansas wheat field, while Toby Keith sang the National Anthem—and they'd still think he was a Kenyan Muslim.
—Jimmy Kimmel, "Top 10 Jokes about Obama's Birth Certificate," About. com (Undated)

It's fine to disagree with Obama on policy. Trying to delegitimize his ability to even hold the office is simply a way of tacitly pandering to the worst racist impulses.
—Brian Lowry, "Fox News' Shep Smith Unloads on Birther Lunacy," *Variety* (April 27, 2009)

BP Gulf Oil Disaster

Fishermen are out of work; shrimp and oyster harvest numbers are way down; marine mammals, especially dolphins, wash in on a daily basis, dead; Gulf fish with lesions consistent with exposure to oil toxins are increasing rapidly . . .
—Jonathan Henderson, "BP [British Petroleum] Oil Disaster: People Still Reeling from Impacts," Aljazeera (March 28, 2012)

Have you been following the big oil spill in the Gulf of Mexico? Or as we call it now, the Dead Sea.
—David Letterman, quoted in "Late-Night Jokes about the BP Oil Spill Disaster in the Gulf," About.com (Undated)

This oil spill is the worst environmental disaster America has ever faced.
—Barack Obama, White House press release (June 15, 2010)

The BP oil "spill." . . . And by the way can we please stop calling it that? A spill
is what happens when the cat knocks over your coffee. Whoops, kitty! What's
going on in the gulf is a disaster.
—Katha Politt, "The BP Oil Disaster: Bringing it All Back Home," *The Nation*
(June 4, 2010)

Buffett Rule

Frankly an economy where my receptionist pays a lot higher tax rate than I do
does not strike me as a just economy.
—Warren Buffett, quoted in "Bill Gates' Dad Wants Him to Pay More Taxes,"
Daily Finance (March 11, 2009)

Explaining a tax code that allows the wealthiest to escape their responsibility
is getting much harder to do.
—Editorial, "Turning the 'Buffett Rule' Into Law," *New York Times* (January 31,
2012)

We don't envy success in this country. We aspire to it. But we also believe that
anyone who does well for themselves should do their fair share in return.
—Barack Obama, "Obama Pushes Lawmakers to Pass 'Buffett Rule' Tax," *Slate*
(March 31, 2012)

Pay A Fair Share Act
—Senator Sheldon Whitehouse, introduced this bill in the U.S. Senate that
would require Americans earning over a million dollars a year to pay at least
a 30 percent effective tax rate, "Buffett Rule Bill Introduced to US Senate,"
News.com.au (February 2, 2012)

Bullies

Based upon the collective behavior of far-right conservative Republicans, we
can only deduce that a considerable number of them are bullies and ought to
be treated as such.
—Bob Cesca, "Right-Wing Bullies Continue to Attack Children," *Huffington
Post* (March 2012)

We are the party that believes we can't let the strong kick aside the weak.
—George McGovern, *What It Means to Be a Democrat* (2011)

Bullies—political bullies, economic bullies, and religious bullies—cannot be appeased; they have to be opposed with courage, clarity, and conviction. This is never easy. These true believers don't fight fair. Robert's Rules of Order is not one of their holy texts.
—Bill Moyers, "Reckoning with the God Squad," *In These Times* (September 24, 2005)

Children are still dying at the hands of bullying.
—Marlo Thomas, "Bully: The Year's Most Important Film," *Huffington Post* (March 29, 2012)

Child Poverty

They have sold food stamps, sold blood, skipped meals, shoplifted, doubled up with friends, scavenged trash bins for bottles and cans and returned to relationships with violent partners—all with children in tow.
—Jason DeParle, what desperate single mothers are forced to do since being dropped from cash assistance in Arizona, "Welfare Limits Left Poor Adrift as Recession Hit," *New York Times* (April 8, 2012)

It is easier to build strong children than to repair broken men.
—Frederick Douglass, "It Is Easier to Build Strong Children Than to Repair Broken Men," *Courier* (February 14, 2012)

Most people who get [food stamps] use them up in the first two weeks of a month, and many turn to food banks by month's end. Cutting benefits so sharply would lead to a significant increase in hunger, particularly among children.
—Editorial, on House Republicans' budget that would cut $90 worth of food a month for a struggling family of four, "A Cruel Budget," *New York Times* (March 29, 2012)

Among the world's advanced nations, we are number one in child poverty.
—Diane Ravitch, "In Defense of Facing Reality," *Huffington Post* (March 18, 2012)

Food stamps the only thing standing between your children and starvation? Listen, we feel your pain. We get it. But we've got more important things to spend money on. Like a new yacht for that guy who only has one yacht.
—Katrina vanden Heuvel, mimicking the GOP, "Republicans Are Causing a Moral Crisis in America," *Washington Post* (March 27, 2012)

Uncovering Kids: 89,000 Poor Pa. Kids Slashed from Medicaid
—Headline, on Republican Governor Corbett's heartless decision to cut poor children from coverage without notice, many with critical health conditions, *Philadelphia Daily News* (April3, 2012)

Citizens United v. Federal Election Commission

[Citizens United] is a major victory for big oil, Wall Street banks, health insurance companies and the other powerful interests that marshal their power every day in Washington to drown out the voices of everyday Americans.
—Barack Obama, quoted in "Justices, 5-4, Reject Corporate Spending Limits," *New York Times* (January 21, 2010)

Rarely have so few imposed such damage on so many.
—Bill Moyers, forward to *Corporations Are Not People* (2012)

Very few believe a corporation is a person, which is what the Supreme Court said in Citizens United. If we do not turn this thing around, you're going to be living in a country where a handful of billionaires and large corporations will be determining who our elected officials are.
—U.S. Sen. Bernie Sanders, quoted in "Super PACs Gone Wild: This Is 'Tip of the Iceberg' If Citizens United Isn't Overturned, Sen. Sanders Warns," Daily Ticker (March 9, 2012)

The rights protected by the Constitution of the United States are the rights of natural persons and do not extend to for-profit corporations, limited liability companies, or other private entities established for business purposes.
—U.S. Sen. Bernie Sanders, from the Saving American Democracy Amendment he introduced, DemocracyIsForPeople.org (Undated)

If our current campaign finance system isn't corrupt, what is? A handful of billionaires can decide who the next president will be.
—Josh Silver, "Citizens United Revisited? Buckle Up, Chief Justice Roberts," *Huffington Post* (February 17, 2012)

While American democracy is imperfect, few outside the majority of this court would have thought its flaws included a dearth of corporate money in politics.
—Supreme Court Justice John Paul Stevens, writing for the dissenters, "Citizens United Decision: 'A Rejection of the Common Sense of the American People,'" Think Progress (January 21, 2010)

There's one word to describe what's going on in the campaign-finance area: The word is "obscene." And it's going to result in scandal and corruption and, eventually, opportunities for reform.
—Fred Wertheimer, president of Democracy 21, a campaign-finance watchdog group, quoted in "Super-PACs and Dark Money: ProPublica's Guide to the New World of Campaign Finance," ProPublica (July 11, 2011)

Climate Change

The defining challenge of our age is to safeguard Earth's natural processes to ensure the well being of civilization.
—Lidia Brito and Mark Stafford Smith, co-chairs of Planet Under Pressure conference, quoted in "Time Is Nigh for Global Action, Manifesto Warns," *New York Times* (March 29, 2012)

Accelerated climate change, driven by human activity, has led to soaring temperatures around the world and the decade between 2001 and 2010 was the warmest ever recorded.
—Common Dreams staff, "Earth Sends Climate Warning by Busting World Heat Records," Common Dreams (March 24, 2010)

Everyone should know the basics: the Earth is heating up because gases produced from vehicles, power plants, deforestation, and other sources are building up in the atmosphere, acting like a thick blanket over our planet.
—"Facts about Climate Change," Nature Conservancy (April 23, 2011)

The United States contains only 5 percent of the world's population, but contributes 22 percent of the world's carbon emissions.
—"Facts about Climate Change," Nature Conservancy (April 23, 2011)

Here is the truth: the Earth is round; Saddam Hussein did not attack us on 9/11; Elvis is dead; Obama was born in the United States; and the climate crisis is real.
—Al Gore, "Al Gore: Climate of Denial," *Rolling Stone* (June 22, 2011)

We are destroying the climate balance that is essential to the survival of our civilization. This is not a distant or abstract threat; it is happening now.
—Al Gore, "Al Gore: Climate of Denial," *Rolling Stone* (June 22, 2011)

This is the moment when we must come together to save this planet. Let us resolve that we will not leave our children a world where the oceans rise and famine spreads and terrible storms devastate our lands.
—Barack Obama, quoted in "Obama Speech: 'We Must Come Together to Save Planet,'" *Independent* (UK) (July 25, 2008)

Conservative Angst

There will be no dynamic, charismatic, Reaganesque Republican presidential nominee this cycle. There won't even be a consistent conservative. There will only be Mitt Romney.
—Charles Blow, "It's Mitt! Oh No," *New York Times* (April 4, 2012)

There's nothing that Democrats can do to satisfy movement conservatives.
—E. J. Dionne, quoted in "The Attack on Liberal Legitimacy," *The Nation* (March 30, 2012)

Conservatives are unhappy because they prefer passive, intimidated liberals to the fighting kind.
—E. J. Dionne, "When Liberals Stop Being Wimps," Truthdig (April 8, 2012)

If conservatives don't want to be seen as bitter people who cling to their guns and religion and anti-immigrant sentiments, they should stop being bitter and clinging to their guns, religion and anti-immigrant sentiments.
—Bill Maher, "For Republicans, Breaking Up is Hard to Do," *Los Angeles Times* (April 24, 2009)

The healthy thing to do is to just get past it and learn to cherish the memories. You'll always have New Orleans and Abu Ghraib.
—Bill Maher, advice to conservatives who will never accept the election of President Obama, "For Republicans, Breaking Up is Hard to Do," *Los Angeles Times* (April 24, 2009)

If it's any consolation, the thieves who run the health insurance companies will still get to deny coverage to adults with pre-existing conditions for the next four years.
—Michael Moore, on the phasing in of Obamacare, "The Great Thing about the Health Care Law That Has Passed? It Will Save Republican Lives, Too," *Huffington Post* (March 22, 2010)

Corporate Control

The corporation is designed to make money without regard to human life, the social good or impact on the environment.
—Chris Hedges, *Empire of Illusion* (2010)

Corporations have intruded into every facet of life. We eat corporate food. We buy corporate clothes. We drive corporate cars. We buy our vehicular fuel and our heating oil from corporations. We borrow from corporate banks. We invest our retirement savings with corporations . . . They are vampires.
—Chris Hedges, "Why I Am a Socialist," Truthdig (December 29, 2008)

If some company is too big to fail, then it's too big to exist. Break it up.
—Bob Herbert, "Safety Nets for the Rich," *New York Times* (October 19, 2009)

Corporations have effectively captured the United States: its judiciary, its political system, and its national wealth, without assuming any of the responsibilities of dominion. Evidence is everywhere.
—Robert A. G. Monks, "The Corporate Capture of the United States," Harvard Law School Forum on Corporate Governance and Financial Regulation (January 5, 2012)

During the same period that CEOs were doubling their own compensation, the "best" CEOs of the "best" companies abrogated the century-old commitment by employers to provide pensions to their workers.
—Robert A. G. Monks, "The Corporate Capture of the United States," Harvard Law School Forum on Corporate Governance and Financial Regulation (January 5, 2012)

Democratic Wing of the Democratic Party

What unites us is our desire to propel our great country onward by meeting the needs of the many, not of the few. A bedrock principle for Democrats is that we bring everyone along.
—George McGovern, *What It Means to Be a Democrat* (2011)

Above all, being a Democrat means having compassion for others. It means putting the government to work for the people who need it.
—George McGovern, *What It Means to Be a Democrat* (2011)

We seek to build a party and government controlled by citizens, not corporate elites—with policies that serve the broad public interest, not just private interests.
—Progressive Democrats of America website (Undated)

You've got to be [an] optimist to be a Democrat, and you've got to be a humorist to remain one.
—Will Rogers, quoted in *Herding Donkeys* (2010)

The freedom to live your life on terms you establish does not mean very much if society is organized in such a way as to deny large numbers of people the possibility of ever realizing that objective.
—Alan Wolfe, *The Future of Liberalism* (2009)

Environmental Abuse

The notion that we can take and take and take and take, waste and waste, without consequences, is driving the biosphere to destruction.
—Ray Anderson, quoted in "Why I Am a Socialist," Truthdig (December 29, 2008)

Nature-Deficit Disorder
—Headline about the increasing disconnect between people and their environment, including the sharp drop in time kids spend outdoors, *New York Times* (March 29, 2012)

What's the use of a fine house if you haven't got a tolerable planet to put it on?
—Henry David Thoreau, *Familiar Letters of Henry David Thoreau* (1894)

The magnificence of mountains, the serenity of nature—nothing is safe from the idiot marks of man's passing.
—Loudon Wainwright, quoted in *Living Green* (2008)

If we continue felling the forests, polluting the earth, and using up all the water, our grandchildren won't have much of a planet left.
—Chip Ward, "50 Years from Now, What Will the World Be Like?" *Mother Jones* (March 27, 2012)

False Equivalency between Left and Right

Here's a real world example of the danger inherent in taking this shortsighted "both sides" view of the political spectrum. Ten years ago, the course of American history was irreversibly skewed, partly because too many liberals believed that Al Gore and George W. Bush were equally as lame.
—Bob Cesca, "Killing the False Equivalency 'Both Sides' Meme," *Huffington Post* (September 29, 2010)

Listen to Rachel Maddow or Keith Olbermann, and you'll hear a lot of caustic remarks and mockery aimed at Republicans. But you won't hear jokes about shooting government officials or beheading a journalist at The Washington Post. Listen to Glenn Beck or Bill O'Reilly, and you will.
—Paul Krugman, "Climate of Hate," *New York Times* (January 9, 2011)

With all due respect to my friends Jon Stewart and Stephen Colbert, it seems to me that if you truly wanted to come down on the side of restoring sanity and reason, you'd side with the sane and reasonable—and not try to pretend the insanity is equally distributed in both parties.
—Bill Maher, *The New New Rules: A Funny Look at How Everybody But Me Has Their Head Up Their Ass* (2011)

The danger of political violence in this country comes overwhelmingly from one direction—the right, not the left. The vitriolic, anti-government hate speech that is spewed on talk radio every day—and, quite regularly, at Tea Party rallies—is calibrated not to inform but to incite.
—Eugene Robinson, "The Hutaree Militia and the Rising Risk of Far-Right Violence," *Washington Post* (March 30, 2010)

Lefties aren't running around shooting people. When was the last time a bleeding-heart liberal went out and killed someone?
—Devona Walker, "In Rhetoric Debate, Media Creates a False Equivalency between Right and Left," AlterNet (January 11, 2011)

God Help Us

Don't tell me you're a Christian. Let me figure it out.
—Anonymous

People see God every day, they just don't recognize him.
—Pearl Bailey, quoted in "Women's History," About.com (Undated)

We are more than cells, synapses and sex drives. We are amazing, mysterious creatures forever in search of something greater than ourselves.
—Charles M. Blow, "Defecting to Faith," *New York Times* (May 1, 2009)

I am at peace with God. My conflict is with Man.
—Charlie Chaplin, quoted in *The Politics of Life* (2012)

The God of the Old Testament is arguably the most unpleasant character in all fiction.
—Richard Dawkins, *The God Delusion* (2006)

You are free to believe that salvation comes only through faith in Jesus Christ and to order your behavior accordingly. You are not free to coerce others, either by physical force or the force of law, to share your faith and behave as you do.
—Stanley Fish, "Religion and the Liberal State Once Again," *New York Times* (November 1, 2010)

The belief that there is an unseen order, and that our supreme good lies in harmoniously adjusting ourselves thereto.
—William James, his definition of religious experience, *TheVarieties of Religious Experience* (1902)

I think the creativity in nature is so stunning and so overwhelming that it's God enough for me.
—Stuart Kauffman, *Atoms and Eden: Conversations on Religion and Science* (2010)

I understand where Bill Maher is coming from when he says, basically, the world is destroying itself over a bunch of fairy tales about talking snakes and men who are alive inside fishes. I'm very sympathetic to it, but at the same time, given the cosmos that we're living in, it's very persuasive, the idea that there is some kind of first cause that's running things.
—Stephen King, interviewed in "Stephen King's God Trip," Salon (October 23, 2008)

We must question the story logic of having an all-knowing all-powerful God, who creates faulty Humans, and then blames them for his own mistakes.
—Gene Roddenberry, quoted in "101 Atheist Quotes," Best Article of the Day (Undated)

No human being escapes the necessity of conceiving some good outside himself towards which his thought turns in a movement of desire, supplication, and hope. Consequently, the only choice is between worshipping the true God or an idol.
—Simone Weil, *The Notebooks of SimoneWeil* (2004)

GOP

The Republicans talk more about the market than about society, more about income than quality of life. They celebrate capitalism, which is a means, and are inarticulate about the good life, which is the end.
—David Brooks, "The Long Journey Home," *NewYork Times* (May 4, 2009)

The new Republicans are utopians, who reacted to a crisis of capitalism by arguing that the fault the calamity revealed was not that America was too capitalist but that it was not capitalist enough.
—Nick Cohen, "Pity the Billionaire: The Hard-Times Swindle and the Unlikely Comeback of the Right by Thomas Frank—Review," *Telegraph* (UK) (January 5, 2012)

The Republicans are now the "How great is it to be stupid?" party.
—Maureen Dowd, "Egghead and Blockheads," *New York Times* (September 17, 2011)

Republicans have a wicked plan for America. They plan to wipe out women's rights. They plan to restrict voting rights. They plan to legalize discrimination against homosexuals and ethnic minorities. They plan to wage endless wars in the name of religious extremism. They plan to eliminate Medicare, Medicaid, Social Security and public education.
—Stephen D. Foster, Jr., "40 Quotes Demonstrating the Conservative Values Republicans Want to Destroy America with," Addicting Info (April 3, 2012)

Republicans originally thought that Fox worked for us and now we're discovering we work for Fox.
—David Frum, former speechwriter to George W. Bush, "David Frum on GOP: Now We Work for Fox," ABC News (March 23, 2010)

I've been watching the Republican debates. I watched these eight clowns on the stage and at the end I wanted to raise my hand and say, "I don't believe in evolution."
—Bill Maher, quoted in "Late-Night Comics' Jokes about Republican Presidential Candidates," *Los Angeles Times* (November 12, 2011)

Their philosophy is simple: you're on your own.
—Barack Obama, quoted in "Obama Blasts GOP 'You're on Your Own Economics,'"Yahoo News (March 30, 2012)

It's not news that the GOP is the anti-abortion party, that it panders to the religious right, and that it's particularly dependent on white men with less education and less income—a displaced demographic that has been as threatened by the rise of the empowered modern woman as it has been by the cosmopolitan multiracial male elites symbolized by Barack Obama.
—Frank Rich, "Stag Party," *New York Magazine* (March 25, 2012)

The GOP has defined itself indelibly as the party of moneyed greed and unfettered imperialism.
—Robert Scheer, "Obama by Default," Common Dream (April 5, 2012)

You have to wonder how it is that the party the Creationists call home is so Darwinian!
—Jon Stewart, quoted in "Jon Stewart Mocks Health Care Reform Hearings with Taiwanese Animation of Supreme Court," *Huffington Post* (March 30, 2012)

You guys [GOP voters] need to take a long hard look in the mirror, and not come away thinking, "You know, there's something wrong with this mirror."
—Jon Stewart, quoted in "Best Jokes about the 2012 GOP Candidates," About.com (Undated)

There is a moral crisis in this country. A horrifyingly, back-breaking, bankrupt-the-core-of-this-nation style crisis. But it isn't women or the poor or the middle class or the gay community or health-care advocates or environmentalists that are causing it. It's you.
—Katrina vanden Heuvel, "Republicans Are Causing a Moral Crisis in America," *Washington Post* (March 27, 2012)

The Great Recession

Considering what conservatives allowed financial markets to do, the fact that the right could be furious with anyone but itself is an astonishing story.
—Nick Cohen, "Pity the Billionaire: The Hard-Times Swindle and the Unlikely Comeback of the Right by Thomas Frank—Review," *Telegraph* (UK) (January 5, 2012)

Democrats did not tell the angry public why their system had run aground and offer an alternative. They allowed the right a free run.
—Nick Cohen, "Pity the Billionaire: The Hard-Times Swindle and the Unlikely Comeback of the Right by Thomas Frank—Review," *Telegraph* (UK) (January 5, 2012)

If ever a financial order deserved a 30s-style repudiation, this one did. Its gods were false. Its taste was bad. Its heroes were oafs and brutes and thieves and bullies. And all of them failed, even on their own stunted terms.
—Thomas Frank, *Pity the Billionaire* (2009)

Americans are learning anew from the financial crisis why it is a mistake to let private firms concentrate more and more power under one management. The failure of megabanks that the government helped create threatens our general well-being, and then government bails them out with taxpayer money because they are "too big to fail."
—William Greider, "The Future of the American Dream," *The Nation* (May 6, 2009)

We must never forget that this economic crisis was caused by the greed, recklessness and illegal behavior of a handful of executives on Wall Street.
—U.S. Sen. Bernie Sanders, "Time to Save the Middle Class," *In These Times* (May 18, 2010)

Guns and Ammo

The "Stand Your Ground" law is a license to kill.
—Former U.S. Attorney Kendall Coffey, on the Florida law that encouraged the killing of Trayvon Martin by a neighborhood gunman, "How ALEC Took Florida's 'License to Kill' Law National," *The Nation* (March 21, 2012)

There is a serious trend toward states letting their residents carry concealed weapons with no more background check than you need to carry a concealed nutcracker.
—Gail Collins, "More Guns, Fewer Hoodies," *New York Times* (March 28, 2012)

There is no way to overstate the horror of gun violence in America. Roughly 16,000 to 17,000 Americans are murdered every year.
—Bob Herbert, "A Culture Soaked in Blood," *New York Times* (April 24, 2009)

Why don't gun buyers have to follow the same rules women are forced to follow? Wait 48 hours after applying. View on ultrasound of a body with a bullet in it. Listen to the heartbeat of someone as they die of a gunshot wound. Get a lecture from a surgeon on what it is like to operate on a gunshot wound. After all that, if a person still wants a gun, he or she can buy one. Why should buying a gun be any easier than having an abortion?
—Linda from Oklahoma, responding to Gail Collin's analysis of events related to the murder of Trayvon Martin, "Best Comment of the Year," Daily Kos (March 29, 2012)

Is the NRA advocating for people who own guns? Or the lucrative companies that make them?

—Siddhartha Mahanta, "Who Does the NRA Advocate for?" *Mother Jones* (January,19, 2011)

You know what they cannot keep on the shelves in America? Guns, and ammo. Even though Obama and every other pussy Democrat has never even mentioned the issue, these people are . . . sure that he and his Negro army are coming for their guns.

—Bill Maher, "But I'm Not Wrong," HBO (February 14, 2010)

Hillary Clinton

I suppose I could have stayed home and baked cookies and had teas, but what I decided to do was to fulfill my profession which I entered before my husband was in public life.

—Hillary Clinton, quoted in "The Great Bush-Kerry Bake-off," *Boston Globe* (July 11, 2004)

In the Bible it says they asked Jesus how many times you should forgive, and he said 70 times 7. Well, I want you all to know that I'm keeping a chart.

—Hillary Clinton, quoted in "Women's History," About.com (Undated)

Life is too short, time is too precious, and the stakes are too high to dwell on what might have been. We have to work together for what still can be.

—Hillary Clinton, Clinton [presidential] concession speech, *Huffington Post* (June 15, 2008)

Gay rights are human rights.

—Hillary Clinton, quoted in *The Week* (December 10, 2011)

You cannot have maternal health without reproductive health. And reproductive health includes contraception and family planning and access to legal, safe abortion.

—Hillary Clinton, quoted in "Planned Parenthood's Canadian Funding Renewed," CBC News (September 22, 2011)

LGBT

Pray the gay away.
—ABC News' apt description of the misguided Christian counseling clinic owned by Republican Congressman Michele and Marcus Bachmann, "Marcus Bachmann Prays the Gay Away," Salon (July 13, 2011)

The male party line concerning Lesbians is that women become Lesbians out of reaction to men. This is a pathetic illustration of the male ego's inflated proportions. I became a Lesbian because of women.
—Rita Mae Brown, quoted in *Out of the Closets: Voices of Gay Liberation* (1992)

Gay people don't actually try to convert people. That's Jehovah's Witnesses you're thinking of.
—Tina Fey, *Bossypants* (2011)

There are so many Republicans in the closet, their symbol shouldn't be an elephant; it should be a moth.
—Bill Maher, *The New New Rules: A Funny Look at How Everybody But Me Has Their Head Up Their Ass* (2011)

Let's make a law that gay people can have birthdays, but straight people get more cake—you know, to send the right message to kids.
—Bill Maher, "Valentine's Day, That Great State Holiday," *Boston Globe* (February 14, 2004)

No matter how I look at the issue, I cannot escape being troubled by the fact that we have in place a policy which forces young men and women to lie about who they are in order to defend their fellow citizens.
—Admiral Mike Mullen, Chairman of the Joint Chiefs of Staff, quoted in "Top Defense Officials Seek to End 'Don't Ask, Don't Tell,'" law, *New York Times* (February 2, 2010)

Religion is far more of a choice than homosexuality . . . . Gay people do not choose to be gay. At what age did you decide not to be gay?
—Jon Stewart, debating Mike Huckabee, *The Daily Show*, Comedy Central (December 9, 2008)

Bisexuality immediately doubles your chances for a date on Saturday night.
—T-shirt

OK4U2BGAY
—T-shirt to fight homophobia featured in *Huffington Post*'s "The Best Gay Moments of the Week," (March 17, 2012)

Liberal Theology

The founders of the republic were Enlightenment thinkers, and in large part philosophically and theologically liberal.
—John M. Buchanan, "Mislabeled," *Christian Century* (October 7, 2008)

I may not believe as Jesus did, but I should dearly hope to love as Jesus did, to forgive and embrace others as unconditionally as he.
—Rev. Forrest Church, *Bringing God Home: A Traveler's Guide* (2002)

Jesus would Occupy.
—Alan Minsky, on a social movement committed to serving the poor and needy, "Would Jesus Occupy?" Common Dreams (April 8, 2012)

In reality, there are no biblical literalists, only selective literalists. By abolishing slavery and ordaining women, millions of Protestants have gone far beyond biblical literalism. It's time we did the same for homophobia.
—Rev. William Sloane Coffin, quoted in "The Rev. William Sloane Coffin on Homosexuality," Democratic Underground (February 15, 2005)

For Christians, the problem is not how to reconcile homosexuality with scriptural passages that condemn it, but how to reconcile the rejection and punishment of homosexuals with the love of Christ.
—Rev. William Sloane Coffin, quoted in "Pre-Inaugural Memo to Rev. Rick Warren: Read Rev. William Sloane," *Huffington Post* (December 19, 2008)

If this is going to be a Christian nation that doesn't help the poor, either we have to pretend that Jesus was just as selfish as we are, or we've got to acknowledge that He commanded us to love the poor and serve the needy without condition and then admit that we just don't want to do it.
—Stephen Colbert, quoted in "Colbert Follows O'Reilly's Logic: 'We've Got to Pretend Jesus Was Just as Selfish as We Are,'" Crooks and Liars (December 20, 2010)

Go. Sell what you own, and give the money to the poor.
—Mark 10:21

Do not judge, so that you may not be judged.
—Matthew 7:1

Whatsoever you do for the least of My people, that you do unto Me.
—Matthew 25:40

Any religion that professes to be concerned about the souls of men and is not concerned about the slums that damn them, the economic conditions that strangle them, and the social conditions that cripple them is a spiritually moribund religion awaiting burial.
—Rev. Scotty McLennan, *Jesus Was a Liberal* (2009)

I believe that Jesus was a religious liberal . . . Instead of an eye for an eye, he asked for us to turn the other cheek. Instead of just loving our neighbors, we were called upon to love our enemies too.
—Rev. Scotty McLennan, *Jesus Was a Liberal* (2009)

Listlessly Liberal

There is no Left left in America. There is only the moderate Right, which is most Democrats, and the merged Religious/Financial Right, which is most Republicans.
—Walter Ellis, "There Is No Proper Left in American Politics—Even Obama Is More Right-Wing Than Cameron," *Telegraph* (UK) (March 7, 2012)

Genteel liberals have allowed American conservatives to all but monopolize political fury since the banks went down.
—Nick Cohen, "Pity the Billionaire: The Hard-Times Swindle and the Unlikely Comeback of the Right by Thomas Frank—Review," *Telegraph* (UK) (January 5, 2012)

The liberal class . . . proclaims its adherence to traditional liberal values while defending and promoting systems of power that mock these values. The pillars of the liberal establishment—the press, the church, culture, the university, labor and the Democratic Party—all honor an unwritten quid pro quo with corporations and the power elite.
—Chris Hedges, "Why Liberals Attack Progressive Heroes Like Cornel West," AlterNet (May 25, 2011)

The most fundamental liberal failure of the current era: the failure to embrace a moral vision of America based on the transcendent faith that human beings are more than the sum of their material appetites, our country is more than an economic machine, and freedom is not license but responsibility.
—Bill Moyers, *Moyers on Democracy* (2008)

There is an astonishing lack of anger among liberals, progressives and radicals who have abandoned emotion to the right.
—Clancy Sigal, "U.S. Liberals Have Lost Their Thunder," *Guardian* (UK) (February 24, 2010)

The problem with socialism—the real kind, not the totalitarian travesty—is, as everyone knows, that it would take too many evenings. The problem with contemporary liberalism is that it takes too few. How many Americans meet regularly with neighbors or co-workers to formulate questions or instructions for their elected representatives?
—George Scialabba, "Only Words: Liberalism, Past and Future," *The Nation* (April 22, 2009)

The point of progressivism is that the people must progress up from their backwardness.
—George Will, conservative columnist, "They Still Don't Get It," *New York Post* (November 4, 2010)

Living Liberally

Economic liberalism is on life-support, while cultural liberalism thrives. The obvious question is why. The simple answer is that cultural liberalism . . . does not cost the wealthy anything.
—Eric Alterman, "Cultural Liberalism Is Not Enough," *New York Times* (April 7, 2012)

I have a love for humankind, a love of truth, and a love of justice.
—Bob Dylan, "Bob Dylan: What's It All About?" *Telegraph* (UK) (April 8, 2009)

The reward of a thing well done is to have done it.
—Ralph Waldo Emerson, quoted in *The Politics of Life* (2012)

Can we envision an economy designed to serve the society, rather than the other way around?
—William Greider, "The Future of the American Dream," *The Nation* (May 6, 2009)

Three things in human life are important: the first is to be kind; the second is to be kind; and the third is to be kind.
—Henry James, quoted in *Henry James: A Life, Vol. V: The Master 1901-1916* (1972)

The ones who are mad to live, mad to talk, mad to be saved, desirous of everything at the same time, the ones who never yawn or say a commonplace thing, burn, burn, burn like fabulous yellow roman candles.
—Jack Kerouac, arguably a definition of a liberal spirit, *On the Road, The Dharma Bums, The Subterraneans* (1993)

Liberals believe that we are better off when we live for each other than when we only live for ourselves.
—Justin Krebs, *538 Ways to Live, Work, and Play Like a Liberal* (2010)

Being liberal is not only a political philosophy—liberal is how you live and interact with neighbors, coworkers, and neighbors.
—Justin Krebs, *538 Ways to Live, Work, and Play Like a Liberal* (2010)

There is no one way to be "liberal,"—of course, that's in the very nature of being liberal.
—Justin Krebs, *538 Ways to Live, Work, and Play Like a Liberal* (2010)

Think globally. Act neighborly.
—Todd Murphy, quoted in "Bill McKibben Says We're Stuffed," Salon (March 23, 2007)

Will we honor that basic American principle that I am my brother's keeper, I am my sister's keeper, and if one of us is hurting, then all of us are hurting? Will we be a country where opportunity is limited to just a few at the top?
—Michele Obama, campaign letter on behalf of Obama for America (March 2012)

I'm pretty sure I'd like you if I got to know you.
—Sign at the Jon Stewart's Rally to Restore Sanity and/or Fear

The core substantive principle of liberalism is this: As many people as possible should have as much say as is feasible over the direction their lives will take.
—Alan Wolfe, *The Future of Liberalism* (2009)

A cornerstone of the liberal sensibility is to extend rights to those who hold ideas with which you disagree.
—Alan Wolfe, *The Future of Liberalism* (2009)

Marriage Equality

Apple-y Ever After
—Ben & Jerry got together with gay rights charity Stonewall and named a new ice cream flavor dedicated to marriage equality, *Huffington Post* "The Best Gay Moments of the Week," (March 17, 2012)

You can't claim you're the party of smaller government, and then clamor to make laws about love. If there's one area I don't want the U.S. government to add to its list of screw-ups, it's love.
—Bill Maher, "Valentine's Day, That Great State Holiday," *Boston Globe* (February 14, 2004)

Gays and lesbians and transgender persons are our brothers, our sisters, our children, our cousins, our friends, our co-workers, and they've got to be treated like every other American.
—Barack Obama, quoted in "Obama Moves Near 'Greater Equality' on Gay Marriage," *New York Times* (June 29, 2011)

Divorce isn't caused because 50% of marriages end in gayness.
—Jon Stewart, debating marriage equality with William Bennett, *Daily Show*, Comedy Central (June 6, 2006)

Fundamental rights may not be submitted to a vote.
—Judge Vaughn Walker, landmark decision overturning California's ban on same-sex marriage, "Marriage Is a Constitutional Right," *New York Times* (August 4, 2010)

Media Coverage

It's astounding to watch the avalanche of hate ooze from conservative media quarters. And why? Because Obama passed an economic recovery bill. Good Lord, imagine if he had failed to win the popular vote and then led the country into a pre-emptive war based on faulty intelligence, a war that lost thousands of American lives, and tens of thousands of foreign lives, while milking the U.S. treasury out of a few trillion dollars in the process.
—Eric Boehlert, "Unhinged in 30 Days: The Right-Wing Media's Obama Era Implosion," Media Matters for America (February 23, 2009)

Wooing the press is an exercise roughly akin to picnicking with a tiger. You might enjoy the meal, but the tiger always eats last.
—Maureen Dowd, quoted in "FBI Director Lightens Up at Press Club," *National Journal* (May 16, 2008)

The political media have accepted the myth of "equivalence" that says political polarization and governmental dysfunction are the result of both parties going to extremes of right and left. It is a myth.
—Gary Hart, "The New Conservatism," *Huffington Post* (March 23, 2012)

New Rule: If one of your news organization's headlines is about who got kicked off *Dancing with the Stars* last night, you're no longer a news organization.
—Bill Maher, *The New New Rules: A Funny Look at How Everybody But Me Has Their Head Up Their Ass* (2011)

[Fox News is] a relentless agenda-driven 24 hours news opinion propaganda delivery system.
—Jon Stewart, quoted in "Jon Stewart's Rare, Unexpectedly Serious Interview with Fox News,'" Atlantic Wire (June 19, 2011)

The press can hold its magnifying up to our problems bringing them into focus, illuminating issues heretofore unseen or they can use that magnifying glass to light ants on fire and then perhaps host a week of shows on the sudden, unexpected dangerous flaming ant epidemic.
—Jon Stewart, on the 24-hour cable news channels, Rally to Restore Sanity and/or Fear (October 30, 2010)

I look at politicians as, they are doing what inherently they need to do to retain power. Their job is to consolidate power. When you go to the zoo and you see a monkey throwing poop, you go, "that's what monkeys do, what are you gonna do?" But what I wish the media would do more frequently is say "bad monkey."
—Jon Stewart, on the failure of the news media, interviewed on *The Charlie Rose Show*, PBS (September 29, 2004)

Military Industrial Complex

You cannot accurately calculate the cost of a decade of war. Start with $1.4 trillion spent so far, 6,390 Americans dead, 47,684 wounded, and more than 150,000 Iraqis and Afghans dead.
—William Falk, Editor's Letter, *This Week* (March 30, 2012)

The U.S. spends almost as much on military spending as the entire rest of the world combined.
—Glenn Greenwald, "The Sanctity of Military Spending," Salon (January 26, 2010)

War perverts and destroys you . . . . We give up individual conscience—maybe even consciousness—for contagion of the crowd.
—Chris Hedges, "Murder Is Not an Anomaly in War," TruthDig (March 19, 2012)

I always knew the Americans would bring electricity to Baghdad. I just never thought they'd be shooting it up my ass.
—Iraqi translator, quoted in "Abu Ghraib: The Hidden Story," *New York Review of Books* (October 7, 2004)

We have been the cowards lobbing cruise missiles from 2,000 miles away. That's cowardly. Staying in the airplane when it hits the building, say what you want about it, it's not cowardly.
—Bill Maher, 9/11 comment that got him fired from *Politically Incorrect*, "The Salon Interview: Bill Maher," Salon (December 11, 2002)

While it is estimated that over 19,000 sexual assaults occurred in the military in 2010, a rate far higher than among civilians, the government has failed systematically to investigate complaints, appropriately punish perpetrators, and treat trauma and other health conditions suffered by survivors.
—Sandra Park, "Note to Military: Sexual Assault Includes Rape," *Huffington Post* (April 2, 2012)

What could that $1 trillion—$745 billion in Iraq and $330 billion so far in Afghanistan—have done instead of war?
—Rev. Jim Wallis, "The War in Iraq: At What Cost?" *Huffington Post* (September 1, 2010)

Net Neutrality

Net neutrality is the First Amendment issue of our time . . . . [Big corporations] want preferred treatment on the Internet like the preferred treatment they get in the rest of their lives.
—U.S. Sen. Al Franken, "Sen. Franken's Speech to Free Press Group in Minneapolis," Al Franken U.S. Senate for Minnesota website (August 19, 2010)

If Republicans have their way [in restricting Internet freedom], large corporations won't just have the loudest voices in the room. They'll be able to effectively silence everyone else.
—U.S. Sen. Al Franken, "Net Neutrality Is Under Attack . . . Again," *Huffington Post* (November 8, 2011)

Letting only the biggest companies and richest individuals have good quality service wreaks havoc with everything that is good about the internet: the freedom of speech, the ability to mobilize people, the entrepreneurial spirit that allows new tech companies to get started.
—Peter Rothberg, "Save Net Neutrality," *The Nation* (August 6, 2010)

Net Neutrality guarantees a level playing field for all websites and Internet users. It ensures that everyone has a voice on the Internet and that no one can be silenced simply because they can't afford to pay.
—U.S. Sen. Mark Udall, "Support Net Neutrality to Preserve a Free and Democratic Internet," *Huffington Post* (November 8, 2011)

Barack Obama

It is thinly veiled social Darwinism.
—Barack Obama, on the House Republican budget that would save millionaires $150,000 a year while gutting Medicaid, Medicare, food stamps, transportation, child nutrition, and college aid, quoted in "The Choice in 2012: Social Darwinism or a Decent Society," *Huffington Post* (April 4, 2010)

For all the cruelty and hardship of our world, we are not mere prisoners of fate. Our actions matter, and can bend history in the direction of justice.
—Barack Obama, "Full Text of Obama's Nobel Peace Prize Speech," MSNBC (December 10, 2009)

As a citizen, and as President, I believe that Muslims have the same right to practice their religion as anyone else in this country.
—Barack Obama, "Obama: Ground Zero Mosque within Muslims' Rights," CBS News (August 13, 2010)

Change will not come if we wait for some other person or some other time. We are the ones we've been waiting for. We are the change that we seek.
—Barack Obama, quoted in "We Are the Ones We've Been Waiting for!" Daily Kos (November 22, 2011)

I don't want to be invited to the family hunting party.
—Barack Obama, on revelations that he and Dick Cheney are eighth cousins, "Late-Night Obama," *New York Times* (October 17, 2007)

Obamacare

Healthcare Not Warfare
—Banner of the Progressive Democrats of America

Obama Is Not A Brown-Skinned Anti-War Socialist Who Gives Away Free Health Care. You're Thinking of Jesus.
—Banner at Occupy protest

If you think it's a socialist plot, then please drop out of the federal employees health program.
—U.S. Sen. Richard Durbin, to Republican lawmakers at health care reform summit, Taegan Goddard's Political Wire (February 25, 2010)

Congress has indisputable authority to regulate national markets and provide for the general welfare through its broad power to tax. Nothing about the mandate [to buy health insurance] falls outside those clearly delineated powers.
—Editorial, "The Supreme Court's Momentous Test," *New York Times* (March 27, 2010)

Our plan is to take away the government-mandated insurance of millions of people under age 65, and replace it with nothing.
—David Frum, former speechwriter for George W. Bush, on the Republican health care plan, "Supremes Won't Save GOP from Itself on Obamacare," Daily Beast (March 27, 2012)

Obamacare Is On Trial. So Is the Supreme Court
—Headline, *The New Republic*, (March 29, 2012)

It's always a bit strange to hear people with government-funded single-payer health plans describe the need for other Americans to be free from health insurance.
—Dahlia Lithwick, on the court's aggressive questions regarding the Affordable Care Act's individual mandate, "The Supreme Court's Dark Vision of Freedom," *Slate* (March 27, 2012)

Thanks to last night's vote, after your cancer returns for the third time—racking up another $200,000 in costs to keep you alive—your insurance company will have to commit a criminal act if they even think of dropping you from their rolls.
—Michael Moore, "The Great Thing about the Health Care Law That Has Passed? It Will Save Republican Lives, Too," *Huffington Post* (March 22, 2010)

Yes, my Republican friends, even though you have opposed this health care bill, we've made sure it is going to cover you, too . . . . So, when you find yourself suddenly broadsided by a life-threatening illness someday, perhaps you'll thank those pinko-socialist, Canadian-loving Democrats and independents for what they did Sunday evening.
—Michael Moore, "The Great Thing about the Health Care Law That Has Passed? It Will Save Republican Lives, Too," *Huffington Post* (March 22, 2010)

I am not the first President to take up this cause, but I am determined to be the last.
—Barack Obama, health care speech to a joint session of Congress, "Obama, Armed with Details, Says Health Plan Is Necessary," *New York Times* (September 9, 2009)

Occupy Movement

When fairness is betrayed, when ordinary people just don't matter to those who get to make the rules, it may be time to break them.
—Lisa Dodson, *The Moral Underground* (2009)

Occupy Wall Street's great problem and great strength is that they're unorganized. They'll have to overcome that somehow, down the line. They'll have to develop some sort of organization like everybody else does.
—Thomas Frank, interviewed in "The American Aftershock," *Los Angeles Review of Books* (March 16, 2012)

Heartfelt actions are, by themselves, not enough to bring down heartless regimes.
—Troy Headrick, "Reading the Revolution," Common Dreams (February 11, 2012)

I'm done being the victim. However long I have left is dedicated heart and soul to this movement, no matter what it takes.
—Miran Istina, 18-year-old denied health coverage by countless providers because she suffers from leukemia and needs a bone marrow transplant, quoted in "Fighting Corporations and a Death Sentence," Truthdig (October 29, 2011)

The original message of Occupy Wall Street is still true now—that banks got bailed out and we got sold out.
—Stewart Leonard, protesting at a Romney fundraiser, Associated Press (March 12, 2012.)

Exercise your right to peaceably assemble; occupy public space; create a process to address the problems we face, and generate solutions accessible to everyone.
—New York City General Assembly, "The Declaration of the Occupation," Occupy.com (Undated)

We are the 99%
—Occupy Wall Street banner

I know where you are coming from. My family was fucked over by foreclosures and predatory loans and the banking industry being twisted . . . but I can't be with you guys because of this badge.
—Police officer arresting protesters on the Brooklyn Bridge, *Occupying Wall Street* (2012)

Capitalism and democracy are incompatible.
—Marina Sitrin, "What Does Democracy Look Like?" *The Nation* (March 14, 2012)

Partisanship

Liberals and conservatives are almost literally living in different worlds with different versions of consensus reality.
—Kevin Drum, "Chart of the Day: Conservatives Don't Trust Science," *Mother Jones* (March 29, 2012)

It is more than a little strange to gaze out over a land laid waste by fantastic corporate fraud and declare that partisanship is what ails us and that reasonableness is the cure.
—Thomas Frank, on Jon Stewart's "Rally to Restore Sanity," *Pity the Billionaire* (2012)

Our political system is designed for vigorous disagreement. It is not designed for irreconcilable contempt.
—Michael Gerson, "A Short Primer on Political Reality," *Times and Democrat*, (February 19, 2010)

We need to figure out how to tone our rhetoric and partisanship down.
—Democratic Rep. Gabrielle Giffords, to a Republican friend the night before she was gunned down, quoted in "Giffords Sent Email on Eve of Shooting Calling for Toned Down Rhetoric," Talking Points Memo (January 10, 2011)

We evolved to be tribal, and politics is a competition among coalitions of tribes.
—Jonathan Haidt, "Viewpoint," *ThisWeek* (March 30, 2012)

Ideology offers human beings the illusion of dignity and morals while making it easier to part with them.
—Vacal Haval, quotes in "Vaclav Havel's Heroic Politics of Truth and Responsibility," Daily Beast (December 19, 2011)

What do you despise? By this are you truly known.
—Frank Herbert, *Dune* (1965)

I never considered a difference of opinion in politics, in region, in philosophy, as cause for withdrawing from a friend.
—Thomas Jefferson, quoted in *What It Means to Be a Democrat* (2011)

We live now in hard times, not end times. And we can have animus and not be enemies.
—Jon Stewart, Rally to Restore Sanity and/or Fear (October 30, 2010)

A civil discourse only works if both sides are civil.
—Ryan Witt, "Keith Olbermann Addresses the 'False Equivalency' of Jon Stewart's Rally Speech" Examiner.com (November 1, 2010)

Political Violence

Much as we do not permit convicted pedophiles to teach kindergarten or convicted hijackers to board airplanes, common sense dictates that individuals who have been imprisoned for plotting violence against abortion clinics should never again be permitted anywhere near such facilities.
—Jacob M. Appel, "The Case for an Anti-Abortion Violence Registry," *Huffington Post* (June 29, 2009)

People get a sense that something is really wrong in government and in our culture. There is a corruption, not only in politics, but of spirit as well, when people are so quick to be violent with one another.
—Jennifer Beals, interviewed by Christina Radish, Collider.com (February 6, 2011)

"Stand Your Ground" or "Shoot First" laws like Florida's expand the so-called castle doctrine . . . sanction reckless vigilantism in the form of self-defense claims.
—Rich Benjamin, "The Gated Community Mentality," *New York Times* (March 29, 2012)

People have always had a right to have a handgun in their home—to protect their homes—then we've seen this breathtaking expansion of the concealed weapons laws in America.
—Bill Clinton, quoted in "President Clinton Hopes Trayvon Martin Case Leads to Reappraisal of 'Stand Your Ground' Laws," ABC News (April 2, 2012)

We're on Sarah Palin's targeted list, but the thing is, the way that she has it depicted has the crosshairs of a gun sight over our district. When people do that, they have to realize that there are consequences to that action.
—Rep. Gabrielle Giffords, Democrat shot in the head at point blank range, quoted in "U.S. Congresswoman Gabrielle Giffords Shot as Six Die in Arizona Massacre," *Guardian* (UK) (January 8, 2011)

When someone like Palin posts a map with cross hairs on the districts of Democrats, when she says "Don't Retreat, Instead—RELOAD!" there are desperate people cleaning their weapons who listen.
—Chris Hedges, quoted in "Glenn Beck and the Yearning for Fascism," *The Progressive* (September 4, 2010)

Politeness may be a virtue, but there's a big difference between bad manners and calls, explicit or implicit, for violence.
—Paul Krugman, "Climate of Hate," *New York Times* (January 9, 2011)

Extreme vocabulary creates a climate of moral permission for extreme acts. This is a movement whose main spokespeople, many of them mantled in clerical or political authority, regularly use words like "baby killers," "murder," "holocaust," and "Nazis," thus legitimizing just about anything.
—Katha Pollitt, "Subject to Debate," *The Nation* (February 5, 2006)

Stand Your Ground laws across the nation must be overturned. These laws are vague and too easily interpreted as condoning violence by those who believe that the simple presence of a person of color in their neighborhood constitutes a threat.
—Sarah van Gelder, "Stand Your Ground to Stop the Violence," *YES! Magazine* (March 28, 2012)

Rightwing extremists have capitalized on the election of the first African American president, and are focusing their efforts to recruit new members, mobilize existing supporters, and broaden their scope and appeal through propaganda.
—"Rightwing Extremism: Current Economic and Political Climate Fueling Resurgence in Radicalization and Recruitment," title of a report from the Department of Homeland Security (April 7, 2009)

There was a time when the far left was a spawning ground for political violence . . . . But for the most part, far-left violence in this country has gone the way of the leisure suit and the AMC Gremlin.
—Eugene Robinson, "The Hutaree Militia and the Rising Risk of Far-Right Violence," *Washington Post* (March 30, 2010)

Pretend it's Obama
—Woman at a campaign stop firing range, while Rick Santorum was firing off some rounds, "As Santorum Fires Gun, Woman Shouts 'Pretend It's Obama,'" ABC News (March 23, 2012)

Pre-Abortion Shaming

Trans-vaginal ultrasounds undertaken without a woman's consent are rape according to the legal definition of the word . . . Women have the right not to be raped by the state.
—Soraya Chemaly, "10 Reasons the Rest of the World Thinks the U.S. Is Nuts," *Huffington Post* (March 15, 2012)

It says that women are incapable of making decisions about their health and wellbeing.
—Rebecca Foley, about a Pennsylvania bill that would mandate pre-abortion ultrasounds, "Mandated Ultrasounds Prior to Abortions, Workplace Gender Inequities Discussed at Council Meeting," News Works (March 8, 2012)

The laws are both about putting obstacles between women and abortion, and most importantly, forcing unwilling doctors to convey the legislators' intent to shame and harass women for getting abortions.
—Amanda Marcotte, "Why Do Right-Wing Extremists Have the Power to Force Doctors to Humiliate Women?" AlterNet (March 6, 2012)

We should leave the practice of medicine to doctors.
—State Sen. A. Donald McEachin, a Virginia Democrat who voted against the mandate, "Senate Approves Ultrasound Abortion Mandate," *Richmond-Times Dispatch* (February 12, 2012)

It is the year 2012, almost 40 years since Roe vs. Wade passed, yet the government is still trying to punish women for legally exercising control over their bodies with state-sanctioned rape. Recent bills requiring a woman to have a trans-vaginal ultrasound before she can have access to an abortion are medically unnecessary and immoral.
—Elaine Wilcox-Cook, "Shameful Abortion Legislation," *Wooster Voice* (March 4, 2012)

Pro-Choice

The right to privacy . . . is broad enough to encompass a woman's decision whether or not to terminate her pregnancy.
—Harry Blackmun, writing for the court, Roe v. Wade, 410 U.S. 113, 153 (1973)

Those of us who are pro-choice are also, passionately, pro-life. Most of us love babies, love children, and love our liberty—not to mention loving sex and our right to have it when, how, and with whomever we choose.
—Rachel Kramer Bussel, "I'm Pro-Choice and I Fuck," *Village Voice* (January 13, 2006)

If [anti-choice advocates] were truly concerned with sustaining life . . . you would begin by having compassion and empathy for living, born people that require and deserve your attention. You feed them, educate them, lift them from poverty and misery.
—Soraya Chemaly, "10 Reasons the Rest of the World Thinks the U.S. Is Nuts," *Huffington Post* (March 15, 2012)

Being pro-choice is not being pro-abortion. Being pro-choice is trusting the individual to make the right decision for herself and her family, and not entrusting that decision to anyone wearing the authority of government.
—Hillary Clinton, quoted in "Women and Children and the Choices We Make," AlterNet (March 24, 2011)

I would love to see a world where abortion doesn't exist—but that's not this world.
—Merle Hoffman, quoted in "Abortion Pioneer: Defend Rights or Lose Them," Salon (January 2, 2012)

Let's be clear here: Women are not an interest group. They're mothers, and daughters, and sisters, and wives. They're half of this country. They're perfectly capable of making their own choices about their health.
—Barack Obama, message to supporters of Planned Parenthood, "This Week in the War on Women: Women Are Not an Interest Group," Daily Kos (March 31, 2012)

As the nation passes the thirty-third anniversary of Roe, it is hard to find anyone who will say a good word in public for abortion rights.
—Katha Pollitt, "Subject to Debate," *The Nation* (February 5, 2006)

What would the alternative be? Abortion by prayer? By edict? Upon seeking consensus? After groveling?
—Suzanne T. Poppema, discussing the strange framing of the common phrase "abortion on demand," *Why I Am an Abortion Doctor* (1996)

The changes we have seen in the status of women in the last forty years in this country would not have been possible without significant numbers of women being able to obtain abortions.
—Linda Weber, *Life Choices* (2011)

There is nothing wrong with having an abortion.
—Linda Weber, *Life Choices* (2011)

Progressive Bumper Stickers

A Vote for Republicans is a Vote against Women
—Bumper sticker

Wag more. Bark less.
—Bumper sticker

No Health Care? Thank a Republican
—Bumper sticker

Unions = Better Wages for All
—Bumper sticker

When Money Talks, Democracy Goes Silent
—Bumper Sticker

Dear 1%, We fell asleep for a while.
Just woke up. Sincerely, the other 99%
—Bumper sticker

Human Need Not Corporate Greed
—Bumper sticker

I'll believe corporations are people when Texas executes one
—Bumper sticker

My marriage is not threatened by love other couples share
—Bumper sticker

Pro-Family, Pro-Obama
—Bumper sticker

Santorum: Just Google It
—Bumper sticker

Public Sector

Medicare is much less costly than private health care. Social Security, which functions with a surplus, would not be in danger of a long-term shortfall if the richest 10% (those making over the $106,800 cutoff) paid their full share.
—Paul Bucheit, "Five Preposterous, Persistent Conservative Myths," Common Dreams (April 2, 2012)

Voters expect government to take an active role in helping rebuild the economy, not to sit back and do nothing.
—Editorial, on Romney's advocacy of government passivity, "Haunted by the Primaries," *New York Times* (April 4, 2012)

The USPS is an unmatched bargain, a civic treasure, a genuine public good that links all people and communities into one nation. So, naturally, it must be destroyed.
—Jim Hightower, regarding right-wing attempts to eliminate the postal service, "The Truth about the U.S. Postal Service," Creators.com (March 28, 2012)

Conservatives hate Social Security for ideological reasons: its success undermines their claim that government is always the problem, never the solution.
—Paul Krugman, "Attacking Social Security," *New York Times* (August 15, 2010)

Social security isn't a Ponzi scheme. It's not bankrupting us. It's not an outrage. It is working.
—Rachel Maddow, advertisement for MSNBC, *New Yorker* (March 19, 2012)

The reflexive belief that government is bad on the face of it, and business good, is not supported by history or theory.
—Jeff Madrick, "Big Government Myths Are Undermining Democracy and America's Future," *Huffington Post* (June 23, 2010)

Radical Right

A study published in the journal *Psychological Science* showed that children who score low on intelligence tests gravitate toward socially conservative political views in adulthood.
—David Freeman, "Conservative Politics, 'Low-Effort' Thinking Linked in New Study," *Huffington Post* (April 9, 2012)

The composite Republican candidate . . . has been harsh on immigration, confrontational on social issues, simplistic in condemning government and silent on the struggles of the poor. How many women would find this profile appealing on eHarmony?
—Michael Gerson, "How Romney Can Solve His Woman Problem," *Washington Post* (April 9, 2012)

Hasn't America seen enough of the exclusionary, prejudicial, vote-suppressing, racial-profiling, inner city-ignoring, confederate flag-waving, Bob Jones University-loving attitudes of the radical right?
—Patrick Kennedy, quoted on *The Mike Malloy Show* (May 17, 2009)

Why Are Obama's Critics So Dumb?
—*Newsweek* cover (January 23, 2012)

It's hard to point to a single priority of the Republican Party these days that isn't steeped in moral failing while being dressed up in moral righteousness.
—Katrina vanden Heuvel, "Republicans Are Causing a Moral Crisis in America," *Washington Post* (March 27, 2012)

Reading

I have always imagined that paradise will be a kind of library.
—Jorge Luis Borges, *Dreamtigers* (1964)

Think before you speak. Read before you think.
—Fran Lebowitz, *The Fran Lebowitz Reader* (1994)

It is not enough to simply teach children to read; we have to give them something worth reading. Something that will stretch their imaginations—something that will help them make sense of their own lives and encourage them to reach out toward people whose lives are quite different from their own.
—Katherine Paterson, quoted in "Banning of Books," *Southern Gazette* (September 15, 2009)

What really knocks me out is a book that, when you're all done reading it, you wish the author that wrote it was a terrific friend of yours and you could call him up on the phone whenever you felt like it.
—J. D. Salinger, *The Catcher in the Rye* (1951)

Fewer people are reading . . . more than 50 million Americans don't read books at all.
—Staff writers, according to the Pew Research Center's Internet & American Life Project, "eReaders, eBooks More Popular than Ever, Survey Finds," *Huffington Post* (April 5, 2012)

How many a man has dated a new era in his life from the reading of a book.
—Henry David Thoreau, *Walden* (1854)

Reason and Science

American conservatives are hostile towards science—climate change, evolution, medical research, etc.—it's not your imagination.
—Steve Benen, "Science Need Not Be a Partisan Issue," Maddow Blog (April 1, 2012)

Your reasonableness is poisoning my fear.
—Stephen Colbert, to rally co-host Jon Stewart, "Thousands Attend 'Rally to Restore Sanity' in Washington," *Telegraph* (UK) (February 1, 2010)

The rule of reason is the true sovereign in the American system . . . . When reason itself comes under assault, American democracy is put at risk.
—Al Gore, *The Assault on Reason* (2007)

The defense of science and reason is the great imperative of our time.
—Christopher Hitchens, *Hitch-22* (2010)

Politically conservative Americans have lost trust in science over the last 40 years.
—Stephanie Pappas, "Conservatives' Trust in Science Weakens, Survey Says," *Huffington Post* (March 30, 2012)

We all have a thirst for wonder. It's a deeply human quality. Science and religion are both bound up with it. What I'm saying is, you don't have to make stories up, you don't have to exaggerate. There's wonder and awe enough in the real world. Nature's a lot better at inventing wonders than we are.
—Carl Sagan, *Contact* (1985)

Schooling

Our education system is going to hell. Average SAT scores are falling, and America is slipping down the list of nations for college completion. And Rick Perry stands up with a smirk to talk to students about how you can get C's, D's and F's and still run for president.
—Maureen Dowd, "Egghead and Blockheads," *New York Times* (September 17, 2011)

The explosion in student debt is a direct outgrowth of the defunding of education in state after state. Unlike corporate and other debt, student debt is excluded from bankruptcy relief, strangling students for life.
—Stephen Lerner, "Horizontal Meets Vertical; Occupy Meets Establishment," *The Nation* (March 14, 2012)

I cannot fathom why we expect so much from teachers and provide them so little in return. In 1940, the average pay of a male teacher was actually 3.6 percent more than what other college-educated men earned. Today it is 60 percent lower. Women teachers now earn 16 percent less than other college-educated women.
—Bill Moyers, *Moyers on Democracy* (2008)

We need to teach our kids that it's not just the winner of the Super Bowl who deserves to be celebrated, but the winner of the science fair.
—Barack Obama, quoted in "Race to the Top of What? Obama on Education," *New York Times* (January 31, 2011)

It's facile to blame schools and teachers, but more realistic to recognize that poverty is a reflection of economic conditions. Schools cannot create jobs, provide homes for the homeless, or change the economy.
—Diane Ravitch, "In Defense of Facing Reality," *Huffington Post* (March 18, 2012)

The amount of student debt owed by Americans exceeded outstanding credit-card debt for the first time . . . The Class of 2010 had an average of $25,250 in student debt.
—Staff writers, "Student Debt Grows to Alarming Levels," *Consumer Reports* (May 2012)

Secular Humanism

It is not hardness of heart or evil passions that drive certain individuals to atheism, but rather a scrupulous intellectual honesty.
—Steve Allen, quoted in *2000 Years of Disbelief, Famous People with the Courage to Doubt* (1996)

Humanism is a progressive philosophy of life that, without theism and other supernatural beliefs, affirms our ability and responsibility to lead ethical lives of personal fulfillment that aspire to the greater good of humanity.
—American Humanist Association website (undated)

Atheists: The Real Ghostbusters
—Anonymous

On the first day, man created God.
—Anonymous

You are an intelligent human being. Your life is valuable for its own sake. You are not second-class in the universe, deriving meaning and purpose from some other mind. You are not inherently evil—you are inherently human, possessing the positive rational potential to help make this a world of morality, peace and joy. Trust yourself.
—Dan Barker, *Losing Faith in Faith: From Preacher to Atheist* (2006)

Be thankful that you have a life, and forsake your vain and presumptuous desire for a second one.
—Richard Dawkins, interviewed in "The Atheist," Salon (April 30, 2005)

The humanist has four leading characteristics—curiosity, a free mind, belief in good taste, and belief in the human race.
—E. M. Forster, *A Companion to E.M. Forster, Volume 1* (2007)

Flying planes into a building was a faith-based initiative.
—Bill Maher, quoted in "101 Atheist Quotes," Best Article of the Day (Undated)

Your religion assumes that people are children and need a boogeyman so they'll behave. You want people to believe in God so they'll obey the law . . . You sell human beings short.
—Carl Sagan, *Contact* (1985)

Strip-Searching America

Driving with a noisy muffler, driving with an inoperable headlight, failing to use a turn signal, or riding a bicycle without an audible bell.
—Supreme Court Justice Stephen Breyer, in dissent, listing some of the infractions that have prompted a strip search, "Supreme Court Upholds Jail Strip Searches, Including for Minor Offenses," *Washington Post* (April 3, 2012)

Lifting his testicles to expose the area behind them and bending over and/or spreading the cheeks of his buttocks to expose his anus. For females, the procedures are similar except females must in addition, squat to expose the vagina.
—Supreme Court Justice Stephen Breyer, describing a typical strip search, "Strip-Searching America: Florence v. County of Burlington," *Huffington Post* (April 4, 2012)

The GOP Five [Alito, Kennedy, Roberts, Scalia, and Thomas, all appointed by Republicans] claimed the extensive use of strip searches was necessary . . . . But strip searches also would give authorities a powerful psychological weapon to use against protesters, like those who have participated in Occupy Wall Street.
—Robert Parry, "GOP Five Like Stripping Americans," *Consortium News* (April 3, 2012)

History shows that the use of forced nudity by a state that is descending into fascism is powerfully effective in controlling and subduing populations.
—Naomi Klein, "How the U.S. Uses Sexual Humiliation as a Political Tool to Control the Masses," Common Dreams (April 6, 2012)

Super PACs

In the old days there were just PACs—political action committees that could accept donations of up to $5,000 . . . Now, there are Super-PACs—committees that, thanks to the court decisions, can raise and spend unlimited sums of money.
—Kim Barker and Marian Wang, "Super-PACs and Dark Money: ProPublica's Guide to the New World of Campaign Finance," ProPublica (July 11, 2011)

One of the many virtues of Super PAC's is they enable people who seek political power to buy disgust by the truckload, and dump it, reeking and steaming, in your living room.
—James Fallows, "The Politics of Disgust," *This Week* (February 4, 2012)

Since the Republican primaries began, the pro-Mitt Romney super PAC Restore Our Future has spent $35 million on commercials attacking Rick Santorum and Newt Gingrich . . . . The group has spent just $1.1 million promoting Romney.
—Taegan Goddard, "Romney Killing Machine," Taegan Goddard's Political Wire (March 28, 2012)

Dark Money
—Secret, unlimited sums that are being donated to Super PACs in the aftermath of the Citizens United decision, "The GOP's New Love of 'Dark Money,'" Salon (March 8, 2012)

Super Rich

The richest 1 percent now owns over 36 percent of all the wealth in the United States.
—Chuck Collins, "The 99 Percent Spring: The People Are Not Powerless," Common Dreams (April 2, 2012)

Romney casually bet a rival $10,000 during a presidential debate, noted that his wife drives a "couple of Cadillacs," and lists owners of professional sports teams among his friends. His personal tax records show investments in the Cayman Islands and a Swiss bank account.
—Beth Fouhy and Steve Peoples, would be one of the richest men ever elected president, "Dems Sharpen Attack as GOP Rallies Behind Romney," Associated Press (April 1, 2012)

Money never seems to be interested in strengthening regulatory agencies . . . but always in subverting them, in making them miss the danger signs in coalmines and in derivatives trading and in deep-sea oil wells.
—Thomas Frank, "How Americans Have Gotten Played—Over and Over and Over Again," AlterNet (March 28, 2012)

The Koch brothers . . . are perfectly out of Central Casting [as typecasts for] rich, arrogant, conservative billionaires.
—Robert Greenwald, on the behind-the-scene funders of many powerful right-wing causes and organizations, interviewed in "Robert Greenwald on the New Film 'Koch Brothers Exposed'—the 1% at Its Very Worst," AlterNet (March 28, 2012)

The vast majority of Americans do not oppose their fellow Americans, simply because they are rich. To the contrary: more than perhaps any other people on this Earth, Americans admire success. What we detest is greed. We like economic winners; we hate economic cheaters.
—Van Jones, "The 99 Percent for the 100 Percent: The Case for Deep Patriotism," *The Nation* (April 2, 2012)

Tax day is the day that ordinary Americans send their money to Washington, D.C., and wealthy Americans send their money to the Cayman Islands.
—Jimmy Kimmel, "Late Night Humor," *Fort Wayne Journal Gazette* (April 23, 2011)

Wall Street's Masters of the Universe realize, deep down, how morally indefensible their position is. . . . They're people who got rich by peddling complex financial schemes that, far from delivering clear benefits to the American people, helped push us into a crisis whose aftereffects continue to blight the lives of tens of millions of their fellow citizens. Yet they have paid no price.
—Paul Krugman, "Panic of the Plutocrats," *New York Times* (October 9, 2001)

Three people have won the Mega Millions lottery. You know what that means—three more votes for Mitt Romney.
—Conan O'Brien, quoted in "Late-Night Political Jokes," About.com (April 2, 2012)

I think when you spread the wealth around it's good for everybody.
—Barack Obama, quoted in, "Spread the Wealth?" ABC News (October 14, 2008)

Rich People More Likely to Cheat, Behave Badly, Research Finds
—Headline about a study published in the Proceedings of the National Academy of Sciences by University of California at Berkeley researchers, MSNBC (February 27, 2012)

Millionaires and billionaires aren't donating to politicians out of generosity.
—Robert Reich, "Big Government Isn't the Problem, Big Money Is," *The Nation* (March 21, 2012)

The Supremes

Rather than allow the state of Florida to continue its recount in the 2000 election, the Supreme Court effectively ruled that Florida should just give the election to George Bush.
—Jamelle Bouie, "The Attack on Liberal Legitimacy," *The Nation* (March 30, 2012)

[The Supreme Court] has squandered even the semi-illusion that it is the unbiased, honest guardian of the Constitution. It is run by hacks dressed up in black robes.
—Maureen Dowd, "Men in Black," *New York Times* (April 4, 2012)

There has been no court less restrained in signaling its willingness to replace law made by Congress with law made by justices.
—Editorial, "The Roberts Court Defined Itself," *New York Times* (March 31, 2012)

When did the right wing dominated United States Supreme Court actually jump the shark? Was it Bush v. Gore or was it their decision in Citizens United?
—Editorial Staff, "The Consequences of a Right Wing Supreme Court," BlackState.com (March 25, 2012)

In case after case, the five hard-core Republicans of the Roberts Court have been chopping furiously at the hard-earned legal rights of workers, consumers, voters, and others who dare to challenge the power of big business elites.
—Jim Hightower, "How a Corporatist Supreme Court Cabal Joined Forces with Right Wing and Kochs to Quietly Sell Out Our Democracy," Alternet (August 5, 2011)

Roberts. Alito. Kennedy. Scalia. Thomas. Memorize these names, for they are thieves.
—Jim Hightower, "How a Corporatist Supreme Court Cabal Joined Forces with Right Wing and Kochs to Quietly Sell Out Our Democracy," Alternet (August 5, 2011)

It's hard not to feel a sense of foreboding—and to worry that the nation's already badly damaged faith in the Supreme Court's ability to stand above politics is about to take another severe hit.
—Paul Krugman, on the likelihood of the court declaring Obamacare unconstitutional, "Broccoli and Bad Faith," *New York Times* (March 29, 2012)

Republicans portray both the Supreme Court and the lower courts as a collective of lefty hippies. And Democrats mainly just look at their fingernails.
—Dahlia Lithwick, "What If Obama Loses?" *Washington Monthly* (January/February 2012)

If you care about the future of abortion rights, stem cell research, worker protections, the death penalty, environmental regulation, torture, presidential power, warrantless surveillance, or any number of other issues, it's worth recalling that the last stop on the answer to each of those matters will probably be before someone in a black robe.
—Dahlia Lithwick, "What If Obama Loses?" *Washington Monthly* (January/February 2012)

We need somebody who's got the heart, the empathy, to recognize what it's like to be a young teenage mom, the empathy to understand what it's like to be poor or African-American or gay or disabled or old—and that's the criterion by which I'll be selecting my judges.
—Barack Obama, quoted in, "Empathy and the Supreme Court," *Los Angeles Times* (April 13, 2010)

I just remind conservative commentators that for years what we have heard is that the biggest problem on the bench was judicial activism or a lack of judicial restraint; that an unelected group of people would somehow overturn a duly constituted and passed law.
—Barack Obama, on his signature Affordable Care Act, quoted in "Barack Obama Confident that Supreme Court Will Let His Health Care Law Stand," *Huffington Post* (April 2, 2012)

Tea Party

He even got a C in gym.
—Maureen Dowd, on Tea Party favorite Rick Perry's scholastic aptitude, "Egghead and Blockheads," *New York Times* (September 17, 2011)

The mob is man voluntarily descending to the nature of the beast.
—Ralph Waldo Emerson, his likely reaction to today's Tea Party, "A Riot Is the Language of the Unheard," *Chicago Tribune* (September 17, 1995)

Expel the bigots and racists in your ranks or take the responsibility for them and their actions.
—Ben Jealous, NAACP president, "NAACP, Tea Party Volley over Racism Claims," NPR (June 14, 2010)

What exactly is the Tea Party plan for America? So far, it seems to consist of screaming at people and working to eliminate the social programs whose checks many of them cash every month.
—Carol Logie, letter to the editor, *New York Times* (March 6, 2010)

There's a word the teabaggers have wanted to use since Obama came on the scene, but they can't because it's not the 1950s. They would love to say this word. It begins with an N and ends with -er, and it's not "nation-builder."
—Bill Maher, *But I'm Not Wrong*, HBO (February 14, 2010)

The problem with the tea party movement, besides their almost universal rejection of dentistry, is that they want money for nothing and chicks for free.
—Bill Maher, "Bill Maher Blasts Tea Baggers for Ignoring Defense Spending," *Huffington Post* (June 23, 2010)

The Tea Party is fundamentally about venting anger at change it doesn't like, not about fixing what's broken.
—Jacob Weisberg, "A Tea Party Taxonomy," Daily Beast (September 18, 2010)

Voter ID Laws

Where are the examples of rampant ballot box stuffing, the hordes of voters with fake IDs voting multiple times in a single election and the out-of-control election fraud? We haven't heard of a single such instance, nor have proponents of the legislation provided any evidence.
—Editorial, "Where's the Evidence of Voter Fraud?" *The News & Advance* (February 3, 2012)

It is more likely that an individual will be struck by lightning than that he will impersonate another voter at the polls.
—Justin Levitt, "The Truth about Voter Fraud," Brennan Center for Justice at New York University School of Law (2007)

In every national American election since Reconstruction, every election since the Voting Rights Act passed in 1965, voters, particularly African American voters and other minorities, have faced calculated and determined efforts at intimidation and suppression.
—*The Long Shadow of Jim Crow: Voter Suppression in America*, People for the American Way Foundation and NAACP (2004)

Government that undermines the very foundation of its existence—the people's inherent, pre-constitutional right to vote—imperils its legitimacy as a government by the people, for the people, and especially of the people.
—Judge Richard Niess, declaring the Wisconsin's photo ID law to be voter suppression, "Wisconsin Voter ID Law Ruled Unconstitutional," Huffington Post (March 12, 2012)

Voter ID laws, as the saying goes, are a solution in search of a problem.
—Andrew Rosenthal, "Voter Fraud: Does It Happen?" *New York Times* (November 7, 2010)

Liberal equality means (or will mean, if we ever get there) that we all have a chance to be heard during the discussion and all have one vote at the end.
—George Scialabba, "Only Words: Liberalism, Past and Future," *The Nation* (April 22, 2009)

War on Women

Georgia State Lawmaker Seeks to Redefine Rape Victims as "Accusers"
—Headline, Republican legislation playing on the myth that rape accusations are fabricated, *Huffington Post* (February 4, 2011)

South Dakota Bill Would Legalize Killing Abortion Doctors
—Headline, about a Republican-sponsored law that would alter the state's legal definition of justifiable homicide, Salon (February 15, 2011)

Patriarchy is not men. Patriarchy is a system in which both women and men participate. It privileges, inter alia, the interests of boys and men over the bodily integrity, autonomy, and dignity of girls and women. It is subtle, insidious, and never more dangerous than when women passionately deny that they themselves are engaging in it.
—Ashley Judd, "Ashley Judd Nails Patriarchy," Feministing (April 9, 2012)

The poorest in this country are women.
—Rep. Marcy Kaptur, quoted in "Rep. Marcy Kaptur Says that the Poorest in America Are Women: PolitiFact Ohio," *Cleveland Plain Dealer* (March 26, 2012)

There's a new Republican-sponsored abortion bill in the House that . . . would allow hospitals to let a pregnant woman die rather than perform the abortion that would save her life.
—Evan McMorris-Santoro, "New GOP Bill Would Allow Hospitals to Let Women Die instead of Having an Abortion," Talking Points Memo (February 4, 2001)

Those states where women do not have access to affordable higher education, reproductive health care and representation in Congress pursue the most regressive, anti-women policies in the country.
—Jessica Pieklo, the states in descending order: Kentucky, West Virginia, Arkansas, Oklahoma, and Mississippi, "Dispatches from the War on Women: The 5 Worst States for Women," Care2 (April 1, 2012)

Without equality there can be no democracy.
—Eleanor Roosevelt, quoted in "Wear the T-Shirt and Make Women's History," *Forbes* (March 13, 2012)

Wing Nuts

Before 2009, the man in the bread line did not ordinarily weep for the man lounging on his yacht.
—Thomas Frank, *Pity the Billionaire* (2012)

A Public Policy Polling study released [today] shows 45 percent of [Republican] voters in Mississippi and Alabama believe Obama is a Muslim.
—Lauren Fox, "Some Southern Voters Still Think Obama Is Muslim," U.S. News Weekly (March 12, 2012)

A new Public Policy Polling survey in New York finds that just 4% of Republican voters support building a mosque near Ground Zero—but 21% say they would support building a strip club in the same place.
—Taegan Goddard, "Ground Zero Strip Club?" Taegan Goddard's Political Wire (October 8, 2010)

Satan's mentally challenged younger brother.
—Stephen King, on Glenn Beck, "Television Impaired," *Entertainment Weekly* (February 1, 2007)

The pretense that the GOP is a reasonable party is no longer sustainable.
—Paul Krugman, "The Republican Party's Long Decline into Irrationality," Truthout (March 13, 2012)

Now that John Boehner has cried while listening to traditional Irish music at the St. Patrick's Day luncheon it's not funny anymore. Seriously, John, tell us: where did the priest touch you? Show me on the doll.
—Bill Maher, quoted in "Late-Night Political Jokes," About.com (March 23, 2012)

This weekend 71-year-old former Vice President Dick Cheney received a heart transplant. The heart is working so well that Cheney has already gone to Whoville and returned all their Christmas presents.
—Conan O'Brien, quoted in Liberal Values blog, (March 29, 2012)

Warmongers
—Republican presidential candidate Ron Paul, characterizing Mitt Romney, Rick Santorum, and Newt Gingrich, "Ron Paul Suggests Republican Rivals Are Warmongers," Associated Press (March 15, 2015)

According to a poll conducted by the Daily Kos . . . 28 percent of Republicans believe that President Obama is not an American citizen. Another 30 percent are undecided.
—John Richardson, "When Did Americans Turn into a Bunch of Raving Lunatics?" *Esquire* (March 17, 2012)

THOSE QUOTED